For Jane, photographer and naturalist, my constant
and observant companion on these walks.

Published by Times Books
An imprint of HarperCollins Publishers
Westerhill Road
Bishopbriggs
Glasgow G64 2QT
www.harpercollins.co.uk

First edition 2016
© HarperCollins Publishers 2016

A catalogue record for this book is available from the British Library

ISBN 978-0-00-820070-1

10 9 8 7 6 5 4 3 2 1

Printed in China by RR Donnelley APS Co Ltd

If you would like to comment on any aspect of this book,
please contact us at the above address or online.
e-mail: timesatlases@harpercollins.co.uk

www.timesatlas.com

facebook.com/thetimesatlas

@TimesAtlas

THE TIMES
BRITAIN'S
BEST WALKS

Contents

Introduction

I started contributing the feature called *A Good Walk* to the Weekend Section of *The Times* in 2009. At the time of writing I've done nearly 400 of these weekly walks, all over the British Isles from the Scilly Isles to Shetland, recording what I've seen, heard, smelt, tasted and thought about along the way.

I can truly say that I have loved every one of these enchanting expeditions. It's an impossible task to choose the 'best' of them. So here are 200 walks I have picked from the list. They range from short strolls in easy country to tough mountain hikes. There's often a pub at the hub. The walk directions are designed to enable you – whether you're an experienced hiker or a complete beginner – to complete the expedition without getting lost. Having said that, you'll find the recommended Ordnance Survey Explorer map, at a scale of 1:25,000, a great help. A good GPS – Satmap (www.satmap.com) is the one I use – takes the worry out of wayfinding, too. My website (see below) contains more details of some of these walks, and many other walks as well.

Whichever walks you follow, you are in for a treat. The coastal walks will introduce you to the great chalk cliffs of the south, the moody shores of the Thames and the pebbly strands and saltmarshes of Suffolk and Norfolk. Here are the great sands and estuaries of the Lancashire coast, the flowery dunes of Scotland's east coast, and the beautiful bays of the islands out west.

Inland there are ancient trackways and level canal towpaths where the walking is slow and easy. If you like your walking with a spice of wildness, try the moorland routes in the Forest of Bowland, the North York Moors or the lonely wastes of the remote Flow Country in Sutherland where you step out of the train at Forsinard and walk, literally, into the middle of nowhere. Upland walks include the Lake District fells and the rolling Cheviot Hills of Northumberland. Go skinny-dipping in Burnmoor Tarn and Loch Neldricken, and climb to the peaks of Mellbreak and Lurcher's Crag and Little Wyvis for the satisfaction and the tremendous views.

Lesser-known pleasures are here for discovery, too - the Lincolnshire Wolds and the Yorkshire Wolds hide secret valleys, and Northern Ireland offers wild uplands, enormous sands and volcanic mountains with hundred-mile views. And of course these walks are rich in wildlife wonders - snake's-head fritillaries by the million beside the infant Thames, portions of wild Cambridgeshire fenland carefully preserved with their orchids, hobbies and dragonflies, and the dazzling springtime display of delicate Ice Age flora in Upper Teesdale where the air is full of the piping of nesting redshank and lapwings.

There are 140,000 miles of public paths in Britain, a network of rights of way that's the envy of the walking world. Stiles and gates make the paths accessible, waymarks indicate the route. But all that is under threat now from financial cutbacks. There's no such thing as the Path Fairy; it takes money and manpower to maintain our rights of way. You can help preserve these wonderful paths by walking them, by knocking aside nettles and brambles, and by reporting obstructions and missing signs to the Ramblers – just go to www.ramblers.org.uk, click on 'Advice' and make your report.

I have walked every step of these 200 walks, but things change from day to day in the countryside. Please let me know if you meet any problems.

Website: www.christophersomerville.co.uk
Twitter: @somerville_c
Facebook: Christopher Somerville

Enjoy these walks, to the hilt!

Christopher Somerville

Key

Key to text pages

Walk title

County

Walk description

Walk information

Page number

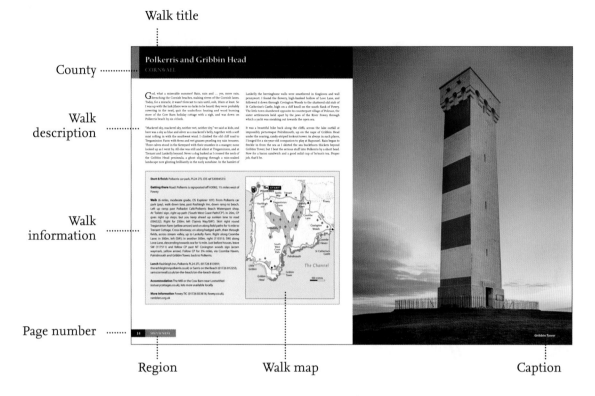

Region

Walk map

Caption

Key to maps

....	Walk route	START 👉	Route start	
→	Walk direction	Ⓟ	Parking	
	Rivers	♀ ♂	Place of worship	
		♜	Castle	
	Built up area			
🌲	Woodland	☀	Viewpoint	
	Moor			
	Sand	🍺	Public house	
	Marsh			
	Rock	⌣	Bridge	

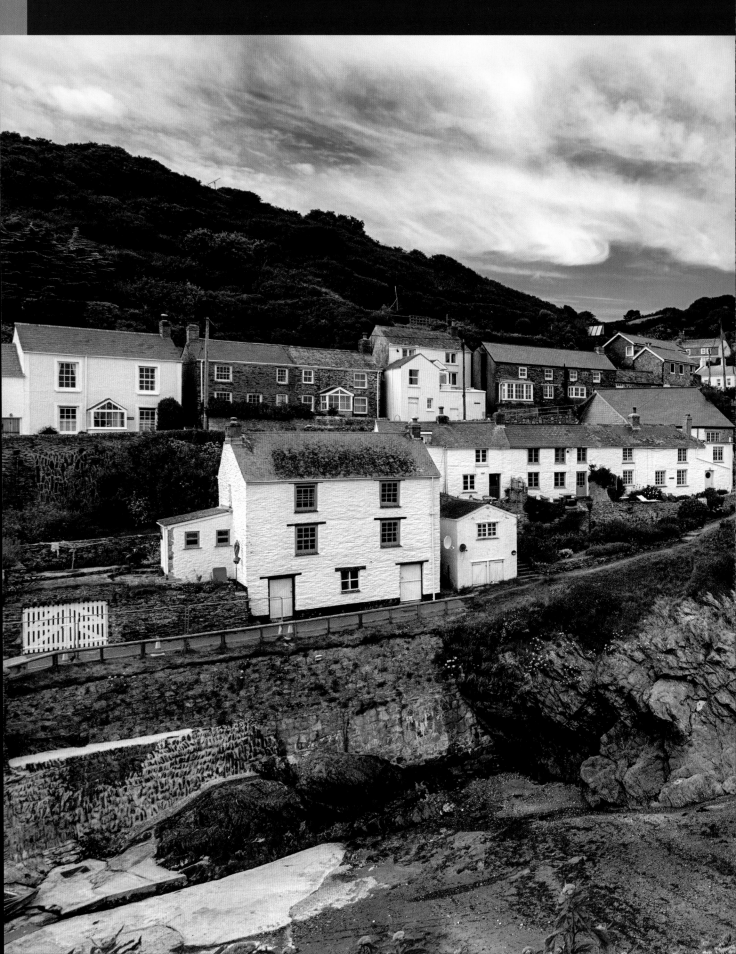

South West

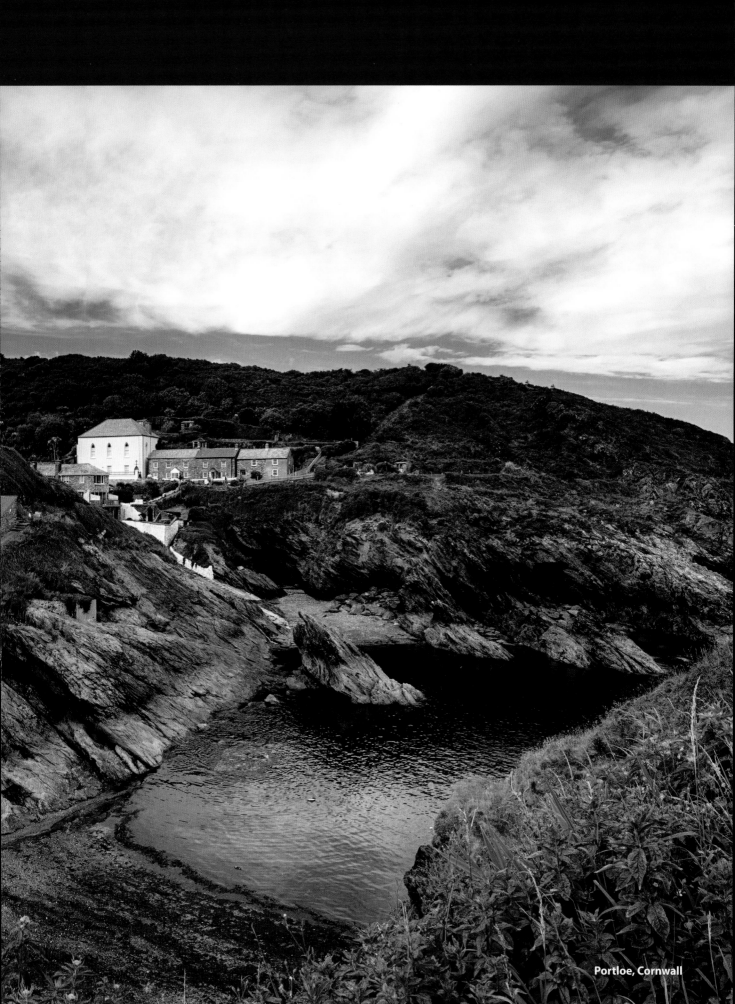

Portloe, Cornwall

Pleinmont to Lihou Island, Guernsey

CHANNEL ISLANDS

The slit opening in the cliff face lay half hidden behind a curtain of creepers. Inside, a chilly tunnel led into blackness — just one of hundreds of half-forgotten bunkers and towers that bear witness to the occupation of Guernsey by the German military during the Second World War. Hitler intended the Channel Islands to be an impregnable bastion against Allied invasion, and the concrete fortifications of his Atlantic Wall still stand stark and massive round the island's coastline.

We followed the undulating path along the southwestern cliffs, where a line of German observation towers stands looking out over a jade-green sea. Bedded on dark gold Guernsey granite among pink drifts of thrift, their flat topped and futuristic profiles stare out blankly, Easter Island heads reimagined by a Bauhaus architect.

A path through neatly drilled potato fields and a tangle of narrow, flowery lanes brought us down to the broad stretch of Rocquaine Bay, where dark bars of rock and pebbles intersect the pale sands. Halfway up the beach we ducked into the Shipwreck Museum in the Martello tower of Fort Grey — tableaux, memorabilia and salvage stories heroic, tragic and hilarious from Guernsey wrecks down the centuries.

Out on L'Erée Headland, our guide Gill Girard was waiting for the tide to ebb far enough to usher a score of clients across the causeway on to Lihou Island. This tiny green strip of islet is the westernmost point of the Channel Islands, a beautiful but rugged world apart. Fishermen in rubber boots, ormering hooks at the ready, were searching the receding tideline for the large, elusive shellfish called ormers that are a proper Guernsey delicacy.

We splashed and skidded across the weed-strewn causeway and made a circuit of Lihou under Girard's expert guidance — the ancient ruin of St Mary's Priory, sea beet and samphire, murders and wrecks, herring gulls on their nests and tales of seaweed munching sheep. And at the westerly tip of Lihou, a view to sum up the reality of island life: harsh shores, bare grazing, a lonely lighthouse warning off shipping and a hungry sea eating inexorably into the granite rocks.

Start & finish Imperial Hotel, Rocquaine Bay, Torteval GY8 0PS. Perry's Guernsey map guide (perrys.gg) widely available locally, p32, D2

Getting there Air: Flights: Aurigny (aurigny.com), Flybe (flybe.com) or Blue Islands (blueislands.com) to Guernsey. Ferry: Poole or Portsmouth with Condor Ferries (condorferries.co.uk). Bus Services 61, 91, 92, 93 (buses.gg) to Portelet Bay.

Road Follow 'Pleinmont' signs from Rue des Landes, adjacent to Guernsey airport. Park near Imperial Hotel.

Walk (8½ miles, moderate, Perry's Guernsey map guide pp32, 26, 20, 12): Pass public WC; follow road to Fort Pezeries (B1). Follow coast path, climbing between outcrops. At top, right to German tower (B2). Cross grass to coast path; follow it to pass another German tower (C4). Halfway between this tower and Watch House seen ahead, turn left off coast path (D5) along wide gravel field track to reach Rue de la Trigale (D4). Right to Route du Crolier; left; in 200m, fork right past Rocque à l'Or house (C3). Pass La Seigneurie; fork right downhill (D3) to Imperial Hotel. North along beach past Fort Grey shipwreck museum (P26, A1) to turn left off Les Sablons ('Lihou Island'; P20, B1) along La Rue du Brave to parking place opposite Lihou Island (P12, A5). Explore L'Erée Headland, then cross causeway (see below) to explore Lihou Island. Return to bus stop on Les Sablons (P20, B1); Bus 61, 91, 92, 93 to Imperial Hotel car park.

Conditions Lihou causeway is open only at low tide for variable lengths of time. Please check first: (01481 717200; gov.gg/lihou; local radio; press; notices at causeway).

Lunch Guernsey Pearl Café opposite Fort Grey, La Rocquaine GY7 9BY (01481 266404; guernseypearl.com)

Accommodation Bella Luce Hotel, La Fosse, St Martins GY4 6EB (01481 238764; bellalucehotel.com) – really comfortable, friendly and stylish

Guide Gill Girard (07781 104094; gillgirardtourguide.com). Fort Grey Shipwreck Museum (01481 265036; museums.gov.gg): March-Oct, 10am-4.30pm. Pleinmont Observation Tower (01481 238205): Sun, April-Oct, 2pm-5pm.

More information Visitor information (01481 723552; visitguernsey.com), satmap.com, ramblers.org.uk

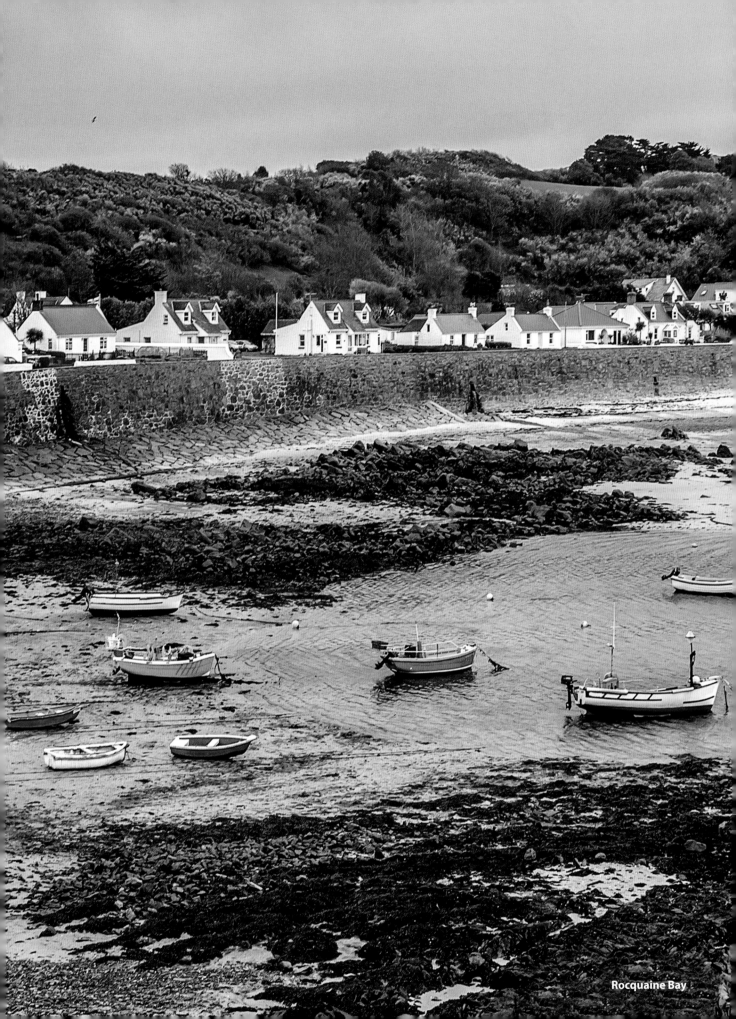

Rocquaine Bay

Logan Rock and Porthcurno
CORNWALL

Whatever you imagine a village pub to be, the Logan Rock Inn in the Penwith hamlet of Treen is pretty much it — warm fire, warm welcome, good talk, good grub. "Thought you might enjoy this," said the landlady, Anita George, proffering Jane and me a bill — not ours, but the reckoning for an extremely costly piece of vandalism in April 1824 by Lieutenant Hugh Goldsmith, RN.

The merry young shaver and the crew of his coastguard cutter had dislodged the famous Logan or rocking stone, the chief tourist attraction of the area, from its perch on a promontory beyond Treen, and sent it crashing to the beach below for a jolly jape. When complaints reached the Admiralty, their lordships were not amused by the bad PR. It cost Goldsmith £130 — a small fortune — and many months' stoppage of pay and a huge and salutary output of anxiety, hard labour and ingenuity to restore the rock to its perch. At last, reported the Royal Society, "in the presence of thousands, amidst ladies waving their handkerchiefs and universal shouts, Mr Goldsmith had the glory of placing the immense rock in its natural position uninjured".

Down on the cliffs, we threaded our way by fly-walk paths out to where the Logan Rock rode high on its outcrop. Climbing the slippery granite stack, shaggy with lichen, proved too much. So we lounged on the turf beneath, watching the sea heaving explosively against the cliffs far below.

The dull gold crescent of the beach at Porthcurno opened ahead as we hunched west into the wind along the coast path. Across the deep cleft where the village lay sheltered, steps climbed past the bowl in the cliffs where Rowena Cade built the Minack Theatre over thirty years. We left its tiered seats and rock gardens behind us, forging on along the cliffs to reach the stone-walled spring of St Levan's Well above the tiny beach of Porth Chapel.

St Levan, a fifth century Irish hermit, was a great fisherman by all accounts. We sat down to admire the thunder of the sea across the saint's favourite beach. In a while it would be time to take the path home by way of St Levan's Church, and then the ancient wheel cross of Rospletha. Not just yet, though.

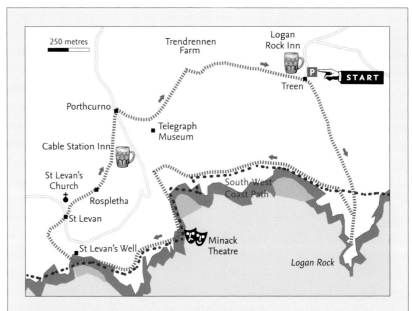

Start & finish Village car park, Treen (OS ref SW395230)

Getting there Road: A30 from Penzance towards Land's End; B3283 through St Buryan to Treen

Walk (4 miles, moderate grade, OS Explorer 102): From car park, left up track; in 10m, left on path (Logan Rock signs) across fields to cross South West Coast Path (397224). Ahead to find Logan Rock (397220). NB, path is hard to make out. Rock is labelled, out beyond first big outcrop. Hazardous climb (up right side as you look at it) is at your own risk! Return to coast path and bear left. Then: Porthcurno (386223); Minack Theatre (386221); St Levan's Well (381219); St Levan's Church (380222); Rospletha (383224); cross road in Porthcurno (383228); Trendrennen Farm (388231); Treen.

Lunch Logan Rock Inn, Treen TR19 6LG (01736 810495; theloganrockinn.co.uk)

Accommodation Rockridge House, Porthcurno TR19 6HL (01736 810410; rockridgehouseporthcurno.co.uk) – very helpful and welcoming

More information Penzance National Trust Visitor Centre (01736 335530), www.visitcornwall.com, purelypenzance.co.uk

Padstow and Harlyn
CORNWALL

On a breezy, blustery day on the North Cornwall coast, a Sunday morning hush hung over Padstow. A herring gull with a crab claw in its beak stood on the harbour wall, observing me with pale, unfriendly eyes.

Up on the coast path to Stepper Point the westerly wind pushed and smacked, shoving roughly, tossing the yellow heads of alexanders vigorously enough to make a hiss that almost drowned the sulky roar of the incoming tide in the mouth of the Camel Estuary.

There was salt on my tongue, and a fish-belly glint of dull silver on the sea. It was fantastically exhilarating walking in such a wind, like fighting a boisterous but essentially friendly troll.

Up on Stepper Point the old daymark tower whistled quietly to itself. Here, stories said, the women of Padstow had paraded in their red cloaks to frighten off the French. What a sight they'd have made on a morning like this, billowing scarlet before the gale sailed them all away over the estuary.

Picturing that, I leant on the wind and plodded west down the black line of the coast, looking ahead along many miles of foam-battered cliff. The rabbit-nibbled turf was spattered with thousands of pale blue stars, the petals of late-flowering spring squill.

Grassy knolls over the sea shook white bells of sea campion, and in a sheltered hollow, unbelievably, I found a bank of primroses still in bloom.

Skirting an enormous blowhole in the cliffs near Trevone, I pushed on to Harlyn, where the thought of breakfast suddenly occurred. Well, brunch, then — a cheeseburger with relish and mustard from the 'Food for Thought' kiosk overlooking Harlyn Bay. Completely delicious, but just what the doctor wouldn't have ordered. "You say that," observed the lady of the van, "but we have a doctor who's a regular customer — and he tells his patients to eat here too!"

I was tired of fighting the wind, and just as well; I had it at my back now. I sauntered like a man in no sort of hurry past sleepy Trevone, through a hamlet too small to have a name, and on among the clucking bantams and stolidly chewing lambs of Trethillick. The wind dropped to a sigh in the hedges and the sun came striding through the clouds to bathe Padstow and the estuary in pure gold.

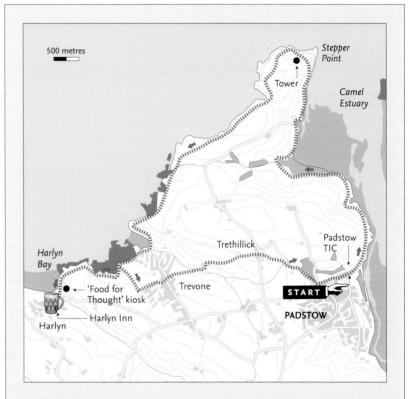

Start & finish Padstow TIC, The Red Brick Building, North Quay, Padstow, Cornwall PL28 8AF (OS ref SW920755)

Getting there Train: (thetrainline.com, railcard.co.uk) to Bodmin Parkway. Bus: (travelinesw.com, cornwallpublictransport.info) Service 219 from Truro/St Columb Major, Service 11A from Bodmin Parkway; Service 56 from Newquay. Road: A30, A39, B3274.

Walk (9 miles, moderate, OS Explorer 106): Pass Shipwright's Arms; up path ('Coast Path, Hawker's Cove'); follow Coast Path arrows/acorns for 6¾ miles to Harlyn, and nearly back to Trevone. At kissing gate (887757 – marked 'Playing Field' on Explorer map), right (footpath sign) up field edge. Dogleg left/right; left along upper field edge to road (893755); left to road in Trevone. Left for 50m; right at left bend (fingerpost) by Hursley house; through gateway, across two fields. In third field, left across stream; on past buildings, over stile at bend of lane; on across fields to lane (905758); right to Trethillick. Right, then left; over stile; cross two fields to road (910757). Right to Padstow.

Lunch 'Food for Thought' kiosk, Harlyn Bay or Harlyn Inn, Harlyn Bay PL28 8SB (01841 520207; www.harlyn-inn.com)

More information Padstow TIC (01841 533449; padstowlive.com), visitcornwall.com, ramblers.org.uk, satmap.com

God, what a miserable summer! Rain, rain and ... yes, more rain, drenching the Cornish beaches, making rivers of the Cornish lanes. Today, for a miracle, it wasn't forecast to rain until, ooh, 10am at least. So I was up with the lark (there were no larks to be heard; they were probably cowering in the nest), quit the underfloor heating and wood burning stove of the Cow Barn holiday cottage with a sigh, and was down on Polkerris beach by six o'clock.

"Mackerel sky, mackerel sky, neither wet, neither dry," we said as kids, and here was a sky as blue and silver as a mackerel's belly, together with a soft mist rolling in with the southwest wind. I climbed the old cliff road to Tregaminion Farm with ferns and wet grasses pearling my rain trousers. Three calves stood in the farmyard with their muzzles in a manger; none looked up as I went by. All else was still and silent at Tregaminion, and at Trenant and Lankelly beyond. Never a dog barked as I crossed the neck of the Gribbin Head peninsula, a ghost slipping through a rain-soaked landscape now glinting brilliantly in the early sunshine. In the hamlet of

Lankelly the herringbone walls were smothered in foxgloves and wall pennywort. I found the flowery, high-banked hollow of Love Lane, and followed it down through Covington Woods to the shattered old stub of St Catherine's Castle, high on a cliff knoll on the south flank of Fowey. The little town slumbered opposite its counterpart village of Polruan, the sister settlements held apart by the jaws of the River Fowey through which a yacht was sneaking out towards the open sea.

It was a beautiful hike back along the cliffs, across the lake outfall at impossibly picturesque Polridmouth, up on the nape of Gribbin Head under the soaring, candy-striped lookout tower. As always in such places, I longed for a six-year-old companion to play at Rapunzel. Rain began to freckle in from the sea as I skirted the sea buckthorn thickets beyond Gribbin Tower, but I beat the serious stuff into Polkerris by a short head. Now for a bacon sandwich and a good solid cup of bo'sun's tea. Proper job, that'd be.

Start & finish Polkerris car park, PL24 2TL (OS ref SX094523)

Getting there Road: Polkerris is signposted off A3082, 1½ miles west of Fowey

Walk (6 miles, moderate grade, OS Explorer 107): From Polkerris car park (pay), walk down lane, past Rashleigh Inn, down ramp to beach. Left up ramp past Polkadot Café/Polkerris Beach Watersport shop. At 'Toilets' sign, right up path ('South West Coast Path/CP'). In 20m, CP goes right up steps, but you keep ahead up sunken lane to road (096522). Right for 250m; left ('Saints Way/SW'). Skirt right round Tregaminion Farm (yellow arrows) and on along field paths for ⅓ mile to Trenant Cottage. Cross driveway; on along hedged path, then through fields, across stream valley, up to Lankelly Farm. Right along Coombe Lane; in 300m, left (SW); in another 300m, right (115515; SW) along Love Lane, descending towards sea for ⅓ mile. Just before houses, leave SW (117511) and follow CP past NT Covington woods sign (acorn waymark, yellow arrow). Follow CP for 3¾ miles, via Coombe Haven, Polridmouth and Gribbin Tower, back to Polkerris.

Lunch Rashleigh Inn, Polkerris PL24 2TL (01726 813991; therashleighinnpolkerris.co.uk) or Sam's on the Beach (01726 812255; samscornwall.co.uk/on-the-beach/on-the-beach-about)

Accommodation The Mill or the Cow Barn near Lostwithiel (estuarycottages.co.uk), lots more available locally

More information Fowey TIC (01726 833616; fowey.co.uk), ramblers.org.uk

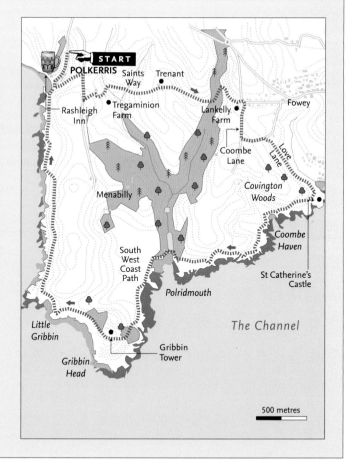

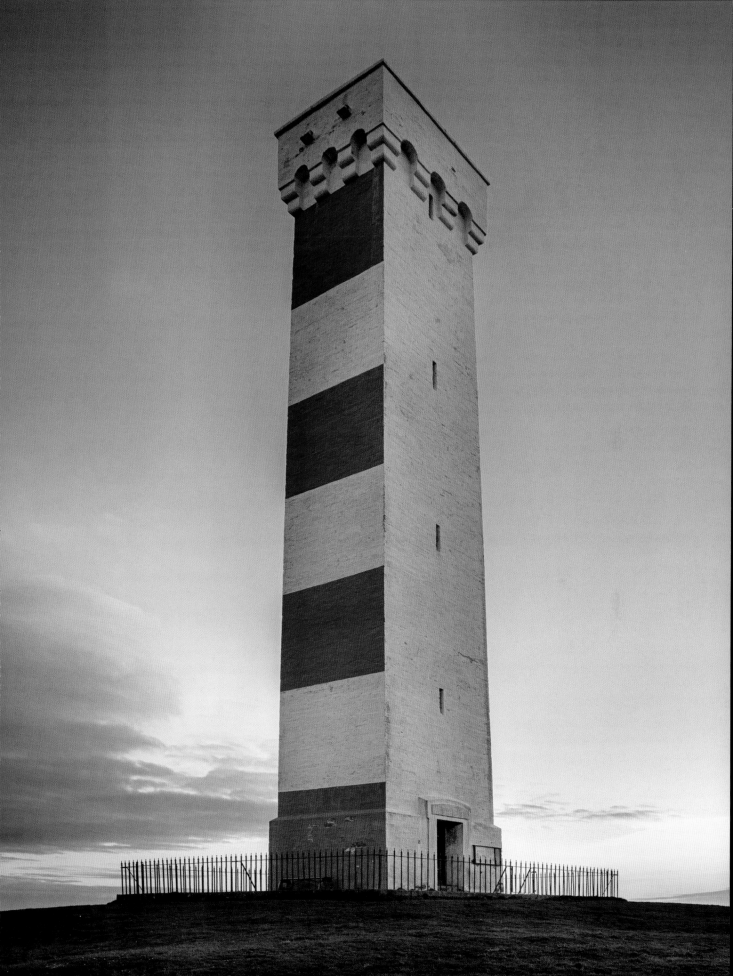

Portloe and Nare Head

CORNWALL

The sleeping-bloodhound profile of Nare Head is veiled in sea fret, and it's tempting to turn back into the comfortable warmth of the Nare Hotel and seek a nice deep armchair. But hang the weather. On with the boots, and out along those misty, seductive cliffs.

From the summit of Nare Head we look back round the great sweep of Gerrans Bay. Portscatho's houses across the bay are a sloping tumble of white. The sea sighs at the feet of the cliffs where fulmars and kittiwakes are sitting hopefully on nests precariously wedged into the narrowest of crevices. Sea campion, gorse in coconut-scented flower, bluebells half bloomed, self heal, celandine, big bushy alexanders and tiny pink cranesbills; the whole power of early summer seems concentrated in brilliant colour along these rugged quartz-veined cliffs.

We walk on slowly over the headlands and round the caves — Rosen Cliff and Kilberick Cove (there's a grey seal there, bobbing sleekly like a well-oiled Channel swimmer), Parc Caragloose and Manare Point, until we stand looking down on Portloe's sprinkle of white fishermen's cottages under grey slate roofs. The neat little slide of houses bends round the tight curve of the valley and down to the slipway with its handful of crab boats.

It's incredible to think that in Victorian times Portloe was a bustling, noisy, stinking pilchard town, catching and salting, packing and shipping the fish to market — notably to Catholic Italy and its Friday fasters. We climb the narrow street, out into the steep fields behind the village. Trewartha Hall farm is scented rich and sweet with silage. The woods above Veryan are pungent with wild garlic. A pint and a sandwich in the New Inn and we're set for the homeward road — a pretty lane between high hedge banks, a sloping valley full of bluebells and birdsong, and a last trudge along the rocky sands of Pendower Beach.

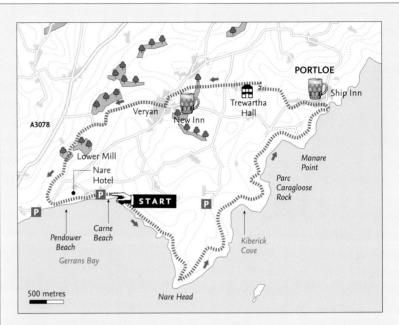

Start & finish National Trust car park, Carne Beach, near Veryan TR2 5PF (OS ref SW905383)

Getting there Road: Car park is 100m from Nare Hotel (signed off A3078 between Tregony and Portscatho)

Walk (9½ miles, moderate, OS Explorer 105): Follow South West Coast Path east for 3¼ miles to Portloe. Left up street, pass Ship Inn, cross stream (934394); in 100m, right ('Veryan'). Pass houses; gate into field; cross field, then stone stile (932396, yellow arrow/YA); left to gate into lane. Follow YAs via Trewartha Hall farm and Trewartha to road (924397). Left; right across road, down 'Roseland Nursery' lane; on (YAs) along green lane, across field, through wood (920397). Half left down to stile (918396); forward past Veryan church to road. Left past New Inn; in 50m right (916395, 'Portscatho') along lane. In ¾ mile cross brook (906392); in 75m left up path, soon descending to Lower Mill (902389). Cross brook; along drive; at left bend, ahead through gate; path to Pendower Beach (898382); left on Coast Path to Carne Beach (NB: Coast Path is narrow, slippery and vertiginous in places).

Accommodation Nare Hotel, Carne Beach, Veryan-in-Roseland, Cornwall TR2 5PF (01872 501111; narehotel.co.uk) – solid, comfortable, friendly, family-run

More information St Austell TIC (01726 879500; visitcornwall), visitengland.com, satmap.com, ramblers.org.uk, exploreincornwall.co.uk (for guided walks)

Tintagel to Boscastle

CORNWALL

I crossed the footbridge slung over the chasm that separates the mainland part of Tintagel Castle from the section that stands on a massive, rock-like promontory, known as Tintagel Island. Here, protected by sheer cliffs on all sides, a prosperous community traded tin for Mediterranean pottery and glassware in post-Roman times. And, if the ancient chroniclers and poets can be believed, Arthur the Once and Future King was conceived here.

Was Arthur born at Tintagel? Or was he washed up there on a tempest-driven wave, to be raised by Merlin in the cave that still underpins Tintagel Island? And what of the ancient stone inscribed 'Artognou' (which is similar to the Welsh name Arthneu), unearthed at Tintagel in 1998? I pondered these signs and wonders as I explored the tiny Dark Ages dwellings and the stark castle ruins on the promontory. Then I set out north along the coast path with the sun on my back and the wind in my face.

It was a spring day in a thousand, under a sky of unbroken blue. The path wound into and out of hidden valleys, swung up flights of steps and slithered down over slaty rocks. Primroses, white sea campion and pink tuffets of thrift trembled in the strong sea breeze. Herring gulls wheeled and wailed above a sea of milky turquoise. Ahead, the cliffs crinkled around tiny rock coves, leading the eye forward to a great curve of coast where Cornwall ran north into Devon.

In the gorse banks at the top of Smith's Cliff, tiny Dartmoor ponies galloped skittishly to and fro. I walked out to the spectacular sheer-sided promontory of Willapark, one among dozens of sections of this precious piece of coastline bought by the National Trust with funds raised through their Neptune Coastline Campaign, launched in 1965. Beyond Benoath Cove's perfect stretch of dull-gold sand lay Rocky Valley, where the Trevillett River jumps down towards the sea over a series of rock steps. I crossed a little grassy saddle near Firebeacon Hill, brilliant with violets and shiny yellow stars of celandine.

Under the white tower of a coastguard lookout, the coal-black cliffs of Western Blackapit stood twisted, contorted and streaked with splashes of quartzite, as though a painter had flicked his brush across them. Beyond the promontory, the white houses of Boscastle lay hidden in their deep narrow cleft, appearing in sight only at the last moment as I turned the corner by the harbour wall — a magical revelation of which Merlin himself might have been proud.

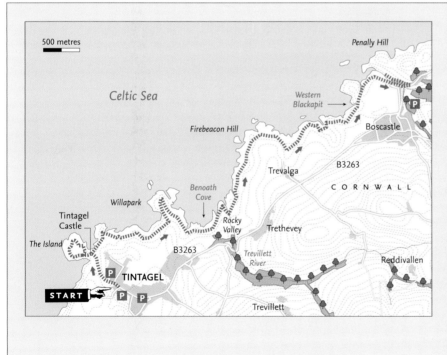

Start Tintagel Castle, near Camelford, Cornwall PL34 0HE (OS ref SX052889)

Getting there Road: A30, A395, B3266; or A39, B3263 to Boscastle. Park in village car park (PL35 0HE) – pay with coins or phone. Then take bus 595, or taxi (Boscars: 07790 983911; boscars.co.uk) to Tintagel. Walk down to castle entrance.

Walk (6 miles, strenuous, many steps and short steep sections, OS Explorer 111): Follow South West Coast Path to Boscastle

Lunch/tea Harbour Light Tea Garden, Boscastle PL35 0HD (01840 250953)

Accommodation Mill House Inn, Trebarwith, near Tintagel PL34 0HD (01840 770200; themillhouseinn.co.uk)

More information Boscastle Visitor Centre (01840 250010; visitboscastleandtintagel.com), visitengland.com, satmap.com, ramblers.org.uk, Tintagel Castle (English Heritage: 01840 770328; english-heritage.org.uk)

Hound Tor and Haytor Rocks, Dartmoor
DEVON

"Mr Holmes, they were the footprints of a gigantic hound!"

I first read this thrilling and chilling line in *The Hound of the Baskervilles* as a ten-year-old, under the bedclothes and with a frisson of pure, delicious fear. I've loved Holmes and Watson's supernatural Dartmoor caper ever since. And though the real Hound Tor isn't quite within howling distance of Conan Doyle's fictional great Grimpen Mire, I couldn't resist that atavistic name when it came to choosing a walk on the moor.

It turned out misty — of course. As soon as Jane and I had climbed from Haytor Vale on to the open moor, ghostly hands began to draw a white woollen blanket across the granite tors and the undulating sea of gorse and heather in which they rode like weathered grey ships. The twin hulks of Haytor Rocks slipped out of sight and a harras of moor mares and their foals faded to insubstantial silhouettes.

But moor mists are funny things, and this one ran up against an invisible barrier. Smallacombe Rocks, our aiming point, remained in sunlight and from the tor we saw the dog's tooth of Hound Tor sharply outlined against blue sky across the steep little valley of the Becka Brook.

We descended among crab apples, sloes and whortleberries, and crossed the brook by a stout old clapper bridge. The path ran past a maze of stone-built dwellings, smothered in bracken and bramble. The high ground of Dartmoor may be deserted today, but in medieval times it was spattered with shepherding and tin-mining settlements such as this.

On the peak of Hound Tor we paused to take in the view. Then it was on, down to ford the Becka Brook, up again to follow the rails and sidings of the Haytor Granite Tramway. Laid down in the 1820s, the solid stone tramway trundled granite from Dartmoor to build some of London's greatest Victorian edifices.

We climbed to the top of Haytor Rocks and surveyed the moor. Snaking away through the purple-gold landscape, the chunky tramway looked endearingly clumsy — as if a troll had taken a peep over George Stephenson's shoulder and decided to do a bit of DIY.

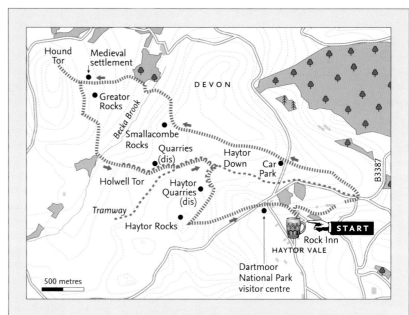

Start & finish The Rock Inn, Haytor Vale, Newton Abbot TQ13 9XP (OS ref SX771772)

Getting there Bus: Haytor Hoppa Service 271 (Sat June-Sep) from Bovey Tracey (dartmoor.gov.uk/visiting/vi-planningyourvisit/vi-gettingarounddartmoor/vi-haytorhoppa). Road: M5, A38, B3344 to Bovey Tracey; B3387 towards Widecombe in the Moor; in 3 miles, Haytor Vale signed to left.

Walk (6½ miles, moderate, OS Explorer OL28): Leaving Rock Inn, right for 50m; on bend, ahead (bridleway fingerpost); in 75m, right ('Moor, Smallacombe'). In 350m, in a dip, fork left through turnstile; follow roadway to cross B3387 (778773). Up path opposite through bracken to ridge; left towards Haytor Rocks for ⅔ mile to cross Manaton road through car park (770778). Follow clear track across Haytor Down, with Haytor Rocks ¾ mile away on your left. Just before reaching Smallacombe Rocks, bear right/north (756782) down rocky path. In 300m, at fork, left downhill past fingerpost (754786; 'Houndtor Down'). Follow bridleway to cross Becka Brook (752787); uphill past medieval settlement (746787) to Hound Tor (742789). Retrace steps for 300m; right (south) along green path just above settlement, with Greator Rocks on left. In 100m pass waymark post, and on. In 300m, through gate (745783); left ('Haytor Down'); descend to ford Becka Brook (747778). Up path opposite, aiming for Holwell Tor, to reach Haytor Granite Tramway track just below it (750778). Left along it. In ⅓ mile, pass branch to right (757777); in another ¼ mile, right (761777) along branch through quarry to climb Haytor Rocks (757771). Aim for Dartmoor National Park centre on B3387 below (767772); left along road; in 100m right, then immediately left to Haytor Vale.

NB In mist this walk is only for map/compass/GPS users.

Lunch/accommodation The Rock Inn, Haytor Vale (01364 661305; rock-inn.co.uk)

More information Ashburton TIC (01364 653426; ashburton.org), dartmoor.co.uk, visitdevon.co.uk, Dartmoor Park Visitor Centre, Haytor (01364 661520; dartmoor.gov.uk), ramblers.org.uk, satmap.com

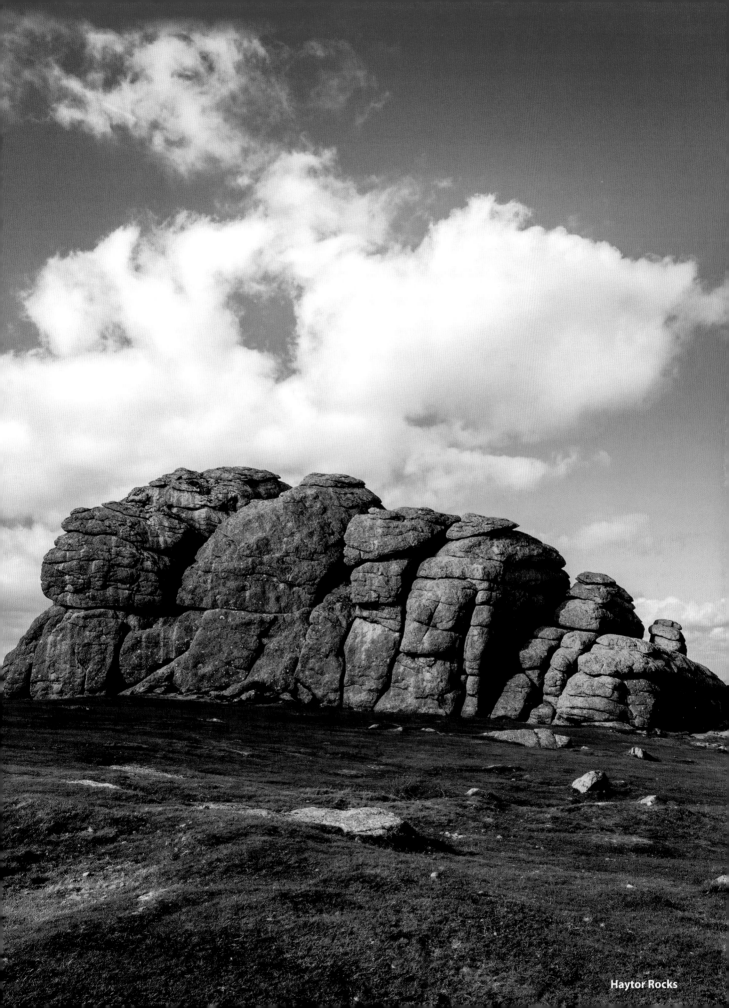

Haytor Rocks

Hartland Point, North Devon

A brisk, blowy, blustering day on the North Devon coast, with a scudding grey sky and big Atlantic waves racing onshore to smash against the black rock of the cliffs. I actually felt the ground quake beneath me as I pushed north into the wind along the line between sea and land, wondering whether leaving the warmth and light of the Hartland Quay Hotel had been a good idea after all.

Tides are strong and cross-currents treacherous out at Hartland Point, where the Devon coast cuts at right angles from north to east at the outer entrance to the Bristol Channel. Curved and contorted bands of sandstone, ground by the sea into upturned razor edges, lie just below the surface; they have brought thousands of sailing ships to grief down the years. I paused by the lighthouse on the point and took in a last breathless prospect of dark sky, dark sea and black rock before heading inland along the high-hedged lanes so characteristic of this part of the world.

In the shelter of the lanes, the wind, roaring high overhead, scarcely trembled a leaf. I threaded past farms with Betjemanic names — Blagdon and Blegberry, Berry and Wargery — with the sounds of trickling water and tentative robin song for company.

In the ridge-top village of Stoke, master craftsmen down the centuries have beautified St Nectan's Church. I admired the Tudor panelling of the rood screen, all slender ribs and exquisite floral detail, and the roof with its coruscating stars and carved bosses. Then it was out and on along the field lanes, dropping down to the cliffs and the roar of the wind once more.

The great waterfall at Speke's Mill Mouth was a lace veil blown to rags, the floor of the cove a seethe of white foam among black rock scars. Above the green shark's tooth of St Catherine's Tor, a raven was struggling to fly north, held at a standstill in mid-air by the counterblast of the wind. I put my head down and shoved on, a midget in motion among the huge forces of nature.

Later, sitting in the warm bar of the Hartland Quay Hotel, I found my cup of tea tasted salty; a legacy of all the sea wind and spray absorbed by my beard on this wild and entrancing walk.

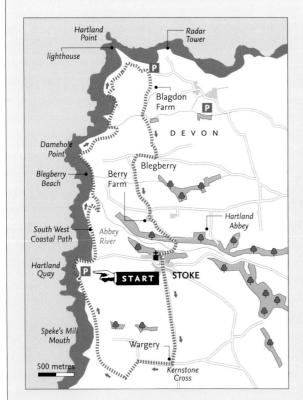

Start & finish Hartland Quay Hotel, Hartland EX39 6DU (OS ref SS222247)

Getting there Road: M5 to junction 27; A361 to Bideford; A39 towards Bude. ¼ mile beyond B3237 Clovelly turning, bear right on minor road to Hartland and Hartland Quay.

Walk (7½ miles, moderate/hard, OS Explorer 126): South West Coast Path/SWCP (fingerposts, acorn symbols) north to Hartland Point. Just before radar station, inland. In 100m, ahead ('bridleway, Blegberry') past Blagdon Farm; bridleway for ¾ mile to road. Right to Blegberry Farm. Left ('unmetalled road'); green lane for ½ mile to road. Ahead past Berry Farm, across Abbey River; road up to Stoke. Left; immediately right up lane by Rose Cottage. In 200m pass 'Unsuitable for Motors'; keep ahead for a good ½ mile. At Wargery, right to road at Kernstone Cross; right ('Kernstone') for 450m to T-junction; left through gate ('Speke's Mill Mouth') on grass path; SWCP north to Hartland Quay Hotel.

Conditions Beware strong wind gusts on exposed clifftops. Many steps, many climbs and descents. Allow 3-4 hours.

Lunch Hartland Quay Hotel (01237 441218; hartlandquayhotel.co.uk) – friendly, characterful and welcoming

More information Bideford TIC (01237 477676; northdevon.com), visitdevon.co.uk, ramblers.org.uk, satmap.co.uk

Kingston and Bigbury-on-Sea
DEVON

Kingston lies shut away in a tangle of high-banked lanes, a South Hams village that retains a vigorous social life in and out of the holiday season. Local families, the Crockers and Terrys, lie companionably in the churchyard of St James the Less, our starting point for a walk along the coast of this isolated region of south Devon. In the ferny banks an astonishing treasury of flowers had responded to the mildness of this winter — herb robert, celandines, primroses, red campion and snowdrops all blooming.

Between the leafless, wind-streamed trees of Furzedown Wood we caught glimpses of the tide-ribbed, dull gold sandflats and milky turquoise water of the Erme estuary, a snaking channel that reached its mouth between wooded headlands of black rock.

Out on the coast a low wind brought a breath of winter in from the sea. The water lay slate-coloured under a grey sky streaked with pearly patches. Contorted cliff faces fell hundreds of feet to secret beaches and coves floored with tight-packed parallel lines of rock scars. A little back from the edge ran the path, swooping a couple of hundred feet into the green grassy dips, then soaring back up and over a succession of headlands.

It was heady walking, with the sea-monster shape of tidal Burgh Island as a target point ahead. The island's Art Deco hotel gleamed in the muted winter light, an exotic morsel much picked over by guests both actual and apocryphal — Noel Coward, Winston Churchill, the Beatles and M. Hercule Poirot among them. We descended to the shore in Bigbury-on-Sea opposite Burgh Island's other hostelry, the tiny old Pilchard Inn. Jane opted to cross the sandy causeway for a bowl of soup and a bit of a sit-down there, while I set off back to Kingston through the switchback fields and stream valleys of the hinterland.

By the time I'd fetched the car and negotiated the narrow lanes back to Bigbury-on-Sea, the tide had risen to cover the causeway. I watched as Jane came ashore on Burgh Island's tall blue sea tractor, riding in state like Queen Suriyothai on her war elephant.

The Dolphin in Kingston is one of those pubs that draws you in on a cold winter's night — a combination of lamp-lit windows, the promise of a pint and a plate of food, a cosy setting and the flicker of a real good fire. It was great to get the weight off our muddy feet and settle down there with the wind and rain shut out, the map spread on the table and a great day's walking to chew over at leisure.

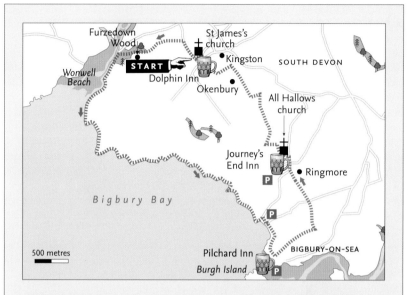

Start & finish Dolphin Inn, Kingston, Bigbury, Devon TQ7 4QE (OS ref SX636478)

Getting there Road: M5, A38 to Ivybridge turn; minor road to Ermington; A3121, A379 to Modbury; minor road to Kingston

Walk (9 miles, strenuous, OS Explorer OL20): From Dolphin Inn, left past church. At crossroads, right ('Wonwell Beach'). In ¼ mile, just past dogleg, left (632481; 'Wonwell Beach'); follow fingerposts and yellow arrows/YAs over fields for ¾ mile, down through Furzedown Wood to road by Erme estuary (620478). Left for 150m; left up steps ('Coast Path, Bigbury-on-Sea'). Follow coast path for 5 miles to Bigbury-on-Sea (if tide allows, cross sand causeway – 651442 – to Pilchard Inn – 648440). In Bigbury-on-Sea, climb Parker Road; at top, through gate (653446; arrow, fingerpost/FP). On across fields; at end of third field (658448), left downhill with fence on right (FP, 'Ringmore'). Follow YAs, crossing lane at 656453, to Ringmore. At road, ahead to T-junction by church (653460). Right, then left up side of church. In 150m, left through kissing gate (653461; 'Kingston' FP). Diagonally right across field and through gate; follow YAs through gates and fields, turning left (650463) to descend to stream in valley. Bear right (648463) along stream, crossing it at ruined Noddonmill (649465); on (YA) along left bank of stream, into wood (very muddy!). In ¼ mile, steeply uphill out of trees; anti-clockwise round field to far right corner (645471; FP). Right along farm track. Round left bend, and turn right (644473; FP) across field to lane (643474). Left (YA) for 50m; right (FP) and follow YAs along field edges and through woodland to road (637476). Right to T-junction in Kingston (636477); right, then left to Dolphin Inn.

Lunch Pilchard Inn, Burgh Island TQ7 4BG (01548 810514; soup and baguettes only; if marooned by high tide, return ashore on Sea Tractor, £2, check times/tides in advance), Journey's End Inn, Ringmore TQ7 4HL (01548 810205; thejourneysendinn.co.uk)

Accommodation Dolphin Inn, Kingston (01548 810314) – low beams, fires, good cheer – a community hub

More information Totnes TIC (01803 863168; totnesinformation.co.uk), visitdevon.co.uk, ramblers.org.uk, satmap.co.uk

Otterton and the Otter Estuary, South Devon

DEVON

Blues and folk music, cream teas, a bakery, story-telling, art exhibitions and a perfect setting by the River Otter at the edge of a village of cob and sandstone cottages under thatch. No wonder Otterton Mill café is as popular in summer as a cold beer on a hot day. We could have squeezed in for a pre-walk cuppa, but the call of riverbank, estuary and rugged red cliffs was too strong on a beautiful afternoon on the south Devon coast. We crossed the three old arches of Otterton Bridge instead, and walked downriver along the slow-flowing Otter.

This is flat green river country bounded by low hills, the Otter running shallow and red over ridges of shillets that trail green hanks of weed, rippling silkily like mermaid hair. "Have you seen the grey mullet?" inquired a fisherman. "In the shallows, look." There they were, a long shoal sinuating with the stream. "I'm going to attempt to catch one, but they're pretty shy." He flicked a lure into the water and drew it wobbling and flashing past the noses of the unmoving mullet.

We crossed the river and went on beside ripe wheat fields glistening in the sun. Down at the river mouth a pebble spit almost closes off the Otter's estuary from the sea. Gulls called mournfully over the piled roofs of Budleigh Salterton, wetsuited youngsters shrieked the echoes out of caves, and surf sighed on the stony ridge — essence of the sounds of summer.

The dusty coast path led north along cliffs striated and weather-bitten, their strata dipping eastward in a mighty curve through the white sprinkle of Sidmouth, the tall red triangle of Dunscombe Cliff and a far white smudge of chalk at distant Beer Head. Fulmars and kittiwakes planed along the line of the cliff edge, and the dark purposeful shape of a peregrine went dashing by at head height. Inland, a bare field of pigs rooted among pink stones, seagulls whirled, and a farmer in a red tractor got his straw bales organised in a newly harvested field.

Above Smallstones Point we pulled up to stare across the great layered rock stacks in Ladram Bay, lambent and crimson in the late sun — a famous view, and one that always delivers a pure jolt of delight. One more glance along the pink and white coast, and we headed along green lanes through the stubble fields towards Otterton and that well-earned cream tea.

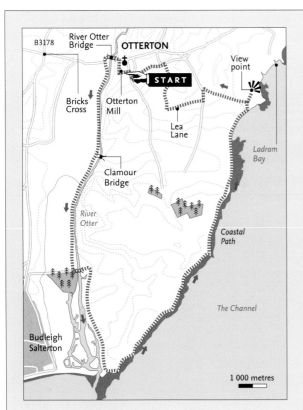

Start & finish Otterton Mill, Otterton, Devon EX9 7HG (OS ref SY080851)

Getting there Road: A3052 (Exeter-Sidmouth); B3178 at Newton Poppleford ('Budleigh Salterton'). In 3 miles, Otterton signposted at Brick Cross. Park in village.

Walk (6 miles, easy grade, Explorer 115): From Otterton Mill cross the River Otter bridge, then go left along riverbank footpath. In 2/3 mile don't cross Clamour Bridge: continue along right bank to cross the next bridge (075830), signposted 'Ladram Bay, Coast Path' (CP). Don't turn right immediately along the river; keep ahead on the road for 100m, then right (CP) on path to coast. Follow CP arrows to the left along cliffs for 2 miles. At 'Otterton ½ mile' fingerpost (094848), go ahead for 50m to view Ladram Bay; return and follow the path (soon a green lane) inland. Turn left at the gate of Monk's Thatch to the road (089849). Left for 100m; then right along Lea Lane ('Unmetalled Road'). Just after right bend, keep ahead (085847; black arrow) to the road in Otterton (085852). Left, then follow lane past church to village.

Lunch Otterton Mill (01395 568521; ottertonmill.com)

More information Budleigh Salterton TIC (01395 445275; visitbudleigh.com), visitdevon.co.uk, ramblers.org.uk, satmap.com

"The peat fires!" rhapsodised Sabine Baring-Gould in his 1900 *Book of Dartmoor*. "What fires can surpass them? They do not flame, but they glow, and diffuse an aroma that fills the lungs with balm."

It wasn't the dream of a lungful of balm that lured so many nineteenth-century prospectors out into the wilds of Dartmoor, but the chance of turning a fat profit by distilling naphtha oil from the 'black gold' of the peat that blanketed the moors. Naphtha oil could be converted into candles and mothballs, as well as the spectrally flickering naphtha flares that lit the evening markets of country towns.

Following the trackbed of the horse-drawn tramway built in 1879 for the Rattlebrook Peat Works, we marvelled at the ingenuity and sheer muscle power that the moorland railway had demanded: the cuttings in the granite rock, the curves and embankments, the granite sleepers hand-bevelled for the rails. A couple of miles out from the Dartmoor Inn, we stopped and took in a mighty view, forty miles across the dun-coloured moor and green farmlands to a broad strip of cobalt Atlantic where the land met the eggshell-blue sky.

Moor ponies grazed the slopes, their long manes and tails streaming wildly in the wind. At the end of the old railway line, 100 men once laboured to dig, dry and load the peat. Here we found a couple of tumbledown peat-drying kilns and two venerable rusty boilers.

Nearby, on the banks of the Rattle Brook stood the ruin of the aptly named Bleak House, home of the peat company's caretaker. All around, the moor slopes had been combed into drainage channels for peat cutting. The ditches, like the ancient packhorse tracks we followed back to the Dartmoor Inn, were already half obliterated by the inexorably growing peat.

Tinning, quarrying, farming, peat cutting — man has tried them all on Dartmoor and the land has swallowed all his endeavours. The meadow pipits, the moor ponies and the ravens are the true masters of these moors.

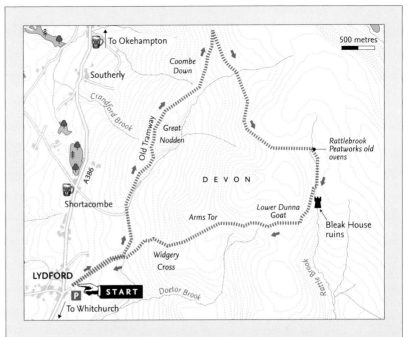

Start & finish Car park off A386 near Dartmoor Inn, Lydford, Okehampton, Devon EX20 4AY (OS ref SX525854)

Getting there Bus: Service 46 (Tavistock-Okehampton). Road: A30 past Okehampton, A386 towards Tavistock. In 4½ miles, 20m before Dartmoor Inn, left up narrow tarmac lane. Car park is beyond gate.

Walk (8 miles, moderate, OS Explorer OL28): Follow stony track by left-hand wall to River Lyd stepping stones/footbridge (532857). Don't cross: turn left beside river for ⅓ mile. Where wall turns left (532863) keep ahead; in 50m, cross old tramway; on up path opposite. In 100m, right (533865) along higher tramway track, passing Great Nodden. In 1¾ miles, reach reversing point/turning circle on Coombe Down (546887). Hairpin back up to right; follow tramway track for 1½ miles to ruined kiln houses (560871). Just before ruin, right on boggy track for 500m. 100m before Bleak House ruin, cross Rattle Brook (560866); follow clear track, bearing away from brook. Pass Lower Dunna Goat tor; in another 250m, turn right/west (557861) on wide, well-walked bridleway path for 1¾ miles to River Lyd footbridge (532857), aiming to descend between Arms Tor and Widgery Cross. Ahead to Dartmoor Inn. NB: Good boots, hill-walking gear, map, compass and GPS are recommended. Not advisable in heavy mist.

Lunch/accommodation Dartmoor Inn, Moorside, Lydford (01822 820221; www.dartmoorinn.com)

More information Museum of Dartmoor Life, Okehampton (01837 52295; museumofdartmoorlife.org.uk) or Princetown Visitor Centre (01822 890414; visitdartmoor.co.uk), visitengland.com, satmap.com, ramblers.org.uk

Portesham and Hardy's Monument

DORSET

A blackbird was singing on the wall of Portesham House, where stone lions guarded the porch. Thomas Masterman Hardy, who lived here as a young boy in 1778, was destined for fame as a much-loved sailor and man of action. Horatio Nelson's close friend and trusted Flag Captain died loaded with honours in September 1839. In that month his namesake, the future novelist and poet Thomas Hardy, became the tiniest of twinkles in his mother's eye at Higher Bockhampton, a few miles to the east. It's not the great writer who is commemorated by the tall stone Hardy's Monument on the downs, but the fighting admiral from little Portesham village.

Near the path to Hardy's Monument crouches the Hell Stone, a Neolithic tomb whose nine massive stone legs support a capstone of flint-studded conglomerate. The Devil, playing a game of quoits, hurled the Hell Stone here from the Isle of Portland ten miles away, so legend says.

Up in a cold wind by the monument, Jane and I savoured that fabulous tale along with an equally fabulous burger of local beef, cooked and served with a relish of friendly banter by the pony-tailed man in the Hobo Catering van. Hobo the Canadian Inuit dog (who lends her name to the admirable fast-food business run by her master) followed every mouthful with the soulful gaze of true cupboard love.

The views over Dorset are sensational.

Even more stunning is the prospect from the steep ridge above Waddon House, where we paused on the way back to Portesham. Downs and farmlands, the shingle bar of Chesil Beach, St Catherine's Chapel on its knoll of strip lynchets, the Devil's quoits pitch of Portland lying like the Gibraltar of Wessex on a bay of molten silver — if any view could entice an adventurous lad to sea, it would be this.

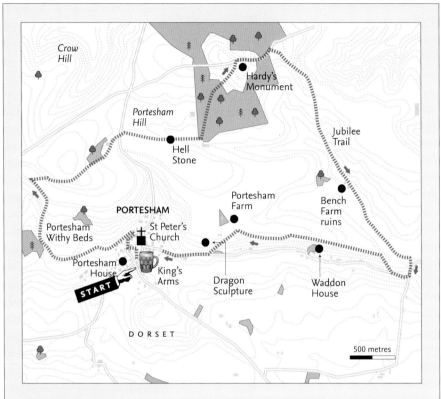

Start & finish King's Arms, Portesham, Dorset DT3 4ET (OS ref SY603857)

Getting there Train: to Upwey – 6 miles (thetrainline.com). Bus: Service X53 from Poole (travelinesw.com). Road: Portesham signed off A35 Dorchester-Bridport at Winterbourne Abbas.

Walk (7½ miles, moderate grade, OS Explorer OL15): From King's Arms, cross street; up Church Lane; right up Back Street; left opposite Manor Close (602860). Follow 'Portesham Withy Beds, White Hill, Abbotsbury Round Walk'/ARW signs/waymark arrows. Pass withy beds; through gate at end of trees (592860). Sharp right up steep bank; follow fence (fingerpost, ARW) for ⅓ mile. Right over stile (592865) by 'South Dorset Ridgeway, Hardy's Monument'/HM marker stone. Follow 'Inland Coast Path'/ICP for ⅔ mile to road (601869). Left (great care!) for 30m; right (HM fingerpost) down fence for two fields. Detour right (605869; 'Hell Stone only') over stone stile to Hell Stone (605867); return to path; follow ICP through wood to Hardy's Monument (613876). Cross road; follow ICP to re-cross road (616877; 'ICP, Jubilee Trail'/JT). In ⅓ mile (620874), right off ICP, following JT for 1¼ miles past Bench Farm ruins (624864) to road (630857). Right; in 100m, right ('Portesham'); in 200m, right over stile (yellow arrow/YA). Diagonally left to ridge top; follow fence (stiles, YAs) for 1 mile. Through gate by Portesham Farm (612861); left down drive; right along lane into Portesham.

Lunch Hobo Catering van at Hardy's Monument (if it's there) or King's Arms, Portesham (01305 871342; kingsarmsportesham.co.uk) – B&B available

More information Dorchester TIC (01305 267992; www.visit-dorset.com), westdorset.com, ramblers.org.uk

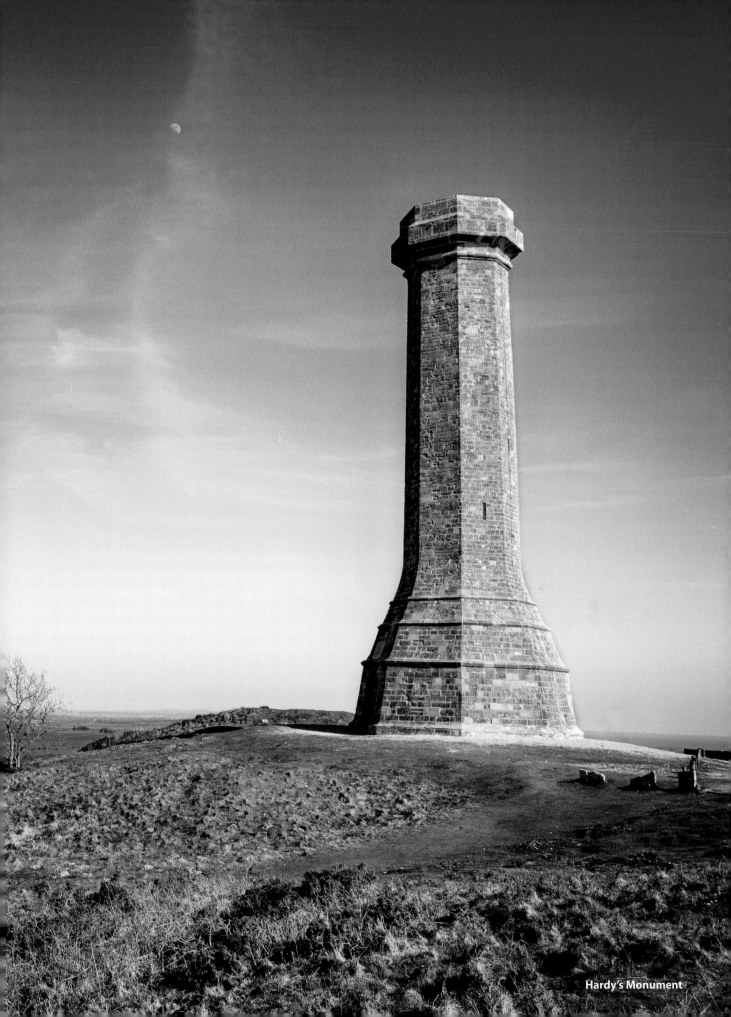

Hardy's Monument

Tyneham and the Jurassic Coast

DORSET

"**P**lease treat the church and houses with care," said the handwritten plea left pinned by the villagers of Tyneham to their church door in the dark days of the Second World War. "We have given up our homes where many of us lived for generations to help win the war to keep men free. We shall return one day," the note ended, poignantly, "and thank you for treating the village kindly."

That return was to remain forever a dream. Evicted by the Army in 1943 so that their homes and lands could be used for training soldiers, the villagers of Tyneham never returned to the lonely valley in the Dorset downs. Lulworth Ranges absorbed the place and threw a cloak of inadmissibility over it. Nowadays only the school, church and great barn of Tyneham remain in good repair, open to the public on certain days. Tyneham's cottages and Post Office are empty shells whose former inhabitants stare from old photographs in the wall displays; the great manor house crumbles unseen and out of bounds among the trees.

We wandered around the skeleton village with dairyman Walter Candy, shepherd James Lucas and a ghostly host of pinafored children and hobnailed farmworkers at our elbow, then made for the grassy track that undulates along the crest of Whiteway Hill, with stunning views west along the chalky, fossil-filled cliffs of Dorset's Jurassic Coast.

A breeze rippled the grassheads like an invisible hand stroking a head of newly-washed hair. We teetered down the steep slope below the ramparts of Flower's Barrow hill fort, and had a quick, ecstatic plunge in the semi-circle of sea under the sloping cliffs of Worbarrow Bay. A stiff climb out of the cove and we were looking down on the Tyneham valley, its green slopes untouched by the intensive agriculture of the past seventy years, its trees concealing their secrets.

The submerged rock ledges far below off Brandy Bay shimmered orange, black and jade green. In the sea haze the long wedge of Portland seemed not so much a peninsula as an island detached from the shore. A last look east to the much-quarried freestone cliffs under St Alban's Head, and we were bowling back to Tyneham along the ridge of Tyneham Cap where sparrowhawks hovered on quivering wings, and a croaky old raven was teaching formation flying to this year's youngsters.

Start & finish Tyneham car park, near East Lulworth, Dorset (OS ref SY882802)

Getting there Road: Tyneham is signposted from East Lulworth (B3070 from A352 near Wareham; or B3071 from Wool, 4½ miles west of Wareham on A352)

Walk (8 miles, moderate/strenuous, OS Explorer OL15): From Tyneham church, track north (yellow markers/YM) to top of down (882810). Left along crest of down (YM) for 1 mile to Flower's Barrow hill fort. At South West Coast Path marker stone, hairpin left (866805); follow Coast Path east for 3 miles via Worbarrow Bay and Brandy Bay to Kimmeridge Bay. At 'Kimmeridge View Point' board and flagpole on right, turn left (904792), following YMs to top of down (905802); left/west for 1¼ miles. Opposite Tyneham, fork right (883797) and follow YMs back to car park.

Lunch Picnic

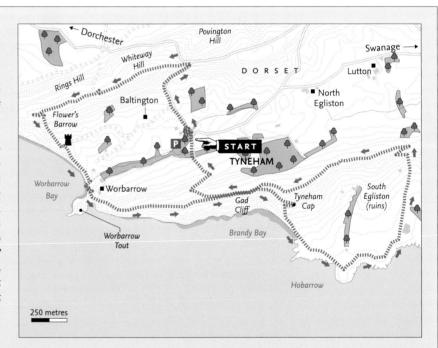

More information Lulworth Range walks and Tyneham are open most weekends and some school holidays/bank holidays (01929 404819; tynehamopc.org.uk). Dorchester TIC (01305 267992; visitdorset.com), visitengland.com, satmap.com, ramblers.org.uk, tynehamvillage.org

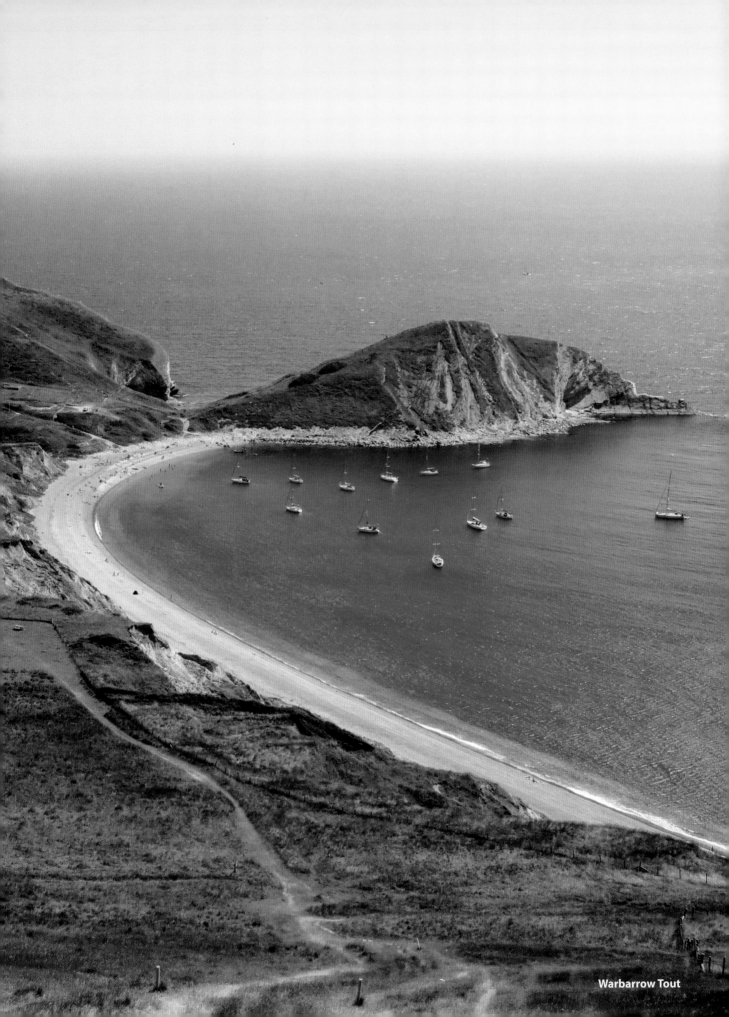

Warbarrow Tout

Sherborne Park & Oborne

DORSET

Sherborne, one of Dorset's most beautiful towns, is full of buildings made of that very distinctive, iron-rich golden limestone called hamstone. Medieval masons worked it to sublime effect in the delicately constructed chapels and lacy fan vaulting of the abbey church that stands at the heart of the town.

From the slopes of Sherborne Park I looked across the meadows to the town's twin castles, an old Norman stronghold in picturesque ruin beyond the trees, its Tudor counterpart beside the long lake. The original lodge, built in brick by Sir Walter Raleigh in 1594 after Queen Elizabeth I had gifted him the land, was enfolded by grand wings added later.

Lit by strong sunshine and framed in fat white cumulus clouds, it looked altogether splendid in its setting of broad parkland studded with magnificent specimen oaks. I imagined Raleigh's ghost sitting smoking, as it's apparently in the habit of doing, in the stone seat that he installed by the lake, puffing out an extra cloud of Virginia-scented satisfaction on this lovely morning.

I walked across the heathy common, where homeless Poles were housed after the Second World War in the cramped and basic Nissen huts of a former field hospital. "People were all in the same circumstances," writes Teresa Stolarczyk-Marshall, who lived there as a child, "in a strange country where they could not speak the language. So they rallied round helping one another. People were very patriotic, observing their traditions and bringing their children up in a Polish spirit. Haydon Park became Little Poland."

I turned north through the parkland trees, looking over the cottage at Pinfold Farm towards the green cap of Crackmore Wood. A quiet moment in a golden stone chancel by the roaring A30, all that's left of the sixteenth-century church of St Cuthbert (one of the last churches built before the Reformation); and then a saunter through Oborne village between hedges netted with pungent-smelling hop bines. The old green road of Underdown Lane dropped me back on to the outskirts of Sherborne, and a path through the sunlit meadows by the River Yeo led easily to the station once more.

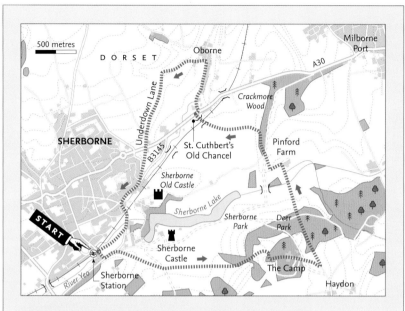

Start & finish Sherborne railway station DT9 3NB (OS ref ST641162)

Getting there Train: to Sherborne. Bus: Services 57, 58 from Yeovil. Road: A30 from Yeovil or Shaftesbury; park at railway station.

Walk (6 miles, easy grade, OS Explorer 129): Cross railway, then B3145; through kissing gate opposite, left on track through Sherborne Park for 1½ miles (yellow arrows/YAs), past thatched lodge (660161) and The Camp depot (665161). In another 400m, left (north) at YA (669160) across field, through Deer Park wood and on to Pinford Farm drive (664172). Dogleg left-right; continue north through ornate gateposts (662173), then west side of wood. West out of wood through kissing gate (661176); across 3 fields (YAs), under railway (654178) to cross A30 at St Cuthbert's Old Chancel (653178). Lane to Oborne; left (655185) past Oborne church; Underdown Lane west, then south to cross A30 (647174). Ahead to farmyard and crossroads beyond (646170). Right along B3145; in 300m, left (644168, 'Dorchester, Blandford') along New Road. Cross railway and river; right (645166, fingerpost) through fields to station.

Lunch Oliver's Coffee House, Cheap Street, Sherborne DT9 3PU (01935 815005; oliverscoffeehouse.co.uk) or the excellent Station Café (01935 814111)

More information Sherborne TIC (01935 815341; sherbornetown.com), visit-dorset.com, visitengland.com, ramblers.org.uk, satmap.co.uk, Haydon Park Polish camp (polishresettlementcampsintheuk.co.uk/haydonpark1)

Blagdon Lake

SOMERSET

A male blackbird, yellow bill a-tremble, was making tentative inquiries of a drab brown female on a bough in the New Inn's garden as I started down the hill towards Blagdon Lake. The celandines were still curled tight and green along the high-banked lane, but there was a breath of warmth in the low sun, more than Somerset had felt for the past three months.

For well over a century Blagdon Lake water has been piped to Bristol's taps, ten miles over the hills to the north. Crossing the broad dam of the lake, I heard the subdued roar of the flood-engorged weir where snowmelt and swollen streams were sending their waters surging down the spillway. I followed the fishermen's path through the trees along the north bank of the lake, then struck out across fields thick with the winter's mud to reach the lane by Bellevue Farm — well named for its prospect of water and hills.

A little way up the lane I was pulled up short by the sight of a large badger squatting on its haunches in a cottage garden. It shouldn't have been out of its sett this early in the year, and it certainly should have fled at sight of me, instead of fixing me with a sleepy stare. It was I who walked away, leaving the badger master of the place.

The southward views grew better and better as the lane rose, until at the top of Awkward Hill I looked down over fields patchworked with green grass and red ploughland, out across the whole expanse of Blagdon Lake to the steep wall of the Mendip Hills beyond in early afternoon shadow.

The late winter light, already beginning to diminish, lay softly on the lake with a blurred sheen more like watered silk than the hard mirrored effect of a summer day's sunshine.

Down by the lake once more, I squelched towards Blagdon over boggy meadows where wild geese went lumbering into the air at my approach, trumpeting reprovingly. It was almost time for them to be off to their mating and brood-rearing, 2000 miles north of these green Somerset fields. Out on the lake the looking-glass surface suddenly fractured as a sturdy body broke into sight from below with a diamond-like spray of droplets. The great crested grebe bobbed and bellied in his own ripples, long beak held low, his nape crest half erected. In a month's time he and his mate would be engaging in the intricate rituals of their courtship dance, all advances, retreats and sinuous writhings like a pair of hot tango dancers.

Back at the New Inn, sitting on the terrace with a cheddar ploughman's and a kingly view over the lake, I heard the love-struck blackbird — or possibly another like him — still singing for spring.

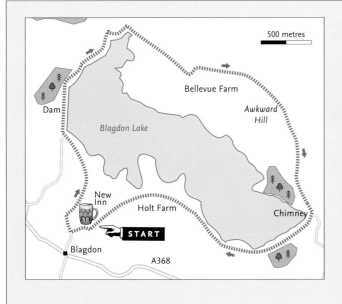

Start & finish New Inn, Blagdon BS40 7SB (OS ref ST505589)

Getting there Road: M5 Jct 21; A371, A368; left in Blagdon down Church Street to New Inn

Walk (5½ miles, easy grade, OS Explorers 141, 154): From New Inn, walk down Park Lane, along the reservoir dam wall. On the far side, go right (504603) beside reservoir for ½ mile, then forward (511608) to Bellevue Farm at West Town (517604). Left for 10m to road, right for ¾ mile; 300m past the top of Awkward Hill (nameplate), right over stile (527600), following path over stiles, down across fields to road (529593). Left for 250m; just before industrial chimney, right (531591 – footpath sign) into damp fields. Follow the footpath close to the reservoir for 1½ miles; 500m past Holt Farm, bear left (510591) on an uphill path back to Blagdon.

Lunch New Inn (01761 462475; newinnblagdon.co.uk) – superb lake views from garden; NB no children under 10 indoors

More informaton Wells TIC (01749 671770; wellssomerset.com), visitsomerset.co.uk

Chelynch and Fosse Way

SOMERSET

A cold north Somerset wind blew like a trumpet across the Mendip Hills as we set out from Chelynch. It's all farming country round here. A couple of porkers came snuffling to the gate at Newman Street Farm, and a bunch of peahens fled down the lane, their speckly grey and white bodies bent forward as they scurried between the hedges like plump little old ladies heading for a bring-and-buy.

We crossed the fields by way of proper Mendip stone stiles, big slabs of limestone a farmer can hop over but a sheep can't. Three Ashes Lane took us west in a tunnel of trees where fallen crab apples littered the trackway, already rotting from blotchy green to soft toffee browns and blacks. At a dip in the lane stood a mighty cast-iron contraption, all bolts and cogs and great spoked wheels.

"It's an early kind of cultivator," explained its owner, emerging from a shed under the hazels. "You'd have a steam traction engine at either side of the field, hauling this thing from one to the other and back again on a rope as it ploughed the soil."

How cumbersome such a monster looked to our modern eyes; but how our forefathers must have blessed its power, its capacity to spare them sore bones and wrenched muscles, back in the dawn of mechanised agriculture.

At a junction of lanes we turned south down the Fosse Way. The military highway where Roman soldiers marched and grumbled is now a beautiful leafy lane, cutting across the grain of the Somerset landscape. In Beacon Hill Wood we veered away from the old road and up through a giant's graveyard of fallen beech boughs to where a standing stone rose at the apex of the hill, already ancient when the legionaries marched by.

Near Shepton Mallet the graceful curve of the Charlton Viaduct, pierced by 27 arches, carried the trackbed of the long-defunct Somerset & Dorset Railway across the infant River Sheppey. Walking back over Ingsdons Hill to Chelynch the view broadened again, north to the green swell of Mendip, south across the green heart of rural Somerset.

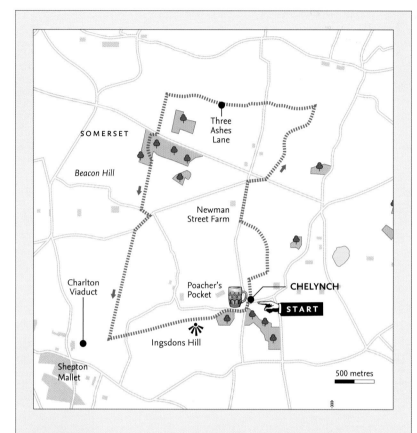

Start & finish Poacher's Pocket PH, Chelynch, Shepton Mallet, Somerset BA4 4PY (OS ref ST649439)

Getting there Road: A37 (Bristol) or A367 (Bath) towards Shepton Mallet. 200m after they merge (2 miles from Shepton Mallet), left at top of Long Hill (signed 'Wagon & Horses') along Old Frome Road. In 1¼ miles, right at the Wagon & Horses PH (signed 'Doulting') to the Poacher's Pocket PH.

Walk (6½ miles, easy/moderate, OS Explorer 142): Chelynch—Newman Street (652444) — King's Road (648450). Right to first crossroads (649455); right to cross Old Frome Road (652455; fast road, so take care). Field path (stiles, yellow arrows) to Three Ashes Lane (658464). Left along lane for 1¼ miles (crossing road at Three Ashes – 652464) to Fosse Way (639466). Left along Fosse Way; cross Old Frome Road (638461); Fosse Way through Beacon Wood to road (636451). Left to T-junction; right; in 200m, left (635449) along Fosse Way for ¾ mile. Pass barn on right (632437); in 200m, left (631435; green arrow, East Mendip Way (EMW); cross Bodden Lane (634436); Ingsdons Hill (638437); EMW to Chelynch.

Lunch Poacher's Pocket (01749 880220; poacherspocketchelynch.co.uk) – good food and friendly atmosphere

More information Shepton Mallet TIC (01749 345258; visitsheptonmallet.co.uk), visitsomerset.co.uk, ramblers.org.uk, satmap.com

The Quantock Hills
SOMERSET

A good friend came up with this tempting route through the Quantock Hills. A sight of the sea, a proper draught of moorland air: it was just what we wanted. Nine of us set off from Beacon Hill, dropping steeply under sweet chestnut trees to Weacombe. The combe sides rose steeply, flushed purple by thousands of foxgloves. From the depths of Bicknoller Combe we looked up to see the western sky a slaty blur of rain. Soon it hit, and soon it passed, leaving us shaking off water.

Up on Black Ball Hill the wind carried a faint sharp hooting. A steam train on the West Somerset Railway was panting its way down the valley towards Minehead, but locomotive and carriages stayed hidden from sight in the steep green countryside.

We sat on the heather among Bronze Age burial mounds to eat our picnic with an imperial view all round, north over the Severn Sea to Wales, east to the camel hump of Brent Knoll, west into Exmoor's heights. By the time we'd serenaded the skylarks with mouth organ tunes and descended among the trees of Slaughterhouse Combe, the sun was backlighting oak leaves and pooling on bracken banks where bilberries and star mosses winked with raindrops.

Thunder ripped across the sky, a last sulk of the weather gods, as we walked west up Sheppard's Combe. A bank of sundews lay pearled with rain, their tiny pale flowers upraised on long stalks above sticky scarlet leaves. One minute blob of a sundew's insect-trapping mucilage is capable of stretching up to a million times its own length.

We climbed to Bicknoller Post on its wide upland with a wonderful prospect northwest to the stepped flank of Porlock Hill and a sea full of shadows and streaks of light. Our steps quickened along the homeward path — not to unload nine souls full of immortal verse, but to beat the clock into Holford by car for the cream tea we suddenly knew we'd earned.

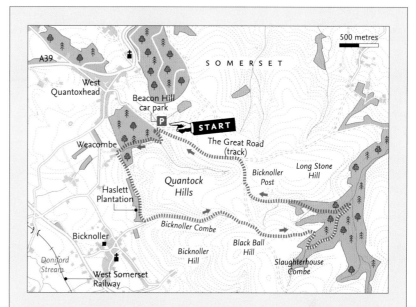

Start & finish Beacon Hill car park, Staple Plain, Hill Lane, West Quantoxhead, Somerset TA4 4DQ approx. (OS ref ST117411)

Getting there Road: M5 Jct 24; A38 then A39 (Bridgwater-Minehead); at West Quantoxhead, just past Windmill Inn, left (Bicknoller). In 350m, left up Hill Lane ('Staple Plain'). Drive for ⅔ mile to car park at end of track.

Walk (5½ miles, moderate, OS Explorer 140): From southwest corner of car park, left downhill (green NT arrow) through trees. At bottom (117408), right to cottage at Weacombe (111408). Left ('Quantock Greenway') through gate; south past Haslett Plantation. In ⅔ mile, arrow points right at junction (115399) but go left here up Bicknoller Combe for 1 mile, climbing to junction of tracks (130398). Ahead on stony track; in 200m, fork left along grass track over Black Ball Hill and descend to bottom of Slaughterhouse Combe (143401). Left (west) for 1 mile to Bicknoller Post (128403). Right (north) for 300m to Great Road track; left to car park.

Lunch picnic, Tea Combe House Hotel, Holford TA5 1RZ (01278 741382; combehouse.co.uk)

Accommodation Rising Sun, West Bagborough TA4 3EF (01823 432575; risingsuninn.info) – excellent pub

More information Taunton Visitor Centre (01823 340470; visitsomerset.co.uk), visitengland.com, satmap.com, ramblers.org.uk

Southstoke and Cam Valley

SOMERSET

The houses of Southstoke, built of the same pale silver and cream oolitic limestone as those in Bath, just over the hill, were lightly dusted with powder snow on this cold winter's morning. Over the porch of the Church of St James the Great, a carving of the much-travelled apostle showed him staring with seer's eyes from the shelter of a pilgrim's scallop shell. With one shoulder bare and a crust of last night's snow for a collar, the hero of Santiago looked a little under-dressed for the weather. Not so the two young girls making snow pancakes outside the church; they were kitted out like crimson-cheeked polar explorers.

From the ridge beyond Southstoke a wonderful vista opened out southwards over deeply cut valleys frosted to lemon yellow and ice green. A smoky grey sky hung low, telling of more snow on the way. I pushed my hands deeper into my pockets and went crunching down the slopes of Horsecombe Vale. The cattle in the fields moved gingerly, sensing the hollows below the ice lids over their own hoof pocks. Warmed by their sweet, cloudy breath, I skittered down through the woods to Tucking Mill.

The tree-knotted track bed of the former Somerset & Dorset Railway led south to Midford. The clanking steam engines of the S&D had carried me to school in the long ago, and I used to look out as we passed over Midford viaduct to see the abandoned tracks of the Somerset Coal Canal and the Cam Valley Railway snaking below. Although the canal was killed off when the railway opened before the First World War, it is the graceful structures of the old waterway that claim attention as you walk the Cam Valley today — a packhorse bridge isolated in a field, and three long, narrow lock basins of beautiful silvery Bath stone, empty and ivy-strangled along a hedge. The bigger, blunter instrument of the abandoned railway eventually came striding in on a tall embankment, shouldering the canal aside into the woods and hurrying me on to Combe Hay.

A proper old lane, stony and tree-lined, led up behind the Wheatsheaf Inn to the crest of the ridge and the field path back to Southstoke. I looked out over whitened fields and blackened woods, a Breughelian scene already half obscured by newly falling snow.

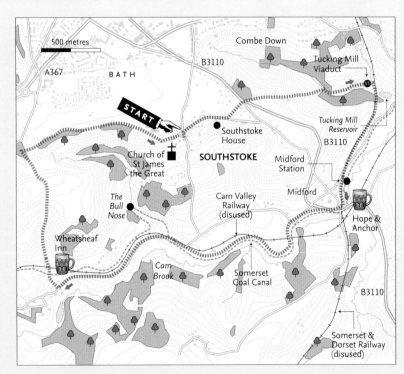

Start & finish Southstoke, Bath BA2 7DU (OS ref ST747613). NB Please park considerately in Southstoke's narrow lane.

Getting there Road: Southstoke is signed from B3110 between Combe Down and Midford

Walk (5½ miles, moderate grade, OS Explorer 155): From church, head east over crossroads. Just past Southstoke House, left through kissing gate (fingerpost) across field. Cross B3110. Descend fields of Horsecombe Vale (yellow arrows/YA); cross brook; follow path to Wessex Water plant. Right; just beyond Tucking Mill viaduct, right up steps (fingerpost); follow old railway to Midford station. Right to road; left through viaduct; cross B3110 (take care!); descend steps opposite Hope & Anchor PH (fingerpost); right along Cam Valley old railway and canal path for 2 miles to Wheatsheaf Inn, Combe Hay. Right beside inn, up lane for ¾ mile to road; right on path (fingerpost) to Southstoke.

Lunch Hope & Anchor Inn, Midford BA2 7DD (01225 832296; hopeandanchormidford.co.uk), Wheatsheaf Inn, Combe Hay BA2 7EG (01225 833504; wheatsheafcombehay.com)

More information Bath Visitor Information Centre (0844 8475256; visitbath.co.uk), ramblers.org.uk

Westhay Moor
SOMERSET

Nothing glows like the skin of a nice ripe cider apple — unless it's the cheeks of a nice ripe cider drinker. You're likely to meet your fair share of both on the Somerset Levels around this time of year, when the windfalls are lying on the ground and so are unwary cider-samplers.

My friends Alan and Joy have the best of views from their house on the ridge in Panborough village: the green whaleback of Mendip, and a glorious prospect over the Levels, grazing moors dented with old flooded peat diggings, bristly with reedbeds, their meadows divided by ditches known as rhynes. On the moors we walked Dagg's Lane Drove over Westhay Moor in a tunnel of willows, Megan the dog chasing sticks in the lush verges.

After centuries of peat digging, Westhay Moor has exactly what wild birds need — open fleets of sheltered water, wet alder woods, reedbeds to hide and nest in, seeds and insects to feed on. We were here a little too early in the afternoon to witness Westhay's most famous spectacle, the dusk sky-dance of a million wintering starlings which floats a thickening and lengthening veil of densely packed birds across half the sky. But from one of the hides we watched a mysterious large bird — not a great northern diver, not a great crested grebe — splashing and diving, lone lord of its reedy pool. A slight movement beyond a screen of alder boughs, and five well-grown cygnets with their parent swans sailed gracefully out of sight.

Turning back up Parson's Drove, we watched a leaden block of rain marching east across the Levels, with a most brilliant rainbow stamped in a perfect arc across it. Such moments mark a walk indelibly in the memory.

Up on the ridge again we followed the lane through Mudgley, past Land's End and Wilkins's cider farm. I've spent a few drowsy afternoons in that fragrant dark cider shed watching Roger Wilkins draw a drop of sweet, a drop of dry from his barrels, blending them into a nectar to suit one's particular palate. Temptation? You just bet. But Roger must have been elsewhere this evening. We walked on, vowing to return, heading along the sloping fields towards home, with the Levels glinting below and Glastonbury Tor intensely sunlit on the south-west horizon, washed in pure cidrous gold, a Somerset Shangri-la.

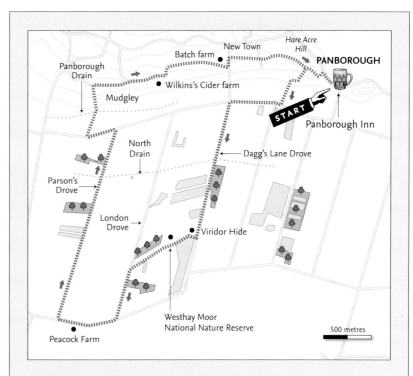

Start & finish Panborough Inn, Panborough, near Wedmore, Somerset BA5 1PN (OS ref ST 471456).

Getting there Bus (webberbus.com) Service 670 (Wells to Burnham-on-Sea). Road: On B3139 between Wells andWedmore

Walk (6½ miles, easy grade, OS Explorer 141): Panborough Inn — right up B3139; in 100m, left up drive; right by house (yellow arrow/YA). In 250m, left (469457, YA) downhill — footbridge (467455) — road (466454). Right; left (461454) down Dagg's Lane Drove. Cross North Drain (459448); in half a mile, left past Viridor Hide (457440) to London Drove (450437). Road (448432) — Peacock Farm — right up Parson's Drove (442432-449451). Left— right (445450) across Panborough Drain, up to road (446456). Right — just past Wilkins's cider farm, left uphill (454456). Path east to Batch Farm (459458)—New Town (465458) —Hare Acre Hill— Panborough Inn.

Left for 300m; right through metal walkers' gate (445450, yellow arrow/YA). Follow field edge, over footbridge (446453), right through gate in hedge; left up hedge for 3 fields (YA) to road (446456). Right through Mudgley for ½ mile. Just past Wilkins's cider farm on right (454456), left (YA, 'Moor View Cottage') up path. In 150m, right over stile (454458). On into dip ahead; follow same contour of hill with hedge on left for ⅓ mile. Near Batch Farm, take right-hand (lower) of 2 gates (459458, YA). Cross field to Dagg's Lane. Right for 1½ miles down Dagg's Lane, then Dagg's Lane Drove, to car park.

Lunch Panborough Inn: (01934-712554; panboroughinn.co.uk). Wilkins's Cider Farm, Mudgley, BS28 4TU (01934-712385; wilkinscider.com): 10-8 Mon-Sat, 10-1 Sun. Westhay Moor Nature Reserve: somersetwildlife.org/westhay_moor.html

More information Wells TIC (01749-671770; visitsomerset.co.uk); ramblers.org.uk; satmap.com

Castle Combe and North Wraxall

WILTSHIRE

In theory you might find a prettier and cosier spot than Castle Combe as a starting point for a cold winter's walk, but in practice, no chance. So I informed myself, anyway, as sloth fought with sense on the doorstep of the warm and cheery Castle Inn Hotel.

Once out under the blue Wiltshire sky, wandering among the gables and tall chimneys, mullioned windows and Cotswold stone roofs of medieval cottages and woolmasters' fine houses, everything was just perfect. The sun struck gleams from the creamy oolitic walls and sparkled in the ripples of the By Brook as it gurgled under miniature bridges along the village street.

I batted my cold hands together and followed the Macmillan Way down the valley, walking between whitethorn hedges where redwings were stripping the berries. The woods were full of dark brown bracket fungi with white frilly edges, like Belgian chocolates scattered prematurely by a careless Father Christmas. A grove of tall old beeches stood in their own crisp litter, their roots gripping the slope like arthritic fingers, the sun painting the smooth trunks in silver verticals.

Two men were burning tree cuttings in a pall of blue smoke. "Just waiting for the fire to die down so we can cook a bit of breakfast," one said.

"Yeah, proper smoky bacon," added his mate with dreamy relish.

A snarl of speeding cars on the main road at Ford, and then the green rutted lane of the Old Coach Road where express four-in-hand stagecoaches once jolted from Bath to Chippenham at 8 miles an hour. Today? One girl walking her dog, a couple of rabbits and a millennium of ghostly travellers at my elbow.

The high-perched houses of North Wraxall looked down from their ridge as I followed a lane that crossed the Romans' Fosse Way high road and slipped into the valley of the Broadmead Brook.

A muddy old bridleway led back east toward Castle Combe beside the twisting brook, past a low clapper bridge whose big decking slabs were supported on sturdy, moss-jacketed piers. Yellow-streaked siskins flocked in the alders, chittering as they picked at the seed cones, and the dipping sun sent a few last bars of silver slanting across the water from which an evening steam was already rising.

Start & finish Castle Inn Hotel, Castle Combe, Wilts SN14 7HN (OS ref ST842772)

Getting there Bus: Service 35 (wiltshire.gov.uk) from Chippenham. Road: M4 (Jct 18); signed from B4039 to village car park

Walk (7½ miles, moderate grade, OS Explorer 156): South down village street; past South Cottage, left over footbridge (841768); follow Macmillan Way (MW arrows) for 1¾ miles via Long Dean mill (851756) to A420 at Ford (843748). Right; past church, right (841749) along Old Coach Road for 1¼ miles to road (822747). Right through North Wraxall. Pass church; right (818750; 'Castle Combe'). In ⅓ mile, left (817757), following yellow arrows/YAs across two roads, then fields for ¾ mile to road (812770). Right along bridleway to road (813771). Right; in 150m left (fingerpost) along bridleway through Broadmead Brook valley via road (823769) for 1 mile to go through gate (829773) by brook. Don't cross clapper bridge; in 30m, right (YA) for ¼ mile to Nettleton Mill (833775). Right through tall iron gate; continue to golf course. Right; left across bridge (838776); right to Castle Combe.

Lunch Castle Inn Hotel, Castle Combe (01249 783030; castle-inn.info) – old inn of nooks and crannies

More information Chippenham TIC (01249 665970; visitwiltshire.co.uk), ramblers.org.uk, satmap.com

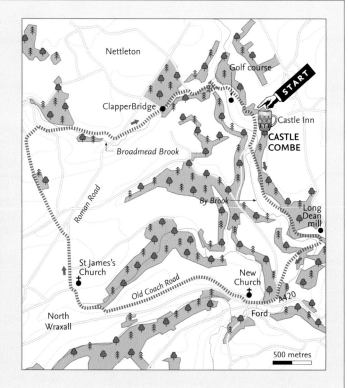

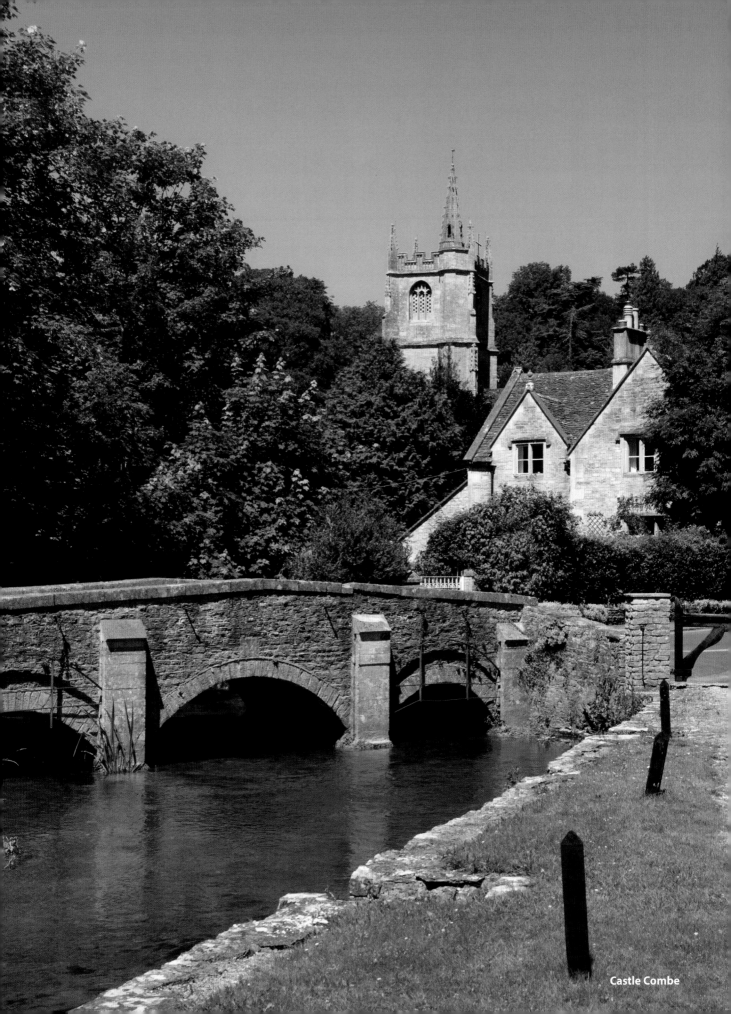

Castle Combe

North Meadow

WILTSHIRE

The infant River Thames links Gloucestershire to Wiltshire at the outer edge of the Cotswolds, in low-lying gravelly country. Setting off along the towpath of the reed-choked old Thames & Severn Canal, we marvelled at how dozens of unsightly old gravel pits have been transformed into the wide, tree-hung lakes of the Cotswold Water Park.

This is a fine example of a conservation landscape; and down beyond the hamlet of Cerney Wick there's another in the lush hundred-acre grassland of North Meadow. This is a beautiful wide hayfield, fringed with greening willows and filled with flowers; a habitat that comes into its own each springtime. Entering the meadow from the old canal, we walked among spatters of wild flowers — golden buttons of dandelions and buttercups, creamy yellow cowslips, the pale blues and pinks of milkmaids, which some call lady's smock or cuckoo flower. And everywhere the large drooping heads of snake's head fritillaries, singly, in pairs or in loose clumps, bobbing and trembling in the wind on their dark red stems.

We got down on our knees, as though in obeisance, to enjoy a close-up look at one of Britain's rarest and most spectacular plants. Some of the downward-hanging flowers were white with green spots inside; the majority were a dusky, deep rose-pink, speckled within in pale pink and rich purple, like stained-glass bells filtering the sunlight. It was astonishing to see them in such numbers — over a million in this one large meadow.

Snake's head fritillaries are particularly choosy about where they colonise. They are nationally scarce — but not here. North Meadow, meticulously managed by Natural England, is home to 80 per cent of the entire British population of these remarkable flowers. The Thames, no wider than a stream, dimples through the meadow, its waters slow and thick with nutritious earth particles, which are spread across the land by winter floods. The silt-enriched grass is left uncut until midsummer or later, by which time the fritillaries and all the other plants have had time to set the seeds of the next generation.

We enjoyed a slice of lemon and lavender cake in the Fritillary Tea Room on the outskirts of Cricklade, and then strolled slowly back through the flowery meadows and along an old railway line, where primroses grow thickly and the breeze carries hints of horses, cattle and that indefinable breath of spring in full flow.

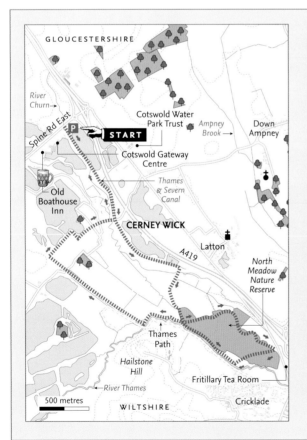

Start & finish Cotswold Gateway Centre car park, Spine Road, South Cerney, Glos GL7 5TL (OS ref SU072971)

Getting there Bus: Service 51 (Swindon-Cirencester). Road: M4 Jct 15; A419 towards Cirencester; B4696 towards South Cerney; in 200m, left into car park (free).

Walk (6½ miles, easy, OS Explorer 169): Past Cotswold Gateway centre to canal; right on towpath for 1½ miles to Latton Basin (088954). Right down road; right along track past lock keeper's cottage; on south along disused canal for 650m. Through gate (087948); left through kissing gate/KG; clockwise circuit of North Meadow, returning to KG. Thames Path on left bank of Thames; in 500m, right along old railway. In ¾ mile, pass under viaduct; in another 250m, right (070956, KG) through fields, crossing two roads. At 2nd road, ahead past Crown Inn to canal (079960); left to car park.

Lunch Old Boathouse Inn, Cotswold Gateway GL7 5FP (01285 864111; oldboathousepub.co.uk), Fritillary Tea Room, Thames Bridge, Cricklade (some weekends in April and May; crickladeinbloom.co.uk/fritillary_tea_room.html)

More information Cotswold Water Park (01793 752413; waterpark.org), North Meadow: Natural England (01452 813982; naturalengland.org.uk), visitengland.com, ramblers.org.uk, satmap.co.uk, Fritillary updates: crickladeinbloom.co.uk/fritillary_watch.html

Wansdyke, Avebury & Silbury Hill

WILTSHIRE

It was a brisk day over Wiltshire, brisker than you'd expect in early spring, with sheepy clouds scudding east and a cold nip under the blue sky. Avebury's stones were warm, though, as I walked a circuit among them — rough and warm to the touch, huge and amiable with their rugged, bear-like shapes sparkling in the sunlight. Unfathomable, as always, the motives of those who in 2000 BC mounded the great circular bank and trench that encloses present-day Avebury village, pairing off one hundred sarsen stones in male and female couples, and building two smaller circles to touch each other within the greater ring.

How much labour must such a work have expended? How much organisation of that 'primitive' society? Our medieval ancestors feared the stones, toppling some and leaving others to fall. One fourteenth-century barber-surgeon incurred the wrath of the stones for such vandalism; his skeleton was discovered under one of the largest in 1938, coins in his purse, scissors by his side. He'd been squashed flat as the great boulder slammed to earth before he could get out of the way.

Field paths led me out of Avebury through paddocks where horses grazed, flicking their tails against the flies. A cock crowed at Durran Farm as I followed a stony track rising for miles to the roof of the downs. The rhythmic crunch of flints under my boots, the sunshine, cold wind and the twitter of sparrows in the hedges combined to give a trance-like feel to the morning.

At the crest of the hills I followed the old ramparted ditch of Wansdyke above the broad flanks of the downs, enormous fields of ploughland and spring wheat all in geometric lines and malleable curves of white and green. Wind in the hair, sun on the cheeks, fantastic exhilaration as I strode out at the hub of a fifty-mile view. But the true focus of this walk lay in the valley of the River Kennet below — the flattened thimble of Silbury Hill.

I stood on the boulder-guarded mound of West Kennet Long Barrow and stared north at Silbury Hill. Why men constructed the long barrow around 3500 BC with its five compartments and its mighty guardian sarsens is clear enough — the dead had to be honoured. But that 40m (130ft)-high, flat-topped hillock with its hidden core of concentric chalk-block walls: what was that about? We'll never know — but we can imagine the feelings of awe that it invoked some 4750 years ago when it first stood dazzling white and dominant between the rolling downs.

Start & finish Avebury village car park, Wilts SN8 1RF (OS ref SU100697)

Getting there Bus: Service 49 (swindonbus.info), Swindon-Devizes. Road: Avebury is on A4361, 12 miles south of Swindon (M4, Jct 16)

Walk (11 miles, easy, OS Explorer 157): From car park, follow signs to stone circle. Walk the circuit of the stones; then follow minor road through village, passing church on right. Opposite Rectory gateway, right (099699) up lane; follow it to the left. Cross 2 footbridges; after second one, left (097698). Through gate (yellow arrow/YA); left along fence. Through gate (096696); immediately right through adjacent gate; up track past thatched cottage to cross road (095696). Pass noticeboard; follow tarred path to road opposite Rose Cottage (094695). Right for ⅓ mile; opposite farmyard, left (089692, 'bridleway') to cross A4361 (090691); on to cross A4 by Waggon & Horses Inn, Beckhampton (091689). Down steps from inn car park; follow road round right bend. Opposite Butler's Cottage, left (087688, 'bridleway') and follow track south for 1¾ miles to join stony track at 084658. In another 750m, just before Manor Farm cattle grid and gate, left (081652). In 150m, bear right and through gate ('Mid Wilts Way'). Follow Wansdyke ditch and bank east. In 1 mile, a broad track comes in on right; 150m before a complex of gates where track converges with Wansdyke, turn left through makeshift gateway in fence (099647, 'White Horse Trail').

Left to fence; follow it NE away from Wansdyke. In 1 mile dogleg right, then left through makeshift gate (109658); on with fence on right. In just over a mile, cross track and keep ahead past ruined barns (114675, 'bridleway') on grassy track. In 300m, left along track (114678); in 15m, right on hedged path; cross stile (YA) and follow left-hand hedge to cross road (110682). On (fingerpost) down fenced track. Cross stile, then follow fence. In ⅓ mile, under oak tree (105681, no waymark) left up field to West Kennet Long Barrow (105677) beyond skyline. Return to cross A4 (104684); take field path ('Avebury' fingerpost) to east of Silbury Hill. In 350m (103687), ignore stile on right, and go through gate and on beside river. At two-arch bridge, don't turn right across it (101689), but keep ahead through gates (blue arrows) to cross A4361 to car park.

Lunch Red Lion Inn, Avebury, Wilts SN8 1RF (01672 539266; oldenglishinns.co.uk).

More information Alexander Keiller Museum, Avebury Manor, shop, café etc contact National Trust (01672 539250; nationaltrust.org.uk/avebury)

Wootton Rivers

WILTSHIRE

I am sure Mary Poppins would declare Wootton Rivers "practically perfect". The little Wiltshire village lies snug under the downs on the edge of the Vale of Pewsey, all thatched roofs and red brick. Sparrows chitter in the thatch as we walk out under a milky blue sky and up along a green lane to the roof of the downs. Up there runs the ancient trackway known as Mud Lane — after recent rain we soon discover why — flanked by old mossy woodbanks and overhung by big beech and ash, and holly trees as substantial as well-grown sycamores. I become aware of a staring pair of eyes in the shadows of an oak, and make out the leafy face of the Green Man, venerable spirit of the greenwood, carved with wonderful skill into the stump of a broken-off bough. The artist has resisted the temptation to give him a jolly grinning countenance; instead he has an expression appropriate to his status as a woodland god, thoughtful, solemn and crafty.

Mud Lane runs out of the trees and over the nape of Martinsell Hill. The promontory down curls away like the flank of a great beast, dimpled with old pits that might have been medieval rabbit warrens, or maybe the clay delvings of the British potters who lived up here 2000 years ago, making their coarse grey Savernake ware for the Roman army. Nowadays cattle munch the downland grass, and walkers stop to sit and stare across the Vale of Pewsey to the far hills, one of southern England's most breathtaking views.

Below Martinsell Hill we follow a track across the high ramparts of the Giant's Grave, an Iron Age hill fort where autumn gentians tremble their glowing purple trumpet flowers in the wind. Here there is a view to challenge the Vale of Pewsey, more intimate but no less stunning, down into the secret cleft of Rainscombe, where a fine Georgian house lies among gold, scarlet and green trees like a promise of earthly delights. A slippery clay path brings us down into the Vale, and we follow the towpath of the Kennet & Avon Canal back to Wootton Rivers in the soft grey light of the autumn evening.

Start & finish Wootton Rivers village hall car park, near Marlborough, Wilts SN8 4NQ (SU197631)

Getting there Rail: Pewsey (⅔ mile from Pains Bridge on Kennet & Avon Canal). Bus: Bookable bus from/to Pewsey (not Sun, Bank Holidays) from/to Royal Oak PH (08456 525255, option 1; wiltshire.gov.uk/connect2wilts-pewsey-vale-guide.pdf). Road: M5 Jct 15; A346 through Marlborough; Wootton Rivers signposted to right in 3 miles.

Walk (8½ miles, moderate, OS Explorer 157): From car park, left past Royal Oak PH. In 200m, pass 'Tregarthen'; keep ahead (197634) up green lane. At top of rise (200642), left, then right ('Mid Wilts Way'/ MWW) to Mud Lane trackway (198646). Right for about 50m to see Green Man; return along Mud Lane. Follow MWW for 4¼ miles via road crossing (183645), Martinsell Hill (177642), left turn off Mud Lane by Withy Copse (171642), Giant's Grave (166632); cross Sunnyhill Lane (161623); follow green lane near Inlands Farm (164616) to Pains Bridge on Kennet & Avon Canal (165612). East along canal for 2½ miles to Bridge 108/lock (198629); cross canal to car park.

Lunch/accommodation Royal Oak PH, Wootton Rivers SN8 4NQ (01672 810322; wiltshire-pubs.co.uk) – friendly local

More information Devizes TIC (01380 800400; devizes.org.uk) visitengland.com, ramblers.org.uk

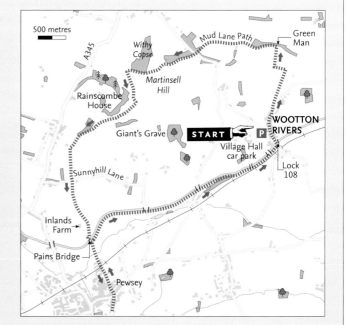

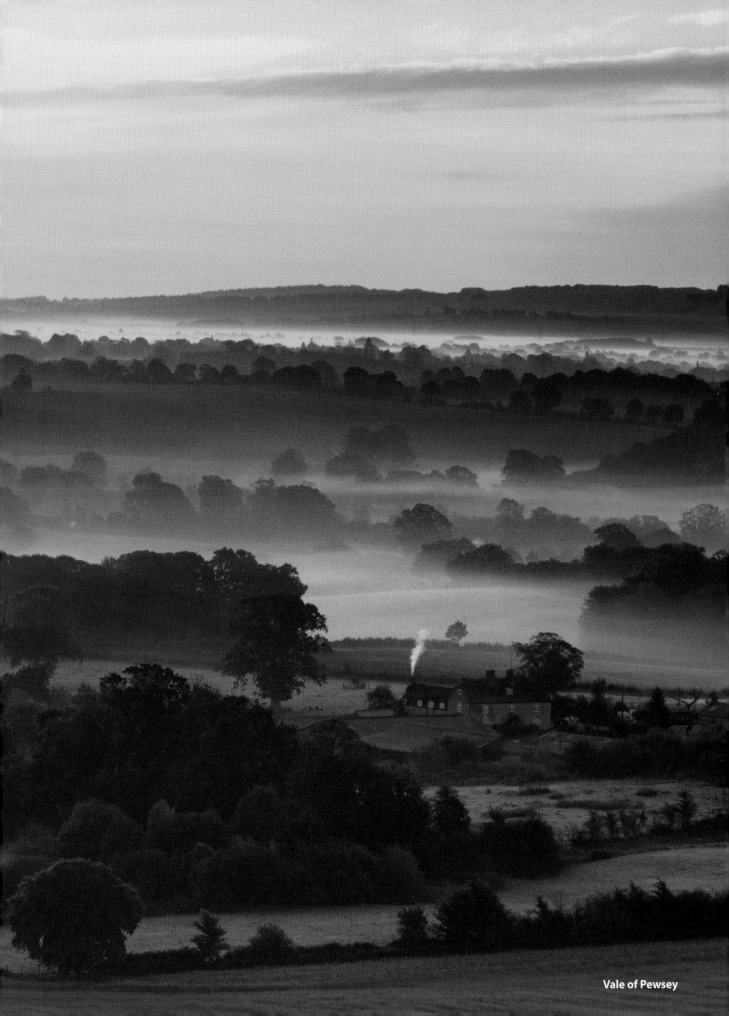

Vale of Pewsey

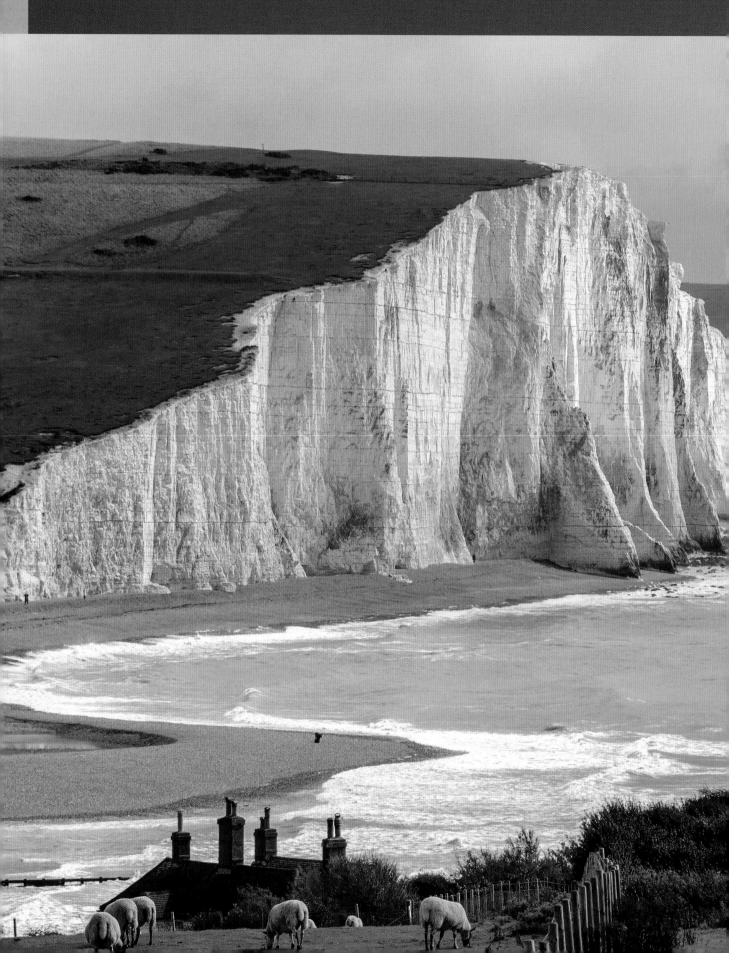

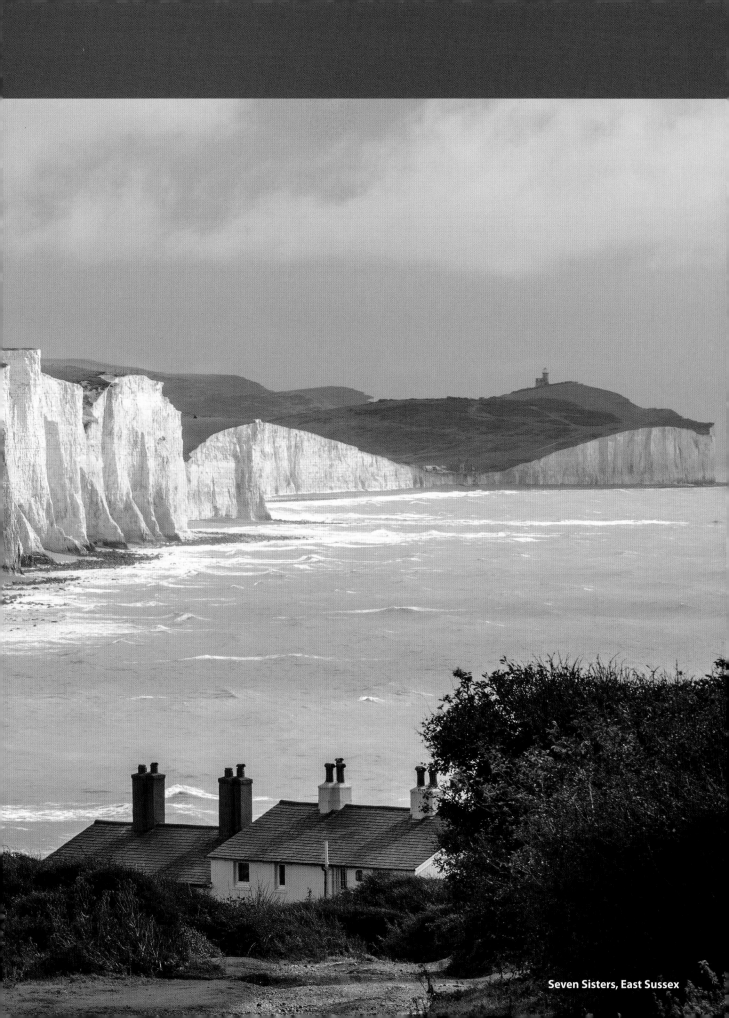

Seven Sisters, East Sussex

Charleston and Firle Beacon
EAST SUSSEX

In 1916 Vanessa Bell and Duncan Grant came to live at Charleston Farmhouse in the shadow of the Sussex downs. This bohemian London couple decorated the farmhouse walls and furniture with primitive designs. Charleston soon became a magnet for such Bloomsbury group illuminati as Virginia Woolf, David Garnett, John Maynard Keynes and EM Forster.

Walking over to Charleston, I was expecting a chocolate-box house in a picture-book setting. Instead, there were grunting tractors, workaday sheds and ordure-spattered dung spreaders busy in the fields around what is still a working farm. It was strange to be guided around the little rooms, with their vividly daubed walls and tables, Grant's nudes and acrobats, Bell's drooping flowers and dotted circle motifs, and then to step out into such a practical farming landscape.

What shapes the scene is the long green arm of the downs behind, enclosing the southern skyline in a simple and perfect undulation. Two young buzzards were riding low across the slopes, to pull up and hang with cat-like cries a couple of feet above the turf as they scanned for small life cowering there.

Up on the spine of the downs a cold wind came rushing in from the north, hammering at my face and tugging my beard like an impatient child. It was quite a prospect: north for many miles over the wooded hollows of the Sussex Weald, south to the spindly arms of Newhaven Harbour embracing the sea.

I pushed on into the wind to the hummock of the long barrow on Firle Beacon, and then found a steep chalk track that descended a slope seamed with pale wrinkles of erosion, like the forehead of an elephant. A fine flint wall accompanied me back to Firle, one of those well-kept estate villages where all seems right with the world.

Peter Owen Jones, vicar of Firle, writes lyrically of his downland walks. Outside St Peter's Church I found a tree festooned in prayer ribbons; inside, a Tree of Life window by John Piper. Its vivid pinks and yellows lit the cloud-shadowed vestry more brightly than any painted room in the Bloomsbury farmhouse across the fields.

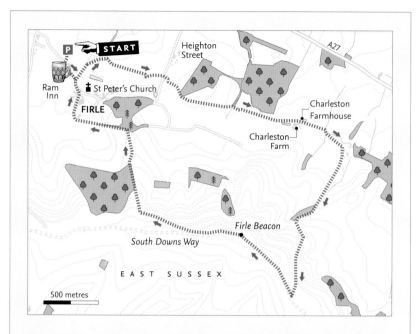

Start & finish Firle village car park, East Sussex BN8 6NS approx (OS ref TQ469074)

Getting there Bus: Service 125 (01903 690025; compass-travel.co.uk), Lewes-Alfriston. Road: Firle is signposted off A27 between Lewes and Eastbourne.

Walk (5 miles, moderate, OS Explorer 123): From car park walk to Ram Inn. Left along street; left at post office (470071) down lane, through gate. Follow track across parkland. In 200m, right up roadway; in 50m, left at post, aiming for flint house halfway along edge of wood ahead. Cross road at cottage (478073); through iron gate; follow bridleway through shank of wood (480071), on over fields to pass Charleston Farm (491069). In 200m, right (493068) along concrete track. At barns (494067), bear right, following track towards downs. In 550m, cross track (492062); on in tunnel of trees; through gate (490060, blue arrow/BA). Bear left up track to top of downs. Right (490054) along South Downs Way to trig pillar on Firle Beacon (485059). In 300m, through gate (482059); in 150m, fork right off SDW, descending path for ¾ mile to T-junction (475068); left beside wall to Firle.

Lunch/accommodation Ram Inn, Firle BN8 6NS (01273 858222; raminn.co.uk)

More information Charleston Farmhouse (charleston.org.uk; 01323 811265 – open March-Oct), Peter Owen Jones *Pathlands – Tranquil Walks Through Britain* (ISBN: 978-1846044434), visitengland.com, satmap.com, ramblers.org.uk

Friston Forest and the Seven Sisters
EAST SUSSEX

The immaculately kept East Sussex village of East Dean, beautifully set up for walkers, lies just inland of the Seven Sisters cliffs at the heart of a superb coast-and-countryside landscape. Ramblers know they'll be welcome at the cosy old Tiger Inn and the Hiker's Rest teashop on the village green, the hub of a network of footpaths. I chose a circuit that would thread woodland, downs and cliffs together, and set out early from the Tiger into a red dawn.

"Morning," said a woman by Friston duckpond, her breath smoking in the cold air. "Saw you yesterday up on the downs, didn't I? Hope you enjoy your walk."

Down in the valley below, ancient Friston Place lay low, pink-faced and many-gabled among beech trees where rooks were cawing lustily. Building low, I noticed; portent of a rainy summer.

Friston Forest sighed gently in the morning wind. A great spotted woodpecker rattled a hollow tree, a pair of racehorses went drumming by like ghosts in the mist on Friston Hill. Sunk in the woods, the medieval rectory and church at West Dean gleamed in dew-wet flint. A long flight of steps, the crest of a hill, and I was looking down over one of England's classic views—the extravagant snake bends of the Cuckmere River sinuating its way seaward through a dead flat littoral between great curves of downland. Their tall chimneys silhouetted against a pale wintry sea, coastguard cottages stood isolated at the brink of the Cuckmere Haven cliffs.

Foxhole Farm, all flint walls and brick-red roofs, lay tucked into a fold of the downs. Beyond the farm the South Downs Way ribboned east along the furrowed brows of the Seven Sisters. Far ahead, the promontory cliff of Belle Tout displayed an elliptical grimace of white chalk like the baleen plates in the mouth of a right whale. At the feet of the cliffs fresh falls of chalk lay scattered, staining the shallows a milky white.

It was hard to tear myself away from this captivating stretch of coast, but my way lay inland, funnelling up Gap Bottom past the old farming hamlet of Crowlink. A last trudge over the downs through a stolid crowd of curly-faced sheep, and I was dipping down the steep slope towards East Dean with a pint of Tiger's Claw in my sights and a head full of wonders to sort through.

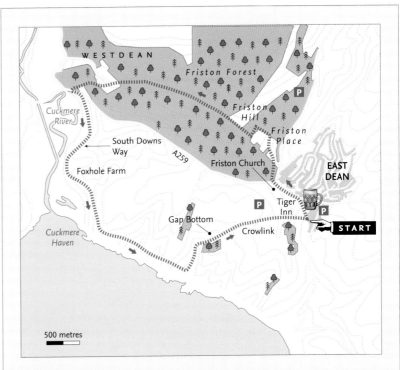

Start & finish Tiger Inn, East Dean, near Eastbourne, East Sussex BN20 0DA (OS ref TV556978)

Getting there Bus: Services 12, 12A (buses.co.uk), Eastbourne-Brighton. Road: East Dean village is signposted off A259 Eastbourne-Seaford.

Walk (8 miles, easy/moderate, OS Explorer 123): Footpath from East Dean (556979) to Friston church (551982); cross A259; footpath (yellow arrow) into trees; right through trees, across field, lane and next field, to lane round Friston Place (550989). Left to corner (548990); left for 100m; right (opposite entrance) on bridleway through woods for 1½ miles to West Dean. Pass church (525997) to T-junction; left along South Downs Way (SDW). Follow SDW south and east along cliffs for 2¾ miles. By NT 'Crowlink' sign (538968) inland to pass Crowlink hamlet. Right here (545975) on footpath east for 600m, to go through kissing gate (551976). Pass right side of triangular woodland; cross stone wall stile (554977 – ahead, not right); downhill to East Dean.

Lunch Tiger Inn, East Dean; The Cuckmere Inn, Exceat Bridge, Seaford BN25 4AB (01323 892247; vintageinn.co.uk/content/vintage-inn/en/restaurants/south-east/thecuckmereinnseaford)

Accommodation Tiger Inn (01323 423209; beachyhead.org.uk/the_tiger_inn) or Beachy Head Cottages (01323 423878) – superb country pub; classy self-catering

More information Eastbourne TIC (01323 415450; www.visiteastbourne.com), visitsussex.org, ramblers.org.uk, satmap.com

A dip in the sea not long after dawn, an early-morning drive into the South Downs and I was away from Fulking as the newly risen sun cast an oblique light along the downland escarpment behind the village. Beans rattled dry and black on their stalks, and the soil lay pale and cracked in this drought summer. To the north rose the downs, a 300ft rampart of turf facing the agricultural lowlands, dull olive patched with white chalk scrapes and dark-green scrub. Near at hand a yellowhammer in the hedge wheedled for "a-little-bit-of-bread-and-no-cheeeese!". The fields stretched breathless and still in an early morning already gathering heat. Up on the downs, though, something was in motion. I stopped and stared as a crowd of bullocks went thundering down the slope, kicking up clouds of powdery chalk dust, mad with delight at the headlong sensation.

In Longlands Wood, a green wilderness of beech and oak, the swearing of a discontented jay broke the stillness. The pastures around Tottington Manor were full of dark chocolate cattle, cows and bull calves slowly grazing together, every muzzle a quivering maze of flies. I leaned over the gate, scratching a couple of handy backs, and then made for the downs. Steeply up through the trees on Tottington Mount, until at the crest I could stop and look back across the flatlands 300ft below — downland slopes and woods leading out to the matt steel eyes of gravel pits and the great floodplain of the River Adur. A few more minutes and I was at the crest of the downs, looking south through beautiful curving valleys to the hazy grey 'V' of the sea.

Three young sparrowhawks hung in the air in line abreast, hunting the downs under the tutelage of their parent birds. I turned east along the ancient track of the South Downs Way, a white chalk thread drawn snaking through the turf. What fantastic elation heading into the penumbra of the sun in this high place among drifts of scrambled-egg toadflax and white campion, passing broad headlands full of poppies and moon daisies left by the farmer around the margins of his barley fields.

By the time I got to Perching Hill the sky ahead over Devil's Dyke was already dotted with hang-gliders, and before I dropped back down the escarpment to Fulking I stood and watched them circling like mythical heroes near the sun.

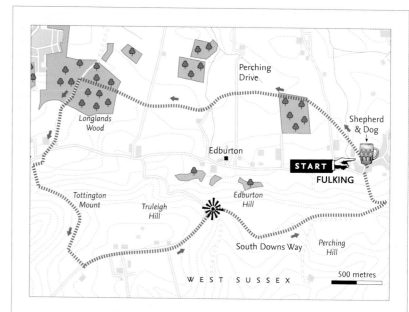

Start & finish Shepherd & Dog PH, Fulking BN5 9LU (OS ref TQ247113)

Getting there Road: Fulking signposted from A281 (Henfield-Brighton) and A2037 (Henfield-Upper Beeding)

Walk (6 miles, moderate/hard grade, OS Explorer 122): Leaving Shepherd & Dog, right along road; in 50m, by fountain, left through gate (fingerpost). Field path (yellow arrows/YA, fingerposts) west for 2 miles via Perching Manor drive, track to Edburton (234121) and track to Truleigh Manor Farm (225120), to path crossing in Longlands Wood (219122, four-way fingerpost). Left to cross road at Tottington Manor (215115). Track steeply up through trees, curving clockwise round Tottington Mount. At top of climb, to post on skyline; left (217106, blue arrow/BA) to road. Left on South Downs Way for 1½ miles to pass under power lines (242109). In another ¼ mile, in a dip, through a gate (246109); left down cleft (YA post). In 250m, sharp left (249111, YA post); steeply down to Fulking.

Lunch Shepherd & Dog PH, Fulking (01273 857382; shepherdanddogpub.co.uk) – lovely old walker-friendly pub

More information Brighton TIC (01273 290337; visitbrighton.com), visitsussex.org, ramblers.org.uk, satmap.co.uk

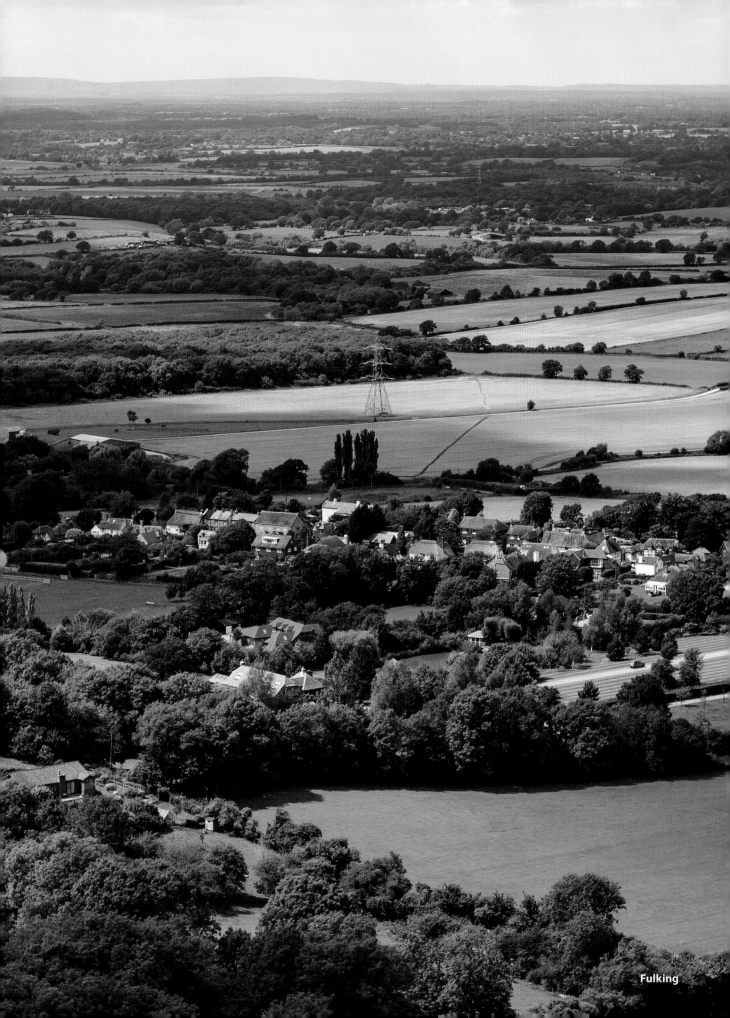

Fulking

Newbridge, Batt's and Dens Wood
EAST SUSSEX

The long, high waves of the East Sussex Weald lay under smoky rolls of grey cloud, through which a pale penumbra of sun came gleaming like a half-dissolved pearl. 'Wild boar, ostrich!' promised the board at the entrance to Birdbrook Farm. 'Bison, zebra, wildebeest!' There were no signs of such exotic creatures in the small-scale hedged fields around Witherenden Farm — just cattle bellowing in the farmyard as they were passed across the scales in a welter of men and dogs before heading out for market.

We squelched along a track of sticky Wealden clay and came into Newbridge Wood, one of the coppice woods that have been tended in these parts since medieval times, when this now quiet and all-but-empty landscape was England's ironmaking centre. The only hint that remains of the smoky, noisy, fiery industry is the large number of woodland ponds — they stored and released the water for the wheels that drove the ironmasters' bellows and drop-hammers — and the woods themselves, harvested to produce the charcoal for the blast-furnaces.

Newbridge Wood, and Batt's Wood and Dens Wood beyond, were thick with hornbeams, the smooth poles of their overshot coppice sprouts seamed with long runnels like withered and witchy arms reaching for the light. Each tree seemed lit from below by the millions of acid green and rich gold leaves that carpeted the forest floor. From the gaps among the woods we had wonderful views across the Weald — the sun-reflecting oasts at Bivelham Farm, thatched roofs among the trees, long low meadows, dark hedges and woods rising to high ridges like green ocean billows.

On the lane into Batt's Wood, seven inkcap fungi rose in a ring beside the hedge, like pixie hats with upturned brims. Dens Wood and the landscaped slopes by Wadhurst Park Lake were full of deer — red stags chasing hinds, roe deer delicately bounding out of the trees, a big pale fallow stag standing stock still under the silver birches, giving us the wary eye. We shuffled hornbeam leaves in the lane to Flattenden Farm and sniffed the sweet scent of applewood fires as we made back across the fields towards Witherenden Farm in the half-light of evening.

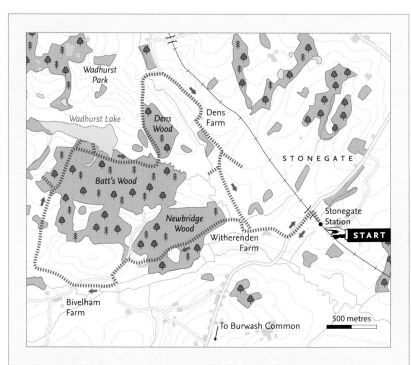

Start & finish Stonegate Station, East Sussex, TN5 7ER (OS ref TQ659272). All day parking £4.70

Getting there Rail: (thetrainline.com, railcard.co.uk) to Stonegate. Road: Stonegate station is off A265 Heathfield-Hurst Green road, just north of Burwash.

Walk (6½ miles, easy, OS Explorer 136): Stonegate Station – left down road – right (655270) to Witherenden Farm. Through farmyard, down track, through metal gate (651271), anticlockwise round field; right to bridleway through Newbridge Wood; past Bivelham Forge Farm (640267) to road (637266). Left; in 80m, right over stile (yellow arrow/YA) across fields to Pound Bridge (633265). Cross road; along track via Gold's Farm into Batt's Wood (630274). Follow YAs – left by interpretive board; immediately right; in 50m, left at junction, down to gate near lake (633278). Right for ½ mile, left to cross stream (642278); left at three-finger post beyond. Track up through Dens Wood; down to T-junction (641286, 'Weir Cottage'). Right; in ⅓ mile, through Dens Farm gate (646283); fork right between sheds, down lane; in 50m, left (YA) across fields. In 350m, cross stream (648279) to gate; don't go through! Right along hedge, across fields for ½ mile (YAs) to track below Witherenden Farm (651271). Left to station.
NB Paths in Batt's Wood are often slippery.

Lunch Picnic

More information Hastings TIC (01424 451111; visit1066country.com), visitsussex.org, ramblers.org.uk, satmap.co.uk

Exton and Beacon Hill

HAMPSHIRE

It was one of those close, steamy mornings when the chalk down country of Hampshire sits very still under a cap of grey vapour, the downs themselves muted into pale hummocks against a leached-out sky. Someone was pruning a fruit tree behind one of Exton's garden walls; the snip-snip of secateurs followed us out of the silent little village like the chipping of two flints.

The South Downs Way took us gradually up between blackberry hedges towards the wooded promontory height of Beacon Hill, the chalk grassland of its steep flanks a pale washy green that suddenly shone a rich olive colour as the hidden sun lowered a beam through the murk. The clouds shredded like mist, exposing a painter's palette sky of forget-me-not blue and mackerel streaks of black and silver. The Beacon itself, a stark iron cresset on a pole with a plaque commemorating the Diamond Jubilee, commanded a wonderful view east over the woods and fields of the Meon Valley.

A potholed country road squirmed along the ridge between the whaleback of Beacon Hill, a National Nature Reserve famous for its summer flowers and butterflies, and the open hull of the Devil's Punch Bowl, a steep and secluded dry chalk valley. Tarmac soon gave way to flint and clay in the green lane that carried us by the humps and bumps where the medieval village of Lomer once stood. The creation of fenced-off sheepwalks in Tudor times caused many a downland village to lose its corn-growing and cattle fields, and Lomer was probably one of these.

A big black bull stood in the field beyond Lomer Farm, staring into space and chewing on unfathomable thoughts. Along the shallow valley charmingly called Betty Mundy's Bottom the stubble ran in parallel zigs and zags. Pungent, lung-clearing wafts came from the freshly creosoted gates around Betty Mundy's Cottage where, peering through the hedge, I glimpsed an enormous bronze horse's head balanced delicately on its muzzle in the grass.

Farther along, near St Clair's Farm, we passed through a plantation of young Northdown clawnuts, a variety of walnut tree, not yet mature enough to produce the sweet-tasting nuts that grow twice the size of a conventional walnut. We put in a mental marker to come back in an autumn ten years from now, and bring a good-sized basket with us.

In Corhampton Forest two roe deer leaped before us across a clearing in three or four graceful bounds. We found a flinty lane and followed it past black sheep bleating at the foot of the Devil's Punch Bowl, through a quiet valley and back to Exton.

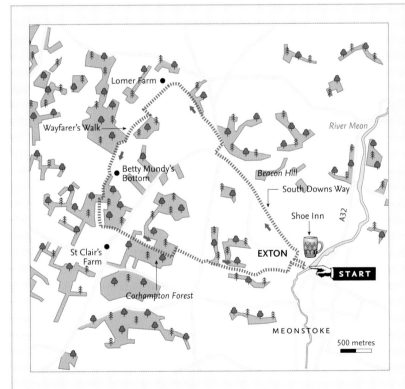

Start & finish Exton village, Southampton, Hants SO32 3NT (OS ref SU612208).
NB Please don't park in the Shoe Inn's tiny car park.

Getting there Road: Exton is signposted off the A32 Fareham-Alton road at Meonstoke/ Corhampton

Walk (7 miles, moderate, OS Explorer 132): From The Shoe Inn, right to corner; right ('South Downs Way'/SDW); right along Church Street; in 100m, left and follow SDW for 2¼ miles via road (603220), entrance to Beacon Hill NNR (598227) and lane (597230) to Lomer Farm (591237). From here, follow Wayfarer's Walk for 1¾ miles via track beside Preshaw Wood (583228), Betty Mundy's Bottom (580222) and Betty Mundy's Cottage (578221) to crossroads of tracks just north of St Clair's Farm (578214). Left here for 2½ miles to Exton via Sailors Lane (582213), Corhampton Forest (589210, 591211), Beacon Hill Lane (595209) and T-junction by Exton Farm (608207).

Lunch The Shoe Inn, Shoe Lane, Exton SO32 3NT (01489 877526; theshoeexton.co.uk)

More information Alton Tourist Information Point (01420 884448), visit-hampshire.co.uk, ramblers.org.uk, satmap.co.uk

Selborne and Noar Hill

HAMPSHIRE

The natural world was a puzzle that eighteenth-century minds longed to put together. From the orgasms of swifts to the submarine breathing of deer, Gilbert White, the curate of the Hampshire village of Selborne, noted and questioned everything around him. The gentle and curious clergyman's letters, published as *The Natural History of Selborne*, have sold countless millions; and thousands of White's admirers and adherents still visit Selborne to look round his house, The Wakes, and to climb the Zig-Zag path cut by White and his brother John into the steep face of the Hanger, the 300ft chalk escarpment behind the village.

Sun was flooding through the stained-glass Gilbert White memorial window in St Mary's Church, back-lighting in glory the heron, the raven, the finches and the warblers waiting their turn to be fed by St Francis. Outside in the sunshine and wind, Jane and I paid our respects at the curate's modest grave, then followed the concertina folds of the Zig-Zag up to the crest of the Hanger. Looking back, we saw the village and its green cornfields framed in beech leaves and bathed in thick shafts of light.

The track led over the ancient wood pasture of Selborne Common, now smothered in trees, but in White's time "a pleasing, park-like spot, commanding a very engaging view". It was one of his favourite places. Here he would come, a notebook in his pocket, alert to all that was going on under, upon and above the Earth. Today a confusion of paths tangles on the common, but we picked out ours with only a modicum of cursing.

Now Noar Hill stood ahead, a high promontory. White wondered whether these downland hills might have been formed by the swelling of their waterlogged chalk, like yeast — a perfect example of his endearing mixture of science and poetry. Here we found, pinned to a tree, a touching quotation by Harry Rustell, a local man who spent the first thirty years of his life, early in the twentieth century, on Noar Hill farms. "If I should happen to know," the note read, "when my last days on this Earth are at hand, I would like to be able to wave a magic wand and be above the beech hangers of Noar Hill among the wild flowers, especially the cowslips, my mother's favourite."

There are still cowslips on Noar Hill, and violets among the mosses in High Wood Hanger. Walking under the beech and hazels back to Selborne, we imagined a meeting on the hill, between farm boy and curate, and guessed that they would not have been short of things to talk about.

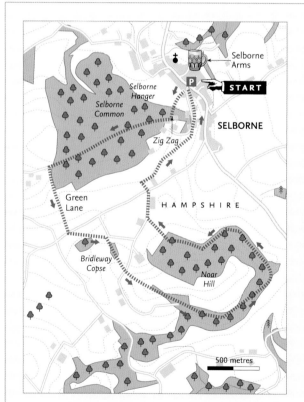

Start & finish Village car park, Selborne GU34 3JR (OS ref SU742335)

Getting there Train: (thetrainline.com, railcard.co.uk) to Alton (5 miles). Bus: 38, Petersfield-Alton (stagecoachbus.com). Road: M3 (Jct 6), A339 to Alton, B3006 to Selborne

Walk (5 miles, moderate grade, OS Explorer 133): From car park, climb Zig-Zag (signposted); path over Selborne Common for ⅔ mile. In open space, fork left (732329) to gate (729328). Green Lane; cross road (731322); left across field to road (734321). Right; cross lane (736318); on for ½ mile to cross tracks at wood edge (742315). Follow Hangers Way/HW for ¼ mile; then descend (747315). At bottom, left (751317) on bridleway for ¾ mile to rejoin HW (740321). Right to road (738323); to T-junction (738325); stiles, HW back to Selborne.

Lunch Selborne Arms, Selborne GU34 3JR (01420 511247; selbornearms.co.uk)

More information Gilbert White's House & The Oates Collections, The Wakes, Selborne GU34 3JH (01420 511275; gilbertwhiteshouse.org.uk), Petersfield TIC (01730 268829; visit-hampshire.co.uk), ramblers.org.uk

Silchester and Calleva

HAMPSHIRE

We'd been longing for a day like this — bright cold sunlight, wall-to-wall blue sky across the Hampshire/Berkshire border, the recently rain-sodden ground frozen hard underfoot on Silchester Common.

The low sun struck glitters out of the frost crusts in the red bracken clumps. We descended towards a wooded stream valley, watching squirrels playing kiss-chase in the birch tops, and turned along a bridleway that threaded the edge of Pamber Forest.

The ancient woodland, a fragment of the once-mighty royal forest of Windsor, lay faintly whispering, its leafless limbs still a month or two short of any hint of leaf-break. Distant cars murmured like waves on a beach. We followed a ruler-straight old woodbank and went on out of the forest to the frost-sparkled lane at Latchmere Green, where the daffodil buds were just beginning to swell. In the fields beyond, hoof pocks left by cattle in the mud were skinned over with white ice. The animals themselves, Highland beasts munching at a rich-smelling hay feeder, looked round at us through thick ginger fringes that hid their eyes.

The woodland boundary near beautiful old Clapper's Farm was labelled 'Park Pale' on our Explorer map. Back at the beginning of the thirteenth century, the Lord of Silchester Manor gave King John a palfrey in exchange for the right to create a deer park inside a pale, an earthen bank topped by a fence. It was cunningly designed so that wild deer could get in but couldn't jump back out. Opposite Clapper's we made out the medieval fishponds and the moated site where the keeper of the park had his fine residence. What status the park keeper enjoyed back then — far more than any of today's gamekeepers.

Field paths brought us back to Silchester by way of the remarkably complete flint walls of the Roman settlement of Calleva Atrebatum. Gridded streets, houses, shops, baths, an ancient Christian basilica and a steep-sided amphitheatre that could hold 3500 seated spectators have all been excavated here. Stories say that Aelle, Saxon King of Sussex, sacked the place around 500 BC, sending sparrows with flaming tails to set fire to the town. There were no sparrows in Calleva today, but we stopped by an oak to watch a treecreeper with a curved back and beak pick hibernating insects from their refuge in the bark cracks — a fate perhaps as terrifying for today's spider as a roaring Saxon warrior's axe-blow for a cowering Callevite 1500 years ago.

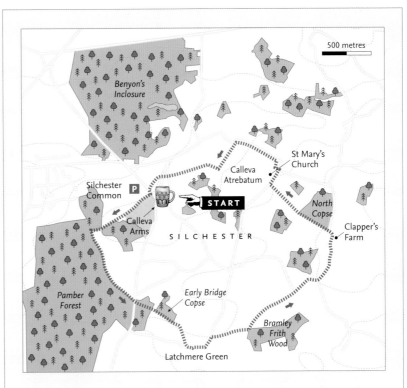

Start & finish Calleva Arms, Silchester, Hants RG7 2PH (OS ref SU627621)

Getting there Bus: Service 14 (stagecoachbus.com) Basingstoke-Tadley. Road: M4 Jct 11; A33 ('Basingstoke'); in 300m, B3349 to Spencers Wood. Left to Beech Hill, Stratfield Mortimer and Silchester. Car park on village green.

Walk (6½ miles, easy, OS Explorer 159): From Calleva Arms down Dukes Ride to 'Brenda Parker Way' across Silchester Common for ½ mile to bridleway crossing (618616). Left for ¾ mile to cross road (624607); on past Early Bridge Copse for ⅔ mile to road at Latchmere Green (632600). Bramley Frith Wood (640603); field edge path to road (647608). Clapper's Farm (651616) to edge of North Copse (647618) then permissive path for ⅓ mile to St Mary's Church (643624). Anti-clockwise half-circuit of Calleva Atrebatum Roman walls; on across end of track bisecting site (637625); in 100m, right for ½ mile to roads at Silchester's village green.

Lunch Calleva Arms, Silchester (01189 700305; callevaarms.co.uk) – popular, cosy, friendly

More information Silchester Trail (hants.gov.uk/rh/walking/silchester-trail.pdf), Pamber Forest (hiwwt.org.uk/sites/default/files/files/Reserves/Pamber_Forest_Leaflet_SW.pdf), Silchester Roman Town (reading.ac.uk/silchester), tourist information (visit-hampshire.co.uk), ramblers.org.uk, satmap.com

Stockbridge and the River Test

HAMPSHIRE

The ruddy-faced man in Stockbridge High Street (flat cap stuck with fishing flies, Barbour, cord breeches, brogues, black labrador strictly to heel) might have been posed there by Central Casting this crisp blue winter's morning. The long, linear Hampshire village is famous for outdoor pursuits in the surrounding countryside, especially fishing. Stockbridge straddles the Test, England's best trout-fishing river bar none. Jane and I hung over the bridge watching the olive green fish sinuating with the water weed. Then we struck out across the roof of Houghton Down, following flinty trackways that might well predate the Romans

Brilliant scarlet rosehips and bryony berries, blush-pink spindle, the soft bloom of unfrosted sloes, crimson haws — the thick hedges flanking the old green roads of the downs were bursting with fruit. Among the bare branches moved darting flocks of fieldfares, buff-breasted thrush cousins over from Scandinavia for the winter, busy gobbling as many berries as they could get down their handsomely spotted necks.

A quick nasty smack of the A30 and we continued our high course along the green lanes. Two horses came cantering towards us, the riders grinning as they passed, their weather-beaten faces cracking into multiple lines like a brace of kindly sea captains. In a trackside copse a wartime pillbox crumbled silently, its cheap utility bricks scalloped by rain and wind into artistic-looking hollows.

Shuffling through drifts of beech leaves, we followed the snaking track down off the ridge into Houghton. The Test gurgled and chuckled under its footbridges, a mazy system of backwaters and sidestreams spreading a net of water through the shallow valley. The sun struck late colours out of the trees along the river — crimson dogwood, acid green willow, yellow birch, vivid against the smeary pearl of a wintry sky.

At Blacklake Farm a tiny terrier, trembling with eagerness, pushed his face through the garden fence and begged us to take him along. We turned for home along the disused Sprat and Winkle railway line, now the Test Way footpath. A final detour through the rushy acres of Common Marsh and we were walking the black peaty banks of the Marshcourt River, with Stockbridge church spire and hot buttered teacakes in Lillies tearoom as twin aiming points.

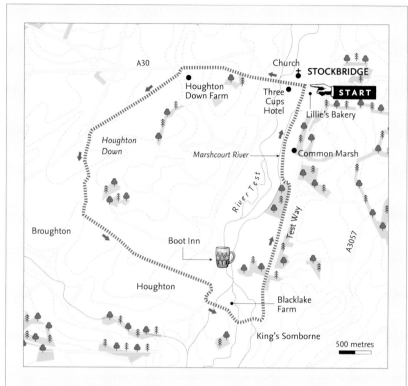

Start & finish High Street, Stockbridge, Hants SO20 6HF (OS ref SU357351)

Getting there Bus: Service 7 Winchester (stagecoachbus.com) or 15 Salisbury (wheelerstravel.co.uk). Road: A30 from Winchester or Salisbury.

Walk (7½ miles, easy, OS Explorer 131): West (Salisbury direction) along Stockbridge High Street (A30). Cross River Test; up hill; at right bend (350352), left up Roman Road. At turning circle, ahead on paved path, then green lane. In ⅔ mile, rejoin A30 (339354); ahead for 200m (take care), then left (337353, 'Byway') on stony roadway for 1 mile. At road (323344), left ('Byway') along green lane. In ¾ mile, left at bench (322331) on green lane down to Houghton. (NB: to reach Boot Inn, left on path by recycling bins.) At road, right (342321); in 300m, left (341319; fingerpost, 'Monarch's Way'). Cross River Test and pass Blacklake Farm. In another ⅓ mile, left (350316) along Test Way. In 1⅓ miles, left through gate (354336; NT sign); bear right across Common Marsh beside Marshcourt River. At north end of Common Marsh, through gate (355347); path to Stockbridge.

Lunch Boot Inn, Houghton SO20 6LH (01794 388310; thebootinn-houghton.co.uk), Tearoom: Lillies of Stockbridge, Stockbridge SO20 6HG (01264 810754; lilliesofstockbridge.com)

Accommodation Three Cups Inn, Stockbridge SO20 6HB (01264 810527; the3cups.co.uk)

More information Winchester TIC (01962 840500; visitwinchester.co.uk), visit-hampshire.co.uk, satmap.com, ramblers.org.uk

Carisbrooke
ISLE OF WIGHT

When King Charles I arrived on the Isle of Wight in November 1647, he was on the run after defeat in the English Civil War. The King believed that the newly appointed governor of Carisbrooke Castle, Robert Hammond, would help him to escape to France, but Hammond, reporting Charles's every move to Oliver Cromwell, held him in the old Norman stronghold like a pearl in an oyster. A year of royal incarceration, of farcical escape attempts and botched deals, ended with the inevitable humiliating journey under guard to London and to public execution in Whitehall in January 1649.

High and handsome on its wooded knoll, its pale stone walls lit with sunshine, Carisbrooke, looked like a dream of a fairytale castle. In the car park a cheerful lady steering a black labrador told us: "Get up on the downs, you'll have a beautiful walk." She couldn't have given us better advice. The Tennyson Trail, a flinty lane in a tunnel of trees, took us up onto the roof of Bowcombe Down, where chalkhill and common blue butterflies were flitting over the last sprigs of wild marjoram.

Views back to the curtain walls, great gatehouse and sloping motte of Carisbrooke Castle were breathtaking. So were the prospects from the ridge track, out across a landscape of corn stubbles squared by hedges, hilltop spinneys, the roll and dip of the island's wide chalk downs, and a gleam of the sky-blue Solent.

A shady green lane dipped down from the ridgeway to a valley, with a wonderful view of Dukem Down quilted with silvery stubbles, green and gold trees, new grass and herby sward. Streamers of chalk dust trailed after the tractors. Up on the crest of Garstons Down buzzards wheeled and jewelled beetles lurched through the turf.

Dropping down the slopes towards distant Carisbrooke, I pictured the captive King's misery. Charles saw himself as God's anointed representative on Earth. It hadn't done him any good. Pacing the quarter-mile circuit of his prison walls and looking out over the downs, how he must have longed for everyman's simple freedom to go for a walk in the country.

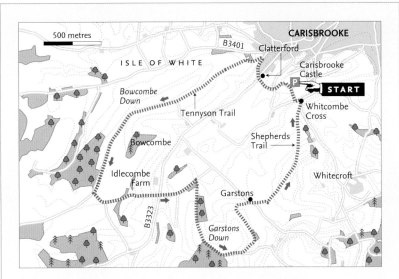

Start & finish Carisbrooke Castle car park PO30 1XY (OS ref SZ485876)

Getting there Ferry: Red Funnel (02380 019192; redfunnel.co.uk) Southampton to East Cowes (vehicles) or West Cowes (foot passengers). Bus: Service 1 (West Cowes) or 5 (East Cowes) to Newport; 6, 7 or 38 to Carisbrooke. Road: A3020 (West Cowes) or A3021/3054 (East Cowes) to Newport; B3341 'Carisbrooke Castle'.

Walk (7 miles, moderate, OS Explorer OL29): From car park, Public Footpath 88 ('Miller's Lane'). Right at Miller's Lane, left along Clatterford Shute (483876); cross ford; cross B3323 Clatterford Lane; up Nodgham Lane and over crest. Hairpin left by 'Little Hill' up Tennyson Trail (481881; fingerpost) across Bowcombe Down for 2¼ miles. At gate, left (455860; 'bridleway N135, Bowcombe Road'). In 250m lane swings right; ahead here and down to cross B3323 Bowcombe Road (465859; fingerpost 'Froglands and The Downs') near Idlecombe Farm. Up field edge left of triangular copse; 100m into next field, right through hedge, left up green lane, over ridge, down to corner of Frogland Copse (471862). Follow stony lane to right; climb field edge; in 50m, ahead up hedged path ('N146 Gatcombe, Shorwell') to Dukem Down. At crest (472852) you'll find a stile with Access Land logo on left, wooden horse jump fence ahead, and a metal rider's gate to the right. Go through this, on among trees. In 400m, left (475850; 'Gatcombe' fingerpost) out of trees; follow fence on left past dewpond on Garstons Down. In 200m, left through gate (478850; 'bridleway G7 Garstons') and down to Garstons farmhouse (479858). Bear right in front of house ('Byway') along stony lane; in 250m, fork left along narrow green lane between hedges. In ⅓ mile, ahead (486864; 'bridleway N108, Whitcombe Road, Carisbrooke') along Shepherds Trail for ½ mile to Whitcombe Cross (487874). Left for 100m; right ('Carisbrooke Castle') along field edge. At top, left to car park.

Lunch Picnic

Carisbrooke Castle Castle Hill, Newport PO30 1XY (01983 522107; english-heritage.org.uk/visit/places/carisbrooke-castle)

More information Isle of Wight Tourism (01983 813813; visitisleofwight.co.uk), ramblers.org.uk, satmap.com

Borough Green and Ightham Mote
KENT

The sun beamed on bean rows and potato ridges in the gardens we passed on our way out of Borough Green. If Kent is the Garden of England, the stretch of countryside around this village on the northern edge of the Weald is a particularly lush corner of the vegetable plot.

The trees are thriving well, too — there are enough deep pockets of forest left to give a flavour of how dense and green the sprawling old Wealden wildwood must have been before the Kentish ironmasters began stripping the ancient forest for charcoal.

A tangle of bluebell woods runs down the twisting Basted valley, skirting the old millpond with its white-browed coots and delicately stepping moorhens. There were mills all down the River Bourne here, all gone now in favour of fabulous new houses.

We walked the woodland paths past long-forgotten watercress beds, then climbed a flinty track onto the roof of the downs, with heat-hazed views over rolling, darkly wooded country.

Near the triplet oasts at Yopps Green — how long since they last dried a load of hops? — we turned onto a bridleway and came down off the ridge to Ightham Mote. A dream of a moated Elizabethan manor, Ightham Mote contains a far older hall house, dark-panelled and timbered. This "vile and papisticall house", as it was styled in a Catholic-bashing report of 1585, is truly a place of secrets, of concealed passages and priest holes.

Tales say that Ightham Mote is haunted by the ghost of Dame Dorothy Selby, who gave away the Gunpowder Plot by warning her cousin not to attend Parliament on 5 November, 1605, and was walled up alive in the house as a punishment. It never happened like that, but who can stop a good Gothic yarn?

We could have stayed all afternoon at Ightham Mote and most of the visitors seemed set to do that.

Tearing ourselves away at last, we climbed steep Raspit Hill and followed the path over an overgrown common and into Oldbury Wood. One of the largest Iron Age hill forts in Britain lies hidden in the wood, its earthen ramparts rooted with oak and sweet chestnut.

The invading Romans captured it from the Belgae warrior tribe in AD 43 as they advanced towards the Thames — perhaps 'with extreme prejudice', if the burnt defences and mounds of slingshots excavated here tell a true tale.

Picturing the mayhem, we followed the ancient trackway through the silent, tree-smothered old fort and out into the late afternoon sun.

Start & finish Borough Green & Wrotham station TN15 8BG (OS ref TQ609574)

Getting there Train: (thetrainline.com; railcard.co.uk) to Borough Green & Wrotham station. Road: M25 (Jct 5), M26 (Jct 2a); A20 to Wrotham Heath, A25 to Borough Green.

Walk (8½ miles, moderate grade, OS Explorer 147): Cross railway; High Street; cross A25; Quarry Hill Road. Opposite church (608572), footpath south to Basted (607563); cross Winfield Lane (606550); Yopps Green (602542). Bridleway west to cross A227 (591451); Ightham Mote (584534). Road north for ⅓ mile; left on bridleway (583539); north to cross road (580546); Raspit Hill; pass ponds to A25 (579555); right for 200m, and cross. Bear right, then north through Oldbury Wood (582560). Oldbury; cross A25 (593565); Sevenoaks Road to A227. Left to George & Dragon Inn; right up Tycewell Lane (595566). In 150m, right by oast; in 200m left (598566), almost to A227; right (599570) on path to Borough Green.

Lunch Mote Café, Ightham Mote TN15 0NT (01732 811314; nationaltrust. org.uk/ightham-mote), George & Dragon Inn, Ightham TN15 9HH (01732 882440; shepherdneame.co.uk/pubs/ightham/george-dragon), Ightham Mote NT (01732 810378; nationaltrust.org.uk/ightham-mote)

More information Sevenoaks TIC (01732 450305), visitkent.co.uk, ramblers.org.uk, satmap.com

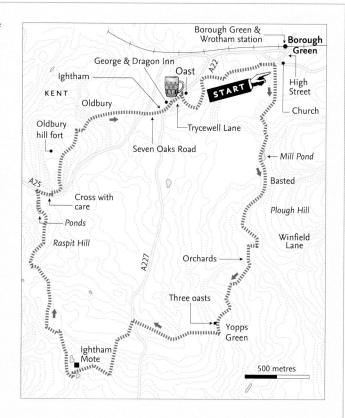

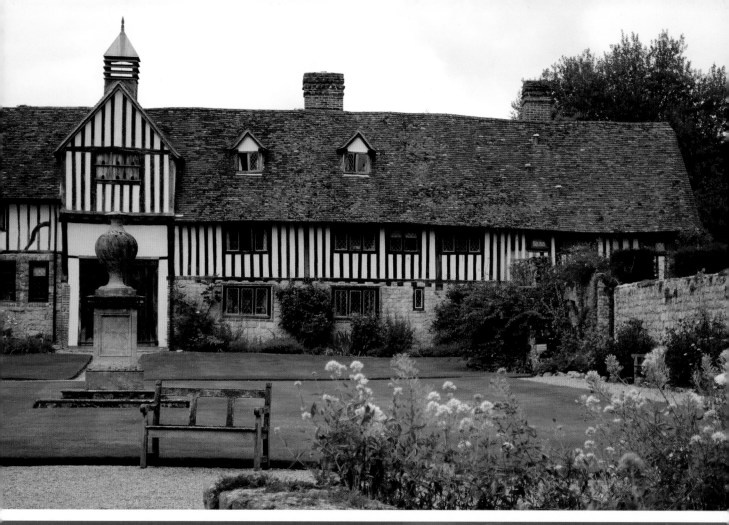

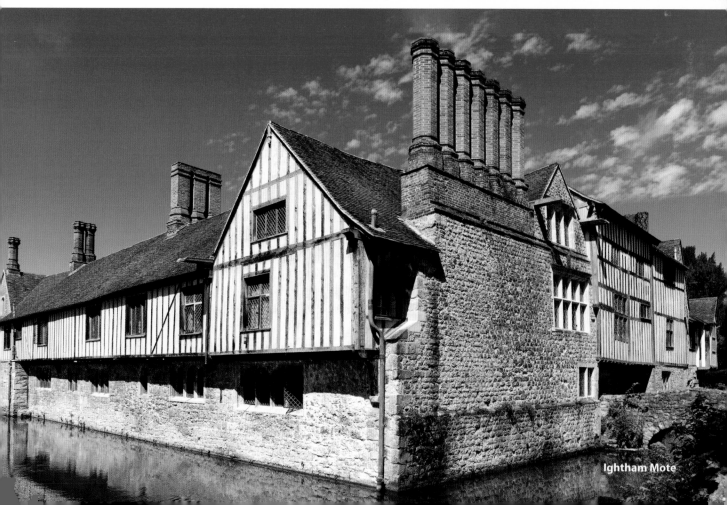

Ightham Mote

Dungeness, Romney Marsh
KENT

Dungeness is one of the great uncommon landscapes of Britain; a vast sheet of pebbles — the greatest in all Europe — studded with tough fleshy and prickly plants, thronged with wild birds. A Kentish pampas that pokes a knobbly nose into the English Channel, Dungeness is a great wilderness, but not unaffected by man — there are fishing boats and tarry fishermen's huts, scattered bungalows, and the giant, pale grey boxes of a nuclear power station.

We followed a grassy path through the RSPB's enormous 800 hectare (2000-acre) reserve, where pools, pastures and reed beds lie at the heart of a great shingle wasteland. Swans sailed with nonchalant grace on the meres. "Look," exclaimed Jane, "marsh harrier!" The big bird of prey got up quite slowly from its stance in a field of stubble and flapped off low over the reeds, the sun glinting among its wing feathers. There was great complaining among the shelduck and coots, and a party of teal sprang into the air and moved away from the vicinity of the dark destroyer as fast as they could. We saw the harrier several times after that, quartering its territory like a king and causing commotion wherever it went.

Among the birds, the yellow-horned poppies, the wide stony wastes and the gentle whisper of the wind, it was easy to forget the strangeness that the nuclear power station and its marching columns of pylons brought to the scene. We turned for home with a two-mile trudge across the pebble sheet in prospect, and there were the ghostly grey boxes and the skeleton pylon army ahead, dwarfed under the blue bowl of the sky.

We headed home, leaving behind us the plants, the birds, the pebbles and the blue sea horizon, with a blood-red sunset spreading in the west.

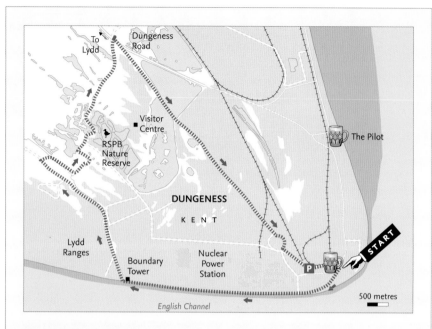

Start & finish Britannia Inn, Dungeness TN29 9ND (OS ref TR092169)

Getting there Rail: Romney, Hythe & Dymchurch Railway (rhdr.org.uk) to Dungeness. Bus: Services 11/11A/11B (stagecoachbus.com) from Ashford via Lydd. Road: from Lydd (signposted off A259, Rye, New Romney), follow signs for 'Dungeness Nature Reserve'; then, near power station, 'Britannia Inn'.

Walk (7½ miles, easy but pebbly, OS Explorer 125): Follow boardwalk near black-and-white lighthouse to shore. Right past power station – the hard-surfaced track by fence makes easier walking! In 1¾ miles, turn right inland by Lydd Ranges boundary tower (065167) on gravel road. In ½ mile, road bends left – in 600m, pass roadway on left (057179). In 400m, right (054181, blue topped post, Footpath No. HL33). Follow grassy path through RSPB reserve. In ⅔ mile, keep ahead at three-finger post (059184, 'Hooker's Pits'); follow bridleway blue arrows to road (063196). Right ('footpath' fingerpost), across shingle (occasional wooden posts) for 2 miles, aiming for black lighthouse. Cross road (083175); beyond old coastguard cottages, road to Britannia Inn.

NB Last section across shingle is hard going! Keep to path – risk of unexploded ordnance.

Lunch Britannia Inn (01797 321959; shepherdneame.co.uk/pubs/dungeness/britannia-inn) or Pilot Inn, Dungeness TN29 9NJ (01797 320314; thepilotdungeness.co.uk)

More information Dungeness RSPB Reserve (01797 320588; rspb.org.uk/Dungeness), visitengland.com, satmap.com, ramblers.org.uk

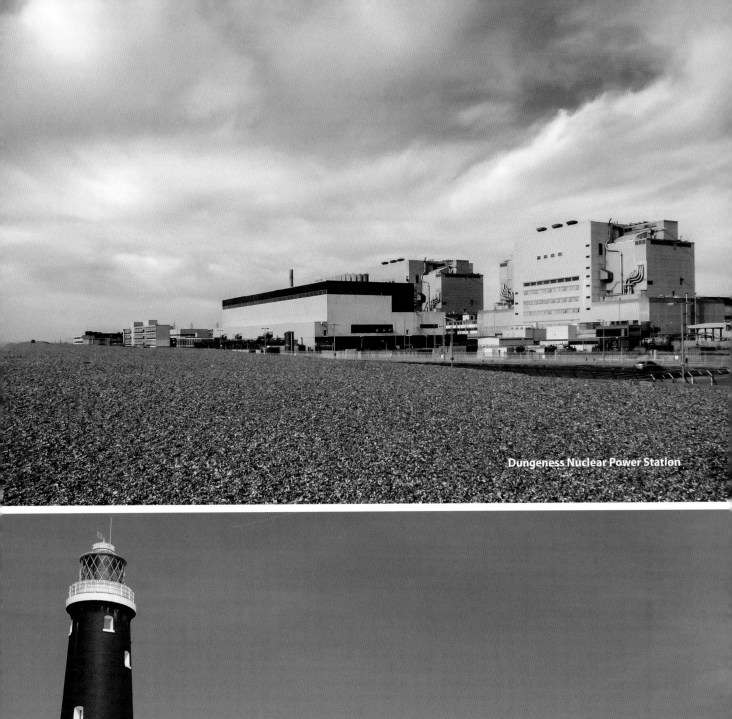

Dungeness Nuclear Power Station

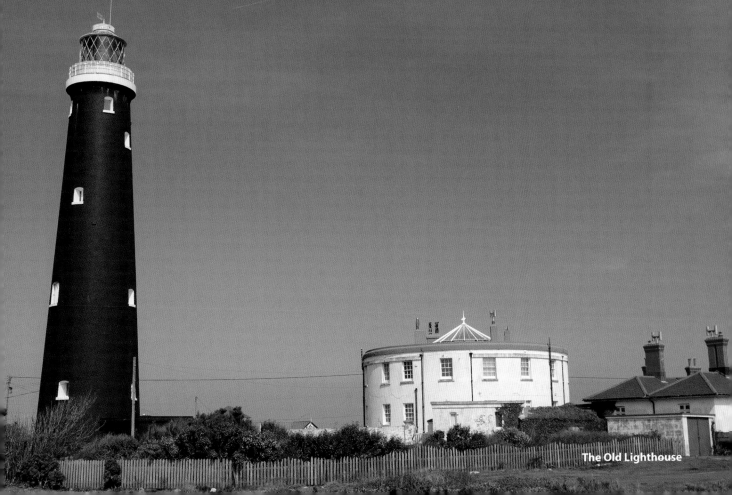

The Old Lighthouse

High Halstow and the Isle of Grain
KENT

The nightingale sang as if its heart would break. The infinitely slow and sweet contralto warbling filled the scrubby wood at the RSPB's High Halstow reserve, an operatic aria against the plainer chorus of blue tits, chiffchaffs and wrens, and the stage-hand knocking and hammering of great and lesser spotted woodpeckers. There can't be a richer, more poignant bird song in England on a misty spring morning, and it held us enchanted on our way down the Isle of Grain's escarpment to the moody Kentish shore of the River Thames.

We followed a path out of the woods through green wheatfields and a blue haze of linseed towards the first glimpse of the Thames — a broad leaden tideway rolling seaward, the tall spindly stacks of an oil refinery on the Essex shore misted out into grey and white spires like a city in a dream. A rough old lane led north between young elm hedges, a puddled track under a thick grey sky that brought us through the dead flat grazing meadows of Halstow Marshes to Egypt Bay in a crook of the sea wall that rims the Isle of Grain.

Yellow cockle shell sands lay at the feet of low black cliffs, leading out to a sheet of bird-haunted tidal mud, slippery and glutinous. In Egypt Bay the overarching imagination of Charles Dickens tethered the dreaded prison hulk from which the convict Magwitch escaped to terrorise young Pip in *Great Expectations*. There really were hulks in Egypt Bay in Dickens's day: stinking, superannuated men-of-war in which convicts were incarcerated to rot away in hellish isolation.

Nowadays Egypt Bay and neighbouring St Mary's Bay hold nothing more threatening than oystercatchers, avocets, curlew and brent geese. They are beautiful, sombre, wild places, destined to be overwhelmed if 'Boris Island', the monstrous Thames Estuary airport that was proposed in the early 2000s, should ever come to pass — because it would be built right here.

Bullocks paced the sea wall, evenly spaced like the wagons of a slow-moving goods train. We left them to it, took a last lungful of salty estuary air, and made inland for the pretty duckpond hamlet of St Mary Hoo and the homeward path.

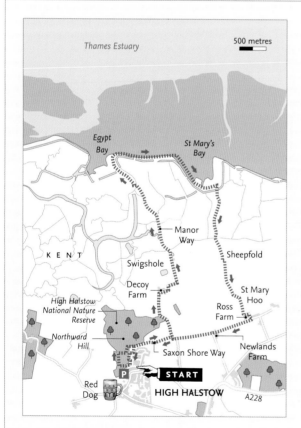

Start & finish RSPB car park, Woodside, High Halstow, Kent ME3 8TQ (OS ref TQ781757)

Getting there Road: from M2 Jct 1, A289, A228 towards Grain. At roundabout on outskirts of Hoo St Werburgh, left down Dux Court Road ('Deangate Ridge'). At High Halstow church, right along The Street past school. Left into Harrison Drive; second left into Northwood Avenue; immediately left down Woodlands to RSPB car park.

Walk (8 miles, easy, OS Explorer 163): Alternative starts: either go through RSPB Northward Hill Reserve woods (see detailed instructions on christophersomerville. co.uk) or return up Woodside; turn left for 200m, left at gate to cross picnic field to edge of wood (783761). Right along Saxon Shore Way for ¼ mile; left (787762; yellow arrow/YA) to Decoy Hill Road (787766). Left past Decoy Farm to Swigshole (788776); Manor Way track for 1 mile to Egypt Bay (778790). Right (east) along sea wall for 1½ miles to St Mary's Bay (796788); right (south) for 1½ miles to St Mary Hoo (803766). Right (west) via Newlands Farm for 1½ miles to car park.

Lunch Red Dog, High Halstow ME3 8SF (01634 253001; reddogdining.blogspot. co.uk), Northward Hill and High Halstow RSPB reserves (01634 222480; rspb.org.uk)

More information Medway Visitor Centre, Rochester ME1 1LX (01634 338141; visitmedway.org), visitkent.co.uk, satmap.com, ramblers.org.uk

Newington, and Lower Halstow

KENT

The Upchurch peninsula sticks up from the North Kent coast into the wide tidal basin of the Medway estuary. This is one of those outposts, remote and full of character, yet amazingly close to London, that one stumbles upon with a thrill of discovery, especially at this time of year when the apple orchards are in full blossom.

Under the 700-year-old roof of St Mary's Church at Newington, the damned bared their teeth in the agonies of Hell while angelic trumpet blasts summoned the righteous from their coffins: the vivid events of Judgment Day depicted by a medieval fresco painter, as admonitory as a slap on the backside. From the candy-striped flint and ragstone tower of St Mary's, we followed a path north over the green upland of Broom Down to Lower Halstow, neatly tucked along its creek beside the great marsh and mud expanse of the Medway estuary.

Black-headed gulls screeched around a brace of beautifully restored Thames barges moored at Halstow Quay. On the seaward horizon, the big blue cranes on the Isle of Grain dipped with majestic slowness like giraffes stooping to graze. A wind scented with salt and mud blew stiffly inland to rustle a million pink and white apple blossoms in the orchards around Ham Green.

Up the seaward edge of the peninsula we went, past the old coasting craft-turned-houseboats lying belly down in Twinney Creek, a curl of smoke rising from a home-made tin chimney. Then inland, past the orchards around Frog Farm, the tiny shoulder-high apple trees frothing with blossom and already beginning to hum with hoverflies and early bees. The tremulous, bubbling cries of a curlew came from the saltmarshes behind us as we followed the narrow lanes through Ham Green and on by the fishing lakes.

As we passed through Upchurch, the village cricket team in well-washed whites was walking out on to Hollywell Meadow. In Chaffes Lane a bunch of lads puzzled over the oily innards of an old scooter. A flat-capped man who must have seen off at least eighty winters gave us a wink as he shuffled into the side door of the Crown Inn, and in St Mary's Church an effigy of the Green Man spewed a mouthful of flowers like a promise of spring.

Start & finish Newington Station, Newington, Kent ME9 7LQ (OS ref TQ859650)

Getting there Train: (thetrainline.com, railcard.co.uk) to Newington. Road: M25 (Jct 2); M2 (Jct 5); A249 towards Sittingbourne; A2 towards London for 1½ miles. Park near Newington Station.

Walk (7 miles, easy, OS Explorer 148): Down Station Road; in 20m, opposite No 41, left along alleyway; left along Church Lane. Under railway; on to crossroads (861653) with Church of St Mary the Virgin to right. From crossroads, ahead ('Lower Halstow') down Wardwell Lane. In 200m on right bend, left (861655; footpath fingerpost); on through valley by footbridges and stiles. At foot of slope (860660), bear left up slope, aiming left of pylon; cross left-hand of two stiles. Follow path under power lines, over Broom Downs to road at Lower Halstow (859669). Left; immediately right along path with stream on left; in 300m, left across footbridge; right at end of alley to T-junction (859672), with Three Tuns PH and St Margaret's Church to right. Across junction by pub; pass 'Private – No Parking' sign, then 'Moorings' house to reach Halstow Wharf. Continue along Saxon Shore Way/ SShW past Halstow and Twinney Creeks for 1½ miles to Shoregate Lane (850691). Inland (SShW) for ¼ mile to Ham Green Farm (847688). Right along road; in 20m, left (SShW) on track through orchards, past riding stables (SShW) to road (844683). Left (SShW); in 250m, right (SShW) across field; through kissing gate (843679) with lake on right. SShW bears right here, but turn left ('public footpath' arrow) along hedge; cross paddocks into housing estate at Upchurch. Left to T-junction; right up The Street, past The Crown PH and St Mary's Church (844675).

Opposite Post Office, left down Chaffes Lane. In 200m, left opposite Bradshaws Close (844672). Take right-hand of two footpaths (stile, 'footpath' fingerpost), across paddocks by kissing gates for ⅓ mile. At far side of paddocks, right over stile (846667); bear left around paddock. On far side, left over a stile (847666, yellow arrow) down path to road (848665). Right to crossroads with Breach Lane (851663). Through a kissing gate opposite; aim for pylon, then keep same line over fields and through an orchard to its top right corner (853658). Left over stile, across field, then between paddocks to cross road (854655). Continue same line across large field; under railway (856650); ahead to A2 in Newington; left to Station Road; left to station.

Lunch Three Tuns, Lower Halstow, Sittingbourne ME9 7DY (01795 842840; thethreetunsrestaurant.co.uk). Church keyholders (please give several days' notice) St Mary's Church, Newington — Canon Alan Amos (01795 842913), St Margaret's Church, Lower Halstow and St Mary's Church, Upchurch — Rev Jacky Davies (01795 842557 jackytd@ halstowmillhouse.eclipse.co.uk).

More information Faversham TIC (01795 534542; visitkent.co.uk), ramblers.org.uk, satmap.com

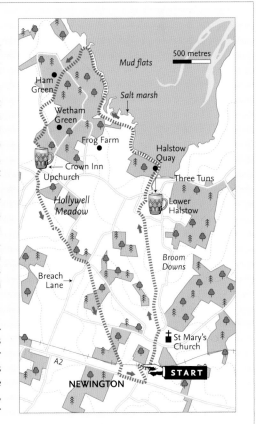

Octavia Hill Trail, Westerham
KENT

Two contrasting but quintessentially English fighters for freedom are celebrated on this walk through the Garden of England: Octavia Hill, one of the founders and pioneering visionaries of the National Trust, and Sir Winston Churchill — now, what did he ever do for us? Hill's large, calm eyes, generous mouth and determined chin are shown to advantage in the portrait featured in the National Trust's leaflet guide to the Centenary Trail, which the Trust has set up in her honour.

We picked up the leaflet from the Toys Hill car park dispenser and set off through the bluebell woods on a misty day, with the Weald of Kent lying veiled in thick dove-grey air. Hill lived locally in Crockham Hill, and her gift of property at Toys Hill in 1898 was one of the first made to the infant National Trust. Since then a big swath of these lovely wooded hills has been acquired by the Trust, a slice of England to be safeguarded forever by the organisation that most of us take for granted and for whose existence all of us should thank our lucky stars.

Twisty old beech pollards, warty and knobbled, stood in the mossy banks of the bridleway, their multiple smooth-skinned arms shooting skywards. Tiny hornbeam and ash suckers grew among them, rooted in rotting tree debris still evincing the terrible destruction of 1987's Great Storm over southern England.

On Toys Hill village notice board a poster written in a child's huge wobbly writing advertised 'Purfyoom For Sale'. We followed Puddledock Lane, a deep hollow way in the soft greensand with sublime misted views across the woods and fields of the Weald, past fields of fat white lambs and a cow pasture where a fox went slinking across the grass between utterly oblivious cattle.

Chartwell was a huddle of red-tiled roofs and white-capped oasts sailing in a frothy pink sea of apple blossom. Here in the big red Victorian house Churchill painted his depressions away, walked the gardens, lived surprisingly modestly and looked out on a view of meadows and wooded ridges as supremely English as any call-to-arms wartime leader could desire in the way of inspiration.

Beyond Chartwell we followed a mesh of beech-shaded country lanes to Crockham Hill, where Hill lies under a yew tree in the churchyard. On through buttercup meadows to high-perched Froghole Farm, all half-timbering, red tiles and oast house caps, and then a final bluebell path over Mariners Hill to descend to Toys Hill once more.

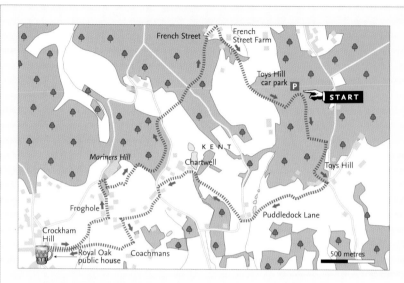

Start & finish Toys Hill National Trust car park, Chart Lane, Brasted, Nr Westerham, Kent TN16 1QG (OS ref TQ469517)

Getting there Road: M25 Jcts 6 or 5; A25 Sevenoaks-Westerham; turn off in Brasted on minor road through Brasted Chart; car park on right, just before Toys Hill

Walk (6 miles, moderate, OS Explorer 147): Go up steps behind information board; follow Olivia Hill Centenary/OHC waymarks through woods. In 300m at junction, turn left (468514/OHC); at lawn area below (469513) bear left down tunnel of hollies to road (470513). Right past phone box along Puddledock Lane. In ²/₃ mile pass foot of lane by 'Windswept' house (462509); in 100m, right over stile (fingerpost, OHC) on fenced path to Chartwell. Pass oasts and Herdsman's Cottage; up lane to road (453513). Left; in 50m, right up Mariners drive (fingerpost). In 200m at sharp right bend, ahead through gate (453510, OHC); in 275m, at three-way fingerpost, bear left down lane and on down green lane. At crossroads near Coachmans bear right (451507, OHC) on lane for ½ mile to Crockham Hill. At B2026 (442506; Royal Oak PH on your left), turn right; in 50m, right past school and church. Go through gate (444507, OHC); on across fields for ¹/₃ mile to Froghole; at top of long flight of steps, left (449509) along lane past Froghole Farm to B2026 (448513). Right here up steps (OHC) and follow OHC through woods and over Mariners Hill for ½ mile. In trees again near road at Chartwell, watch for left turn uphill (453514, OHC) on path. In ¼ mile, descend to cross road at Chartwell entrance gates (453519).
Ahead along bridleway (OHC). In ¼ mile cross road (456522, OHC) and on for ²/₃ mile to French Street. At road, right (459527, OHC) along road for ½ mile past Frenchstreet Farm. At a fork, left uphill (463521, OHC) into Toy's Hill Woods. Follow track (ignore side turns) and OHC past site of Weardale House (468518). In 100m, fork left; in another 20m, right (OHC) to car park.

The National Trust has devised two waymarked Octavia Hill Walk trails around Toys Hill – West and East. Download pdf leaflets at nationaltrust.org.uk/toys-hill, or pick up trail leaflets at Chartwell Visitor Centre or from Toys Hill car park dispensers.

Lunch Royal Oak, Crockham Hill, Edenbridge TN8 6RD (01732 866335; royaloakcrockhamhill.co.uk, westerhambrewery.co.uk), Landemare Café (run by the National Trust) at Chartwell (01732 863087)

Accommodation King's Arms, Market Square, Westerham, Kent TN16 1AN (01959 562990; oldenglishinns.co.uk/westerham), Chartwell – National Trust (01732 868381; nationaltrust.org.uk/chartwell)

Burpham
WEST SUSSEX

A perfect summer's morning over West Sussex — blue heavens with huge white cumulonimbus clouds reaching up from the South Downs skyline, warm sunshine spreading across the countryside like butter and wood pigeons sleepily cooing in the beech trees around Burpham. "Good morning!" quoth a man in a pink and white striped shirt, with that very British crispness that means, "Glad to see you in our beautiful village, but don't drop any sweet papers, will you? Thank you so much!"

The old valley track of Coombe Lane brought us up from the village to the downs, its elder bushes and guelder rose and spindle all beginning to come into fruit. The sun released warm, spicy wafts from tuffets of wild marjoram where meadow brown butterflies staggered, half drunk on the smell. A clump of thistles seethed with hungry goldfinches. Chalkhill blue butterflies clung to the nettles that grew along the chalky banks of pale grey soil, burrowed into a powdery tissue by rabbits. Two marsh harriers had come up from the wetlands by the River Arun, and we watched them making slow passes through the valley on their long dark wings.

The downland slopes were a maze of pale gold stubble fields where big straw bales lay doubled over like blankets in a giant's linen cupboard. The view widened back south from Wepham Down to a flat gleam of the distant sea, the Isle of Wight lying long in a grey haze on the south-west horizon. Up on the roof of the downs the ramparts of Rackham Banks — a Bronze Age cross dyke, probably a boundary marker, and a hill settlement in a hollow — were spattered with scabious, knapweed and poppies. We sat idling there, the chalk-white South Downs Way ribboning east and west, the ground plunging away north to the Arun snaking through the Sussex lowlands among woods and pastures.

The ancient ridge track dipped to Downs Farm, a pretty old farmhouse marooned in a monstrous muddle of harsh modern barns and silos. Here we turn off south, dropping into a steep, silent and nameless valley where sheep nibbled the turf and red kites turned on the thermals with crooked wings and subtly balancing tails. Then a last stretch beside the Arun, past an old tree-grown moated site that might well be part of the burh or fortified village established here by Alfred the Great 1100 years ago. A timeless walk, where now and then join hands seamlessly.

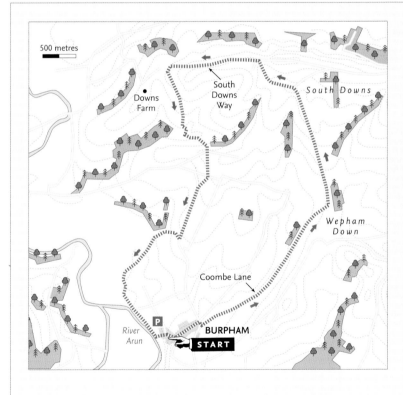

Start & finish Burpham village car park, BN18 9RR (OS ref TQ039089)

Getting there Train: (thetrainline.com, railcard.co.uk) to Arundel (2½ miles). Road: Burpham is signed off A27 just east of Arundel station.

Walk (7 miles, moderate, OS Explorer 121): Right along village street; in ⅓ mile, left up Coombe Lane (044090; fingerpost, blue arrow/BA). In 1½ miles at T-junction of tracks (061106), left (north) for 1½ miles to South Downs Way (051125). Left for ¾ mile. Just before Downs Farm, left (038125, 'Restricted Byway'). In 100m fork right ('bridleway' fingerpost, BA). South into valley bottom (041116); up and across tracks (044114, yellow arrow/YA) to corner of wood (044110, YA). South for ½ mile; at gateway with BAs (040102), take footpath beside it (YA) down to bottom of steps (039103). Left (BA). In ⅓ mile, right over stile (035099, YA); left across fields (stiles, YAs); keep right of moat (033094, YA); along river, back to Burpham.

Lunch The George at Burpham, Main Street, Burpham BN18 9RR (01903 883131; georgeatburpham.co.uk)

More information Arundel tourist information point in Arundel Museum (01903 882456), visitsussex.org, visitengland.com, ramblers.org.uk, satmap.com

Charlton and Goodwood
WEST SUSSEX

The Fox Goes Free at deep-sunk Charlton is one of my favourite Sussex pubs, especially when it's warm enough to sit in the garden with a pie and a pint, looking out across the flint wall and over the grazing sheep in the meadow beyond to the double swell of Levin Down and North Down.

Those seductive hills soon called Jane and me away, up along North Lane and past open sheds at Ware Barn full of hay bales and sacks of wool from last year's clip. Loose flints chinked under our boots as we climbed a dark holloway through an old yew grove.

From the broad whaleback of Levin Down we had a wonderful southward prospect across Singleton's grey houses huddled in their valley, over to the flags and white pavilions of Goodwood racecourse and the round knoll of the Trundle, crowned with the ramparts of an Iron Age hillfort.

It's a view from a patriotic wartime poster, a landscape worth fighting for, thousands of years of history rolling out in plain view. And if this is one of southern England's great views, it's outdone by the panorama from the Trundle itself — Chichester Cathedral spire, the twin grandstands of the racecourse, the sails of Halnaker windmill, the silvery windings of Chichester harbour, the Isle of Wight lying like a cloud along the smoky blue bar of the sea.

On the ramparts of the fort we sat and stared. At the height of summer the race meeting aptly nicknamed 'Glorious Goodwood' fills the course with noise and colour, but today it lay quiet, a green snake of grassy track rolling below us between its white railings. A childhood memory came to Jane — watching an excavation at the foot of the Trundle, a female skeleton being unearthed and the archaeologist pointing out her excellent teeth, "because there were no sweeties in those days".

The Trundle's embanked fort was built more than 2000 years ago, but the remnants of an enclosure three times as old underlie the stronghold. It's a resonant place with a most stupendous view.

Two sparrowhawks skimmed the ramparts, scanning the banks, and a couple lay in the long grass at the summit, talking quietly, as people have surely been doing here since long before men fortified the hill.

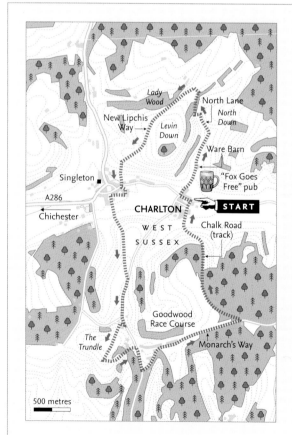

Start & finish Fox Goes Free Inn, Charlton, West Sussex PO18 0HU (OS ref SU889130)

Getting there Bus: Service 99 Petworth-Chichester (pre-book on 01903 264776; compass-travel.co.uk). Road: Charlton is signed off A286 Chichester-Midhurst road at Singleton.

Walk (7 miles, easy/moderate, OS Explorer 120): From Fox Goes Free, right along road; in 150m, right up North Lane. In ¾ mile, left (890141, bridleway fingerpost) up track through trees for ¼ mile to T-junction (889145). Left ('Singleton') through gate; over Levin Down via corner of Lady Wood (886143) for ⅔ mile to gate (883138). Bear right past fingerpost to kissing gate (880135, 'New Lipchis Way'); down to cross road in Singleton (879132). Cross green; follow 'The Leys' through houses (880131), past recreation ground and churchyard; left (878190, 'The Trundle') on path to lane (880119), across road (880113), climbing to summit of the Trundle (877111). Left (east) on Monarch's Way via woodland track and road; east past Goodwood racecourse (882110, 883107); then Chalk Road track north to Charlton.

Lunch The Fox Goes Free, Charlton PO18 0HU (01243 811461; thefoxgoesfree.com)

More information Chichester TIC (01243 775888; chichesterweb.co.uk), visitsussex.org, visitengland.com, satmap.com, ramblers.org.uk, Goodwood Racecourse (goodwood.co.uk)

Stoughton and Kingley Vale
WEST SUSSEX

A still, sunny day lay over West Sussex. Pigeons were loud and throaty in the beeches around Stoughton. The rumble of harrow and roller sounded faint and far off from the stubble fields around Old Bartons farmhouse, where a crowd of wailing seagulls followed the gleaming disks as they turned grubs and worms into the sunlight. A Hereford bull stood dazed with sleepiness against the fence and permitted me to scratch his woolly poll and stroke his warm, dusty coat.

Up on the crest of Stoughton Down the woods hung dense and silent, darkened with summer heat. I threaded the pine plantations and oak groves on Bow Hill, with sensational views opening to the south over the sinuous tidal channels of Chichester Harbour, as blue and rippled as silk. Tree-lined tracks led on to the brow of Kingley Vale National Nature Reserve and the rounded green Bronze Age burial mounds of the Devil's Humps.

Here, I was lucky enough to bump into Richard Williamson, for thirty years the manager of Kingley Vale, now its dedicated archivist and guardian angel. "The chalkhill blues are out," he confided. Following his directions, I found the brilliant silver-blue butterflies on the tiny patch they favoured at the edge of the reserve, and spent half an hour watching them feed, sunbathe and mate — heaven for butterflies, and pretty close to it for human beings, too. At last I got up from the sward of marjoram and harebells, shook out the cramps and went off to see the venerable yews of Kingley Vale. Visiting these bulbous trees with their arthritic limbs, all but naked of bark and extremely aged — some were old when the Romans arrived in Sussex — is like paying a call on a roomful of dignified, rather aloof Chelsea Pensioners in their birthday suits.

When eventually I tore myself away from their spell, it was to follow the path dreamily up through the flower-rich meadows of Kingley Vale, before resuming the downland ridge and the flinty trackway back to Stoughton in its sun-soaked hollow.

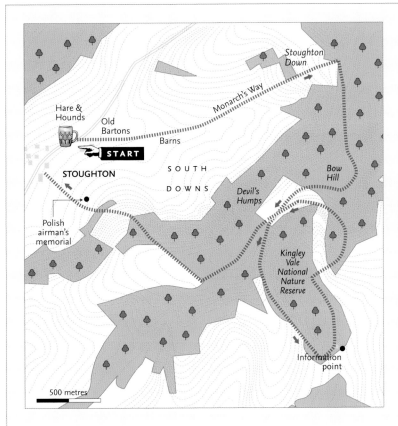

Start & finish Hare & Hounds, Stoughton PO18 9JQ (OS ref SU803115)

Getting there Train: (thetrainline.com, railcard.co.uk) to Chichester (8.3 miles). Road: A27 to Chichester; B2178 to Funtington; right by Fox & Hounds to Walderton; right to Stoughton.

Walk (6 miles, moderate grade, OS Explorer 120): Leaving Hare & Hounds, left up road. In 200m, right at Old Bartons (fingerpost, yellow arrow/YA); then fork left on gravelled track ('Monarch's Way' arrow). Pass barns (809115); on for 1 mile to three-way bridleway fingerpost (824121). Right; in 200m, fork left (blue arrow/BA) on narrower path through fir grove. In 600m pass BA on right; in 350m, reach track crossing by Kingley Vale NNR notice (825113; four-way fingerpost). Right along track for ½ mile. Just past Devil's Humps barrows, left by 'Nature Trail' post (819109), through gate. Follow numbered posts anticlockwise round Nature Trail, passing information shelter at 824100, for 2 miles to return to Devil's Humps. Resume walk along track. In 300m, keep ahead by Kingley Vale NNR notice (817107; bridleway fingerpost, BA). In ¼ mile, reach edge of wood (813105); right on track for 1 mile to road in Stoughton; right to Hare & Hounds.

Lunch Hare & Hounds, Stoughton (02392 631433; hareandhoundspub.co.uk) – a pub that knows it's a pub with excellent food, too

More information Tourist Information Point in Novium Museum, Tower Street, Chichester PO19 1QH (01243 775888; visitchichester.org), ramblers.org.uk

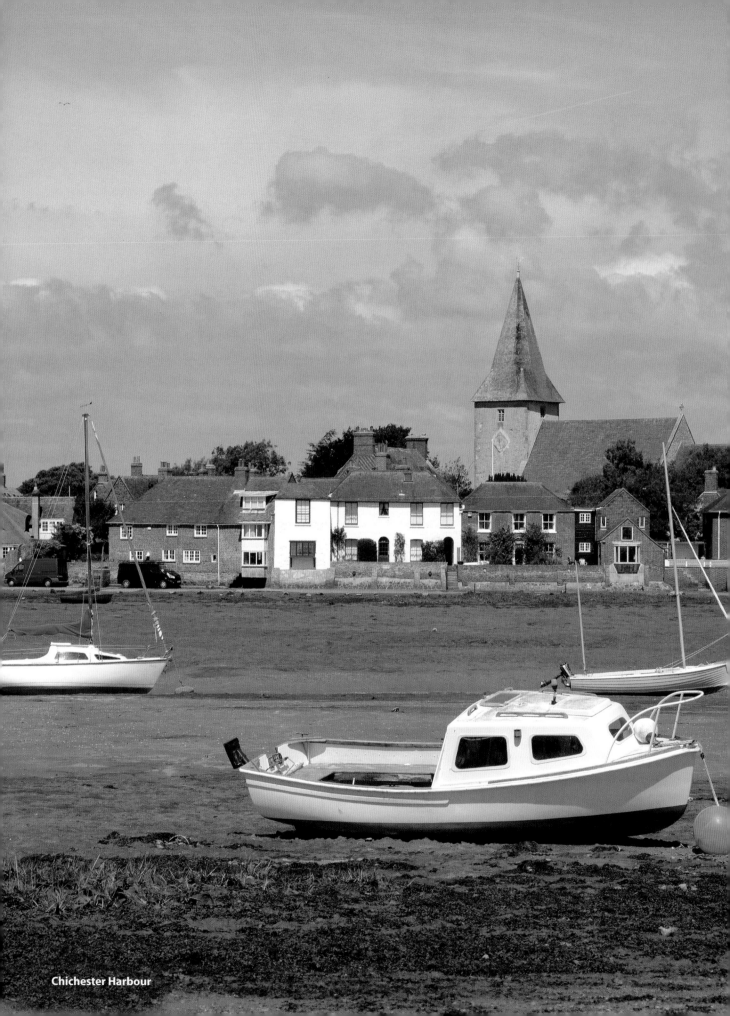

Chichester Harbour

Thorney Island
WEST SUSSEX

Wild plums, green and purple, hung heavy above the path as Jane and I began our circuit of Thorney Island, a narrow-necked peninsula suspended like a bulbous fruit from the inner shoreline of Chichester Harbour. A memorable feature of my wife's childhood in this low-lying coastal country had been the V-shaped bomber planes from Thorney Island's RAF base — long since closed — that would rumble overhead, low and dark in the sky.

Black-headed gulls screamed peevishly from the mud banks exposed at low water; oystercatchers piped and curlews made their melancholy bubbling cry. Salt, mud, seaweed — the smells were of tidal country under a drying wind.

As for the views, they widened over mud flats green with algae and weed, seamed with wriggling creeks known locally as rithes, out west to the low, wooded coastline of Hayling Island. Inland, hissing beds of reeds lined the waters of the broad ditch romantically named Great Deep.

Sea lavender lay in purple mats on the salt marshes. Leopard-spotted comma butterflies alighted on fleabane flowers and opened their scalloped wings to the sun. From the seawall path, the army establishment that replaced Thorney's RAF base in 1984 was so well hidden among the

trees it might not have been there. The only clue as to where those great triangular bombers had taken to the skies was a grey smear of runway tarmac, long disused.

We watched a lovely old wooden sailing boat scudding down Sweare Deep under a white bulge of jib, the mainsail rattling up as the boat heeled into Emsworth Channel. By the time we had reached Longmere Point at the nethermost tip of Thorney, the tide had crept in to cover mud flats, shell banks and rithes in a rippling world of water that spread south towards the open mouth of Chichester Harbour.

St Nicholas Church at West Thorney, "the least known and altogether uttermost church in Sussex", has stood here on the remote eastern coast of the island for 800 years. Wartime allied and German servicemen share the graveyard, foes in life, brothers in death.

Under the seawall, an unseen fish hunted the flood-tide shallows, dorsal fin and tail cutting the surface. Far to the east the spire of Chichester Cathedral glowed ghostly white in the evening sun, the South Downs ran in black and gold along the northern skyline, and from the marina moorings came the music of halyards blown by the wind against yacht masts, chinking and chiming like miniature bells.

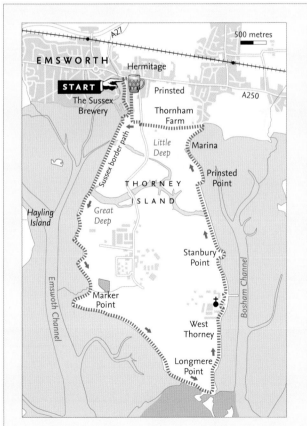

Start & finish Sussex Brewers PH, 36 Main Road, Hermitage, Emsworth PO10 8AU (OS ref SU755057)

Getting there Road: A27/A259 to Emsworth. Park in village; follow A259 to Sussex Brewery PH.

Walk (9 miles, easy, OS Explorer 120): Follow footpath down side of pub (fingerpost), then field edges south to boatyard. Right (755053, fingerpost) through Emsworth Yacht Harbour to sea wall. Left (753052, fingerpost) anticlockwise round Thorney Island for 7 miles, passing Little Deep (752047), Great Deep (749040), Marker Point (746023), Longmere Point (768011), West Thorney Church (770025), Stanbury Point (770031) and Prinsted Point (766042). At foot of road above Thornham Marina (766051), turn left inland along Sussex Border Path past Thornham Farm for ½ mile to cross Thorney Road (756051). Over stile (fingerpost), across field and opposite stile. Right (fingerpost) past stilt houses, and retrace path to Sussex Brewery PH.

Lunch Sussex Brewery PH, Hermitage (01243 371533; sussexbrewery.com) – a really friendly, clean and welcoming pub. Chichester Harbour Conservancy, Itchenor PO20 7AW (01243 512301; conservancy.co.uk) – walks, information and much more.

More information Tourist Information Point in Novium Museum, Tower Street, Chichester PO19 1QH (01243 775888; visitchichester.org), visitsussex.org, visitengland.com, satmap.com, ramblers.org.uk

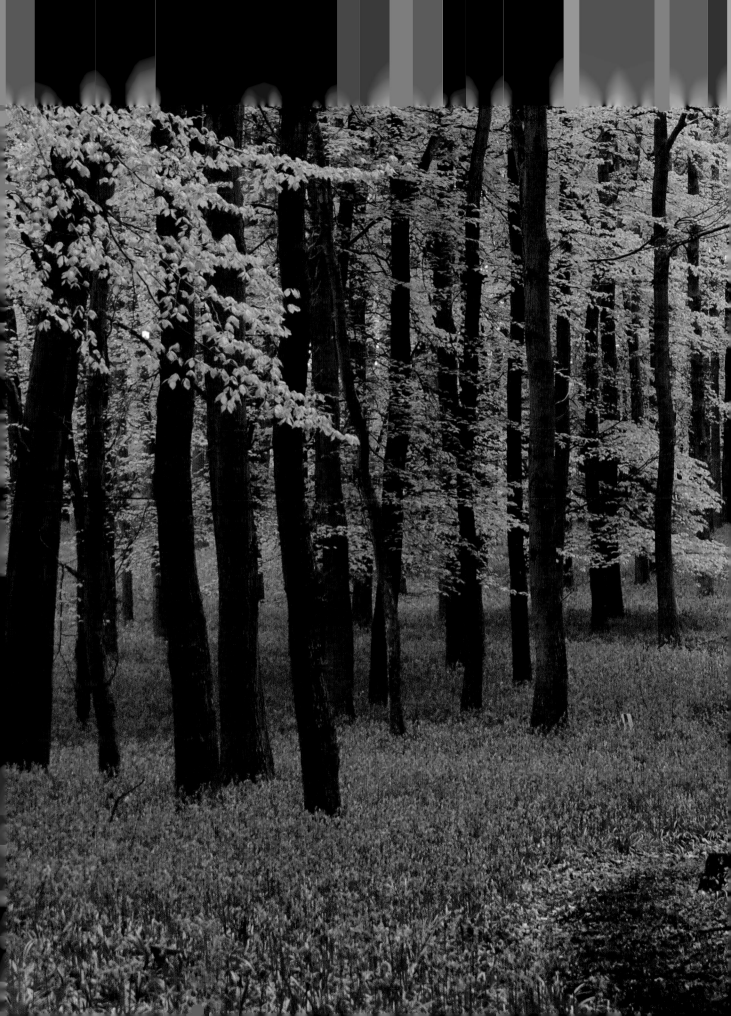

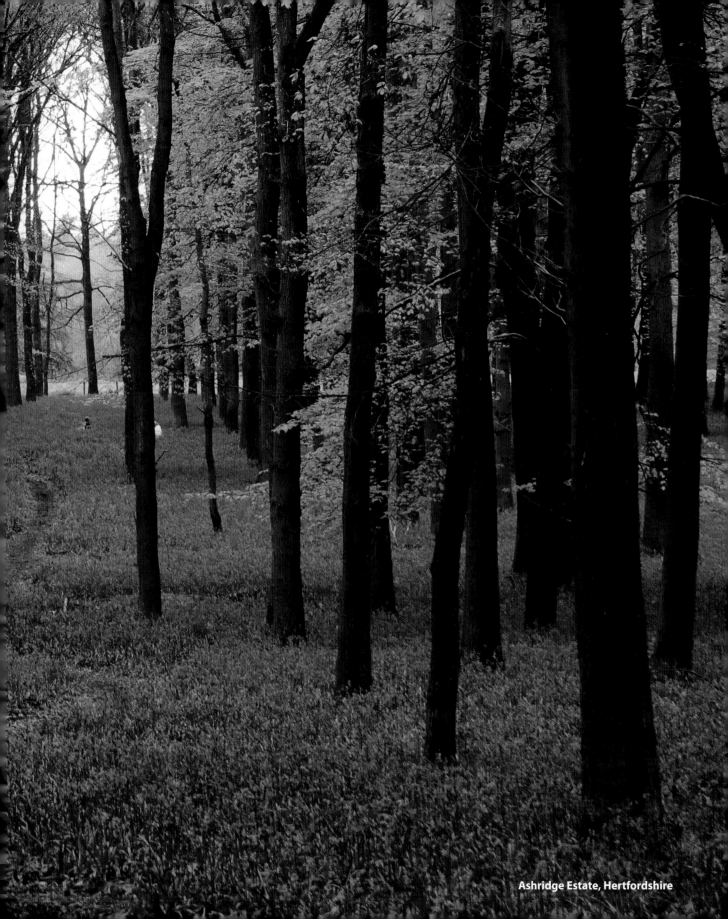

Ashridge Estate, Hertfordshire

The hedge roots around Hexton were spangled sherbet-yellow with primroses and the catkin-laden hazels were loud with explosive bursts of chaffinch song as I set out along Mill Lane from the Raven Inn. Across the north Hertfordshire fields, a skyline of sinuous chalk hills looked out towards the great clay plains of Bedfordshire, misty and cool on this fresh March morning.

Hexton's neighbouring hamlet of Pegsdon lies in a southward-bulging salient of Bedfordshire. The signboard of the Live and Let Live pub showed a dove and a peregrine falcon sitting amicably together beside an unloaded shotgun. So there are miracles still in the borderlands, just as the Bedfordshire tinker, fiddler and outlawed nonconformist preacher John Bunyan saw in visions when he roamed these hills in Restoration times — visions that drove him to compose *The Pilgrim's Progress* in the prison cells he was so long confined in.

In the south rose the Pegsdon Hills, the "Delectable Mountains" of Bunyan's fable. A winding path and hollow field lanes brought me to where the ancient Icknield Way rose along the nape of the hills, deeply sunken in a tunnel of beech and hornbeams studded with green buds. The 6000-year-old highway ran rutted, grassy and sun-splashed past Telegraph Hill, where a gaunt semaphore mast was once sited by the Admiralty, one of a chain that passed signals between London and far-off Great Yarmouth. A little farther along rose Galley or Gallows Hill, a place of ill-omen in Bunyan's time, where witches were buried and the tar-soaked bodies of executed criminals hung to terrify passers-by.

I turned off the old track, heading north over the rounded sprawl of Barton Hills. A nature reserve with dry chalk valleys too steep to plough, the hills remain a beautiful stretch of unspoilt chalk grassland. Trees disguised the ramparts of Ravensburgh Castle, the largest hillfort in southeast England. Beyond lay Bonefirehill Knoll, in former days the scene of the Hocktide Revels shortly after Easter. It doesn't take much post-Freudian analysis to work out the symbolism of Pulling the Pole, a game in which the men of Hexton tried to keep an ash pole erect on the hill, while the women strove to collapse it and drag it down into the village. Strange to relate, the women were always triumphant. I made my way down the hill and over the fields to Hexton, with plenty to ponder.

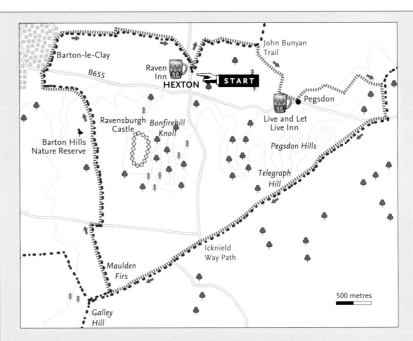

Start & finish Raven Inn, Hexton, Hitchin, Herts SG5 3JB (OS ref TL106307)

Getting there Train: (thetrainline.com) to Harlington (5 miles). Road: M1, Junction 12; A5120, then minor road to Harlington and Barton-le-Clay; B655 to Hexton.

Walk (10 miles, easy grade, OS Explorer 193): Leaving Raven Inn, turn left; walk up road past 'No Through Road' sign and continue for ½ mile, along Mill Lane, past Hexton Mill (blue bridleway waymarks), to pass between Green End and Bury Farm, and on to meet road (120306). Right for 300m, then left to pass Live & Let Live Inn (121303). In 100m, just before B655, left up Pegsdon Common Farm drive (fingerpost, 'Private Road'). Rounding a left bend, go right (125305 – fingerpost) up grass path and up steps, then on up right side of conifer plantation. At end of trees, continue along rim of dry valley to waymark post (129304 – Chiltern Way/CW waymark). Left along edge of escarpment for 300m; right along sunken lane (CW). Pass entrance to Knocking Hoe NNR and go over stile by gate (133305). Left (CW) for 150m, then right along field edge path (blue arrow, 'Walk on the Wild Side' waymark) for 500m to B655. Right for 250m along grass verge, then through car park and through gates and stiles to join the Icknield Way (132300).

Icknield Way climbs for nearly ¾ mile, then levels off. In another 400m, look on your right for kissing-gate with brown 'Access Land man' logo (121291). Continue along Icknield Way; at a fork in 150m, keep ahead for ¾ mile to meet a road (109282). Forward along verge for 500m; where road bends left under power lines, forward along Icknield Way for ⅔ mile to cross John Bunyan Trail (unmarked on ground) on edge of Maulden Firs (096275). Ahead for another 300m, then fork left (093273) to ascend Galley Hill.

From Galley Hill return to Icknield Way; retrace steps for 300m to edge of Maulden Firs wood; left along John Bunyan Trail, under power lines for ⅔ mile to road (093284). Right for 150m; left (fingerpost) through trees on path past Barton Hill Farm for ⅔ mile to pass gate of Barton Hills National Nature Reserve on your left (092296). Continue along track, noticing on your right the thickly wooded rampart of Ravensburgh Castle, and beyond it the tree-smothered Bonfirehill Knoll.

Follow track down slope for ⅔ mile to T-junction with lane (085303). Right past church to B655 in Barton-le-Clay (085305). Right for 50m, left along Manor Road. 100m past gates of Ramsey Manor School, right (086310 – fingerpost) down path, over footbridge and follow field edge. In 100m, ignore arrow pointing left; keep ahead for 1 mile along field edges, to cross footbridge (104311) and the final field into Hexton. Turn right to Raven Inn.

Lunch Raven Inn, Hexton (01582 881209; theraven.co.uk) or Live & Let Live, Pegsdon, Beds SG5 3JX (01582 881739; liveandletlive.co)

More information Letchworth TIC (01462 487868; letchworthgc.com), hertfordshire.com

Marston Vale
BEDFORDSHIRE

In the 1670s, John Bunyan modelled the sinner-snaring 'Slough of Despond' in his moral fable *Pilgrim's Progress* on the Bedfordshire morass of Marston Vale. Three centuries later, Marston Vale was still a waste landscape, albeit of an industrial nature. Its sticky clay expanses encompassed the world's most active brickfields, and thousands of acres were stripped and dug for the raw material of brickmaking. Since the 2008 closure of the Stewartby brickworks, though, a green transformation has been wrought in these unpromising flatlands.

We set off from Marston Vale Forest Centre, at 9am already lively with youngsters gathering for a mucky day out. The centre is the hub of the Forest of Marston Vale, a community forest that has seen a million trees planted across the old brickmaking wasteland. There are lakes, ponds, trails and woods where the clay was dug, and fantastic enthusiasm for their use among local people.

The thirteen-mile Marston Vale Timberland Trail leads across enormous cornfields towards an undulating greensand ridge. The path switchbacks through the woods on the ridge slope. Up on the open heights of Ampthill Park stands a memorial cross to Katherine of Aragon, wronged wife of King Henry VIII — she was incarcerated here while Henry wrangled to divorce her.

We stood looking out north across many sunlit miles of the Bedfordshire plain, before skirting the tall and haunted ruin of Houghton House — 'House Beautiful' in *The Pilgrim's Progress*. From here the cornfield paths returned us to the model village of Stewartby, flagged by the four mighty chimneys that still overshadow the redundant brickworks.

In their 1930s heyday the works produced 500 million bricks a year for the London Brick Company. Now the grey brickfields are turning green once more, and Stewartby's chimneys stand smokeless and gaunt over a beautiful lake, where the giant clay pits once lay in all their desolation.

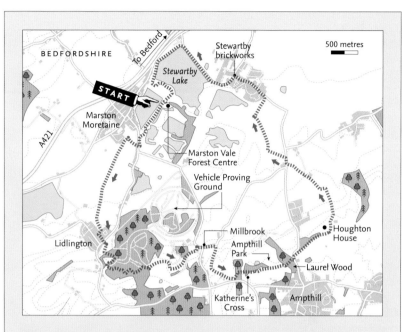

Start & finish Marston Vale Forest Centre, Marston Moretaine, Beds MK43 0PR (OS ref TL004418)

Getting there Train: to Millbrook or Stewartby (1 mile on foot). Bus: Service 52 from Bedford (bedford.gov.uk/transport_and_streets/public_transport/timetables). Road: M1 Jct 13; A421 towards Bedford. In 5 miles, 'Marston Moretaine, Sports Centre' signed to right. At T-junction in Marston, left; right at Co-op and follow 'Forest Centre'.

Walk (12½ miles, easy but long; OS Explorers 192, 193, 208): Outside Forest Centre, fingerpost points to Marston Vale Timberland Trail (TT). Follow excellently waymarked TT for 5½ miles to Katherine's Cross, Ampthill Park (025384). To visit Ampthill village, continue on TT. To bypass village – 250m past cross, fork left off TT by dog bin (028385). Follow Greensand Ridge Way through Laurel Wood to B530 (032387). Left for 100m; right (cross with care) on farm track, passing top of drive to Houghton House ruin (040393). Continue to gates of Houghton Park House; right over stile; footpath down 3 fields to plank footbridge (039401). Don't cross; turn left on TT and follow it for 4¼ miles back to Forest Centre.

NB: Sticky clay underfoot – mucky after rain.

Lunch Picnic; café at Forest Centre

Accommodation Black Horse, Ireland, Shefford, Beds SG17 5QL (01462 811398; blackhorseireland.com) – excellent restaurant with rooms

More information Forest Centre, Marston Moretaine (01234 767037; marstonvale.org), experiencebedfordshire.co.uk, visitengland.com, satmap.com, ramblers.org.uk

Cookham and the Wild Wood

BERKSHIRE

"It was a cold still afternoon with a hard steely sky overhead, when he slipped out of the warm parlour into the open air. The country lay bare and entirely leafless around him, and he thought that he had never seen so far and so intimately into the insides of things."

Crunching through the snowy fields to Cookham Dean, I caught myself looking out for the short, intent figure of Mole scurrying along in his newly bought goloshes. Kenneth Grahame was living in the Berkshire village at the turn of the twentieth century when he wrote *The Wind In The Willows* for his son, Alastair, who was nicknamed 'Mouse'. That story immortalised the landscape of the River Thames, its fine houses and meadows — and especially its woods. How thrilling to my childish imagination were the adventures of Mole and Ratty in the Wild Wood! Now, leaving Cookham Dean's whitened village green and entering snow-bound Quarry Wood, I found myself in the thick of that sinister forest.

A sunken cart track led down to the bottom of the wood. I turned back along a path between bushes of spindle whose brilliant orange seeds pushed through splits in bright pink fruit cases, the brightest colours in the sombre wood. With the muted winter sun already setting and shadows lying long on the snow under the trees, I was visited by a frisson from childhood, the thing that Rat had tried to shield poor Mole from, "the Terror of the Wild Wood".

A stunning panorama from Winter Hill over the graceful curves of the Thames; then a peaceful stretch under frozen willows along the riverbank in the half-light of dusk. I got into Cookham just in time to catch the Stanley Spencer Gallery, a treasure-house of the fabulous art of another celebrated Cookham resident. What an odd, complicated and ecstatic vision this kind-of-naive painter brought to his work, most of it rooted in his beloved native village. And how strange to walk from the black hollows and snow-crusted trees of Grahame's Wild Wood into Spencer's summery Cookham of picnickers in short sleeves, girls in bathing dresses, and the figure of Christ in a black straw boater preaching with fiery fury from a punt at Cookham Regatta.

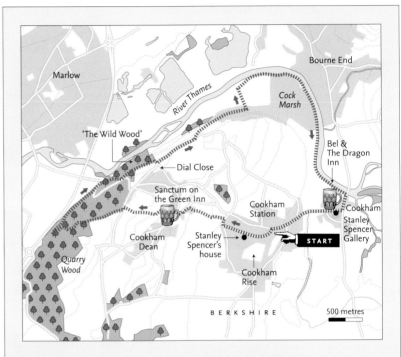

Start & finish Cookham Station, Berks SL6 9BP (OS ref SU886850)

Getting there Train: (thetrainline.com; railcard.co.uk) to Cookham. Bus: Arriva (arrivabus.co.uk) service 35/37. Road: M40, A404 Marlow; A4155, A4095 Cookham; B4447 to station.

Walk (7½ miles, easy/moderate, OS Explorer 172): From station, left, then first left along High Road for ½ mile to T-junction (879851). Right for 75m; field path (yellow arrows/YA) to Cookham Dean (874853). Village green; pub sign – Sanctum on the Green (871853). Path west for ⅓ mile, through dip to road (864853). Bridleway west for ¾ mile through Quarry Wood. At 'Restricted Byway' sign (854849), back along bottom of wood for ⅔ mile. Cross Quarry Wood Road (861857); right up fenced path to road (864857); don't cross! Left on path for ⅓ mile to road at Dial Close (870860). Left beside road for ⅓ mile; left down Stonehouse Lane (874863); in 20m, right along Chiltern Way/CW. At fork beyond gate, leave CW; downhill to foot of slope; left (882867, fingerpost) across field to Thames; right to Cookham Bridge; right into Cookham High Street. Pass Stanley Spencer Gallery (896853); path beside B4447 to station.

Lunch Sanctum on the Green, Cookham Dean SL6 9NZ (01628 482638, sanctumonthegreen.com), Bel & the Dragon, Cookham SL6 9SQ (01628 521263; belandthedragon-cookham.co.uk)

More information Stanley Spencer Gallery: winter opening Thurs-Sun, 11am-4.30pm; summer opening every day 10.30am-5.30pm (01628 471885; stanleyspencer.org.uk), satmap.co.uk, ramblers.org.uk

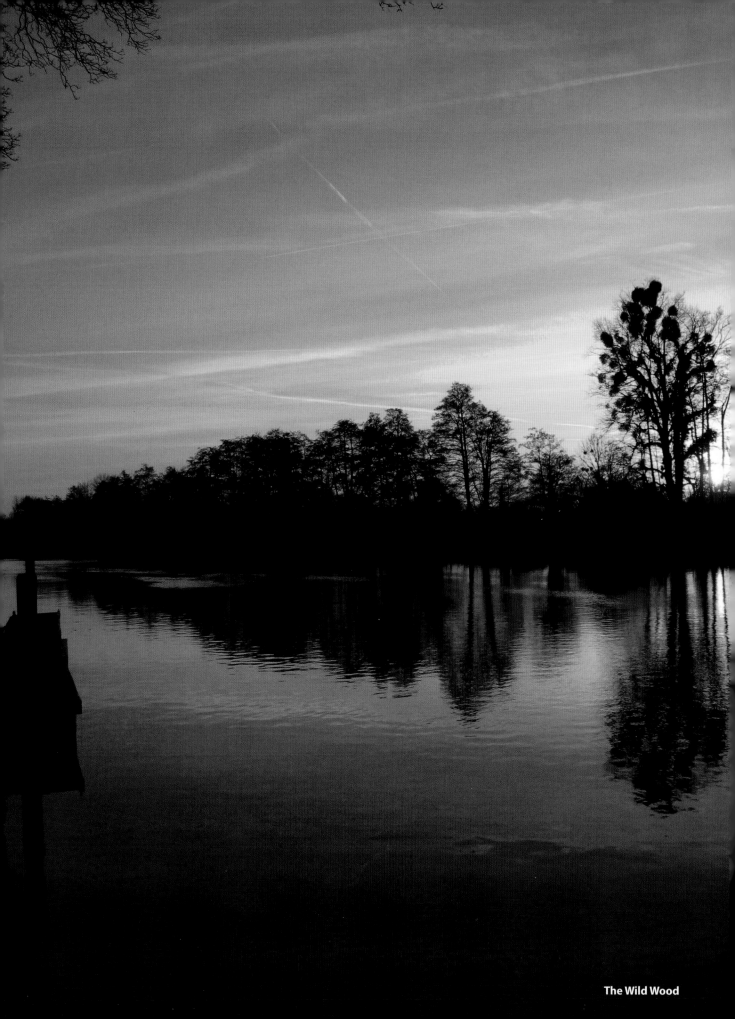

The Wild Wood

Hurley and the River Thames

BERKSHIRE

Hurley lies modestly beside the Thames a little west of London, a quiet village of handsome red-brick houses. The single road ends just before the river at the remnants of a Benedictine priory — church, house and barn made of flint, infilled with that soft blocky building chalk known as clunch.

Jane and I set out under a sky opaque with cold milky light. A scraping of snow clung to the field slopes. Big burly sheep cropped the grass, their fleeces dark with winter mud. Under the sycamores and beeches in High Wood at the top of the down, little Eeyore-style shelters of propped-up sticks showed where local children had been hiding out in their own make-believe world.

A horse-gallop as wide as a main road led like a green highway towards thickly wooded Ashley Hill, where bare trees stood knotted with mistletoe clumps — a skeletal landscape as thin and stark as this midwinter season. By contrast we found the chimney of the Dew Drop Inn smoking cheerfully. The secluded pub exuded a seductive smell of burning beech

and hazel logs. What a siren note a good pub fire sings out to winter walkers. We stepped inside out of the cold air and spatter of rain, and found soft lamplight, low chatter and the growl of sweet soul music on the sound system. A quick one, eh?

Back outside in a nipping wind we went on along a muddy bridleway that wound through green country, gently rolling, generously wooded. From a nature reserve coppice we got a stunning view out over a swooping field where seven dark horses walked slowly in line abreast up the slope, tossing their heads conversationally together. On the squared-off stump of a fence-post lay the greeny-white skull of a squirrel, clean and feather-light, the long incisors seeming too large for the narrow face.

Down in the valley, the Thames ran swollen and brassy brown, a muscular arm of water flexing towards London and the sea. We followed it back to Hurley through flooded meadows where Canada geese sailed with dignity and black-headed gulls screeched over their feast of drowned insects like greedy clubmen over the port and stilton.

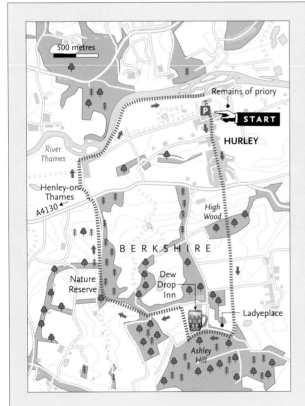

Start & finish Hurley village car park, High Street, Hurley SL6 5NB approx. (OS ref SU825840)

Getting there Bus: Services 239/239 (courtneybuses.com), Henley-on-Thames-Maidenhead. Road: Hurley is signposted off the A4130 between Maidenhead and Henley-on-Thames.

Walk (5½ miles, easy, OS Explorer 172): From car park, right along village street to cross A4130 (827831). Ahead up fenced path. At top of rise, ahead (828827) through High Wood, then on along horse gallop (yellow arrow/YA). In 600m cross track (828820); ahead (YA) across field and along green lane past Ladye Place to road (828815). Right; follow 'Dew Drop Inn' past end of Honey Lane (825815). In 250m, right (823814; 'Knowl Hill Bridleway Circuit'/KHBC) past Dew Drop Inn. In 400m, left at T-junction (822818; KHBC). In 400m, right (818817) along track. In 600m, enter nature reserve (813819). At far end KHBC turns left (813822), but go right here ('bridleway') for ½ mile to cross A4130 (812830). Down Black Boy Lane to River Thames (810835). Right on Thames Path for 1¼ miles. At tall footbridge (825842), right to car park.

Lunch Dew Drop Inn, Honey Lane, Hurley, SL6 6RB (01628 315662; dewdrophurley.co.uk) – warm and welcoming

More information Maidenhead TIC (01628 796502; windsor.gov.uk), visitengland.com, satmap.com, ramblers.org.uk

Kintbury and Hamstead Park

BERKSHIRE

A blustery afternoon with a driving sky and reports of trees down across Berkshire. It was a day just like this, according to an anonymous poet of the school of William McGonagall, when the old church tower at Kintbury blew down:

> "Fate had decreed, come down he must,
> And Boreas then gave him an extra gust,
> And down he went with a crashing fall,
> Clocks, birds, bats, the green ivy and all."

The church bell, often cursed by the villagers for its loudness, rolled into the River Kennet and tolls there still — according to legend. However, all we heard as we set out was the ting-ting of the level-crossing bell and the rattle of a London-bound train.

It's a very long time since the Kennet & Avon Canal provided 'logistics solutions' to the broad green countryside of the Kennet Valley. We walked its muddy towpath by still waters through a tangle of willows, reeds and marshy ground. A fisherman had hooked a rainbow trout, but it got away with a mighty splashing as he drew it to the bank. "That's the trickiest bit," he said, ruefully, "when they catch sight of the net!"

At Hamstead Lock we crossed the canal bridge and entered the green spaces of Hamstead Park. Fine specimen oaks and chestnuts, some very old and storm-blasted, raised skeletal limbs to the racing clouds. A pair of red kites hung on their elbow crooks and bounced in the wind over our heads, craning their necks to assess us from on high.

We came up from the pools and lakes along the Kennet and followed a path beside an ash coppice, where ripe sloes hung from blackthorn twigs.

In the rutted fields around Barr's Farm, friesian heifers came cantering up to check us out. The silvery light of a stormy winter's evening streaked the west as we turned away from the long line of the Berkshire Downs and dropped back down to Shepherd's Bridge and the homeward path along the old canal.

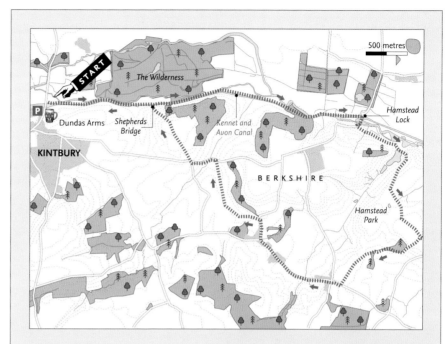

Start & finish Kintbury Station, Berkshire RG17 9UT (OS ref SU386672)

Getting there Rail: to Kintbury. Road: Kintbury is signed off A4 between Hungerford and Newbury. Use The Dundas Arms car park opposite station (ticket from pub).

Walk (7½ miles, easy, OS Explorer 158): Left (east) along north bank of canal for 2½ miles to Hamstead Lock (423670). Cross bridge; at right bend of road, left (yellow arrow/ YA) into Hamstead Park. Follow drive for ¾ mile; at right bend into The Mews, ahead off drive through kissing gate (428661, YA). Ahead across grass to drive (428659). Left; at left bend by memorial, right through gate (431657, YA). Aim a little right to gate into trees (429656, YA). Path/YAs for ¾ mile to road (421651). Right along road (take care on road) through Hamstead Marshall. In ¾ mile, right (412657, 'Marsh Benham'); in 250m, left (411659, stile, YA). Half left across field to track (407659); right for 700m to lane (406665). Left past Peartree Cottage; in 100m, right (403665, stile, YA). Path across field to conifer plantation (401668); right on grassy track; down to cross Shepherd's Bridge (398672). Left to Kintbury.

Lunch/accommodation The Dundas Arms, Kintbury RG17 9UT (01488 658263, dundasarms. co.uk) – a warm, stylish stopover

More information Newbury TIC (01635 30267; visitnewbury.org.uk), visitengland.com, satmap.com, ramblers.org.uk, The Kintbury Great Bell ballad (berkshirehistory.com/legends/kintburybell_bal.html)

Windsor Great Park

BERKSHIRE

Gentlemen in cream linen jackets and white hats, ladies in floral dresses. A solitary zephyr that stirred this baking summer morning in the southern end of Windsor Great Park. Lord, what a beautiful day!

The Royal Landscape (Savill Garden, Valley Gardens and Virginia Water) was at its peak, the Savill Garden especially. Its many decades of scrupulous landscaping, planting and pruning were bursting out in this sensational weather in a carefully crafted 'sweet disorder' of rhododendrons — purple, pink, orange, peach, white, mauve.

The gardens, created in the 1930s, only occupy 14 hectares (35 acres), but I could happily have lost myself all day following the trails to the Hidden Gardens and the intensely scented Rose Garden, through Spring Wood and Summer Wood, past the coot sailing in the Obelisk Pond and the flood of psychedelic colour from the Senetti magenta in the Queen Elizabeth Temperate House.

At last I tore myself away, paused in the Savill Building for a glass of lemonade that hardly touched the sides going down, and set out through the glades and lawns of Windsor's wider Great Park. This is one of England's oldest parks, founded by William the Conqueror and embellished over a thousand years by his successors.

After the beautifully sculpted formality and simmering heat of the Savill Garden, it was like throwing off a heavy cloak to wander in the shade of the oaks and sweet chestnuts, past Cow Pond (a unique Baroque water feature, recently restored from dereliction), and to see what artless nature had scattered in the grass — bluebells, milkmaids, red campion, buttercups. Up at Snow Hill, King George III in green bronze looked out from his seat on a pawing horse over the Great Park, where the Long Walk ran arrow-straight between newly mown verges towards the distant towers and battlements of Windsor Castle nearly three miles away.

Back south through the woods and down beside the wide empty polo field, and a final saunter through hilly Valley Gardens and along the tree-lined banks of Virginia Water, that vast man-made lake, in a blue simmering haze of heat so arcadian I might just have dreamed the whole walk up.

Start & finish Savill Garden car park, Englefield Green, Berks TW20 0UJ (OS ref SU977707)

Getting there Train: to Egham: 2½ miles (thetrainline.com; railcard.co.uk). Road: Savill Garden (car park: free to Savill Garden visitors, charges for non-visitors) signposted from A30 (M25 Jct 13).

Walk (7½ miles, easy grade, OS Explorer 160): Start with circuit of Savill Garden (check windsorgreatpark.co.uk for charges). Return to car park; leaving Savill Building, left (north) along tarmac track. In 300m, ahead past 'No Cycling' notice (977710). In 400m, left past end of Cow Pond. Left on track from pond's left (west) edge; in 300m, right (972715) up tarmac drive. In ½ mile pass pink lodge (976722); through gates (press button); over Spring Hill to equestrian statue on Snow Hill (967727). Left (south) on grassy ride for ½ mile into trees. In 250m, seven tracks meet (967717); left on gravel path bisecting two tarmac drives. In 400m, at five-way junction (971715), right on gravel path; on beside Smith's Lawn for 1 mile. Just before bridge over Virginia Water, bear left (966695; 'Lakeside Walk'). Follow along shore for 1½ miles; left past Totem Pole (980696); follow 'Savill Gardens' to car park.

Lunch Savill Garden Restaurant in the Savill Building (01784 485402)

More information Windsor TIC (01753 743900; windsor.gov.uk), windsorgreatpark.co.uk, thecrownestate.co.uk/Windsor

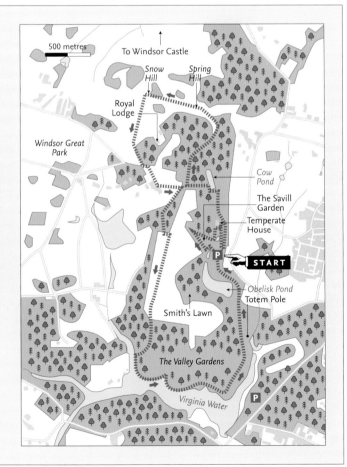

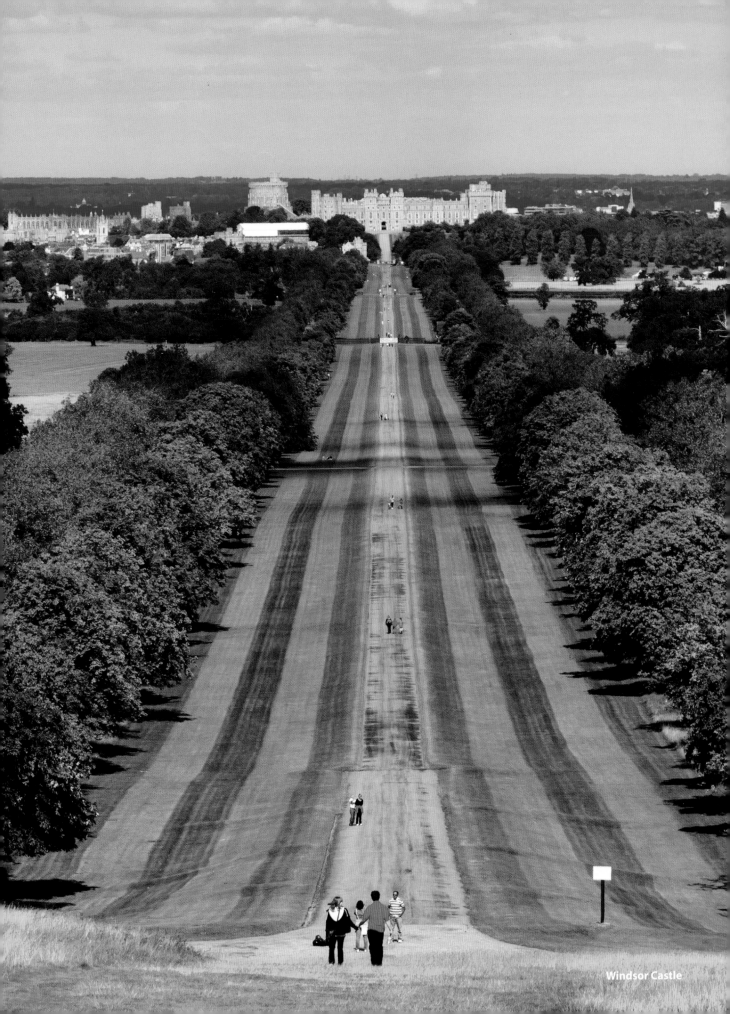

Windsor Castle

It was hard to leave the comfort and good cheer of the Plough at Cadsden, but the sound of rooks cawing among the blossoming treetops fetched us out at last along the Ridgeway into a cool, cloudy Buckinghamshire afternoon. Large edible snails were crawling on the grassy slopes of Grangelands Hill, where half a dozen hungry red kites wheeled overhead.

What a fantastic success story the reintroduction of red kites to the Chiltern Hills has been. Thirty years ago there were none of the big fork-tailed birds here; today there are so many pairs — 300 at least — that they can't be counted accurately.

If you are looking for a wildflower walk, this circuit is a slice of heaven. In the beech and oak woods, where the new leaves gleamed a shiny lime green, we found yellow archangel, woodsorrel, delicate white anemones and carpets of blue and white bluebells. Out in the cornfields we spotted groundsel, scarlet pimpernel and beautiful yellow and violet heartsease. As for the chalky grassland of the open downs — cowslips and primroses, jack-by-the-hedge and herb Robert, speedwell and forget-me-not, guelder rose and early purple orchids ...

Rounding the corner of Whorley Wood we came suddenly on the sublime prospect of the shallow valley where Chequers sits, the handsome red brick Elizabethan manor house making a centrepiece for some subtle landscaping. It seems extraordinary, and admirably English, to be able to stroll across the driveway of the Prime Minister's country retreat without so much as a by-your-leave — though the CCTV cameras tell you that any private enterprise in the shape of a detour would likely be discouraged with extreme prejudice.

Up through Goodmerhill Wood we went, following the Ridgeway to the tall Boer War monument at the prow of Coombe Hill. A pause here for a glug of water and a stare over what must be a 100-mile view over fields, woods and hill ranges, as far as Salisbury Plain and the Malvern Hills on a good clear day. Then we quit the Ridgeway for a woodland track along the edges of Low Scrubs, where twisted beech and hornbeam made a dark and mysterious Grimm's fairytale of the old coppice wood.

Peewits were tumbling over the beanfields around Dirtywood Farm and a pair of crows swooped on a red kite like fighter boys from Biggin Hill. Bandits at Angels Five!

We dropped steeply down through Ninn Wood, brilliant in late afternoon sunshine, until the Plough Inn hove up ahead, a cosy port in a green sea of leaves.

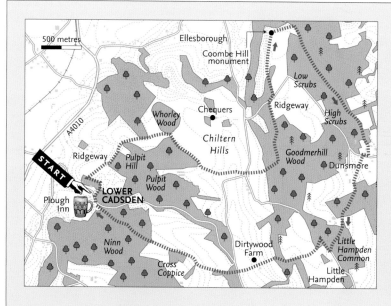

Start & finish Plough Inn, Lower Cadsden, Princes Risborough HP27 0NB (OS ref SP826045). Pub car parking only for walkers who are customers; please ring, book a table and ask about parking.

Getting there Train: (thetrainline.com, railcard.co.uk) to Monks Risborough (1½ miles). Bus: (arrivabus.co.uk) Service 300 Aylesbury-High Wycombe to Askett roundabout (⅔ mile). Road: Cadsden signed from Askett roundabout on A4010 (Princes Risborough-Wendover).

Walk (7½ miles, moderate, OS Explorer 181): From Plough, left along road; in 10m, right; Ridgeway (fingerposts, white acorns) for 3¼ miles to pass Coombe Hill monument (849067). In 300m, right off Ridgeway ('Bridleway') for 150m to wide crossing track. Left for 100m; right (853067) along wide track. In 200m, left on woodland track (yellow arrows/ YAs on trees) for 1 mile past Low and High Scrubs to Dunsmore (862052); Little Hampden Common (857040); Dirtywood Farm (848038); past Cross Coppice; through Ninn Wood to Plough Inn.

Lunch/B&B Plough Inn (01844 343302; ploughatcadsden.com) – it welcomes walkers

More information Princes Risborough TIC (01844 274795), visitbuckinghamshire.org, chilternsaonb.org, ramblers.org.uk

Cuddington and the Winchendons
BUCKINGHAMSHIRE

It is a bleak and blowy winter's day, with a sky full of those bruised clouds that foretell heavy rain. Even the charms of Cuddington — thatched houses of silver-gold stone, an excellent village shop and a gorgeous church on a knoll — can't hold us. We long to be out in the subtle, low-rolling landscape, walking off sloth, that insidious old enemy, before the Clerk of the Weather spies us.

The River Thame bubbles full of snow-melt floods. It races under its flimsy footbridge and laps into the fields around Old Mill. Out along the Thame Valley path, swans paddle in the flooded aspen groves and a big red kite balances over them, adjusting its crooked wings and forked tail to each nuance of the wind.

The whole land lies muted, still and beautiful. This is a countryside swept and sailed through by winter. Giant old oaks stand stark and bare in the fields of winter wheat. The close-shaven hedges guard ditches brimming with brown water. The field paths clog and bog us so that we wear what seems to be two pairs of boots apiece, our own encased in huge clown boots of mud and flood-scattered straw.

At Eythrope Park the river surges with a soft roar under the bridge beside a fabulous fantasy house of carved wood, fishtail tiles and Tudor chimneys. The splendidly individualistic Alice de Rothschild built it in the 1870s as the lodge for her nearby country house, The Pavilion. She laid her hand decisively on the stable block along the drive, too, with lashings of half-timbering, bright red brick and candlesnuffer roofs.

Long paths through parkland and fields bring us up to the church and manor house at Upper Winchendon, down again over ridges and silent little dells to church and manor at Nether Winchendon. What a contrast to the garish gloriosities of Eythrope, these settled and graceful old compositions of house, church, gardens and trees.

If you wanted to show visitors from abroad the essence of England, you'd probably show them Nether Winchendon.

Back across the eddying, still rising Thame; back over the fields to beat the rain into Cuddington by a short head, with the lights of the Crown shining through the dusk like welcoming beacons at the harbour mouth.

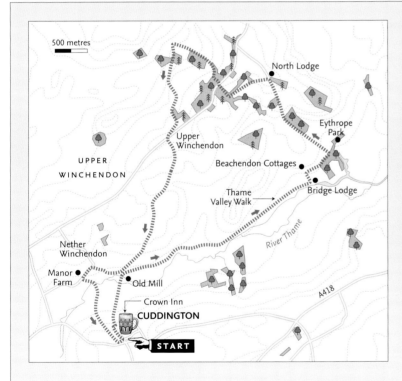

Start & finish Crown Inn, Cuddington, Bucks HP18 0BB (OS ref SP738111)

Getting there Rail: (thetrainline.com; railcard.co.uk) to Haddenham (2 miles). Bus: Service 110 (redlinebuses.com), Aylesbury-Thame. Road: Cuddington is signed off A418 between Aylesbury and Thame.

Walk (9 miles, easy grade, OS Explorer 181): Crown Inn, Cuddington; Upper Church Street, Tibbys Lane (737112), footpath across River Thame to Old Mill (738121). Right ('Thame Valley Walk') for 2½ miles to Bridge Lodge (767135). Beachendon Cottages; Eythrope Park gate (770140); Swan's Way for 1 mile to North Lodge (760151). Left; in ½ mile, right at post before reaching drive (754148; no arrow). Cross road; through trees; right, and follow drive for ½ mile; left through gate (745156); yellow arrow waymarks (YAs) for 1 mile south; cross road in Upper Winchendon (744141). Pass to right of cottage; cross stile (745140); follow top of bank to stile (746139; YA); diagonally right, and follow YAs/ stiles for 1¼ miles across fields (743133-742129-741125) to Old Mill. Right to road in Nether Winchendon (733122). Left past Manor Farm, left (731120) on path to Cuddington.

Lunch Crown Inn, Cuddington (01844 292222; thecrowncuddington.co.uk) – warm, friendly, welcoming

More information Thame TIC (01844 212833), visitbuckinghamshire.org, ramblers.org.uk, satmap.co.uk

Latimer, Chenies and Chess Valley

BUCKINGHAMSHIRE

Mr William Liberty of Chorleywood, nonconformist brickmaker, died in 1777. In his will he had categorically stated that he was not to be buried anywhere within the bounds of a church. His wife, Alice, was of the same mind. And so for well over 200 years the freethinking and aptly named Liberties have lain in modest state in their brick-built tomb by the field path to Chenies Bottom.

Passing the tomb, I wondered whether Mr Liberty would have sucked his teeth at last night's Midsummer Music festival — celestially beautiful music, sublimely played, within the bounds of Latimer's Victorian church. There were certainly wings to my heels and tunes at the back of my head as I followed the Chess Valley Walk through head-high grasses and champagne-scented elderflower blossom, past Mill Farm and on to Tyler's watercress farm at the ford on Holloway Lane. The dimpling Chess, a gin-clear stream over a clean gravel bed, raises wonderful crops of cress, and a couple of pounds secured me a crunchy and eye-wateringly peppery bunch to chew as I went on over the fields to Holy Cross church at Church End.

William Liberty might have approved the craftsmanship, if not the location, of the fourteenth-century paintings under the dark timber roof of Holy Cross. Here are a slim young Virgin astonished before the angel Gabriel and his remarkable news, a shepherd carrying a lamb to Bethlehem, and a musical angel blowing a celebratory blast on a shawm with twin pipes.

Back down the field slope, and on west across the Chess on a lush wet path, then up under the shade of hornbeam and bird cherry into Chenies village. History lies thick on the great Tudor mansion of Chenies Manor where King Henry VIII still walks at night, a limping ghost.

In the adjacent church, generations of Russells, dukes and duchesses of Bedford, lie entombed. I found something a little oppressive about the pomp and grandeur of the monuments looming in the Bedford chapel. It was a relief to be out under the cool grey sky again, walking the ridge path back to Latimer and looking across the river valley to where the Liberties lay free and easy among the nettles and dog roses.

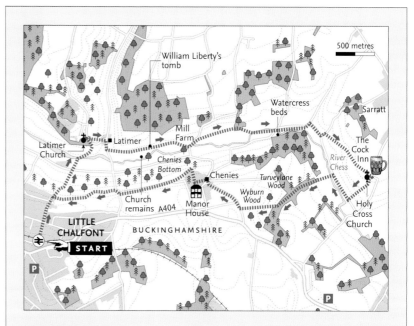

Start & finish Chalfont & Latimer Tube station, Bucks, HP7 9PR (OS ref SU997975)

Getting there Rail: Metropolitan Tube. Road: A404 to Little Chalfont.

Walk (7 miles, easy, OS Explorer 172): Chalfont & Latimer station; left along Bedford Avenue; right along Chenies Avenue (996976). Where it bends left into Beechwood Avenue (996981), ahead into woods. At junction (997981, blue arrows/BA, yellow arrows/YA), ahead downhill to bottom of wood and kissing gate (998983). Cross road (999985) and river (000986); right to cross road (004987; 'Chess Valley Walk'/CVW, fish waymark). Follow CVW for 1¾ miles to road (031990); right; round left bend, right (033989) on path to Sarratt church and Cock Inn (039984). South gate of churchyard — valley bottom (035981); right for 400m, left across River Chess (034984; NB: wet and muddy). Chiltern Way to road (021980); right to Chenies church (016983); right at Manor, into woods. At tree with three arrows, left along upper edge of wood; ridge track to cross Stony Lane (005982); track for ½ mile to junction in woods (997981, BA, YA); left to station.

Lunch Cock Inn, Sarratt, Herts WD3 6HH (01923 282908; cockinn.net)

Accommodation Latimer Place, Latimer, Chesham HP5 1UG (0871 2224810; deverevenues.co.uk). Chenies Manor Tours, Chenies, Bucks WD3 6ER (01494 762888; cheniesmanorhouse.co.uk)

More information Midsummer Music festival, Latimer – every June (01494 783643, midsummermusic.org.uk), Chalfont St Giles TIC (01494 874732), visitbuckinghamshire.org, satmap.com, ramblers.org.uk

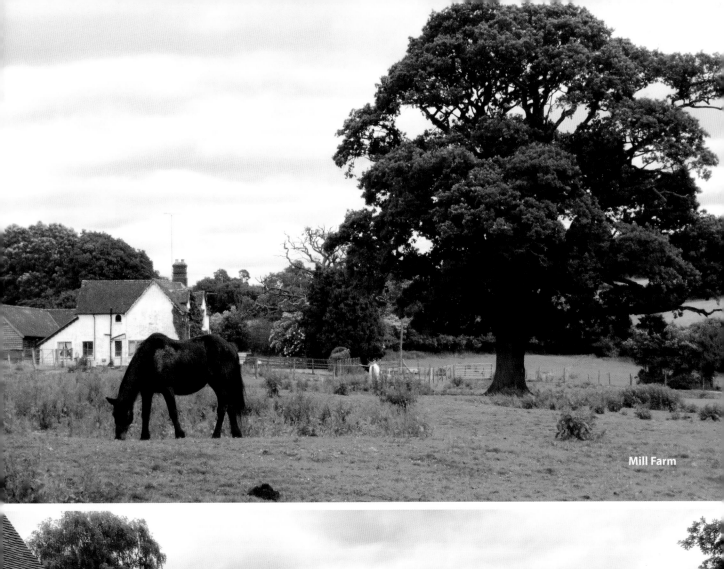

Mill Farm

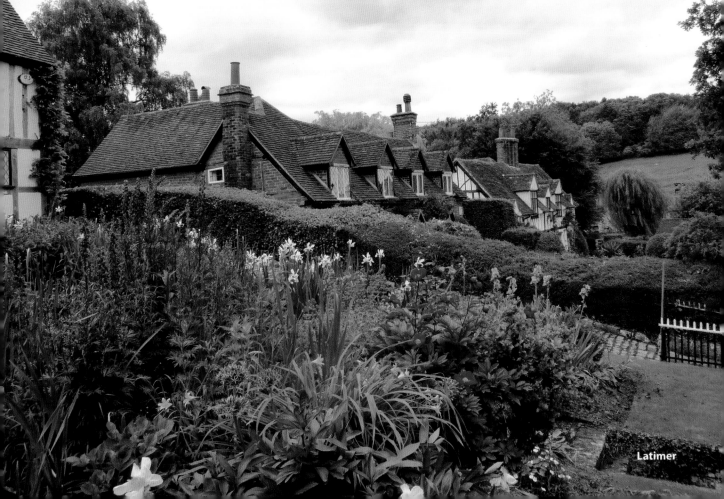

Latimer

The sun had just risen over Hatchet Wood as we left the Frog Inn, pursued by the raucous "Get-up-and-at-'em!" of Skirmett's alarm-cock. Blackthorn and field maple, bramble bushes and wayfaring trees edged the track that climbed Elmdown to reach the skirts of Great Wood. Here we sat on a fallen beech, its trunk rotted and eaten by insects into bare sinews of black and brown, to watch two red kites circling and talking to each other with staccato, kitten-like mews.

The long, narrow valley of the Hamble Brook, running north-to-south to meet the River Thames near Henley, is thick with beautiful mature Buckinghamshire woodland, easy to get lost in if you don't keep your wits (and your GPS device) about you. Roe deer haunted the trackways of Great Wood, slipping away into the shadows as soon as glimpsed. Between beech trunks streaming with dusty sunlight we caught glimpses of the crossed sails of Turville Windmill, high and mighty on a sharp-cut ridge. Great tits went chasing through the pines. And, at the edge of the wood, a burst of feathers edged with blue and black showed where a jay

had come to a sudden full stop — fox, peregrine or shotgun.

We emerged at last from the woods to a superb prospect over Hambleden and its valley — the pale chalky green-and-white of ploughed fields; green pasture in squares and lozenges; the hanging woods above; and the red brick walls and tiled roofs of the village clustered round the grey church, half hidden among its trees. If you ever have to illustrate 'essence of rural England' to a Martian, here's the view.

Down among the half-timbered Arts & Crafts gables, terracotta chimneys and flint cobble walls of the village, a herd of pedigree cattle stood under a massive beech. I put my hand over the fence, and one of them licked it with a pale muscular tongue as abrasive as sandpaper. Out along the valley, red kites had gathered over the pastures; we counted eighteen in the air at the same time, their red, white and chocolate forms brilliantly lit in strong sunlight. Under these fork-tailed guardian angels we followed the field paths back to Skirmett.

Start & finish Frog Inn, Skirmett, Henley-on-Thames, Oxon RG9 6TG (OS ref SU775902). NB – alternative start at Hambleden (more parking). If starting from the Frog Inn, please ask permission, and please give the inn your custom.

Getting there Road: M40 Jct 5, and minor roads via Ibstone; or A4155 (Henley-on-Thames to Marlow) to Mill End, then minor road to Skirmett.

Walk (9 miles, moderate, OS Explorer 171): From Frog PH, right along road (take care!). Round right bend (776899; 'Hambleden'), then left bend. In 30m, right (775898) over stile, up hill path. At top of rise, follow path to right along ridge. In ¾ mile it curves right to top of ridge (766897), then begins to descend (footpath sign on tree). In 200m, at fork with footpath sign, keep downhill. In 200m path forks (766900); keep ahead (not left downhill). In 150m, where track bends sharp left along bottom of wood (766901) keep ahead, forking immediately left (yellow arrow/YA) across open field. Through woodland to road (765905). Left for 100m to bend, left ('bridleway') along wood bottom. In 1¼ miles, just before green 'Bridleway Users' notice and wooden railings (757891), left uphill (YA) through Gussetts Wood. Cross stile (758889) and field to road junction (758887). Ahead downhill for ¼ mile. At Upper Woodend Farm, left (578883; bridleway fingerpost) up driveway (ignore 'Private Road' notices). In 150m, before gate, right (759882; bridleway blue arrow/BA) down hedged green lane between fields. In 150m cross footpath (760881); continue on bridleway. In ¼ mile it re-enters wood (762878); follow it as a hollow way, then a path, close to wood edge. Follow path and hollow way down to major track crossing in wood bottom

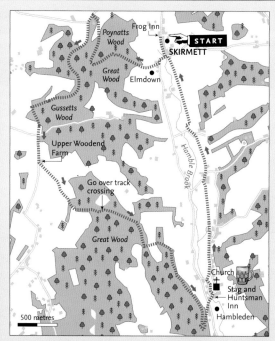

(767877). Go over crossing (uphill) on path which bends right. Now follow 'Shakespeare's Way'/SW arrows. In 500m pass a yew grove and fork right (772875; white arrow/WA on tree). In 100m fork left (SW). In 300m, reach track crossing (773872); turn left out of wood, on path across field and down left side of wood (SW) to track at bottom (778871). SW crosses it, but you turn right (WA on tree) on bridleway which bends immediately left to run inside wood edge. Follow BAs. In ¾ mile path bends right (782860); go left here (bent BA) on bridleway. In 50m, left (YA) on path. Descend to cross road (783864) into Hambleden. Cross churchyard; leave by far left (NW) corner; follow road. In 100m, right through kissing gate/KG (783867; fingerpost). Cross 3 fields (KGs), then hedged path past Pheasant's Hill, then 4 fields (KGs) to road at Colstrope Farm (782881). Forward to bend; forward here along Chiltern Way/CW (782882; 'bridleway'). Cross road at The Hyde (781887); forward on CW (YA) for 5 fields (KGs) to road (777899). Left, then right to Frog Inn. NB - many unmarked paths in woods.

Lunch Stag & Huntsman Inn, Hambleden, Oxon RG9 6RP (01491 571227; thestagandhuntsman.co.uk)

Lunch/accommodation Frog Inn, Skirmett (01491 638996; thefrogatskirmett.co.uk) – friendly. Tea – Hambleden Village Shop.

More information Henley-on-Thames TIC (01491 578034; visit-henley.com), ramblers.org.uk, satmap.co.uk

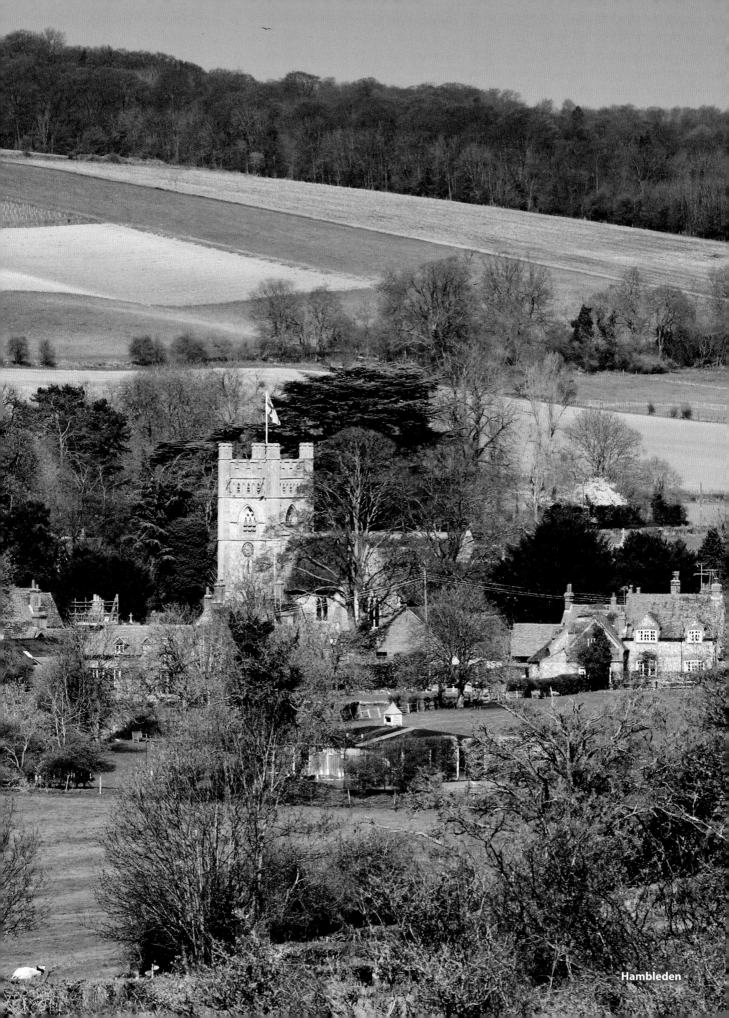

Hambleden

A cold, cloudy morning had settled over Hertfordshire, but that hadn't stopped the thrushes fluting their triple phrases in the trees around Aspenden. What a pretty place, all plastered cottages and deep-thatched roofs. The bells of St Mary's rang us out of the village, past park-like paddocks and west between hedges thick with crab-apple blossom and dog roses. We stooped to sift flints out of the dark earth of the fields, looking for the bevelled edges that might betray a scraper or arrow-head worked thousands of years ago.

Beyond Tannis Court lay a thicket full of early purple orchids and silverweed fronds. 'Moat,' the map said, and there it was, a shadowy dip behind the trees, full of mossy boughs and a glint of water. Site of the old manor house? Bruno, the black labrador who came to inspect us, couldn't have cared less. Curiosity satisfied, he turned his attention to a rank piece of fox-stinking hedge, while his owner gave us a cheery hello.

We turned down a lane past impossibly pretty Rumbolds under its thatch, and came to Back Lane. The rutted green lane was far too long and unwavering to be anything other than a Roman road — Stane Street, in fact. The road from St Albans to Colchester had been made 2,000 years ago by men who left thick red tile fragments and oyster shells to be kicked out of the earth by today's walkers.

The Sunday rambling club of the Letchworth Arts and Leisure Group came shouting and laughing along Back Lane. Where were they heading? "Haven't a clue," they chortled, "we've left our leader back there and he hasn't caught up yet!" Forget-me-nots, the blue trumpets of self-heal, white stars of stitchwort — this was a really delightful old highway, hedged and ditched, passing in secret through the countryside. We left it near Cherry Green and followed the path to Button Snap.

In the early nineteenth century the curiously named cottage belonged to the poet and essayist Charles Lamb. Poor dutiful Lamb, with his crippling stutter and his failed love affairs, claustrophobically entwined with Mary, his bipolar sister who had stabbed their mother to death in a fit of mania. Walking along the lane to Aspenden, it was good to think of the twitchy poet striding the garden at Button Snap, liberated from mental strife for a few hours amid the wide green fields of Hertfordshire.

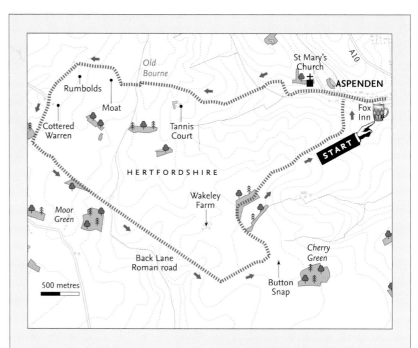

Start & finish Fox Inn, Aspenden, Hertfordshire SG9 9PD (OS ref TL361282)

Getting there Bus: Richmond's Coaches (bustimes.org.uk) Service 386 (Stevenage-Bishop's Stortford) to Buntingford (1 mile). Road: A10 to Buntingford, minor road to Aspenden.

Walk (7 miles, easy grade, OS Explorer 194): Leaving Fox Inn, left along road. Ahead at bend near church ('Bridleway 003'). In 400m follow 001/Buttermilk Farm, then 007/Tannis Court. At 'Private Property' notice in ⅔ mile, right (yellow arrows/YA) past Tannis Court, over Old Bourne stream (333283) and through thicket with moat. Emerging (319285), cross field to road. Left past Rumbolds to Cottered Warren. Right opposite The Lodge, then left (014/Moor Green) between converted barn houses, through gate (YA) and on (YA) to Back Lane Roman road (320277). Left (red arrow) for 1¾ miles. Cross valley bottom; through gate; in 300m, left (blue arrows) to Button Snap (348265). Left, passing Wakeley Farm entrance, on track for 1½ miles to Aspenden.

Lunch Fox Inn, Aspenden (01763 271886) – really good, friendly place

More information Hertford TIC (01992 584322), enjoyhertfordshire.com, ramblers.org.uk

Berkhamsted Common

HERTFORDSHIRE

An old favourite, this Hertfordshire walk and — like many such — a delight whatever the season. Last time out the trees of Berkhamsted Common had been of that rich, juicy gold that you get only after a long hot summer. Today I was looking forward to seeing what a long cold winter had done to the hedgerows and woods. Through Berkhamsted snaked the Grand Union Canal, smoking with early mist. Chaffinches were trolling on the broken walls of Berkhamsted Castle where William the Conqueror accepted the homage of the Saxon nobility of Britain after riding here through the autumn of 1066, flushed with his victory at Hastings.

Picturing the chaos and terror that the Norman invaders brought with them, I headed up the fields from Berkhamsted along hedgerows where the celandines, usually heralds of spring, lay tightly curled in waxy green spear blades. There was something grand and bracing about this uphill march through the sleeping Hertfordshire landscape, from memories of one famous battle to the site of another, all but forgotten, that lovers of access to open country ought to have as an equally red-letter day in history.

Berkhamsted Common occupies the ridge north of the town, a sprawl of open ground where locals had always enjoyed the right to roam. When Lord Brownlow arbitrarily railed off a great chunk and added it to his Ashridge Estate in 1866, he thought that he would encounter little opposition. But an equally autocratic and bloody-minded grandee, Augustus Smith, took exception. Smith paid a gang of tough London navvies to tear down the three miles of railings by night — and leave them neatly rolled up for Brownlow to collect in the morning. The locals reclaimed their common land, and Lord Brownlow had to 'retire hurt'.

Today Berkhamsted Common is a thick wood with a maze of footpaths. I trod its tangled ways as far as Lord Brownlow's country seat of Ashridge House, a vast Georgian mansion modelled by James Wyatt for the 7th Earl of Bridgewater as a Gothic extravaganza with battlements, turrets and a 300m (1000ft)-wide frontage. From the house it was back into the trees, among the grey old seniors of Frithsden Beeches. These wonderfully gnarled beech trees of the Chiltern slopes were already ancient when Ashridge House was built. I stood under their pale, contorted limbs, looking up. Over the meadow beyond the trees a lark was spilling out song like seed — spring's favourite doorkeeper.

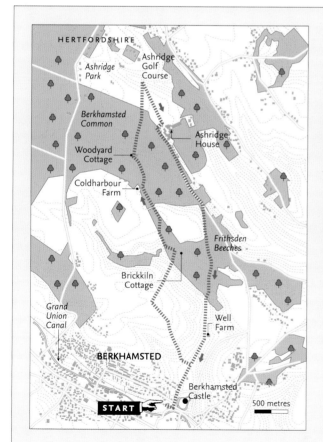

Start & finish Berkhamsted station, Herts HP4 2JU (OS ref TR015660)

Getting there Train: (thetrainline.com; railcard.co.uk) to Berkhamsted. Road: M25 (Jct 20); A41.

Walk (6½ miles, moderate grade, OS Explorer 181): Left out of station; Berkhamsted Castle (995082); north up Brownlow Road; path towards Well Farm; in 400m, left (996088 – FP fingerpost). NW up hedge paths for ¾ mile; through hedge, turn right (991097 – post with three yellow arrows/YA), heading NNE past pond; into Berkhamsted Common woods (993102). Just before Brickkiln Cottage, left on bridleway (post; blue arrows/BA). Follow south wood edge; right (991107) to north edge. Left (992108; BA); Coldharbour Farm (989113; BA); Woodyard Cottage (987117). Just beyond cottage, left over stile (YA); north through trees to Ashridge Park golf course. Turn right; aim right of Ashridge House (994122); road for ¾ mile; 300m beyond Crome Hill entrance, right (four-finger post; take left-hand of two bridleways); south through Frithsden Beeches ('bridleway', then 'Grand Union Canal Circular Walk' arrows); Well Farm; Berkhamsted.

Lunch Picnic

More information Hemel Hempstead TIC (01442 234222), www.hertfordshirelep.com/enjoy/tourist-info, ramblers.org.uk

Flamstead, Markyate & Jockey End

HERTFORDSHIRE

Flamstead sits in the gently undulating clay-and-flint country where Hertfordshire slips over into Bedfordshire. Bright sunlight played on the tile-hung houses and the pleasing jumble of brick and flint and thin old tiles that composes the Church of St Leonard at the heart of the village. It was a day in a thousand, woods and fields all bursting into life under the warm sun. Central London lay less than an hour away — how could that possibly be? Luton-bound aeroplanes passed silently like silver fish across the blue pool of the sky; but down here, walking through the spring wheat with flints jingling under our boots, we felt as remote from them as could be.

Beyond the busy main street of Markyate we came into more rolling ploughlands where beans were beginning to push up dark green leaves in neatly drilled rows. A faint heat ripple shimmered above the sun-warmed clay. In the woods around Roe End the beeches were just coming into leaf, their upper works a froth of tender translucent green, a contrast to the sombre density of the storm-tattered cedars in the former parkland of Beechwood House.

Some of the ancient oaks standing barkless like dry ghosts might be old enough to have sheltered the wicked Lady of Markyate. The legend that attaches to Lady Katherine Ferrers is well known hereabouts — her marriage in 1648 at the age of fourteen to the heir of Beechwood, the robbing expeditions she embarked on with her highwayman lover, their hideout in Beechwood Park, and the bullet that ended her life at twenty-six. Are the youngsters who attend school in the great mansion nowadays taught that racy tale? Let's hope so.

Beyond Beechwood Park we followed the stony old trackway of Dean Lane, where two blackcaps were conducting a song battle from the hedges. Dean Wood is a magical sort of place, sun-silvered and wren-haunted. We drifted on in a daze of sunlight, past the duck pond at The Lane House, a tumbling old cottage of many corners and nooks, and back toward Flamstead through woods hazed with bluebells, where wild cherry trees lifted a froth of pink blossom against the deep blue sky.

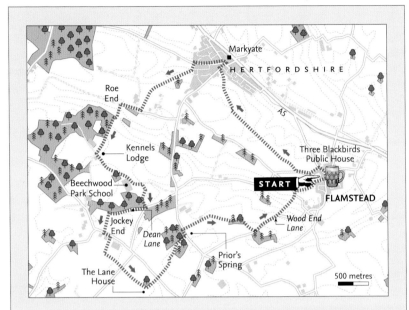

Start & finish Three Blackbirds PH, Flamstead, Herts, AL3 8BS (OS ref TL078146)

Getting there Bus: (Centrebus; centrebus.info) Service 34 (St Albans-Dunstable), 46 (Hemel Hempstead-Luton). Road: Flamstead is signed off the A5 Dunstable road, just west of M1 Jct 9.

Walk (8½ miles, easy, OS Explorer 182): Right along Chapel Road, left down Friendless Lane. At fork with Mill Lane, right; in 200m, right (073146, Hertfordshire Way/HW). Follow HW waymarks to Markyate. At road, right to village street (662164). Left for 50m; left along Buckwood Road. By last house on left, left (057164, HW); follow HW waymarks for 3 miles to Jockey End via Roe End (048156), Kennels Lodge (040149), Beechwood House (046145) and Dean Lane (048141-042140). In Jockey End, left along road (041137); in 150m, right past allotments. At gate, leave HW and turn left (041134, yellow arrow). Fenced path through paddocks, across road (044131); field, paddocks, white arrow to The Lane House drive (048128). Left here on Chiltern Way/CW; follow CW waymarks to Flamstead via road at Prior's Spring (055136), Little Woodend Cottages (058136), Wood End Lane (067137) and Pietley Hill (073142).

Lunch Three Blackbirds PH (01582 840330; threeblackbirdsflamstead.co.uk) or Spotted Dog, Flamstead, Herts AL3 8BS (01582 841004; thespotteddog.co.uk)

More information St Albans TIC (01727 864511; enjoystalbans.com), visitengland.com, satmap.com, ramblers.org.uk

Stagenhoe and St Paul's Walden

HERTFORDSHIRE

Two skylarks sprang out of a stubble field as we climbed its gentle slope towards Poynders End. They ascended, blithely singing as though it were sunny April and not a cold and cloudy winter's day. Such little incidents inject a welcome shot of joy into these gloomy months when all nature seems to have curled up and pulled the blankets over its head.

The sticky ochreous clay under our boots was studded with flints. We picked up one with a delicately bevelled edge — whether by man or natural process wasn't easy to decide, but we stood looking out over the wide fields of north Hertfordshire and pictured the men who hunted here when it was all forest. Our companion Milo the mad spaniel, meanwhile, went on running in circles and pointing at pheasants flying overhead.

In the margins of Hitch Wood, twisted green-barked hornbeams pointed their witchy limbs along the trackway that took us south towards the Palladian house of Stagenhoe. Its mid-Victorian owner, the 14th Earl of Caithness, was a genial soul who would drink whisky with his tenants and whose Spanish wife, 'massive and theatrical', believed she was the reincarnation of Mary, Queen of Scots.

From the track through Stagenhoe's grounds we caught a glimpse of St Paul's Walden Bury at the far end of its long avenue, another splendid eighteenth-century house, childhood home of the late Queen Mother. We stopped to admire the gurning gargoyles at All Saints' Church, and then turned north again along the Chiltern Way, heading across wide fields and down a tree-hung lane at Langley End where a flock of jaunty yellow-cheeked siskins bounced and twittered in the branches overhead.

Out of bounds in a thicket at the crest of the last hill crouched the broken flint walls of Minsden Chapel. It was built in the fourteenth century as a staging post for pilgrims on their way to St Albans, but the Reformation swept away its raison d'être. Now it stands forgotten among the trees, a ruin haunted by the wraith of a monk. Some claim to have seen the shapes of men and women here, hiding in a phantom cart full of spectral barrels. An eerie place. We went quickly on down the hill, with something more substantial in our sights — the Rusty Gun pub, and a damn good lunch.

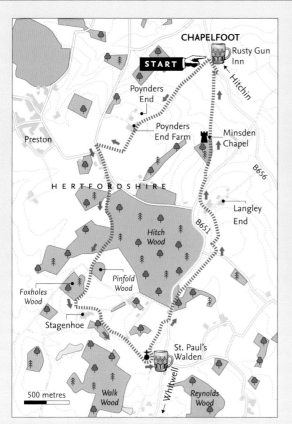

Start & finish Rusty Gun Inn, London Rd, St Ippolyts, Herts SG4 7PG (OS ref TL199253)

Getting there Road: From A1(M) Jct 8, follow Little Wymondley, Todds Green, St Ippolyts and Preston. At B656 cross roads, left for ⅓ mile to Rusty Gun PH

Walk (5½ miles, easy, OS Explorer 193): From Rusty Gun, left along B656; in 150m, left ('Preston', Chiltern Way/CW) on field path to Poynders End Farm. 300m past farm, right (190245, CW) past reservoir to road (186245). Left; on down Hitchwood Lane. In 350m, right (188242, 'Whitwell') on track south for ¾ mile past Hitch Wood, Pinfold Wood and Foxholes Wood (yellow arrows/YA). At south end of Foxholes Wood (184229, post with 2 YAs), left to driveway (186228); left for 70m; right past lodge/garden wall, following track to St Paul's Walden Church (192223). Chiltern Way north for 2¼ miles via Stagenhoe gatehouse (195228), B651 at Langley End (198241) and past Minsden Chapel ruin (198246) to Rusty Gun.

Lunch Rusty Gun (01462 432653; therustygun.co.uk)

More information Stevenage TIC (0300 1234049), visitengland.com, satmap.com, ramblers.org.uk

Coulsdon Commons

SURREY

Riddlesdown rises opposite Kenley railway station, a steep slope of rough grassland dotted with buttercups and speedwell, and scrub woods thick with yew, oak and ash. Wrens whirr, blackcaps flute, squirrels scuttle up the tree trunks. Walkers stride the grassy paths of Riddlesdown as though they own the place — and, in effect, they do.

If the Corporation of the City of London hadn't bought the 'Coulsdon Commons' — Riddlesdown and its neighbouring 'wastes' of Kenley Common, Coulsdon Common and Farthing Downs — for £7000 in 1883 (nearly £1 million today), there's little doubt what would have happened. All four high green spaces would have been gobbled up in London's inexorable southward expansion. As it was, the City of London dedicated the 140 hectares (350 acres) of Coulsdon Commons, "fine, open, breezy downs, already largely used for purposes of recreation by the public, and now for all time secured for those purposes".

Along the crest of Riddlesdown I followed a flinty track. It was a shock to descend from the open countryside to find the A22 snarling and stinking in the valley bottom. A minute's wrestling with this monster and I had left the houses behind, climbing up through woods again to the yellow buttercups and blue speedwell drifts of Kenley Common.

And then a pint of Lancaster Bomber in the Wattenden Arms, whose walls were hung with photographs of fresh-faced fighter aces from nearby Kenley Aerodrome, who used to drink here in between aerial duels with their German counterparts. I moved on, dipping down into suburbia at Old Coulsdon, rising again to the tangled woodland paths on Coulsdon Common.

The local landowner's enclosure of portions of Coulsdon Common in the 1870s provoked two brothers into taking him to court. Lobbying and legal advice from the Commons Preservation Society helped the pair to win their case, and pressurised the Corporation of London into making its philanthropic move. The society (now the OSS, the Open Spaces Society), is 150 years old this year, and still working to preserve our open green spaces. What would we do without campaigners like these?

I crossed the steep-sided combes of Happy Valley. Then a last long descent through the buttercups and fairy flax of Farthing Downs, with the outlandish monoliths of twenty-first-century London rising on the northern skyline, like a nightmare warning of what might have been done with our green spaces — and what could still be done — without the vigilance of the OSS and other groups like it.

Start Kenley station, Kenley Lane, Surrey CR8 5JA (OS ref TQ324601)

Getting there Rail: to Kenley. Bus: Service 434 (Coulsdon-Whyteleafe). Road: Kenley station signposted off A22 between Purley and Whyteleafe (M25, Jct 6).

Walk (7 miles, moderate, some steep steps, OS Explorer 161): Down station approach; right to cross A22; up steps and hill path opposite. In ¼ mile, at clearing with 4 gates (327603), go through uppermost gate. Bear right on grass path to join main gravel track, Riddlesdown Road. In ½ mile London Loop path ('LL') joins, before track crosses railway and descends to A22 (336593). Left along road; in 50m, right across A22 (LL), across railway, and up New Barn Lane, then up steps through wood (LL, 'Hayes Lane'). By Kenley Common notice at top (333590) ahead with wood edge on right. In 150m, into wood (332589). Ahead over path crossing, past Kenley Common notice, on through wood. In 250m, main path bends right (330588); but keep ahead on lesser path to reach open field. Diagonally left across field to fenceless gate and fingerpost in far corner (329585). Ahead ('Hayes Lane') past bench; follow path through wood. In 100m, right along lane (LL, 'Hayes Lane') for 300m to road (325583). Right (LL); in 150m, left (LL, 'Old Lodge Lane') and follow LL signs through corner of Betts Mead and on to road (323582). To visit Wattenden Arms PH, turn left for 100m. To continue walk, cross road; bear left (LL) along left edge of field. Across next paddock to

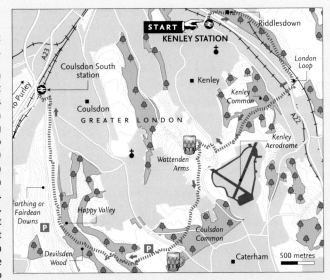

stile (LL); ahead along lane ('Waterhouse Lane' fingerpost). At T-junction, right (323578, LL). Descend to cross Caterham Drive (323576); on up Rydons Lane for 500m to cross road (321571). Ahead (LL, 'Coulsdon Road') to cross B2030 (319569). Ahead down Fox Lane. At Fox Inn, bear right round sports field and past Happy Valley notice (317568, LL, 'Farthing Downs'). Follow lane along right side of field. In 400m pass bench at corner (313566); on through woodland. Bear right along side of next grassland valley; through neck of woodland; descend slope of next open valley ('Happy Valley') diagonally right to bottom (308568). Keep same direction up far slope to top right corner (306569; LL, 'Farthing Downs'). Ahead on track through Devilsden Wood (LL) to emerge by notice on Farthing Down (302572). Bear right; follow path parallel with road north for 1 mile towards Coulsdon. Where it joins B276, turn left along Reddown Road (300590). In 150m, right across railway to Coulsdon South station. Return to Kenley by rail via Purley station; or District Cars taxi from Coulsdon South station (0208 6686686; £7 approx).

Lunch Wattenden Arms, Kenley CR8 5EU (0208 6604926; thewattendenarmskenley.co.uk) – cheerful place with wartime memorabilia

London Loop: Download leaflet guides at https://tfl.gov.uk/modes/walking/loop-walk; or follow directions in 'The London Loop' by David Sharp with Colin Saunders (Aurum Press).

More information Open Spaces Society (01491 573535; oss.org.uk), visitengland.com, satmap.com, ramblers.org.uk

Devil's Punch Bowl and Old Roads

SURREY

Geologists say that the Devil's Punch Bowl is the sandstone roof of a giant cavern that collapsed after springs had hollowed it out, while folklorists say that it's the imprint of the Prince of Evil's bottom when he landed there after a mighty jump from Devil's Dyke near Brighton. Whatever its origin, this great green hollow in the Surrey Hills is packed with wildlife — slow worms and lizards, butterflies and beetles, flowers and trees. We followed a path down under silver birches, through a boggy green dell and on across heathland of ling and bell heather gleaming purple in the strong midday sunlight.

A short climb to the lip of the Punch Bowl and we were walking the A3 London-Portsmouth trunk road — not the modern version, which has been buried far underground in twin tunnels since 2011, but the old road that was left abandoned. Where single-file traffic once queued and fumed, a wide green pathway now sweeps round the rim of the Devil's Punch Bowl, subtly landscaped, edged with silvery grasses and wild flowers. Common blue butterflies opened their gorgeous wings to the sun, and a pair of clouded yellows enacted a crazy chase as we strolled the grass-grown track.

Just above the abandoned road runs another, an ancient highway that once linked the capital with the Royal Navy's home port of Portsmouth. On a September day in 1786 three ruthless rogues murdered a sailor here for the price of his clothes. We found a memorial stone beside the track "erected in detestation of a barbarous Murder", its reverse face bearing a faded inscription calling down a curse on anyone "who injureth or removeth this Stone".

On Gibbet Hill nearby, the three malefactors were hung in chains for all to see. It's a haunted place and a sensationally beautiful one, with a view that stretches out across the Sussex Weald from the South Downs to the ghostly towers of London, 40 miles off. We sat to take it all in, then followed the National Trust's Hidden Hindhead walk through woods of oak and sweet chestnut coppice, up hollow chalk ways under bulbous pollarded beeches filtering green light, and back across an open heath where the wind was sweetened with pine resin and our finger tips grew purple with the juice of ripe little bilberries.

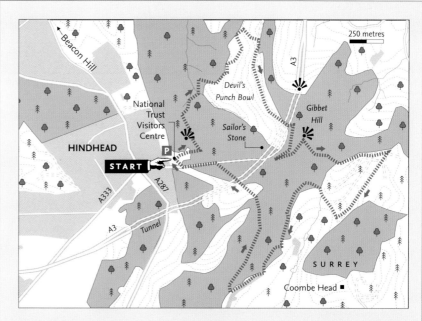

Start & finish Devil's Punch Bowl car park, Hindhead, Surrey GU26 6AG (OS ref SU890358)

Getting there Bus: Stagecoach (stagecoachbus.com) service 18, 19 (Aldershot-Haslemere); Road: A3 or A287 to Hindhead; car park signed in village

Walk (5 miles, easy, OS Explorer 133): From car park walk to viewpoint; right ('Hidden Hindhead'/HH fingerpost). In 150m fork left through gate; immediately left (892358) down track into Devil's Punch Bowl. In 350m, right (891361, yellow arrow/YA on post) down to cross stream (892363). Up slope, follow YAs across heath. In 250m go over path crossing (894364). In 400m, through kissing gate beside road on left (895367); right on gravel path to former A3; right along old road (896366) at lip of Devil's Punch Bowl. In 650m, on right bend, left (898360) up track through trees to cycle track; right for 300m to Sailor's Stone (897358) on right. Return for 100m; right ('Sailor's Stroll'); follow cross symbol to Gibbet Hill viewpoint (900359). From here follow HH for 2½ miles back to car park.

Lunch Devil's Punch Bowl Café, NT. Hidden Hindhead Walk and local info downloadable at nationaltrust.org.uk

Accommodation Devil's Punch Bowl Hotel, Hindhead GU26 6AG (01428 606565; devilspunchbowlhotel.co.uk)

More information Guildford TIC (01483 444333; visitsurrey.com), visitengland.com, satmap.com, ramblers.org.uk

It was a chilly February morning in Ewhurst, in the lee of the Surrey hills. Snowdrop clumps were still full and white down in the sheltered hollow of Coneyhurst Gill where the sharp, sweet song of a robin laid the archetypal soundtrack for a wintry walk in the woods.

We followed a muddy path up towards the tree-hung escarpment of the great Greensand Ridge that cradles the lowlands of the Surrey Weald. This was all loud and smoky ironworking country in the late Middle Ages, but these days the fine large houses of the stockbroker belt look out from their hillside eyries on to paddocks and pastures that lie silent and unblemished.

Signs of spring were already infiltrating the closed doors of winter — lamb's-tail catkins and tiny scarlet flowers on hazel twigs, rushy spears of bluebell leaves under the oaks, and an insistent bubbling of birdsong up in the high woods along the ridge. A stream stained orange by iron leachings had cut deeply into the greensand, and the golden ball of a crab apple bobbed endlessly in a back eddy where the brook had trapped it for a plaything.

The Greensand Way trail strings together the promontories and heights of the escarpment, and we followed its knobbly yellow track to Holmbury Hill. In the century before the Romans invaded Kent, a Belgic tribe built a mighty fort here with ramparts and ditches as tall as three men. From its southern lip a wonderful view opens out across the Weald and away towards the South Downs about 20 miles off. On clear days walkers on Holmbury Hill can spot the semaphore flashes of the sea at Shoreham on the Sussex coast. Yet today, all was muted and misty down there.

Using gorse branches as banisters, we groped our way down a precipitous slope below the hill fort. At the foot of the escarpment the mud-squelching track of Sherborne Lane led us back through the fields towards Ewhurst, between hedges where primroses were already beginning to cluster among the hawthorn roots.

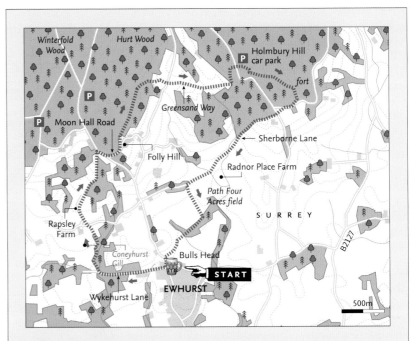

Start & finish The Bulls Head, Ewhurst, Surrey GU6 7QD (OS ref TQ090408)

Getting there Bus: Service 63 from Horsham or Guildford then 53 Cranleigh to Ewhurst (arrivabus.co.uk). Road: Ewhurst is on B2127 between Forest Green and Cranleigh.

Walk (6 miles, moderate grade, OS Explorer 145, 146): Cross B2127; follow Wykehurst Lane. In ½ mile cross Coneyhurst Gill (082407); in 50m, right (FP, stile) through trees. In 600m, left along road (081413); in 50m, right ('Rapsley') on bridleway north for ½ mile to road (081422). Right; in 100m, left up Moon Hall Road. In 200m, left opposite Folly Hill (084422, FP) on bridleway to turn right along Greensand Way/GW (085425). Follow waymarked GW for 1½ miles via Duke of Kent School (089430) and Holmbury Hill car park (098431) to Holmbury Hill fort (104429). At 150m beyond trig pillar, right (105429; warning notice) very steeply down slope to road (105428). Right; in 200m, left off road; fork right on path to left of 'Wayfarers' gate (FP). Cross road (103426); down drive with staddle stones (FP). By pond, fork left (FP) along Sherborne Lane bridleway. In ¾ mile, left (093418) across driveway; footpath (FP) across Path Four Acres field, into wood (094414). Right (FP) to Ewhurst.

Conditions Muddy/wet paths; very steep slope down from Holmbury Hill fort

Lunch/accommodation The Bulls Head, Ewhurst (01483 277447; bullsheadewhurst.co.uk)

More information Guildford TIC (01483 444333; visitsurrey.com), visitengland.com, satmap.com

Thorncombe Street, Bramley

SURREY

A group of us set out from The Jolly Farmer at Bramley. This is just what you want a village pub to be: cheerful, bouncy, well-kept, a bit eccentric; a place where the landlord tends the flowerbeds and the barmaid sees herself as a member of 'the Jolly Farmer Family'.

You know you're in deepest stockbroker Surrey when the wind-vanes on the stables are topped, not by foxes or cocks, but by bonus-friendly helicopters. This is beautifully maintained countryside — the fields all smooth, green grazing, the woods coppiced, the driveway gates enormous, the paddocks full of glossy thoroughbreds. The secret glory of this corner of Surrey is its ancient lanes, old trackways winding through the woods that have never known a tarmac-spreader. Hooves and boots have worn them hollow down the centuries. They lie deeply sunken into the sandy landscape, a network of shady holloways dappled with sun.

We went west from Bramley along a lane bordered with white stars of stitchwort and bells of pungent wild garlic. The spring sunlight reached down, fingering sycamore leaves so intensely green that the woods appeared lit from within. Brick gables and the tall stalks of ornamental chimneys poked out of the treetops at Catteshall and Thorncombe Street, telltale signs of splendid houses hidden away.

On the steep hillside above Thorncombe Street we sat on a weather-furrowed beech log to gaze around the valley with its string of old millponds and lakes ribboning south to the treasury of trees at Winkworth Arboretum. Horses grazed paddocks between copses of hornbeam and oak, all cradled in a perfect bowl of hills.

We dipped down through a bluebell wood with a floor more blue than green and found a straight holloway leading northward back to Bramley. Up on the crest, in the paddock at Hurst Hill Farm, a young god in a pink shirt and a warrior topknot cantered by on a gleaming steed with two other horses on loose reins as outriders. Watching the careless grace of the youth and his animals, I could understand why men of old believed in centaurs.

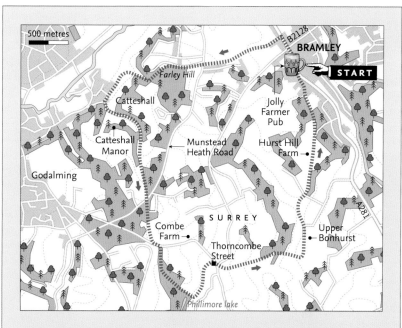

Start & finish Jolly Farmer PH, Bramley, Surrey GU5 0HB (OS ref TQ008448)

Getting there Bus: Services 53/63/63X Guildford-Ewhurst (arrivabus.co.uk). Road: Bramley is on A281, Guildford-Horsham (M25, Jct 10).

Walk (7 miles, easy/moderate, OS Explorer 145): From Jolly Farmer, left along A281; cross end of B2128; in 200m, left (007451); follow bridleway to Catteshall via road crossing (997477), T-junction of holloways on Farley Hill (990445), five-way junction of tracks (987446). Bridleway south to lane (991424) near Combe Farm, via Catteshall Manor gates (984441) and Munstead Heath Road (990430). Footpath to cottage at north end of Phillimore lake (997417); follow field edges to road at Thorncombe Street (999422). Footpath steeply up (003422); on west for ½ mile to bridleway (011423); north on bridleway for 1½ miles to Bramley via Upper Bonhurst (011426) and Hurst Hill Farm (012438).

Lunch Jolly Farmer PH, Bramley (01483 893355; jollyfarmer.co.uk) – a cheerful, characterful, family-run pub

More information Guildford TIC (01483 444333; visitsurrey.com), visitengland.com, satmap.com, ramblers.org.uk, Winkworth Arboretum (01483 208477; nationaltrust.org.uk)

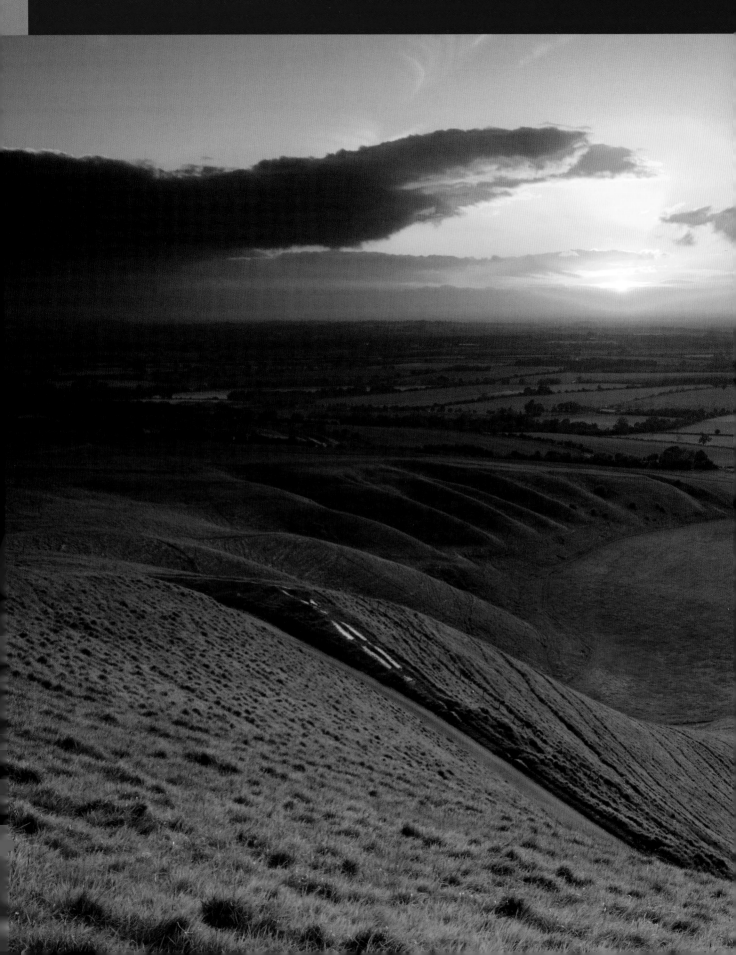

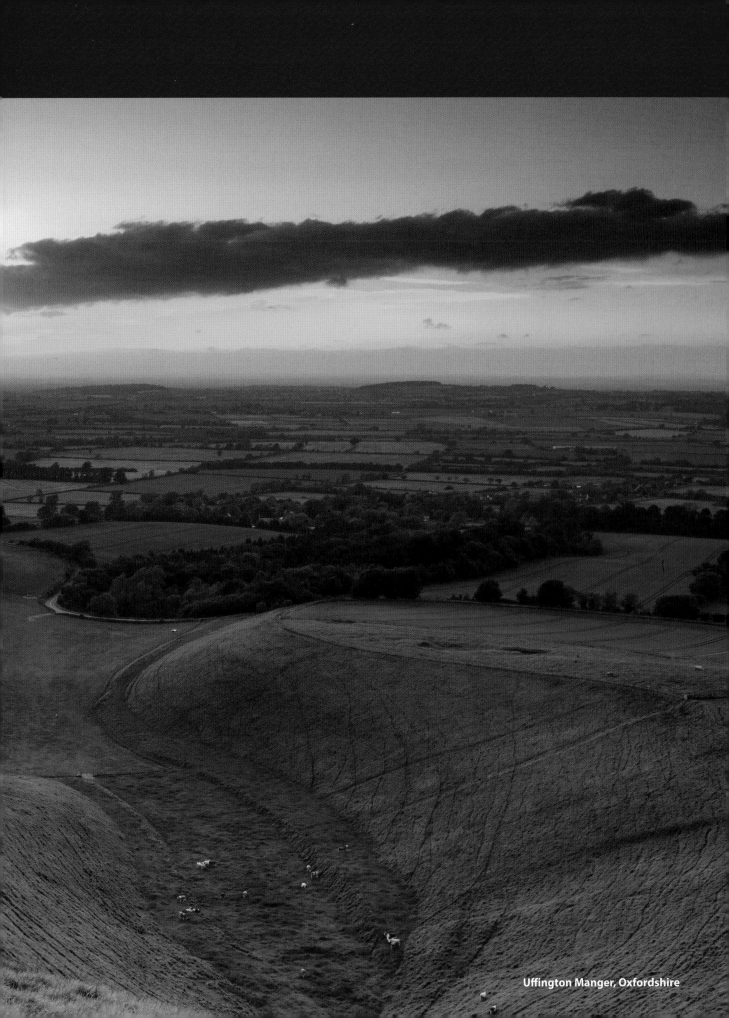

Uffington Manger, Oxfordshire

Forest of Dean Sculpture Trail

GLOUCESTERSHIRE

The Sculpture Trail in the heart of the Forest of Dean was a pioneering project when it opened in 1986. The artists' brief was to respond to the forest, an ancient mineral-rich woodland between the Wye and the Severn whose atmosphere is full of latency and 'otherness'.

Some of those initial works have been absorbed organically by the place; sixteen remain with more planned, strung out along a winding path — charred boats in an old coal mine drain, a house in the trees on spindly legs, a whole oak tree felled, sawn and reconfigured into a neat Jenga-style pile. These artefacts in such a natural setting could be an intrusive annoyance, but somehow they work together to reinforce the air of mystery that the forest exudes so powerfully.

On a cold winter day under a blue sky netted with the bare limbs of oak, beech and silver birch, we walked the circuit as far as the installation named *Cathedral*, a big stained-glass window suspended between the pine trees and glowing with sunlight. From here we crossed the road that bisects the forest and headed south past Speech House Lake among the inclosures — areas where the growing trees were once fenced off against grazing animals. The Forest of Dean has its own laws and customs, enforced by wardens known as Verderers, and forest-born locals — the 'Foresters' — guard their rights to graze their animals and to mine for coal, iron and stone as, when and where they see fit.

We followed forest paths and the trackbeds of old railways between the trees to New Fancy Colliery, where the great spoil tip is now a greened-over hillock with a superb view from its summit across an ocean of treetops. The goshawks that hunt hereabouts were elsewhere today, but by the side of the homeward path we saw what looked like a tight coil of rope, patterned with black diamonds — a male adder, sunk deep in hibernatory half-consciousness as it waited for spring and the mating season.

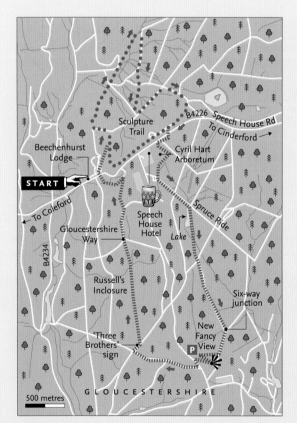

Start & finish Beechenhurst Lodge Visitor Centre, Speech House Road (B4226), near Coleford, Glos GL16 7EJ (OS ref SO614121)

Getting there Bus: Service 30 (Cinderford-Coleford). Road: Beechenhurst Lodge is on B4226 between Cinderford (A4151) and Coleford (A4136).

Walk (9 miles, easy, OS Explorer OL14): From Visitor Centre follow Sculpture Trail (leaflet map/guide available from Centre; blue-ringed posts/waymarks). From 'Hanging Fire' (624126), walk to B4226. Right for 100m; left into car park just east of Speech House Hotel. Ahead through gate (623122) into Cyril Hart Arboretum. Ahead for 150m to next gate; don't go through, but turn right along path. In 400m, through gate (622118); left (SE) along Spruce Ride. In 300m, over a crossroads; in another 300m, right (627115) on path along left (east) shore of Speech House Lake. At end of lake fork left with ditch, then fence on left for 400m to T-jct (628109); right for 100m, then left for 300m to meet cycleway (628105). Path runs beside it for ½ mile to 6-way junction of tracks (631099). Right here along surfaced track. In 300m, right (630096, 'New Fancy Picnic Site'); in 200m, fork left into car park. Follow 'Viewpoint' to summit lookout (629095).
Back to car park, and to road entrance (627095). Left along road for 150m; right through gate, and on west along trackway. In ½ mile descend to track (619097); left for 30m; at 'Three Brothers' sign, right (north) along rising grass track for nearly 1 mile. At junction, take 2nd right (618111) along waymarked 'Gloucestershire Way'/GW. In 400m it forks left (618114, GW, yellow arrow/YA) off hard-surfaced track onto grassy/muddy ride. Continue north for 400m to cross stile (618119); left on path through trees, down to track; right to cross B4226 (take care!) to car park and Visitor Centre.

Lunch Speech House Hotel (on B4226), Coleford GL16 7EL – ½ mile east of Beechenhurst Lodge (01594 822607; thespeechhouse.co.uk)

More information Beechenhurst Lodge (0300 0674800; forestry.gov.uk), ramblers.org.uk, satmap.com

Lasborough
GLOUCESTERSHIRE

On a cold dewy morning we set off from the Hunter's Hall Inn, a cheerful chattering crowd of friends happy to be up and away from post-Christmas lethargy. The wide south Cotswold fields are heavy with meltwater, their winter wheat flattened like a giant's crewcut by weeks of lying under snow. Hereabouts the Gloucestershire landscape revolves around a network of delectable hidden valleys, snaking unseen a hundred feet below the upland fields.

Down in Hay Bottom we meet a trio of disdainful llamas being led reluctantly across a footbridge. They resist until a coaxing word from their owner melts their intransigence. "People just love to go walking with them," says the llama leader. "They've got lovely natures — haven't you, Two Tone?" Two Tone flutters a pair of eyelashes that a Fifties starlet would have killed for and nuzzles our hands with his baby-soft lips.

We climb to the closed and shuttered Church of St Bartholomew, alone and lonely on its ridge. Nearby rises a little round tuffet of rough grass surrounded by a ditch, all that remains of some Norman lord's motte-and-bailey castle. Diminutive settlements shelter here, gorgeous in golden stone: the farmhouses and barns of Newington Bagpath, the battlemented Georgian mansion of Lasborough House and, between them, the gardens of medieval Lasborough Manor, a Jilly Cooper dream of gables and tall chimneys. We gaze and speculate — "There's Rupert Campbell-Black eyeing up the au pair!" — before dropping down into the woods along Ozleworth Bottom.

Frozen lakes where we skim twigs across the ice; a zee-zee-zee of long-tailed tits in the fir tops; the sense of winding deeper into secret country. A quick halt for hot chocolate and biscuits (New Year Resolutions come into force tomorrow, we decide), then a stiff climb to reach Scrubbett's Lane and the gambolling pigs of Scrubbett's Farm. "The black ones are Hampshires," says the farmer, "and those gingery ones are Durocs from New England. They love dashing about — must be happy."

Back at the Hunter's Hall we sit down to lunch, nearly twenty strong. A cheery pub, a lowering afternoon outside and a post-walk glow — ye canna whack that, man.

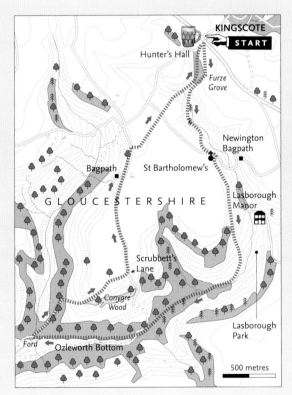

Start & finish Hunter's Hall Inn, Kingscote, near Tetbury GL8 8XZ (OS ref ST814960)

Getting there Road: Hunter's Hall is on A4135 Dursley-Tetbury road (M4 Jct 18/17, M5 Jct 14/13)

Walk (5½ miles, easy/moderate, OS Explorer 168): Turn right along A4135 outside Hunter's Hall; cross mouth of side road; right into field; follow left-hand of two fingerposts across field. On far side, through hedge (814956; yellow arrow/YA); in 50m, where fence bears left, continue downhill (YA) with wall on right. At end of wall, bear half left across slope to go through gate (813953; 'public right of way'); up woodland track to road; left past St Bartholomew's Church (815948). Immediately right (fingerpost); pass motte (816947); bear left along track by wall. In 200m, through gate; bear left up to continue along edge of escarpment. In 400m, descend; cross Lasborough House drive (819938); through gate; follow grass track below house, on into wood in valley bottom (816935).
Follow valley-bottom path for 1¼ miles, passing ponds (815934) and a flat area with a pond at far end (809930). Continue, soon passing through a gate along Ozleworth Bottom. At next gate/stile, where path slopes downward (798929), don't go through gate, but bear sharp right up slope to go through gate with waymark (799931). Steeply up woodland path. In 300m, meet gravelled track on bend; bear right uphill along track for 800m to Scrubbett's Lane (808936). Left to pass Scrubbett's Farm, then pass left turn to Bagpath (807946). In 200m, right over stile (807949; fingerpost); cross field (YAs) and road (810952). Descend to cross footbridge (812954); up through gate; follow track to Hunter's Hall.

Lunch Hunter's Hall Inn (01453 860393; huntershallinn.co.uk) – friendly staff, good walkers' grub

More information Tetbury TIC (01666 503552), cotswolds.com, ramblers.org.uk, satmap.com

Naunton and the Slaughters

GLOUCESTERSHIRE

They've seen a few winners at the Hollow Bottom; a few losers, too. The walls of this famous horse-racing pub in the north Gloucestershire Cotswolds are hung with jockeys' silks, snapshots of grinning owners, racing mementoes and photos of our four-legged, long-faced chums in action. It's a great place to stay the night if you're after local atmosphere, because this is horse country nonpareil. If we saw one horse on our walk through the Cotswolds' most delectable corner, we saw a hundred.

After a night of rain the woods were full of cold mist above the valley where Naunton lay, a dream of rich gold stone houses and snowdrop gardens. Horses in blue blankets cropped the paddocks. Every hawthorn twig held a line of raindrops suspended, each drop reflecting a miniature world of inverted trees and walls. Up on the roof of the Cotswolds it was a wintry scene of sombre beauty, all bright colours leached away by the mist. A group of bullocks grazing at a mountain of silage in an isolated barnyard turned their muddy faces towards us as we walked by. "Hey, hey!" soothed a hawk-faced little man leading a nervously shying colt along the lane, gentle authority in each of his gestures.

The sky began to clear as we came down towards Upper Slaughter. The view broadened to reveal wide upland fields dipping to hidden valleys. The horizons rolled with smoking cloud, and a weak sun came through to frost lichen-encrusted ash trees with cold silver light.

Upper Slaughter is everyone's Cotswold dream made manifest — a gorgeous manor house with peaked gables, mullioned windows and tall chimneys, the church high on a bank like a ship on a billow, the whole village scented with applewood smoke, a mellow fantasy. In Lower Slaughter the channelled waters of the River Eye ran under a diminutive stone footbridge. The plain red brick chimney of the old mill came as a relief to the eye after so much beautiful gold stone.

In a green lane beyond we stopped to hear a song thrush fluting his twice and thrice-repeated phrases from the hedge. The lane took us twisting down to follow the River Windrush in its tightly curving valley. Goldcrests swung in the treetops — gold seemed to be the theme today. We skirted the skittish horses beyond Lower Harford Farm, and came over the hill and down to Naunton with the evening song of a blackbird echoing through the valley below.

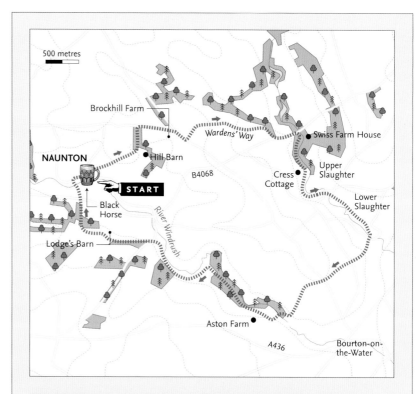

Start & finish Black Horse PH, Naunton, Glos GL54 3AD (OS ref SP119235)

Getting there Road: M5, Jct 11a; A40, A436, B4068 towards Stow-on-the-Wold, Naunton signposted on left. Park in village street.

Walk (9 miles; easy/moderate; OS Explorer OL45): Black Horse PH, Naunton; follow well-signposted Wardens Way for 4½ miles via Hill Barn (126239), Brockhill Farm drive (131242), B4068 (148241-152242), view of Swiss Farm House (153241) and Cress Cottage (153236) to Upper Slaughter (155233) and Lower Slaughter (164225). Follow Macmillan Way for 1¼ miles into Windrush Valley (151213). Follow Windrush Way for 1¾ miles via River Windrush crossing (149213) and Aston Farm (147213) to road at Lower Harford Farm (129225). Continue on Windrush Way for nearly ⅔ mile; below Lodge's Barn, right across river (119226); cross B4068 (17231); return to Naunton.

Lunch Picnic or Black Horse Inn, Naunton (01451 850565; theblackhorsenaunton.co.uk)

Accommodation The Hollow Bottom, Guiting Power GL54 5UX (01451 850392; hollowbottom.com) – famous horse-racing pub, refurbished rooms, warm and friendly, especially around Cheltenham Festival races.

More information Stow-on-the-Wold TIC (01451 870998), visitcotswolds.co.uk, satmap.com, ramblers.org.uk

Purton and Sharpness
GLOUCESTERSHIRE

There's something other-worldly about the river country along the Severn Estuary. Setting out from Brookend I thought of the landscape as flat, so close to such a big river. It came as a shock to top the rise near Purton and find a twenty-mile view unrolling — to the east the long South Cotswold ridge; May Hill and the heavy tree cover of the Forest of Dean swelling in the west; between them the Severn hurrying seaward in a muscular double bend of low-tide tan and silver. Jane and I halted, gazing our fill.

When the Gloucester & Sharpness Canal opened in the 1820s, Purton became a busy little place. Nowadays it's a sleepy canal-side hamlet, full of charm and possessed of a true classic of a never-changing pub. No food, no late opening and no nonsense at the Berkeley Arms under the admirable guidance of Mrs Wendy Lord — just a huge fire, stone floors, comfortable old settles, and beer so good it sits up and begs to be drunk. Resistance is useless.

Just down the river path we found an extraordinary elephant's graveyard of redundant boats — dozens of concrete barges and wooden Severn colliers, rammed into the mud during the late years of the twentieth century to stabilise the tide-burrowed bank between river and canal. Lovingly labelled by the 'Friends of Purton', they cluster the margins of Severn in death as in life – *Orby*, *Abbey*, *Huntley* and *Harriett*, their timbers shivered, their sides split, tillers and hawseholes still bravely held aloft, a poignant gathering.

On down the canal, and through the abutments of a mighty railway bridge that spanned the Severn until the night of 25 October 1960. Then, in a thick autumn fog and pitch darkness, two tankers — one loaded with oil, the other with petrol — collided with the bridge piers and exploded, sheeting the river in flame, killing five of the eight crewmen and wrecking the bridge.

Plenty of people around Sharpness retain vivid memories of that awful night. Sharpness is a rare survival, a river port still handling cement, fertilizer and scrap metal far up the tidal Severn. We stopped to watch the cranes swinging bags of fertiliser out of the hold of *Shetland Trader*, then crossed the canal and made for the field path to Brookend with a sharp appetite apiece. "Try the antelope and ginger sauce," suggested cheery Dan in the Lammastide Inn. I thought he was pulling my leg, till I looked at the menu board. You're not in Kansas now, Toto.

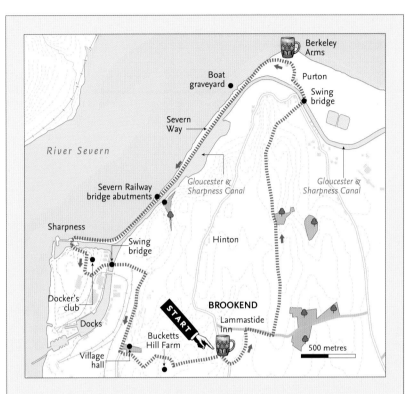

Start & finish Lammastide PH, Brookend, Sharpness GL13 9SF (OS ref SO684021)

Getting there Train: (thetrainline.com; railcard.co.uk) to Cam & Dursley (7 miles); several buses to Sharpness (carlberry.co.uk). Road: M5 (Jct 14); A38 ('Gloucester'); B4066 ('Sharpness'); right to Brookend. Park at Lammastide PH (please ask permission, and give the pub your custom!).

Walk (6½ miles, easy, OS Explorer OL14): Right from pub; left on bend ('bridleway') to green lane T-jct; right (686023 – blue arrow) along Lip Lane. In 300m, left (689022 – 'footpath' stone) across fields for 1 mile to Purton (682042). Cross canal; past Berkeley Arms PH (691045). Riverside path joins canal towpath (687044). NB For beached boats, detour right here. Towpath into Sharpness; cross canal (670030). 'Severn Way' up steps; ahead past Dockers' Club (671029) to road. Left across left-hand of 2 swing bridges (673029). Ahead to road (677026); right ('Sharpness'). Left beside Village Hall (674021 – fingerpost); paths via Buckett's Hill Farm to Brookend.

Lunch Lammastide Inn (01453 811337; lammastideinn.co.uk) – friendly and handy.

Drink Berkeley Arms, Purton (open Wed-Sun, 7-10; Sat-Sun 12-2)

More information Stroud TIC (01453 760960), exploregloucestershire.co.uk, ramblers.org.uk

Winchcombe and Belas Knap
GLOUCESTERSHIRE

A church bell was ringing nine in the morning as we set out from Winchcombe, one of Gloucestershire's nicest towns in which to linger, with its chic little shops and golden houses of oolitic Cotswold limestone.

The pretty estate cottages of Vineyard Street looked out to a green ridge of hills on the southern skyline. We passed the tall gatehouse of Sudeley Castle and struck out across squelchy fields of medieval ridge-and-furrow, the mud under our boots as pale and thin as batter. The view eastward opened over the deep valley where Sudeley Castle lay set with towers like a cathedral among well-kept pastures and woods of pale wintry mauve and brown.

The sun was a greasy button of silver in a thick grey cloak of cloud as we passed Wadfield Farm, a hedge of holly and beech whistling in the wind. A track flecked with dull gold stone led up past Humblebee Cottages, and from the road above we followed the well-trodden path up to Belas Knap.

Belas Knap is truly impressive, a magnificent neolithic barrow nearly 60m (200ft) in length, lying north-south. Its northern portal, deliberately blocked with an enormous chockstone, lies between walls that curve outwards like the flippers of a giant turtle. What those who built the great tomb 5000 or so years ago intended when they constructed the dummy entrance is unclear — perhaps to deter robbers, or maybe as a spirit door to allow the dead free passage.

We walked a circuit of Belas Knap. Then it was back to Humblebee Cottages and a slippery track to New Meadow Farm, where dung and straw were being shifted from the cattle shed to a steaming muck heap in the yard.

A muddy path led on north past the intriguingly named wood of No Man's Patch towards the broad green parkland around Sudeley Castle. Henry VIII's sixth wife, Catherine Parr, remarried and lived here. Sometimes she's seen at one of the windows, a wan figure in a green dress, watching the world pass by.

Start & finish Back Lane car park, Winchcombe, Gloucestershire GL54 5PZ (OS ref SP024284)

Getting there Bus: Service 606 or W1 from Cheltenham. Road: M5 Jct 11, A40 to Cheltenham, B4632 via Prestbury and Cleeve Hill to Winchcombe.

Walk (6 miles, easy, OS Explorer OL45): Follow 'town centre' to High Street. Right; left down Vineyard Street ('Sudeley Castle'). Follow road past castle gates; in 300m, right (025278); follow 'Winchcombe Way' for 1¼ miles across fields, past Wadfield Farm (026264) and Humblebee Cottages (023259) to road. Right for 600m; left at car park (020262, 'Belas Knap') on well-trodden path to Belas Knap long barrow (021255). Return to Humblebee Cottages. Just below cottages, right (yellow arrow); in 300m, through gate and left (025257, 'Gustav Holst Way'/ GHW) down to Newmeadow Farm (029261). Right on track (GHW); in 700m, left at fingerpost (035259, 'Windrush Way'/WW). Follow WW north for 1 mile via northwest corner of No Man's Patch wood (032265) to Sudeley Castle. Aim left of castle; beside castle, through double gates (030276); half left to drive (028278); left to gatehouse and Winchcombe. Conditions can be wet and muddy.

Lunch The Plaisterers Arms, Abbey Terrace, Winchcombe GL54 5LL (01242 602358; plaisterersarms.co.uk)

More information Sudeley Castle (01242 604357; sudeleycastle.co.uk) – open early March-end Oct; Cheltenham TIC (01242 237431), visitengland.com, satmap.com, ramblers.org.uk

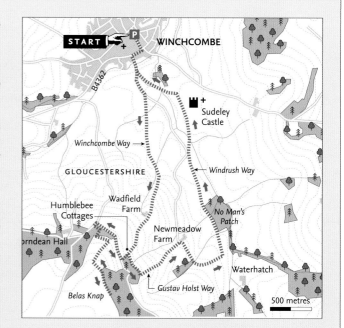

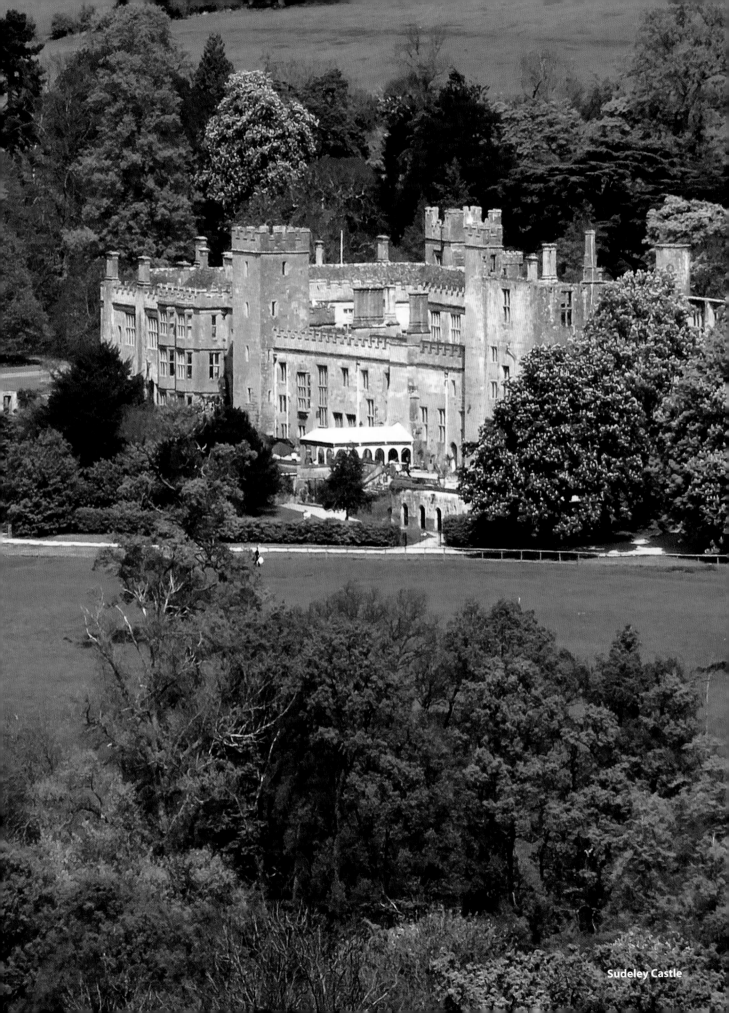

Sudeley Castle

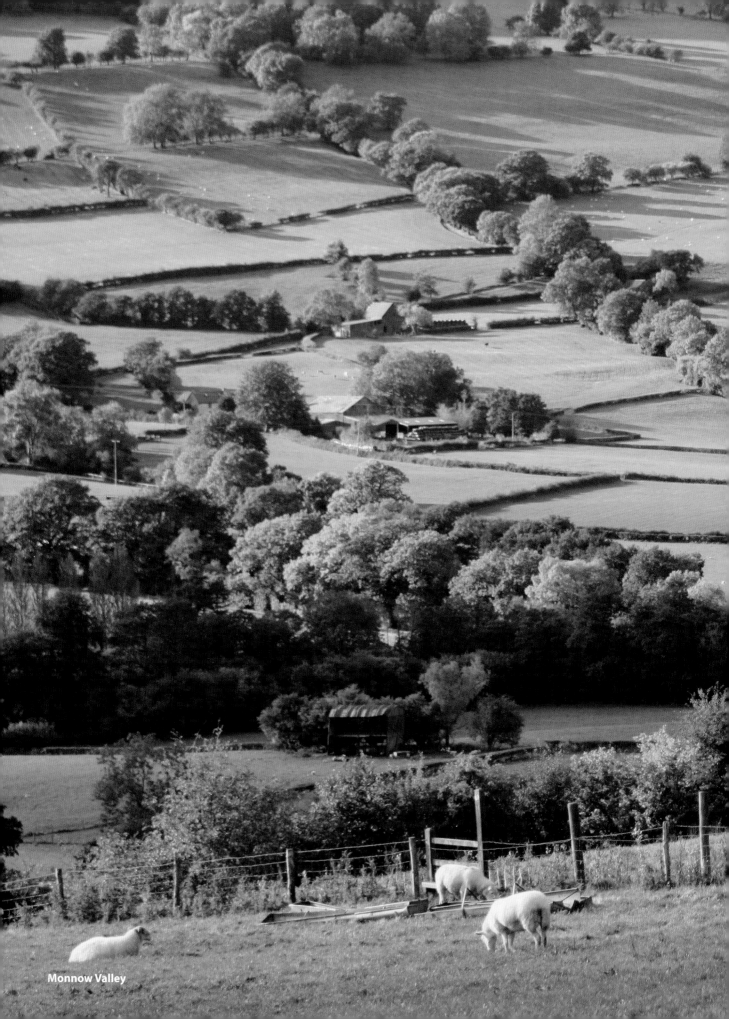

Monnow Valley

Craswall and Monnow Valley

HEREFORDSHIRE

Two tiny terriers came barking to their fence in Craswall, a tiny hamlet in a remote cleft of the hilly border country where Powys frowns down on Herefordshire. A pale sun was trying its best to draw aside the blankets of mist that the Black Mountains had pulled across their shoulders overnight. Celandines and daffodils were struggling out in the roadside verges, chaffinches burbled, catkins hung long and yellow from the hazels – everything spoke of spring just around the corner.

Craswall's modest Church of St Mary crouched in its ring of trees. Inside, everything was plain and simple – a tiny gallery, beams shaped and bevelled by some nameless medieval village carpenter, hard upright pews. The sunken grassy hollow on the north side was an arena for cockfights not so long ago, and Craswall boys would play fives against the church wall.

We followed a bridleway through sheep pastures, heading north to cross the infant River Monnow in a dell under alders and low-growing oaks. The dogs of Abbey Farm barked us in and out of the farmyard. Down in the cleft beyond, sunk deep into grassy turf banks, lay the silent and time-shattered ruins of Craswall Priory. The Order of Grandmont monks ran it in medieval times with a severe rule and harsh discipline. They could not have chosen a bleaker or more remote spot to build their refuge, or a more beautiful one to a modern walker's eyes. The curved apse still holds its rough altar, sandstone sedilia and triple piscina complete with stone bowls and drain holes. Over all is a profound sense of peace, and an echo of melancholy.

Up on the ridge we strode out. Suddenly the mist curtain shredded away and a stunning view lay ahead – the great steep prow of Hay Bluff and the upturned boat keel of its long south-going ridge, towering 700 feet above us but completely hidden until now. We stood and stared, entranced, before turning back to follow old green lanes that led down to Craswall over a succession of rushing mountain fords.

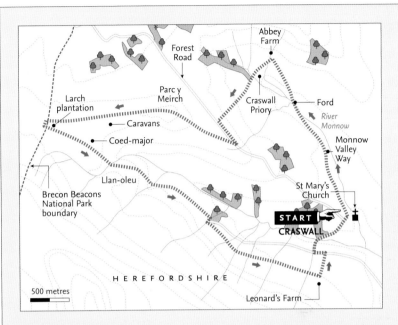

Start & finish St Mary's Church, Craswall, near Hay-on-Wye, Herefordshire HR2 0PX (OS ref SO 281363).

Getting there A438, B4351 to Hay-on-Wye. Follow B4350 west out of town; on outskirts, left up Forest Road (Capel-y-ffin). In 2½ miles fork left ('Craswall 4'). In Craswall, right at phone box to St Mary's Church (please park neatly!).

Walk From Craswall Church (281363), right along road; immediately right, then left (blue arrow/BA; 'Monnow Valley Walk'/MVW). Follow BAs along hillside for nearly 1 mile; ford River Monnow (276375); aim across field to far top corner (275378); on through gates to Abbey Farm (274379). Left down drive to Craswall Abbey ruins (273377); on up drive to road (268373). Left; in 300 m, right (271370; 'bridleway' fingerpost/BFP). Follow BA and MVW through fields for nearly 1 mile. Through gates, over stile at caravans (257374; BA); on through gate on skyline (255373). On for ¼ mile through 2 gates; at 2nd one (251373, at Brecon Beacons National Park boundary) turn left up end of larch plantation. At top of wood, left along its south side. Pass Coed Major on left (256371), down to cross stream (257369), and follow green lane/path through gates. In ⊠ mile it becomes metalled lane. At gate (268363), right (BFP) for 50 m; left (BFP) on bridleway through gates. In ¾ mile, at post with 2 BAs (278357), left to road; left, and in 100m right to church.

Lunch Picnic

Accommodation Pandy Inn B&B, Dorstone HR3 6AN (01981 551199; pandyinnbandb.co.uk) – lovely friendly pub with fabulous wooden chalet for B&B

More information Hay-on-Wye TIC (01497 820144; visitherefordshire.co.uk), satmap.com, ramblers.org.uk

Fownhope and Wye Valley Walk
HEREFORDSHIRE

The steeply folded countryside of the Wye Valley lay deep in the cold season, with strings of scarlet bryony berries festooning the hedges. Up in the trees above Fownhope the Wye Valley Walk traced the long ridge of Common Hill, looking south towards the rainy hills of the Forest of Dean. Fieldfares from Scandinavia were pillaging the windfalls in long-abandoned cider orchards, their pale spotted breasts and smoky grey heads bobbing among the brown and yellow fruit.

"We used to send all our cider apples to Bulmers," said the farmer who stopped for a chat. "But then they said, 'Tisn't enough, don't bother.' So now we just leaves 'em for the birds and the deer."

Through the ancient woodland of Lea and Paget's Woods went the Wye Valley Walk, past old limekilns half buried among the tree roots. On the grassy slope beyond the woods a potbellied pig was champing the greenery with splayed tusks and plenty of squelching, his sagging stomach trailing along the ground.

A short, sharp climb to the elliptical rampart of Capler Camp, an Iron Age hill fort commanding a wonderful southward view across the Wye Valley. Down through pines and larches and we were finally at close quarters with the Wye itself, walking the bankside footpath round the wide bends of the river. The water raced by, swirling and bubbling, carrying a flock of Canada geese who trumpeted to one another as the river swept them away round a bend.

Back at Fownhope, the crooked broach spire of St Mary's Church beckoned us. The twelfth-century tympanum of the Virgin and Child inside the church displays all the idiosyncratic brilliance of the style known as the Herefordshire School of Sculpture. The wide-eyed Virgin delicately balances a mysterious fruit between thumb and forefinger. A Wye Valley cider apple? I'd like to think so.

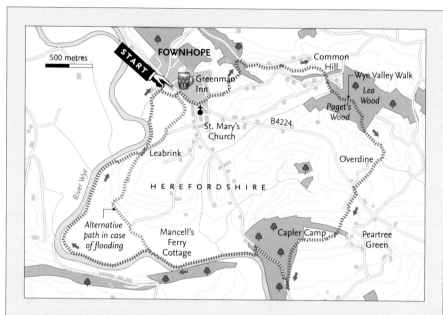

Start & finish Greenman Inn, Fownhope, Herefordshire HR1 4PE (OS ref SO578345)

Getting there Bus: Service 453 from Hereford. Road: M50, Jct 4; A449 ('Ledbury'); in 1¾ miles, Fownhope signed to left on B4224.

Walk (6½ miles, moderate, OS Explorer 189): Right along B4224; at church, left up Common Hill Lane; 200m past Medical Centre, left through gate (584345). Dogleg right-left-right round 2 field edges, up to cross lane (585347, yellow arrow/YA). Up bank; in 50m, left (YA); in 30m fork right (YA); in 200m, right by electricity pole (YA) to turn right on ridge along waymarked Wye Valley Walk/WVW (586348). Follow WVW for 2½ miles via road crossing on Common Hill (595346), Lea and Paget's Woods (599342), Overdine (600336), B4224 road crossing (598334), Caplor Farm (597332), Capler Camp hill fort (596329) and road at Capler Lodge (591324). Right to bottom of hill (587328). Left on path; in 30m, right downhill (YA); at foot, right along River Wye. In ¾ mile, cross Mancell's Ferry cottage garden (576328).
If riverbank path clear: Continue along riverbank for 1¼ miles. At entrance to wood (572337) bear right along southern edge of woodland to rejoin riverbank at Leabrink (575339). On between house and river; ahead along river for 300m, then inland (575342) to Fownhope.
If riverbank path flooded: Keep ahead from Mancell's Ferry cottage (NW) across field, soon with a bank on right, to metal gate, then kissing gate (YA). Cross farm track (573330) and keep ahead with bank on right. In 300m, right over stile (571333, YA); uphill with hedge on right. In 150m, at tree with YA, cross field to barn (573335). Pass to left of barn, cross 2 stiles (no waymarks) and field to kissing gate (574338, YA). Bear right down slope to stile (YA) on left of gate above Leabrink (575339). Follow hedge on left to cross lane by sewage works (577340, YA). Follow footpath (YA) back to Fownhope.

Conditions Wye riverbank path can flood in winter – ring Greenman Inn to check

Lunch/Accommodation Greenman, Fownhope (01432 860243; thegreenman.co) – very smart, stylish place

More information Hereford TIC (01432 268430), visitengland.com, satmap.com, ramblers.org.uk

Yarpole and Croft Ambrey

HEREFORDSHIRE

Around the church tower at Yarpole the fading snowdrops and swelling daffodils made contrasting notes in the tentative chorus of spring just beginning along the lanes of north Herefordshire. It was hard to picture the raw mayhem of border warfare here, the bitter atmosphere of bloodshed and anger between Welsh and English neighbours that caused the medieval builders to raise the tower of St Leonard's as a separate structure from the body of the church, a refuge for besieged villagers as much as a belfry to call the faithful to worship.

Under the oaks at the bottom of Fishpool Valley lay a string of medieval fishponds, their water petrol-blue from the chemicals exuded by the rotting leaves that lined them. Jane and I strolled through the valley and on up a side dingle, sniffing damp air richly scented with leaf-mould and moss. At the top a sentinel avenue of weather-blasted sweet chestnuts fell away with the lie of the land towards fourteenth-century Croft Castle, tucked away below. Crofts have lived here since the Norman Conquest in a succession broken only once. King Edward IV sent Thomas Croft off across the western ocean on a secret mission in the early 1480s to confirm the existence of rich fishing grounds at the edge of the world. Did the Herefordshire man beat Christopher Columbus to the discovery of the New World? The family believe he did.

We left Croft Castle to its mysteries and turned north through Croft Wood, where a flock of redpolls with chestnut wings and scarlet caps was flirting and swinging in the bare birch branches. From the high ramparts of the Iron Age hillfort of Croft Ambrey, exhilarated by the cold wind and the climb, we gazed over thirty miles of tumbled border hills from sharp-prowed Titterstone Clee in the northeast to the Powys mountains out west. The bones of this wonderful panorama can hardly have changed in the 2000 years since the last native British inhabitants quit Croft Ambrey after 600 years of occupation. Perhaps they were forced out by the invading Romans, or maybe they simply thought it safe at last, under Pax Romanus, to colonise the lower and easier lands.

Since the revolutionary CROW (Countryside and Rights of Way) Act passed into law in 2000 AD, nearly two million acres of upland, moor and mountain in England and Wales have been opened to walkers to wander where they will — a right and privilege to be treasured. Through Oaker Coppice and across Bircher Common we tramped, revelling in the freedom of picking our own path across this large swath of Access Land. Then it was on down the field slopes towards Yarpole, looking south over lowlands washed with muted blues and greys under the heavy cold afternoon light of a late winter's day.

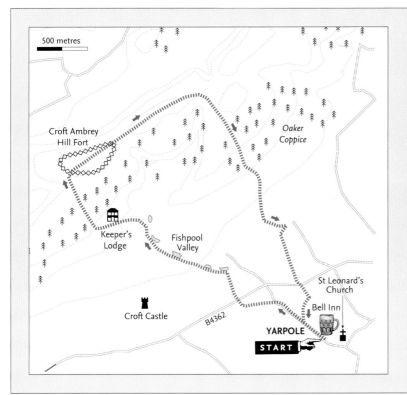

Start & finish Bell Inn, Yarpole, Herefordshire HR6 0BD (OS ref SO467649)

Getting there Road: A49 to Leominster, B4361 to Luston, minor road to Yarpole

Walk (5 miles, easy/moderate grade, OS Explorer 203): Bell Inn; footpath crossing B4362 (459653); pond (458656); up Fishpool Valley for ⅔ mile. Left (450662; post marked 8); Keeper's Lodge (446661); Croft Wood; forward along Mortimer Trail (443666). Croft Ambrey hillfort (444668); Whiteway Head (457675); through Oaker Coppice (459672-462667). Across Bircher Common past cottages (462663); left to Beechall Cottage (464661); right up bank; re-cross B4362 (466655). Left for 50m (take care!); right through garden gate ('shut gate' sign); left along stream; stiles and waymark arrows to Yarpole.

Lunch Bell Inn (01568 780537) – stylish, wonderful food, Croft Castle, Yarpole HR6 9PW (01568 780246; nationaltrust.org.uk/croft-castle-and-parkland)

More information Leominster TIC (01568 616460, visitherefordshire.co.uk)

Ardington and the Ridgeway
OXFORDSHIRE

It's a cold sunny morning among the peerless estate villages of south Oxfordshire. If you're looking for red tiles, spreading chestnut trees, gravelled drives and leafy lanes, here's the spot. On our way out of Ardington, Jane and I pass cottages sunk in fabulously pretty gardens. From the field track we look back to admire the mellow brick frontage of Ardington House among its trees, with the stumpy spire of the church crouched alongside like a curate at the elbow of a squire.

Glossy horses gallop the trackways, and hares chase each other in circles over the milky-grey ploughlands. We cross the shallow, chalk-bedded Ginge Brook and follow the deep canyon that it has cut for itself between the thatched and whitewashed cottages of East and West Ginge. A sunken track climbs south to the roof of the downs, crossing the puckered green scar of Grim's Ditch. Iron Age folk dug the ditch and mounded its rampart about 300 BC, but what for is anyone's guess. Anglo-Saxon settlers took it to be the work of giants and named it after their god Grim.

The ancient downland track of the Ridgeway could predate Grim's Ditch by 3,000 years or more. We follow its rutted course along the crest of the Downs, looking out over sunlit Oxfordshire to reach the tall stone cross that commemorates Robert Loyd-Lindsay, Lord Wantage. A Crimean War hero, Loyd-Lindsay was a founder of the British Red Cross and a great local benefactor.

If the woods on his Lockinge estate were laid out, as stories say, in the formation employed by his troops at the Battle of the Alma, it's hard to make out on the ground. But there's no mistaking the order and good taste that he brought to the building of the estate village of East Lockinge. On the immaculately kept village green stands a bronze statue of Best Mate, winner of the Cheltenham Gold Cup in three successive years from 2002, who was trained nearby.

On the duck pond near Ardington, coots feed their crimson-faced chicks and a blackbird sings in a horse chestnut tree; all really does seem right with this corner of the world.

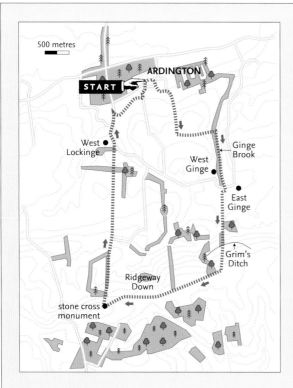

Start & finish Boar's Head, Ardington, Wantage, Oxon OX12 8QA (OS ref SU432883)

Getting there Train: (thetrainline.com; railcard.co.uk) to Didcot (8 miles). Bus: Service 32 Wantage-Didcot (thames-travel.co.uk). Road: Ardington signposted off A417 Wantage-Didcot road.

Walk (7 miles, moderate, OS Explorer 170): From Boar's Head, right; past Ardington House entrance gates, right through arch; path to road. Right; cross brook; ahead past barns (437879). At gate, left (437875; blue arrow) to cross Ginge Brook (444875). Right by brook for ⅔ mile to road in East Ginge (446866). Dog-leg right and left ('bridleway'); track for 1 mile, past Upper Farm, to Ridgeway (445851). Right for 1⅓ miles to monument (424844). Right downhill on footpath to track crossing (424846). Take track to right of one marked 'No Public Right of Way', down right side of field; follow it for 1¾ miles past Chalkhill Barn and Bitham Farm to road (425873). Left through East Lockinge, passing West Lockinge turn; by Lockinge village nameplate, right (425878; yellow arrow) across bridge; follow path. Where it forks, left ('permissive path') to road; left, then right to Boar's Head.

Lunch & accommodation Boar's Head (01235 835466; tbhardington.co.uk) – friendly and comfortable

More information Wantage TIC, Vale & Downland Museum, Church Street, Wantage OX12 8BL (01235 760176), visitsouthoxfordshire.co.uk, ramblers.org.uk, satmap.com

Sibford Gower, Banbury
OXFORDSHIRE

A beautiful winter morning, piercingly cold, under a blue porcelain sky spread across the gently undulating landscape where northernmost Oxfordshire runs hand-in-hand with Warwickshire. This is ironstone country, reflected in the burnt-orange hue of the cottage walls in Sibford Gower. As we left the village, the low wintry sun washed the fields. It was a morning to savour and we felt more than ready for it — incessant rainstorms had been drowning the country for the past month and another was forecast for this afternoon.

Green ranks of winter wheat squelched underfoot and a stodge of puddles flanked every stile and gateway. We strode out with all the energy that a brisk wind lends, across stubble gleaming with sunlight in gold and cream. A flock of sheep lay at ease in a turnip field, slicing and chewing the sweet white flesh of the roots with their strong teeth. Down in Epwell we leant on the churchyard gate and admired the scene, everyone's dream of an English village setting, the mellow stone church with centrally placed tower leading the eye along to a row of sunlit cottages.

Little hard green crab apples spattered the hedged path that took us on from Epwell over the fields to find the rutted thoroughfare of Beggar's Lane. This ancient track runs under many names — Ditchedge Lane and Traitor's Ford Lane are two more — connecting with other old green roads, reputedly linking York and the West Country at its extremities. Hereabouts it runs as a snaking lane twenty strides broad between hedges of oak and sycamore, devoid of leaves in this cold season, but with tiny scarlet buds on every twig as a promise of spring.

A horse came dashing by with a clatter of hooves and a splatter of divots, its rider's crab-claw profile reddened with wind and weather. "Hope you don't mind us cantering past," he called. "Only it's nice to give him practice at not shying at everyone he meets." We didn't mind at all: it seemed a timeless image, the muddy horse and rider pelting along the ancient greenway, a moment snatched from any winter day in the past 5000 years.

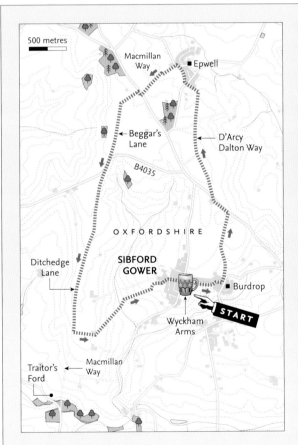

Start Wykham Arms, Sibford Gower, Banbury, Oxon OX15 5RX (OS ref SP352378). Customers can park at pub.

Getting there Bus: Service S3 (stagecoachbus.com); Stratford-upon-Avon-Chipping Norton. Road: Sibford Gower is signposted from B4035 between Lower Brailes and Swalcliffe.

Walk (6 miles, easy, OS Explorer 191): From Sibford Gower, road to Burdrop. Left ('Swalcliffe'), in 100m (358379), take D'Arcy Dalton Way (DDW). Follow DDW for 1½ miles to Epwell (354403). Left past Chandlers Arms, right (DDW) to road by church (352405). Left; in 100m, left (Macmillan Way/MW, fingerpost) up path. Through gate (MW); anti-clockwise round field edge to road (348401). Right; in 50m, left ('Beggar's Lane') across field to stile into Beggar's Lane (345401, MW). Left to B4035 (344394). Right; in 250m, left (MW) along Ditchedge Lane for 1¼ miles. Left over hedge stile (339373, yellow-top post, blue arrow) across field. At 50m beyond Haynes's Barn, left through hedge (342372, fingerpost); follow path (yellow arrows/YA) down to cross stream (345376), up to top corner of next field (349378). Left for 100m; right over stile (YA) into lane; left; first right through gateway; follow lane into Sibford Gower.

Lunch Wykham Arms, Sibford Gower (01295 788808; wykhamarms.co.uk) – a well-kept, friendly pub

Accommodation Gate Hangs High inn, Hook Norton OX15 5DF (01608 737387; gatehangshigh.co.uk)

More information Banbury TIC (01295 753752; visitnorthoxfordshire.com), visitengland.com, satmap.com, ramblers.org.uk

Stonesfield and the North Cotswolds

OXFORDSHIRE

The rolling landscape where Gloucestershire shades into Oxfordshire is thickly woven with footpaths and studded with villages of mellow gold stone. In this northeast corner of these delectable hills you can walk in classic Cotswold countryside, but without those camera-clicking Cotswold crowds.

On a brilliant day of blue sky and balmy weather Jane and I set out to explore this corner of the Cotswolds. From Stonesfield, gorgeous among its trees, the Oxfordshire Way took us among oilseed rape fields where yellowhammers in the hedges wheedled for "a-little-bit-of-bread-and-no-cheeeese". A lark poured out song like the trickle of a brook. Views were big and broad, with a heat haze softening the dark green of spinneys and windbreak woods.

In the valley of the River Evenlode, swallows skimmed the stone-tiled roofs of Fawler. Dark Lane led us between hedges carefully tended by the Friends of Wychwood hedge-laying group, up a cowslip-sprinkled valley to Finstock and on through the environmentally friendly farmland of Wilcote Farm. All around lay evidence of a countryside that is loved and cared for.

At North Leigh we went into St Mary's Church to admire the north chapel with its fan vaulting and richly carved fifteenth-century alabaster tomb of Sir William Wilcote and his wife Elizabeth. Over the chancel arch hung a splendid medieval Doom (painting), with a coal-black Devil and his red-faced acolytes jeering the damned into eternal fire. Outside, all seemed a dream of peace — horses cropping the meadows near Holly Court Farm, the smooth gurgle of the Evenlode round its meandering bends, and the splashing and laughter of picnicking families by the river as we made our way back up the old cart track to Stonesfield.

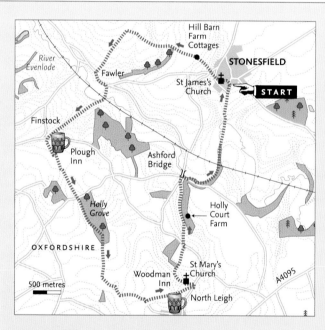

Start & finish Near St James's Church, Stonesfield OX29 8PT (OS ref SP394171)

Getting there Train: (thetrainline.com; railcard.co.uk) to Charlbury. Bus: (stagecoachbus.com) service S3 (Charlbury-Oxford). Road: Stonesfield is signed off A44 Woodstock-Chipping Norton.

Walk (8½ miles, easy, OS Explorer 180): Park in 'square' (actually a triangle!) by St James's Church, Stonesfield. With your back to church, bear left along High Street. Opposite Methodist chapel, left down walled lane ('bridleway'). At bottom, cross road and go up stony bridleway (390173; 'Oxfordshire Way/OW'). In 400m, ahead over crossroads along tarmac lane. In another 400m pass end of woodland belt. Road bends right by Hall Barn Farm Cottages, but keep ahead here (383177; blue arrow/BA) through gate (OW) and on down right side of hedge. In ½ mile, at crossing of bridleways, left off OW (375180) on

bridleway (BA) descending to Fawler. Left along road. Opposite bus stop, right down lane (372170; 'Finstock 1' fingerpost). Cross under railway and over River Evenlode. Follow path on far bank and through shallow valley. Keep ahead at 'Right of Way' arrow among trees (368166); on up Dark Lane to Finstock.

Right past Plough Inn (362161); left up side of Plough (fingerpost) on path on right side of pub car park. On (yellow arrow/YA) through kissing gate, up field edge. At far end, through kissing gate (362159); don't turn right here, but keep ahead with hedge on left. Path doglegs left and right, then crosses field; through Ramsden Mill Longcut woodland strip (364156); on along wide field paths to road (367151). Left for 20m; right ('Wychwood Way'/WW fingerpost) through Holly Grove wood. At end of wood (372143), on along hedgeside track (YA) for 2 fields to turn left along North Leigh Lane. In 300m pass footpath diverging to left (374136; fingerpost); on next bend, bear left ('WW' YA) along path in tunnel of trees. In 400m, right along End Farm drive (379134); in 20m, left ('Church ½' fingerpost) across fields (kissing gates, YAs) to St Mary's Church, North Leigh. (NB For Woodman Inn or Mason's Arms, turn right from church to top of hill, then right to pubs).

Continuing walk from church – left along road; in 20m, left ('bridleway' fingerpost) along farm drive. In 400m, right over stile and down hedge; cross brook (385140), through gate and up fence to road (386143). Left for 50m; right down Holly Court drive ('Bridleway, Ashford Bridge 1'). At buildings bear right to T-junction (386147); left and continue, following BAs by brook for ½ mile to road near Ashford Bridge (385154). Right to crossroads by bridge; right ('East End, Hanborough'), following path on right bank of Evenlode ('Stonesfield 1½' fingerpost). Under railway; on to kissing gate; aim across meadow to cross footbridge (383164). Up cart track opposite; at road, forward to Stonesfield 'square'.

Lunch Plough Inn, Finstock OX7 3BY (01993 868333; theplough-inn.co.uk), Woodman Inn, North Leigh OX29 6TH (01993 881790; thewoodmaninn-norlye.com), Mason's Arms, North Leigh OX29 6RZ (01993 882005) – right from church to top of hill, then right to pubs.

More information ramblers.org.uk

102   SOUTH MIDLANDS

Wayland's Smithy
OXFORDSHIRE

A clear morning after a night of steady rain, with the sun diffusing a pearly light over the Vale of White Horse. Crossing the sodden paddocks on the outskirts of Woolstone, we caught a glimpse of the chalk-cut White Horse herself, cavorting with dismembered limbs across a hilltop above the vale at full and gleeful tilt as she has done for 3000 years or more.

By Compton Beauchamp church, a pot-bellied Shetland pony tried to squeeze through the paddock gate behind us to join his long-legged cousins in the next field. From Odstone Farm — another tremendously handsome house of brick and chalk clunch — an old road took us south up the steep face of the downs to join the Ridgeway. The ancient track ran broad and pale along the crest between hedges of pink spindle berries where scarlet bryony fruit hung tangled in long necklaces.

The great neolithic tomb of Wayland's Smithy lay beside the Ridgeway in a ring of tall beeches, its southern portal guarded by four immense, roughly shaped boulders. The gold and silver trees, the weighty stones and the sigh of the wind made this a solemn place. Here the blacksmith Wayland would shoe the horses of travellers if they left a silver coin with their steeds. Wayland, a figure from Norse mythology, was a murderer, rapist and drinker of blood from his enemies' skulls, and something of his dark spirit seems to cling to the old tomb in the trees.

The Ridgeway forged on east, hollowed and slick with trodden chalk as it rose to the crest of Whitehorse Hill and the ramparts of the Iron Age camp built up here to command a fifty-mile view north over the vale. We stopped to stare at the enormous prospect, with the chalky squiggles that compose the white horse entrenched in the turf at our feet. Once every hundred years, old tales say, the horse leaps up and gallops across the sky to Wayland's Smithy to be shod by the bloodthirsty blacksmith. Now that would be something to see.

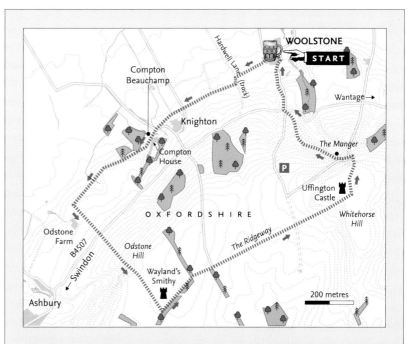

Start White Horse PH, Woolstone, Oxon SN7 7QL (OS ref SU293878)

Getting there Bus: Service X47 (Swindon-Wantage). Road: M4 to Jct 15; A419 towards Swindon; in 1 mile, right on minor road via Bishopstone to Ashbury; B4507 towards Wantage; in 2½ miles, left to Woolstone.

Walk (6 miles, moderate, OS Explorer 170): Leaving White Horse PH, left for 150m; at right bend, ahead ('Knighton') across two fields. Dogleg left/right across Hardwell Lane (289875); on across fields (yellow arrows/YA) to cross road at Knighton (283873). On (D'arcy Dalton Way) to road at Compton Beauchamp (281871). Follow 'To the Church' past barns and church; across two paddocks (YA, red discs), then field edges (276876) towards Odstone Farm. Just short of farm, left (270863) up track; across B4507 (273860); up for ⅔ mile to the Ridgeway (280851). Left, following Ridgeway east past Wayland's Smithy (281854) for 1½ miles to Whitehorse Hill. At summit, left through gate (301862, 'Bridleway') past NT sign to trig pillar. Fork right beyond on grass path to White Horse (301866). Left above Horse on path, down to cross Dragonhill Road at map board (298865, gate). Half left down to gate; over left-hand of two stiles; downhill with fence on right. At bottom, left to gate into road (294871); right across B4507, down to Woolstone.

Lunch/accommodation White Horse, Woolstone (01367 820726; whitehorsewoolstone.co.uk)

More information Abingdon TIC (01235 522711), visitengland.com, satmap.com, ramblers.org.uk

Brailes Hill
WARWICKSHIRE

All the birds in Warwickshire were singing their little heads off as we climbed away from Upper Brailes and up Gilletts Hill. Ben the black labrador barked an unavailing plea from behind his gate to be taken walkies: 'Oh come on, have a heart…!' But his owner shouted him down and waved us through with a smile.

On top of the hill, a great swath of green bearded barley glistened in the sunlight. We dropped down through Ashen Coppice to a wonderful westward view — cornfields, oilseed rapefields, hedges, pastures and red-roofed farms stretching away for 15 miles or more. Cloud shadow darkened the nearer ground, but a single pale church spire rose to the northwest, brilliantly lit in a ray of sun.

Chiffchaffs, whitethroats and blackbirds warbled fit to beat the band. We skirted above handsome old Famington Farm and climbed the wooded southwesterly flank of Brailes Hill. On the hill's upper slope an old cart track ran by pastures full of bouncing black and white lambs. We followed it down to Lower Brailes, looking out between veteran sycamores towards the church tower and its zigzag backdrop of green and yellow fields rising to the long ridge of Mine Hill.

St George's Church in Lower Brailes is a glorious confection of dark gold limestone. The fourteenth-century masons had massive fun with the grotesques they fashioned under the eaves — a mad nun, a bearded demon, a man with three faces, a wolfman with pricked-up ears — some of them blurred with weathering as though breaking through the stone. Inside, overlooking the nave, I found an old friend, the Green Man, with tendrils sprouting from his mouth and bursting into leaf around his cheeks.

Out in the fields north of St George's we climbed Lower Brailes's famed '99 steps', some of them formed of recycled grave slabs. On across medieval ridge-and-furrow farmland, a circuit of the ramparted mound of Castle Hill, and we were threading our way back into Upper Brailes between neat allotments of beans, peas, showy globe artichokes and humble spuds.

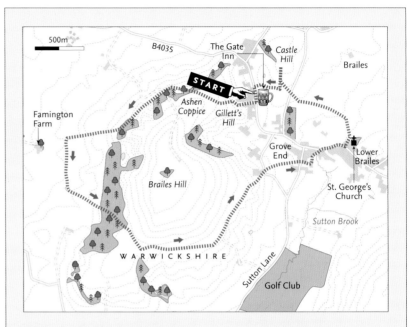

Start Gate Inn, Upper Brailes, Warwickshire OX15 5AX (OS ref SP305398)

Getting there Bus: Service 50A (stagecoachbus.com), Stratford-upon-Avon to Banbury. Road: Upper Brailes is on B4035, 3 miles east of Shipston-on-Stour.

Walk (6 miles, moderate, OS Explorer 191): From The Gate PH left; in 100m, right up Gilletts Lane. Past last house, right (303397, yellow arrow/YA) uphill. At T-junction at top, right; in 50m, fork left on path 58b. In 100m, across stile (300398); path 58 on and down through Ashen Coppice. At foot of steps, diagonally left (298399, YA) downhill; then left along lower edge of wood, following blue arrows/BA. At 'Private' gate (292396), fork right down field; at bottom, left (285393, YA). In 500m, left (285389, YA) across field; up through wood; at top (289386, YA), right. Pass two gates, then left through gate (292382, BA) on bridleway for 1 mile to Grove End (306390) and B4035 in Lower Brailes (312393). Right; opposite George Inn, left up Butcher's Lane. In 100m, left; Path 52 across footbridge (314396); on across 3 fields to cross Castle Hill Lane (309398). On across stile to Castle Hill; return across stile. Right for 70m; through gate (307399); ahead through allotments to road; left to The Gate.

Lunch The George Inn, Lower Brailes OX15 5HN (01608 685788; georgeinnbrailes.com)

Accommodation The Gate, Upper Brailes OX15 5AX (01608 685212; thegateatbrailes.co.uk) — clean and friendly village B&B

More information Warwick TIC (01926 492212), visitengland.com, satmap.com, ramblers.org.uk

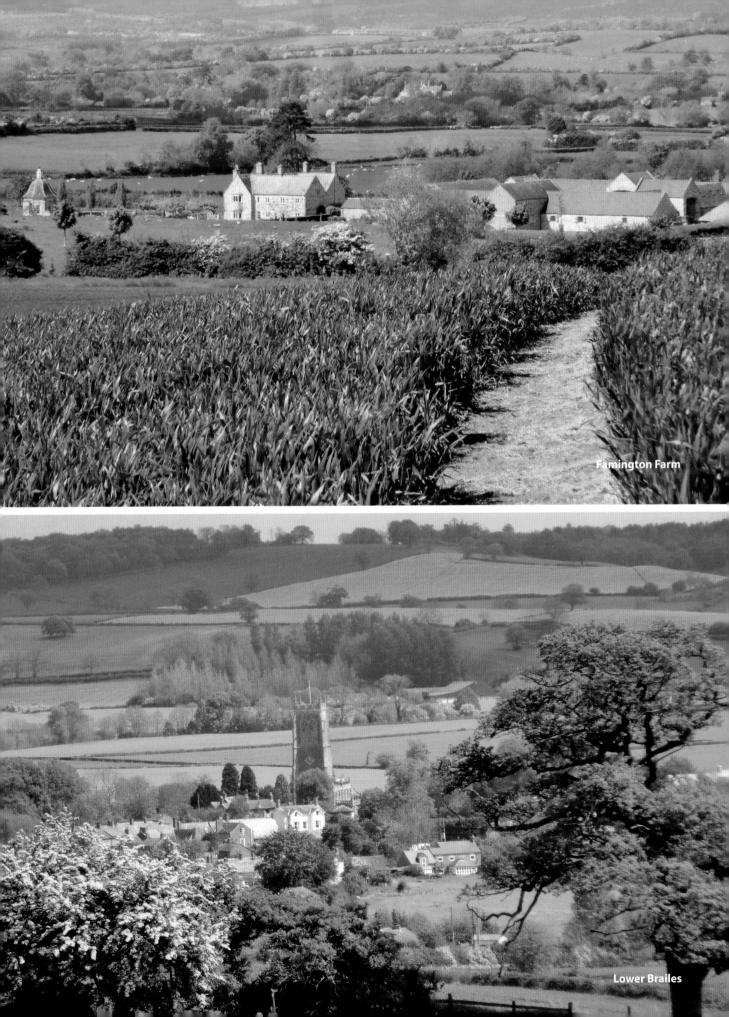

Famington Farm

Lower Brailes

A brilliant blue day of wind, with big clouds sailing over Warwickshire, building and dissolving in towers of rain and blurry shafts of sunlight. Jane and I were planning on a quick circuit of the fields and woods around Coughton, but we hadn't reckoned with the seductive powers of Coughton Court. This handsome house, seat of the staunchly Catholic Throckmorton family, was one of the centres of conspiracy of the Gunpowder Plotters in 1605.

The explosive old story, its heroes and villains twisted topsy-turvy by the distorting mirror of religion, held us spellbound. One peep down the secret alcove of the Tower Room into the deep, chilly refuge of the priest's hole was enough to summon up all the desperation and paranoia of that mistrustful age.

Walking away from the grand old house, we crossed thick clay ploughland studded with flood-smoothed pebbles. Big, centuries-old oaks in the hedges, rooks sailing with the wind, and lacy curtains of rain sifting sideways across the gently rolling landscape. We crossed the River Arrow, red with mud as it coiled lazily through the fields near Spernall, and went on over a little hill sown with thousands of young poplars and cherries, silver birch and sweet chestnut. These dense plantations of infant trees are a wonderful feature of this walk, an ambitious reseeding of William Shakespeare's sadly diminished Forest of Arden.

We passed the neat brick house and the immaculately kept garden of St Giles Farm, and found ourselves forging through head-high rushes and reeds on a squelchy path with young aspen leaves quivering a translucent cherry-red against the blue sky. A group of buzzards rode the wind over Spernall Park Wood, their cat-like calls cutting across the continual, wind-generated susurration of the oaks on the knoll.

From Round Hill the path ran south with the Cotswolds folding gracefully in sunlight far ahead, and then made west over the hump of Windmill Hill along an old green lane. Blackthorn, hawthorn, guelder rose and spindle spattered the hedges with their varying berry shades of crimson, pink and scarlet, and the sky raced vigorously overhead until we came back to Coughton.

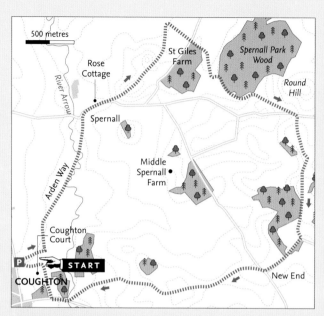

Start Coughton Court, Coughton, Warwickshire B49 5JA (OS ref SP082607). NB this is a NT car park – non-members pay. Park in Coughton village if not visiting Coughton Court.

Getting there Bus: Service 26 Redditch-Stratford (stagecoachbus.com). Road: Coughton Court is signposted in Coughton, on A435 between Alcester and Studley.

Walk (6 miles, easy, OS Explorer 220): *Starting from Coughton Court NT car park* – Turn left (away from house) through gates and across overflow car park field. Through kissing gate (083608) to join Arden Way/AW.

Starting in Coughton village – go north along A435; pass car entrance to Coughton Court; turn right ('Arden Way'/AW) across field to kissing gate at 083608. Turn left here along AW.

Both routes now keep ahead along field edge. At far end (082612; AW, Millennium Way/MW), right for 50m; then left through kissing gate (no waymarks). Cross field, through kissing gate (085615; AW, MW); on to cross River Arrow (086618). On to road by Spernall Church (087621). Ahead (AW, MW) to T-junction; right along road (MW) for 300m. Pass Rose Cottage on left; through kissing gate just beyond (089624, MW) and on, up and over a hill, following MW. On far side, under power lines (092626), a broad grass path forks right, but keep ahead here (MW yellow arrow on telegraph pole) with hedge on left, down to cross drive (095629). Through wicket gate (yellow arrow/YA); along edge of St Giles Farm garden; through another gate (MW) and on under power lines. Through gate on far side of field (095631, MW); cross stream and turn right off MW (YA) along rushy path, under power lines again to cross road (098630).

Through pedestrian gate (YA); on with wood on right. Through kissing gate; bear right between plantation and hedge (YA), then across field to corner of Spernall Park Wood (101626). Follow path round right-hand edge of wood. Where it curves into trees (104624), keep ahead down grassy ride, then through kissing gate. Keep ahead (YA) across a field, through kissing gate (106624); across next field, aiming to left of tree. In top left corner of field, turn right down steps onto lane (108623). Left for 150m; right through gate; left (YA) along hedge for 2 big fields, into trees (110618). Through gates; in 15m, right (YA) out of trees and along hedge. Follow field edge to go through kissing gate by a house (110613). Right down drive ('Heart of England Way') to road (109610). Right for 30m; left along green lane (AW) for 1½ miles to road (085603). Right to cross river by footbridge beside ford. In 200m, right (083604, 'Coughton Court') to car park.

Lunch Picnic or Coughton Court restaurant/tea room (01789 400777; nationaltrust.org.uk/coughton-court)

More information Redditch TIC (01527 60806), visitengland.com, ramblers.org.uk, satmap.com

Napton-on-the-Hill

WARWICKSHIRE

A cold breeze and a milky sky foretold winter, but the trees of Warwickshire still rustled autumn coats of gold and russet. St Lawrence's Church stood squarely at the nape of Napton Hill, its iron-rich stonework smoothed and hollowed by eight centuries of wind and weather. Inside, a fragment of stained glass showed a stern-faced, bare-breasted goddess crowned with a headdress of harvest fruits. Along the lane to Napton windmill the hedges were bright with rosehips and haw berries. If autumn was being shoved to one side by winter, she was evidently still resisting pretty stoutly.

The old tower mill holds a vantage point right in the path of the wind on the escarpment edge. We looked out west across the tumbled ground and pools of the former village brickyard, away over many miles of Warwickshire. Then we dropped down the hill to follow the Oxford Canal to its confluence with the Grand Union on the northern outskirts of Napton.

Canals shaped the Midlands early in the Industrial Revolution, snaking their way from town to town through the low-lying countryside. From the towpaths of the two man-made waterways the views were telescoped, an intimate prospect of grazing ponies, green and scarlet hedges and wind-ruffled water. Narrowboats with aspirational names — *Free Spirit, Dancer to the Drum* — went puttering by. A tang of woodsmoke from the chimney of *Kelly Lee*, a waft of music from *Saucy Lady*.

How many worlds one slips into and out of during a country walk! Up in the Shuckburgh Hills, eight centuries of residency by the Shuckburgh family have left their mark in a landscaped park full of fallow deer, lakes with islands, and beautiful woods, a hall and church peeping among the trees. One family's gradually developed vision of heaven on earth, sublime at any season, today the park lay drenched in a spectrum of autumn colour from pale lemon to fiery crimson.

We followed the edge of the wood up to the peak of Beacon Hill, then descended the slope into the green vale once more. A streaky afternoon sky, the rackety shout of pheasants, and a brisk wind to nudge us back towards Napton-on-the-Hill, spread below church and windmill along its patchwork hillside.

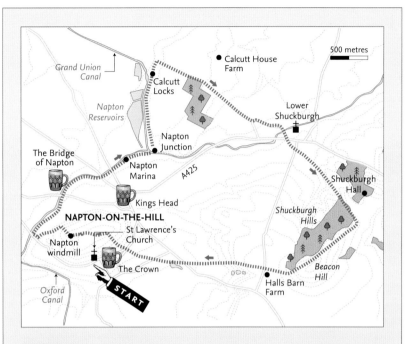

Start & finish St Lawrence's Church, Napton-on-the-Hill CV47 8NP (OS ref SP463613)

Getting there Train: (thetrainline.com; railcard.co.uk) to Leamington Spa (10 miles). Bus: Services 214, 503. Road: 'Napton village' from A425 Leamington-Daventry; then 'church only'.

Walk (7½ miles, moderate, OS Explorer 222): From church, track west to windmill; yellow arrows (YA) down scarp, across stile, bear left to road. Right across Oxford Canal; right to towpath, left for 1¼ miles to Napton Junction. Left up Grand Union Canal to Calcutt Locks. Right (YA) through hedge and gate; left up hedge to kissing gate; right for 1¼ miles, south of Calcutt House Farm, to Oxford Canal. Left to footbridge; right to Lower Shuckburgh church. Cross A425; YAs diagonally left uphill across fields, aiming SE between woods. Through gate by lake; at crest, right over stile (arrow); follow wood edge to Beacon Hill. Through gate; right along wood edge; YAs to road at Halls Barn Farm. Left through gate; right through double gates. Follow YAs due west, keeping same line, through fields for 1¼ miles, crossing two roads, to road in Napton. At foot of School Hill opposite, footpath (white notice) uphill; left at top to church.

Lunch The Bridge at Napton (on canal), Napton-on-the-Hill CV47 8NQ (01926 257575; naptonbridgeinn.co.uk), Kings Head (on A425), Napton-on-the-Hill CV47 8NG (01926 812202; thekingsheadnapton.co.uk), Crown Inn, Napton (on the village green), Napton-on-the-Hill CV47 8LZ (01926 812484)

More information Leamington Spa TIC (01926 742762), www.visitcoventryandwarwickshire.co.uk, ramblers.org.uk, satmap.com

Bredon Hill
WORCESTERSHIRE

The poet A. E. Housman was probably sublimating when he wrote in A Shropshire Lad of lying with a girl in summertime on Bredon Hill. He wasn't really that sort of chap, by all accounts. Jane and I would have got pretty wet if we had tried it under the troubled sky that the weather forecaster was glooming over today, with rain showers scudding in from the Bristol Channel.

But you just can't abandon an expedition up Bredon, however ominous the forecast. The hill tugs at you like an impatient companion — Housman got that right. And everything turned out bright and breezy anyway, as it happened.

Above the village of Elmley Castle we climbed smooth parkland fields past tremendous storm-shattered old oaks. Up the back slope of the hill past the high bracken-smothered earthworks of Elmley Castle itself — the Norman castle's stones were recycled to mend Pershore Bridge in Tudor times. Up through ancient woods full of the tall spikes of pungent woundwort and lace-like enchanter's nightshade. Up to the ridge that curls round the edge of Bredon Hill's 270m (900ft) escarpment, and along to the flowery ramparts of a sprawling Iron Age hill fort.

There's no exhilaration on earth like striding the walls of a hill fort with the wind bashing you and a fifty-mile view to stun you speechless.

The Cotswolds in the east, the Malverns in the west. South to Oxenton Knoll, down which they used to roll a fiery wheel to see if the new year would bring good luck. North-west to the Clents and the far-off Clee Hills that so enchanted Housman — a Worcestershire lad, in unromantic fact.

The larks he wrote about were up on Bredon Hill today, and so were masses of wild flowers: yellow and white lady's bedstraw, mats of wild thyme, rockroses with papery yellow petals; harebells, scabious, a pyramidal orchid in the ditch between the ancient fort's ramparts.

Up at the summit of the hill we found the Banbury Stone, shaped like a crusty old elephant couchant, and the grim little tower called Parson's Folly that a local squire built for himself.

One more gaze around the best view in the Three Counties, and we were bowling back down the slopes to Elmley Castle and the neat parlour of the Queen Elizabeth Inn, everyone's dream of a proper country pub.

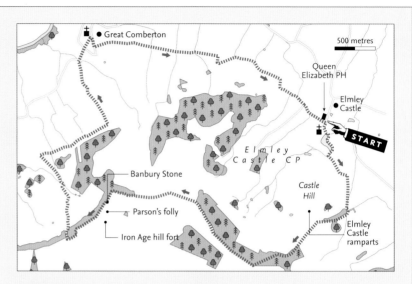

Start & finish Queen Elizabeth public house (PH), Elmley Castle, Worcs WR10 3HS (OS ref SO982411)

Getting there Bus: Service 565 Evesham-Worcester. Road: M5, Jct 9; A46 ('Evesham'); just after junction with B4078, left to Elmley Castle.

Walk (7 miles, moderate grade, OS Explorer 190): From Queen Elizabeth PH into churchyard. Keeping church on right, follow wattle fence to cross foot of pond (982410). Cross stile (yellow arrow/YA), follow field edge round 3 angles. In 500m, just before corner, turn right over plank bridge and stile (985405). Aim for far left corner of parkland field (985402). Left over stile and footbridge; right (blue arrow/BA) through metal gate and up grassy track. In 100m, right across footbridge (984401). Don't fork left up bank, but keep ahead on clear dirt track. In 400m cross footbridge (981400); bear left (BA) uphill. Keep fence on right, up through woods to T-junction of tracks at top of hill (974395). Right beside wood; keep to ridge track, ignoring side tracks. At end of wood, keep ahead with fence on left (967403, BA) for ¾ mile to pass Elephant Stone and Parson's Folly (957402). Continue beside wall to enter trees. In 100m, on right bend with BAs, turn even sharper right (952398, YA) down through trees, over gate stile and on down slope. Follow YAs on posts for ¼ mile to gravel drive (952405); left downhill for 2 fields, then right (949408; 'Private Estate – footpath') along stony track (YAs) for ½ mile. At water trough, left (957411, YA) downhill with fence on left. At kissing gate (954415) leave fence and fork a little right; follow hedge on right down to road (953418); right into Great Comberton. At top of hill by 'Pershore, Bredon' road sign (954420), ahead along footpath (fingerpost) to enter churchyard. Right along wall to road; right for 50m past Bredon House; left (955420; 'Elmley Castle 1½') on footpath through fields (YAs). After nearly 1 mile, ignoring all side tracks, reach a bridleway (970418; BAs left and right). Right for 30m; left through kissing gate (YA) and on. After 3 more fields, pass through kissing gate (976416); in 4th field, keep to right hedge; in 100m, right over stile (YA). Follow YAs for 3 more fields and through farmyard. Through 2 gates to left of barn; right behind barn to road (980413); left to Queen Elizabeth PH.

Conditions Many stiles, some tall and awkward

Lunch Queen Elizabeth PH (01386 710251; elmleycastle.com)

More information Evesham TIC (01386 446944), visitworcestershire.org, ramblers.org.uk, satmap.com

Clifton upon Teme
WORCESTERSHIRE

A cold, still day of early spring, with the clouds layered in motionless lines over the Worcestershire hills. The low whine of an organ from the red sandstone St Kenelm's Church heralded the end of matins as we left Clifton upon Teme and headed out over pale pink ploughland. Down in the steep wooded cleft of Witchery Hole, dog's mercury had taken over the world, a brief flush of tiny green flowers at the crack of spring before the primroses and wood anemones had got properly into their stride.

The Teme is a beautiful river. AE Housman called its landscape "The country for easy livers/ The quietest under the sun", and there's something leisurely and seductive about the slow green flow of the river, the miniature red cliffs of its steep banks and the winding valley it has smoothed out under high ridges of hard limestone. We walked upstream along the river to Brockhill Court, with its stumpy old oasts (this was hop-growing country once upon a time) and red brick barns, where a tawny owl was softly hooting.

A series of shallow billowing valleys led up to a little wood. We sat to eat our buns and cheese, watching a pair of treecreepers scuttling up an ash trunk, their neckless heads tucked down into their shoulders as they picked insects from their winter shelter in the cracks of the bark.

On up past Hillside Farm, with its architecture from three eras all jammed improbably together; a steep little burst up to the ridge, and then three glorious south-going miles along the Worcestershire Way, hurdling the dips and striding along the crests with a broad plain stretching out eastwards, and the Teme to the west running unseen in its lumpy green valley far below. We saw frogspawn in thick clumps in a pond at Woodbury Old Farm, smelt a whiff of wild garlic on the rim of a petrol-blue flooded quarry, and heard the first chiffchaff of the year in the woods on Pudford Hill.

Down in the valley we recrossed the dully glinting Teme and went up a long bridleway towards Clifton upon Teme, with the pocket mountain range of the Malvern Hills rising in the south, smoky grey and insubstantial in the last sunlight of the March evening.

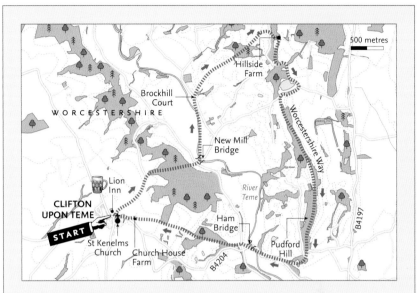

Start Lion Inn, Clifton upon Teme, Worcestershire WR6 6DH (OS ref SO714616)

Getting there Bus: Services 308, 310 from Worcester. Road: Clifton upon Teme is on the B4204 between Martley and Sapey Common (M5, Jct 7; A44 west).

Walk (9 miles, strenuous, OS Explorer 204): Take signed footpath between Lion Inn and church. Follow yellow arrows (YA) into field. On far side, over left-hand of 2 stiles (716617). Ahead with hedge on left. At field end, left over stile (718619); follow hedge on right. In 50m, right over stile (YA); on to cross lower stile (YA). Aim across field to right-hand corner of Harrisfield house (719621); bear left around house, and on down to cross stile into woodland (720623). Right along waymarked track, steeply down Witchery Hole for ½ mile to road (728624). Right, then left across New Mill Bridge. Left (729625) along east bank of River Teme for ¾ mile to road at Brockhill Court (728635).
Right at foot of drive (YA) through gate. Up and through next gate; right (YA) into shallow valley. Bear half right to gate (731639, faded YA). Follow valley bottom NE to stile into wood (735642). Follow path clockwise to cross stream (736642); 50m up the far bank, bear right to leave wood over stile (737643). Aim for far top corner of field (738644); over stile, and follow fence on left. Just past Hillside Farm house, left through gate (739645) onto drive; right to road (741646).
Cross road onto waymarked Worcestershire Way/WW; follow it south for 3 miles to B4204 (743608). Right (take care!) for ½ mile to cross River Teme by Ham Bridge (737611). First right after bridge ('Shelsleys'); pass 2 houses, then left (736611) up bridleway. Climb through wood; in 400m, at top of first rise, dogleg left/right through gate (732612, blue arrow, 'Sabrina Way'). Continue uphill with fence on right for 1 mile to Church House Farm. Left to road (717615); right to Lion Inn.

Conditions Strenuous walking, plenty of up-and-down. Steep, slippery and many steps in Witchery Hole wood.

Lunch/accommodation Lion Inn, Clifton upon Teme (01886 812975; thelionclifton.co.uk) – friendly, clean village inn

More information temetriangle.net, visitengland.com, satmap.com, ramblers.org.uk

Nine o'clock on a Sunday morning, with streamers of cloud hiding the top of Worcestershire Beacon and the whole Malvern range spread under a cool and cloudy sky. Dew soaked our trousers as we brushed through the pastures and corn stubbles, walking north in a patchwork countryside of green and gold with the Malverns bulking on our right hand.

In the straggly hamlet of Evendine, a screech among the masses of petunias in a beautiful cottage garden made us jump. "Oh, that's Harry our young bantam cockerel," chuckled the lady of the house, leaning out of her window. "That's his little trick, startling people as they go by. A blonde with highlights, he is. We're getting him a couple of lady friends to shut him up!"

We struck off down a farm lane towards the high-wrinkled ramparts of the British Camp, one of several ancient forts and strongholds along the ridge of the Malverns. Long-tailed tits and blackbirds lifted their voices among the oaks and overshot hazels of Hatfield Coppice as we trod the broad track of the Worcestershire Way southwards along the foot of the hills.

We fingered the green, apricot-like fruit of a bullace tree that leant across the path, making one of those fantasy resolutions never actually to be fulfilled, to return and pick the ripened yield for a Christmas of bullace gin around the fire.

Following the medieval Shire Ditch up the spine of Broad Down, then on up the magnificent quadruple ramparts of the British Camp, I thought of proud Caractacus defying the Romans from these heights in 51 AD. The last stand of the Catuvellaunian king probably didn't happen here, despite what legends say. But watching children in bright football shirts swooping like buzzards down the slopes, and looking away into Wales and up over the Midland plains — a hundred-mile view — it seemed a place where old spirits might linger. Looking down, we made out the churchyard of St Wulstan's at Little Malvern, where Edward Elgar lies. "If ever you're walking on the hills and hear this," said Elgar of the cello concerto he composed below the Malverns, "don't be frightened — it's only me."

Start & finish British Camp car park, on A449 opposite Malvern Hills Hotel, Wynds Point, Jubilee Drive, Malvern WR13 6DW (OS ref SO763404)

Getting there Train: (thetrainline.com; railcard.co.uk) to Colwall (¾ mile from Evendine by footpath). Bus: (herefordshire.gov.uk) service 44B or Malvern Hills Hopper. Road: M5, M50 (Jct 1); A38, A4104 via Upton-on-Severn to Little Malvern; A449 towards Ledbury.

Walk (3½ miles, moderate grade, OS Explorer 190): Cross A449 (take care!); up B4232 ('West Malvern'). In 10m, by public lavatories on left, are 2 fingerposts; follow right-hand one (past WCs). In 50m, cross stile; keep ahead downhill, across field and over stile with 2 yellow arrows/YA; keep ahead to cross stream and stile (760409); ahead (YAs) to road by Upper House in Evendine (759413). Left for ¼ mile; just past Lower House Farm, left (755412; fingerpost, YA) along lane. In ⅓ mile, left over stile by Oldcastle Farm gates (756406; YA), then 2 more stiles, before aiming diagonally left uphill (757405) to cross stile at corner of Hatfield Coppice (758404; YA). In 30m, right over stile (YA); follow Worcestershire Way/WW through trees to cross A449.
Continue south on WW. In ⅓ mile cross steep track (758396); in another ⅓ mile, cross stile with reservoir on right (761392). In 200m, left (YA) off WW up track for 100m to saddle of ground where 5 paths meet (762390). Sharp left uphill on broad gravelly track; in 30m, at 'Hangman's Hill, Broad Down' marker stone, bear right uphill on track which swings left to follow Malvern ridge northwards. In ¼ mile descend left to toposcope on saddle (762395); follow 'British Camp Earthworks' sign to summit. Continue on track to second summit (760400), and down to car park.

Lunch Malvern Hills Hotel (01684 540690; malvernhillshotel.co.uk); café/kiosk at car park

More information Malvern TIC, 21 Church Street, Malvern WR14 2AA (01684 892289), malvernhills.org.uk, malvernhillsaonb.org.uk

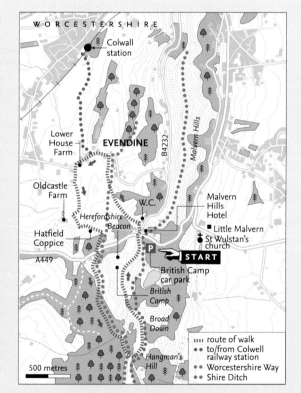

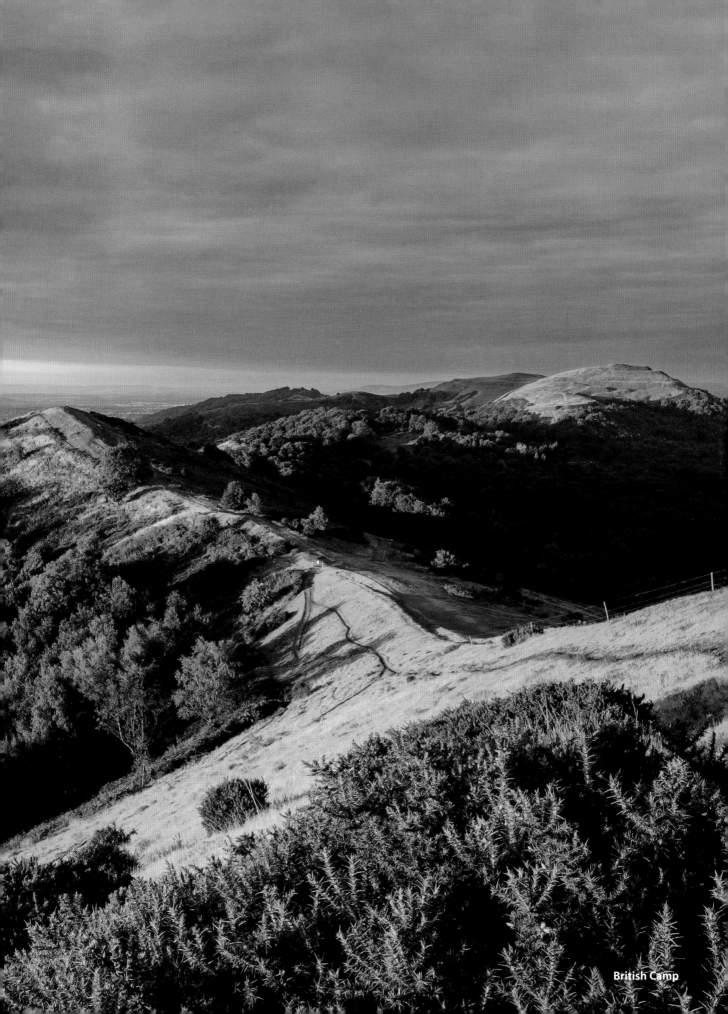
British Camp

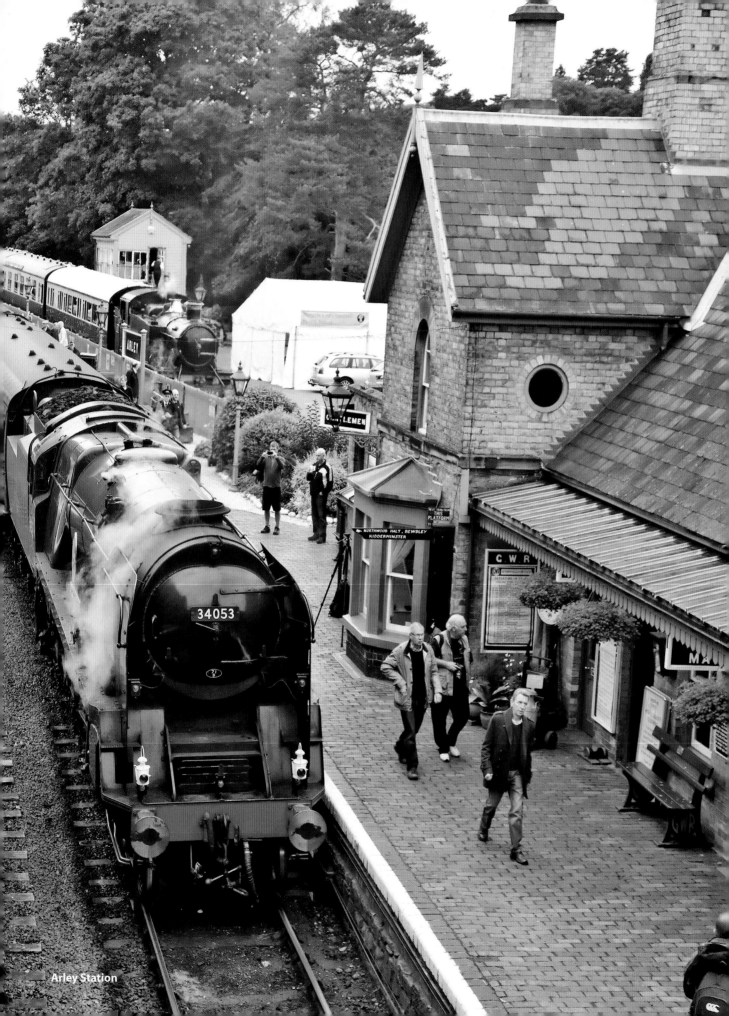

Arley Station

Wyre Forest
WORCESTERSHIRE

The last time I found myself at the Harbour Inn, I'd sat back in the sunny garden at noon and rejoiced as follows: (a) it was a beautiful morning, (b) there was a gorgeous walk up the River Severn in prospect, and (c) it was the first day of the rest of my life (I'd just given up teaching after ten years at the chalk face). Now here I was, a load of years later, setting out once more up the hill past Arley station. Around the hanging flower-baskets wreathed a whiff of train smoke — the Severn Valley Railway's gleaming green GWR locomotive 7812 *Erlestoke Manor* had just pulled out with the 10.54 for Bewdley.

I walked up through a grove of young ash and poplar trees, their long-stalked leaves helicoptering in the wind, and on through horse paddocks to Pound Green, where a flock of sheep quietly grazed the village green. A short sharp shock of the B4194, and I was walking through the cool green shade of the Wyre Forest. Six thousand acres of this ancient hunting forest stretch west of Birmingham along the Severn and the borders of Worcestershire and Shropshire, a resource and refuge for families, mountain bikers and walkers.

Today's cloudy sunlight lit patches of purple heather, showing where the trees had encroached on old heaths. Golden bursts of St John's wort and the pink 'fairy fingernails' of centaury lined the woodland path that ran easily down to Dowles Brook. The little river rushed sparkling around its bend in the heart of the forest, a sibilant guide that carried me east to the brink of the Severn.

The broken abutments of the Wyre Forest's own long-abandoned branch railway line rose mid-river, like relics of a vanished civilisation. I turned upstream and idled the three miles back to Arley and the Harbour Inn past riverbank houses and purple drifts of meadow cranesbills, looking across the river to the brambly embankment of the Severn Valley Railway. A mournful owl hoot, a clatter of wheels on the mighty cast-iron bow of Victoria Bridge, and *Erlestoke Manor* went thundering over the river with a flash of polished brass and an evanescent plume of smoke.

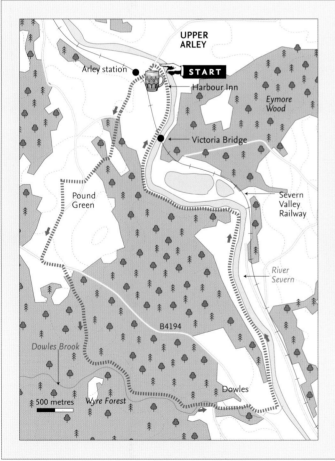

Start & finish Harbour Inn, Arley DY12 3NF (OS ref SO765800)

Getting there Rail: Severn Valley Railway (01299 403816; svr.co.uk) to Arley. Road: A456 to Bewdley, B4194 towards Kinlet; in Buttonoak, right (Pound Green, Arley). Follow 'Arley Footbridge' to car park beyond Harbour Inn.

Walk (7½ miles, easy, OS Explorer 218): Up road past Arley station. On right bend, left (762795); fork right past pond, off gravel road and up bank. Take middle of three paths uphill between trees. At top, through metal kissing gate (761792), up field, right at top past houses to road (758788). Right for 20m; left (fingerpost) down field to bottom right corner (755789). Over stile (yellow arrow/YA), left to road in Pound Green (755785). Forward to B4194 (753780); left for 250m (keep to left-hand grass verge, take care!). Cross road at St Andrew's Church (755779); right (fingerpost); follow YAs into Wyre Forest (756778). In 350m, at five-way meeting of tracks (758775), ignore track on left and fainter track ahead; take next one on right, a stony roadway, down towards Dowles Brook. Towards bottom, join concrete track; just before foot of slope, left (758768) on dirt track. In ¾ mile cross brook, in another 200m, left through gate (772764, Geopark Way). Follow to road (777763). Right for 100m; left to River Severn (779764). Left for 3 miles to Arley.

Lunch Harbour Inn, Arley (01299 401204)

Accommodation Hallmark Stourport Manor, Stourport DY13 9JA (0330 0283421; hallmarkhotels.co.uk)

More information Bewdley TIC (08456 077819; bewdley.org.uk), visitworcestershire.org, satmap.com, ramblers.org.uk

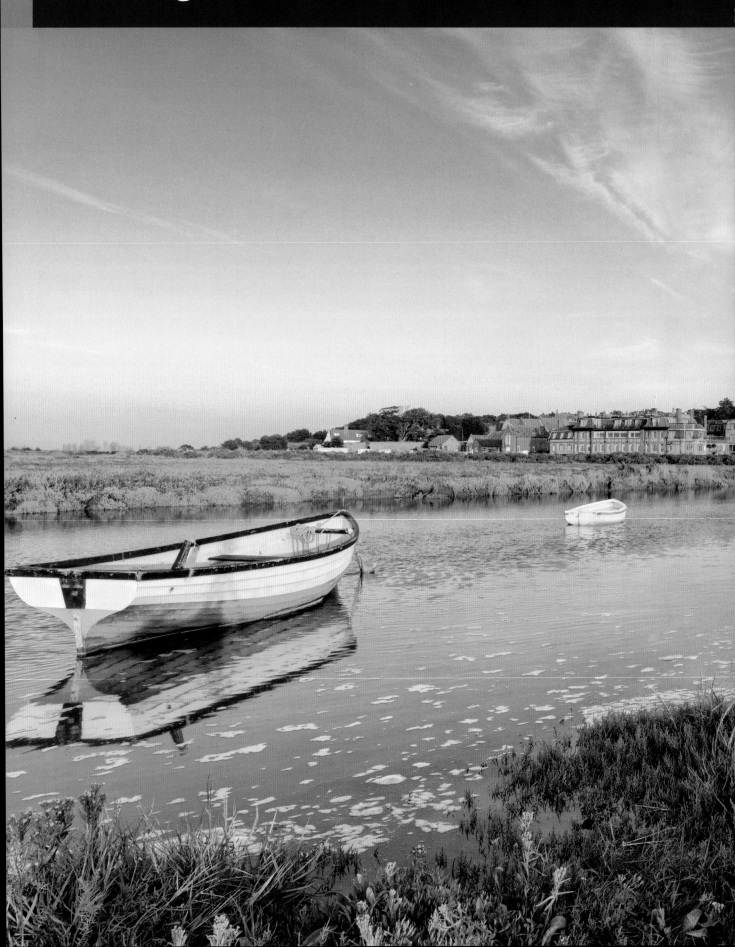

East Anglia

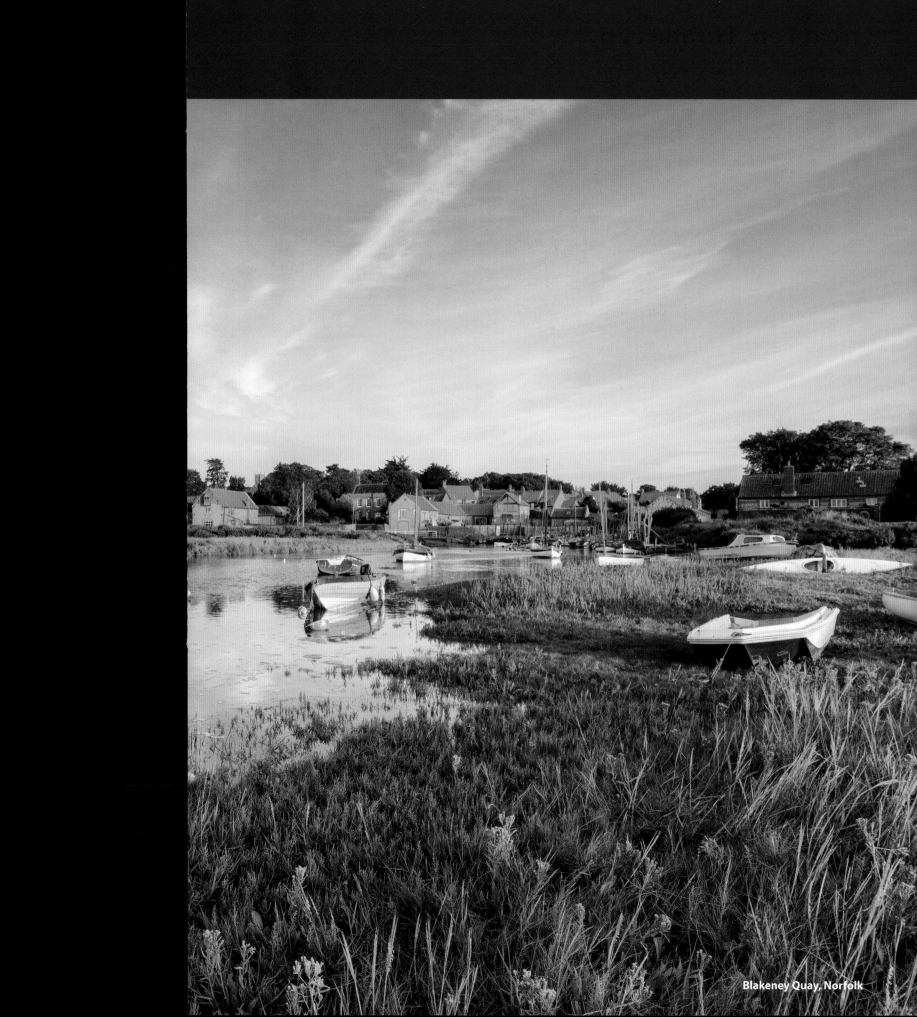

Blakeney Quay, Norfolk

Great Fen, Holme Fen
CAMBRIDGESHIRE

Bright sun slanted across the Cambridgeshire flatlands, silvering the tree trunks of Holme Fen as we stepped from a bumpy old drove road into the green heart of the nature reserve. "The largest silver birch wood in lowland Britain," said Carry Akroyd, leading the way. "I just love this place."

The East Anglian fens have a passionate champion in Carry Akroyd, an artist with sharp eyes who works in vivid colours and bold, decisive shapes. I'd long admired the observant realism of her fenland paintings — straight dykes running to the skyline, square arable fields sinuating with tractor tracks, tangled marshes where lapwings flicker in black and white, and level horizons pierced by wind turbines and smoking brickfield chimneys. It was a huge pleasure to be walking with Carry through the landscape that inspired such striking images.

Holme Fen National Nature Reserve is a lush place, as damp as a sponge. Yet the land that the trees and plants stand on has been shrinking, its level dropping, ever since drainage for agriculture began to suck the black peat dry. Beside a drove road we came to the cast-iron columns of the Holme Posts that mark Britain's lowest point, 2.7m (9ft) below sea level. In 1851 the older of the two posts was rammed into the peat until its top was flush with the ground. Today it stands 4m (13ft) tall, a measure of how far the dried-out land has shrunk around it.

The path led on beside an insect-riddled dyke. A beautiful little falcon came dancing down the ditch — a hobby with spotted chest and yellow talons, snatching dragonflies to dismember and eat on the wing. At the corner of Trundle Mere we climbed into a bird hide and looked out from on high across the broad empty fens to a skyline of wind turbines and silos — a Carry Akroyd scene stretched out before us. "I try to make a portrait of a place," she said, "that's more than the sum of what you can see. But it has to be honest."

There's an ongoing scheme, the Great Fen project, to return all this countryside, nearly 15 square miles of intensively farmed land, to native fenland, managed for wildlife. What a superb vision.

We turned back through the silver birches of Stilton Roughs, the willows of Caldecote Fen and the great oaks of Home Lode Covert, to reach open flatlands once more. Cattle were chomping rich grass where wheat had grown only three years ago. "It's happening, the Great Fen," said Carry, looking over the new meadows, "and it's so exciting to see it coming alive."

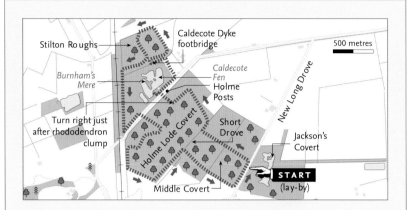

Start & finish Lay-by on New Long Drove (OS ref TL214885)

Getting there Road: A1(M) Jct 16; A15 to Yaxley; minor road to Holme; B660 towards Ramsey St Mary's. In 1 mile, left up New Long Drove; lay-by on right in ¼ mile, by reserve barrier. NB: limited space.

Walk (6 miles, easy, OS Explorer 227): Continue along road for 100m; left over footbridge, right on path, first left through wood for ½ mile. At T-junction on Short Drove, right (208890); in 150m, left across footbridge (209891); path bends right to T-junction; left on grass path. In 450m by 'Discovery Trail' post (206895), bear left. In 250m, at big patch of rhododendrons, bear right; in 50m, right on unmarked path between trees (204893) for 200m to reach Holme Posts (203894).
Cross road; left along fenced path to bird hide on Burnham's Mere (202895). Return to road; left for 250m. Where trees end just before Holme Lode Farm (204896), left past NNR sign along path. In 300m, just before T-junction of drains, left (203898). In 250m, right over footbridge across Caldicote Dyke (201898). Right for 20m; left into trees; fork immediately right, and in 30m right again, to continue parallel with Caldicote Dyke for 300m to south-east corner of wood (203899). Left on grass ride to Trundle Mere Hide (201903), where you turn left along wood edge. In 250m (199902), left into wood. At T-junction, right; in 100m, left; at 200899 fork right to T-junction with Caldicote Dyke (201898 – hidden by bank ahead). Right for 350m to T-junction with railway just ahead (197896). Left across Caldicote Dyke (footbridge) for ½ mile to gate onto road (198889). Left along road; in 300m, right across Holme Lode (200891), past NNR sign and on, south-east along grass path. In 300m path widens into clearing; pass crooked oak on right, then in 70m turn right by pine tree with 'withered arm' branch (203889). Follow grass track which winds for over ½ mile to south-west corner of wood near railway (199884). Turn left along grass track; follow wood edge. In 700m, pass footbridge across drain on right (204886); keep ahead along Short Drove into wood. In 250m, right (206887) on track south-east for ½ mile to ditch with cottage on your right (212883). Left for 10m; right across ditch onto New Long Drove; left to car.

Lunch Picnic

Accommodation Stilton Cheese Inn, Stilton PE7 3RP (01733 240546; stiltoncheesepublichouse.co.uk)

More information greatfen.org.uk, www.naturalengland.org.uk, visitengland.com, satmap.com, ramblers.org.uk, see Carry Aykroyd's work at carryakroyd.co.uk

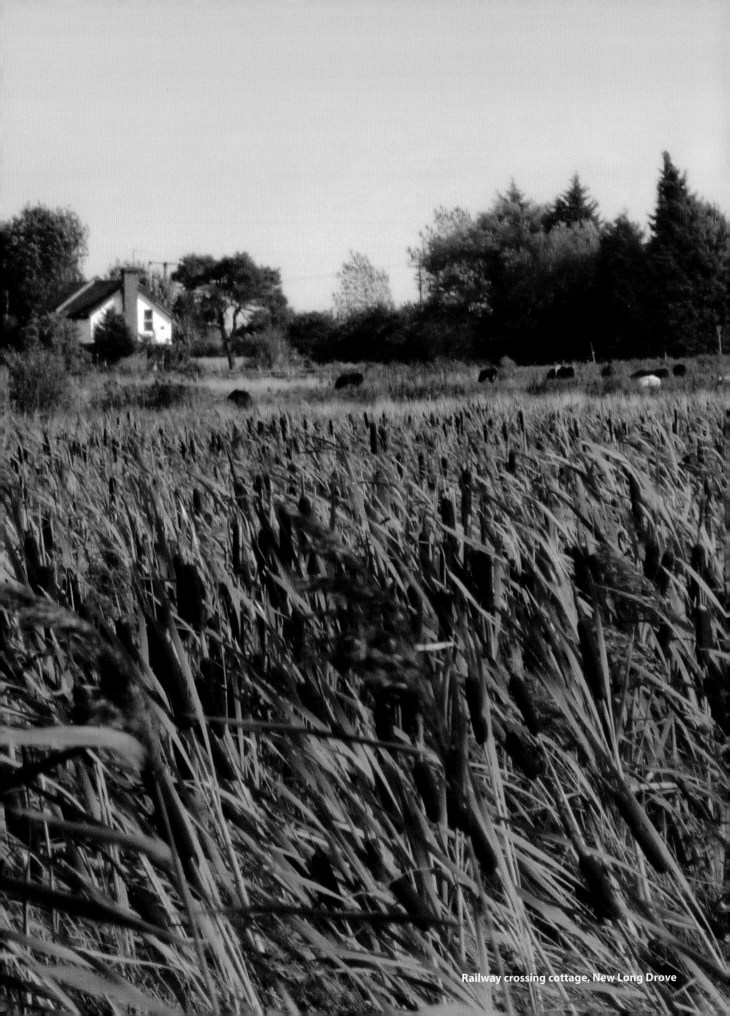

Railway crossing cottage, New Long Drove

A cuckoo was calling, faint and far, across Wicken Fen National Nature Reserve. Unlike the rest of these Cambridgeshire flatlands, Wicken Fen has never been drained for agriculture. Under the National Trust's expert care for the past 100 years, it remains a flourishing, sodden, teeming green jungle, supporting wildlife that has died out or greatly diminished everywhere else.

In front of one hide, greenfinches cavorted, vivid in their spring jackets of intense green; from another we watched a beautiful chocolate and red marsh harrier swooping and quartering the reedbeds on long, feather-fingered wings. Then we set out to follow a cycleway across Adventurers' Fen. What a contrast! On the east of the path, intensive agriculture in drilled green rows to the flat horizon; to the west, the lush pastures of the reserve where highland cattle and springy muntjac deer grazed, sedgy pools stood full of geese and egrets, and swallows and hobbies zipped about the sky.

We crossed the long silver finger of Burwell Lode, a man-made drainage channel, and followed Reach Lode west to Upware on a high green embankment with grandstand views across both wild fen and intensively farmed fields. The National Trust's 100-year plan, named 'Wicken Fen Vision', would see the nature reserve stretch all the way from Wicken to Cambridge — a restoration of the landscape so beloved of Richard Fielder, king of Upware, who ruled this fenland realm with his fists and foul (but classically trained) tongue in the 1860s.

Fielder, a Cambridge undergraduate and black sheep of a well-heeled family, would smoke, drink and fight with anyone who came to his 'court' at Upware's riverside pub, the charmingly titled 'Five Miles From Anywhere — No Hurry!' He pitched bargees into the river, blackened friends' eyes and dispensed punch from his private seven-gallon gotch, a giant jug.

When the railways brought the outside world to Fenland, Fielder and his wild courtiers melted away into oblivion. But at Wicken Fen — these days extending across Adventurers' Fen and beyond — a corner of the ancient fenland environment in which the king of Upware once reigned as Lord of Misrule, has survived and is prospering.

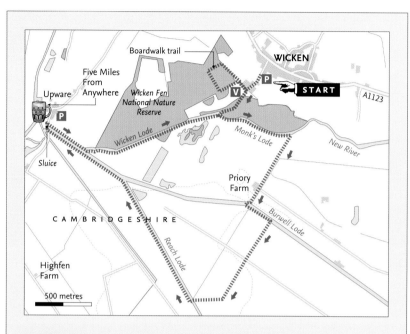

Start & finish Wicken Fen NNR, Wicken, Cambs CB7 5XP (OS ref TL565706)

Getting there Bicycle: National Cycle Route 11 from Ely. Road: Wicken Fen is signed from Wicken village, on A1123 between A142 (Newmarket) and A10 (Cambridge). Park in NT car park (£2.50/day, NT members free).

Walk (8 miles – 7 excluding NT Wicken Fen, easy, OS Explorer 226): Walk circuit of Wicken Fen NNR boardwalk trail (optional). From visitor centre, right along left bank of Wicken Lode. In 500m bear left, then right across footbridge (560701, Adventurers' Fen); left along right bank of Monk's Lode. In ½ mile, right (539700, Cycleway post 11). Pass Priory Farm (565693) and cross Burwell Lode (564690); left along south bank of lode. Track bends south to cross Cycleway 51 (564684); on to cross Reach Lode (557678). Right along its left bank for 1¾ miles to turn right across lode at Upware sluice (537699). Back along north bank of lode. In 600m cross mouth of Wicken Lode (542696); left (yellow arrow, 'Wicken Fen') up its south bank for more than a mile. Left across Monk's Lode footbridge (560701), and then return to car park.

Lunch Wicken Fen NNR café; Maid's Head, Wicken (01353 720727; maidsheadwicken.com), Five Miles From Anywhere PH, Upware (01353 721654; fivemilesinn.com)

More information Wicken Fen NNR (NT) (01353 720274; nationaltrust.org.uk/wicken-fen-nature-reserve) £6.80 adult, NT member free, visitengland.com, satmap.com, ramblers.org.uk

Witcham and Bedford Rivers
CAMBRIDGESHIRE

A peerless midwinter day of wall-to-wall blue sky, like a Ming bowl upturned over the Cambridgeshire flatlands. On Witcham village green we huddled into gloves and scarves. Hereabouts they call the fen wind a 'lazy wind', because it goes straight through you rather than taking the trouble to go round you. It was lively enough to make our eyes water on this piercingly cold morning.

Like all the other established settlements in Fenland, Witcham is footed on an island. This almost imperceptible hummock of clay stands marooned among enormous, saucer-flat fields, reclaimed by constant drainage, labour and bank-building from what was formerly a fenny, marshy and flood-prone landscape. We slogged our way with clay-weighted boots along the margins of waterlogged fields, then turned north-east along the raised bank of the New Bedford River, a broad highway of steel-blue water rippled by the wind.

The twin Bedford Rivers, Old and New, were dug ruler-straight and half a mile apart for more than twenty miles across the face of Fenland in the mid-seventeenth century, to prevent disastrous flooding and to drain the land for agriculture. We followed the New Bedford River for a couple of miles, the wind pouring into our faces as cold and sharp as glass, looking out over pale clay fields that suddenly gave way to a patchwork of chocolate-dark peat ploughland interspersed with winter wheat glinting green in the low sunshine. The exhilaration and sense of space were intoxicating, the views immense, especially to the east where the great central lantern and twin west towers of Ely Cathedral rose on the skyline like a celestial city.

At last we dropped down off the river bank and made our way back to Witcham by way of sticky black drove roads, the cathedral glimmering ghostly pale beyond the sunlit fields. A big flock of Bewick's swans, over from the frozen Siberian tundra for the winter, was feeding on potato and sugarbeet fragments, the white bodies and yellow nebs contrasting brilliantly with the dark peat soil. Their restless piping and honking followed us a long while, a haunting keynote of winter in Fenland.

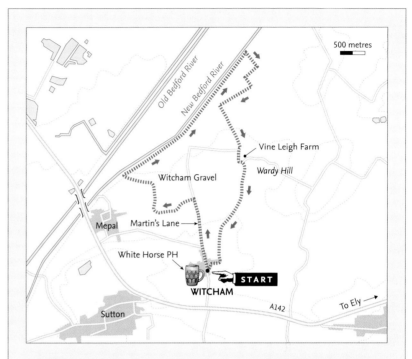

Start & finish Witcham village green, near Ely, Cambs, CB6 2LB (OS ref TL463800)

Getting there Bus: Service 106 from Ely. Road: Witcham is signposted off A142 between Ely and Chatteris.

Walk (8 miles, easy, OS Explorer 228): North up village street. Where Mepal Road bends left (462803), head along Martin's Lane for ⅔ mile. At bridge, left (460813, fingerpost) beside ditch for 1⅓ miles to New Bedford River (445817). Right along bank for ¾ mile to pass house at Witcham Gravel (456825). In 1¼ miles go through fence (469841); down bank, left along path for 200m; right (470843) through gate; ahead along drove. In 300m, right (473840); in 350m, left (471837); in 200m, right (472836). In ½ mile, bear left at fork (465832) for ⅔ mile to road in Wardy Hill (462823). Left along The Green, round left bend; at next bend (470820) ahead (fingerpost) through Vine Leigh Farm gate. Right beside house, through gate, on beside hedge to crossing of droves (471818). Ahead for ¾ mile to Witcham. At T-junction (466802), right through second of two gates; left through kissing gate; path to road (465800); right to village green. NB: droves can be muddy after rain.

Lunch White Horse, Silver Street, Witcham (01353 775368), closed Monday; food Thurs-Sun, lunchtimes and evenings; opening times negotiable for groups

Accommodation Anchor Inn, Sutton Gault (01353 778537; anchor-inn-restaurant.co.uk)

More information Ely TIC (01353 662062), visitcambridgeshire.org, satmap.com, ramblers.org.uk

Canvey Island

ESSEX

Before I ever set foot on Canvey Island I'd thoroughly explored this dead-flat offshoot of the Thames Estuary's Essex shore in my imagination — washed up there on the tides of Wilko Johnson's gritty lyrics and Lee Brilleaux's gravelly bark. If the tough-looking, fist-punching Brilleaux was the voice and face of Dr Feelgood, Canvey Island's crunchy home-grown R&B band, guitarist Johnson was its heart and soul, with a unique song-writing talent for depicting the mean streets and hard men and women of a place he called 'Oil City'. It wasn't the real Canvey Island, but it was a real enough place to me and thousands more fans of the "greatest local band in the world".

Setting out across Benfleet Creek to walk a circuit of the Canvey sea walls, I found myself immediately in acres of green marshes where piebald horses grazed and skylarks sang overhead. This western sector of the island houses one of the most diverse bird reserves in Britain — marsh harriers over the reedbeds, lapwings in the fields, curlews on the muddy foreshore — more RSPB than R&B.

Where was the Feelgoods' Oil City? I looked ahead and saw the burning flare stacks and mad scientist's chemistry set of Shell Haven oil refinery across the creek. Farther round the island a giant black jetty, a remnant of a never-built refinery on Canvey itself, rose out of the fields and hurdled the mud flats of Hole Haven to curve into the River Thames.

"I've been searching, all thru' the city," growled Brilleaux on Dr Feelgood's debut album, "see you in the morning, down by the jetty." Here it was, as skeletal and ominous as I'd always imagined.

Now the Thames lay in full view, nearly two miles wide, the green and yellow escarpment of the North Kent shore rising on the southern skyline. A great concrete sea wall 4.5m (15ft) high keeps the tides out of Canvey these days — it was built after the East Coast flood disaster of 1953 when the island, which lies below sea level, was inundated and fifty-eight people lost their lives.

I followed the sea wall under the jetty and on above the white weatherboarded Lobster Smack pub, a notorious haunt of smugglers back in the day, where Charles Dickens had Pip and Magwitch hiding out in *Great Expectations*. On along the Thames shore among sunbathing Canveyites; past the Art Deco cylinder of the Labworth Café; round the eastern point of the island, a maze of ramshackle wooden jetties with a glimpse of Southend Pier far ahead.

The northern side of Canvey is all saltmarshes and creeks. I strolled the seawall path and hummed the tunes that brought the 'Canvey Delta' to life in my imagination, back when the Feelgoods ruled the world.

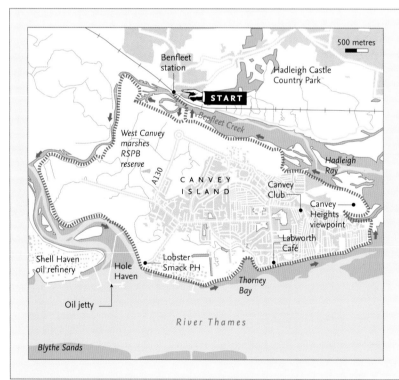

Start & finish Benfleet station, South Benfleet, Essex SS7 1NF (OS ref TQ778859)

Getting there Train: (thetrainline.com) to Benfleet. Road: M25 Jct 29, A127, A130 to Waterside Farm roundabout on Canvey Island, left on B1014 to Benfleet.

Walk (14 miles, easy, OS Explorer 175): From Benfleet station turn left along B1014 on to Canvey Island; turn right (west) along the sea wall and follow it, and the outer edge of the island, anticlockwise all the way round.

Lunch Lobster Smack PH, Haven Road, Canvey Island SS8 0NR (01268 514297; thelobstersmackcanveyisland.co.uk)

Accommodation Oysterfleet Hotel, 21 Knightswick Road, Canvey Island SS8 9PA (01268 510111; oysterfleethotel.com) – friendly, welcoming and very helpful

More information Southend-on-Sea TIC (01702 215620), visitessex.com, ramblers.org.uk, satmap.com

Jane's amazement — "Is it really Essex?" — was easy to understand. Essex simply isn't associated with scenes like this. Thatched, colourwashed, timber-framed houses line Ashdon's village street; the River Bourn courses dimpling under diminutive brick bridges; gentle farmlands rise all around. A place that wears its 'Best Kept Village' trophies up on its walls, with pride, for all to admire. Go to the Thames Estuary shore of Essex to have your prejudices confirmed (or challenged — but that's for another walk); but come to the northwest corner of England's most maligned county to have them scattered to the four winds.

Here are rolling green hills, catkin-laden copses and delectably situated medieval hall houses enough to delight any country walker with all five senses alert.

Children's shouts drifted from the village school playground as we climbed past beet fields with flapping scarecrows to the crest where Ashdon windmill raised its white sails. Crossing the ridge to walk the descending field path into Steventon End, we gazed ahead at what must be the most perfect juxtaposition of two houses in all Essex — the beautiful half-timbered Tudor house of Ashdon Place, pink-washed, sheltered under a wooded slope; and beyond it the mellow red-brick Waltons, its ranks of windows flashing back the sun, every inch an early Georgian country house, but with an Elizabethan hall buried inside it.

The way led through the Waltons parkland, where drifts of winter aconite with yellow hairdryer hoods and ruffs of green grew under the trees. Six chestnut foals watched us with wary curiosity from a paddock. Out among the wheat and bean fields, their hedges white with old man's beard, we crossed the wide roof of the hill and came down by Bowsers End with its farmhouse standing quiet among willows.

Back in Ashdon's little sub-hamlet of Church End we found the lumps and bumps of a former village abandoned at the time of the Black Death, its remnants a couple of old cottages and a crooked, timber-framed old Guildhall. Here stands All Saints, one of those rural Essex churches cobbled together over the centuries out of bricks, flints, timber chunks and blocks of limestone. A splendid mish-mash with round porthole windows on high, the whole building a bit skew-whiff and out of kilter. And in one of the south windows a few fragments of delicate, ancient glass — leaves and flowers, angels' faces, wings, hands, and a wight with mournful countenance and golden hair.

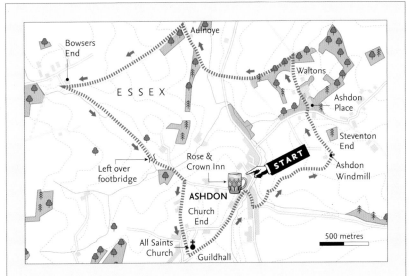

Start & finish Rose & Crown, Ashdon, Saffron Walden CB10 2HB (OS ref TL587421)

Getting there Bus: Four Counties Buses (01799 516878; www.cambridgeshire.gov.uk) Service 59 (Haverhill-Clavering). Road: Bartlow, then Ashdon, signed from A1307 Cambridge-Haverhill at Linton.

Walk (5½ miles, easy grade, OS Explorer 209): From Rose & Crown take road opposite ('Radwinter'). In 200m, left up Kates Lane. In 100m, left (fingerpost); at top of bank bear right past bench (589421; yellow arrow/YA) and follow YAs (Harcamlow Way on map). At next bench don't turn right; keep ahead to Ashdon Windmill (595425). Left along road. Don't take first 2 paths on right (black fingerposts); keep on round bend and turn right on path (concrete fingerpost) diagonally across field, aiming to left of buildings below. Cross road in Steventon End (593429); up drive (fingerpost), past Waltons house and on. Through shank of woodland; at its end, sharp left (591434; no waymark) on bridleway along its north edge. Cross road (584432; NB blind bend! take care!). Down lane opposite; follow it for ½ mile. Opposite Aulnoye, left (580437, 'bridleway') up wood edge and on for nearly a mile to Bowsers End. Sharp left here (568431, fingerpost) along broad footpath. In ⅔ mile pass woodland; through gate; in another 150m, left over footbridge (577424, YA). Cross stile; aim half left for bottom left corner of wood; cross stile with waymark here (579423). Up steps to lane; right; at top of hill, right (581422; fingerpost) past cottage and along farm track. In 50m, left through hedge (YA); right along field edge past Hall Farm to road (580417). Cross; down lane to All Saints Church (581415). On far side of church pass to left of Guildhall; bear left past gate. In 20m, left at crossing of paths; follow fence past east end of church and on to gap in hedge (582415). Diagonally left across big field to far bottom corner (585418). Left to road by village museum; right to Rose & Crown.

Lunch Rose & Crown, Ashdon (01799 584337); Ashdon village museum (tea and WI cakes) (01799 584253; ashdonvillagemuseum.co.uk): Open 2-5pm; Sun, Wed, BH Mon, Easter to end Sept; Sep-Christmas, Sun only

More information Saffron Walden TIC (01799 524002), www.visitessex.com, ramblers.org.uk, satmap.com

The Swan Inn at Great Easton made a perfect base for our leg-stretch through the rolling landscape of rural northwest Essex. Great Easton is full of lovely old houses, half-timbered and whitewashed, with some fine pargeting plasterwork on the walls of the former Bell Inn – a beaky gryphon, a sun in splendour, a bell enfolded by its ropes.

Broad fields of rape surrounded the village, and crossing them felt like walking in a *Sgt Pepper*-style dream of intense, opiate yellow, all the more sense-scrambling for lying under a sky full of sharply defined grey clouds from which issued the occasional grumble and whine of a Stansted-bound jet.

Apple blossom frothed in pink and white along the path to Tilty Mill, a witchy ruin caught with its curly spoked flywheels in a thicket of ivy. In the adjacent field lay the crumbling walls of Tilty Abbey. Just beyond, the magnificent rose window and chequerboard flint flushwork of today's

parish church are the only reminders of the glories of the twelfth-century Cistercian foundation. "Allelu-alleluia," sang the congregation, their harmony floating past us and away over the billowing cornfields.

Sleek horses were grazing the paddocks at Brook End Stables. "There are wartime American air force runways hidden under these crops," said a man over his garden gate. "You'll find a window to those brave young men down in Little Easton church."

That wasn't the only memorial in the church. Beautiful medieval frescoes adorned the nave walls, and the south chapel was packed with monuments to local gentry: the Bourchiers and Maynards — ruffs and beards, armour and silks, faces lean or podgy, all lent authority and in some cases arrogance by their whiteness and immobility. Yet it was those young Americans, far from home, daily facing death, who filled my mind as we walked the fields under the growling airliners of the modern age.

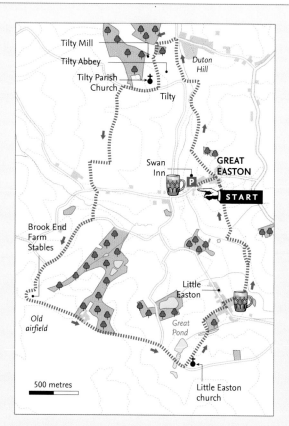

Start & finish The Swan, Great Easton, Essex CM6 2HG (OS ref TL606255)

Getting there Bus: Service 313, Saffron Walden-Great Dunmow. Road: M11, Jct 8; A120 to Great Dunmow; B184 to Great Easton; left to church and Swan Inn.

Walk (7 miles, easy, OS Explorer 195): From Swan Inn, left; left by The Bell; field path NW to footbridge (604258), don't cross, but turn right (north) for ½ mile; left (604265) to road. Right for ¼ mile; opposite side road, left (602269) to Tilty Mill (600267); left to Tilty Abbey (600265) and road. Right for 400m; left (597264, black fingerpost) along Harcamlow Way for ½ mile; dogleg right and left (595256) to cross road (594253). On through paddocks (yellow arrows, white arrows), up field edge to road (594250). Right for ½ mile; at right bend (589245), ahead along green lane. In 100m, fork left along paddock edges to Brook End Stables (587242); left along driveway for over a mile to Little Easton church (604235). Left through Little Easton Manor gates, on past manor, through far gates, down field between ponds (606239). Up past garden fence, right to road in Little Easton (608241). Left; right down Butchers Pasture, through gate, across footbridge; half left to cross next footbridge (610245). Ahead; in 50m, right across footbridge; left to cross stile (610247). Left for 300m; right (608248) up ditch; left (yellow arrow) across ditch and field to Great Easton.

Lunch The Swan, Great Easton CM6 2HG (01371 870359; swangreateaston.co.uk), Stag Inn, Little Easton CM6 2JE (01371 870214)

Accommodation The Swan, as above

More information Saffron Walden TIC (01799 524002), visitessex.com, ramblers.org.uk, satmap.com

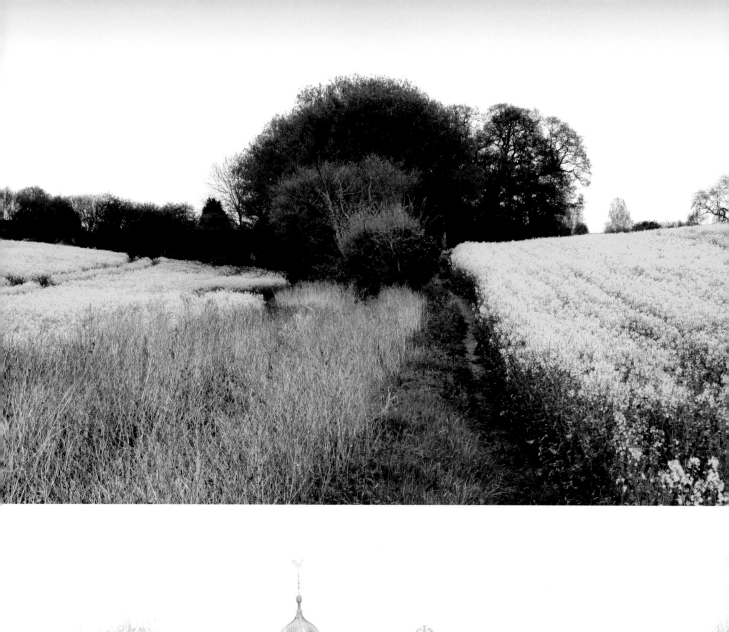

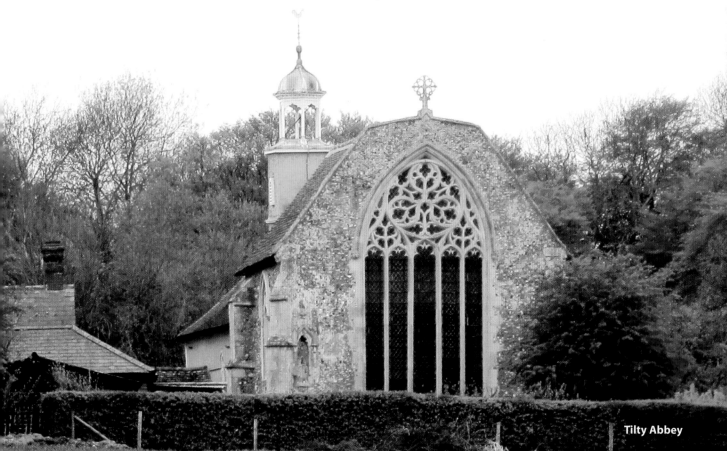

Tilty Abbey

"Lincolnshire?" say friends who've never been there. "Flat as a pancake; just boring." More fool them. The westernmost corner of the county, along the River Witham, is wonderful for rambling, threaded by immaculately maintained and waymarked footpaths. There's a subtle dip and roll to the landscape. Medieval sites, villages with vigorous community lives, woods, ponds, moats, green lanes; west Lincolnshire has it all. Nonetheless, you rarely see another soul about the fields. What a pleasure it is to have such an undiscovered piece of walking country to oneself, especially on a drowsy afternoon after a pint and a sandwich in the flower-bedecked Royal Oak at Aubourn.

In a thistly field beyond the village, Jane and I found the Anglo-Saxon manor site of Hall Close, all lumps and bumps of grassed-over earthwork, half-dried moats and masonry. In a thicket by the river, broken fragments of wall and dragonfly-haunted pools showed where a monastic settlement once thrived among its fish ponds. Up the bank stood a fifteenth-century dovecote of creamy oolitic stone with nesting holes for 500 birds — the last remnant of Haddington Hall, seat of the ancient Meres family.

On the far side of a quiet green lane we went on across pastures heavy with meadowsweet, over-pungent beanfields, through the slumbrous hamlet of Thurlby, where mulberries and horse chestnuts half-smothered the houses. As we crossed the River Witham and came into Bassingham, the tower of St Michael and All Angels was striking three over a fantastic collection of gargoyles grinning and gurning from the church eaves. Did Walt Disney, on a visit to his ancestral village of Norton Disney a mile away, come here taking notes? Certainly more than one of the Bassingham grotesques put us in mind of Mickey Mouse's cock-eyed pup Pluto.

Schoolchildren queued up politely in Green's Stores to buy sherbet lemons. Walking back along the well-kept field paths to Aubourn, watching swans on the river and listening to yellowhammers, Jane and I began to wonder if we had slipped through a crack in the space-time continuum and wandered into some improbable land of lost content.

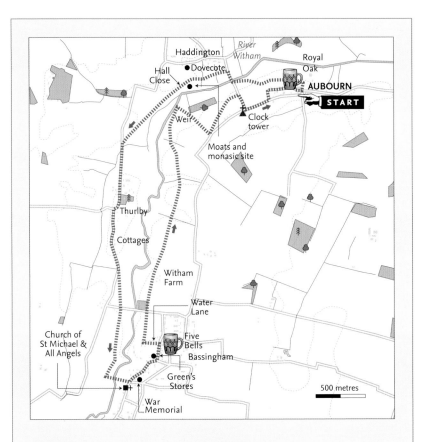

Start & finish Royal Oak PH, Aubourn LN5 9DT (OS ref SK925628)

Getting there Road: A1 to Newark, A46 towards Lincoln; right through Haddington to Aubourn

Walk (6 miles, easy grade, OS Explorer 272): From Royal Oak, left; in 70m, left (fingerpost) up path. Through kissing gate at end; left; follow yellow arrows (YA) to road (918628). Right across bridge; in 100m, left over footbridge. Follow YA across 3 fields, then Hall Close historic site, to cross green lane (912626). Continue same line for ½ mile to road (907622); left into Thurlby. Beyond bend, left ('Bassingham') along pavement. 200m past cottages, left (907609) across field; cross road (908605), and on across fields. Opposite Bassingham church, left (906598) across river to road (909598). Right to church. Return up road; left at war memorial ('Thurlby, Lincoln'); left by Green's Stores. Just past Five Bells PH, left (912602) down Water Lane. In 100m, right (fingerpost) down path and on through fields. Cross road (910605); on past Witham Farm, following YA. for 1¼ miles to weir (913625). Right to end of green lane (916623); left along road; immediately left (fingerpost) across two fields to road (919626). Right to clock tower; left into Aubourn.

Lunch Royal Oak, Aubourn (01522 788291; www.royaloakaubourn.co.uk)

More information Lincoln TIC (01522 545458), www.visitlincolnshire.com, ramblers.org.uk

An enormous sky of blue and silver wheeled above west Lincolnshire as we set out from Swinstead to wander the paths and rides of Grimsthorpe Park. The de Eresby family has held Grimsthorpe Castle since before the Reformation. Their seat and stronghold stands on a green ridge overlooking a long lake set perfectly in its valley.

We crossed the wide fields west of the lake, whose alders and willows framed a picture-book view of the castle. Dozens of partridge poults went scurrying frantically before us as we turned from the lakeside into the woods. The track led us east to Edenham for a pint in the Five Bells and a sandwich in the shade of the churchyard trees. Then it was off down Scottlethorpe Road, where stickily pungent hops hung in the hedges and naked ladies posed in miniature statue form among the geraniums at Cowman's Cottage.

Alongside the lane ran the overgrown cutting of Lord Willoughby's Railway. It didn't exactly fulfil the dreams of its founder, Lord Willoughby de Eresby. He opened it in 1856 to connect two bigger railways on either flank of his estate, but his tiny branch line closed only seventeen years later, scuppered by its limitations — mainly the speed of the trains, which at a maximum of 8 mph was not all that attractive to paying customers.

From Scottlethorpe Road we went west across the park, following the green way of Steel's Riding through woodland full of majestic old oaks, then over the fields to Creeton and a railway with a history rather more magnificent than that of Lord Willoughby's Railway. A mile or two north of this stretch of the East Coast main line, on 3 July 1938, the A4 locomotive Mallard flew into history at 126 mph, the fastest speed ever recorded by a steam train.

The racing railway has a companion through the countryside, the ancient drove road of the Drift, where cattle and sheep would meander to distant markets at two miles an hour. We sauntered its ribbony course before turning aside to cross the Swinstead Valley — a deep-sunk and beautiful hollow of calcareous grassland never ploughed or fertilised. All lay gilded by the low evening sun as we climbed to the ploughlands and turned for home.

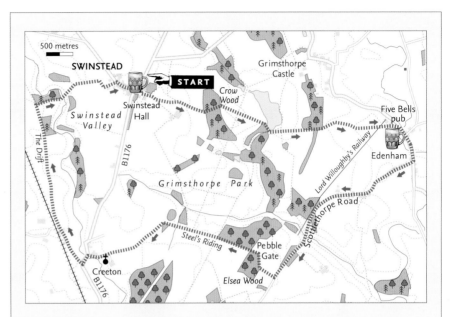

Start & finish High Street, Swinstead, near Bourne, Lincs NG33 4PA (OS ref TF019225)

Getting there Bus: Service 4 (centrebus.info), Grantham-Stamford. Road: Swinstead is on the B1176, signed off A151 Bourne-Colsterworth.

Walk (11 miles, easy, OS Explorer 248): Up Park Road past Swinstead Hall gates and Park Farm notice; left (yellow arrow/YA) across field; at crossroads of tracks (025223), right (east) along track. At end of Crow Wood (032222, Grimsthorpe Castle ahead), half right to cross end of lake (039220). East on path for 1⅓ miles to A151 at Edenham Bridge (060220); right through Edenham. Right down Scottlethorpe Road (062215) for 2 miles; right (041197, fingerpost) to Elsea Wood (038199) and Pebble Gate (037201). Steel's Riding through woods and fields for 1½ miles to Creeton (015200). Right to B1176; left to corner (010198); right ('Counthorpe'). In 700m (006204, fingerpost) up The Drift green lane. In a little over a mile, at start of descent, right (003222) into valley. Cross footbridge (007223); dog left/right up slope; left over stile at top (009226); path to B1176 at Swinstead.

Lunch The Five Bells, Edenham PE10 0LL (01778 591111; the-five-bells.co.uk)

Accommodation Toft Country House Hotel and Golf Club, Toft PE10 0JT (01778 590614; tofthotelgolf.co.uk)

More information Stamford TIC (01780 755611), visitlincolnshire.com, visitengland.com, satmap.com, ramblers.org.uk

A blustery cold day at the start of spring, with bursts of snow racing across the Lincolnshire Wolds. Seen from afar, they are a modest green bar on the horizon, but as you get closer, the Wolds loom up as a considerable wall. This long whaleback of limestone and ironstone rises some 90m (300ft) above the Lincolnshire plains, a height lent grandeur by the flatness of the surrounding landscape.

'Tealby, Claxby, Normanby, Otby, Walesby, Risby,' said the map. So many 'bys' in this part of the world — bý is the Norse word for a farmstead or village, denoting where ninth-century Danish invaders settled and beat their swords into ploughshares (to some extent).

Outside Tealby, the Viking Way long-distance path handed me over to a footpath running through Walesby and on through the wind-whistle fields. From Claxby I went steeply up the grassy escarpment, picturing the village's founder, one Klakkr — rather a fierce fighter, I guessed, carrying the smack and clatter of swords in his name. Up in the wind, on the wold top at Normanby, I rejoined the Viking Way and followed its horned helmet symbols down to lonely Otby on its ridge, then back to Walesby, tucked into the valley below.

Walesby folk have not always dwelt in the vale. In the Middle Ages the village lay high on the Wolds, but when the Black Death arrived in 1348 the inhabitants fled their plague-ridden settlement and its church.

I found snowdrops and daffodils growing on the ancient foundations of houses and fields around St Andrew's — known to generations as 'The Ramblers' Church'. It became the focus of local walkers' expeditions in the 1930s, when it stood in romantic ruins. Nowadays, there's a beautiful stained glass window depicting a red-robed Jesus Christ beckoning across a cornfield to a trio of clean-limbed young ramblers of the old school, while a brace of 1950s cyclists wait to attract his attention.

Medieval masons carved a jostle of cheeky, coarse-featured faces among the stone foliage of the nave pillars. I took some snaps and had a chuckle, then followed the Viking Way along the ridge.

Near Walesby Top a herd of forty red deer watched me pass. The flock of pedigree Lincoln Longwool sheep at Risby — hefty beasts with a llama-like hauteur — stared through their floppy fringes as if mesmerised. And I stared back beyond them, west, where an apocalyptic sunburst sent Blakean shafts from blackening clouds to pick out the two towers of Lincoln Cathedral on their ridge some twenty miles away.

Start & finish King's Head, Tealby, Lincolnshire LN8 3YA (OS ref TF156905)

Getting there Road: Tealby is on the B1203 near Market Rasen (A46, Lincoln-Caistor)

Walk (10 miles, moderate, OS Explorer 282): From the B1203 in Tealby, northwest on Viking Way (VW) (157905). In the second field, left (152911); footpath to Catskin Lane (142917); ahead, then footpath (136919) to Walesby. VW along Moor Road; right (130924; 'Mill House Farm'). Left at fork (129926; 'Byway'); in ⅓ mile, left (127931, 'Byway') to road (113942) into Claxby. Up Normanby Rise; right by reservoir (118948) up fields (yellow arrows/YA) to Normanby le Wold church (123947). VW south for three fields; footpath (125936, YA) to valley bottom. Left (130930; fingerpost) to end of paddock (133933); uphill to Otby House drive (139935). Right to road and Walesby. VW for 1¾ miles to Tealby.

Lunch King's Head, Tealby (01673 838347; thekingsheadtealby.co.uk)

Accommodation Advocate Arms, Queen Street, Market Rasen LN8 3EH (01673 842364; advocatearms.co.uk) – stylish and very welcoming

More information Lincoln TIC (01522 873256), visitlincolnshire.com, satmap.com, ramblers.org.uk

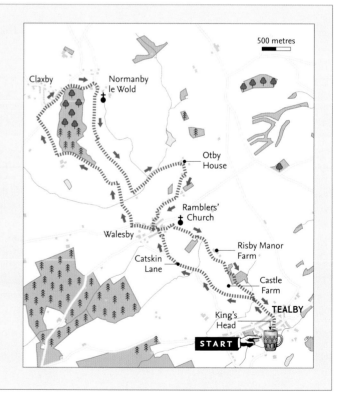

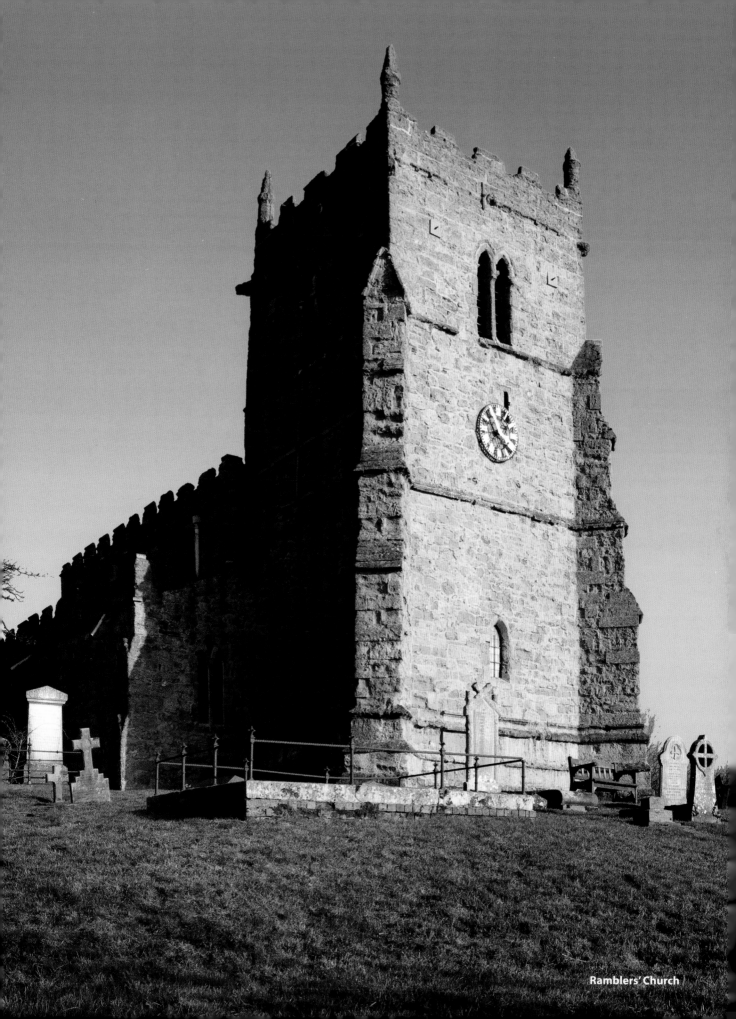

Ramblers' Church

Blakeney to Salthouse
NORFOLK

The black-backed gull was having a real struggle with its breakfast down on the muddy banks of Blakeney Quay. We stopped to watch it battle a flapping flatfish that kept writhing out of its beak like a monstrous silver tongue. Eventually gull had fish subdued, and we turned our steps seaward along the mile-long creek that connects Blakeney with the North Sea.

Looking back from the shingly shore at the distant red roofs and flint-and-brick walls of Blakeney, it seemed incredible that the town was once abutted by the sea. The enormous apron of salt and freshwater marshes that has grown through silt deposition along the north Norfolk coast has cut Blakeney off from the sea, but it has also made the former port a wonderful place for birdwatchers and walkers.

Redshanks piped nervously among the marsh pools. A flock of dark-bellied brent geese, newly arrived for the winter from northern Russia, scoured the grassy marshes for food. Wigeon in twos and threes went hurrying across the sky with fast wingbeats. Canada and greylag geese sailed in company on a stretch of water.

We turned the corner by the sea and made for the white cap and sails of the great coastal windmill at Cley next the Sea. Like its neighbour, Cley is now separated from the sea by a long mile of marshes. It too is entirely charming, with its flint walls, red roofs and narrow, curving street round whose blind corners bus drivers and pedestrians dice with one another. You can get homemade lavender bread, and spinach-and ricotta filo parcels in Cley's picnic shop — not exactly traditional Norfolk fare, but a good indicator of the change that has come to these pretty villages.

We passed under the sails of the windmill and went seaward along the floodwall towards journey's end at Salthouse. Along the marsh edge, samphire was changing colour to scarlet and yellow. A black brant goose, a rarity in from America, bobbed its white shirt-tail. Pink-footed geese in long skeins passed across the cloudy sky, and a grey seal swam off the shingle beach while he checked us over.

Beach pebbles laid a carpet of many colours along the strand. Goldfinches jockeyed among yellow-horned poppies whose long seedpods quivered in the wind off the sea. Hundreds of golden plover stood huddled by a pool, close-packed like one wind-ruffled organism. All nature seemed intent on its own business in the marshes, indifferent as to whether we were walking there or not.

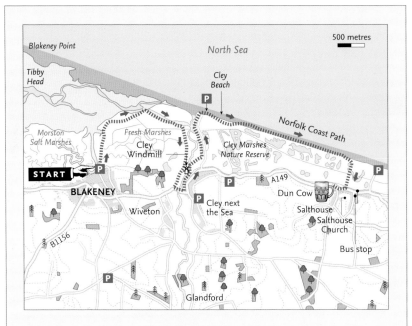

Start Blakeney Quay car park, NR25 7ND (OS ref TG028441)

Getting there Bus: Coasthopper (Hunstanton-Cromer). Road: A149 from Hunstanton.

Walk (6½ miles, easy, OS Explorer 251): From car park, climb steps and walk seaward along floodbank ('Norfolk Coast Path'/NCP), following path for 2¾ miles to Cley next the Sea. Follow road through village (take care; narrow, sharp, blind corners). In 500m, left (045439, signed) to Cley Windmill. Follow NCP seaward along floodwall to Cley Beach for 1 mile, then right (east) along shingle bank for nearly 2 miles. Opposite Salthouse Church, inland (078444, yellow arrow) to A149 (076437). Left to bus stop/ right to Dun Cow PH. Return to Blakeney by Coasthopper bus.

Lunch Dun Cow pub, Salthouse NR25 7XA (01263 740467; salthouseduncow.com)

Accommodation Blakeney Hotel, The Quay, Blakeney, Norfolk NR25 7NE (01263 740797; blakeney-hotel.co.uk) – comfortable, classy and obliging

More information Wells-next-the-Sea TIC (01328 710885; visitnorfolk.co.uk), visitengland.com, satmap.com, ramblers.org.uk

Great Bircham and Fring
NORFOLK

The wolfman of Great Bircham stared down from his vantage point high above the chancel arch in St Mary's Church. With his pointed ears, blank eyes and thick-lipped oval mouth, he looked altogether too malevolent to be the resident spirit of such a gloriously light and airy building. Not for the first time I found myself wondering what was in the minds of the medieval masons who carved such vivid and disturbing creatures in the parish churches of these islands.

I wandered through the churchyard where Second World War airmen, Allied and German alike, lay buried. Then I set out into the cold, bright light of a north Norfolk morning, following a green lane through the sugar beet fields. Partridges skimmed away with hoarse squeaks over the leathery green leaves, and a hare went lolloping along the rows of a stubble field at a slow canter.

Soon the lane met the ancient trackway of Peddars Way, arrowing northwest across the low, rolling landscape. I stepped out along the wide, grassy trackway, with a view eastward to Bircham's tall windmill on its ridge. The iconic East Anglian hellhound known as Black Shuck haunts Peddars Way, and I wondered whether the mason of St Mary's had had that demon dog in mind when he did his carving.

A tremendous commotion in a stubble field beside the track made me jump. A couple of hundred pink-footed geese, gobbling the grain left behind after harvest, had been panicked. With a tremendous honking and complaining and a roar of wings, they took off and wheeled away with flashing white rumps.

I left Peddars Way and came down into the hamlet of Fring, all brick and flint under red-pantiled roofs. Along the lane the beet harvesters were roaring in the fields, stacking giant mounds of roots for the lorries. Bircham Windmill stood proud, its fantail revolving to keep the ladder-shaped sails to the wind.

There was no sign of Black Shuck on the way back to Bircham, but I did meet a dog at the entrance to the village — a soppy old labrador, who was only too pleased to be chucked under the chin.

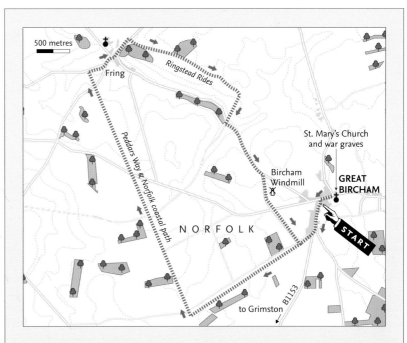

Start & finish Great Bircham Social Club car park, Church Lane, Great Bircham, Norfolk, PE31 6QW (OS ref TF769325)

Getting there Road: Great Bircham is signed from Snettisham, off the A149 between King's Lynn and Hunstanton

Walk (8¾ miles, easy, OS Explorer 250): Right along Church Lane to St Mary's Church. Return past car park to B1153; left along pavement past Bircham Country Stores and King's Head Hotel. Opposite village sign, right (767321) along lane. In 1¼ miles, right along Peddars Way (748309, signposted). In 2½ miles, at third road crossing (733345), right into Fring. Ahead across bridge (Docking). In 350m, right up track (739350, Ringstead Rides). In 1¼ miles, right (756342) on footpath to road (754337). Left; in ⅔ mile, turn right (760330) past Bircham Windmill. Cross road beyond (761324); green lane to junction (765320); left to King's Head on B1153; left to return to car park.

Lunch Bircham Country Stores; Kings Head, Bircham PE31 6RJ (01485 578265; the-kings-head-bircham.co.uk)

Dinner/accommodation Rose & Crown, Snettisham PE31 7LX (01485 541382; roseandcrownsnettisham.co.uk) – wholly delightful, friendly village inn

More information Hunstanton TIC (01485 532610), visitengland.com, satmap.com, ramblers.org.uk

Holkham Park

NORFOLK

In 1776, twenty-two-year-old Thomas Coke inherited the Holkham Estate, 12100 hectares (30000 acres) of sandy, salty, windblasted and flinty land along the North Norfolk coast. The young owner dedicated himself with a passion to improving the agriculture of this barren countryside. When he died in 1842, hugely famous as a sheep and cattle breeder, grass and turnip pioneer and all-round agricultural reformer, he was known universally as 'Coke of Norfolk'.

On a glorious afternoon, the tall column of the Coke Monument glows brilliantly in strong winter sunlight among the bare trees of Holkham Park. Guarded by stone sheep and long-horned cattle, embellished with bas-reliefs of sheep shearers, horses and dogs, diggers and seed planters, the inscription names Thomas Coke "Father, Friend and Landlord", and declares: "Of such a man contemporaries needed no memorial. His Deeds were before them: His Praise in their hearts."

Grand sentiments, and a grand artificial landscape to wander through, a gentle forest of old sweet chestnuts and beeches in which a long lake lies like a dark jewel. Pink-footed geese honk and chatter as they rest on the water. On a green knoll the Church of St Withburga catches the sun and throws it back dazzlingly from windows and flint cobble walls.

Across the lake lies the grand Palladian palace of Holkham Hall, built of yellow brick by Coke's uncle, the Earl of Leicester. Fallow deer roamed its parkland, their big branchy antlers occasionally clashing as they grazed.

From this miniature land of content, the trail extends into the southern half of Holkham Park with its more agricultural feel; open fields of beet, carrots and winter wheat, bounded by conifer belts and pheasant coverts. Coke of Norfolk would have appreciated the Holkham of today, a subtle balance of commercial and utopian landscapes.

Coke took a barren countryside and made it tremendously productive, literally sowing the seeds of North Norfolk's agricultural success. People are not the only beneficiaries of this transformation. The pink-footed geese that come from Iceland and Greenland to winter on the Norfolk coast spend each day in the fields, feeding on sugar beet fragments, before flying seaward at dusk to roost on the marshes and mudflats. That's where I find them towards nightfall, gabbling and jostling in their hundreds, a seething carpet of big rustling birds. I watch them from a hide, entranced, as the sky turns apple green, then gold and pink, before darkening to the indigo of night.

Start & finish Holkham, North Norfolk NR23 1RG (OS ref TF892440)

Getting there Bus: Coasthopper Bus (01553 776980), King's Lynn–Cromer. Road: On A149 between Brancaster and Wells-next-the-Sea.

Walk (6½ miles from Holkham or 8½ miles with hide extension, easy, OS Explorer 251): Up Holkham Hall drive, through gateway (892435); right, following Farm Walk (red posts) to Coke Monument (884436). Ahead to lake; right (anti-clockwise) round lake (Lake Walk, yellow posts) via St Withburga's Church (878436). At T-junction at foot of lake (880427), left past Ice House, right along The Avenue to pass obelisk (884420). In 300m, left (883416; Park Walk, green posts) back to gateway at Holkham.

Hide extension Start walk from car park at north end of Lady Anne's Drive (891448; £5 all day, coins or card). To reach easy access bird hide (883452, signposted) turn left on forest track beyond car park.

Lunch/accommodation The Victoria Inn, Holkham (01328 711008; www.holkham.co.uk/victoria) – friendly, warm and welcoming.

More information Holkham Estate (01328 710227; www.holkham.co.uk), Wells-next-the-Sea TIC, closes in winter (01328 710885; visitnorfolk.co.uk), satmap.com, ramblers.org.uk

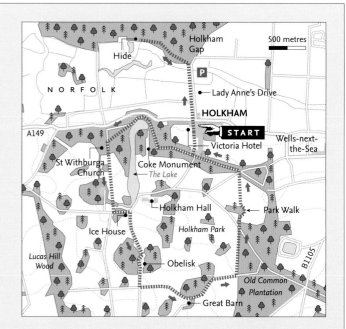

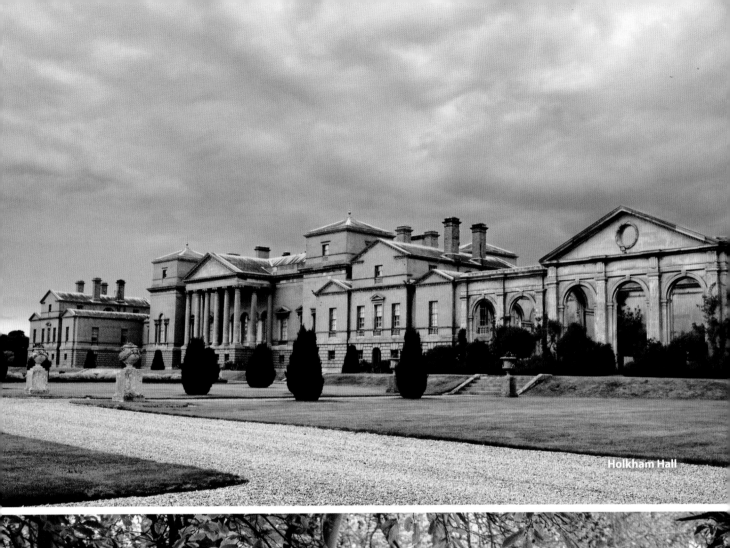

Holkham Hall

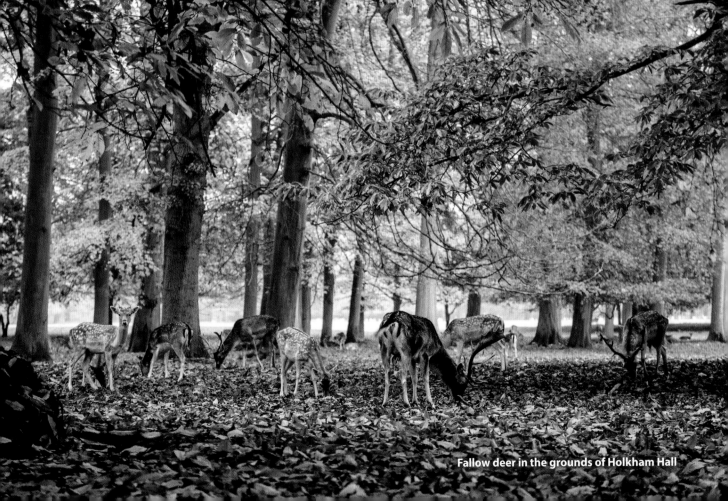

Fallow deer in the grounds of Holkham Hall

Under the silver birch and oaks of Stow Bedon covert, shallow ponds lay dotted across the peaty ground, their mirror-still dark water skinned across with pondweed and tufted with clumps of rushes. They have lain here in the flat, dry landscape of Breckland, southwest Norfolk's great belt of sand and pebbles, since the end of the last glaciation 10 000 years ago — these are pingos, Ice Age holes where ice blocks melted and left a string of lakelets behind.

We followed the Great Eastern Pingo Trail as it wound between them. They lay absolutely still, like pieces of polished sky dropped in among the trees. The trail snaked over former commons, now grazed for wildlife conservation. We passed a group of Highland cattle with extravagant horns that stared at us from their bower of apple blossom with utter indifference before resuming the grooming of their nostrils with long, pale tongues.

This maze of pingos and flowery fields is made for sauntering. At last we found ourselves on a country road that declined to a flint-pebble track and then a green lane where an avenue of big old oaks and willows formed a double guard of honour for travellers. Chiffchaffs chirped out their two-tone calls, wrens chattered, great spotted woodpeckers rattled the hollow trees, and some unseen and unidentified sweet singer glorified a may-bush right beside us as we sat on a stump to take it all in.

We followed a sluggish little river, petrol-blue with peat iridescence, and came to Thompson Water, where a cramped little bird hide gave us an Attenborough's-eye view of the reedy lake. A swan sat on her eggs 6m (20ft) away; another sailed by with her six fluffy grey cygnets. Over the water, swallows circled like circus acrobats around a flight of hobbies, small dark raptors that zipped across the mere, every now and then hunching their heads between their legs to pick a dragonfly from their claws and eat it in mid-glide.

The puddled track of the Peddars Way, an ancient high road through Breckland, brought us south past MoD ranges of sheep-grazed heaths and sombre blocks of conifers. Then we swung north along the track bed of the Great Eastern Railway's old Thetford-Swaffham branch line, a homeward path by Breckles Heath and Cranberry Rough where the pingos lay thick with water violets. Along the way we discovered that crab apple blossom smells of roses. A day of wonders, truly.

Start & finish Great Eastern Pingo Trail car park on A1075 near Stow Bedon, Norfolk NR17 1DP approx. (OS ref TL941966)

Getting there Road: Car park is on A1075 Watton-Thetford road, on west side, 3 miles south of Watton

Walk (7 miles, easy, OS Explorer 237): Walk away from A1075 to Old Station Yard notice. Turn right through car park; on through kissing gate ('Thompson Common nature reserve'). Cross boardwalk and follow Great Eastern Pingo Trail/GEPT arrows through trees for ½ mile to road (934966). Left, and follow GEPT for 2 miles to pass Thompson Water and reach Peddars Way (913948). Left (Stow Bedon 7). In 1 mile pass chicken farm on left to reach crossing of tracks (921933). Left off Peddars Way/GEPT; follow fence on left for 500m. At 'Peddars Way Circular Walk' arrow (926936), right down grassy ride; ahead to old railway line (928931). Left for 2¼ miles to car park.

Lunch Chequers Inn, Thompson IP24 1PX (01953 483360; thompsonchequers.co.uk)

Accommodation Olde Windmill Inn, Great Cressingham IP25 6NN (01760 756232; oldewindmillinn.co.uk)

More information visitengland.com, satmap.com, ramblers.org.uk

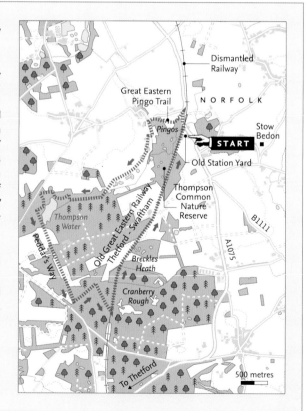

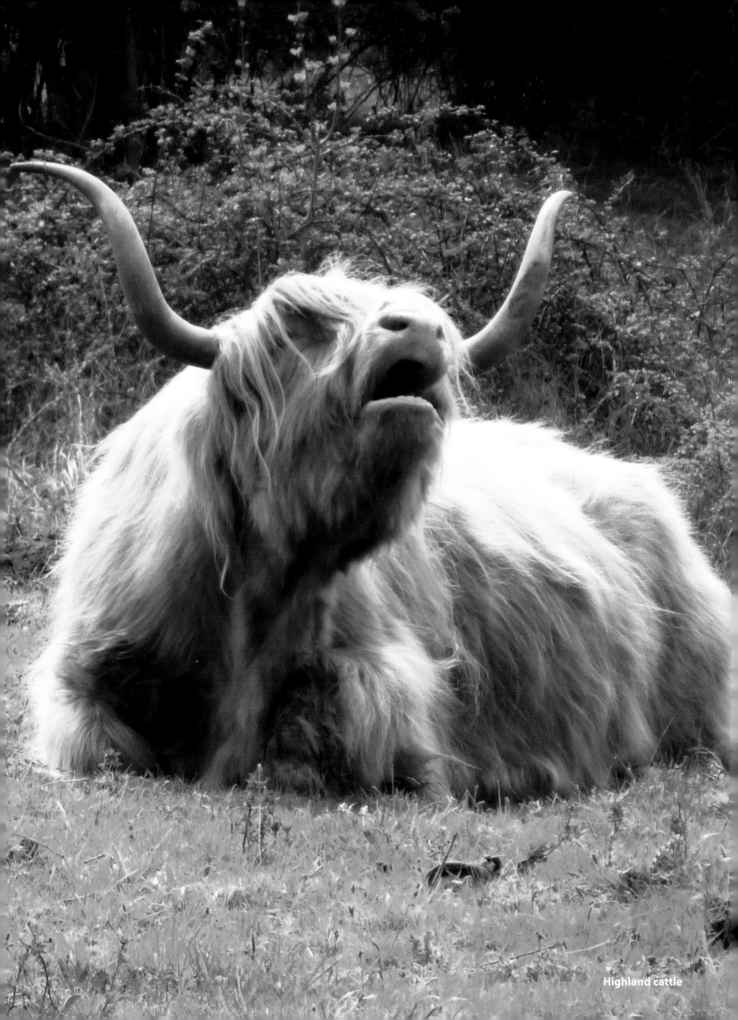

Highland cattle

Cavendish and Clare

SUFFOLK

Cavendish lies perfectly arranged for a painter's canvas. Why John Constable never got himself along here to capture the thatched and pink-faced cottages on the village green and the flint tower of St Mary's Church peeping over their shoulders is a mystery. Even on this blowy winter's morning, under a scudding grey sky, the composition seemed flawless.

We passed crooked old Tumbleweed Cottage, half pink and half green, and turned down a path among poplars to cross the slow-flowing River Stour.

Out in the fields a green bridleway led through gently rolling country, the meandering of the invisible Stour marked by grey and gold willows. Wide ploughed fields slanted up from the river, their crests bristling with hedge oaks. From this high ground we looked back to see Cavendish church tower poking above the trees. Then it was down again over the sticky fields to a wandering green lane between banks of iron-rich, burnt orange soil across which burrowing badgers had spread their bedding.

On the outskirts of Clare the grounds and ancient flint buildings of the Priory lay very quiet and still. Opposite rose the castle mound, with its tall fragment of Norman masonry. In 1865 local 'detectorist' Walter Lorking unearthed a gold cross and chain in the castle grounds. It had been lost there 500 years earlier by King Edward III and contained a fragment of the true cross in a tiny compartment. Walter was more than happy to sell it to his sovereign, Queen Victoria, for the rather appropriate sum of three gold sovereigns.

There was beautiful pargetting — ornate plasterwork — on many of the houses in Clare and a host of scowling and howling Green Men to guard the doorway of the village church, the 'cathedral of the Stour Valley'. I left my companions to linger among the antique shops of Clare and hurried back to Cavendish along the high ground north of the river. The cold wind tousled me all the way, pouring out of a sky ridged with grey billows of cloud, a wintry ceiling for the furrowed ploughland below.

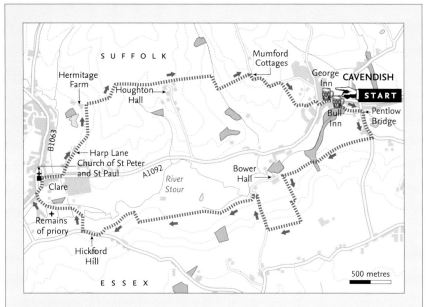

Start & finish The George, Cavendish, Suffolk CO10 8BA (OS ref TL805465)

Getting there Bus: Service 236 (Haverhill-Sudbury). Road: Cavendish is on A1092 between Long Melford (A134) and Haverhill (A143).

Walk (8 miles, easy, OS Explorers 196, 210): In Cavendish, right opposite the Bull Inn (807465, yellow arrows/YA) on path to road (810464). Right across Pentlow Bridge; in 300m, right (812461) on bridleway. In ¾ mile, just before first barn at Bower Hall, left (800455) up field edge; 50m before top, right (803450, YA) to hedge end of green lane. Follow it to road (799449); right to bottom; left by brick hut (797453) on bridleway (green lanes, field edges) for 1½ miles to road at Hickford Hill (777447). Right; in 200m, right across field to cross river (775450). Fork left to cross weir (774451); on along New Cut. In 400m, left through stone gateway (770451) to Clare Priory. Return to cross footbridge into village; right to church (770455). A1092 Cavendish road out of Clare. In 300m, left up Harp Lane (773454) and follow 'Stour Valley Path' yellow arrows and 'Heritage Trail' purple arrows for 3 miles to Cavendish via Hermitage Farm (775463), Houghton Hall (785466) and road at Mumford Cottages (796468).

Lunch Plenty of cafés and pubs in Clare and Cavendish

Accommodation The George, Cavendish (01787 280248; thecavendishgeorge.co.uk) – smart, stylish, comfortable

More information Sudbury TIC (01787 881320), visitengland.com, satmap.com, ramblers.org.uk

Dunwich and Dingle Marshes
SUFFOLK

A tangle of trees has almost smothered Dunwich's famous 'last grave'. The solitary curly-topped headstone of Jacob Forster, however, still clings to the cliff edge above the hamlet on the Suffolk coast, the last relic of the church of All Saints that toppled to the beach in 1922. Just inland, the grand flint walls and gateways of Greyfriars priory enclose an empty square of grass.

These remains are all that speak to us today of medieval Dunwich, the great trading port whose churches, hospitals, squares and houses were consumed by the sea. A model in the village's excellent small museum shows the extent of what was lost, and it made a sobering image to take with us as we set out across the green hinterland of Dingle Marshes.

A brisk wind pushed us along the flinty tracks through copses of old oak and pine trees. The grazing meadows, dotted with black cattle, stretched away east towards a dun-brown line of marshes below the long bar of the shingle-banked sea wall. There's a feeling of country walked by many, but known by few.

Beyond Dingle Stone House stretched the great reedbeds of Westwood Marshes, burnt orange and green, whispering in a million scratchy sibilants. A flock of pink-footed geese lined the edge of a fleet of still water. Tiny bearded tits bounced and flitted through the reed heads, trailing their long tails low and emitting pinging noises like overstretched wire fences. Over all floated the kingly black silhouette of a marsh harrier, circling with deliberate flaps of its wings as it scanned the reeds for mice and frogs.

We crossed the Dunwich river and came up on to the shingle bank. An instant switch of view and perspective, out over a slate-grey sea and round the curve of the bay to Dunwich under its sloping cliff and the distant white sphere of Sizewell nuclear power station. Sea inundations are increasingly common here, overtopping the shingle bank and flooding the freshwater marshes — part of the ongoing dynamism of this coast and its all-devouring neighbour, the sea.

Among the shore pebbles, a flat black stone caught my eye. It was a worked flint tool, dark and ribbed, snugly fitting in my palm, its edges scalloped by some ancient maker. Dunwich Museum has it now — one more stage on its journey from hand to hand through the millennia.

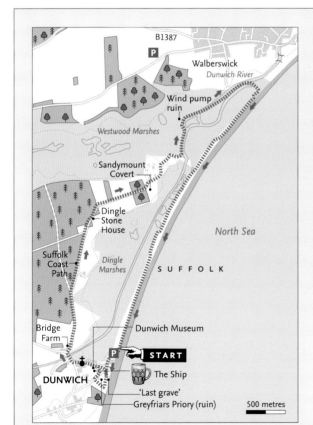

Start & finish Dunwich car park, Suffolk, IP17 3EN (OS ref TM478706)

Getting there Road: Dunwich is signed from A12 between Yoxford and Blythburgh

Walk (6¾ miles – final 2½ miles is on shingle – easy, OS Explorer 231): At car park entrance, left up footpath (fingerpost, 'Suffolk Coast Path'/SCP arrow). Just past 'last grave' on left (479704), turn right through Greyfriars wall, across monastery site, through archway. Right along road; in 100m, left down footpath (fingerpost) to road with Dunwich Museum on right (477706). Left; fork right at church ('Blythburgh'). In 150m, right past Bridge Farm (474707) along SCP. In 1½ miles, leaving Sandymount Covert (483728), fork right along marsh path. In ¾ mile, just past the wind pump ruin (487737), right down steps, over footbridge, along boardwalk. In ⅔ mile, right across footbridge (495742, SCP) to shingle bank; right to Dunwich.

Lunch/accommodation The Ship at Dunwich IP17 3DT (01728 648219; shipatdunwich.co.uk) – a cosy, friendly village inn

More information Southwold TIC (01502 724729), thesuffolkcoast.co.uk, satmap.com, ramblers.org.uk, Dunwich Museum: open March-October, varying times (01728 648796; dunwichmuseum.org.uk)

Fressingfield, Weybread & Wingfield
SUFFOLK

Suffolk is the land of beautiful parish churches, par excellence. So much money was poured out by well-to-do medieval wool-masters intent on glorifying the Lord and saving their own souls (and showing the neighbours how well they were doing; a pleasing by-product of piety) that every village possesses a miniature masterpiece. Setting out on a sunny morning from Fressingfield, we stopped to admire the handsome knapped flint of the south porch of St Peter and St Paul's Church, and the carved bench-ends within — maidens with flowing hair, priests and beasts, their faces hacked off by Puritan zealots, but their intrinsic beauty complete.

We walked out into one of those wide, flat-seeming, entirely agricultural Suffolk landscapes whose subtler curves hide shallow valleys. Farm and barn roofs made red squares against the dark blocks of copses under a sky of fat silver clouds lumbering their way across the blue. The handsome old houses of Viponds Farm and Willow Farm faced their ploughlands square-on. But neighbouring Church Farm, extant on the map, had vanished under the stiff Suffolk clay as though it had never been.

Weybread's church of St Andrew, with its cylindrical Saxon tower, had wonderful carved corbels of angels, lions and a leafy-faced Green Man. South of Weybread the landscape changed abruptly from wide, open arable fields to steep, intimate grazing valleys cut with streams and with oaks full of the sleepy cawing of rooks. Near Syleham Hall we leaned on a gate, munching bread and cheese, speculating on what a land of milk and honey this must have been in medieval times, with its castles and halls, moats and farms, priories and abbeys and marvellous new churches.

It was the De la Poles, Earls of Suffolk, kinsfolk and friends of the Plantagenet kings, who built Wingfield's gorgeous church, a stately ship of flint that today dominates a tiny hamlet — the De La Pole Arms, a couple of cottages and a fourteenth-century college for priests that stands beside the church in disguise as a Georgian farmhouse. Inside the church, De la Poles and Wingfields lie in effigy, their weathered old faces full of character.

From tiny Wingfield we joined the cornfield paths once more, making east for Fressingfield. The sun came out, putting a pale dazzle on the fields and spotlighting the scarlet necklaces of bryony berries strewn by nature across the skeletal winter hedges with careless grandeur.

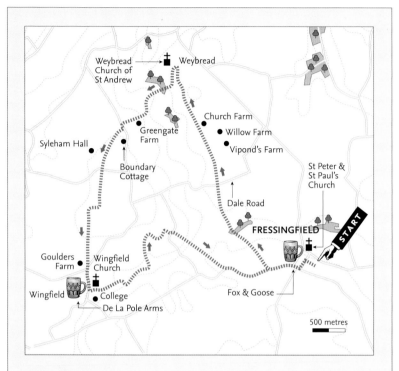

Start & finish Fressingfield village car park, near Harleston, Suffolk IP21 5QQ (OS ref TM263773)

Getting there Bus: Sat only (convenient for walk) Service 40 Diss–Norwich (01379 647300; www.simonds.co.uk). Road: A143 to Harleston, B1116 to Fressingfield.

Walk (8½ miles, easy, OS Explorer 230): Fressingfield car park to Diss road then right on path just beyond Post Mill Lane (256773). Northwest for 1 mile – cross Dale Road (248784). On northwest for more than a mile to Weybread Church (241801). Southwest by Greengate Farm to road (233793). Left for 100m; right by Boundary Cottage; on south across fields to cross road (231786). South through fields for 1 mile to road at Goulder's Farm (229772). On to Wingfield Church, Wingfield College and the De La Pole Arms PH. Opposite pub (230768), east on footpath for ¾ mile to 239772; north, clockwise around big field to gazebo (239776). Through orchard, wicket gate and paddocks to reach stile in left hedge of field (240778); don't cross, but turn right across field; cross road (241777). Southeast for ½ mile to road (250773); left into Fressingfield.

Lunch Fox & Goose, Fressingfield IP21 5PB (01379 586247; foxandgoose.net; closed Mondays), Swan Inn, Fressingfield IP21 5PE (01379 586280; fressingfieldswan.co.uk)

More information Southwold TIC (01502 724729), visitsuffolk.com

Stoke-by-Nayland
SUFFOLK

Low over the undulating countryside where southernmost Suffolk tips over into northern Essex, rainclouds rolled heavy and grey. At the crossroads in ridge-top Stoke-by-Nayland, the village's brace of inns, the Crown and the Angel, faced each other like mutually suspicious cats. I had a pint of Adnams in one and a ploughman's in the other, in the interests of good neighbourliness. Then I set out under dripping ash and hazel along roads glistening from a midday downpour, into a landscape smoky and insubstantial behind the golden sheen of a vaporous, sun-splashed winter afternoon.

The deeply furrowed landscape hereabouts would astonish believers in the old canard about East Anglia being pancake flat. I crossed grazing fields sloping sharply into oakwoods that lifted and swung back up to the ridges. Farms founded before the Reformation stood under expanses of red pantiles. This timeless landscape of rural England on the borders of Suffolk and Essex gave expression to the genius of the local lad John Constable, and there wasn't a prospect in sight that might not have come from one of his canvases.

Down in the valley of the River Box the ploughed stiff clay lay dark and flat. How strange it felt to be walking empty handed through fields where, twenty-five years ago, I never strolled without a child's mouse-like paw in my fist. The sinuous Box was one of our favourite family walks when we lived in Nayland, just up the valley. On one of those expeditions a chance

kick at a clod of earth had uncovered a Stone Age scraping tool, its delicately scalloped cutting edge still sharp as a razor.

Time moves on. Wrens, roses and thistles still adorned the pargeted walls of Farthings house at Thorington Street, but I found that the Rose Inn had closed and been turned into a private dwelling. Back in the day, a big treat for the children was lunch in the Rose's garden, where a straw-stuffed cage marked 'Silverwater 'otter' fascinated them. A tug on the chain brought forth nothing more exotic than an aluminium kettle — the landlord's little jest.

In the grounds of Tendring Hall estate shotguns were popping. A cock pheasant scuttled across the path with head and tail strained high, like a brightly coloured barge scudding before a breeze.

Neighbouring churches framed the walk — St James's at Nayland low in the south near the River Stour, its stumpy spire rising among leafless trees, and on the ridge to the north the great brick tower of St Mary's. I steered for the latter by way of Poplar Farm, a gorgeous old tall-chimneyed house tucked away in the trees. Looking up, the Stoke-by-Nayland ridge stood innocent of buildings, as though village and church had been magically drawn down into the earth. But as I climbed the field path the tower of St Mary's appeared again, rising in apricot light as the sun went down over the valley.

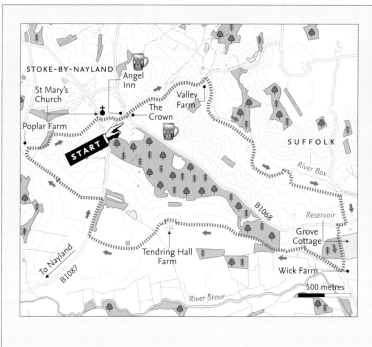

Start & finish Crown Inn, Stoke-by-Nayland CO6 4SE (OS ref TL989363)

Getting there Bus: Chambers Coaches' service 84 from Colchester or Sudbury. Road: M25; A12 to Colchester; A134 to Nayland; B1087.

Walk (5½ miles, easy, OS Explorer 196): Lane opposite Angel Inn ('Hadleigh, Shelley'); in 400m, right (992365; fingerpost) up path. Through kissing gate, left and follow field edge, then yellow arrows/YA for ½ mile to Valley Farm (001361). Ahead along River Box (YA) for ⅓ mile; then (005358) follow YAs away from river to lane (010356); right to B1068 in Thorington Street. Right for 50m, then left (010353; fingerpost) past reservoir to Wick Farm (011349). Right along road; left between barn and Grove Cottage (007351; fingerpost) along farm drive. Skirt right of Tendring Hall Farm (994353); follow drive to B1087. Right (take care!) for ¼ mile; left opposite 'fishing temple' (986355) along farm track to Poplar Farm (978359). At 3-finger post, right up track into Stoke-by-Nayland. Through churchyard to crossroads and Crown Inn.

Lunch/accommodation Crown Inn, Stoke-by-Nayland (01206 262001; crowninn.net), Angel Inn, Stoke-by-Nayland (01206 263245; angelinnsuffolk.co.uk)

More information Sudbury TIC (01787 881320), visitsuffolk.com, visiteastofengland.com, ramblers.org.uk

Wales

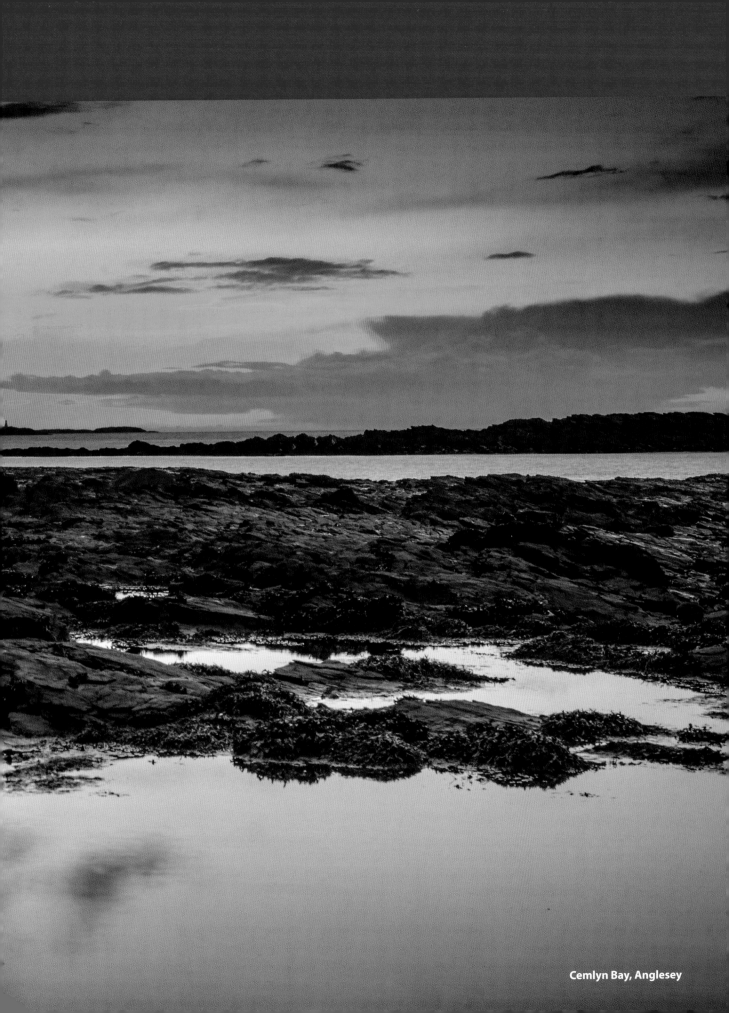

Cemlyn Bay, Anglesey

Cemlyn Bay & Carmel Head
ANGLESEY

Out in the remote northwest corner of the Isle of Anglesey, the shingle bank of Esgair Gemlyn runs west in a shapely curve, guarding a brackish lagoon where hundreds of sandwich terns raise their young each year. As we walked the beach, our boots crunched smooth flat pebbles — grey and crimson, jade-green, apricot and snow white, enough shapes and colours to gladden the heart of any princess who might peep over the castle-like walls of Bryn Aber.

Bryn Aber lies low beyond the beach, a house in a brambly piece of land surrounded by sturdy double walls of sun-paled brick. The walls were built in the 1930s by Captain Vivian Hewitt, flying ace and passionate ornithologist. Hewitt planned to conceal himself in the space between the walls, to observe without scaring the terns, gulls and waders breeding in the lagoon he created for their benefit and his own pleasure.

Sea kale's leathery pale leaves and the big crinkled flowers of yellow horned-poppy shivered in the breeze along the shingle. The slim shapes of grey mullet flickered through the gaps of the causeway below Bryn Aber. We crossed the inlet and made west along the coast path, looking forward to the prominent seamarks of the White Ladies on Carmel Head, and the squat red and white lighthouse out on the long reef of the Skerries a couple of miles offshore.

Up close the White Ladies proved an angular pair, tall and thin, their triangular buttresses like grey cloaks held out to catch the wind. Below them the point of Carmel Head was a jumble of quartz and rusty iron rock, and of ancient gneiss pushed up and over the underlying rocks — the oldest exposed rock in Wales. Out at sea a pair of porpoises were hunting in the agitated waters of the tide-ripped sound, and we sat to watch their curving backs and thorn-shaped fins breaking the sea.

On past a series of deep, dark coves, the path narrow and vertiginous round their unguarded edges. By the rock stack islet of Ynys y Fydlyn with its black wave-cut arches, we turned inland between fields of sheep and cattle, a landscape rolling south to the crumpled peak of Mynydd y Garn. Over the pastures to Tyn Llan and its little chapel tucked behind a field wall, and down again to Bryn Aber and the bird cries in Captain Hewitt's lagoon.

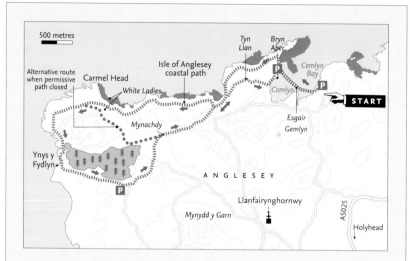

Start & finish Cemlyn Bay car park (east side), near Cemaes, Anglesey, LL67 0DY approx. (OS ref SH336932)

Getting there Road: Cemlyn is signed from A5025 Holyhead-Cemaes road between Llanrhyddlad and Tregele

Walk (9½ miles, moderate, OS Explorer 262): Walk Esgair Gemlyn shingle bank to west end at Bryn Aber (329936); follow coast path for 4 miles via Carmel Head to beach at Ynys y Fydlyn (292917). NB closures – see below. From beach, head inland (yellow arrow) with trees on left; over open land for ½ mile to car park (303914). Left along road. In ½ mile, at right bend (308918), keep ahead ('Mynachdy, Private Road'). At Mynachdy, through gate (309923); right along wall by barns; on along stony track, past derelict lodge on left, to gate/stile (314925). Ahead to gate into road (317926). Immediately left through iron kissing gate ('NT'); path to coast (319929). Right on coast path round Hen Borth, through gate at far end and on to next gate (321931). Half right to gate near chapel (322932); across field to kissing gate to left of Tyn Llan farmhouse (323933). Ahead down lane; in 500m, left (328932) across causeway and past Bryn Aber; across Esgair Gemlyn to car park.

Conditions Esgair Gemlyn shingle bank, April-August – please walk seaward of wooden posts to avoid disturbing nesting birds.

NB: Coast Path immediately north of Ynys y Fydlyn is narrow, slippery and vertiginous, with sheer drops. Walk this section at your own risk. It is a permissive path, courtesy of the landowner, and is closed between September 15 and January 31. Alternative return route from Carmel Head: footpath SE to Mynachdy, then as detailed above.

Lunch Picnic

Accommodation Harbour Hotel, Cemaes Bay LL67 0NN (01407 710273; angleseyharbour.co.uk)

More information Conwy TIC (01492 577566), visitanglesey.co.uk, satmap.com, ramblers.org.uk

Plynlimon
CEREDIGION

When the supreme egotist and ferocious walker George Borrow ascended Plynlimon in 1854, he called at the Castell Dyffryn Inn to engage a guide, "a tall athletic fellow, dressed in a brown coat, round bluff hat, corduroy trowsers, linen leggings and highlows". This splendid chap proved reluctant to take the East Anglian writer to the source of the River Rheidol — "the path, sir, as you see, is rather steep and dangerous". But Borrow, researching his classic travelogue Wild Wales, would not be gainsaid. "It is not only necessary for me to see the sources of the rivers," he told his guide, "but to drink from them, that in after times I may be able to harangue about them with a tone of confidence and authority."

Three rivers have their source close together on Plynlimon's rough summit — Rheidol, Wye and Severn. Jane and I, having no need to harangue, were aiming simply to get to the top of the mountain. Our companion for today's walk, Liz Fleming-Williams, is an expertise in the ecology of peat bogs, a fascnation that led her to the kind of revelation that Burrow would have recognised; a sense of how closely Welsh poetry, music, art and language are bound up with this beautiful and sombre landscape.

We strode up the old miners' track towards a long-abandoned lead mine in the southern flank of the mountain; then on up a faint track through heather and bilberry, reindeer moss, black peat hags and bent grass. "Listen!" Liz said, holding up a finger. Not a sound, bar the complaints of sheep and the hiss of wind.

Up in the summit shelter, two Cornish surfies had arrived from their camp on the shores of Nant-y-Moch reservoir below. Hospitably they poured us tea, and we took in the 100-mile view: the Preseli Hills in far-off Pembrokeshire, a huge arc of Cardigan Bay, the Llŷn Peninsula misty on the horizon; Cader Idris, the Brecon Beacons, the mountains of Snowdonia.

Only the semaphore arms of a wind farm far below, sited smack in the middle of an ecologically sensitive peat bog, told of the greedy crassness of Man. Borrow would have had a crisp harangue suitable for the subject at his fingertips. But for now we had to make do with the cheep of pipits and the sigh of the cold mountain wind.

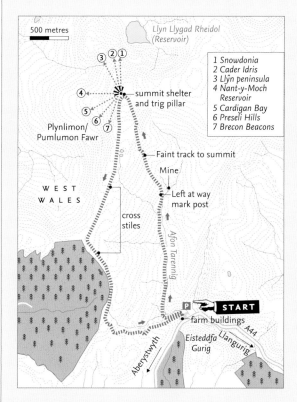

1 Snowdonia
2 Cader Idris
3 Llŷn peninsula
4 Nant-y-Moch Reservoir
5 Cardigan Bay
6 Preseli Hills
7 Brecon Beacons

Start & finish Eisteddfa-Gurig car park SY23 3LE (OS ref SN799841) – moderate charge

Getting there Road: 4½ miles east of Ponterwyd on A44, Aberystwyth-Llangurig.

Walk (5 miles, moderate, OS Explorer 213): From car park, up farm drive past 'Caution, children playing' notice. Right through yard past dog kennels. In 30m, bridleway sign points left; bear right through gate (797841) along stony track. Ignore first right turn; follow track as it curves right over stream and climbs for 1 mile to old mine. Just before it swings right to cross Afon Tarennig (795897), white arrow/green background on post points left up faint track. Follow this for ¾ mile to summit of Plynlimon (789869). Descending keep close to fence on your right. Cross stile at 787857. Left at forestry (784851): follow fence with trees on your right. Cross stile at 786849; continue along fence to meet rough road back to car park.

NB Family-friendly. Wear hill-walking gear. Track from mine to summit can be hard to find in mist.

Lunch Picnic

Accommodation Ffynnon Cadno Guest House, Ponterwyd SY23 3AD (01970 890224; ffynnoncadno.co.uk)

Dinner George Borrow Hotel, Ponterwyd SY23 3AD (01970 890230; www.thegeorgeborrowhotel.co.uk)

More information Aberystwyth TIC (01970 612125), visitwales.co.uk, Wild Wales by George Borrow (Nabu Press)

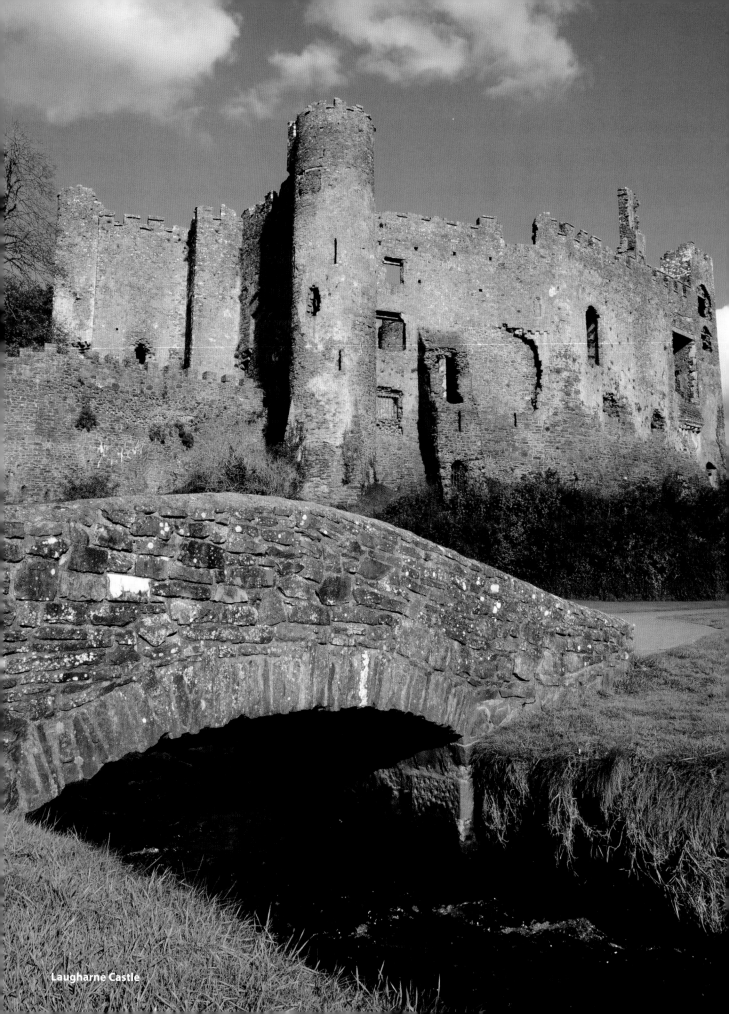

Laugharne Castle

Dylan Thomas's Laugharne
CARMARTHENSHIRE

It was a most beautiful morning of blue sky and crisp spring weather over Laugharne. Fresh flowers had been laid on Dylan Thomas's grave in the sloping churchyard. Following the town trail map along the village street, we picked out the everyday waymarks of the poet's life here in the 1930s and 1940s — Browns Hotel where he drank (and drank), the green-faced Pelican house where his parents lived, the baker's where Thomas came for bread each morning. Here we filled the backpack with Welsh cakes and went on our way, down past the big jagged ruin of Laugharne Castle and up Sir John's Hill along a cliff path above the great dun apron of salt marsh that separates the village from the sea.

On his thirtieth birthday, Thomas noted in *Poem in October*, he felt himself summoned out and over Sir John's Hill by "water praying and call of seagull and rook/And the knock of sailing boats on the net webbed wall". He had a rainy view that October morning in 1944, but ours today was laid out in sunlight — marsh, dunes, a crawling silver sea rough with surf, and Worm's Head promontory a string of grey islets at the edge of sight.

The path soon swung inland, up and over a ridge of pastures, down into a green valley. A holloway stodgy with red mud brought us to the back lanes of Laugharne, from where stony byways led via the Wales Coast Path to the lonely farm of Delacorse.

Back along the edge of the Taf estuary we found the Boathouse where Dylan and Caitlin Thomas and their three children lived for the last four years of the poet's life, and the tiny shed where he sat and wrote and looked out on a sublime view of sea and sky. You have only to sit on the Boathouse terrace, looking out over the estuary towards Sir John's Hill, and read *Poem in October* to see exactly why Wales so fervently celebrates its national poet in all his wayward genius.

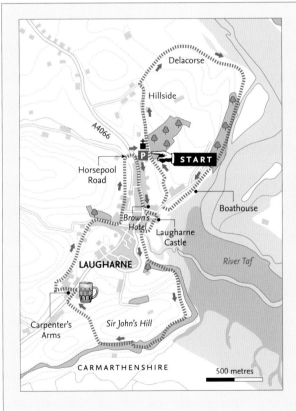

Start & finish Church car park, Laugharne, SA33 4QD (OS ref SN301114)

Getting there Bus: Service 222 (tafvalleycoaches.co.uk), Carmarthen-Pendine. Road: Laugharne is on the A4066 (signed from St Clears on A40).

Walk (6½ miles, easy, OS Explorer 177): From the car park, left along road through Laugharne (town trail downloadable at discovercarmarthenshire.com/dylan-thomas). By castle on waterfront (302107) right, following Wales Coast Path (WCP) and Dylan's Birthday Walk (DBW) along shore, then up cliff path. In ½ mile WCP, DBW fork left by bench (306100). Leave WCP/DBW here, keeping ahead along cliff path. In ⅓ mile at fork (301097), right up steps on WCP for 50m; don't cross stiles; left through unmarked fence gap. Cliff path for 350m; stile (297098, yellow arrow); field path to A4066 in Broadway (294101). Right; left by Carpenter's Arms; across stile at lane end (294103); right to hedge corner; right along path/lane for 700m to road (297108). Right; left at '30' sign; in 150m, left along Holloway Lane, then field path to Horsepool Road (300114). Right to A4066. Up cobbled lane by church car park; on via Hillside (302117) to Delacorse (308122). WCP to Boathouse and Writing Shed (306110), then road (304109). Right on bridleway to church.

Lunch Dylan Thomas Boathouse, Laugharne SA33 4SD (01994 427420; dylanthomasboathouse.com/tearooms) – snack with a view; open 10.30am-2.45pm

Accommodation Browns Hotel, Laugharne SA33 4RY (01994 427688; browns-hotel.co.uk)

More information Carmarthen TIC (01267 231557; discovercarmarthenshire.com), dylanthomasbirthdaywalk.co.uk, satmap.com, ramblers.co.uk

Carreg Cennen Castle
CARMARTHENSHIRE

Sometimes you just have to go with the flow. Jane and I arrived in Carmarthenshire determined to puzzle out an original walk around Carreg Cennen Castle. But then we found that Carreg Cennen was infuriatingly positioned at the junction of three OS Explorer maps. And once we'd visited the café-shop and picked up the county council's superb leaflet of walks based on the castle itself, we simply thanked our lucky stars and set out into the day, a gloriously sunny one under a blue summer sky spread all across the southern hills of Wales.

Among green waves of lowland slopes, the jagged walls of Carreg Cennen Castle rose like a dark island. We walked down the path through the oakwood of Coed y Cennen in a bubble of birdsong, crossed the shallow brown river and climbed southward up a stony track with a most magnificent view of the castle clinging to the very lip of its 100m (300ft) crags. Out at the top into a wide, sedgy upland, with a prospect to the distant humps of the Preseli Hills forty miles off in the west.

A flock of sheep lay panting like woolly steam engines under a rowan tree. From the moorland road we turned back towards the castle, dipping into dells formed by the collapse of underground caverns. Whole trees grew in the depths, their canopies on a level with the rim of the hollows. Down there under a bank of orchids we found a shadowy cave mouth spewing forth a broad gush of water — the infant Loughor River, destined for greatness in its broad estuary 20 miles away. On we went through damp bogland, bright with pink beaks of lousewort and the trembling blue flowers of insect-digesting butterwort, a beautiful wetland full of frogs and spiders.

Back at Carreg Cennen we roamed over the castle, its towers and baileys. Steps descended to a sinister twist of a passage, rough-floored and pitch black. By the light of Jane's torch we followed its course below the castle, bending and slithering until we crouched at the very heart of the crag. Not a lamb's cry or child's shout penetrated the rock. The original purpose of this black chamber in Carreg Cennen is obscure. But one couldn't help but picture a desperate man of the garrison crouching there, waiting with beating heart for a victorious enemy, screwing up his courage in the dark to kill or be killed.

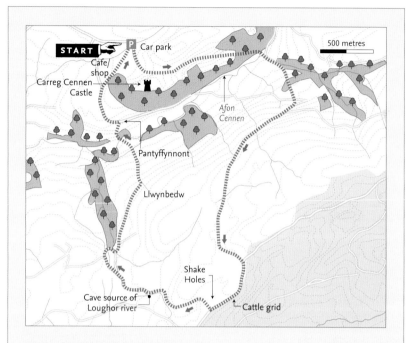

Start & finish Carreg Cennen Castle car park, Trapp, Llandeilo, Carmarthenshire SA19 6UA (OS ref SN666193)

Getting there Train: (thetrainline.com; railcard.co.uk) to Ffairfach (3½ miles). Road: From Llandeilo, A483 ('Ammanford'); left at crossroads in Ffairfach; right after bridge to Trapp; don't cross bridge, but keep ahead to Carreg Cennen.

Walk (3½ miles, moderate, OS Explorers OL12, 178, 186; NB; excellent map leaflet at castle): From shop-café follow Carreg Cennen Circular/CCC fingerposts (red castle symbols) past castle, through wood, across Afon Cennen (675193). Follow CCC and Beacons Way/BW up stony path for ¾ mile to road (673180). Right to cross cattle grid; in 200m, right across stile (671177; CCC); follow CCC and yellow arrows (YA) to pass source of Loughor River (668178). Continue (YA, CCC) to Llwyn-bedw; down field to cross Afon Cennen (666188); stile and steep path (YA) to road at Pantyffynont. Left; in 300m, right (665191; CCC) across field to car park.

Lunch Carreg Cennen café (01558 822291; carregcennencastle.com), Cennen Arms, Trapp, Llandeilo SA19 6TP (01558 822330)

Accommodation Cawdor Hotel, Llandeilo SA19 6EN (01558 823500; thecawdor.com) – friendly boutique hotel

More information Carmarthen TIC (01267 231557; discovercarmarthenshire.com), Brecon Beacons National Park (01874 623366; breconbeacons.org), ramblers.org.uk

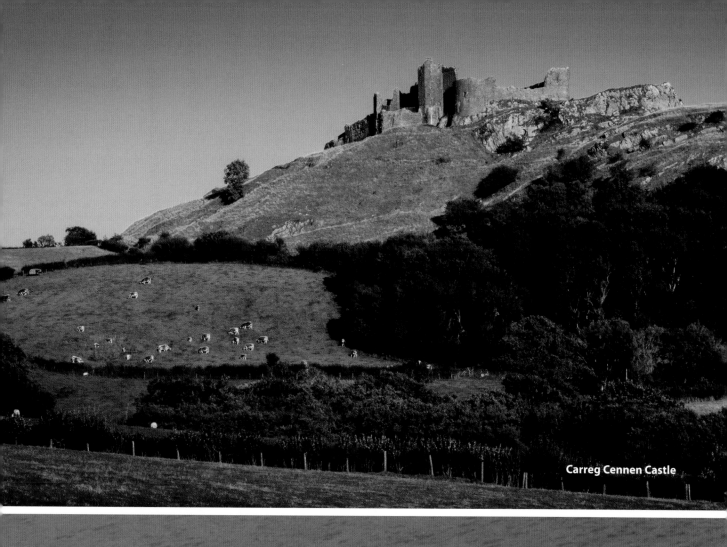

Carreg Cennen Castle

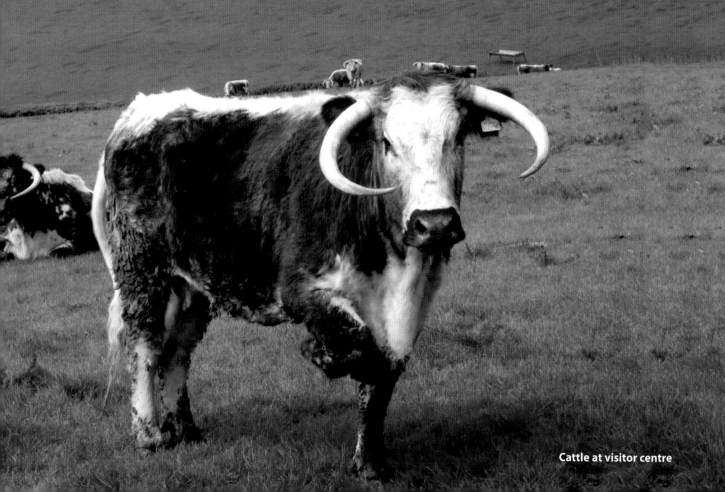

Cattle at visitor centre

Crimpiau
CONWY

Capel Curig on a cloudless morning: the sky upturned like a blue porcelain bowl above Snowdonia, the air as fresh as spring water, full of light and clarity. In the west, Snowdon thrust up its crown of peaks round a shadowy hollow. Moel Siabod rose like a rocket to the south. What a morning for exploring the rugged uplands that lie north of Capel Curig, the walkers' and climbers' mecca in the mountains.

We crossed the stile by the chapel and were away up the fields with tumbled rocks and hillocks rising all round. A well-trodden path led through a mossy oakwood and out into a patch of sun-warmed bog myrtle. We picked a handful of the olive-shaped leaves and sniffed their sweetly spicy fragrance as we climbed on round a great bog in a rocky hollow, northwards towards the pass under the peak of Crimpiau.

"Go on a bit down the other side, there's a great view," the man in Capel Curig's Moel Siabod café had urged us. We did so, and were rewarded with a wonderful prospect northeast over the blue waters of Llyn Crafnant

framed in a cleft of hills. Back up to the pass, and a meandering climb up to the pale quartz rocks of Crimpiau's summit. Snowdon stood up dramatically in the west, with Tryfan's stegosaurus back arched to the sky alongside.

Mountains and uplands were all lit as though by a stage designer granting the dearest wish of every walker out in the hills today. "Tryfan," said a cheery man as we sat drinking it all in like thirsty travellers in a bar. "Up there yesterday, and couldn't see a thing for the mist. Wayfinding was… interesting." He smiled. "Back to Bedfordshire tomorrow — worst place in the world if you love hills!"

A very rugged and rough path led south off the ridge and down past Llyn y Coryn, gleaming in its dark peaty bed like a splash of mercury. A pair of mating dragonflies flew away, banking like biplanes. We descended through heather and gorse, with Snowdon and its cohorts beyond the double lakes of Mymbyr a feast for eyes and soul the whole way down.

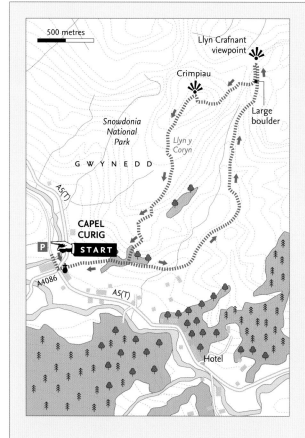

Start & finish Car park behind Pinnacle Stores, Capel Curig, LL24 0EN (OS ref SH721582)

Getting there Bus: Snowdon Sherpa (gwynedd.llyw.cymru) service S2 (Llanberis-Betws-y-Coed), service 6B (Bethesda-Betws-y-Coed). Road: Pinnacle Stores is at crossroads of A5 (Betws-y-Coed-Bangor) and A4086 (Llanberis).

Walk (4½ miles, strenuous, OS Explorer OL17): Cross A5; stile beside chapel ('Crafnant' fingerpost). In 200m, between trees, ahead on stony path. Gate/stile into wood (725582); out of trees to gate/stile (729581); on to cross wooden footbridge (732581). Left ('walking man' waymark); on (stiles) for 1¼ miles, up to pass beside large boulder (738596). On downhill for 200m to Llyn Crafnant viewpoint (738598). Back to pass and boulder; right up path to Crimpiau summit (733596). Path descends south along ridge, aiming for figure-of-eight lakes (Llynnau Mymbyr). Llyn y Coryn soon in sight; keep left of lake (731591) to fence on saddle beyond (731590). Keeping fence on right, down to cross stile (730587). Steeply down to cross stile by stone wall in hollow (729586). Turn right between fence and stone wall; follow fence to cross two more stiles (727583). Steeply down to path (727582); right to Capel Curig.

Conditions Steep and rough in places

Lunch Picnic

Accommodation Tyn-y-Coed Hotel, Capel Curig, LL24 0EE (01690 720331; tyn-y-coed.co.uk) – comfortable, helpful, walker-friendly

More information www.eryri-npa.gov.uk, visitsnowdonia.info/walking-85.aspx, satmap.com, ramblers.org.uk

Moel Famau and the Clwydian Hills
DENBIGHSHIRE/FLINTSHIRE

Rain and gales over northeast Wales, with the Clwydian Hills bathed one moment in brilliant sunshine, the next in grey showers chased northwards by the wind. We watched the squalls marching through the Vale of Clwyd far below as we followed the broad stony track of Offa's Dyke Path north along the ridge.

The Clwydian Hills make a hugely popular day out for local walkers; and Moel Famau, at 554m (1818ft) the summit of the twenty-mile range, is the natural target, with the stump of its ruined Jubilee Tower as an aiming point. Hikers, runners, strollers, dog-walkers, all were out striding the path in the buffeting wind, children running and tumbling in the heather, their parents crunching across the snow banks of last month's unseasonable blizzards.

The Jubilee Tower was erected in 1810 for King George III's Golden Jubilee and blown down in a storm in 1862. Its blockhouse foundations sit across the peak of Moel Famau like a double-crowned cardinal's hat. Up on its walls we found we couldn't keep our feet — the wind literally pushed us off that hilltop, tears in our eyes, the breath rammed back in our throats. There was time for a glimpse of the snow-streaked crests of the Berwyn Mountains in the south, and then we had left the Offa's Dyke Path and the wind-blasted ridge, and were skeltering down a green hillside into the calm airs of the Vale of Clwyd.

A string of small sheep farms runs north to south in the shelter of the Clwydian Hills. Above Tyn-y-Celyn we crossed a fast-running hill torrent, ice-cold from snowmelt, and turned back along a path through sheep pastures. Ewes issued their throaty, peremptory calls to the lambs that came in pairs to look us over, their large ears sticking out and filtering the sun into a pink glow. We crossed a patch of unmelted snow, stamping our boots into the icy crust to get a grip, and went on south above the slate-roofed farms that crouched among shelter trees — Tyddyn Norbury, Bron-y-felin, Fron Goch, Fron Ganol, Fron-bellaf, ringing names to a Saesneg ear.

At Fron-bellaf we crossed a stream where daffodils were still in bud and took the old green road up over the shoulder of the hill, climbing back towards Offa's Dyke Path once more. The gale came rushing to meet us, the sky raced from peak to peak, and an old crow's nest rocked in the fork of a weather-skinned thorn tree, seething to itself in the wind.

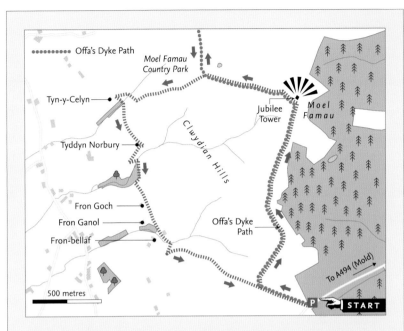

Start & finish Bwlch Pen Barras car park, Llanbedr-Dyffryn-Clwyd, LL15 1US approx. (OS ref SJ161606)

Getting there Bus: free shuttle bus from Loggerheads (clwydianrangeanddeevalleyaonb.org.uk/buses) in summer. Road: A494 from Mold towards Ruthin. In Llanbedr-Dyffryn-Clwyd, just before church, right up Lôn Cae Glas. Bear left along Lôn y Mynydd to Bwlch Pen Barras car park at top of road.

Walk (5 miles, moderate, OS Explorer 265): From car park follow Offa's Dyke Path/ODP to Moel Famau tower (162626) and on. In ⅓ mile cross side track in dip (156628); in next dip, left off ODP (152630, fingerpost, yellow arrow/YA). Descend slope, looking to left for marker posts on a clear downward track. Follow it down. At bottom, cross stream (143628); in 200m, above Tyn-y-Celyn farm, sharp left (142627, waymark post) back along wall. Recross stream; on beside wall/fence. In ⅓ mile, YA points ahead (144622), but you hairpin right to cross stile; ahead along drive. At entrance to Bron-y-felin farmyard (144620), left through gate; bear right above and round farm; ahead through field gate and on with hedge on right. Keep same contour above Fron Goch (144616, stile, YA). At Fron Bellaf cross stream; left to cross stile (YA); climb bank ahead. Ignore first green track you cross, and YA pointing right; keep climbing to fence (147612). Turn left here, following fence on green track. In 200m cross stile; up slope for 50m, then left on grassy track, climbing for ½ mile. At top, ignore first stile on right (154609); ahead with fence on right for 200m to cross next stile. Ahead to join ODP (157608); right to car park.

Lunch Griffin Inn, Llanbedr-Dyffryn-Clwyd, Ruthin LL15 1UP (01824 702792; robinsonsbrewery.com) – cosy and friendly

Moel Famau Country Park moelfamau.co.uk

More information Ruthin tourist information point in Ruthin Craft Centre (01824 704774), visitwales.co.uk, satmap.com, ramblers.org.uk

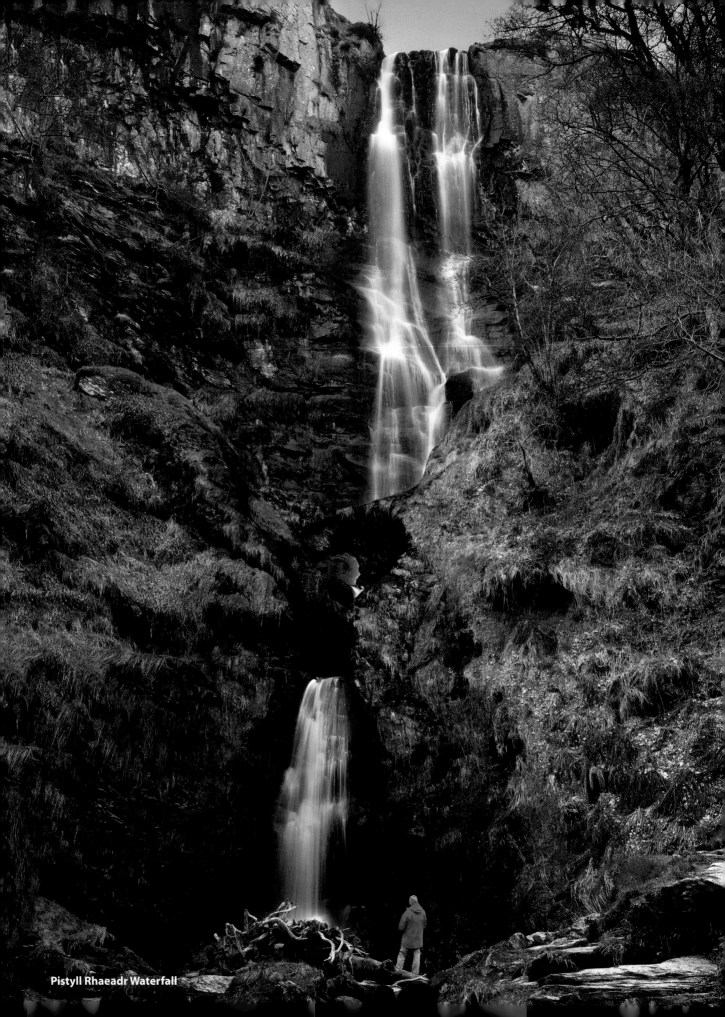

Pistyll Rhaeadr Waterfall

The Afon Disgynfa rushed toward the 60m (200ft) cliff, gathered into a bulge of glass-clear water at the very rim, then hurled itself into space. Prone on a spur of beaten earth beside the cliff, I watched the cascade drop away. Then I raised my gaze to take in the view down the U-shaped valley into which the river was tumbling — grazing meadows and small farms between towering hillsides and naked rock crags. Up here at the top of Pistyll Rhaeadr, the tallest waterfall in Wales, everything — mossy rocks, slippery stones, lichen-encrusted larch and hazel — spoke of the damp, clean air of the surrounding Berwyn Hills.

Down on the footbridge at the base of the cliff, the waterfall itself is all the view one needs. Is there a more stupendous and humbling spectacle in all Wales than this mighty cataract seen from below? I watched spellbound as the fall came hissing lazily out of the mist-whitened sky in lacy skeins, toppling gracefully into a half-way basin before bounding out through a natural bridge of polished black rock and crashing on down towards the spray-shrouded pool at the bottom.

I lingered a long time on the bridge, till eyes and ears were sated with the movement and noise of falling water. Then I turned and followed a path between mossy trees scarred with ancient penknife carvings of lovers' names. Out on the hillside the path dropped between house-high boulders fallen from the sharp ramparts of Craig y Mwn, the Mine Rock cliffs far above. Here in times past quarrymen dug out slate and miners delved for lead and silver, leaving levels, tramway trackbeds and spoil heaps to litter the mountain.

The path threaded the hillsides where lambs tottered after their mothers. Smoke whirled from the chimneys of Tan-y-graig, where the farm dogs gave me a tongue-lashing at the ends of their chains. I stopped for a word with the farmer at Tyn-y-wern — the cost of feed, the price of lambs, the hard winter of 1982 when Pistyll Rhaeadr froze solid and daring souls went ice-climbing up its face. Fondling the head of Nell the ancient sheepdog of Tyn-y-wern, I leant on the farmyard gate and sniffed woodsmoke, silage and wet grass, the essence of spring in the Berwyns, all underpinned by the distant murmur of the great fall.

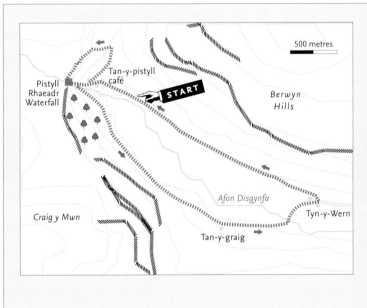

Start & finish Pistyll Rhaeadr car park, SY10 0BZ approx. near Llanrhaeadr-ym-Mochnant (OS ref 075294)

Getting there A5 from Shrewsbury towards Oswestry; B4396 to Llanrhaeadr-ym-Mochnant; 'Waterfall' (4 miles) signed on right in village

Walk (3 miles, moderate grade with one steep climb/descent, OS Explorer 255): From car park, down road to end; right behind public lavatories, up signed path (yellow arrows) that zigzags steeply uphill. At top, track continues to arrow pointing through gate (fingerpost) to top of waterfall. Please take great care: slippery rocks, unfenced 60m (200ft) drop! Return same way to foot of fall; cross by footbridge; follow path through trees, over fields, across mining spoil to Tan-y-graig and road at Tyn-y-wern. Left to car park.

Lunch Tan-y-Pistyll Café (01691-780392; www.pistyllrhaeadr.co.uk)

Accommodation Wynnstay Arms, Llanrhaeadr-ym-Mochnant (01691 780210; www.wynnstay-arms-hotel.com) – simple, comfortable, very friendly and helpful

More information Llangollen TIC (01978 860828), www.visitwales.co.uk

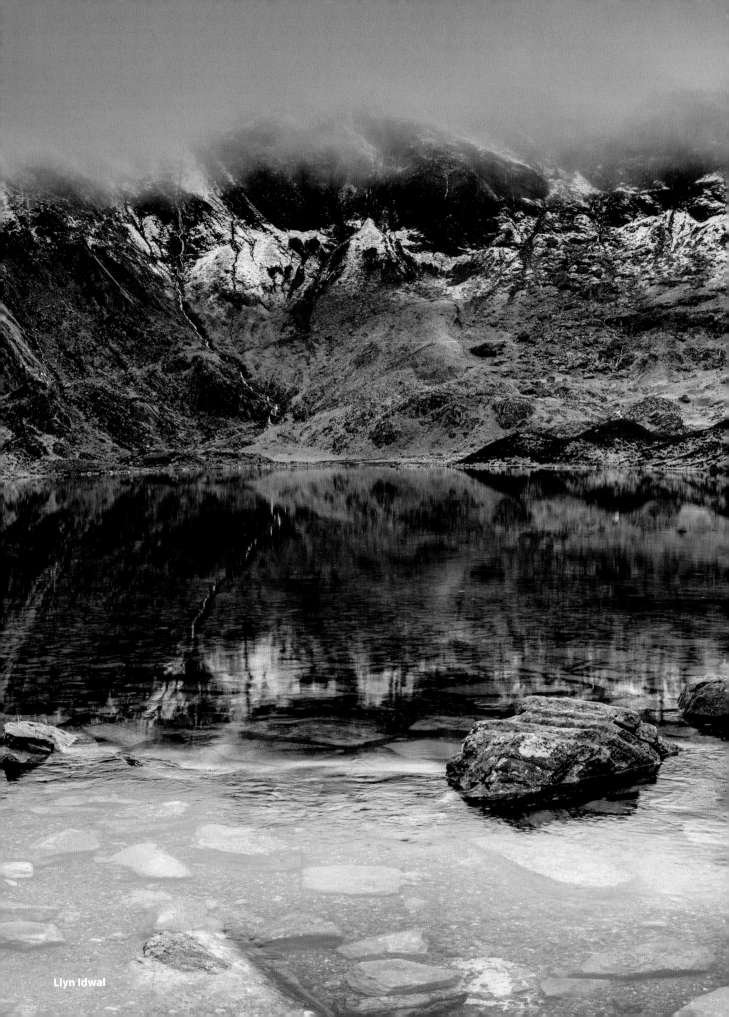

Llyn Idwal

Llyn Bochlwyd and Llyn Idwal

GWYNEDD

Cwm Idwal is a very popular place, and here was the proof in a procession of sturdy, bare calves, red rolled-down socks, big boots and sticks clattering up the stone-pitched path towards Llyn Idwal, lying hidden in its dark, dramatic bowl of cliffs.

Soon we struck off the main path and followed a stony trod across bog feathery with cotton grass, then up the steep mountain cleft where Nant Bochlwyd came jumping down from rock to rock in a rush of foam and flying water. Up over the rim of the cleft we found Llyn Bochlwyd lying flat under the sombre cliffs of Glyder Fach, a wind-rippled mountain lake in a hollow of green bilberry, as quiet and lonely as could be.

The outline of Llyn Bochlwyd mirrors almost exactly that of Australia. We took great delight in walking the Gold Coast from Sydney to Cairns — so to speak — before making for the saddle of ground that looks down on Llyn Idwal lying as dark as tarnished copper 180m (600ft) below. A sudden harsh rattle of alarm brought both our heads up, and there was a ring ouzel, a rarely seen mountain blackbird with a big white bib, alert on a rock as it waited for us to clear out of its high and wild territory.

A very steep rocky chute of a path landed us on the shore of Llyn Idwal, and from there we took the high road south, a slanting path rising under the tremendous crags of Glyder Fawr to reach a tumbled boulder field. Delicate starry saxifrages grew here, their white flowers powdered with bright scarlet dots of anthers. Along with royal blue butterwort and tiny green stars of alpine lady's mantle, they made a delightful mountain meadow to walk through before we descended the rough path to Llyn Idwal.

Some say that Prince Idwal the Bald was drowned here by his foster father, Nefydd the Handsome; others hold that the prince was cremated on its shores in AD 942 after falling in battle against the Saxon foe.

We walked its gritty beach and looked our last on the Glyder cliffs, now wreathed in curls of mist, before turning down the homeward path in a whirl of flitting meadow pipits.

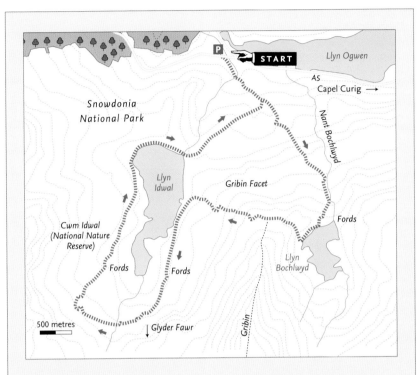

Start & finish Ogwen Warden Centre, Nant Ffrancon, Cwm Idwal car park, LL57 3LZ (OS ref SH649603)

Getting there Bus: Snowdon Sherpa (gwynedd.gov.uk) service 6B. Road: On the A5 between Capel Curig and Bethesda.

Walk (4½ miles, hard, OS Explorer OL17): Up stone-pitched path at left side of warden centre. In 350m path bends right (652601); ahead here on stony track across bog; steeply up right side of Nant Bochlwyd to Llyn Bochlwyd (655594). Right (west) on path for 400m to saddle (652594); pitched path to Gribin climbs to left, but you keep ahead, then very steeply down to Llyn Idwal (647596). Left along lake. At south end take higher path (646593) slanting up to boulder field; take care fording torrent at 642589. Arriving face to face with a very big boulder (640589), go right down the side of it, then left across rocky grass to find downward path (640590), steep in places, to Llyn Idwal and visitor centre.

Conditions steep and slippery in places; a strenuous hike for surefooted and confident hill walkers

Lunch Picnic

Accommodation Tyn-y-Coed Inn, Capel Curig LL24 0EE (01690 720331; tyn-y-coed.co.uk) – really helpful, walker friendly inn

More information Ogwen Warden Centre (01248 602080) or Betws-y-Coed TIC (01690 710426), eryri-npa.gov.uk

St Arvans and the Eagle's Nest

MONMOUTHSHIRE

The two cast-iron infants on St Arvans village fountain discharged streams of water from their urns for well over a century. The fountain stands dry these days, and on this cold St David's Day its twin cherubs looked distinctly underdressed and half frozen. We left them to their invisible pouring, and followed a wide grassy ride west across the fields to where the barns of Rogerstone Grange overlooked stud farm paddocks of horses in thick winter coats. Field paths led us on through a broad, undulating landscape typical of these southernmost Welsh Borders.

In the margins of Chepstow Park Wood a buzzard mewed like a frightened kitten as it side-slipped the dive-bombing attacks of a pair of angry crows. Turning back east through the conifer wood, all was still and windless, though the tree tops roared a hundred feet above our heads.

At the forest edge we sat on a bench and looked out across sunlit slopes and the first yellow-green buds of this year's daffodils to a wide silver streak of the Severn Estuary. Then we plodged on along puddly lanes and paths to Gaer Hill, trenched with the concentric ramparts of a magnificent Iron Age hill fort. It was built by the Silures, a curly-haired and dark-complexioned people, famous for fierceness in battle.

With the flat, tree-encircled crowns of the Forest of Dean ahead, we dropped downhill and went west to where sheer limestone cliffs formed the walls of the Wye Valley's winding gorge. From the Eagle's Nest lookout on Wyndcliff there was a spectacular view over the deserted village, ruined church and working farm of Lancaut, cradled in a great meander of the flood-reddened Wye far below. Then we plunged down the steep metal stairways and slippery, worn-away stone treads of the 365 Steps, a nineteenth-century tourist attraction.

At the foot of the cliffs, a last stretch through sunlit meadows brought us back to St Arvans, where the wintry afternoon sun had brought a touch of warmth to the fountain cherubs' cold iron limbs, if not a rosy glow to their green-painted cheeks.

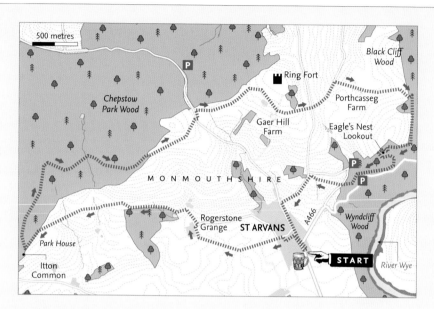

Start & finish The Piercefield, St Arvans, Chepstow, Monmouthshire NP16 6EJ (OS ref ST519963)

Getting there Bus: Service 69 (monmouthshire.gov.uk), Chepstow-Monmouth. Road: St Arvans is on A466 Chepstow-Monmouth road.

Walk (8 miles, moderate, OS Explorer OL14): By fountain on A466, ahead up Devauden Road; left along Church Lane; right past church; left to kissing gate (516965, yellow arrows/YA). West to Rogerstone Grange (507965); right past barns to road; dogleg right/left ('Tewdrig Trail'/TT). In 200m, left through gate (506968, YA); field path west for 1 mile to road at Park House (489966). Right into Chepstow Park Wood (488964); forest road north and east for 1½ miles to leave wood by benches (502974). Lane to road (507978); path east for 700m; right (513981) past barn (515980, TT) to Gaer Hill Farm (516979). East beside hill fort ramparts; down to cross road (520979). No Through Road for ¼ mile, then right (522982) past Porthcasseg Farm to Black Cliff Wood (531980). Right ('Wye Valley Walk'/WVW) for ½ mile to waymark post (528975); left to Eagle's Nest Lookout. Rejoin WVW; in 200m, left (527974, YA, footprint symbol) steeply down the 365 Steps. At bottom, right, parallel with A466, for 700m to cross minor road (523971). Path west to road by house (519972); left to St Arvans.

NB: The 365 Steps are steep, badly worn and slippery.

Lunch The Piercefield, St Arvans (01291 622614; piercefieldgwent.co.uk)

More information Chepstow TIC (01291 623772; chepstowtowncrier.org.uk), visitwales.com, satmap.com, ramblers.org.uk

Aberedw and Llandeilo Hill

POWYS

Not so long ago the Seven Stars at Aberedw lay closed down, boarded up and despaired of by all and sundry. These days it's a thriving little place — a testament to how a tiny mid-Wales community and a lively-minded landlord can rally round a moribund pub and breathe life into it once more.

The Seven Stars Inn sits next to one of the most appealing churches in Wales, dedicated to St Cewydd (a rainmaker, like St Swithun). Inside, a glass case displays the two flutes of William Williams, church flautist in Victorian times — he'd also play for dancing, seated in the timber-framed porch while the local swains and damsels footed it on the church green.

With such bucolic images as sauce for the day, we set off into a big blowy morning. Enormous clouds marched east across blue sky fields, with sunbursts at their trailing edges. A stony track beyond the River Edw took us up the tiers of a giant natural amphitheatre, a curved hillside of stepped cliffs facing northwest across the Edw's valley. Here in the winter of 1282 Llywelyn ap Gruffydd, last true prince of Wales, spent his final night on earth in a dark slit of a cave among the hazels, a fugitive from the might and wrath of King Edward I. Next day Llywelyn was caught and killed, his severed head was paraded in London, and Welsh dreams of freedom were snuffed out with the prince evermore to be known as 'Llywelyn the Last'.

We contoured the curved valley on a grassy path, then climbed to the broad back of Llandeilo Hill, a sombre sea of dark heather beyond which the graceful peaks of the Brecon Beacons, Pen y Fan and Cribyn, rose pale and ghostly in the south, with the long prows of the Black Mountains low on the southeast horizon, marinated in sunlight. We passed the low stone cairn that marks the grave of Twm Tobacco — maybe a hanged felon, maybe a much-loved pedlar, depending on who's relaying the tale — and went steeply down through the bracken. A muddy path along the Edw among incurious long-horned cattle, and we were heading up the road towards the Seven Stars in the last sunshine of the day.

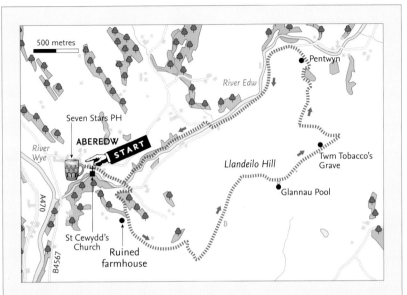

Start & finish Seven Stars Inn, Aberedw, Builth Wells LD2 3UW (OS ref SO080474)

Getting there Road: Aberedw is signed off A470 Talgarth-Builth Wells just beyond Erwood

Walk (7½ miles, moderate, OS Explorer 188): From Seven Stars pub, right along road past church to cross River Edw (085471). In 50m, fork right up 'No Through Road' lane. In 100m, hairpin right up track, through gate and on up track. In ⅓ mile, pass a ruined farmhouse (085467). In another 100m track forks; bear left and follow the grassy stony track, ignoring side tracks. In 250m, track forks again (087465); go right, and follow this track anticlockwise round curve of hillside. In ⅓ mile go under power lines; in another 100m, turn right uphill on track (092464). At top of rise, ahead for 150m; then left along grassy bridleway (094462).

Follow edge of ridge for ⅔ mile; then veer east away from ridge (100472) to meet bridleway at Glannau Pool (104471). Left (blue arrow/BA); follow BAs for nearly ½ mile to Twm Tobacco's Grave (109475; small cairn). Keep ahead (white arrow on green disc) for 250m; hairpin back to left (112476) along lower track. In ⅓ mile, just past triangular pond on right, bear right on path (106478) past pond and on downhill. Follow this path down through bracken for ⅓ mile to T-junction of tracks (108482). Left downhill to go through gate; follow right-hand side of field downhill and through gate to 3-way junction of tracks (108484). Left here, down through Pentwyn Farm to road (106487). Left for 1 mile. Pass white-painted Glan Dwr house on left; right here to cross river (094478). In 20m, left through gate; in 30m, left across stile (yellow arrow, fingerpost) and follow riverside path (very boggy!). In ⅔ mile where path forks (086473), keep left beside river across field to stile onto road (085471). Right into Aberedw.

NB: riverside path is very boggy. Drier alternative between the two bridges is by road.

Lunch/accommodation Seven Stars Inn, Aberedw, Builth Wells LD2 3UW (01982 560494)

More information Builth Wells TIC (01982 552253), visitwales.co.uk, tourism.powys.gov.uk, ramblers.org.uk, satmap.co.uk

Breidden Hills

POWYS

Lord, what a beautiful Welsh Borders day; one of those fabulous cold afternoons when the sky is untroubled blue, the air's as clean as a whistle and you just know that from the heights of the Shropshire/Powys border you can see for a hundred miles. Absolutely the day to explore the three peaks of the Breidden Hills with my godson Andy Harrison, enthusiastic walker and geologist.

"It's always amazed me," mused Andy at the summit of Moel y Golfa, "how you can have three hills so close but so totally different in geology. Where we're standing is what's left of a huge volcanic body that erupted about 450 million years ago. Then Middletown Hill," — he pointed across to a smooth rounded dome — "is the tuff, the ashes and waste, chucked out by the volcano. And that rough, crumpled hill to the north, Breidden Hill itself — it's dolerite, a tongue of magma that pushed out from the volcanic chamber and cooled."

We gazed across the green plain where the River Severn lay in meanders and oxbows of brilliant enamelled blue, out to Cadair Idris nearly 40 miles off on the coast of West Wales, to the whaleback of the Wrekin, to the minuscule bump of Helsby Hill 40 miles to the north and the shallow ridge of the Long Mynd and Wenlock Edge to the south. Here was my 100-mile view, and food for speculation, too, in the blocky stone pillar on the summit of Moel y Golfa. Its inscription eulogised the Romany Chell or leader Uriah Burton ("Big Just") — "a fighter for the weak, good to the poor, never beaten in fisty cuffs from the age of five to sixty, a man who led his people into the twentieth century". What more fulsome obituary could anyone want?

We dipped and swooped up to Rodney's Pillar on Breidden Hill, erected in 1787 to honour Sir George Brydges Rodney, Admiral of the White. What might he and Big Just have found to say to each other, supposing that they had met? I'd like to think they would have blacked one another's eye, and then shared a glass of something convivial.

Whether anyone of note is buried in the Iron Age fort on Middletown Hill, neither history nor grand monuments relate. But the third Breidden summit gave Andy and me a last prospect over the Midlands and Welsh Borders, bathed in evening sunlight and looking good enough to eat.

Start & finish Middletown car park, near The Breidden PH, Middletown, Powys SY21 8EL (OS ref SJ301125)

Getting there Train: (thetrainline.com; railcard.co.uk) to Welshpool (5 miles). Bus: Service X3 (www.tanat.co.uk) Welshpool-Shrewsbury. Road: M50, M54, A5 to Shrewsbury; Middletown is on A458 Welshpool road. Car park beyond Breidden Hotel.

Walk (6½ miles, hard, OS Explorer 240): From car park turn left along A458. In 100m take tarmac track on left of road. In 100m, cross road (298123); up path to right of house; in 70m left through gate (yellow arrow/YA) and up slope of field to cross stile (296124). Path hairpins to right and climbs. In 200m, sharp left (297125, YA), steeply up through trees, aiming for ridge (occasional YAs). Once there (293127 approx), bear left along ridge to Romany monument (291125) on Moel y Golfa. Continue along crest of ridge, then scramble down rocks; on down through trees, soon following white arrows, for a good ½ mile. Where track steepens and bends left on Golfa Bank, look for cairn of stones on right; turn right here (285117) on level path through trees. In 200m fork right (fingerpost) to house and road (284121). Right along road for ¾ mile; then left (292130), following bridleway up to crossing of paths at New Pieces (293134). Continue on bridleway; in ¼ mile, at footpath crossing, left (295137, YA), up and over saddle to T-junction of paths. Right to forest road (296141). Left; in 250m fork right; through gate, and zigzag left and right up to Rodney's Pillar (295144).
Bear right off summit from pillar, steeply down grass path (YA), through fence in dip (297143); on east (YA). In 200m, through kissing gate; on down into valley. At saddle under Brimford Wood (303144) bear right (YAs) down to cross track (blue arrows); on down to cross stream (305142 – very muddy!). In 30m right through gateway; on with hedge on left, to follow lane to Belle Eisle Farm (307137). Right along road; in 50m, left to skirt Belle Isle Cottage; fork right (YAs) up very steep path to saddle between Bulthy Hill and Middletown Hill (308135). Right to summit of Middletown Hill (305133). On down to saddle between Middletown Hill and Moel y Golfa (301131). Ignore YA pointing ahead, and turn sharp left, steeply down to A458 and Breidden Hotel.

Conditions Steep, muddy; not waymarked throughout; for confident map and GPS/compass walkers

Lunch The Breidden PH (01938 570880; thebreidden.co.uk)

Accommodation Old Hand & Diamond, Coedway, Shropshire SY5 9AR (01743 884379; oldhandanddiamond. co.uk)

More information Welshpool TIC (01938 552043; welshpool.org), visitmidwales.co.uk, ramblers.org.uk, satmap.co.uk

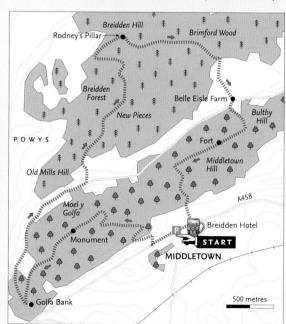

Caerfanell Horseshoe

POWYS

The Nant Bwrefwr waterfall came sparkling down from the heights of Craig y Fan Ddu, chuckling over its gleaming black and red rocks as though at the folly of walkers who'd bust a sweat climbing the Brecon Beacons on a glorious summer morning as hot and sunny as this.

Wild thyme and tiny white flowers of heath bedstraw jewelled the sedgy grass as we went slowly up towards the ridge. Up there a welcome breeze was blowing from the precipitous valley of the Afon Caerfanell. We circled the rim to where the infant river tipped over the edge and cascaded down through a clutter of boulders. Bog cotton trembled like trapped swansdown over the surface of a pool framed in sphagnum moss as green and cool as a freshly cut lime.

The flat high heads of Fan y Big and Cribyn looked over the moorland to the northwest. We went on along the cliffs, past shaggy hill ponies and newly shorn sheep, to the far side of the valley. Here two jumbles of weather-pitted aluminium and a memorial cairn marked the site of a wartime air crash. Five Canadian airmen — Sergeants Beatty, Hayes, Mittle and Yuill, and their skipper, Flight-Sergeant JB Kemp — died on 6 July 1942, when their Wellington bomber lost direction on a training flight in low cloud and slammed into this hillside. Today it couldn't be a more peaceful place, looking south through the jaws of the cleft to the blue ridges of the South Wales valleys, one behind another till they merge into the sky.

From the cairn at the end of the ridge we dropped steeply off the promontory, making across a grassy upland to descend beside the Afon Caerfanell. Following it down the valley and back to the car we found orchids in the bogs, blue butterwort under the rocks, and a whole rake of families splashing and swimming and making the most of the waterfalls of the hastening, beautiful Caerfanell.

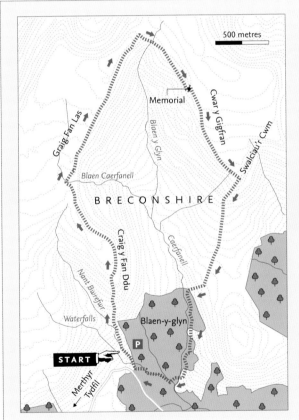

500 metres

Start & finish Upper Blaen-y-glyn car park, near Pontsticill, Powys CF48 2UT approx. (OS ref SO056176)

Getting there Bus: From Merthyr Tydfil (A465, A470), follow Pontsticill and Talybont-on-Usk. After 7 miles, beyond road summit, left (signed) into car park.

Walk (5½ miles, moderate/hard, OS Explorer OL12): Return across cattle grid, immediately right on stepped path, steeply up to ridge (054183). Where path flattens, bear right; follow rim of valley clockwise for 1½ miles to saddle at head of valley where Blaen-y-Glyn cleft descends (057206). Right on path to aircraft crash memorial (062200). Steep path ascends on left of stream gully; right along top of Cwar y Gigfran crags to cairn (067192). Bear half right, steeply down; on across upland plateau to wall; right down to Afon Caerfanell (062183). Left over stile; follow riverside path. In ½ mile, just before valley bends left (east), turn right by footpath fingerpost across footbridge (061174). On through kissing gate; in 50m, left at junction; in another 50m, before concrete footbridge, right up steep path between two streams. At top, where trees open to left, turn left on wider track, which bends right to car park.

Conditions Steep climbs and descents; boggy path by Afon Caerfanell

Lunch Red Cow, Pontsticill (01685 384828). Pubs/tearoom in Talybont-on-Usk. Nearest tearoom (March-Oct): Old Barn, Ystradgynwyn, Merthyr Tydfil CF48 2UT (01685 373175)

More information Brecon Beacons National Park (01874 623366; breconbeacons.org), visitwales.com, satmap.com, ramblers.org.uk, theaa.com/walk-and-bike-ride

Sugar Loaf
POWYS

On a still afternoon in the Brecon Beacons the Grwyne Fawr River ran dark and noisy under the single arch of Llangenny bridge. The landlady of the Dragon's Head Inn worked on her flowerbeds in the sunshine, and all seemed right with the little world folded into its valley in the eastern skirts of the mountains.

It was a stiff pull up the hill out of Llangenny, following a wet green lane full of cress and pennywort. Lost lambs scampered in front of us, calling "Ma-a-aaa!" as their mothers answered gruffly from beyond the hedges. A buzzard went mewing in wobbly circles, its steady flight pattern shaken up by a pair of dive-bombing and furiously croaking ravens. Soon the Sugar Loaf stood ahead, a green hill rising to a broad domed top, the kind of mountain that beckons rather than threatens.

Up above Cwm-cegyr — 'hemlock valley' — a wide green cart track left the shelter of the larch groves and headed for the craggy summit of the Sugar Loaf. What a fabulous view from the top: the upturned longboat shapes of the Black Mountains along the northern skyline, the whaleback

of Ysgyryd Fawr rising on the east, the rippling spines of the Valleys' hills in the southwest, and farther in the west the ground climbing towards the Brecon Beacons proper. Two centuries of hill walkers have come up here to admire the prospect, and many carved their names and the date of their ascent into the grey crags that pepper the summit of the Sugar Loaf.

A bunch of beautiful semi-wild horses with wind-tossed manes and tails followed us off the Sugar Loaf, one cheeky fellow nibbling at Jane's hat and hair. Soon they rollicked off to a water hole, plunging their muzzles in with loud sighs of satisfaction, while we went on down through fields honeyed by the declining sun.

What the hell is a sugar loaf? Well, children, if you're sitting comfortably … that's how granny used to buy her sugar, in tall conical blocks with rounded tops. They came out of the moulds in the sugar factory that way; it was easier to slide the crystallised lump out of a cone than a cylinder or cube. Bingo! That simple!

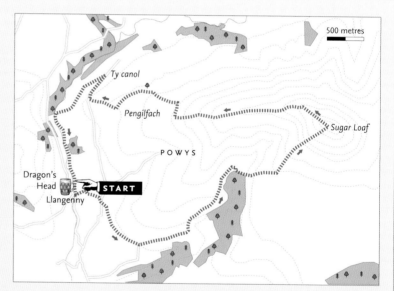

Start & finish Dragon's Head Inn, Llangenny, near Crickhowell, Powys NP8 1HD (OS ref SO240180)

Getting there Train: (thetrainline.com, railcard.co.uk) to Abergavenny (6 miles). Taxi: Crickhowell Taxi Express (01873 811764; crickhowelltaxis.com) service on demand, Tuesdays only, Llanbedr-Llangenny-Crickhowell. Road: Llangenny signposted off A40 (Abergavenny-Crickhowell).

Walk (6½ miles, moderate/hard, OS Explorer OL13): Cross bridge; left uphill past Pendarren gatehouse. In 150m, right ('Castell Corryn'). Ahead for 100m, over stile, left uphill to cross stile. Right (yellow arrow/YA) to stile into road (244179). Cross road; follow green lane (fingerpost, then YAs) for ¾ mile, first along lane, then with fence on left. By Cwm-cegyr, track comes in on right (254175); follow it, rising for 200m, then bearing right along fence and on uphill for ½ mile to corner of larch grove (260183). Bear right into dip; steeply uphill for 500m to where main track to Sugar Loaf crosses path (265182). Left to summit (272188). Left along ridge to end; follow broad path off ridge. In ¾ mile keep ahead (right) at fork (260190). In another 300m, fork right again. At foot of slope, follow wall to right. At bottom right corner, through gate above Gob-pwllau (blue arrow); follow stony lane through wood and on to Pengilfach (246190). Right along lane; in 50m, ahead (right) down to road (242191). Right for 350m to Ty-canol (244194). Left here (fingerpost); cross 2 stiles; follow path downhill through orchard and on (YAs), taking right forks downhill to Grwyne Fawr river (238190). Left for ¾ mile to Llangenny.

Lunch Dragon's Head Inn (01873 810350) – delightful, welcoming country pub

More information Crickhowell TIC (01873 811970; www.visitcrickhowell.co.uk), ramblers.org.uk, satmap.com

Llanarmon Dyffryn Ceiriog and Upper Ceiriog Way
WREXHAM

Leaving The Hand Inn, we found a sky of luminescent silver patches and grey clouds drifting over Llanarmon Dyffryn Ceiriog. The little village with the big name lies in a cleft of the Berwyn foothills, a corner of northeast Wales not exactly unknown, but out of the main tourist stream by quite a long way. The valley of Afon Ceiriog winds between bulgy slopes of sheep pasture and high moor tops, with forested ridges marching against the sky — wonderful walking country, especially on a bright and blustery day.

They would have flooded the valley in 1923, drowning Llanarmon DC and its neighbouring villages, if the former Prime Minister David Lloyd George hadn't headed a huge Welsh protest against a scheme that the locals saw as being for the benefit of foreigners, specifically the brewers of Warrington.

"The English are taking the Water out of Wales and turning it into Ales", was the clunky, but effective slogan that helped to kill off the scheme. We gave thanks for that as we halted at a gateway in the long lane leading up to the hilltops and looked down over Tregeiriog village, nestling deep and dry at the foot of a wooded cleft — picturesque Wales encapsulated in one perfect view.

Harebells trembled in royal-blue clumps, yarrow's tiny white blooms massed in wide flowerheads. A clutch of young pheasants scuttered ahead, wheezing plaintively.

Up near the ridge we turned west into the wind along the Upper Ceiriog Way, a rutted and puddled old track surfing the uplands. Ahead stood the crests of the Berwyn Hills, a sombre brown wave breaking from the west in a wall of 200m (700ft) cliffs revealing themselves slowly as we advanced — Moel Sych and Cadair Bronwen flanking Cadair Berwyn, the summit of the range at 830m (2723ft). The last time I was up there it had been in a rainy mist so thick that I'd had to turn back. Today the cloud army was marching northeast, well clear of the peaks.

We stopped in a sheltered hollow for a cup of tea and then went down the old hill track to the farm at Cyrchynan-Uchaf.

The house and barns lie sunken in the head of the valley, a very lonely spot. Two chained dogs barked us in and out, their sore-throat complaints soon overlain by the bleating of sheep as we topped the hill beyond and looked down on Llanarmon DC once more.

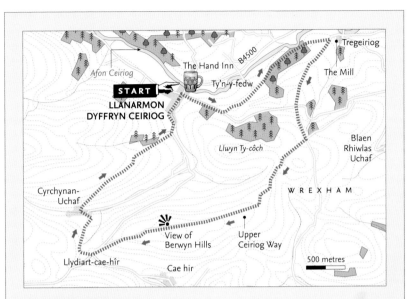

Start & finish The Hand, Llanarmon Dyffryn Ceiriog, Llangollen LL20 7LD (OS ref SJ157328)

Getting there Bus: Services 64, 65 from Oswestry and Chirk (01978 820820; www.ghacoaches.co.uk). Road: A5, A483 to Oswestry, B4679 to Glyn Ceiriog, B4500 to Llanarmon DC.

Walk (6 miles, moderate, OS Explorer 255): From The Hand, right along road ('Oswestry'). By plantation on right, fork left through gate (161326, yellow arrow/YA). Track past stone building (YA). Through gate, across hillside, over stile, across field and through gate (165328). Ignore 'footpath closed' notice; right over stile, left along fence above Ty'n-y-fedw. At gate (166329) white/red arrow (WRA) points right. Don't go through gate; keep fence on your left, into and along lower edge of wood (WRA), then across field to gate (176335). Right up lane. In 100m, tarmac forks left; but keep ahead up stony lane. In ½ mile cross road (171327); on up lane. Cross stream with wood on left (172323); in 100m, right along broad rutted Upper Ceiriog Way track for 2 miles to road (146309). Left; over stile by gate; diagonally left over field to gate. Boggy stretch joins track curving right along hillside. Through gate (144310); descend track to Cyrchynan-Uchaf farm (145314). Bear right across road-head, up through farmyard (vociferous but chained dogs!); right round barn, through gate (145315), up cart track. It rises through gates (follow YAs) to join another track at hill crest (151320). Follow YAs down hill slope. At bottom, through left-hand of 2 gates (155323), down green lane to road. Left to Llanarmon DC.

NB: No dogs – sheep country.

Lunch & accommodation The Hand, Llanarmon DC (01691 600666; thehandhotel.co.uk) – a warm, friendly inn, very helpful to walkers, with its own walks booklet for sale

More information Llangollen TIC (01978 860828), visitwales.co.uk, satmap.com, ramblers.org.uk

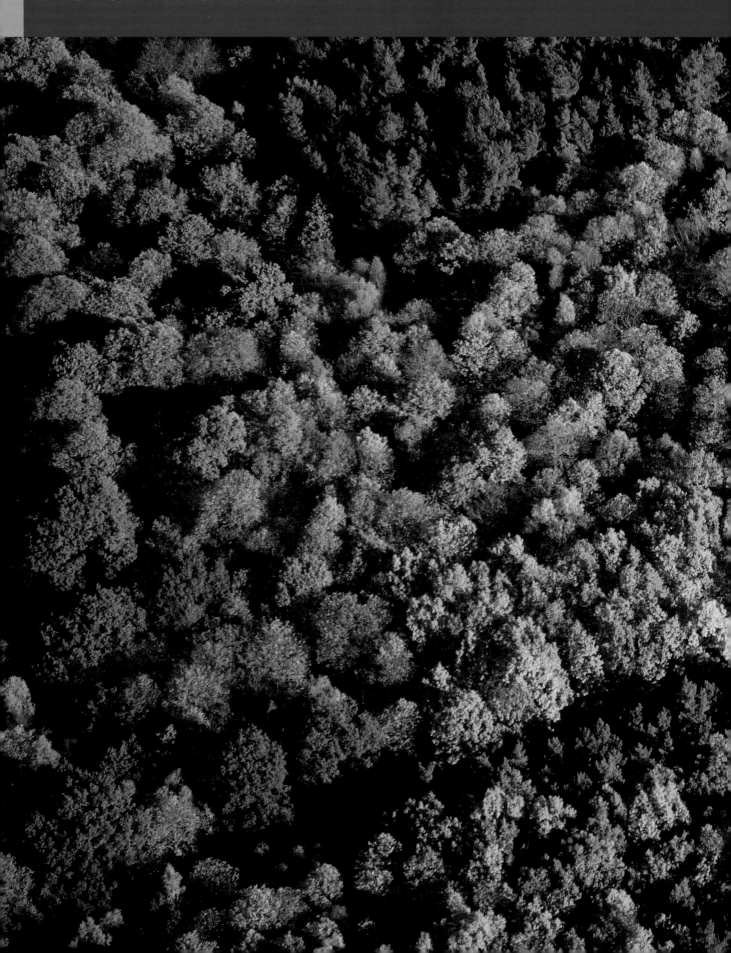

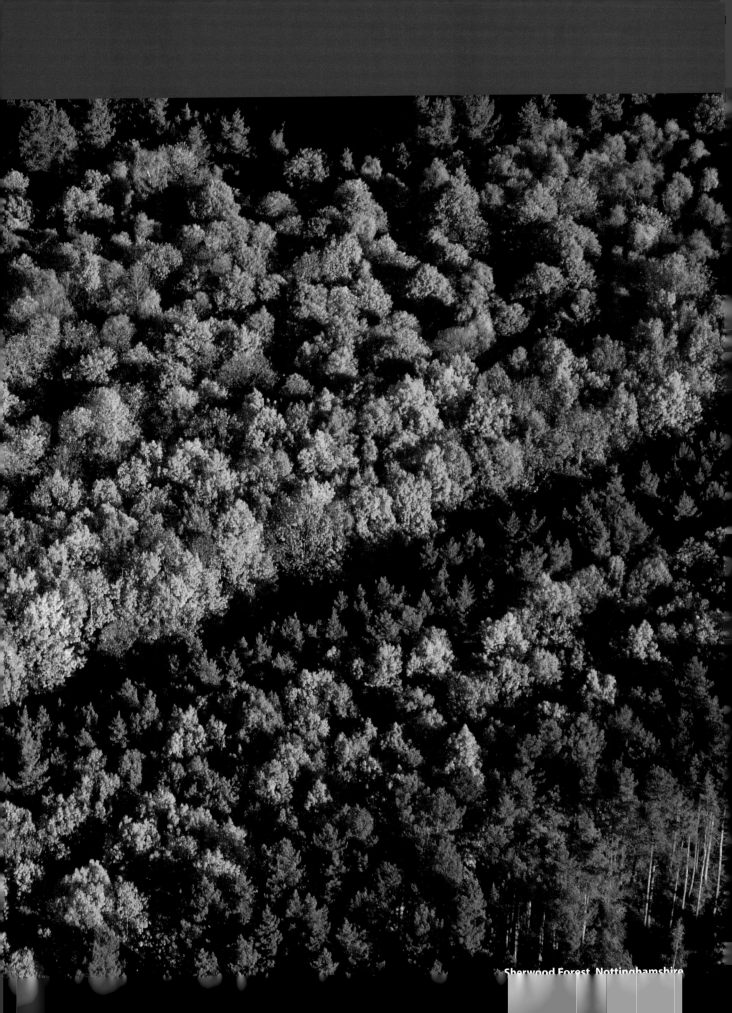

Sherwood Forest, Nottinghamshire

Calke Park, near Ticknall

DERBYSHIRE

Soft autumn sunlight lay over southwest Derbyshire, tipping the hedges with scarlet berries and showing up the medieval ridge-and-furrow in the fields around Ticknall. Once across the old limestone tramway and into the broad acres of Calke Park, it was a wonderful landscape of graceful old oaks and chestnuts, in whose shade fat white sheep grazed the parkland meadows.

Acres of land and quarries of limestone made the Harpur family's fortune, and the park that they laid out around their Palladian house of Calke Abbey in the eighteenth century is a dream-like place in which to wander on an autumn day. We followed the National Forest Way as it wound past enormous gold-crowned oaks, bulbous with age, and the long ponds below the house and stables. When the National Trust acquired the Harpurs' property in 1985 it was as a time capsule, perfectly illustrating the decline of the English country house in the twentieth century. There's no Downton Abbey glamour or polish to Calke Abbey. This is a family house where spending trickled to a stop. Low-wattage bulbs dimly light the mounted heads of favourite cattle, mineral collections and ancient cartoons pasted on to the wallpaper. It's all tremendously subfusc and poignant.

From the great house in its hollow we found our way along a back road to the shores of Staunton Harold reservoir, a lion-shaped sheet of water where hundreds of greylag geese trumpeted to the cloudy heavens. In Calke Abbey's deer enclosure a couple of magnificently antlered fallow bucks were restlessly pawing the ground in anticipation of the rutting season.

We walked out across stubble fields, and in among the iridescent grey ponds, and the steep hummocks and canyons of Ticknall Limeyards, where limeburners once slaved at the kilns for the Harpur-Crewe family. We ducked through a tramway tunnel and came out into fields around Ticknall where medieval peasants ploughed the ridge-and-furrow when monks still sang their vespers at Calke Abbey, long centuries before the Harpurs had been heard of.

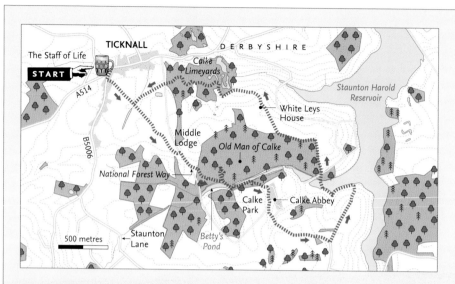

Start & finish Staff of Life pub, Ticknall, Derbyshire DE73 7JH (OS ref SK351238)

Getting there Bus: Service 61, Derby-Swadlincote. Road: Ticknall is on the A514 between Derby and Swadlincote. Staff of Life is on corner of A514 and B5006 roads ('Smisby').

Walk (6 miles, easy, OS Explorer 245): From Staff of Life PH, left along B5006. In 100m, left (fingerpost) across 2 fields (yellow arrows/YA) to cross tramway path (353235). Cross next field; turn right along gravelled cyclepath. In 250m, opposite Middle Lodge, through gate (357232, 'National Trust' sign): emerge from woodland; bear right down left side of driveway. In 200m, pass yellow-topped post/YTP (359229, 'National Forest Way'/NFW); follow path through trees. In 400m, just before Betty's Pond, hairpin back on your left at YTP (363228; yellow, blue, pink arrows) up path and steps. At top, right for 100m to 'Old Man of Calke' oak (363229).

Return to pass east end of Betty's Pond. Through gate; bear left on narrow path beside long pond. In 250m, bear right at gate (365228) up steps. In 100m, hairpin left, through gate and car park to Calke Abbey.

Follow path down right side of stable block (NB shop, restaurant). Through gate (367226); on down drive with wall on left; pass church (369223) and on to road (373223). Left; in 450m, at end of road, ahead through wall gap (375226, 'Maroon Walk', NFW), down to Staunton Harold reservoir. Left along shore; right across weir (372228). Follow path anticlockwise round edge of deer enclosure. In 700m, through gate; ahead past info board (368233); in 50m, right through gate (YA); left over stile.

Half-right across fields past White Leys house. At far side of second field, path enters hedge. Follow path to right; continue with hedge on left. Over stile (YA) and on with hedge on right. In 300m, path bends right into trees (362236). In 200m look left for gate and stile down a slope. Through gate (NT); follow trail (NT markers) through Calke Limeyards. In 400m, through arch; continue along trail to go through Ticknall Tramway Tunnel (356237). In 200m, right through gate (353235); retrace steps to Ticknall.

Lunch/accommodation Staff of Life, Ticknall (01332 862479; thestaffoflife.co.uk) – excellent village pub with rooms

More information Swadlincote TIC (01283 222848), visitengland.com, satmap.com, ramblers.org. uk, Calke Abbey (01332 863822; nationaltrust.org.uk) house open mid Feb-end Oct; park, restaurant, shop open all year

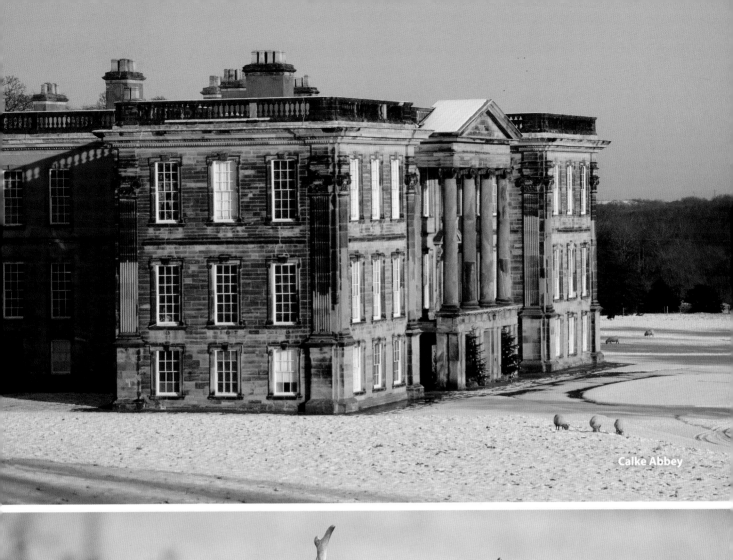

Calke Abbey

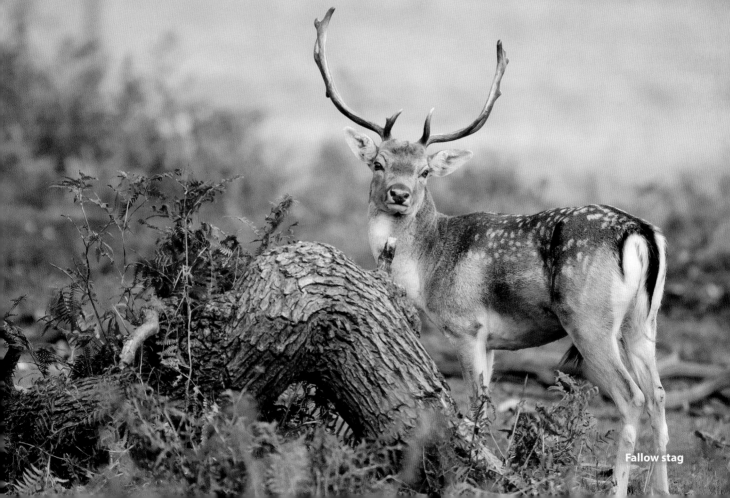

Fallow stag

Castleton and Lose Hill, Peak District
DERBYSHIRE

A milky sky, a cold wind, and the chaffinches going crazy in the trees around Castleton. Maybe it was the promise of a long-delayed spring implicit in the tender leaf buds sprouting at the tip of every twig, or perhaps they were just getting their mating chops together. Whatever about the birds, the nip of the wind and the scud of the morning sky had Jane and me stepping out sharply enough as the church clock chimed half-past eleven.

Castleton lies cradled in a natural amphitheatre of hills whose rocks are seamed with rich deposits of lead. The mineral was mined from a series of caverns along the line of the hills — Peak, Speedwell, Treak Cliff and Blue John itself, its name derived from the beautiful pale purple Blue John stone so popular with jewellery makers and ornamental carvers. This early in the year there were few visitors in the show caves and Blue John shops. Most folk moving in the hills around Castleton were walkers such as ourselves, only too delighted to be stretching the winter slackness away.

Below the rocky gorge of Winnats we looked back across fell sides striped with dark stone walls and dotted with small stone barns, to see the black ruin of Peveril Castle perched like a raven on its crag above the huddled houses of Castleton. In the chill dark mouth of Peak Cavern, below the stronghold, once squatted a whole tribe of rope-spinners, their lungs and joints sacrificed to the dampness they needed to tease the fibres together. Lead miners lived and died in even worse case. What desperate conditions our ancestors put up with, just because they had to.

A bunch of schoolchildren were munching sandwiches at tables outside Treak Cliff Cavern. "We've done our big walk already!" they squeaked proudly. Tired? "Naah! We're going to play football when we get back to the hostel!"

We crossed the bumpy old mine-spoil ground with its velvety nap below the striated cliff of Mam Tor, and went crabwise up the long slope to Hollins Cross on the ridge, where ant-like figures were striding. Up there the wind blew at double strength, smacking and shoving us along the flagged pathway towards the big dark cliff of Back Tor. Here with a KitKat apiece we snuggled down in the lee of a handy peat hag and took in the view north up the long valley of the River Noe. Edale village was a scatter of toy houses far below and the old purgatorial start of the Pennine Way up Grindsbrook Clough cut a deep dark scar into the fellside. A step more along the ridge to the summit point of Lose Hill, and we were looking down on the glorious length of the Castleton valley — our forward view for the homeward path.

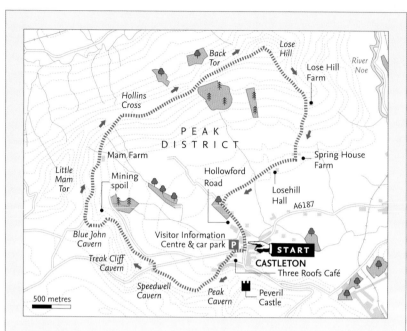

Start & finish Castleton Visitor Information Centre, Castleton S33 8WN (OS ref SK149830)

Getting there Rail: (thetrainline.com; railcard.co.uk) to Hope (2 miles).
Bus: (derbysbus.info/times) from Bakewell, Matlock, Sheffield.
Road: From A57 at Ladybower Reservoir – A6013, A6187.

Walk (5½ miles, moderate grade, OS Explorer OL1): Cross road; up lane by 3 Roofs Café. At road, right (148828); uphill ('Speedwell Cavern'), then field path to cross road at Speedwell Cavern (140827). Left-hand path (yellow arrows) above Treak Cliff Cavern (136831) to Blue John Cavern (132832). Right to road; right to car park; across waste ground under Mam Tor Cliff to Mam Farm (133840); up hillside to Hollins Cross (136845); ridge to Back Tor and Lose Hill (153854). Paved path down to cross stile (155851); bear right for 100m to cross another stile; left along fence, then downhill through trees (157848). In 30m, just before fingerpost, right downhill to bypass Losehill Farm. Lane downhill to Spring House Farm. Just past house, right along lane (156840, 'Castleton' fingerpost) past Losehill Hall. Where drive swings left, keep ahead through wicket gate (152838). Ahead across fields, then along lane to road (148835). Ahead into Castleton.

Lunch Picnic on Back Tor

More information Castleton Visitor Information Centre (01629 816572; peakdistrict.gov.uk), peak-experience.org.uk, ramblers.org.uk, Peak District walking festivals: www.visitpeakdistrict.com/walkingfestivals

Derwent Edge and Ladybower Reservoir
DERBYSHIRE

It was one of those Peak District days you can only dream of: a gauzy blur of sunlight over moors and pastures, enough bite in the wind to fill the blood with oxygen, and the great reservoirs of Ladybower and Derwent winking cheerfully to fishermen and walkers alike. "I've been absolutely longing for this," Jane said, looking up at the Derwent Moors, "a day up somewhere high and wild."

The broad moor paths glittered with mica, their sandy gritstone pebbles rumbling quietly under our boots as we climbed to Whinstone Lee gap and a most stupendous view up Ladybower Reservoir, a long blue tongue caught in the lips of the hills. The wind blew like a mad thing, making the tears fly from our eyes as we followed a dark stone wall north towards the tors of Derwent Edge. Wheel Stones and White Tor, they stood out in drama on the skyline, piled towers of rocks shaped and slit by wind and frost.

We passed a shallow pool full of mating frogs, the males piggyback on the females in a bubble bath of spawn. Climbing across Access Land through trackless heather up to the Edge tested our leg muscles and lungs, but once up there in the wind and sun we grinned like fools at a thirty-mile view streaming away in all directions, a magically spinning topography.

Red grouse whirred like clockwork projectiles across the heather, landing with a plump bounce to give out their manic giggle of a call, followed by a staccato go-back! go-back! go-back! Warning calls, I thought. "No," Jane said, "that's definitely a party animal's shout: Where's-the-action? Where's-it-at?"

A paved path led north up the length of Derwent Edge and we followed it past the outcrop of Dovestone Tor, where weathering had sculpted a pair of monstrous lovers' heads, forever petrified, their protruding lips fated never to touch. Beyond stood the Cakes of Bread, flat folds of stone like giant piles of pancakes. It was quite a wrench to leave these outlandish stones, but a great wide moor was beckoning to the northwest, a dun and black blanket of utterly empty country.

The moor lay spread to the horizon, an invitation to roam and explore. These uplands, with their enormous spaces, promote exhilaration and a sense of one's own insignificance. Heather, grouse, gritstone boulder, snail, pipit, human — each of equal significance under a giant sky.

A clotted mass of brown fur and weather-stained white bones lay beside the path. We puzzled over it until the disparate elements resolved themselves into the corpse of a mountain hare. It was a shock to remember these creatures as we'd last seen them up here, mottled white and brown at the end of the snow season, dashing and leaping over the skyline in full and randy vigour.

Mountain hares are rare in England. In fact, these remote moors of the Dark Peak are the only place they survive — the last remnants of a nineteenth-century craze among landowners for transplanting them from their native Scotland to prettify the grouse moors. What a temptation to anthropomorphize over this sad little rag of skin and pelt in the heather. "But", Jane said, "for every dead hare there's a satisfied fox." That was a true word, as well as a philosophical one.

The moors are the antithesis of virgin country. The hand of Man lies emphatically on them. Through deforestation, sheep grazing, mining and abandonment they have been stripped to the barest of elements — heather, moor grass, rock, water. By rights they should be dismal, frightening places. But for a walker in search of huge horizons, of absolutely nothing between him and his maker, they are sublime. Descending the rough lane to Ladybower Reservoir and the long walk home, I felt like a man in the company of friends.

Start & finish Ladybower Inn, Ladybower Reservoir, Bamford S33 0AX (OS ref SK205865). NB Please ask permission to park, and give the inn your custom.

Getting there Bus Services: 51A, 241, 242 (travelsouthyorkshire.com) from Sheffield, Castleton, Bakewell, Chesterfield. Road: Ladybower Inn is on the A57, at its junction with the A6013 on Ladybower Reservoir.

Walk (9 miles, hard grade, OS Explorer OL1): From Ladybower Inn climb steep path to north-east. At top of incline, don't fork left; keep ahead, to descend almost to A57 at Cutthroat Bridge (213875). Turn left uphill, then left (west) along bridleway for 1 mile to Whinstone Lee gap (198874). Path splits in 5 here; take marked bridleway to right of National Trust 'Whinstone Lee Fields' sign, following wall north along fell side. In ¾ mile pass 'Derwent, Moscar' sign (198884); aim half right uphill across trackless Access Land to White Tor on ridge (198888). Left along ridge track for 1⅓ miles by Dovestone Tor to Bradfield Gate Head. 200m before trig pillar on Back Tor, left at stone marker pillar (198907) on stony path going NW over moor. In 1 mile (185912) join wide grassy track on Green Sitches. Go through ruined wall; in 100m fork left (182911); almost immediately left again, aiming for fingerpost (180905). Follow 'Ladybower' and 'Footpath' fingerposts, with tumbled wall as guide, past plantation (182903) and on for ¾ mile to Lanehead Farm (184892). Descend (yellow arrow) to road at Wellhead (184887). Left on lakeside track for 1⅔ miles to bridge (195865). Left fork uphill between houses becomes hillside track, descending to Ladybower Inn.

Lunch Ladybower Inn (01433 651241; ladybower-inn.co.uk) or picnic on Derwent Edge

More information www.visitpeakdistrict.com/walkingfestivals, ramblers.org.uk

Flash and the Dane Valley

DERBYSHIRE

Where Cheshire, Staffordshire and Derbyshire rub up against one another, it's beautiful walking country. Wild moors, steep little valleys, sparkling rivers, lonely sheep farms and villages; the western edge of the Peak District has them all. We didn't really know the area well, but we didn't need to; a random jab of the thumb on the map alighted on the hilltop settlement of Flash, and we were in for an absolute treat of a walk.

In spite of its racy name, Flash is a modest place. In 1820 Sir George Crewe judged this moorland hamlet "dirty, bearing marks of Poverty, Sloth and Ignorance". Nowadays The New Inn's sign proudly proclaims that it is the "highest village pub in the British Isles, 1518ft". The views from here across the Staffordshire moors are immense, a curve of green meadows rising to sombre uplands of bracken and heather, their skyline broken by jagged, wind-sculpted sandstone tors.

This morning the sky raced blue and silver, trailing thick grey belts of rain. The wind shoved us impatiently away from Flash, scurrying us up and over Wolf Edge with its canted rock outcrop. A dip on a rubbly path through dark heather and we were skirting Knotbury Common, where peewits creaked and tumbled like toy stunting planes. The road to high-perched Blackclough

farm lay gleaming with water and humpy with rain-pearled sheep.

Blue sky now, glints of sun and a big boisterous wind. Huge grassy spoil heaps and an ancient industrial chimney marked the long-defunct quarry and colliery at Danebower. We dropped down the steep, winding valley of the infant River Dane, a lovely green dell with a flagstone path across rushy bogs, the hills tightly enclosing the river, which sparkled and gushed over step-high falls that it had shaped in its sandstone bed. By the twin bridges at Panniers Pool, the Dane dashed in cascades through a miniature gorge, a perfect picnic spot.

We crossed the open moor, its walls as loosely assembled as Connemara stone walls, and came down to Gradbach bridge. A handsome cream-washed house; a Methodist chapel beyond, very plain and dignified; the stone-built bridge over the rushing river. Simple and perfect. Back through pony paddocks and sheep pasture where a Swaledale ram with tremendous curly horns followed us a good step of the way.

Then a last stretch where the wind, now at our backs like a comrade rather than in our faces like a bully, pushed us all the way up the lane to Flash.

Start & finish New Inn, Flash, Staffordshire SK17 0SW (OS ref SK025671)

Getting there Road: At Rose & Crown, Allgreave (on A54 Buxton-Congleton), take side road ('Quarnford') to Flash

Walk (8½ miles, moderate, OS Explorer OL24): With your back to the church, take lane that forks right past New Inn. In 150m, right (fingerpost, yellow arrow/YA) to pass houses; right (YA) up field, aiming for post. Continue over wall stiles (YAs). In ¼ mile, left (024676; YA) past stone outcrop and over Wolf Edge. Aim for fence; follow it down to road (020681). Left; in 100m, right up farm lane. Opposite Knotbury farm, right through gate (017682; fingerpost) on gravel track that bears left over Knotbury Common, down to road (015689). Left over cattle grid; up road past Blackclough farm. Follow track north beside wall for ½ mile to walk through Reeve-Edge and Danebower quarries. Descend to cross stream by stepping stones (014699; YA). Up bank and turn left (fingerpost, 'Dane Valley Way'/DVW). Follow track nearly to road, then slant left downhill by chimney (010700). Path by River Dane (stiles, YAs, DVW) for ¾ mile to the two bridges at Pannier's Pool (009685).

Here DVW crosses bridge; but you keep ahead on right bank of river on permissive path under Three Shires Head. In ⅓ mile ignore YA pointing left; continue uphill on main track to road at Cut-thorn (002681). Forward past house; left over stile ('Access Land'). Follow wall, then path over moor. In ¼ mile, just short of gate in wall ahead, fork left to cross stile (998683). Follow left-hand of two YAs by fence, following track as it curves left across Robin's Clough stream and runs south over moor. In ¾ mile follow track past house and down to road at Hole-edge (001671). Right past Bennettshitch house. In 100m, left off road (fingerpost), steeply down to road by Methodist chapel (001664).

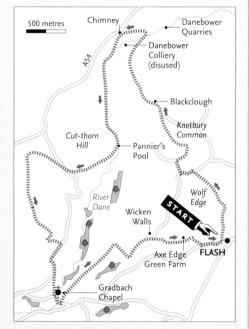

Left across River Dane; round left bend; immediately left (fingerpost) past Dane View House. Through gate (fingerpost) and follow path with wall on left for ¾ mile through 6 walls. Just before corner of 7th wall, by a 'Peak & Northern Footpath Society' notice on pole (009671), turn right downhill. In 200m, left at another PNFS notice ('Flash'); aim across fields to pass Wicken Walls farm (014672). Ahead with wall on left; down across stile; steeply down rocks to river (016672). Cross footbridge ('Flash'); steeply up bank, over stile; bear right up path which curves to left with wall on right (YAs). Follow path to drive of Axe Edge Green farm (020672). Right for 100m; left up to road (021671); left to Flash.

Lunch The New Inn, Flash (01298 22941) – open daily evenings, Fri-Sun lunchtimes and evenings (no food, BYO sandwiches)

More information Staffordshire Moorlands TIC (01538 483741; visitpeakdistrict.com)

Monk's Dale and Chee Dale
DERBYSHIRE

Excited youngsters scoot around the old railway station at Miller's Dale, learning to ride their bikes on a Sunday afternoon in the safe surroundings of the Monsal Trail while their mothers become quietly frantic. "Tom! Tom! Just wait there, please!" "But Mum, I can do it, look…"

The Peak Park has done a wonderful conversion job on the old railway line between Buxton and Bakewell. It's hard to credit that trains once rattled under the sheer limestone cliffs and hanging woods where cyclists, walkers and riders now enjoy themselves. But once we drop down the bank into adjoining Monk's Dale, the leisure crowds melt away and we have the snaking dale and its slippery stone path to ourselves.

Monk's Dale is just one of dozens of narrow clefts in the limestone countryside of Derbyshire's White Peak. You'd never know that the dale was there until you're on its brink.

Down in the depths a long damp wood of ash and oak carries us north, until we turn aside to climb the walled lane of the Pennine Bridleway between weather-twisted thorn trees, up to the roof of Wormhill Hill. Up here the whole feel of the country changes dramatically, from a prospect hemmed in by towering cliffs to huge views over rain-swept countryside squared by stone walls and dotted with sheep.

Over the crest beyond Old Hall Farm, a monstrous limestone quarry is soon hidden by screening trees. Fat white rams crop the pastures with their characteristic, impatient jerks of the head. At Mosley Farm a trio of young sheepdogs rushes out to sniff us over. Then it's down the zigzag path into Chee Dale and another sudden stunning view at the brink of the gorge — sheer pale-grey cliffs thick with jackdaws, dreadnought prows of limestone jutting into the dale where handsome arched viaducts carry the old railway line across the River Wye.

Narrowly avoiding death by a hurtling cyclist (where's your bloody bell, boy?) we turn along the Monsal Trail, through lamp-lit tunnels and over bridges where daredevils abseil into the depths, until the old station at Miller's Dale appears once more around the bend.

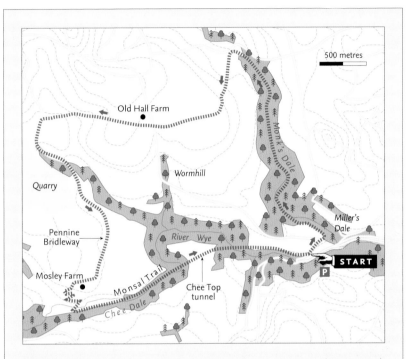

Start & finish Miller's Dale car park, near Tideswell, Derbys SK17 8SN (OS ref SK138733)

Getting there Bus: Service 68 (Buxton-Castleton) to Miller's Dale car park; 65, 66, 193 to Miller's Dale on B6049, just below. Road: A6 (Buxton-Matlock); B6049 to Miller's Dale. Turn up side road ('Wormhill') to car park (moderate charge).

Walk (7½ miles, moderate, OS Explorer OL24): Left up road for about 100m; right over stile (140734; fingerpost). Through gate; left into Monk's Dale. Valley floor path for 1½ miles to road (131753). Left. In 50m, left up steep path; follow 'Pennine Bridleway'/ PBW. At top of rise, right at T-junction (129747) along walled lane to road (122745). Right for 50m; left (PBW) into Old Hall farmyard. Left ('bridleway') through gate. Pass old barn on right; through left-hand of two gates; on with wall on right. Keep ahead through hunting gates for about ⅔ mile to road (110746). Follow PBW for 1¼ miles to Mosley Farm (115730). Through farmyard ('footpath' signs); just beyond, left through gate (PBW); descend into Chee Dale; left, and follow Monsal Trail to Miller's Dale car park. NB Slippery path in Monk's Dale!

Lunch Picnic or the Red Lion, Litton SK17 8QU (01298 871458; theredlionlitton.co.uk)

Accommodation George Hotel, Tideswell SK17 8NU (01298 871382; georgeinn-tideswell.com), Ravenstor Youth Hostel, Miller's Dale SK17 8SS (0845 3719655; yha.org.uk/hostel/ravenstor)

Bradgate Park

LEICESTERSHIRE

Snow had fallen across Leicestershire overnight, and hundreds of people were out walking, sledging and sliding in the open 320 hectares (800 acres) of Bradgate Park beyond the northern boundary of Leicester city.

I followed the path beside the icy pools and spillways of the River Lyn, where a couple were building a seated snowman on a park bench. Above the path sprawled the ruins of the great Tudor mansion of Bradgate House, its red brick towers and chapel set off against the white of the snow. Henry Grey, Duke of Suffolk, built it early in the Tudor dynasty, and here his eldest daughter, Jane, grew up, a distant heir to the throne through her mother.

Poor Jane! Strictly brought up, resentful over the 'pinches, nips and bobs' with which her parents disciplined her, she was shovelled on to the throne when the boy king Edward VI died in July 1553, in an attempt to prevent Edward's Catholic half-sister Mary acceding. The Privy Council deserted her, and within nine days Mary had been proclaimed queen. Jane was clapped into the Tower, and seven months later the 16-year-old was executed by beheading for a treason she had never intended.

Beyond the house young fallow deer were grazing, their spotted coats and white bellies well camouflaged against the russet winter-dry bracken and the snowy parkland. Up by Hallgate Hill Spinney beyond the steel-grey waters of Cropston Reservoir, Scots pines stood tall, their ramrod trunks marbled and scaled like dragon skin.

Up on the crest of a knoll stood Old John Tower, a crenellated turret with a curious arched buttress alongside, making the shape of a giant beer tankard. It was built in 1784 by the Earl of Stamford; legend says he named it and added the 'handle' in memory of an old retainer who had been fond of a pint or ten. A strong northerly blew like a fury up there. I sheltered in the arm of the buttress and savoured the prospect of forty miles of countryside transfigured by the beauty of newly fallen snow. Then I let the gale shove me off the tump, and all the way down to the ruined house in the valley once more.

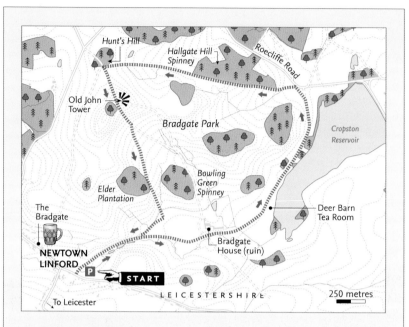

Start & finish Bradgate Park car park, Newtown Linford, Leics LE6 0HB (OS ref SK523098)

Getting there Bus: Service 120, Coalville-Leicester. Road: M1 Jct 22; A50 towards Leicester; follow 'Newtown Linford'. In village, brown signs to Bradgate Park.

Walk (5 miles, easy, OS Explorer 246): From car park, go through kissing gate to right of tall iron gates. Follow tarmac track for 2 miles, past Bradgate House ruin (534102) and Deer Barn Tea Room (539104) to gate into car park and Roecliffe Road (542114). Left along road for 100m; left (footpath fingerpost) up drive, then walled lane beside Hallgate Hill Spinney for 1 mile. Just before wooden hut opposite public toilet at Hunt's Hill, left through kissing gate (525115); climb to Old John Tower (526112). Aim southward between Elder Plantation and Bowling Green Spinney in valley; through gap in wall (530102), right to car park.

Lunch Deer Barn Tea Room, Bradgate Park; The Bradgate PH, Newtown Linford (01530 242239; thebradgate.com)

Accommodation Mercure Grand Hotel, Granby Street, Leicester LE1 6ES (0844 815 9012; mercure.com) – large, comfortable city-centre hotel

More information Leicester TIC (0116 2994444), visitengland.com, satmap.com, ramblers.org.uk, Bradgate Park (0116 2362713; bradgatepark.org)

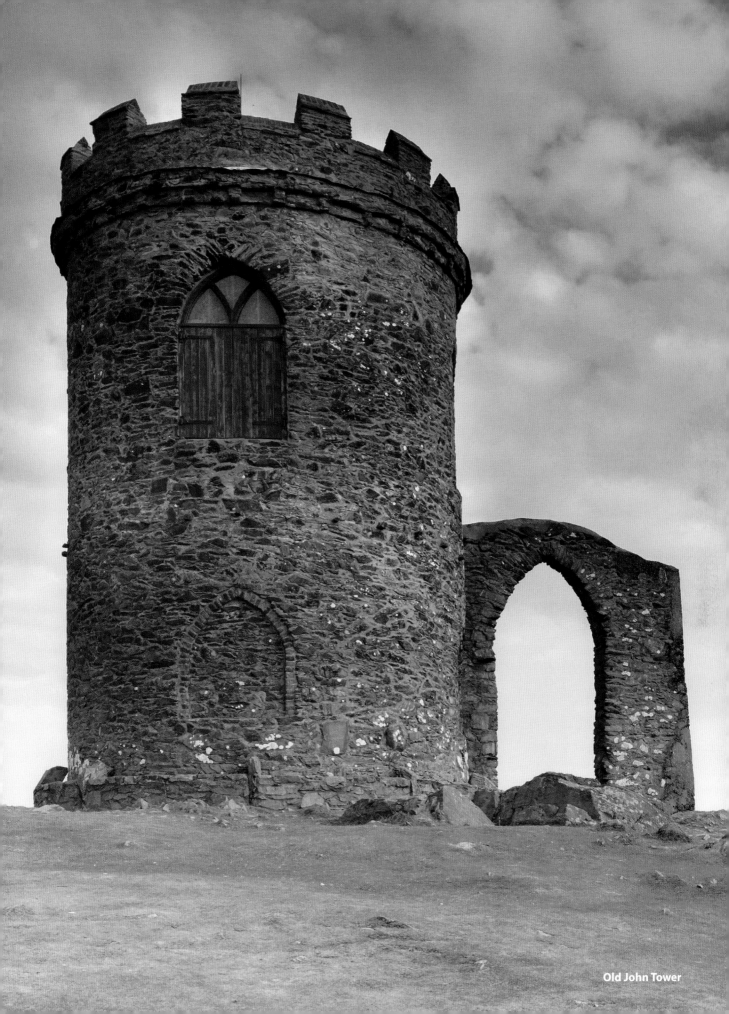

Old John Tower

Hallaton and Medbourne
LEICESTERSHIRE

Hallaton is a beautiful village, all thatched roofs and golden walls, set in the rolling wolds of east Leicestershire. But there's more to it than meets the eye. Setting off from the Bewicke Arms past the Buttercross on a windy spring morning, I glanced up the road to St Michael's Church. In a couple of weeks' time Hallaton's great Easter Monday procession would gather at the church gates for the ceremonial cutting of a giant hare pie, the gentler half of the village's annual ritual, Hare Pie Scramble and Bottle Kicking.

If you don't like rough play, beer drinking and large muddy men, stay away from Hallaton's Hare Pie Bank on Easter Monday afternoon. It's there that the dismembered pie is sent flying into the crowd. After that the Master of the Stowe launches a painted wooden cylinder, or Bottle, into the air. Hundreds of men and one or two women hurl themselves on top of it, and each other, and battle begins. The rough aim (and rough's the word) is for Hallaton to score by getting the 5.5kg (12lb) Bottle — a wooden keg filled with beer — across to its bank of the Medbourne brook through fair means or foul, while the neighbouring villagers of Medbourne do their damnedest to force it across to their side. Best of three Bottles wins. And that's it. Unlimited numbers can take part, with no time limit and no rules.

Picturing the mayhem, I walked fast over fields of fresh spring wheat. From Keythorpe Hall the Midshires Way long-distance path led me south between pastures where the ewes brought their newborn lambs to stare at the stranger. Hunting fences separated the fields, their upper rails smoothed by the friction of passing horse legs — a reminder that I was tramping the 'Galloping Shires'.

Amid the immaculate gardens of Medbourne daffodils were out along the brook. Another Bottle stood above the bar of the Nevill Arms. Which village had gained the victory last Bottle Kicking? "They did," mumbled a tough guy in a T-shirt, "but not next time, mate!" A spring hailstorm marched across the wolds as I walked back to Hallaton by way of Blaston Chapel. Hailstones pattered on my coat. Blackbirds sang. Nature seemed bursting with life; and people, too, were preparing in their own rough-and-tumble way to celebrate health, strength and vigour.

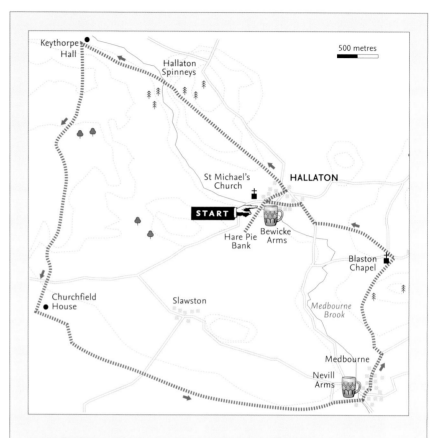

Start & finish Bewicke Arms, Hallaton LE16 8UB (OS ref SP788965)

Getting there Road: A47 Leicester towards Uppingham; minor road East Norton-Hallaton. Park near Bewicke Arms.

Walk (11½ miles, easy grade, OS Explorer 233): From Bewicke Arms take bridleway north-west for 2 miles by Hallaton Spinneys to Keythorpe Lakes Farm (766994); south for 3 miles by Midshires Way, through Cranoe to Churchfield House (760945) then bridleway east for 2¾ miles across Welham Road and Green Lane to Medbourne and Nevill Arms (798929). Along Uppingham Road for ½ mile; then left/north (802938 – 'Blaston, Field Road') for 1 mile to Blaston; left at foot of Horninghold Lane (803956) across fields to Medbourne Road (794961) and right to Hallaton.

Lunch Nevill Arms, Medbourne LE16 8EE (01858 565288; nevillarms.co.uk)

Accommodation Bewicke Arms, Hallaton (01858 555734; thebewicke.com)

More information Leicester TIC (0116 2994444; goleicestershire.com)

Hungarton
LEICESTERSHIRE

Early morning in the Leicestershire wolds, cold and foggy, with a Sunday morning slumber over the golden stone village of Hungarton. Rose Cottage, Pear Tree Cottage, Lilac Cottage: they snoozed, one and all. The cat-like gargoyle on the tower of St John the Baptist's church lifted a silent howl into the mist as I slipped out of the village past grazing horses and over a kale field, my boots already clotted with dark clay soil. Sheep came running up to lick my fingers with their stiff tongues and butt my knees gently with their woolly foreheads.

The fifteenth-century moated manor of Ingarsby Old Hall, its house and barns beautiful in rich gold and pale silver oolitic stone, presides in isolation over a field of hummocks and hollows, seamed across with deep old trackways — all that's left of the deserted village of Ingarsby, the property of the canons of Leicester Abbey in medieval times. In 1469, in the middle of a wool boom, the abbey enclosed and hedged the land for sheep, forcing the crop-growers of Ingarsby to abandon their homes and fields. It was a ghostly place in which to wander, the grassy humps sparkling with dew and buttered with sunlight cutting through the mist.

Ingarsby is one of half a dozen abandoned medieval villages in this rolling corner of Leicestershire. From Ingarsby I followed a slowly plodding horse across fields trenched with the ridge-and-furrow of strip farming, up to Quenby Hall. This magnificent red-brick Jacobean pile, a palace in the wolds, is a more showy order of architecture than the domestic enclave of Old Ingarsby. The village of Quenby lay reduced to a patch of ridge and furrow in the smooth, lawn-like parkland. Beyond, the abandoned settlement of Cold Newton echoed the Ingarsby model, all slopes, humps and slanting house platforms.

I followed the gentle green valley of the Queniborough Brook. A bedlam of cawing from the rookery in Carr Bridge Spinney; seven horses nosing an ancient oak tree at Bell Dip Farm; the handsome pale stone Baggrave Hall on a knoll above its still lake. The park still carried faint ridges of the vanished fields of Baggrave village. There is deep poignancy in such landscapes. But the well-laid hedges around Waterloo Lodge Farm, and the beautifully looked-after sheep in the homeward fields, were proof that not all the old agricultural traditions are gone from this countryside.

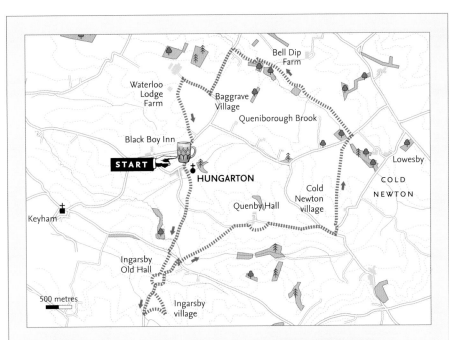

Start & finish Black Boy Inn, Hungarton, Leicestershire LE7 9JR (OS ref SK690075)

Getting there Train: (thetrainline.com; railcard.co.uk) to Leicester (7 miles). Bus: (rutnet.co.uk): Rutland Bus Rural Rider 5, 6, 11 (Saturday and Wednesday) to Black Boy, Hungarton. Road: Hungarton signposted off A47 at Houghton-on-the-Hill, between Leicester and Uppingham.

Walk (8½ miles, moderate, OS Explorer 233): From Black Boy Inn, follow main street south through Hungarton. Left along Church Lane; on along path (fingerpost) to road (691066). Ahead ('Ingarsby') to T-junction (688059). Ahead over fields (fingerposts, stiles, yellow posts/YP). Cross brook (686055); bear right for 50m (yellow arrow/YA), then left (YP, YA) over stile. Follow YA through farmyard to road (686054). Right past Ingarsby Old Hall. In another ¼ mile, just before bridge, left (684050, fingerpost, YP) on path through Ingarsby deserted village. Aim for tree on skyline; left here to road by Old Hall (685053). Forward for ½ mile to cross road (689058, YP); follow bridleway for 1½ miles, up field slopes (YPs), passing right of Quenby Hall and following drive to road (713064). Right; first left ('Lowesby'); fork left past cottage, through gate (YA), down through Cold Newton deserted village. Through gate at bottom of slope (716067); follow YPs north beside stream. In 300m, look for YP and YA on right. Cross stream; in 150m don't recross brook where blue arrow indicates (716072), but keep ahead (YA) on right of stream. In 200m, left across stream (YA); right to road (717077). Right; in 150m, left (YA) up right bank of Queniborough Brook for ¾ mile (YAs, YPs).
At corner of Carr Bridge Spinney (708086), YA points left downhill to cross brook; don't take this! Instead, keep on right side of brook and go ahead through hedge opposite (YP) and on. In ⅓ mile, cross track to Bell Dip Farm (704089). In corner of next field, left over stile (YA) to cross brook. Right along far bank (YA) to road (698091). Left past Baggrave Hall. At top of rise, right (695085; 'bridleway') up Waterloo Lodge Farm drive. Just before farm, left over stile (690087; YP). Aim for far left corner of field; over stile in hedge (YA, YP); aim left of buildings; follow YPs to cross drive (691079). Diagonally left across field to road (692077); right to Black Boy Inn

Lunch Black Boy Inn, Hungarton (0116 2595410; theblackboyhungarton.co.uk)

Accommodation Nevill Arms, Medbourne LE16 8EE (01858 565288; nevillarms.co.uk) – a delightful, friendly village inn.

More information Leicester TIC (0116 2994444; goleicestershire.com), ramblers.org.uk, satmap.com

Fotheringhay and Elton
NORTHAMPTONSHIRE

Elton lies on the borders of Northamptonshire and Cambridgeshire, a postcard picture of an English village, its cottage walls of creamy limestone packed with fossils, sturdy and enduring under heavy brows of thatch. I walked out beside the slow-flowing Nene on a rainy morning, with wrens loud and persistent in the willows. By the river I met a flock of cheerful youngsters on a Duke of Edinburgh Award trudge, wrapped like small parcels against the wind and rain.

Low-rolling countryside like this catches plenty of exhilarating weather — one moment a bright blaze of sunlight bringing skylarks out in full voice over the barley, the next a slash of rain and a burst of wind to silence the birds and turn the field paths sticky. I went on, whistling, towards Nassington's graceful church spire. King Cnut dined and played chess at Nassington in a great wooden hall a thousand years ago. The Time Team discovered remnants of the structure in 2003, under and around the ancient stone-built manor house opposite the church.

History lies thick on this corner of the countryside. It was at Fotheringhay, a couple of miles to the south, that Mary, Queen of Scots met her end in 1587 in the castle by the River Nene. Mired in Catholic plots, real or imaginary, Mary was too much of a threat to her cousin, Queen Elizabeth I, to be permitted to live.

I came into Fotheringhay along the Nene Way, a beautiful pathway across yellow rape fields and between hedges laden with May blossom. The bare castle mound, innocent of all masonry, lay isolated in a field beyond the village's mellow stone houses. I climbed to the top of the mound and found it thick with self-heal and scotch thistles — a poignant flora; for here in the early morning above the sinuating bends of the Nene, the pale and self-controlled Queen of the Scots knelt for the two axe blows that severed her head.

Walking back to Elton across the fields, a flash of red and white stopped me in my tracks. A magnificent red kite hung in the wind on elbow-crooked wings as it searched the barley for prey, utterly indifferent to my existence — a lordly presence above the rain-pearled land.

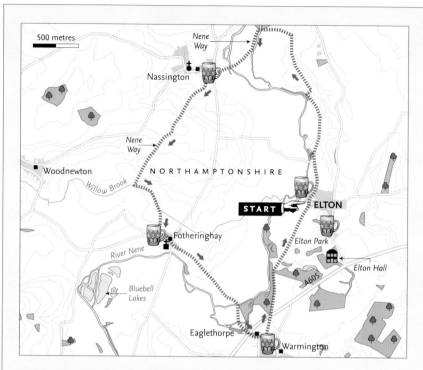

Start & finish Elton, Cambs PE8 6RQ (OS ref TL086940)

Getting there Bus: Service 24 (Oundle-Peterborough). Road: Elton is signed off A605 (Oundle-Peterborough). Park (neatly, please) on village green.

Walk (9 miles, easy, OS Explorer 227): From village green walk north up Duck Street passing Crown Inn on your right (pavement along road). In 450m, fork right on left bend (086945; 'Yarwell Mill, Silson'). Follow this track north for 1½ miles; then left (081968) for 700m to meet Nene Way (076969). Left to meet Fotheringhay Road in Nassington (068961).

Right to pass Black Horse Inn; left along Nassington village street. Opposite church, and just short of Nassington Manor, left (064961, fingerpost) down path and on over field. In 400m, right along Nene Way/NW (065958). Follow NW (black arrow/BLAs) for 4 miles via Model Cottages (052937), Falcon Inn (059933) and castle mound (062930) at Fotheringhay, and mill at Eaglethorpe (074916) to go under A605 and on to road at Eaglethorpe sign (076915). Left round right bend; in 100m, left (fingerpost) through kissing gate/KG; right over stile; left between fence and polytunnels. In 300m, left through KG to cross A605 (077918 – please take care!).

Right; in 50m, left through KG; then another. Right up slope; in 50m, left through KG (079919). Follow path north for 1⅓ miles, past quarry heaps, then across Elton Park (occasional BLA) to road in Elton (085939). Left to reach village centre.

Lunch Black Horse, Nassington PE8 6QU (01780 784835; blackhorsenassington.co.uk), Falcon Inn, Fotheringhay PE8 5HZ (01832 226254; thefalcon-inn.co.uk)

Accommodation Crown Inn, Elton PE8 6RQ (01832 280232; thecrowninn.org)

More information Oundle TIC (01832 274333), visitengland.com, satmap.com, ramblers.org.uk

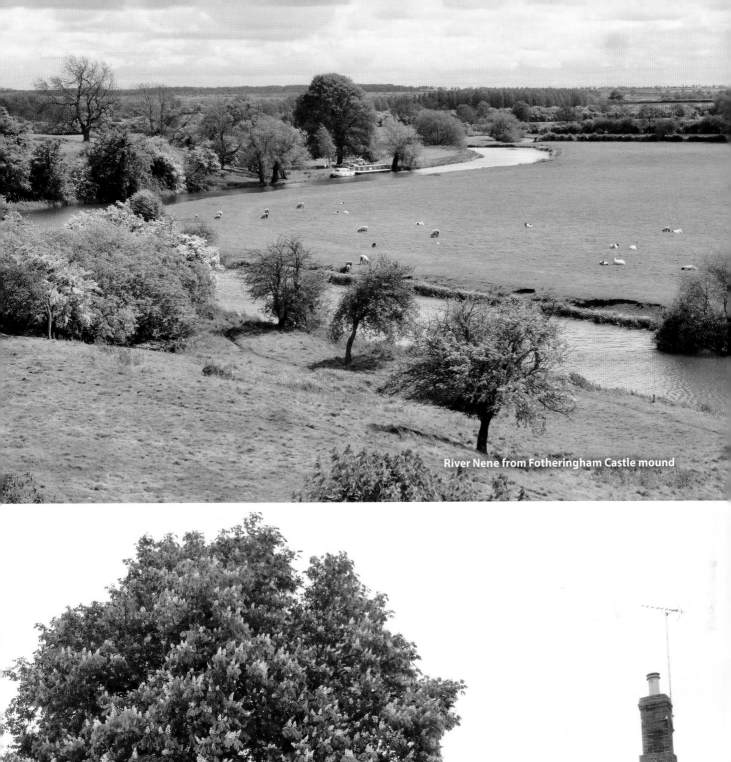

River Nene from Fotheringham Castle mound

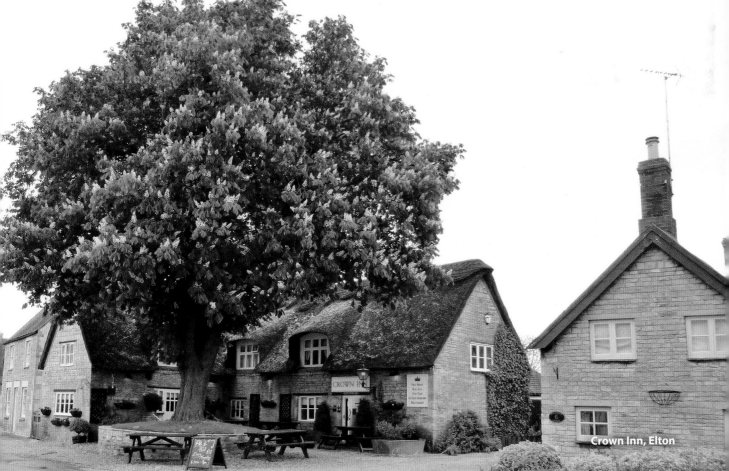

Crown Inn, Elton

Badby, Everdon and Fawsley Park

NORTHAMPTONSHIRE

A late winter sky of chilly blue lay over Northamptonshire, lending a glow to the deep orange ironstone of Badby's houses. Children were rushing to school as we set off out of the village, and we heard their playground squeals as we followed the Nene Way through green fields. Mention of the River Nene usually brings to mind an image of the broad, mud-choked tideway that empties into the Wash, but here, a hundred miles away, the Nene crawls below overshot willows, an infant stream narrow enough to jump across.

Trees shaded the golden houses of Newnham along the village green. The path ran through the churchyard where the arcaded memorial to Eric Newzam Nicholson of the 12th Lancers (died 1917 "in the service of his country") stood wrapped in creepers and ivy tendrils, looking out of its thicket over classic English countryside of sheep pastures corrugated by medieval ploughing, wooded ridges and well laid hedges.

Rooks cawed in the oaks around the farming enclave of Little Everdon with its handsome buttery gold houses. Three fields away, hounds were singing. In the lane we met four-year-old Grace, dolled up in immaculate jodhpurs and just about big enough to stay on board Stumpy, her Shetland pony. Grace was not happy. "She wanted to follow the hounds," her mother explained, "but she couldn't really have kept up." Grace cracked a watery smile as Stumpy bore her away home.

There were big views all round from the summit of Everdon Hill. Storm-battered cedars and wide gleams of water heralded Fawsley Park, the two slender arms of its man-made lake cradling the estate church on a knoll — another dream of settled tranquillity in the heart of England.

The peaceful woods of the Fawsley Estate provided a refuge and haven for Joseph Merrick, the Elephant Man, during the late 1880s, in the last stages of the mysterious affliction that grotesquely distorted his face and body. Travelling from London in a private railway carriage to avoid the public consternation caused by his appearance, Merrick stayed in the gamekeeper's cottage as the guest of Lady Louisa Knightley. Walking back to Badby we pictured the outcast man in these bluebell woods, free to stroll among the trees, pick flowers and feel at ease for the only time in his life.

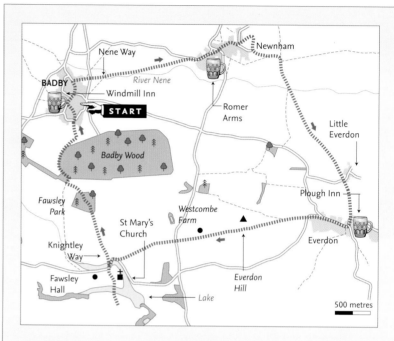

Start & finish Windmill Inn, Badby, Northants NN11 3AN (OS ref SP559589)

Getting there Bus: Service 200 Banbury-Daventry (stagecoachbus.com). Road: M1 Jct 16, A45 towards Daventry, B4037 to Badby.

Walk (7½ miles, easy, OS Explorer 207): From Windmill Inn, left through Badby. Opposite Maltsters Inn, right down Court Yard Lane (560592). Follow well waymarked Nene Way for 3 miles via Newnham to road at Little Everdon (594580). Forward; in 150m Nene Way goes left (595579), but keep ahead on road to Everdon, past church and on. At top of village, left ('Fawsley'). In 100m, right (590576; fingerpost, black arrow/BLA); follow BLAs for 1 mile to cross road near Westcombe Farm (573573). Through gate, up field to gate (570572); follow BLAs to road (566570). Right, round bend to Fawsley Church (565568); return to bend; left on Knightley Way (KW). Follow KW for 1 mile through Fawsley Park and inside west edge of Badby Wood (559580). Leaving wood (559584), aim diagonally right across field; follow KW to Badby Church (560587). Right to Windmill Inn.

Lunch/accommodation Romer Arms, Newnham NN11 3HB (01327 705416; romerarms.co.uk), Plough Inn, Everdon NN11 3BL (01327 361606; theploughinneverdon.com), Windmill Inn, Badby NN11 3AN (01327 311070; windmillinn-badby.com)

More information Daventry TIC (01327 300277), satmap.com, ramblers.org.uk

Clumber Park

NOTTINGHAMSHIRE

"There'd be forty gardeners here back in Victorian times," said the National Trust volunteer, digging the rhododendron verges at Clumber Park, "and not one of them was to be seen by the lords and ladies. They'd hide in the bushes and creep out with the shears — snip, snip! — when the fine folk had gone."

Henry Douglas, 7th Duke of Newcastle-under-Lyme, founded the Chapel of St Mary the Virgin by the lake at his family seat of Clumber in 1889. The church of deep pink sandstone stands as tall and elegant as many a cathedral, full of glorious stained glass by Charles Kempe, delicate wood carving, and enough stone demons to keep the Devil good company.

It was the 2nd Duke, handsome Henry Pelham-Clinton, who poured out his money on landscaping Clumber Park and creating its great serpentine lake in the mid eighteenth-century. We walked the lake as far as the dock where the 4th Duke once kept a miniature frigate, with a sailor employed full-time to tend it. The path looped inland and back to the water, where tufted duck sailed with brilliant white flanks and intense golden eyes. A mother coot scooped seeds from the lake surface to feed her tiny scarlet-faced chick, beak tip to beak tip.

Beyond the lake we turned off across a belt of heather, broom and silver birch — a wild contrast to the neatly contrived artificiality of the landscaped park. A bridleway led through the birch and pine of Hardwick Wood to the outskirts of Hardwick, built as an estate village for the park, its cottages with steep ornamental gables and giant chimney stacks. In the E-shaped yard of the model farm, a peep through a chink in a barn door disclosed a collection of beautiful old agricultural wagons in the gloom.

A long stretch by the southern shore of the lake, looking across to the chapel spire, and we were crossing the Palladian arches of Clumber Bridge. Coot sat tight on their domed nests in the shallows, and a duck of mixed parentage ducked its head ecstatically in the lake, sending showers of diamond droplets flying in all directions.

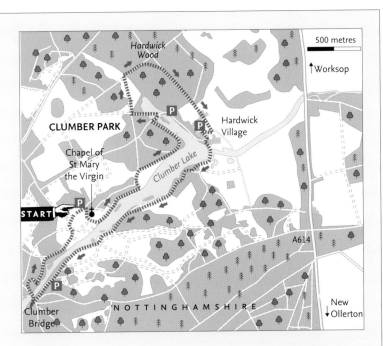

Start & finish Clumber Park main car park, near Worksop, Notts S80 3AZ (OS ref SK625746)

Getting there Road: Clumber Park is signed from B6034, off A616 between Ollerton and Cuckney

Walk (6 miles, easy, OS Explorer 270): From car park follow 'Chapel'. From chapel (627746), left along lakeside path. At Boat House dock, left (632748), heading north close to fence. In 150m, right through stone gateway; pass gate on right; at pair of stone gateposts, right on gravel path. At 'In The Wood' info board (633755) right across neck of lake, then left along causeway road. In 300m, beyond lake, right off road (631756, '16' marker on left side of turning) on gravel path. In 400m, right along road (630759); in 200m, right ('Bridleway') on bridleway. At road (634760), right into and through Hardwick. At T-junction, right (639754); opposite farmyard, left past log barrier and NT 'No Parking' sign ('Route 5'). In 50m, left across water (639752); follow path along south side of Clumber Lake. In 1¼ miles, meet road at a car park (623740); continue along road. In 300m, right across Clumber Bridge (621738). Fork right along road. In 150m, right past log barrier on woodland path. At road with barrier, right to car park.

Lunch Clumber Park tea rooms

Accommodation Forest Lodge Hotel, Edwinstowe, Notts NG21 9QA (01623 824443; forestlodgehotel.co.uk), Clumber Park (01909 544917; nationaltrust.org. uk/clumber-park)

More information experiencenottinghamshire.com, satmap.com, ramblers.org.uk

Creswell Crags and Welbeck Abbey

In the caverns of Creswell Crags they left the bones of arctic hare and reindeer, along with the tools that cut-marked the bones — black and white flint, delicately slivered and still razor sharp. What they felt and dreamt, these ancient ancestors of ours, was expressed in the shapes of antlered stags, bears, bison and long-billed birds that they incised some 13 000 years ago into the cave roof that sheltered them from Ice Age winds and snows.

As Jane and I walked down the leafy tunnel of the Robin Hood Way on a sunny evening, our heads were full of bears and bones. As we strolled the green acres of the Welbeck Estate, though, other wild imaginings took over. The splendidly eccentric 5th Duke of Portland — a kindly man, known as the 'workman's friend' — created employment far and wide in this district by having an extraordinary series of tunnels constructed in the mid-nineteenth century. Two led to a vast equestrian school built by the Duke; another, wide enough for two carriages to pass, ran for well over a mile to the South Lodge.

The Robin Hood Way wound through the cornfields and grasslands of Welbeck Estate. A few feet below our boots ran the South Lodge tunnel, hidden in the ground. 'Tunnel Skylights' the Explorer map said, teasingly. It proved impossible to find them in the grass; but there was a wonderful view of the pepperpot turrets and fantasy towers of Welbeck Abbey, peeping over the trees beyond a lawn where archers were busy at target practice. Give or take a Chelsea tractor or two, it could have been a scene from the life of the celebrated greenwood hoody of nearby Sherwood Forest.

At the gates of Welbeck were the coal mines that made the Dukes of Portland rich and provided the 5th Duke with his expert tunnellers. Now the mines lie abandoned, with their spoil heaps as memorials. Towards sunset Jane and I threaded a tiny sunken lane to the hamlet of Penny Green, then crossed the vast tip of Belph Colliery. Cavemen incising by firelight, the Duke of Portland in his echoing chambers, the miners of Belph: our evening walk had turned out to be all about the underground.

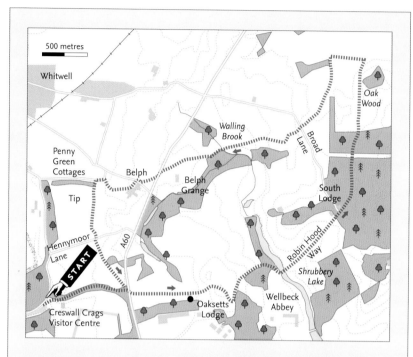

Start & finish Creswell Crags Visitor Centre, Creswell S80 3LH (OS ref SK538744)

Getting there Train (www.thetrainline.com; www.railcard.co.uk) or bus (Stagecoach 77 or First 150) to Creswell (1 mile from Centre). Road: M1 (Jct 30); A616 to Creswell; follow 'Creswell Crags' signs.

Walk (7½ miles, easy grade, OS Explorer 270): From Visitor Centre take the Robin Hood Way/RHW to cross A60 (546744 – take care!). RHW via Oaksetts Lodge (552745) and Shrubbery Lake to South Lodge (568754). Continue north for 1 mile. Past Oak Wood, left (571770) down green lane. At end, left over stile (yellow arrow). Follow yellow posts across brook (567767), then over fields, across Broad Lane (564763), then Walling Brook (555760). Waymark arrows, passing Belph Grange to A60 (548757). Left for 100m; cross (take care!); path to lane. Right for 50m; left (545756 – fingerpost) down field edge. Left across stream; right to road at Penny Green Cottages (543756). Left for 100m; left over stile (fingerpost). Follow path south over tip, then across Hennymoor Lane (542750) to A60 (546745). Right for 100m; right up RHW to Visitor Centre.

Lunch Creswell Crags coffee shop
Creswell Crags Museum, tours etc: 01909 720378; www.creswell-crags.org.uk

More information Worksop TIC (01909 501148); experiencenottinghamshire.com
Pack of eight circular Notts walks – order from Nottingham TIC (0844 4775678)

Sherwood & Budby Forests

NOTTINGHAMSHIRE

The two children came pelting out of the trees near Sherwood Forest Visitor Centre, home-made bows in hand. "Look!" shouted the girl in the green peaked hat, and sent her stick arrow flying across the clearing. "No, look at me!" squealed the little boy behind her. He stopped to bend his bow, the string snapped, and his sister fell around in heartless laughter. Robin Hood would have had something to say to her on the subject of looking after the weak and misfortunate, I'm sure.

Whether bold Robyn Hode, the forest outlaw of the early medieval ballads, really existed or not is open to question. He certainly lives on in the imaginations of dozens of kids in Lincoln green hats who were dashing about and shooting the tree trunks in the outskirts of Sherwood. A fair number of them had made it as far as the Major Oak, a colossal veteran with a golden crown that could well be old enough to have dropped an acorn on Robin's head as he sat at parliament with his Merry Men in its shelter — one of uncountable legends about the greenwood hero.

Once past the Major Oak, the clamour of young voices fell behind. The wide woodland track of Robin Hood Way took us west through the heart of Sherwood Forest, where immensely distorted and swollen old oaks raised arthritic limbs in the shadows. These tremendously characterful trees owe their survival to their imperfections. Had they stood straighter and taller, they would have been cut down for timber long ago. In the carpet of red and gold leaves at their feet grew clusters of fly agaric with white-spotted scarlet caps, fungi so potently psychotropic that even the most reckless outlaw would steer clear of them.

When fugitives from justice such as Robin Hood lived in Sherwood, the Forest was 100 times its current size and covered 150 square miles of country. Nowadays it all fits comfortable into two square miles. Somewhere toward the middle we found the Centre Tree and turned north along a grassy bridleway into Sherwood's northerly neighbour, Budby Forest. Here the trees opened out into a broad heathland of golden bracken and purple heather.

The track swung south again through a stretch of wood pasture grazed by long-horned cattle with chocolate-brown coats and white streaks up their backs, a stylish combination. We stopped to admire their sleepy stolidity, and reckoned that the Merry Men would have been exceptionally pleased to encounter such slow-moving lunches on the hoof. Hollywood has dandified the doings of such as Robyn Hode, but the life of a Sherwood Forest outlaw must have been pretty tough. You had to grab your opportunities when every man's hand was against you.

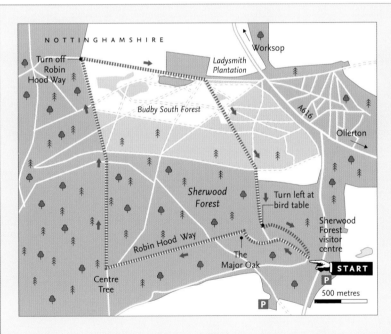

Start & finish Sherwood Forest Visitor Centre, Edwinstowe, Notts NG21 9HN (OS ref SK627677)

Getting there Road: Visitor Centre signed off B6034 just north of Edwinstowe (A6075)

Walk (5 miles, good forest tracks, OS Explorer 149): From Visitor Centre, follow signposted Major Oak walk. Just beyond Major Oak, fork left (not through gate) and follow Robin Hood Way/RHW green arrows. In ¾ mile at Centre Tree, right (607676, 'public bridleway') on RHW for 1¼ miles. At crossing with 7-finger post, right (604695, 'Budby'). In ¾ mile at crossing (616694), right through kissing gate; fork left on grassy bridleway for 1 mile. At bird table on left (622680), left to Visitor Centre.

Lunch/Accommodation Forest Lodge, Edwinstowe NG21 9QA (01623 824443; forestlodgehotel.co.uk) – friendly, comfortable village stopover

More information Sherwood Forest Visitor Centre (01623 823202; nottinghamshire.gov.uk), experiencenottinghamshire.com, satmap.com, ramblers.org.uk

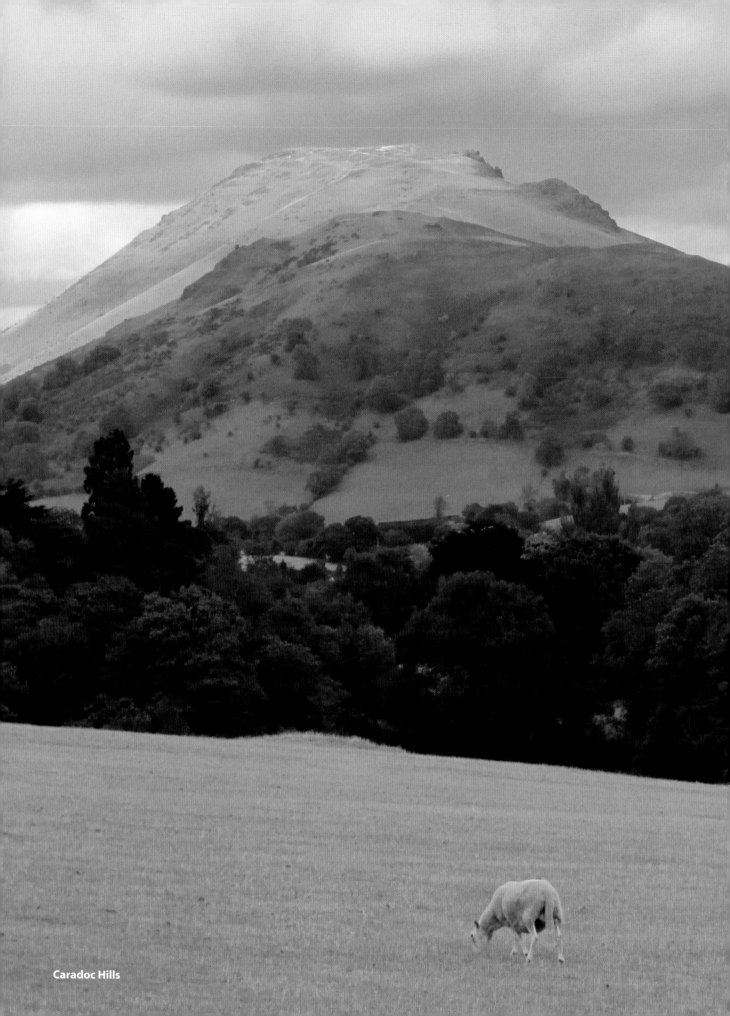

Caradoc Hills

Caradoc and Hope Bowdler

SHROPSHIRE

It's not often that I have the pleasure of a weekend's walking with my London-based daughter, Ruth. We'd fixed our sights on Shropshire and the Caradoc Hills, and today was exactly the kind of bright day we'd been hoping for, with a buffeting wind sending cloud shadows and floods of sunlight chasing across the land.

Climbing the steep slope to Three Fingers Rock from the secret valley under Helmeth Hill was all sweat and effort, but once we'd got up there it was as though we had been lent the keys of Heaven. How else to describe the pure exhilaration of this moment when the view and the wind burst on you in a single instant?

We scrambled up to perch on the rocky crest called the Fingers, and gazed round, gasping.

The ancient volcanic upthrust of the Caradoc Hills, with its naked rock outcrops, stretches north like a recumbent dinosaur, the double-humped back of Caer Caradoc and Little Caradoc dropping to a low neck before rising again northward into the long domed head of The Lawley.

A mile to the west rolls the great rounded whaleback of the Long Mynd, and squeezed between them lies Church Stretton, Shropshire's own alpine village. Up on the breezy spine of the Caradocs you feel you could lob a pebble straight down the chimney of Dudgeley Mill a thousand feet below.

We strode north on the short mossy turf of the ridge. Near the summit of Caer Caradoc the marbled wall of a volcanic dyke merged with the ramparts of an Iron Age hill fort, fabled scene of the last stand of Prince Caradoc, or Caractacus, against the all-conquering Romans.

A last linger over the immense view — the roll of the Long Mynd, the sharp cone of the Wrekin rising out of the Shropshire plains, The Lawley a mere hummock in the foreground — and we were bowling downhill over Little Caradoc. The homeward path was a tangled and squelchy one by lost orchards, abandoned coppice groves and the mossy yard of tumbledown Hill House where abandoned dishes lay among wind-tumbled roof tiles.

A climb over the bracken-smothered common of Hope Bowdler Hill among witchily twisted elder trees, and we descended to Hope Bowdler, with the Shropshire fields and woods spread out for contemplation at our feet.

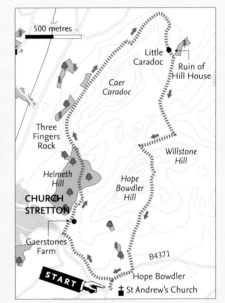

Start & finish St Andrew's Church, Hope Bowdler, near Church Stretton SY6 7EN (OS ref SO476924)

Getting there Train: to Church Stretton – 1½ miles (thetrainline.com; railcard.co.uk). Road: A49 to Church Stretton; B4371 to Hope Bowdler. Park (neatly, please) near church.

Walk (6 miles, hard grade, OS Explorer 217): Right along B4371; in 100m, left up driveway (475925; yellow arrow/YA). In 30m, bear left ('Church Stretton, Gaerstones') on path under trees and through fields for ⅔ mile, to kissing gate on left onto B4371 (468932). Right for 40m; right up farm track ('Hope Bowdler, Gaerstones Farm') past Gaerstones Farm. In ⅓ mile cross stile (472937; blue/orange arrow); in 50m, left over stile (YA), left along fence, then down track through wood for ⅓ mile. At bottom, right along track (471943). In 50m, bear left up green track; immediately sharp left, and straight up steep slope, crossing kissing gate (471944) to reach Three Fingers Rock (471947). On along spine of hills for ⅔ mile to Caer Caradoc summit (478954).

Steeply down, on over Little Caradoc (481960) and down to turn right along fence (483963). In ¼ mile, where it doglegs right and left (484960), cross stile (YA); ahead through bracken, aiming halfway down fence on far side of field, past YA post. Turn left past ruined Hill House (484957) to roadway below. Just before reaching it, turn right past 'footpath' post; on along grass path with hedge on right. In ¼ mile, over stile (484953; YA), and on with fence on left. At cross fence, over stile (483951; YA) and cross track, aiming towards Battle Stones rocky peak ahead. Descend with fence on left; at bottom, cross stile (484948; YA); down through trees and over stream. Up path, then over brackeny wet hillside, aiming for Battle Stones. Cross wired-up stile (485946; YA, 'Access Land'); turn right along grass track, with hedge on right and brackeny Willstone Hill on left. In ¼ mile cross stile (481945); in 200m, sharp left at 'Ride UK1' post, diagonally left up hillside, aiming for rock outcrops. At saddle (482942) don't go left, but keep ahead on grassy bridleway through bracken across Hope Bowdler Hill for 1 mile, down to B4371 in Hope Bowdler (478927). Right to church.

Lunch Royal Oak, Cardington SY6 7JZ (01694 771266; at-the-oak.com)

Accommodation Raven Hotel, Much Wenlock TF13 6EN (01952 727251; ravenhotel.com) – comfortable, friendly hotel in the heart of walking country

More information Shrewsbury TIC (01743 258888; shropshiretourism.co.uk), ramblers.org.uk, satmap.com; Walking with Offa: 12 walks with pubs in Shropshire AONB; Twitter @ShropHillsAONB

Booklets 01588 674095; shropshirewalking.co.uk/walking-with-offa

Offa's Dyke & Kerry Ridgeway

SHROPSHIRE

On a bright winter afternoon we studied the big OS map in the hall of the Castle Hotel at Bishop's Castle. We were looking for a short, sharp walk, something to work off some excellent bangers and mash. Churchtown, a few miles west, looked just the job — the rollercoaster ups and downs of Offa's Dyke for exercise, and the ancient Kerry Ridgeway for the views.

There's no town at Churchtown, just a church and a house or two sunk in a deep valley. We headed north up the knee-cracking rampart of Offa's Dyke, a good stiff puff uphill. When Offa, the eighth-century king of Mercia, ordered the great boundary built between his country and the badlands of the wild Welsh, he meant it to last, and it has — a solid raised bank and attendant ditches, running north and south like a green scar across the face of the Welsh border.

We plunged into the Edenhope Valley, crossed the stream and plodded up another steep stretch of dyke to where the Kerry Ridgeway ran along the crest of the hills. Sunlight and hail showers chased each other, the wind roared in the holly hedges, and the view northwards swung from the distant whaleback peaks of the Berwyns and the green knuckles of the Breidden Hills round to the craggy Stiperstone outcrops of the Long Mynd and the radar globes on Titterstone Clee. A fifty-mile view under sun, storm and a rainbow.

This is tumbled country, overlooked from on high by the Kerry Ridgeway. We followed the former drover's road to the few houses of Pantglas, then headed south across sheep pastures and steeply down to where the neat slate-roofed farm of Lower Dolfawr lay tucked out of sight in its roadless valley.

Across the little rushing stream, up around the silent farmhouse and sheds, and up again along a holloway all but choked with gorse and broom, to the broad pastures on Edenhope Hill. A last battering from the wind, a scud along a rutted trackway, and we were descending into Churchtown down King Offa's mighty landmark and memorial.

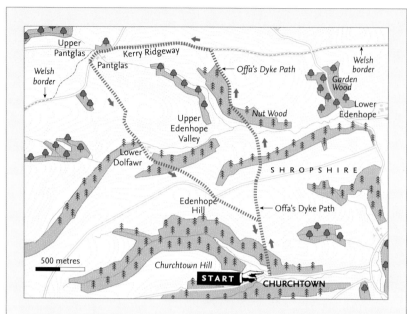

Start & finish St John's Church, Churchtown, near Bishop's Castle, Shropshire SY9 5LZ (OS ref SO264873)

Getting there Road: From A488 Clun road, 3½ miles south of Bishop's Castle, turn right, following 'Bryn', 'Cefn Einion', 'Mainstone' and then 'Churchtown'

Walk (4½ miles, strenuous, OS Explorer 216): From car park, cross road; follow Offa's Dyke Path north for 1½ miles to Kerry Ridgeway/KR (258896).

Left along KR. At Pantglas, fork left (247896, KR); in 150m, just past Upper Pantglas cottage, left (fingerpost) through gate. 100m up track, right over stile (yellow arrow/YA); left along fence; left over stile at far end (248892, YA); right along fence past pond. Through gate at field end (not right over stile); down slope through next gate (249889). Left (YA) downhill; in 300m, hairpin right to bottom of track (251887), to cross river.

30m after crossing river, before farm buildings at Lower Dolfawr, right up bank. Through gate (YA); skirt to left around farm and along conifer hedge. Right up bank, through gate (251885, YA). Up hollow path to gate (YA). On up hollow path among broom and gorse bushes through felled plantation. At top, through gate (255884); keep same line across field to road near pump house on Edenhope Hill (258881). Left; in 50m, at left bend, keep ahead on green trackway for 600m to meet Offa's Dyke (263878). Right to Churchtown.

NB Steep ascents/descents on Offa's Dyke; path through felled plantation above Lower Dolfawr overgrown

Lunch Picnic

Accommodation Castle Hotel, Bishop's Castle, Shropshire SY9 5BN (01588 638403; thecastlehotelbishopscastle.co.uk)

More information Church Stretton TIC (01694 723133), visitengland.com, satmap.com, ramblers.org.uk

Picklescott & The Portway

SHROPSHIRE

It was a cold late winter's afternoon over the Shropshire hills when I set off from the Bottle and Glass at Picklescott; so cold that the cows in their sheds were making the air foggy with their soft silage-sweetened breath. The broad lowlands of the great Shropshire and Cheshire plain stretched out green and sunlit as I climbed the lane from the village. But there was a frosting of white along the upper bulwarks of the Wrekin, fifteen miles off, and when I got out into the high fields I found that the slopes of Cothercott Hill were still blanketed in snow, freshly dinted with bootprints.

I followed the bootmarks southwest up the broad nape of the Long Mynd where it rose from the lowlands. This enormous whaleback upland dominates the north Shropshire landscape from afar, a billowing presence full of hidden valleys known as 'beaches' which only sheep and walkers know.

The sheep were still out in the fields, hardy endurers of the cold, staring incredulously as I trudged by, as though they had never seen a human before. It was wonderfully exhilarating walking, with the Welsh hills in the west white-capped and whirling with localised snowstorms, and a bullying north wind to shove me roughly on and up to the ancient Portway on the crest of Wilderley Hill.

Men have been travelling the ridgeway route known as the Portway for perhaps 5000 years, traversing the length of the Long Mynd by way of this broad green thoroughfare. The Portway was white this afternoon, its black hedges knee-deep in wind-sculpted snow.

My boots creaked and crunched in the drifts as I followed the old way south, with Brueghelian vistas of black-and-white winter landscapes on either hand.

At last my homeward path diverged from the Portway, and I went slipping and sliding down through the fields towards Picklescott with the temperature dropping, the afternoon light draining and the cold nipping at my fingers.

In the firelit bar of the Bottle and Glass, I found a cheerful party of walkers. It was their bootprints I had been treading in all the way round.

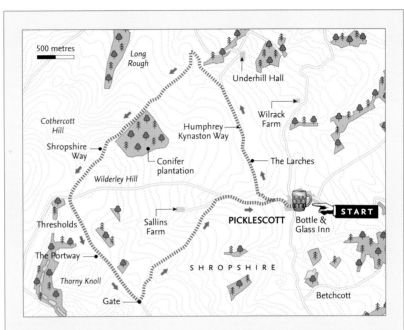

Start & finish Bottle and Glass Inn, Picklescott, near Shrewsbury, Shropshire SY6 6NR (OS ref SO435994)

Getting there Road: M54, A5 to Shrewsbury; A49 towards Leominster; minor road to Picklescott from A49 at Dorrington

Walk (4¾ miles, moderate, OS Explorer 217, 241; download map/guide leaflet at bottleandglass.co.uk): From Bottle and Glass, left to crossroads, right ('Ratlinghope'). In 200m, right (No Through Road, 'Humphrey Kynaston Way'/HKW) up lane. In ¾ mile, left through gate (428005, HKW, 'Walking With Offa'/WWO). Half right across field, through dip to bridleway gate (426007, HKW, WWO). Half right across field, left on Shropshire Way/SW (unmarked here) at hedgebank with thorn trees (426009). Follow SW with hedge on right, up along right side of conifer wood to crest (417000). Aim for another wood ahead; in 400m through gate (414997; SW, WWO), half left to cross road (413995). Follow lane opposite (SW, WWO) for just over ½ mile to gate across lane (420985). Left through another gate (WWO, HKW), follow fence on right to gate (421988, HKW) at corner of wood. Right through gate, follow hedge to next gate (424990), farm drive down to road (428995), right to Picklescott.

Lunch & accommodation Bottle and Glass, Picklescott (01694 751252; bottleandglass.co.uk) – a cosy, lively and friendly place

More information Shrewsbury TIC (01743 258888), visitengland.com, satmap.com, ramblers.org.uk

Kinver Edge
STAFFORDSHIRE

The view from the sandstone peak of Kinver Edge on this brisk, sunny morning was utterly sensational. It was all there, spread at our feet like butter on a roughly crumpled pancake: the Worcestershire plains stretching away south east, the quarried prow of Titterstone Clee and the amorphous lump of Brown Clee standing up far to the west, and, dead in the south, the pale blue humps of the Malvern range floating on a surf of mist.

Eventually we tore ourselves away and went south along the ridge, following the broad, pebbly track of the Staffordshire Way as it wound between the mossy tree trunks with tremendous views over the precipitous drop of Kinver Edge's west flank. A side path brought us down through conifers, and on along a green lane by the balustraded Italianate tower of Blakehall House. Two horses with beautiful feathery legs went snorting impatiently by. "Irish cobs," said their owner. "They don't like to stand still."

Just here, hidden in the ground somewhere under our boots, ran the three-mile complex of Drakelow Tunnels, ghost-haunted by local reputation – the remnants of a Second World War 'shadow factory' built well away from the bombed-out Black Country to make Rover aircraft engines. Climbing back to Kinver Edge we fancied we could hear the hollow boom of the tunnels.

A northward stretch past the well-concealed cave called Nanny's Rock, once home to a 'cunning woman' who could cure your ailments and tell your fortune, and we were dropping down towards the remarkable cliff dwellings of Holy Austin rock houses.

Burrowed into the rich red sandstone, their outer surfaces smoothed into house walls, windows and doors cut out and floors quarry-tiled, the Holy Austin houses have been dwellings since time out of mind. Certainly they have been that way since pre-Reformation days, when resident Augustinian hermits gave them their name. At the turn of the twentieth century Rose and Harry Shaw raised ten children here, mostly boys, so boisterous that Mrs Shaw would banish them outside during the day. J. R. R. Tolkien knew the place and it may have prompted him to imagine the tunnel homes of Hobbiton. The children playing Bilbo Baggins and Smaug the dragon around the rock houses this afternoon certainly seemed to think so.

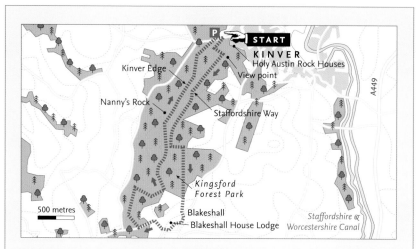

Start & finish National Trust car park on Compton Road, just west of Kinver DY7 6DL approx. (OS ref SO836836)

Getting there Bus: Service 228 (networkwestmidlands.com) Stourbridge-Kinver. Road: Kinver is off A458, three miles west of Stourbridge.

Walk (4½ miles, moderate, OS Explorer 219): From NT car park, cross clearing with oak tree. Uphill to right – not path with red arrow, but with post labelled 'Car Park'. At top of slope (834835), left ('Viewpoint' fingerpost, 'Staffordshire Way'/SW) up path and steps to viewpoint (836834). Right (south) along SW (red and orange waymarks). In ¾ mile, go through barrier (829822). By seat, North Worcs Path/NWP continues ahead (fingerpost); but bear left downhill here (angled yellow arrow/YA). In 150m, right (831822, YA) on track through conifers. In 300m, 5 paths meet (831820) – there's a seat on your right and a post pointing left to a path marked 'Woodpecker, Nuthatch Trails'. Take path immediately to right of this one – i.e. straight ahead. In 200m, through barrier (831818; 'No cycling, no horses'); in 250m, ahead ('Cookley 1') to road in Blakeshall (831813).

Turn right; in 30m, right along green lane with houses on left, to road (829812). Right; in 50m, fork right on sandy track past lodge of Blakeshall House. On along sandy track. In 500m, right through barrier (825812; NWP), along path through conifers. In 500m, in a dip, right through barrier (825817; NWP). At top of slope, left through barrier (828817; YA, NWP, 'Coal Tit Trail'). In 200m, at grassy reservoir (828819), right; in 30m, left (YAs, NWP). In 300m NWP meets SW at fingerpost (829822). Left here down slope; in 50m bear right (north) keeping parallel with SW above and passing Nanny's Rock cave (830826). In another ⅓ mile (832831), ahead over crossing of tracks (not left downhill, or right up steps), up slope ahead, over brow and down to path crossing. Fork left (orange waymark). In 400m fork right ('Rock Houses'/RH post); follow RH to car park. Rock Houses (836836) are just beyond.

NB Excellent directions of a very similar walk at walkingbritain.co.uk

Lunch Bell & Cross pub, Holy Cross, Clent DY9 9QL (01562 730319; bellandcrossclent.co.uk); Holy Austin Rock Houses Tea Rooms: 11am-4pm, Thurs-Sun; Holy Austin Rock Houses (NT): 2pm-4pm, Thurs, Fri; 11am-4pm, Sat, Sun

More information nationaltrust.org.uk/kinver-edge, enjoystaffordshire.com, ramblers.org.uk

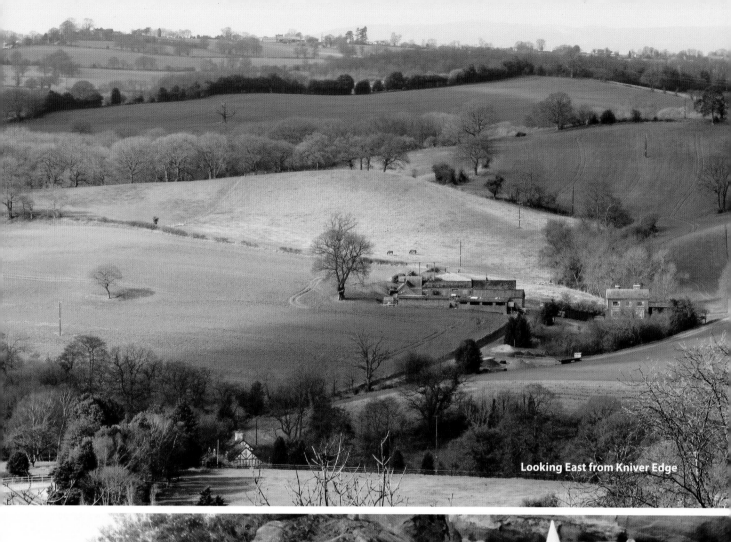

Looking East from Kniver Edge

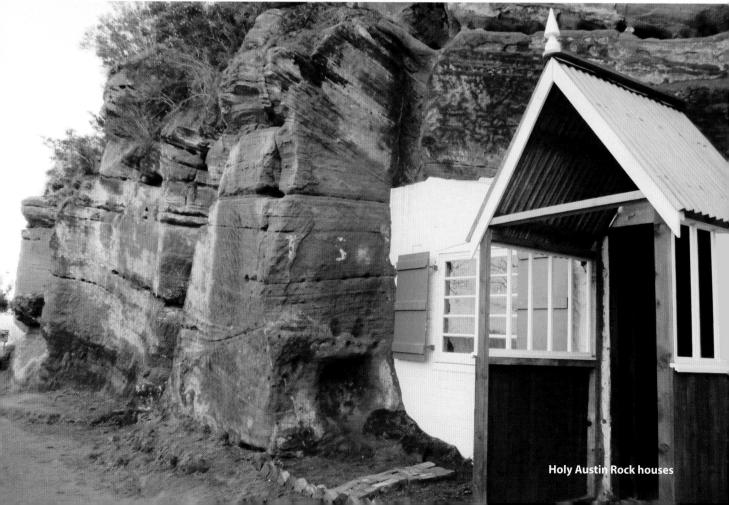

Holy Austin Rock houses

Cannock Chase and the Trent Canals

STAFFORDSHIRE

A table full of cheery Midlands pensioners were getting to work on their ice-cream sundaes as Jane and I left the Barley Mow and set off across Milford Common into the woods of Cannock Chase. Tits and finches whistled in the treetops, and our boots stirred weightless leaves.

The woodland ponds lay cold and black, mirrors of a long winter sent packing by a few days of spring that had brought sticky buds to the ash trees and a gleaming sheen to the leaves of as yet unbroken daffodils.

Cannock Chase, an ancient no man's land of hummocks and hollows, mine heaps and quarry scoops, has been greening over for centuries. This is what the neighbouring Black Country would look like if the Industrial Revolution had not ravaged it. Nowadays the diggings and delvings of the Chase hold a mosaic of spring-fed meres and tussocky bogs, threaded by a maze of paths.

We followed the Heart of England Way, then the Staffordshire Way, up sandy rides flanked by venerable, deeply fissured silver birches, and by bilberry bushes whose green shoots had been nibbled down to the woody root by hungry deer.

The Chase is a place in which to get lost, a wanderer's paradise where a million West Midlanders come for recreation and are never seen again — not by Jane and me today, anyway. We sat on a bilberry bank to admire a haze of purple and gold willow shoots, lingered under the slopes of Harts Hill to hear a wren boldly chittering for a mate, and hopped the stepping stones in the Sher Brook to our hearts' content. Dogs splashed after sticks in the pools of Sherbrook Valley, and over in Abraham's Valley a great spotted woodpecker flashed scarlet, white and black as he gave a hollow oak a battering.

From the green enclosures of Cannock Chase we emerged into the open country through which the River Trent snakes round the northern edge of the Chase. The sky expanded, the ground smoothed out into broad, flat river meadows in which the mansion of Shugborough Hall lay like a giant wedding cake on a croquet lawn.

You can't have a Midland scene without canals, and so it turned out here; the Trent & Mersey to carry us north along its towpath to Haywood Junction, the Staffordshire & Worcestershire to lead us past grebe-haunted reedbeds and fields of spring lambs to the Barley Mow and the borders of Cannock Chase once more.

Start & finish Barley Mow PH, Milford, Stafford ST17 0UW (OS ref SJ973212)

Getting there Train: (thetrainline.com; railcard.co.uk) to Stafford (4 miles). Bus: Arriva 825 (Stafford-Rugeley) to Barley Mow (0871 200 2233; arrivabus.co.uk). Road: on A513, Stafford-Rugeley.

Walk (8½ miles, easy, OS Explorer 244): Cross A513; left along Milford Common. Opposite Shugborough Park gates, 2 paths diverge (975210); take farther one (bridleway fingerpost) past one pond to another (974207). 'Heart of England Way' (fingerposts) to Mere Pits (978201); left ('Trail 5, Punchbowl'); in 250m, right on Staffordshire Way (981202) for 1⅓ miles. At pools (986186) left across Sher Brook; up and over into Abraham's Valley. Left (999186) for 1⅓ miles (blue arrows) to car park. Follow road across A513 (004207) to Navigation Farm bridge (004213). Left along Trent & Mersey Canal to Great Haywood Junction (995229); left along Staffs & Worcs Canal to Tixall Bridge (975216). Left down road to Milford Common and Barley Mow PH.

Lunch Barley Mow PH (01785 665230)

More information Stafford TIC (01785 619619; enjoystaffordshire.com), cannockchasedc.gov.uk/visitors, ramblers.org.uk

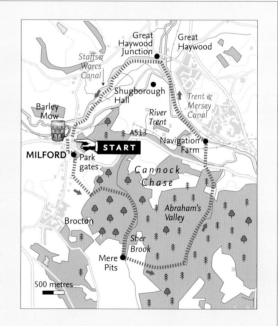

Oakamoor and Churnet Valley

STAFFORDSHIRE

A cool day over Staffordshire, with blue chinks in a milky, almost static sky. Down in the thickly wooded Churnet Valley, Oakamoor was full of vigorous white-maned ramblers greeting each other with the easy familiarity of those who've walked for decades in company: "Now then, Stan! How do, Bet! Got your legs on today, then!"

Oakamoor is a centre for walkers these days, a peaceful little town where the Churnet rushes down a stepped weir and under the bridge. It's hard to picture the industrial past here, the copper and iron foundries, the steam and furnaces, the clangour and fumes. Now the once-blackened houses stand pink-faced among their trees. We climbed the lane out of the village, and were soon high over the cleft of Cotton Dell in quiet woods that might never have echoed to hammer or axe.

At Side Farm a kennel full of foxhounds greeted us the best way they knew how, with fierce howls and contradictorily wagging sterns. Tall foxgloves and flimsy wands of yellow-flowered wall lettuce fringed the lane, which yielded to a side path and a sudden, tremendous view west over ten miles of Staffordshire hills and woods. We passed Rock Cottage,

a handsome pink stone folly with a giant sandstone boulder for an end wall, and came across Whiston golf course to descend to the dark stone house of Whiston.

The flowery old green lane of Ross Road brought us down the valley slopes to find the Staffordshire Way shadowing the extravagant meanders of the River Churnet in the dale bottom. These riverside meadows are a wanderer's dream in late summer: head-high meadowsweet, grasses and Himalayan balsam to walk through, every flower head and grass stalk a holding pen for jewel-coated beetles, snails and spiders, and the chuckle of the river as a lazy guide.

East Wall Farm, handsome in red brick, lay at ease in the roadless valley. Before tackling the woodland paths homeward, we leaned on a gate and savoured the scene: geese and ducks on the pond, bean sticks and a marrow patch in the garden, smoke trickling from the chimney. A tenant of East Wall in Victorian times, returning through a crack in time, would find — give or take a tractor and a plastic tub or two — not too much changed in this view of the farm he knew.

Start & finish Oakamoor car park, Oakamoor, Staffs ST10 3AB approx. (OS ref SK053447)

Getting there Bus: Service 32A Uttoxeter-Stoke (firstgroup.com) Road: A52 Stoke-on-Trent-Ashbourne; B5417 to Oakamoor. Cross bridge, 1st left ('Ramblers Retreat') to car park.

Walk (7½ miles, moderate grade, OS Explorer 259): Recross bridge; left by Cricketer's Arms; right by Lord Nelson PH, up road. In ¼ mile on left bend, ahead past gate (055454; 'Orchard Farm, footpath'). Up steps to left of house; on up walled lane. At gate into wood, right (057457, yellow arrow/YA). In 150m fork left (YA; 'Moorland Walk'/MW). In 350m pass Weaver Walk waymark; go through stone gateway (059460). Ignore left fork; keep ahead over crest and along hillside lane (MW) above Side Farm (059464). At cattle grid enter Access Land (055469); in 100m look out for post on left with 2 YAs pointing ahead. Hairpin back left here up track through bracken; through squeeze stile at top (054470). Ahead by wall for 2 fields; left (YA) along walled path to road (052466). Right past Rock Cottage; left (fingerpost, YA) across field, through wall gap, over stile in wall opposite (049466). Keep ahead with trees on left. On through fields with wall on right; cross Whiston golf course to road (041471). Left to A52 at (037472).Left up road for 200m; left down Ross Road (036471), then Ross Lane, for ¾ mile, past Eavesford Farm, to join Churnet Way/CW (031460). Cross railway (030459) and River Churnet. Ignore right fork in meadow beyond. Keep ahead across stream; left along Staffordshire Way (SW/CW). In ¾ mile at East Wall Farm, aim right of buildings; cross stile (035448; SW/CW) and go uphill with fence on left. Follow farm drive; in 200m, fork right (037447; CW/SW) through Hawksmoor Wood to B5417 (039442). Left for 150m, right by bus shelter (CW/SW); through Sutton's Wood to road in Stoney Dale (045440). Right (SW) for 200m; at summit of road, left up lane (SW). In ½ mile pass huge sycamore; in another 50m, left over cattle grid along drive (052438). In 10m, left along walled lane, through gate into wood (SW). Keep ahead, steeply down Moss's Banks. Cross 2 forest tracks in quick succession, and keep ahead on steep path down to lane (053441). Left to road (053442); right to car park.

Lunch Picnic

More information Stoke-on-Trent TIC (01782 236000; visitstoke.co.uk), churnet.co.uk, enjoystaffordshire.com, satmap.com, ramblers.org.uk

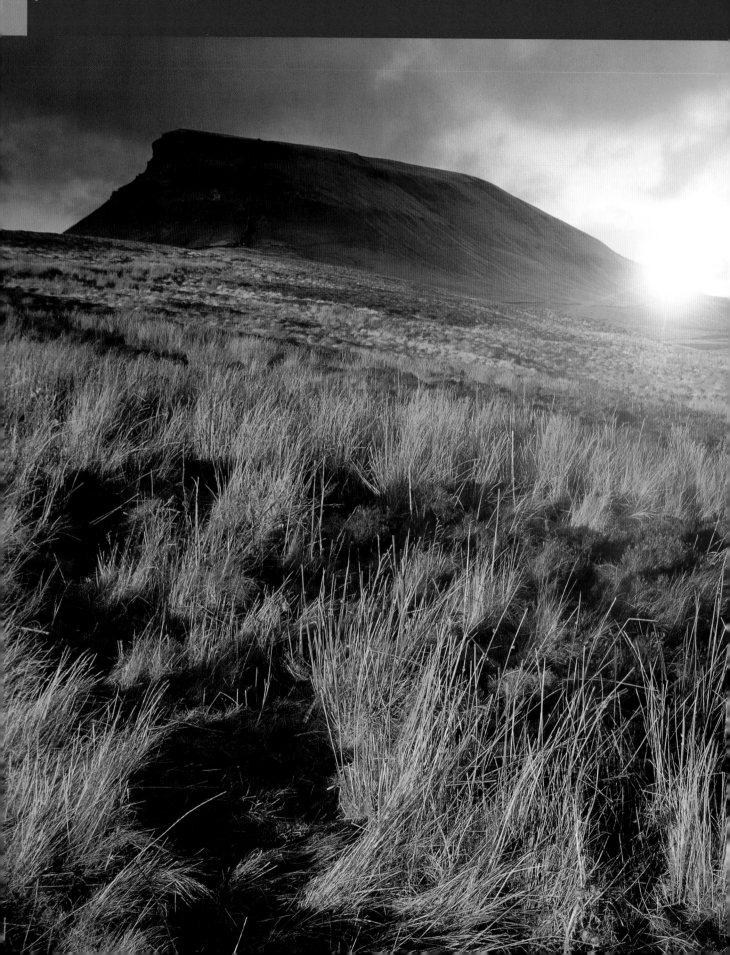

Yorkshire

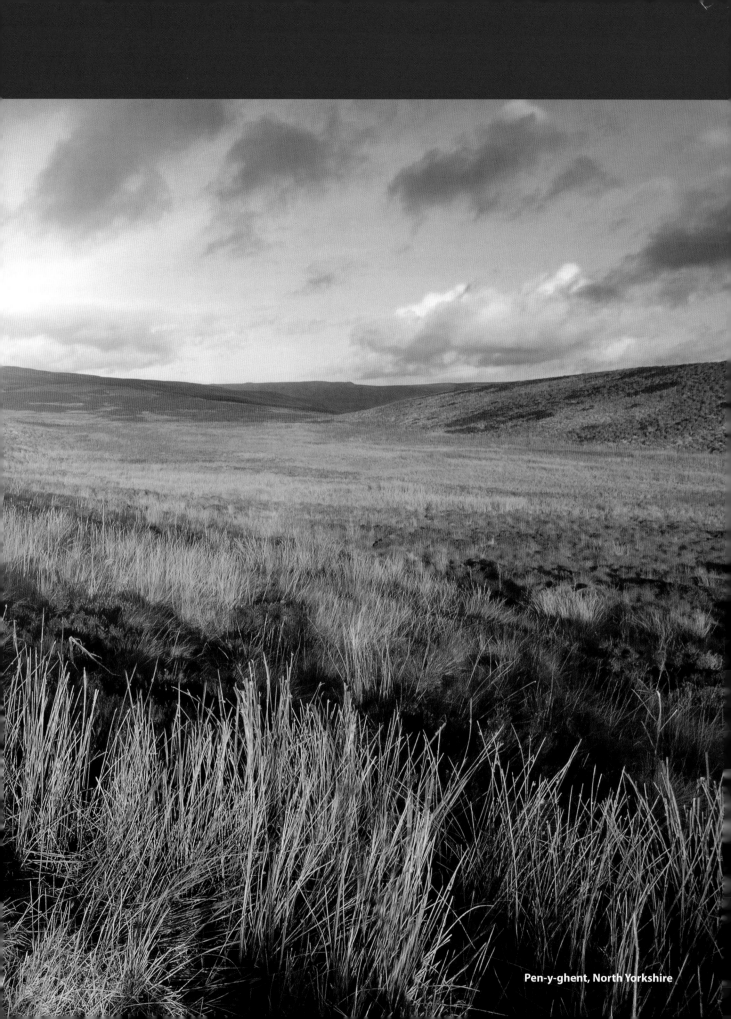

Pen-y-ghent, North Yorkshire

Clapham & Ingleborough Cave
NORTH YORKSHIRE

Reginald Farrer of Ingleborough Hall, the intrepid and dedicated Victorian plantsman, travelled all over the wild lands of China, Tibet and Upper Burma to collect seeds for the out-of-doors plant collection he established around his family home in the North Yorkshire village of Clapham. Some thought him mad, especially when he took to firing seed out of a shotgun to scatter it evenly along the crevices of Clapdale. It was a pleasing picture to have in the mind on our way up the cobbled lane that travels in tunnels and artificial stone-walled canyons through the grounds of Ingleborough Hall and on up to the limestone fells beyond.

Beyond the sullen grey cliffs of Robin Proctor's Scar we crossed the sloping fields and found the path up to Norber, a slanted upland where retreating glaciers dumped hundreds of sandstone erratics — square boulders as big as tanks — on the limestone pavements 10 000 years ago. One boulder had been left delicately perched on limestone blocks like a barn on staddle-stones.

Pen-y-ghent's lion face poked out of a welter of dark grey cloud ahead as we made for the lane up Crummack Dale in a spatter of rain. A heavily muscled bull lay beside the lane but, although he cocked his ears towards us, he didn't deign to turn his head. A grass track brought us up to the ridge at Long Scar, where the tremendous view encompassed Pen-y-ghent, the elongated purple back of Ingleborough ahead in the north, and away to the south the bulk of what we guessed to be Pendle Hill far off in Lancashire.

On the way down to Clapham we stopped off for a tour of Ingleborough Cave. Down in the depths our young guide Sam blew out his candle and plunged us into the profoundest blackness. Candles were all those first explorers had to light their way in 1837 when they first ventured into this now famous tangle of caves and cramped passages. Brave as lions, or mad as hatters? Like Reginald Farrer, probably — a good stiff helping of both.

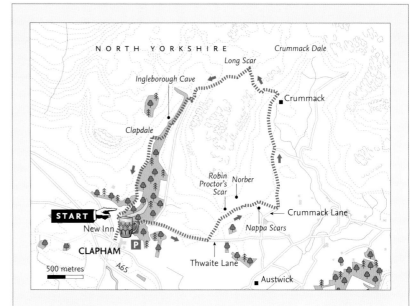

Start & finish National Park car park, Church Avenue, Clapham, N. Yorks LA2 8EF (OS ref SD745692); pay and display

Getting there Bus: Malham Tarn shuttle service 881 (Sun, BH Mon, May-Sept). Road: Clapham is signed off A65 Ingleton-Settle road.

Walk (7½ miles, moderate, OS Explorer OL2): From car park, right up Church Lane; fork right by church, up cobbled lane. Follow 'Austwick' for 1 mile along Thwaite Lane. Where field wall angles in on left, turn left over stile (760692, 'Norber'). Half right to far wall corner (763695, stile); on to fingerpost (766697); left ('Norber') to plateau and erratic boulders (766700). Back to fingerpost; left, downhill to cross wall (768698); under Nappa Scars to Crummack Lane (772697). Left for 1¼ miles to Crummack. Pass 'Bridleway' fingerpost; at next fingerpost (772715, 'Sulber') left uphill. Follow grassy track; in 300m, bear right below scar; at crest (768719), left on track for 900m past cairn, downhill to gate into lane (758716). Left down lane; in 250m, right over wall; down to lane in valley; left past Ingleborough Cave Centre (754711). In 250m, right (blue arrow) through gate, up to Clapdale farm (751708); left on track to Clapham.

Lunch Reading Room Café, Clapham (01524 251144; claphambunk.com)

Accommodation New Inn, Clapham, N. Yorks LA2 8HH (01524 251203; newinn-clapham.co.uk) – stylishly refurbished; friendly and comfortable

More information Ingleborough Cave (01524 251242; ingleboroughcave.co.uk), Ingleton TIC (01524 241049; www.ingleton.co.uk/inginfo.asp), yorkshire.com, visitengland.com, satmap.com, ramblers.org.uk

Farndale and Rudland Rigg

NORTH YORKSHIRE

Brilliant sun on the high ridges of the North York Moors, a flush of purple heather up the heights of Farndale, and Low Mill's handful of houses slumbering in a Saturday morning hush.

The River Dove, shallow and copper-brown, went sparkling in a tunnel of alders through the meadows I followed upstream to High Mill. These fields, cropped close and green by blackface sheep, will be a riot of wild daffodils in spring.

'You are only three fields away from the Daffy Caffy,' said the notice on a gate. 'Can you smell the bacon? We have the kettle on.' A tiny curly terrier stood sentinel on the Daffy's doorstop. He was an interested spectator as I made short work of the world's best bacon sandwich and a cup of tea. Care to lick my greasy fingers? Well, he signalled, don't mind if I do.

I climbed grassy fields full of eyebright, then on up through black hummocks of coalmining spoil. It's always an astonishment to remember what smoky and clangorous hives of industry these quiet dales once were, their lead, iron and coal prised out and processed by men who lived as a tribe apart.

Up on the moor's rolling back, distant walkers appeared to be wading shin-deep in a purple sea. "Never seen the heather bloom like this," said a man in very short shorts. "Every year it's like a miracle, and this one in particular."

The old moor track called Westside Road rides the spine of the long north-south upland of Rudland Rigg, a broad stony way just made for a good step-out. I rattled along, watching slate-grey clouds rolling on the wide horizons, blotting up the colours from the adjacent dales and stretching their shadow west across the Vale of York.

Bright sunshine had cracked out of hiding and bathed the moors in rich gold and purple by the time I had come down off Rudland Rigg into the fields of Lower Farndale. Black thunderflies reeled above the grass, amorously clasped two by two to claim membership of the Yard High Club, and the silly sheep stopped and stared like shocked spinsters, as they've always done and will do until Farndale is under the sea once more.

Start & finish Low Mill car park, near Kirkbymoorside, North Yorks YO62 7UY (OS ref SE673952); pay and display

Getting there Road: From Kirkbymoorside (on A170 Pickering-Helmsley), follow 'Gillamoor' and 'Farndale'. In Gillamoor, right at T-junction; in 1 mile, left ('Farndale') to Low Mill

Walk (9½ miles, moderate, OS Explorer OL26) Take footpath next to car park ('High Mill'). Cross River Dove, left along river (yellow arrows/YAs) to High Mill and Daffy Caffy (668971). Up lane to Church Houses and Feversham Arms PH; or to continue walk, left over stile (YA). Along river for 100m, left over footbridge, right up 2 fields ('Low Bank') to road (664970). Right; ahead at junction ('Dale End'). Just past Monket House, left through gate (660972; 'Bransdale'), up track through spoil heaps. Ignore left fork (655971); continue for nearly 1 mile to crossing of wide tracks with motorcycle prohibition notices (641974). Left (south) along Rudland Rigg for 3¼ miles to road (659927).
Ahead across cattle grid; in ¼ mile on right bend, left (662920; 'footpath') through wood to gate (665923, YA). Aim ahead to angle of tumbledown walls; right along path, which bends left to cross Harland Beck (667925). Through gateway; bear left along wall parallel to beck. At gate (666927), don't go through; bear right up wall and through fence gap (YA). Follow wall up through gate, on up through another gate (YA) to stony lane (668930). Left to Harland Farm. By farm gate, right up wall through successive gates (YAs). Left over ladder stile (668933), right beside wall (YA). At wall end, forward through heather (aim for post); continue along clear path, bending left to run parallel with Farndale. In ¾ mile, pass YA on pole (667944); in 150m pass tall cairn; then fork right downhill. At bottom of slope, right through gate (666946, YA). Down through wood, then gate (667947, YA). Down through next gate to cross road (668948). Down 3 fields (fingerpost) to road; forward to Low Mill.

Lunch Daffy Caffy, High Mill (01751 430363; 9am-5pm, Fri-Sun, May-September; daily, March-April) or Feversham Arms PH, Church Houses (01751 433206; fevershamarmsinn.co.uk)

Accommodation King's Head, Kirkbymoorside, North Yorks YO62 6AT (01751 431340; thekingsheadkirkbymoorside.co.uk) – very friendly and helpful

More information Pickering TIC (01751 473791), discovernorthyorkshire.co.uk, ramblers.org.uk, satmap.com

Hawnby and Bilsdale

NORTH YORKSHIRE

In this southern corner of the North York Moors, every heathery summit seems only to lead you to another higher crest, each wooded dale bottom to precipitate you into one even lower. Within five minutes of setting out from the Inn at Hawnby I looked up to find the hamlet high above me; ten minutes later Hawnby had been swallowed by the landscape, not to be seen again till the last few steps of this beautiful walk.

The land hereabouts is hard on its farmers. Little and Low Banniscue have vanished as though they had never existed. At Crow Nest I found a roofless ruin in a zigzag tumble of yard walls. A boulder-strewn moor loud with the complaint of curlews and lapwings led down into the in-bye fields of Bilsdale. Across the dale fat lambs cried in the fields around Carr Cote, where they were gathering the sheep for shearing. "Good weather for it," said the farmer at Helm House as he hauled hay bales from the field to be sealed for silage in a plastic skin. A golden labrador at Fangdale Beck thought so, too — he cavorted under his master's hosepipe, shaking the water into rainbows and barking like a maniac.

I climbed up through bracken, then away across the purpling moor where red grouse chicks scuttered off, their mothers whirring low over the heather as they shrieked: "Back! Back! Back!" Up on the crest a broad yellow sand road led south past the lonely moorland farm of Low Thwaites towards Easterside Hill and Hawnby Hill.

Up on the thyme-scented summit of Hawnby Hill I sat by the conical cairn, looking down the precipitous slopes into Ryedale and picturing the Hawnby Dreamers. Three modest local men, Chapman, Cornforth and Hugill by name, fell asleep upon these moors one day in the 1740s, and dreamed identical dreams of repentance and salvation. They sacrificed their reputations, their livelihoods and the tied cottages they lived in to set out immediately and walk 100 miles to hear John Wesley preach. To borrow Thomas Hughes's words from *Tom Brown's Schooldays*, Hawnby Hill is "altogether a place to open a man's soul, and make him prophesy".

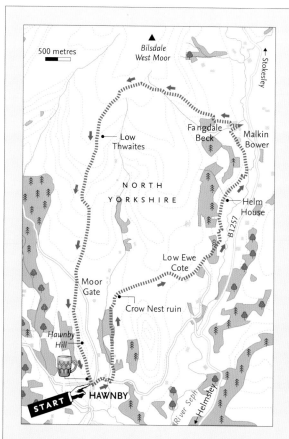

Start & finish Inn at Hawnby, North Yorkshire YO62 5QS (OS ref SE542898)

Getting there Road: Hawnby is signposted from Osmotherley (A19/A172, Thirsk to Middlesbrough)

Walk (10 miles, moderate, OS Explorer OL26): Follow 'Osmotherley', then 'Laskill' on tarmac to cross stream. In 100m, left/north (547899) on bridleway (occasional blue arrows/BA) for 1 mile to Crow Nest ruin (547914). Track east-north-east for 1 mile across moor to Low Ewe Cote (561918). Green lanes north-east, then north up Bilsdale for 2¼ miles via Helm House (569934) and Malkin Bower (570944) to Fangdale Beck. Left by Chapel Garth (570946) across footbridge; left through garden gate, right between buildings, into lane rising west uphill through gates (BAs) for ⅓ mile to final gate (563949). Trackless path west-north-west (aim slightly left of mast) for ¾ mile to line of grouse butts (552954). Left along them, then continue same direction to sandy moor road (548954). Left; 200m past Low Thwaites, fork right (543942); track south for 1½ miles to Moor Gate (540917); ahead up path to top of Hawnby Hill (540910). South, and descend to Inn at Hawnby.

Lunch Picnic

Accommodation Inn at Hawnby (01439 798202, innathawnby.co.uk) – classy and characterful

More information Thirsk TIC (01845 522755; www.visitthirsk.org.uk), visitengland.com, satmap.com, ramblers.org.uk

Muker and Keld, Swaledale

NORTH YORKSHIRE

A brisk west wind, a chink of sun in the Swaledale clouds after days of rain over North Yorkshire, and the clatter of walking sticks on the road outside Muker Teashop where Jane and I were finishing our Yorkshire rarebits. Out in the village street a hairy-kneed rambler of the old school frowned at our Satmap device. "Get you lost, will that," was his pithy judgement.

A walled lane led up the sloping fellsides behind the village, the grazing fields dotted with the square-built farmhouses and small stone barns so characteristic of the Yorkshire Dales. Sun splashes and cloud shadows chased across them.

It was a joy to be alive and walking up there in the face of the wind, climbing the old stony road to the crest of Kisdon Hill and following it down to Skeb Skeugh ford and the huddle of grey stone houses at Keld, the Norsemen's well-named 'place by the river'. On the outskirts of Keld,

Jane and I joined the glorious and notorious long-distance treadmill of the Pennine Way, but only to cross the rain-engorged Swale. East Gill Force jetted down its black rock staircase and into the river with a muted rumble and hiss, and here we swung away from the Pennine Way and made for Crackpot Hall's dolorous ruins.

"Don't miss Swinner Gill," we'd been advised by Nick and Alison Turner, the owners of Muker Teashop. "It's really something special." It was lead-mining subsidence that put an end to Crackpot Hall, and the ruins and spoil heaps of the Dales' great lost industry lie all around — stone-arched mine levels, a tumbledown smelt mill deep in the cleft of Swinner Gill, and the precarious trods or tracks of the lead miners. All lay silent this afternoon, with the dale sides rising sharply to the sky, the beck sluicing below, and a breathtakingly beautiful prospect opening southward towards Muker down the sunlit floor of Swaledale.

Start & finish Muker Teashop, Muker, Richmond, N. Yorks DL11 6QG (OS ref SO910979)

Getting there Bus: (getdown.org.uk) service 30 (Richmond-Muker-Keld, Mon-Sat) or 830/832 (Richmond-Muker-Hawes, Sun & BH). Road: A1; A6108 or A6136 to Richmond; A6108, B6270 to Muker

Walk (6½ miles, moderate/hard grade, OS Explorer OL30): Leaving Muker Teashop, left; left again up lane by Literary Institute. Forward; right by Grange Farm, left up its side ('footpath to Keld'). Follow lane; then 'Bridleway Keld' (909982) up walled lane for ½ mile. Pennine Way/PW forks right, but continue for 30m, then bear right uphill by wall (903986; 'Keld 2 miles'). At top of slope follow wall to left; continue climbing to open hilltop. Follow green road (fingerposts) over hill, down to ford beck, right along road. On left bend, right (893009; 'Keld only') into Keld.

Right down gravelled lane (893012; 'footpath to Muker'). In 300m, left downhill ('PW'). To return direct to Muker, turn right and follow PW. To continue walk, cross River Swale footbridge; left to reach top of waterfall. Where PW forks left, turn right along track (896011; 'bridleway' fingerpost). In ½ mile pass stone barn; in another 100m pass engine and steering wheel sunk in ground (!). In 50m fork left (904009) on stony track to Crackpot Hall. Aim for house above; then follow path (progressively narrower) into Swinner Gill. Where path forks opposite ruined lead mine buildings, take lower fork to fingerpost; turn back sharp right (911012; 'Muker') down narrow path to ford beck (911008; NB – if beck too swollen to ford safely, retrace steps to Crackpot Hall and follow main track south towards Muker).

Continue along path for ¼ mile to join main track; continue down Swaledale on left (east) bank of river for 1 mile. Cross Swale by footbridge (910986); right (yellow arrow) for 50m, then left along meadow path for ½ mile back to Muker.

Conditions Narrow, slippery paths in Swinner Gill. Beck could be impassable after heavy rain.

Lunch Farmer's Arms, Muker DL11 6QG (01748 886297; farmersarmsmuker.co.uk)

Tea & accommodation Muker Teashop (01748 886409; www.mukervillage.co.uk) – really warm and welcoming

More information Richmond TIC (01748 828742), www.yorkshire.com, www.ramblers.org.uk

Pateley Bridge
NORTH YORKSHIRE

Business-like bunches of walkers were assembling in Pateley Bridge car park in a clatter of boots and sticks. Everyone wants to grab hold of a day such as this, with enormous white clouds slowly drifting in a blue sky across Nidderdale. Yet this steep, rolling country has a mysterious way of swallowing its walkers, and we scarcely saw another soul all day.

The spring wind came down from the moors, full of the baby cries of newborn lambs and cold enough to prickle the nose. We followed the waymarked Nidderdale Way west along a narrow farm road between carefully maintained stone walls that sparkled with minute, intense winks of sunlight. Farms lay along the higher contours of the green inbye land. The steep fields were striped with walls that wriggled like snakes up the undulations of the daleside and vanished over the top into sombre coloured moorland, where heather burning operations were sending up curling towers of oily smoke.

We sat to eat our snack on a fallen stone lintel opposite the bankside cottage of Throstle Nest. A gang of ewes still heavy with unborn lambs came up bleating for crisps. They soon settled to cropping the grass with short, decisive jerks of their teeth — gentle company, and a peaceful sound to picnic by.

We followed the lane down to Ashfold Side Beck through a tremendous slump of old lead-mine workings. Below the ashen tips a cluster of tumbledown buildings and a great rusty cogwheel and shaft showed where nineteenth-century miners had processed the precious and poisonous ore. Cornishmen, Irishmen, Scots and Welsh laboured here for the Prosperous and Providence Lead Mining Company, working the Wonderful and Perseverance Levels — names that say everything about the triumph of hope over experience.

Back along the beck and up over the fields to Stripe Head Farm, where the farmer in cap and gumboots was helping a ewe newly delivered of twins. "I'm out at 11pm to check on them this time of year," he said, "and out at 5.30am too." The newborn lambs staggered about and cried until they found what they were looking for under their mother's shaggy pelmet of wool stained dark by the winter. Then you couldn't hear a sound out of them.

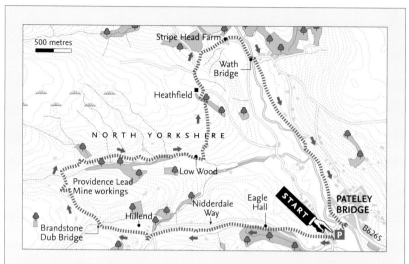

Start & finish Showground car park, Pateley Bridge, North Yorkshire HG3 5HW (OS ref SE157654); pay and display

Getting there Bus: Service 24 from Harrogate. Road: Pateley Bridge is on the B6265 between Grassington and Ripon.

Walk (7 miles, easy/moderate, OS Explorer 298): From car park, left along B6265. Pass turning to Ramsgill; in 50m, right (fingerpost, yellow arrow) up laneway to road (155654). Dogleg right/left ('Ladies Rigg'), and follow path through fields past Eagle Hall, following left-hand hedge/fence to meet Nidderdale Way/NiW at corner of wood (147655). Turn right along road, following NiW.

In 1 mile, fork right at Hillend along lower lane (131653, 'Ashfold Side, Cockhill'; NiW). In 700m cross Brandstone Dub Bridge (124655); follow stony lane to left. In ½ mile follow path down through ruin of Providence Lead Mine workings to cross Ashfold Side Beck (119611). Follow NiW downstream for 1¼ miles. Beyond Low Wood, left off lane (138664, NiW, 'Heathfield'). Up field edge, through Spring House farmyard (138665); half right across next field to gate; on along track by wall. In 500m pass Highfield Farm; on down to Heathfield and Grange Lane (138673).

Left along road. In 250m, 100m before Pie Gill drive, right through gate (137676, fingerpost). Follow left-hand wall; cross stile; half right between garage and wall. Keep wall on left till it bends left; aim half right for gate below (139679). Down track to Stripe Head Farm; through gate to right of buildings; down to road (141680). Right; in 500m, left ('Wath') across bridge (145677); right on NiW along River Nidd for 1¾ miles to Pateley Bridge.

Lunch The Sportsman's Arms, Wath (01423 711306; sportsmans-arms.co.uk)

Accommodation High Green Farm, Wath, Pateley Bridge, North Yorkshire HG3 5PJ (01423 715958; highgreen-nidderdale.co.uk) – first-class B&B or self-catering

More information Nidderdale Museum, King Street, Pateley Bridge (01423 711225; nidderdalemuseum.com), Pateley Bridge TIC (01423 714953), visitharrogate.co.uk; nidderdaleaonb.org.uk, visitengland.com, satmap.com, ramblers.org.uk

Pen-y-ghent
NORTH YORKSHIRE

When you get a crisp, clear day in a long North Yorkshire winter, it's a case of grabbing it with both hands. I caught the early train to Horton-in-Ribblesdale and was striding through the stone-built village with smoking breath and tingling fingers as the clock said ten. A clear sky lay over Ribblesdale, a backdrop of intense blue for the leonine profile of Pen-y-ghent hill.

Up in Horton Scar Lane the stone walls sparkled with hoar frost, and the sheep in the whitened fields nosed the stiff grasses suspiciously, as if nature had played a nasty trick on them. The old packhorse track rose straight and steady up the fellside, bordered with kerbstones cut and shaped centuries ago by the drovers and wool transporters who used this ancient way to cross from dale to dale. The Pennine Way, Britain's first designated National Trail, climbs the old thoroughfare, and now it is walkers' boots that keep Horton Scar Lane well trodden.

The limestone of these hills is riddled with pot holes, and the Pennine Way runs near two tremendous examples up on the flanks of Pen-y-ghent. I stepped aside to stare into the crag-lined gash of Hull Pot, as broad and deep as a city block. Hunt Pot, by contrast, a tight black slit in a rock terrace, was a door to a dark dwelling for one of the boggarts or goblins that haunted the imaginings of dales-dwellers in times past.

The path ran on eastwards, steepening as it climbed, to turn south along the sharp ridge crest of Pen-y-ghent. Nobody knows the meaning of this hill's Welsh-sounding name. 'The hill of the…' Of the what? The great steps, perhaps. The south-facing profile of Pen-y-ghent resembles a recumbent lion, gazing south towards the Lancashire border, 15 miles off. The beast's face is composed of two enormous steps in the rock, a pair of terraces, the upper one of dark gritstone rough to the touch, the lower of smooth light-grey limestone. From the lion's forehead at 693m (2273ft) there was an immense prospect this morning over a wide, frost-gripped landscape from which rose Pen-y-ghent's two neighbouring summits, bulky Whernside and tent-shaped Ingleborough.

One of the great challenges of these islands, the twenty-five-mile Three Peaks Walk, involves surmounting the three sister hills and returning to Horton within twelve hours, having climbed more than 1500m (5000ft). Descending Pen-y-ghent's steps, I vividly remembered stumbling into the Pen-y-ghent Café at Horton, stiff-legged, sweat sodden and smeared with peat after completing the circuit — and the blissful taste of that first mug of tea.

The broad walker's highway of the Pennine Way dropped gently from the terrace steps to Churn Milk Hole. Here the drover's track of Long Lane led away from the National Trail, descending the hillside by easy stages, a long two miles under the blue sky in a pinching wind, the view across Ribblesdale dominated by the grey bowl of a giant quarry. Down in the dale bottom, a winding path led me back to Horton through the frozen meadows, with the rush and babble of the River Ribble for a wintry marching song.

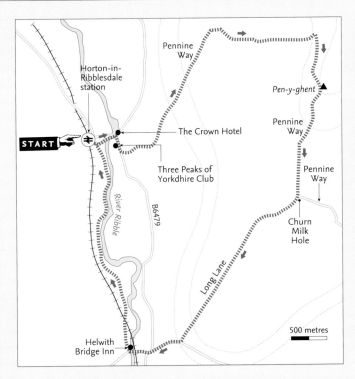

Start & finish Horton-in-Ribblesdale station BD24 0HH (OS ref SD803727)

Getting there Train: (www.thetrainline. com) to Horton-in-Ribblesdale. Road: A65, B6480 to Settle; B6479 to Horton-in-Ribblesdale.

Walk (8 miles, moderate/steep grade, OS ExplorerOL2): Follow Pennine Way/PW from Horton to climb to Pen-y-ghent summit (OS ref 838733). Descend south on PW for 1 mile to Churn Milk Hole (835718); right down Long Lane for 2 miles to Helwith Bridge; follow Ribble Way beside river back to Horton.

Lunch Pen-y-ghent Café (01729 860333) – famous for walker-friendliness and mugs of tea. Golden Lion Hotel, Horton-in-Ribblesdale (01729 860206; goldenlionhotel.co.uk) – warm and welcoming.

More information Settle TIC (01729 825192; www.settle.org.uk/settle-tourist-information-centre)

Reeth, Swaledale and Arkengarthdale
NORTH YORKSHIRE

As we drove into Reeth at seven in the evening, the quoits players were out on the village green, getting in their game before the forecast rain arrived. The solid clink of the hefty horseshoe quoits, the joking voices of the players and the sunset view beyond the pubs and houses of Reeth to the high bare bulk of Harkerside Moor were all just as Dales as could be.

The next day, I got into everything waterproof I could find and went out into the damp day. The rain didn't deter the blackbirds among the wet gardens of Reeth, nor the hatless, coatless, careless schoolchildren carrying out a survey of the village with incredible cheerfulness in the drizzle. In the meadows along the River Swale, rain-pearled Swaledale sheep watched me go by, their curly horns twisted each side of their heads like a wartime telephonist's hairdo. Swallows dipped low over the wide Swale, and the barking of a dog up at a farm high on the fellside

came clearly down to me. I found a lane in the hamlet of Healaugh that took me up around the back of Calver Hill, out onto the moor where everything except the creaky-voiced lapwings was silent and still in the rain seething in from the west.

Out on the moor an ancient hut circle lay pinpointed on the OS Explorer Map. It measured seven strides across. Who knows how many inhabitants it sheltered from the rain all those thousands of years ago?

The path dipped over the saddle and wound down into remote Arkengarthdale, the dale sides scarred with mounds of lead-mining spoil, the moor tops empty and magnificent. By West Raw Croft and East Raw Croft I found the homeward path, through narrow stone stiles and along the rushing Arkle Beck. It never stopped raining all day; and I wouldn't have missed one moment of it.

Start & finish Reeth village green, near Richmond, N. Yorks DL11 6SZ (OS ref NZ039993)

Getting there Bus: (getdown.org.uk) Service 30 (Richmond–Keld). Road: A1; A6136 or A6108 to Richmond; A6108 ('Leyburn'), B6270 to Reeth.

Walk (8 miles, moderate, OS Explorer OL30): From Reeth village green, take alleyway just to right of chapel, beside Holmlea. At T-jct opposite Heatherdale Bungalow (038991), right along lane. In ¼ mile, left down walled lane (034991, 'Harkerside & Grinton'). At River Swale, right (034990) along bank path. Pass end of Reeth swing bridge (032989 – don't cross!); on along north bank of Swale. In ¾ mile, right (021988; 'meadowland, single file') to B6270 (020991). Left into village.

By three stone troughs, right up lane (019990). Steeply up to Thirns farmhouse (012995). Tarmac ends; forward on stony lane. In about 200m, fork right uphill (010996) on a clear stony track. In 150m, wall on right makes right-angle turn uphill. In another 50m (008997) look for small cairn of stones on right; fork right here up grassy track between angle of wall and lower stony track. Follow grassy track (fairly clear, occasionally cairned) for 1 mile, over saddle (004004), past hut circle (005006 – detour) to meet a stony track (004009). Right for ½ mile to road (010015). Right; in ½ mile, left down gravel track (018012; fingerpost) to West Raw Croft farm (023016).

Don't follow stony track in front of house, but keep right of wire fence, through gate. Bear half right up field, aiming for right end of line of trees. Through stone stile (yellow blobs/YB); follow stone wall on your left. At end of field go through gate (025012); over stream, past rock with YB; on through 2 more stiles, then left down farm track (027008, 'Fremmington' fingerpost) to cross Arkle Beck. Up farm track; bear right to go through gate just to right of Castle Farm House (030008; YB). Cross garden in front of house; through opposite gate/stile; on through fields by stiles (YB).

In ¼ mile, nearing Arkle Beck, follow 'bridleway' sign uphill (035005). In 250m go through stone wall (037004); in another 250m, through another wall (039003) and slant right downhill to track below. Turn left along it, through gate; follow fence on right downhill above Arkle Beck. At bottom, right through stile (040997; fingerpost); left along field path parallel with Arkle Beck. Through wall gaps and stiles for ½ mile to B6270 (042992); right across Reeth Bridge into Reeth.

Conditions Moor path over Calver Hill is not advisable in mist

Lunch Picnic. Many pubs, cafés in Reeth

Accommodation Burgoyne Hotel, Reeth (01748-884292; theburgoyne.co.uk) – immaculately kept and run

More information Reeth National Park Centre (01748-884059; www.yorkshiredales.org.uk), yorkshire.com, ramblers.org.uk, satmap.co.uk

Robin Hood's Bay to Whitby

NORTH YORKSHIRE

Robin Hood's Bay is one of those coastal villages so intrinsically beautiful and full of character that it draws you back again and again. Mazy lanes tangle on either side of the precipitous main street. Cobbled or flagged, twisting and turning, plunging from one level to another by worn stone stairs, wriggling between tiny gardens, climbing and falling, framing views of sea and cliff under crooked archways … Fisherhead, Sunny Place and Bakehouse Steps, they seduced me into lingering long after I should have been away.

The tide had slipped in to cover the great scars or eroded rock layers that floor the bay in extravagant arcs. I turned my back on the red pantiled roofs of Robin Hood's Bay at last and set out along the cliffs with a good stiff northwesterly breeze in my face. I hadn't walked this stretch of the North Yorkshire coast in years, but I well remembered the jagged out-thrust of the headlands with their horizontal bands of mineral-bearing rock, and the black boulders that carpeted the tiny bays.

The map names held magic — Craze Naze and Clock Case Nab, Pursglove Stye Batts and Maw Wyke Hole. Angular names for angular places, where men wriggled into the most awkward of holes to win the fossilised wood which, properly shaped and polished, transformed itself into Whitby jet. A hard job for hard times — but, as they told over-romantic visitors lamenting the mining scars, "You can't eat scenery."

The sun came through the mackerel sky and shone a silver shaft as thick as a searchlight beam on the sea where lobster pot buoys and flags were bobbing. A jaunty gang of jackdaws went chakkering off inland. Fulmars rode the thermals along the cliffs with upturned tails and slender wings stiffened at right angles to their bodies. I marvelled yet again at these seabirds' precision of flight, every movement as economical and graceful as a dancer's.

I passed the stubby white lighthouse on Whitestone Point and skirted Saltwick Bay with its fast-eroding sea stacks and gull-dotted rock pavements. The black skeleton of Whitby Abbey stood ahead on its cliff, forever haunted by the ghastly shade of Count Dracula — one of many scenes in his horror novel *Dracula* that Bram Stoker set in Whitby, to the delight of today's nation of goths who hang whey-faced around the town.

A wildly steep cobbled alley precipitated me from the abbey down to Whitby harbour. The town where Captain Cook learnt his sea trade was under attack by jovial pretend pirates today, one of Whitby's frequent festivals of fun. I dodged Bluebeard and Blackbeard and Short John Silver, and went off to find a fish pie with a nice sea view.

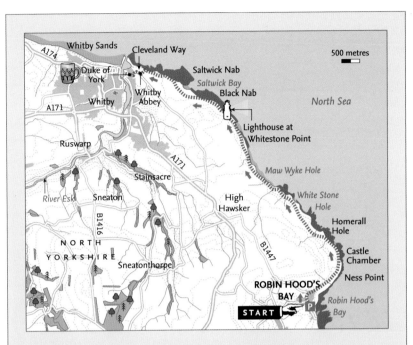

Start Upper car park, Station Road, Robin Hood's Bay, North Yorkshire YO22 4RE (OS ref NZ949055); pay and display

Getting there Bus: Service X93, Whitby-Scarborough. Road: Robin Hood's Bay (B1447) is signed from A171 Whitby-Scarborough road at Hawsker.

Walk (7 miles, easy/moderate, OS Explorer OL27): Right along B1447 towards village; on right bend, left along Mount Pleasant North (951055, Cleveland Way). From here, follow well-waymarked Cleveland Way to Whitby. Return by bus X93, or taxi from Whitby railway station (£10-£15).

Conditions Unguarded cliff edges; some steep flights of steps

Lunch Duke of York, Whitby (01947 600324; dukeofyork.co.uk) – at bottom of 199 steps from St Mary's Church

Accommodation Victoria Hotel, Station Street, Robin Hood's Bay YO22 4RL (01947 880205; victoriarhb.com) – a long-established hotel, characterful, helpful and friendly

More information Whitby TIC (01723 383636), www.visitwhitby.com, visitengland.com, satmap.com, ramblers.org.uk

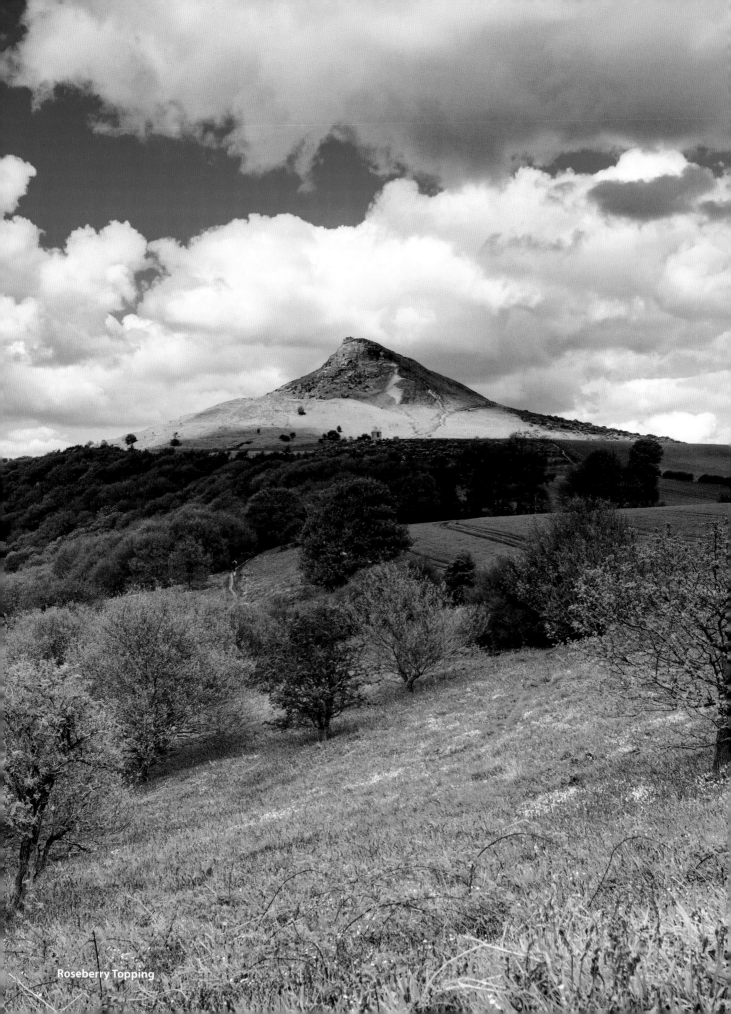

Roseberry Topping

Roseberry Topping
NORTH YORKSHIRE

A pale grey, windy sky streamed south over the North York Moors. Well wrapped against the foul weather, Jane and I followed a bowed but sprightly old lady up the lane to Aireyholme Farm. Cows lowed, a spade scraped on a stone floor and barn doors banged.

Captain James Cook would have recognised the sounds that echoed round the buildings; it was here that the farm foreman's son spent his boyhood in the late 1730s, dreaming of the sea and faraway places.

Roseberry Topping was a whalehead of a hill above Aireyholme Farm back then. Now it takes the shape of a tsunami wave in a classical Japanese painting, a convex green back rising to tip suddenly over at the summit in a great vertical cliff face of rugged broken rock. It was a giant landslip in 1912 that sent the western half of the hill crashing and sliding into ruin.

A yellowhammer in the hedge broke out with a wheezy request for "a-little-bit-of-bread-and-no … cheeese". We followed a zigzag path, well patched with stones, steeply up to the crest of Roseberry Topping and one of the best views in the north of England — the long escarpment of the Cleveland Hills pushing out their ship-prow profiles one behind the other into the great wide vale of the River Tees. A mess of chimneys lazily emitting coils of smoke showed where Teesside lay, still a heartbeat of industry in the northeast.

We followed the Cleveland Way down off the hill and up again to skirt the edge of a sombre dark moor at Great Ayton, all the way south to where the thick sandstone needle of the Captain Cook monument rose on its ridge.

"A man of nautical knowledge inferior to none, in zeal, prudence and energy superior to most" eulogised the inscription. "Long will the name of Capt. Cook stand out among the most celebrated and most admired benefactors of the human race."

We drank to that with bottled water as we sheltered under the obelisk and watched the moors and hills smoking under a rolling sea of cloud.

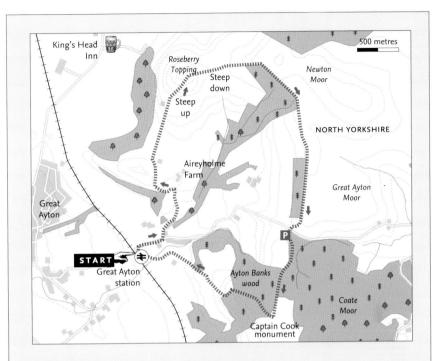

Start & finish Great Ayton Station, TS9 6HR (OS ref NZ574108)

Getting there Rail: (thetrainline.co.uk) to Great Ayton. Road: Great Ayton is on A172 between Gainsborough and Stokesley. Follow High Street, then Station Road for 1 mile to station.

Walk (5½ miles, hard, OS Explorer OL26): From station, cross bridge; on up road. Left at White House Farm down lane (577110); in ⅓ mile, nearing Aireyholme Farm, left over stile (578115; 'footpath'); over next stile; ahead with wood on left. Ignore stile on left; over stile in corner of field (576115); right on path towards, then up Roseberry Topping. From summit (579126) follow Cleveland Way (CW) pitched path east, down and up to gate at edge of plantation (588127); right (blue, yellow arrows) on CW for 1¾ miles to Captain Cook monument (590101).

Face back the way you came up CW, and take next path to left, aiming to go between two prominent gateposts. Follow path (yellow arrows) down through Ayton Banks wood; cross track near bottom (585104); continue down out of trees to angle of wall on right (584104). Right along sunken lane. In ½ mile, nearing Dikes Lane, left down stony track (578108; 'Fir-Brook'); in 200m, right through gate; cross field to farm track (576107); left to station.

Conditions Steep climb up to Roseberry Topping and Captain Cook monument. Steep descent through Ayton Banks wood.

Lunch Picnic

Accommodation Chapters Hotel, Stokesley, North Yorkshire TS9 5AD (01642 711888; chaptershotel.co.uk)

More information Great Ayton TIC (01642 722835), yorkshire.com, ramblers.org.uk; satmap.com

Runswick Bay

NORTH YORKSHIRE

Runswick Bay, pride of the North Yorkshire coast, is an utterly charming, easel-friendly jumble of red-roofed, white-walled houses. They stand piled in one corner of a perfectly semicircular bay whose cliffs have been assiduously quarried and mined over the centuries. The steep green slopes are patched with the black scars of landslips and at their foot lie pebbles of black, red, ochre, cream and chocolate — colours that betray the presence of a treasury of minerals. You can still pick up pieces of raw jet or lignite on the beach after cliff falls, not to mention the ammonites and remains of prehistoric reptiles for which these bays are famous.

This is a dangerous coast for contrary currents and winds. Runswick Bay's lifeboat is not just there for show. The crew were always traditionally drawn from local fishermen. On one occasion in 1901, all the able-bodied men of Runswick Bay — including the lifeboatmen themselves — were out at sea fishing when a storm blew up and threatened them. It was the women on shore who launched the lifeboat, and the old and infirm men of the village who clambered in and rowed it to the rescue.

Beyond Hob Holes caves we climbed a steep flight of stairs and were away along the cliffs, looking ahead to where Whitby Abbey stood in Dracula-style ghostliness on the headland, eight miles off as the fulmar flies. The red pantiled roofs of Kettleness hamlet rose high above the bulbous snout of Kettleness, eroded by alum mining to a blunt stump of land.

We skirted above landslip bays where dense undercliffs of heather and grass never see a human footfall, and turned back inland through fields corrugated with medieval ridges and furrows. The grassy foundations of a Roman lookout tower lay low on a hump of ground. The tower's minders evidently came to a bloody end at the hands of German barbarian pirates; archaeologists unearthed their skeletons, together with that of their dog, crushed in the ruins.

Lapwings wheeled and tumbled over the meadows, brown hares scampered in the long grass. We followed the track of an old railway on a great curve through the fields, and dipped down through the trees to Runswick Bay once more, a shining strand scattered with sea-smoothed stones, tide-rinsed and gleaming in our fingers.

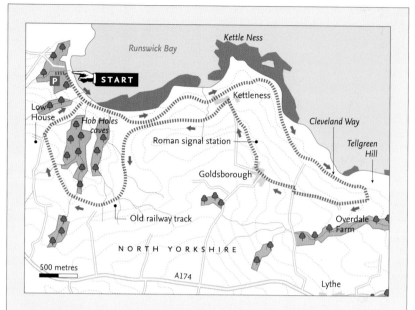

Start & finish Runswick Bay car park, N. Yorks TS13 5HT (OS ref NZ810160); pay and display

Getting there Bus: Service 4 (getdown.org.uk/bus/bus/4-x4.shtml). Road: Car park is signed from Cliffemount Hotel at Runswick Bank Top (signed as 'Runswick' from A174 Whitby-Loftus road).

Walk (9 miles, moderate, OS Explorer OL27): Right along beach. In ½ mile, just past Hob Holes caves, right (815154, Cleveland Way/CW acorn symbol) up rock, then wooden steps to cliff top. Follow CW for 2¾ miles. At Tellgreen Hill headland, right inland (850145; 'Lythe' fingerpost). In 150m, yellow arrow/YA points ahead, but go right here to Overdale Farm drive (847143): ahead to road (840144). Right to Goldsborough (836147). Follow 'Kettleness'; in 50m, right ('footpath') through farmyard; on through gate (YA) down green lane. Through gate (836148, YA); half left via Roman lookout tower mound (835151) to shed in field corner. Over stile (YA); down to chapel (833153); over 2 stiles to road; right into Kettleness. Left along old railway track (832155) for 2½ miles. Beside Low House, right off railway (807151) on track down to beach (812156); left to Runswick Bay.

Lunch Royal Hotel Runswick (01947 840215) or beach café, Runswick Bay

Accommodation Cliffemount Hotel, Runswick Bay (01947 840103; cliffemounthotel.co.uk) – welcoming hotel perched above Runswick Bay

More information yorkshire.com, visitengland.com, satmap.com, ramblers.org.uk

Thixendale
NORTH YORKSHIRE

With the air of one who'd heard it a thousand times before, the landlord of the Cross Keys echoed: "What's a Painslackfull? Listen, if I have to tell you, I've got to kill you to keep the secret." I ordered one sight unseen, and went out into the garden of Thixendale's little pub to wait for it and to savour the cold, bright, windy day that had descended over the Yorkshire Wolds.

That evocative name of 'wolds' brings to mind the gentle felicities of the Cotswolds, near where I grew up in Gloucestershire. The wolds of East Yorkshire are a different kind of countryside; steeper, deeper, more remote, wilder in feeling and aspect. The village of Thixendale, near the deserted medieval village of Wharram Percy, lies down at the junction of half a dozen of the small, snaking, flat-bottomed valleys, called 'dales' hereabouts, that hide so effectively in these chalky uplands. Driving from York to Bridlington through the modestly rolling cornfields of East Riding, you'd never guess village or dales were there at all.

My Painslackfull turned out to consist of … well, I couldn't possibly reveal that. But it was fantastically delicious. Wiping my mouth and burping pleasurably, I made my way up the adjoining valleys of Thixen Dale and Milham Dale.

Sheep had grazed the steep dales sides into a beautiful sward bright with pale blue scabious, wild thyme and delicately trembling harebells. The view west from the Roman road on the ridge above was sensational, and quite unexpected in these apparently flat lands: forty or fifty miles across the Vale of York towards the hazy outlines of the Pennine Hills.

I walked down into the silent, sleepy and perfectly ordered village of Kirby Underdale, whose Norman church held a strange surprise: a blurred sandstone carving of Mercury, Roman god of good luck and swift action. Setting back by way of Painsthorpe Dale and Worm Dale, I pictured the sculptor at work with careful devotion, long before Christianity first blew like a breeze across these secret dales.

Down in the green cleft of Thixendale I came across fifty heavy-coated sheep barging frantically round a pen, watched with fixed intensity by a brace of collies. The farmer and his boy were opening their Thermos on the dale side above. "Rained off from shearing 'em yesterday," observed the farmer phlegmatically, "but we'll get 'em done tonight," and he sipped his tea with quiet relish.

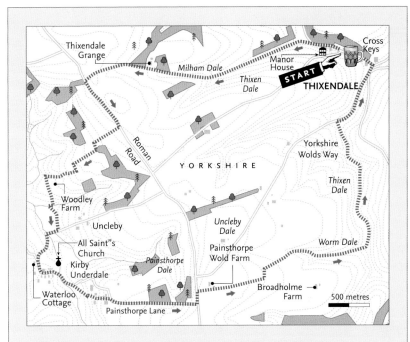

Start & finish Cross Keys Inn, Thixendale YO17 9TG (OS ref SE845610)

Getting there Road: Thixendale is signed off A166 York-Driffield road. Entering village, turn left ('Birdsall, Malton') to find Cross Keys on right.

Walk (8½ miles, moderate, OS Explorers 300, 294). From Cross Keys Inn turn left for 50m, to road; right through village past Uncleby turning. 50m beyond village sign, left through gateway (838612, 'bridleway'). In 50m, bear left (blue arrow/BA) up Thixen Dale. In ¾ mile fork right through gate (826608, 'Chalkland Way') up Milham Dale. At Thixendale Grange (819609), left along drive to Roman road (811607). Left for ⅓ mile; at fingerpost on left of road, turn right (815602) down left side of hedge. At bottom of field, left to cross stile. Down hedge, through gate (812599); on down through next gate; follow left hedge down past Woodley Farm. At bottom of field, left through gate (807596; yellow arrow/YA). Follow hedge; on across field to join track (YA); follow it for ¼ mile to road (808590); right to pass Waterloo Cottage. At T-junction, left into Kirby Underdale.

Left by phone box to pass church. Beyond church road bends left; right here over stile (811584; fingerpost, YA). Cross paddock; through gate (812583); left (YA) past Beech Farm; right (815583) up Painsthorpe Lane for ⅔ mile to Roman road (825582). Left ('Malton') for 150m; right ('bridleway' fingerpost) along farm track past Painsthorpe Wold Farm. In ½ mile, track bends left, then right. On this right bend (833586) keep forward (BA) for 30m, then right with hedge on right. Through gate (835588, BA), bear right for ½ mile down Wormdale. At junction with Thixen Dale (845589), left (fingerpost, YA) along Thixen Dale bottom for 1 mile to road (841603); right to Thixendale village.

Lunch & Accommodation Cross Keys Inn, Thixendale (01377 288272) – B&B

More information www.yorkshire.com

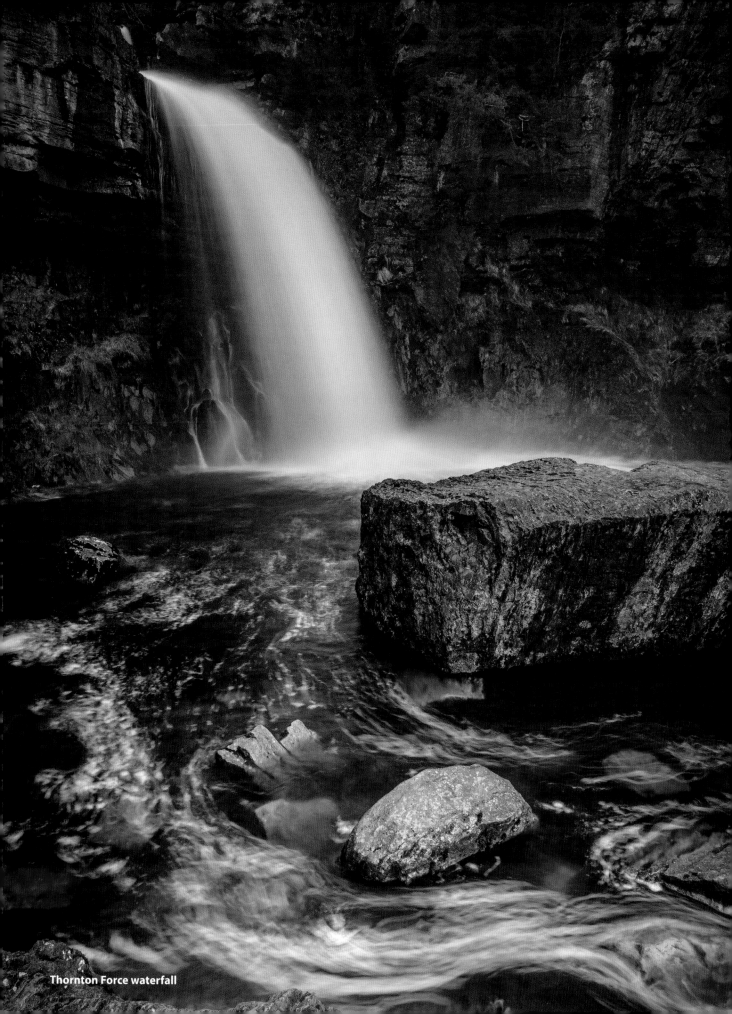

Thornton Force waterfall

Waterfalls Trail, Ingleton
NORTH YORKSHIRE

People have been doing the Waterfalls Trail since the days of stovepipe hats and crinolines, and this steep, tree-hung circuit of the two moorland rivers that rush together in Ingleton village to form the River Greta continues to be one of Yorkshire's prime outdoor attractions. I'd always assumed that any walk so popular must be a bit tame — but not at all. The twin gorges of the rivers Twiss and Doe may be well trodden, but they're far from commodified. The combination of thick woods, waterfalls, churning narrows and thread-like paths exerts as much magic on today's walkers as it did on Victorian holidaymakers in search of swoonsome thrills.

Setting off from Ingleton along the narrow path that shadows the River Twiss, we were almost at once enclosed in the dark walls of a gorge, with the river running fast among mossy stones splashed with dipper droppings. Beside the path lay a money tree, its hide as scaly as a lizard's with tens of thousands of copper coins hammered into the boughs for luck. The trail climbed the wall of a canyon above swirling holes where the south-going river chased round and round before escaping, sculpting semi-circular hollows in the rock walls with a continuous swallow and gurgle. Its cold breath and smell of stone and earth came up to us as we crossed the gorge on lattice footbridges under which the peat-charged water sluiced as dark and frothy as a gush of porter.

A roe deer went bounding up the bank, its white scut bobbing a warning. A long view upriver showed Pecca Falls crashing down a staircase of slippery rock steps. Beyond the cascade the trail left the trees and followed a curve of the Twiss. A wonderful view opened ahead towards Thornton Force, pride of the walk, descending a series of rapids before hurling itself in a 15m (50ft) free fall into a smoking pool. Above this thunderous weight of water we followed a walled lane into the mist. Unseen and offstage, sheep bleated, a farmer whistled and a quad went puttering over an invisible field by Twisleton Hall.

Below the farm the River Doe echoed and hissed in its own steep-walled canyon, leaping down towards Ingleton and its confluence with the Twiss through S-shaped channels carved through the shale by the force of water alone. We crossed above potholes boiling with toffee-coloured bubbles, and skirted backwaters where the surface lay marbled with scarcely moving patterns of foam. Below the white wall of Snow Falls the path snaked past another money tree and on through mossy old quarry workings, to emerge at the foot of the gorge with the church and houses of Ingleton lying beyond, as muted and dreamy as any faded Victorian lithograph.

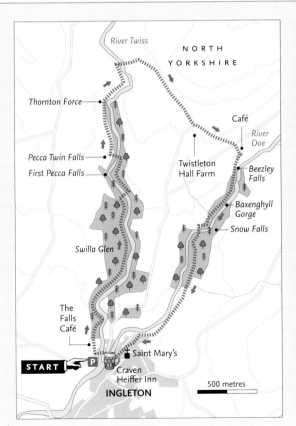

Start & finish Waterfalls Walk car park, Ingleton, North Yorks LA6 3ET (OS ref SD693733)

Getting there Bus: Service 80 (Lancaster- Ingleton), 581 (Ingleton-Settle). Road: M6 Jct 34 (A683, A687) or Jct 36 (A65) to Ingleton. The Waterfalls Trail is signed in the village.

Walk (4½ miles, moderate/strenuous, Explorer OL2): From car park follow waymark arrows up River Twiss, along lane via Twisleton Hall Farm (702751) and down River Doe.

Conditions Continuous slippery paths and steps

Lunch Falls Café (www.thefallscafe.co.uk)

Accommodation Croft Gate, Chapel-le-Dale, Ingleton (01524 242664; croft-gate.co.uk) – quiet, friendly and immaculate B&B

Waterfalls Trail Open 9am daily; £6 entrance/car park pp; £15 family; complimentary leaflet guide

More information Ingleton TIC (01524 241049); www.ingleton.co.uk/inginfo.asp; ingletonwaterfallstrail.co.uk, yorkshire.com

Back in 1965, when the Pennine Way was officially opened, Britain's first National Trail gave a wide berth to Hebden Bridge — a smoky mill town, famous for its fustians and corduroys, but nobody's idea of a pleasant stopover for holiday-makers.

Times have changed — and so has the town after a big smartening up. A new detour route, the Hebden Bridge Loop, was opened to coincide with the Pennine Way's fiftieth anniversary, beckoning walkers to savour the organic cafés, artisan bakers and boutique shops of the newly sparkling gritstone town in the depths of Calderdale.

On a brisk day with newborn lambs jumping in the fields, I climbed the cobbled lane to Horsehold Farm, where the Hebden Bridge Loop led me along the edge of a steep beech wood. A strong, cold wind blew in from the west with a spatter of snowflakes in its skirts. I dropped down through the tender new green leaves of Callis Wood to where road, railway, canal and river ran squashed close together by the tight geography of the Calder Valley.

The Hebden Bridge Loop rose very steeply up the northern flank of Calderdale by way of narrow cobbled lanes between green gritstone walls footed in daffodils. In the fields high above the valley bottom, nesting curlews and golden plover flew away with wild bubbling cries, the haunting sound of spring in the northern dales. Back across Calderdale the slim finger of the monument on Stoodley Pike stood high, pointing into a sky swirling with snow and sunshine.

From the ridge I descended, with a superb view ahead over Colden Clough to far moors painted chocolate and cream. Down through fields of pregnant ewes to Hebble Hole and the ancient stone footbridge over the Colden Water, a perfect picnic spot for some warm summer's day. Today, though, it was upwards and onwards with the wind at my back to Heptonstall, and a vertiginous path all the way back down through Mytholm Woods to Hebden Bridge.

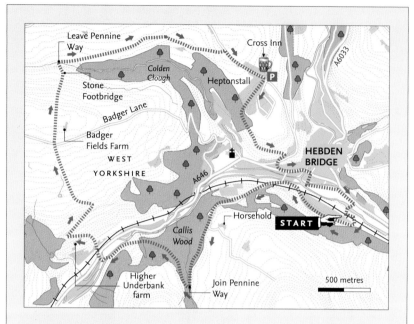

Start & finish Hebden Bridge Station, West Yorkshire HX7 6JE (OS ref SD996268)

Getting there Rail: to Hebden Bridge. Bus: Service 500 (Keighley), services 590, 592 (Halifax- Todmorden), service 900 (Huddersfield). Road: M62, Jct 20; A58, A6033 to Todmorden; A46 to Hebden Bridge.

Walk (7 miles, strenuous, OS Explorer OL21): Right under railway; right along Palace Hill Road. Recross railway; first left (989271, Horsehold) up to Horsehold Farm (982267). Hebden Bridge Loop /HBL to Mankinholes fingerpost (980261); right across stream; follow Pennine Way/PW down through Callis Wood to cross A646 (971264). Right for 50m; left, and follow PW for 1½ miles, uphill via Higher Underbank Farm, then 'Official Route' waymark (968266) to cross Badger Lane (967674), over crest and downhill to cross Hebble Hole footbridge (968282). Leave PW here; turn right (east) for 1 mile, parallel to Colden Water (HBL) to road (983283) into Heptonstall. First right past Cross Inn; follow HBL past church, steeply down through woods to road in Hebden Bridge (989273). Right; in 100m, left down steps to A646. Left to traffic lights (991272); right across canal; left on towpath to bridge 16 (995270) and station.

Conditions Short, steep climbs; vertiginous path from Heptonstall to Hebden Bridge

Lunch Cross Inn, Towngate, Heptonstall HX7 7NB (01422 843284)

Accommodation Hare and Hounds, Old Town, Hebden Bridge HX7 8TN (01422 842671; hareandhounds.me.uk) – friendly, cosy country pub

More information hbwalkersaction.org.uk, nationaltrail.co.uk/pennine-way, Hebden Bridge TIC (01422 843831; hebdenbridge.co.uk/tourist-info), yorkshire.com, visitengland.com, satmap.com, ramblers.org.uk

Meltham and Marsden Clough

WEST YORKSHIRE

Snow flurries were scudding across the sedgy fellsides above Meltham as we started up Royd Lane towards the open moor. This part of West Yorkshire, the very northernmost tip of the Peak District National Park, is Last of the Summer Wine country; but if Compo, Clegg and Foggy had been out and about today, they'd have needed their caps and comforters. This was the Yorkshire Moors at winter's end — bleak, harsh and compelling.

Royd Lane gave way to Magdalen Road, a noble name for a rugged old horse track that hurdles the low hill between Meltham and the twin reservoirs of Marsden Clough. Moor farms stood hunched along the lane, their windowless backs to the weather — Fox Royd, Upper Royd, Ash Royd. A 'royd' is a piece of land cleared of its roots, stones and trees for agriculture, but a lot of the royd land on these hills is going back out of keeping. One by one the hill farms are being abandoned in the face of pickings too slim to survive on.

Curls of snow still lay in the lee of the stone walls. A stray bullock was wandering in the lane, but when he caught sight of us he plunged with a twang straight through a barbed-wire fence and cantered off to join his chums.

Beyond the Holmfirth road we dropped into Marsden Clough by way of Springs Road, a walled track whose beautifully cut sandstone paving-slabs had been grooved to guide the wheels of quarry wagons. Down along Nether Lane the stone-built farmhouses stood empty, solid old dwellings each in its own strip of fields — Goodbent, Bartin and Greaves Head.

Our ancestors did not always build solidly and well. Before climbing out of Marsden Clough and on back to Meltham, we leant on the wall and looked down over the twin waters of Bilberry and Digley Reservoirs. When the poorly constructed embankment of Bilberry Reservoir collapsed in February 1852, a giant wall of water rushed down the valley and devastated Holmfirth, "throwing a four storey mill down like a thing of nought, tossing boilers about like feathers, and carrying amongst the wreck of houses, mills and other buildings, men, women and children".

Rural tradition says that the cries of plovers are the lamentations of lost souls. The air was full of them today, wailing and piping us away from the lakes and that dark old tragedy.

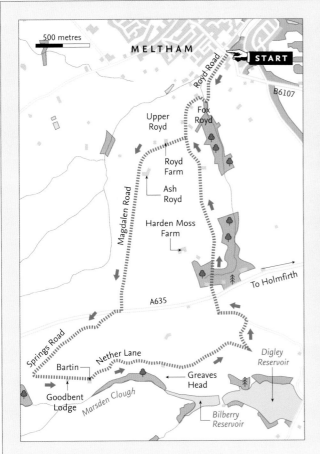

Start & finish Royd Road, off Holmfirth Road, Meltham HD9 4BE approx (OS ref SE104102)

Getting there Bus: Service 335 (stottscoaches.co.uk), Holmfirth-Meltham, or service 911 (wymetro.com), Honley Rail Station-Meltham, to Royd Road bus stop (at foot of Royd Road). Road: Royd Road is off B6107 Meltham-Holmfirth road on the southern edge of Meltham.

Walk (6 miles, moderate, OS Explorers OL1, 288): Walk up Royd Road. In ½ mile pass Fox Royd; in 200m fork right (100094, 'bridleway' fingerpost), past Royd Farm and on for 1 mile to A635 (094078). Right; in 50m, left through gate, down track (Springs Road) for ⅔ mile. At gate with ladder stile (086073) don't cross, but swing left along Nether Lane; follow it for ¾ mile past Goodbent Lodge and Bartin to Greaves Head farmhouse (098074). In another ½ mile, turn left (106075) up grassy lane, over stile by gate (yellow waymark). On up between walls to road (106077); left to cross A635 (103080); ahead for 1¾ miles along Harden Moss Road (track), then Royd Road to B6107.

Lunch Plenty of pubs/cafés in Meltham

Accommodation Durker Roods Hotel, Meltham HD9 4JA (01484 851413; durkerroodshotel.co.uk)

More information Holmfirth TIC (01484 414868), yorkshire.com, ramblers.org.uk

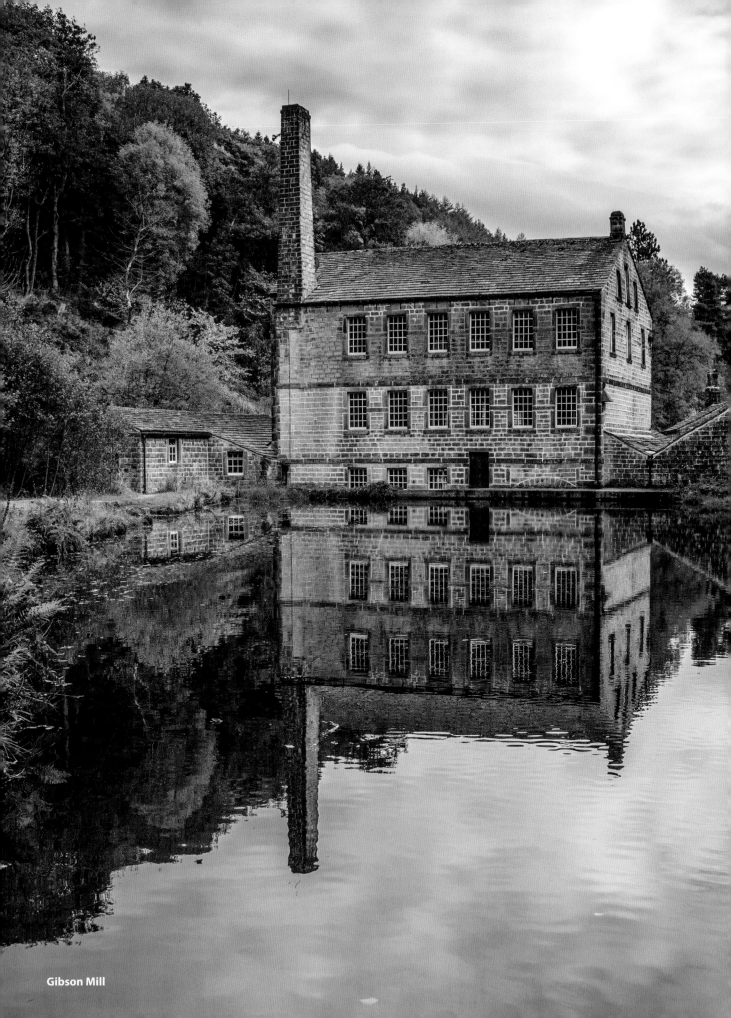

Gibson Mill

Hebden Water
WEST YORKSHIRE

The chaffinches of Hebden Dale certainly seemed pleased with the day. They were practicing their 'fast bowler doing his run-up' songs from every oak and sycamore in the deep, sun-struck valley on this beautiful spring morning — or so it seemed as I descended the gravelly path to where the Hebden Water sparkled among its gritstone rocks.

Hebden Dale winds down to Hebden Bridge, one of West Yorkshire's most productive weaving towns not so long ago, nowadays all cleaned up and classy. Walking by the river up this quiet cleft in the flank of the Brontë moors, I pictured the smoke and pollution, the roar and clatter of milling that filled the town and its satellite dale scarcely more than a century ago, and found such scenes almost impossible to credit.

Last time I'd walked the dale, the Hebden Water had been charged with storm water and rushed viscous and peat-brown down from the moors. Today the river ran slow and limpid, its dimpled surface reflecting an electric blue flash as a kingfisher streaked by. Broken walls and the remnants of old sluices showed where the mills had once lined the banks. One remains in the dale, the queen of them all, the handsome neo-classical Gibson Mill, beautifully restored by the National Trust.

I stopped in at the mill café for a cuppa and a bit of cake, and then went on up the dale with the chaffinches singing me over the bridges and through the miniature alps of Hardcastle Crags. A steep little climb up the dale side and I was walking up a meadow full of lambs towards the dark stone house of Walshaw.

The long, low farmhouses of these moors, many of them built all of a piece with their cattle barns, always put me in mind of John Wesley and the other passionate nonconformist preachers who set the gunpowder trail of Methodism alight around West Yorkshire in the mid eighteenth-century. I don't know if Wesley preached in the barns or outhouses at Walshaw or Lady Royd or Shackleton, the farms that stand along the lane which runs back towards Hebden Bridge. But I pictured him there, travel-stained and weary, uplifting congregations of ploughmen and weavers with glimpses of a promised land.

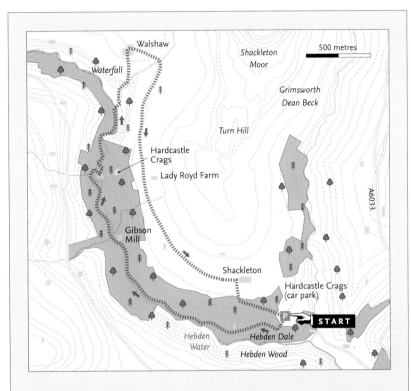

Start & finish Hardcastle Crags car park, Midgehole, HX7 7AA approx (OS ref SD987292)

Getting there Train: (www.thetrainline.com; www.railcard.co.uk) to Hebden Bridge (2 miles). Bus: Service 500 (from Keighley-Hebden Bridge); services 590, 592 (from Halifax); services 900, 901 (from Huddersfield). Road: M65 Junction 9, A646 to Hebden Bridge; A6033 towards Haworth; in ¾ mile, left to car park.

Walk (4½ miles, moderate grade; OS Explorer OL21): Follow red-and-white, then red waymark poles down to the river's edge, then upstream to Gibson Mill (973298). Cross river here; on along left (west bank). In ⅓ mile cross, then recross by adjacent footbridges (971304) to continue on left bank; in another ⅓ mile cross to right bank beside weir and stone hut (973309). Cross side beck by stone bridge; right through stone wall gap; climb steep path on left of beck to farmyard (974313). Right by Walshaw Cottage along stony lane for 1½ miles to Shackleton (983295); right here (footpath fingerpost) down crumbling walled field track. Cross stile at bottom; bear left and down through woodland for ⅓ mile to reach upper car park; steps to lower car park and bus stop.

Lunch Weaving Shed Café, Gibson Mill (01422 844518)

More information Hebden Bridge TIC (01422 843831; hebdenbridge.co.uk/tourist-info)

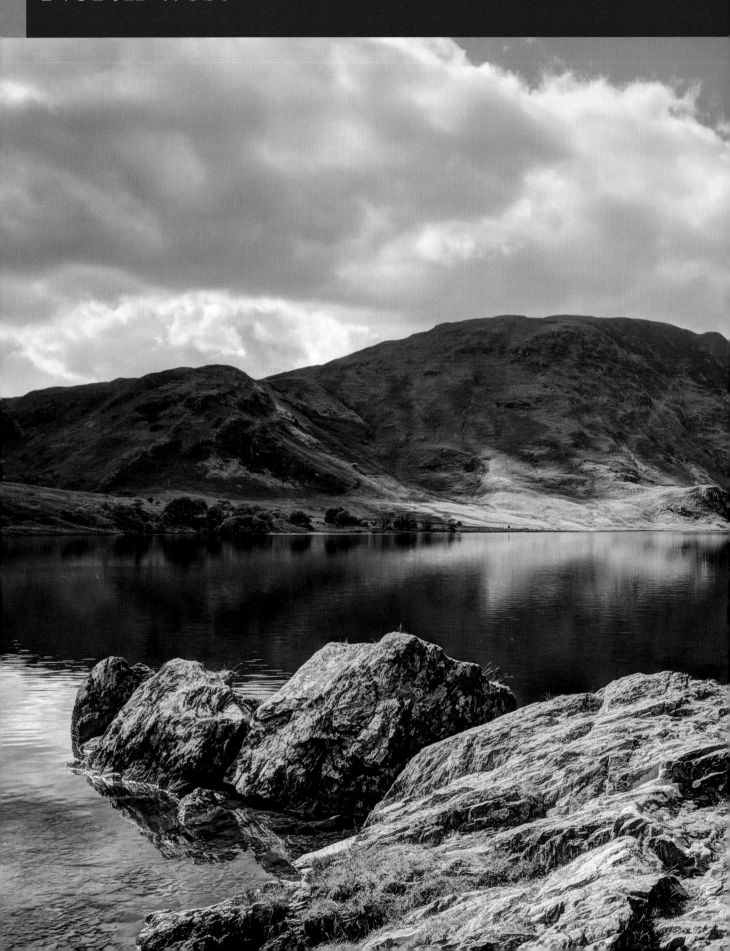

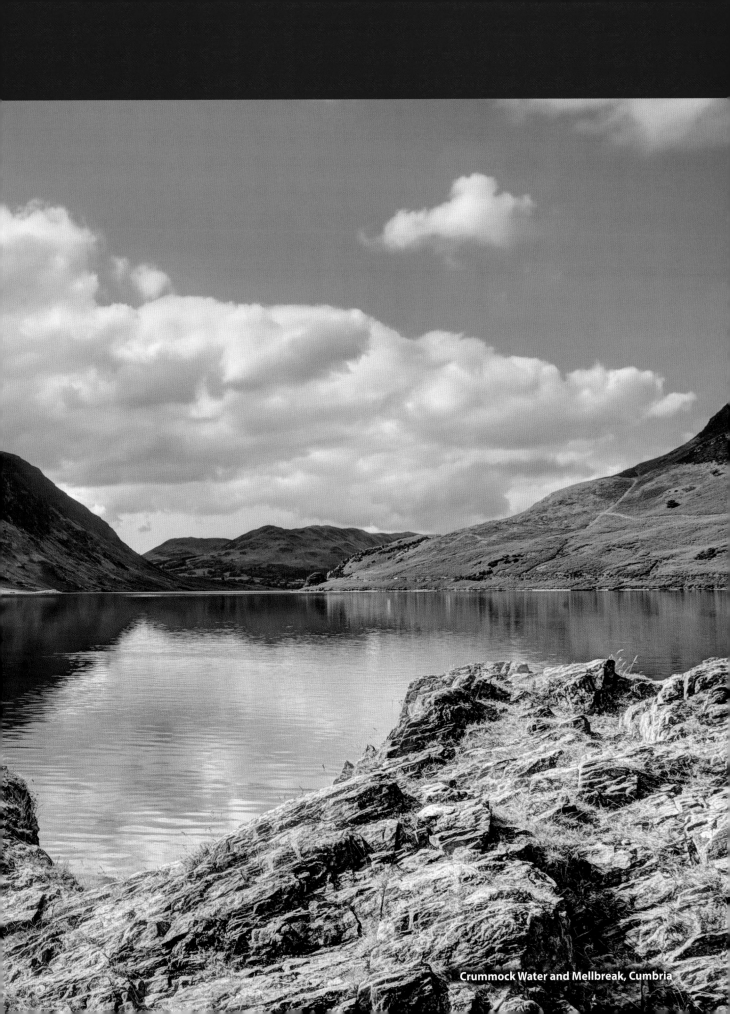

Crummock Water and Mellbreak, Cumbria

Higher Burwardsley
CHESHIRE

As we left the Pheasant Inn at Higher Burwardsley, a Sunday cavalcade of veteran tractors was spluttering up the hill — red, blue, orange, green and yellow; Fordson, Ferguson and Field Marshall. It was a salutary reminder that here is working farming country. Walkers exploring this beautifully kept, beautifully ordered corner of Cheshire have a great wooded ridge at their elbow, sheltering a scatter of lovely old half-timbered farmhouses, and a view sweeping west into Wales and the distant blue line of the Clwydian mountains.

The cattle at Wood Farm were frisking in their pastures. Bull calves shoved their blunt little heads together in play-fights, then kicked up heels and tails as they went bucketing away at the gallop.

Walking the walled lane at the foot of the Peckforton Hills, we found crinkle-edged hart's-tongue ferns sprouting from chinks between the sandstone blocks. It's sandstone that shapes this landscape, particularly the great ridge that undulates north to its outermost crag where Beeston Castle stands. The castle occupies one of the most sensational sites in England, right at the lip of a 100m (330ft) crag, with a superb prospect across thirty miles of country in all directions.

We looked around the exhibition down at the castle gateway (bronze axe heads and stone spinning weights, Civil War bullets and drinking flagons), then climbed through the massive sandstone gatehouse and wall towers of the outer ward, and on up through pine trees to the inner ward gatehouse and the tiny, lumpy stronghold at the peak. Pennine and Welsh hills, Liverpool Cathedral, the Wrekin and Chester — all lay there in open view, with the Victorian folly of Peckforton Castle rising on its crag a mile away southward.

It's claimed that in December 1643 eight Royalist desperadoes forced the surrender of the Roundhead garrison after they climbed the western crags. Some say the treasure of King Richard II lies at the bottom of the castle's well. It's certainly a hauntingly beautiful spot. Walking back to Burwardsley I kept turning round to gaze at the castle on the crag, an image to fix in the inner eye and carry away with me.

Start & finish Pheasant Inn, Higher Burwardsley, Tattenhall, Cheshire CH3 9PF (OS ref SJ523566)

Getting there Road: Burwardsley is signed from A534 between Ridley (A49 junction) and Broxton (A41 junction)

Walk (6½ miles, moderate, OS Explorer 257): Right out of Pheasant car park; along lane. In 300m, left down field (524568, fingerpost, yellow arrow/YA) with hedge on left. Over stile (Eddisbury Way/EW); down to road (522571). Right; follow EW round Outlanes Farm; on across fields. Approaching Wood Farm, cross double stile (519577, EW); half left across stile by gate; right along field edge. Over stile at far end (522578); half left across field, through boggy dell (YAs). Half left across field beyond, to fingerpost at far top left corner (527580). Follow lane to join Sandstone Trail/ST (533583). Ahead on ST for 1 mile, crossing road (539588), to reach next road (540590). Ahead to Beeston Castle (537593). Return along ST for 2¼ miles to road just east of Higher Burwardsley (529567). Right to Pheasant Inn.

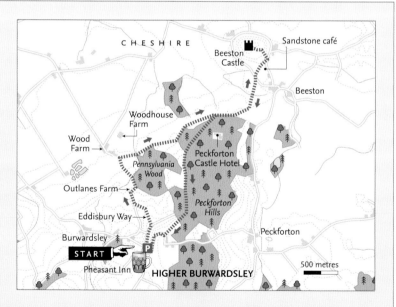

Lunch/accommodation Pheasant Inn, Higher Burwardsley (01829 770434; thepheasantinn.co.uk) – comfortable and popular inn. Also, try the Sandstone Café near Beeston Castle gatehouse.

Walking Cheshire's Sandstone Trail by Tony Bowerman (Northern Eye Books); sandstonetrail.com

More information Chester TIC (0845 6477868), visitcheshire.com, visitengland.com, Beeston Castle (01829 260464; english-heritage.org.uk/beeston), sandstonetrail.com

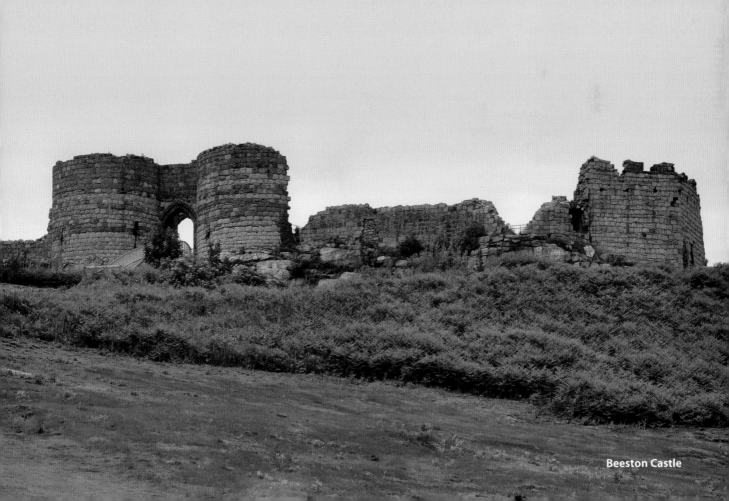

Beeston Castle

Grindley Brook & Llangollen Canal
CHESHIRE

On a stormy night the worst of winter was trying to outdo itself. We sat huddled by candlelight round the log fire of the Cholmondeley Arms in the throes of a power blackout across south Cheshire with hurricane winds sucking at the doors, rain lashing the darkness outside, and toppled trees cutting off the roads in all directions. Drama and chaos everywhere, and a cosy fatalism round the fireside.

In the morning, all change — gentle breeze, blue sky, cold sunshine, the hedges littered with broken branches, the fields streaked with silver fleets of flood water. "You could actually see the barn roof trying to lift off," said the farmer at Grindley Brook Farm as he cleared his drive of timber.

This countryside, a maze of small drumlin hills and kettle-hole lakelets, was shaped by melting glaciers about 10000 years ago. As we gained height up the hummocky ground around Hinton Bank Farm, we were treated to a panorama of the hills across the Welsh border, from the knobbly volcanic upthrust of the Breiddens in the south to the broad cones of the Clwydian Hills out west. Between them rose the high cliffs of the Berwyn range, painted dazzling white by last night's terrific blizzards.

Storm-bedraggled sheep lay soaking up the temporary sunshine in the fields round Wirswall. This is rolling, bumpy, hard-riding country. I thought of Randolph Caldecott, the Victorian bank clerk and graphic genius who lived at Wirswall. As a child I loved his illustrations for favourite books such as *The House That Jack Built* and *The Diverting History of John Gilpin*, full of broad-bottomed old gents courting pretty fair maids and getting tossed into ditches by stampeding nags.

We squelched and slithered across red mud fields from Wicksted Old Hall down to the glacial kettle-hole of Big Mere, where great crested grebes with glistening chestnut cheeks bobbed on the steel-grey water in pre-courtship practice. We passed Marbury's pink sandstone church, sunlit on its knoll, and went on to Marbury Lock and a great arc of towpath beside the Llangollen Canal.

The copper-brown canal ran glinting between the inundated fields. Three hungry buzzards circled, mewing over a waterlogged marsh; a flotilla of swans sailed as white as snow on the floods below; and green catkins hung from hazel twigs and wriggled in the wind like lambs' tails, a whisper of spring somewhere beyond these winter storms.

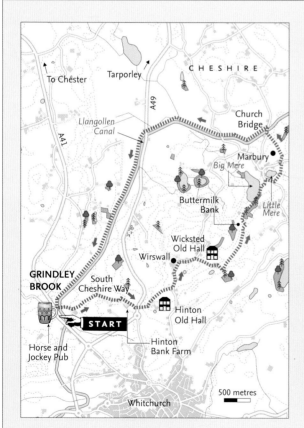

Start & finish Horse & Jockey, Grindley Brook, Cheshire SY13 4QJ (OS ref SJ522432) – park at pub; please give them your custom!

Getting there Bus: Service 41 (shropshire.gov.uk/bustimes), Whitchurch-Chester. Road: Grindley Brook is on A41 Chester road, just NW of Whitchurch.

Walk (8½ miles, easy, OS Explorer 257): From Horse & Jockey cross A41 (be careful); follow Bishop Bennet Way left of garage; over canal, through railway arch; through gate on left ('South Cheshire Way/SCW'). From here, follow waymarked SCW for 4 miles via Hinton Bank Farm, A49 crossing (538432), Hinton Old Hall cottages (540433), road through Wirswall (544436-548441), Wicksted Old Hall (554439), Buttermilk Bank, stile to right of The Knowles house (558450), east bank of Big Mere, road near Marbury church (562455), and road northeast of Little Mere (565459). From here, footpath north (yellow arrows) across four fields to Llangollen Canal at Church Bridge (562464); left along towpath for 4 miles to Grindley Brook.

Conditions Some very boggy patches

Lunch Horse & Jockey, Grindley Brook (01948 662723)

Accommodation Cholmondeley Arms, Cholmondeley, Cheshire SY14 8HN (01829 720300; cholmondeleyarms.co.uk) – friendly, characterful pub in a former school

More information Chester TIC (0845 6477868), visitengland.com, satmap.com, ramblers.org.uk

Barbon and Brownthwaite
CUMBRIA

A lovely day over the western Dales, with plenty of hot sun and those big drifting white clouds that herald a beautiful afternoon. "And going to get even better," prophesied the lady walking her terrier through Barbon village. The green bulk of Barbon Low Fell stood on the eastern skyline like an invitation, and I couldn't resist its summons.

The woods of pine, beech and chestnut above Barbon Beck were drowsy with insect hum and shimmer. Speckled wood butterflies opened their cream and brown wings on warm stones, hoverflies hung suspended as if on invisible wires and the beech leaves cradled flies in gorgeous glossy jackets of enamelled green. Leaving the trees, I looked ahead up the remote high-sided cleft of Barbondale, one of the least walked and loneliest dales. Its green flanks rose to open moor tops shot with cloud shadows under the blue and white sky.

Giant convulsions of the earth's crust hundreds of millions of years ago ripped the great Pennine Fault through here, shoving Lake District gritstones on the west of Barbondale 800 feet into the air, while pushing the east side limestones up on end. Hence the steep west side of Barbondale, and the more weathered, rounded and ragged limestone tops to the east of the dale where I was headed.

At Blindbeck Bridge a couple of young girls were playing in the beck. The smell of their picnic fire, thick and sweet, drifted across the stream. The scent of the fire and the girls' shouts and laughter followed me along the sedgy old bridleway up the fellside to Bullpot Farm. The limestone hereabouts has been eaten by rain, frost and floods into thousands of holes, caves and underground passages, some with witchy reputations. Did a bull fall down one of the potholes near Bullpot Farm, drawn there by a maleficent hag?

From the solid old house, tucked down in its cleft among shelter trees, I followed a moor road edged with bilberry and heath bedstraw, then a grassy fellside track that wound up and over the shoulder of Brownthwaite to a jaw-dropper of a view.

From this highpoint you look west over the tight grey huddle of Kirkby Lonsdale, out to the sea in Morecambe Bay, round to the fells of southern Lakeland, more sharply cut and mountainous than anything the Dales can show. The view owns grandeur, vast scale and intimate rural detail in one sweep.

The rough cobbled lane of Fellfoot Road carried me most of the way back to Barbon. I could have taken a short cut across the meadows. But the afternoon felt timeless; a walk to spin out as long as I wished.

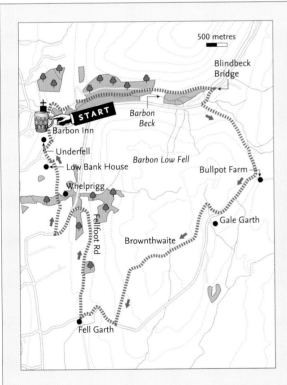

Start & finish Barbon Inn, Barbon, Cumbria LA6 2LJ (OS ref SD629824)

Getting there Road: Barbon is signposted from A683, 3 miles north of Kirkby Lonsdale

Walk (8 miles, moderate, OS Explorer OL2): From Barbon Inn, right up road. Beyond Barbon Church, left (fingerpost) to cross Barbon Beck (631825); follow roadway round right bend and on. In ¼ mile on left bend, keep ahead (635826, blue arrow) through gate. Follow bridleway to Blindbeck Bridge. Right along road (656828); cross bridge; in 50m, left (654826, 'Bullpot'); follow bridleway 1 mile uphill to road at Bullpot Farm (662815). Right for ½ mile. Above Gale Garth, right (657809, fingerpost, yellow arrow/ YA) up green moor track for 1¾ miles by Brownthwaite Pike to road (641793). Right; at foot of steep slope, opposite 'Wandales Lane' fingerpost, right (635794) along stony Fellfoot Road for 1¼ miles to road (634810). Left; opposite Fell Garth, right through gate (632646, 'Barbon'). Cross fields through gates (YAs); cross Whelprigg drive (632812); aim for far left corner of big parkland meadow; through gate (632817); follow track (YA) through gate into Low Bank House farmyard (631818). Before buildings, right through squeeze stile; aim for far left corner of field; through stiles to road (639819). Right for 150m; through Underfell driveway gate (631821); through 2 more gates (YAs) into lane (631822). Left; in 30m, right over stile; cross field back to Barbon.

Lunch Barbon Inn (01524 276233; barbon-inn.co.uk)

More information Kirkby Lonsdale TIC (01524 271437), ramblers.org.uk, satmap.com

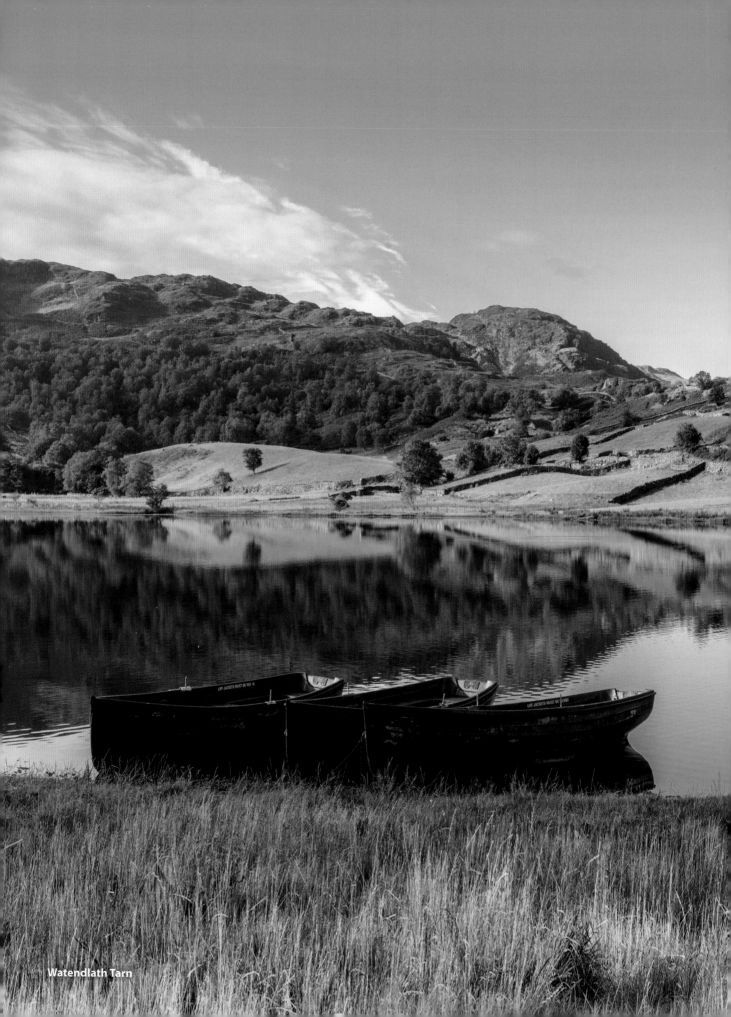

Watendlath Tarn

Dock Tarn and Watendlath

CUMBRIA

A warm and muggy morning in Borrowdale, with low cloud brushing the hilltops and the weatherman muttering of thunderstorms. The side dale of Langstrath was full of the bleating of Herdwick sheep, white-faced with blue-grey coats, the black-coated and black-muzzled lambs stolidly chewing alongside their dams.

From the fellside above Stonethwaite we climbed steeply away through oakwoods, the stepped and stone-flagged path rising under trees mottled with gleams of sunshine, rags of blue and smears of grey sailing overhead among the branches. The stream of Willygrass Gill tinkled and rustled down a narrow channel of gleaming black rocks, the water falling in a succession of leaps, jumps and pauses for reflection. We sat to watch a jay hopping from branch to branch, roguish in chestnut, black and white with a flash of blue — a handsome and swaggering buccaneer of a bird.

At the treeline the view opened tremendously, a stand-and-gasp moment — the steep converging clefts of Greenup Gill and Langstrath under their twin crowns of Eagle Crag and Heron Crag, and away in the west the enormous eroded cliffs that hang ominously over Honister Hause and its slate mine workings, the old tramway running straight as a die up the hill behind and the road snaking steeply down into Borrowdale.

Dock Tarn lies sheltered in a ring of little craggy hills. The water lily blooms were out, white crowns scattered on green mats of leaves. The tarn lay perfectly still, emitting a faint shimmer as the wind crumpled the wavelets around a rocky islet crowned with a handful of rowans. You could easily stay all day in such a place, searching for frogs and orchids, dreaming your dreams.

Eventually the stony path called us on, through a pass and down over a broad rushy upland, gold-spotted with bog asphodel and heavy with the scent of wet peat and sun-warmed bog myrtle. We came down to Watendlath Farm along the shore of Watendlath Tarn, where families were swimming and picnicking. We could have murdered a cuppa there, but the cosy-looking tearoom was cash only, no cards. Hellfire and damnation!

A rough and rocky old bridleway leads over from Watendlath to Borrowdale, with classic lakeland views ahead over the green meadows of the flat-bottomed dale to the heights of the Borrowdale Fells. Down in Rosthwaite, before setting back to Stonethwaite, we looked into the Royal Oak. I did my first ever Lake District walks from this little inn when I was fifteen. My boots bit into my heels, I was sulky with my Dad and sore-legged each morning, but it instilled a love of these enchanting hills that has never gone away.

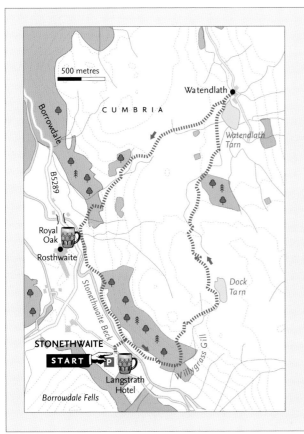

Start & finish Langstrath Country Inn, Stonethwaite, Borrowdale, Cumbria CA12 5XG (OS ref NY263137)

Getting there Bus: Services 77,78 (Arriva). Road: Stonethwaite is signed off B5289 Borrowdale road just south of Rosthwaite.

Walk (6 miles, moderate/hard, OS Explorer OL4): From Langstrath Country Inn, right along road. Right ('Greenup Edge') across beck; right ('Greenup Edge'); in 200m, left (265137, post with yellow arrow) up slope. Cross stone stile in wall (268136); very steeply up through woods, then across moorland to Dock Tarn (274143). Continue north on good stony track for 1½ miles to Watendlath (274163). Right across bridge to tearoom, or left ('Rosthwaite'), following signs to Rosthwaite. At bridge (259150), right into village, or forward ('Stonethwaite') to Stonethwaite.

NB: steep climb through woods below Dock Tarn!

Lunch/accommodation Watendlath tearoom (cash only), Langstrath Country Inn, Stonethwaite (01768 777239; thelangstrath.co.uk) – lively, friendly country inn

More information Keswick TIC (0845 9010845), visitengland.com, satmap.com, ramblers.org.uk

Dufton and Threlkeld Side

CUMBRIA

A cold wind over Cumbria, blowing across the fells around Dufton. The last time I was here, walking the Pennine Way, I had fallen in love with the trim little farming village in its neat green dale. Today there was time for a cup of coffee in the Post Box Pantry and a saunter around the long village green before Jane and I donned scarves and headed for the hills.

Goldfinches were tentatively cheeping in the leafless sycamores of the stone-walled lane up Pus Gill's cleft, and the bubbling cry of curlews, so hauntingly evocative, came down from the moors where they would be pairing up for nesting and rearing. Spring was moving in curlew blood, but its green fingers hadn't yet stirred much response in the trees or wayside plants of these high Pennines.

Looking back above Pusgill House, we saw Dufton cradled in green, the wide vale of the River Eden beyond and, standing magnificently on the western skyline, the humpy backs of the Lakeland fells. We watched a snow shower move across the landscape in Blakean shafts of sunlight, trailing a white hem that clung to the highest peaks and ridges in the thinnest of skins.

Once we had skirted the sharp cone of Dufton Pike and turned up the narrow side dale of Threlkeld Side towards the moors, the green road we were following became rocky and dark, and the sides of the dale sloped thick with tumbled boulders and charcoal-coloured slack. Lead miners of former days had burrowed the cleft into a warren of pitch-black levels, and their smelting kilns, spillways and spoil hummocks lay all around. Above the desolation lay the high moor, where we found a stone-built shooting box on the bank of cold and steely Great Rundale Tarn. Coming unexpectedly over the skyline, we shocked a pair of Canada geese who were sailing in the tarn, contemplating connubiality; frantic honking and splashing signalled their displeasure.

It was too damn cold to hang about. We turned about, put our heads down into the buffeting half-gale and pushed back downhill, the fifty-mile view before us blurred by wind tears. We turned along the beautiful wooded valley that lies like a secret behind the nape of Dufton Pike, and were soon back on the Pennine Way and bowling down to Dufton.

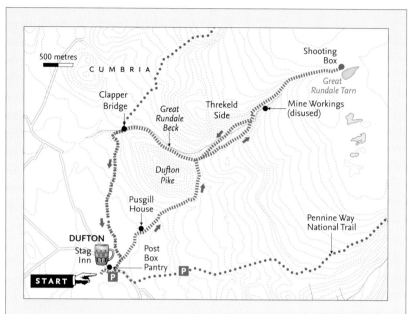

Start & finish Dufton car park, near Appleby-in-Westmorland, Cumbria CA16 6DB (OS ref NY690250)

Getting there Road: Dufton is signposted from Appleby-in-Westmorland (A66)

Walk (8½ miles, moderate, OS Explorer OL19): Right along road from car park, round left bend; on following right bend by Old Dufton Hall, ahead on stony lane ('Pennine Way'/PW). In 150m, at foot of slope, PW forks left; but keep right here (692252; 'bridleway') and up walled lane for 3½ miles, passing Pusgill House (696257) and mine workings of Threlkeld Side, to reach shooting box by Great Rundale Tarn (729283). Return for 2 miles past mines. Under Dufton Pike, right over wall stile at yellow-topped post (704268); down to another post; over stile, and right along track through Great Rundale Beck valley (yellow arrows). At clapper bridge (692273), left on PW to Dufton.

Conditions Upper moors can be cold, wet and inhospitable – dress appropriately!

Lunch Stag Inn, Dufton CA16 6DB (01768 351608; thestagdufton.co.uk), Post Box Pantry, Dufton (07903 358081; postboxpantry.co.uk)

Accommodation Brow Farm B&B, Dufton CA16 6DF (01768 352865; browfarm.com)

More information Appleby-in-Westmorland TIC (01768 351177), visitcumbria.com, ramblers.org.uk, satmap.com

Eel Tarn and Burnmoor Tarn

CUMBRIA

The tiny narrow-gauge Ravenglass and Eskdale steam railway, known to all as 'Ratty', winds its way up from Ravenglass on the Cumbrian coast deep into Eskdale in the western flanks of the Lake District. On a damp, steamy morning we set out from the Boot Inn to piece together three of the walks in Alfred Wainwright's little booklet, *Walks from Ratty*, and make a good day in the hills.

St Catherine's Church lay low and dusky pink beside the River Esk. In the churchyard we paid our respects to Tommy Dobson, master of Eskdale and Ennerdale Foxhounds for fifty-three years until his death in 1910. His carved stone likeness, radiating humour and pugnacity, looked out from the grave slab, flanked by the heads of a fox and a hound.

We followed the glassy Esk through miniature gorges and past rocky rapids where grey wagtails bobbed rhythmically on the water-sculpted boulders, up to the graceful old packhorse span of Doctor Bridge.

Above the nearby Woolpack Inn a gate led on to the brackeny hillside. High above, we found Eel Tarn spread under mats of water lilies and ruffles of wind — one of the quietest and loveliest spots in Lakeland.

The path led on over a wide upland of marshy ground and bracken. A pale smoky light lay on Eskdale. Ahead, Eskdale Fell hid its face in cloud. We squelched over wet ground full of golden stars of bog asphodel, and crossed loud little Whillan Beck to come to Burnmoor Tarn, a steely oval in a hollow under great fells. We stripped off and went in, sliding over the pebbles into water full of peat-flecks, warm and silky on the skin.

We swam in lonely delight, before dressing on the tarn bank and making our way back down the old corpse road to Boot. Eskdale's hay meadows gleamed pale green, and the shouts and whistles of the farmer at Gill Bank, busy training a young dog to muster the sheep, came faintly up to us from the fields around the farm.

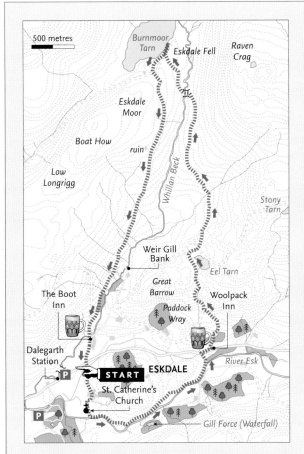

Start & finish Dalegarth station, Ravenglass & Eskdale Railway CA19 1TF (OS ref NY174007)

Getting there Rail: mainline service to Ravenglass (thetrainline.com); Ravenglass and Eskdale Railway (01229 717171; ravenglass-railway.co.uk) to Dalegarth station. Road: Boot is signposted from Eskdale Green (minor roads from A595 at Duddon Bridge or Holmrook).

Walk (7 miles, moderate, OS Explorer OL6): From Dalegarth station, left along road. At Brook House Inn (126008), right ('St Catherine's') on stony lane to Eskdale Church (176003). Left along River Esk to Doctor Bridge (189007) and road (189009). Right for 200m; left before Woolpack Inn (yellow arrow, 'Burnmoor, Wasdale Head'). Up track behind house, through gate (190011); up path through bracken with wall close on left. At gate/ladder stile (189014; 'Boot, Woolpack') don't cross; continue uphill, leaving wall on left. By ruined house (188015) bear right and head north. Above house cross bog; bear right and go anti-clockwise round knoll, and on north. Skirt round left side of Eel Tarn (188019); right along north shore; at far side bear left/north (189021) towards Eskdale Fell, passing two lone trees. Cross Brockshaw Beck (190027); keep left of rock outcrops; descend to cross Whillan Beck by Lambford Bridge (188038). Bear right to Burnmoor Tarn (186043). Follow path back past (but not across) Lambford Bridge, down to Boot and Dalegarth Station.

Lunch/accommodation Boot Inn, Eskdale CA19 1TG (01946 723711; thebooteskdale.co.uk), Brook House Inn, Eskdale CA19 1TG (01946 723288; brookhouseinn.co.uk), Woolpack Inn, Eskdale CA19 1TH (01946 723230; woolpack.co.uk)

More information *Walks from Ratty* by A. Wainwright is available from 'Ratty', £3. Ravenglass TIC (01229 717278), visitengland.com, satmap.com, ramblers.org.uk

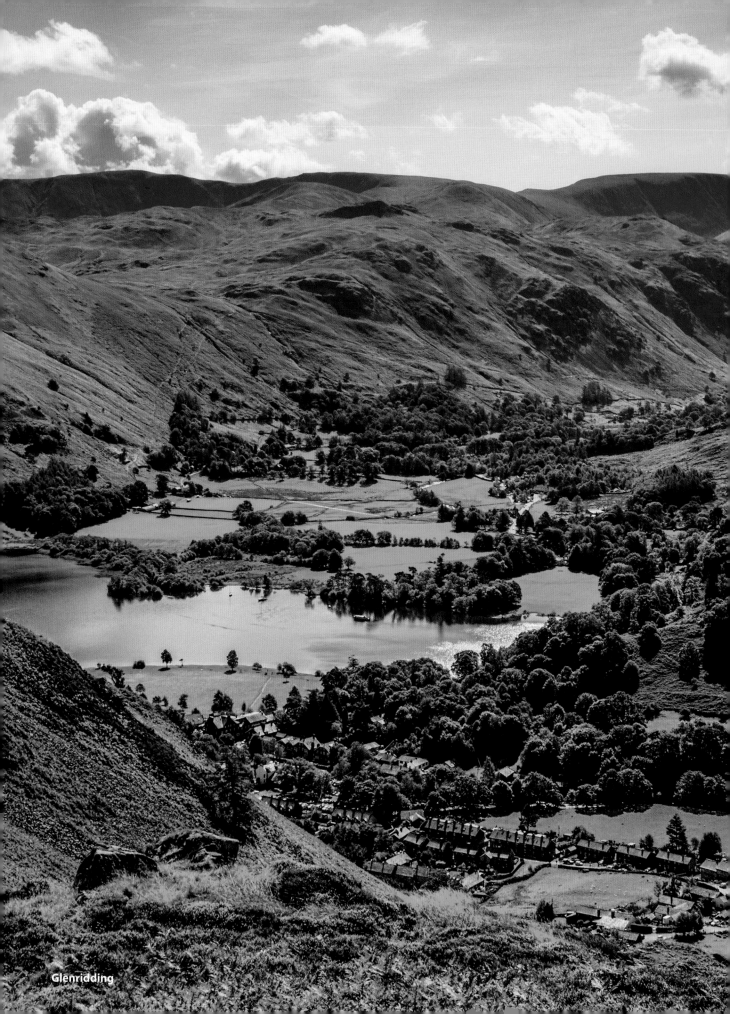
Glenridding

Glenridding Dodd and Sheffield Pike

CUMBRIA

Mark Hook pointed out of the dining room window at Mosscrag Guest House — "That's Glenridding Dodd. It's a shame people don't go up there from Glenridding any more. The Victorians did, and they knew a good view when they saw one. It's a beautiful little fell. And here's how you can link it up with Sheffield Pike…"

In the Lake District it's handy to have a B&B host who knows the local fells inside out. Within five minutes Mark had pencilled out the route on my map. It didn't seem too fearsome, even though some of the contours looked a little close-packed for comfort. After all, if Victorian ladies and gentlemen had managed it in their crinolines and well-polished high-lows …

Half an hour into the walk I paused to catch my breath, not for the first time. If our genteel ancestors really did 'ascend' Glenridding Dodd (it was always 'ascending', never 'climbing') by this 45° channel of rubbly stones, they must have been made of stern stuff. In an era when high fells such as Helvellyn and Scafell Pike were still considered alpine in difficulty, Glenridding Dodd was a worthy objective for a family 'ascent'. At the summit of the Dodd, a towering lump of rock scabbed with pale outcrops, I saw what they had perspired to see, a fabulous prospect down the southern length of Ullswater.

Nowadays, with better boots and weatherproof gear, we nonchalantly tackle mountains all over the world. Celebrity mountaineers and their TV heroics can make the humbler fells of Lakeland seem unworthy of attention. Alfred Wainwright wouldn't have had any truck with such notions. He commends the modest delights of Glenridding Dodd to his disciples and points approvingly towards the scrambly crag-top climb up the ridge of Heron Pike to the moor leading to Sheffield Pike.

With a travel-stained copy of the master's guide to *The Eastern Fells* in hand, I negotiated the steep and rugged pathway, splashed between the peaty tarns and stood by the cairn on Sheffield Pike, lord of a most superb view — north up Ullswater, east to the long line of the High Street ridge, west into the great green clefts under Glencoyne Head, and south to the blade-like profile of Helvellyn, standing dark and threatening like a lead weight against the clouds.

Wainwright hated the lead mines whose remnants scar the upper end of Glenridding. But I enjoyed the descent through those incredible banks of multicoloured spoil, hanging in the sky like the sword of Damocles over the former smelting mills dwarfed at their feet.

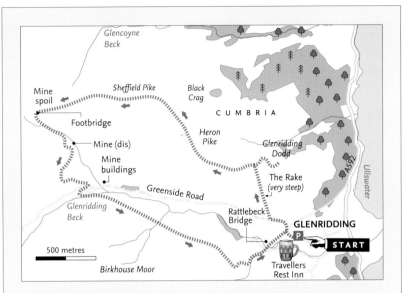

Start & finish Glenridding car park CA11 0PD (OS ref NY386170)

Getting there Bus: Service 108 (Penrith – stagecoachbus.com), 208 (Keswick, summer only – albatravelcumbria.co.uk), 517 (Windermere, summer only – stagecoachbus.com) Road: A592, beside Glenridding Bridge.

Walk (7 miles, hard, OS Explorer OL5): From car park follow signs to Traveller's Rest PH (382170). 100m past pub, right ('Greenside Road'). Fork left ('Greenside Mine'); past 2 cottage terraces, through gate at cattle grid, then right up zigzag path; in 100m, right (yellow arrow) up steep stony track to wall at saddle (378175). Don't go through gate; follow wall to right; in 150m, right up track to summit of Glenridding Dodd (381175).

Return to gate; don't go through, but keep ahead, with wall on right, along path (grass, then stones). Steeply up ridge of Heron Pike, then across boggy grass for ¼ mile to summit of Sheffield Pike (369182).

From summit aim west for long ridge of mine spoil. Cross Swart Beck by footbridge (359179); left along mine track; steeply down to mine buildings. Just before buildings, right (364174; 'Red Tarn, Helvellyn'). In 200m, left across Glenridding Beck; left along hillside path for almost a mile. At fork by big boulder with wall, left downhill; follow wall; through gate by ladder stile (376167). Down stony path; cross Glenridding Beck by Rattlebeck Bridge; Traveller's Rest; car park.

NB: very steep path up to the saddle below Glenridding Dodd, and up the ridge of Heron Pike. Boots, fell-walking gear and stick are advisable. A walk for fit, energetic fell-walkers. Not recommended in mist.

Lunch Traveller's Rest Inn, Greenside Road, Glenridding CA11 0QQ (01768 482298)

Accommodation and advice Mosscrag Guest House, Glenridding CA11 0PA (01768 482500; mosscrag.co.uk)

More information Ullswater TIC, Glenridding car park (01768 482414), golakes.co.uk, ramblers.org.uk, satmap.com

Green Quarter and Kentmere Pike
CUMBRIA

Looking back from the old fell path from Kentmere over to Long Sleddale, the Kentmere Valley on this gorgeous, clear morning looked almost too good to be true. Church, houses and scattered farms lay in a dale bottom so richly and uniformly green it might have been stroked there with a painter's brush. A farmer went bouncing down the fields on her quad bike, shouting "C'm-aan!" to the madly bleating sheep chasing her trailer with its load of feed. Near the crest of the path we were following, a just-born black Herdwick lamb wobbled on splayed legs, sniffing along its mother's blue-grey body to locate the bulging udder that awaited it.

We found the steep upward path to Wray Crag and set our boots to it, pushing upwards under lark song that poured from invisible performers overhead. Up on Shipman Knotts we sat to catch our breath, looking east to the long back of Sleddale Fell and a gleam of Windermere down in the southwest.

Now the rocks and crags gave way to a smooth saddle of moor grass, the dark stain of the path leading on and up the long nape of Kentmere Pike to the summit cairn at 730m (2,395ft). Up here the wind was blowing strong and cold. We huddled down and gazed our fill at the westward view — Coniston Old Man and Windermere, Great End and Bowfell beyond the breaking wave of Ill Bell, and a shoulder of Helvellyn crusted with snow.

A long descent over bogs and crags, down to Hallow Bank and the walled and cobbled lane back to Green Quarter. We chatted with a farmer looking over the wall at his sheep — tales of winter storms, lost lambs and ewes covered by snowdrifts. "We'd forty lambs indoors being bottle fed," he said, "and forty ewes looking for 'em once the snow went! But we got 'em all matched," and he smiled with satisfaction as if it had only happened yesterday.

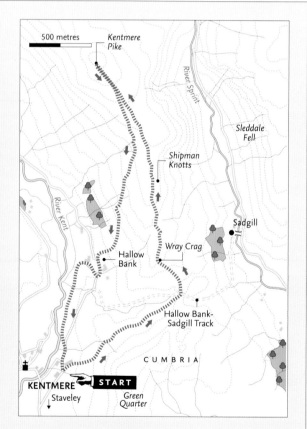

Start & finish Green Quarter, Kentmere, near Staveley, Cumbria LA8 9JP approx (OS ref NY461040)

Getting there Road: Staveley is signed off the A591 (Windermere-Kendal). Follow road to Kentmere. Just before village, right ('Hallow Bank, Green Quarter'). Limited car parking at Green Quarter (four spaces on left before triangular green). If none available, park in Kentmere and walk to Green Quarter.

Walk (6½ miles, strenuous, OS Explorer OL7): From triangular green, right up lane ('Longsleddale'). At Old Forge gate, right through gate (yellow arrow, 'Longsleddale'). Bear left; through gate at wall angle; follow track (public right of way) across fields north-east for 1 mile. Through kissing gate (476050) onto Hallow Bank-Sadgill track. Left through gate; right up track, following wall on right steeply uphill northwards for 1¼ miles over Wray Crag (473054) and Shipman Knotts (472062) to ladder stile across wall (472067). From here, clear path up Kentmere Pike (fence soon coming in on right) to summit cairn (465078).

Return in poor weather/mist – back the way you came. Otherwise – return to where wall meets fence on left (468075). Fork a little right away from ascent path, following clear path. Cross ladder stile 250m north-west of ascent stile (470069). Follow path (sometimes faint, but well trodden) south-south-west downhill for 1 mile to farm lane gate at Hallow Bank (466055). Through gate, down track; in 50m, left through gateway beside parking area; fork right down stony track. In 200m cross stream; next right (465052, 'Mardale'), down road, through gate, and on to where farm buildings are in front of you. Bear left (not sharp left) past barn and on downhill. Track bends left; don't bear right through gate (463053), but keep ahead along Low Lane. In ²/₃ mile join road (461044); right to Green Quarter.

Conditions A moderately hard fell walk; appropriate clothing and boots recommended.

Lunch Picnic

Accommodation Eagle & Child, Staveley LA8 9LP (01539 821320; eaglechildinn.co.uk) – very cheerful, walker-friendly inn

Reading *Wainwright Book 2 – The Far Eastern Fells* (Frances Lincoln)

More information Kendal TIC (01539 735891), golakes.co.uk, visitengland.com, satmap.com, ramblers.org.uk

Haweswater and Swindale

CUMBRIA

First-time guests at the hospitable Mardale Inn in Bampton, Cumbria, should take heed: the bar game of Nails is not for the faint-hearted, nor the over-refreshed. It involves a massive tree stump, a sharp hatchet blow, a flat-headed nail and more hand-eye co-ordination than I usually possess. As things turned out, a lucky whack put me in the winner's enclosure and I set out for Haweswater reservoir next morning with my fingers still attached to my person.

A quiet, still, cold winter day, with distance and incipient mist laying a milky gauze across the east Cumbrian fells, muting the fiery red of the bracken to a soft fox-brown and melding together ridge line and sky. The long curve of Haweswater lay flat in its cleft, its water stained yellow with the reflections of larches and stirred by wind too slight to feel on the cheek.

A bridleway through mossy woods brought me down to Naddle Farm, where the farmer, his sheepdog and shepherd's crook all jolted up the fellside together on a spluttering quad bike. I crossed Naddle Beck and climbed a stony track into bare moorland. A solitary, sinewy old thorn tree stood at the crest, bent nearly double by the blasts of many hundred winters. On over an upland of sphagnum and pale moor grass, then down into narrow Swindale, with a memorable view of Swindale Beck snaking in extravagant curves through neat green inbye fields and a swathe of dun-coloured bogland under craggy red dale sides. Swindale is a lonely dale, where farming is as hard as the landscape is beautiful. Few make their way here, even to walk — it is a little outside the Lake District's charmed inner circle. A scatter of stone-built barns and farmhouses, a muck-spreader parked on the road verge, Swaledale ewes in the bracken and the chattering rumble of the beck over its dipper-whitened stones, all enclosed by a mighty half-moon of crags at the dale head.

I could happily have idled away the short winter afternoon under Swindale's enchantment, but already the light was draining out of the day. A green track took me up under Trussgap Brow, then across a squelchy moor to Tailbert Farm. A teeter along the rim of Tailbert Gill's precipitous little cleft and I was walking the old concrete track back towards Haweswater with the rocky jaws of Swindale closing behind me.

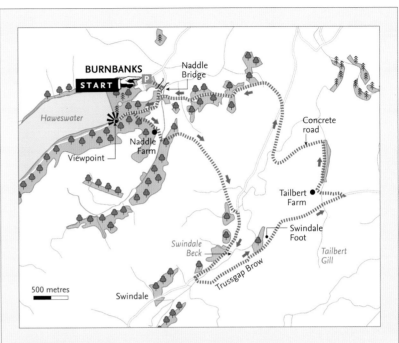

Start & finish Burnbanks car park, Haweswater, Cumbria CA10 2RP approx (OS ref NY508161)

Getting there Road: M6 to Jct 39; A6 through Shap; left at north end of Shap through Bampton Grange and Bampton towards Haweswater. At Naddle Gate (510162), road bends left to cross Naddle Bridge; keep ahead here ('No Through Road') to car park in Burnbanks (507161).

Walk (8½ miles, moderate, OS Explorer OL5): From Burnbanks car park, follow footpath (Naddle Farm') through woods to road (510160). Right across Naddle Bridge; follow road ('Hawsewater Hotel') to dam for reservoir views (503155). Return along road; in 250m right up bridleway (506156; fingerpost) through woods to descend to Naddle Farm (509153). Right along house; follow 'Swindale' across beck (510152); up fellside on stony track. In ½ mile at ridge, ahead through metal gate at junction of walls (516151); ahead across moor on path, aiming for peak dead ahead. Descend to road in Swindale (521142); right up dale. In ¾ mile pass a dam; in another 100m, left across Swindale Beck (515132). Forward for 100m (very wet!) to turn left up green track. At top, ahead over crossing of tracks (528140); bear right (ENE) across wet moor to corner of wall (534143). Ahead over moor for ¼ mile to road (537144). Left to Tailbert Farm (534145). Right along back of farmhouse; through gate (yellow arrow); ahead along west rim of Tailbert Gill to meet concrete road (534152). Left for 2¼ miles to road (510159); right across Naddle Bridge; left to car park.

Lunch/accommodation Mardale Inn, Bampton, Cumbria CA10 2RQ (01931 713244; mardaleinn.co.uk) — friendly inn at the heart of its community

More information Penrith TIC (01768 867466), golakes.co.uk, ramblers.org.uk, satmap.com

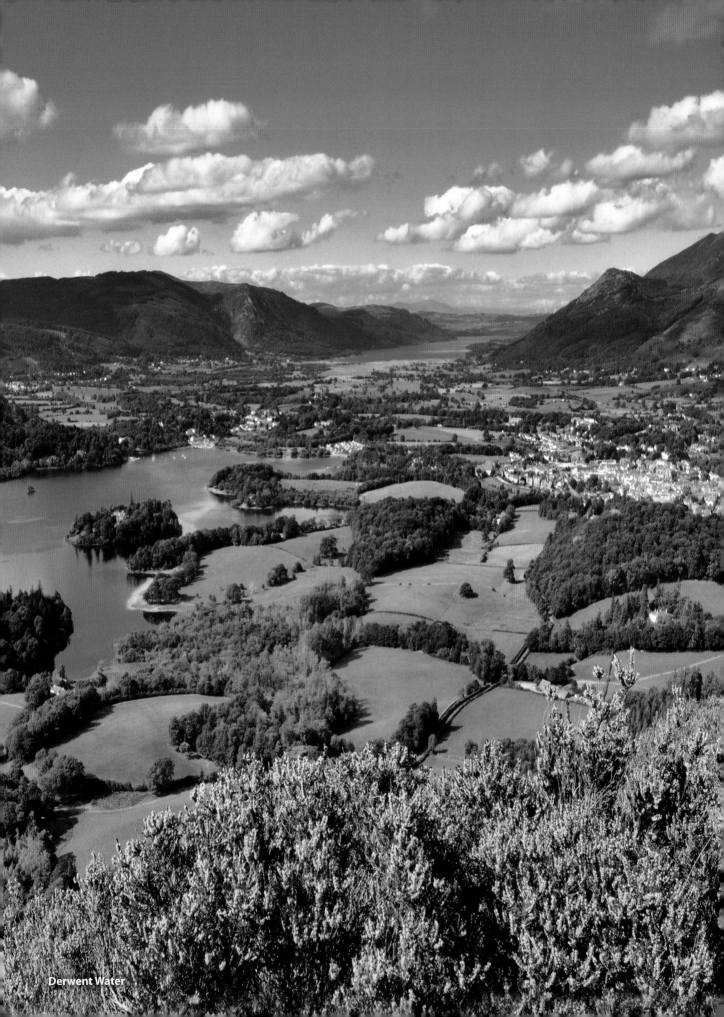
Derwent Water

Walla Crag and Derwent Water
CUMBRIA

I hadn't seen Fi since we were trainee teachers together in Somerset, but her energy was instantly familiar when we met up at Keswick's Theatre by the Lake. What a day for walking, as cold as anything, with high cloud over the Lake District and lemon-yellow sunlight streaming across the crumpled faces of Skiddaw and Blencathra. It was wonderful to be kicking up showers of leaves in Cockshot and Castlehead woods like teenagers, chattering away as you do when you have a few decades to catch up on.

Up by Springs Farm the chaffinches were trying out short explosive phrases in the silver birch coppice. A stony lane led us up beside a loud little stream with the big dark bulge of Walla Crag looming ahead, its crown feathery with larches.

"An eminence of intermingled rocks and trees," pronounced Alfred Wainwright's *Pictorial Guide to the Lakeland Fells* (Book 3) in my hand, "of moderate elevation, yet steep, romantic, challenging." We passed Rakefoot Farm, its chimneys pushing up columns of woodsmoke behind a screen of leafless sycamores, and turned uphill and out on to the open fellside leading up towards Walla Crag.

A "braided path" as Fi described it, an in-and-out tangle of footways beside the wall, with a sensational view behind us northward towards hollow-shouldered Blencathra and the rising waves of the Skiddaw range, the sun picking out the monoliths of Castlerigg stone circle in the foreground.

"Dear thoughts are in my mind
And my soul soars enchanted,
As I hear the sweet lark sing
In the clear air of the day."

So sang Fi as we crunched the ice in the puddles and followed the braided path along the edge of the crag. A quick stop in a sheltered hollow out of the clear (but bloody cold) air for oatcakes and mango chunks, and we were at the summit cairn admiring the deep glacial scratches in the rocks and looking out over the islands and bays of Derwent Water. Clouds went marching through the valleys beyond, but all the tops to the west were clear.

On along the escarpment with an incomparable view southward towards the jostling hills enclosing Borrowdale, the peaks of Great Gable, Scafell Pike and Glaramara dipping in and out of the cloud sea like so many dark topsails. Then a steep skelter down the fellside among juniper bushes, and we turned back along the stumbly path under Falcon Crag.

It was a vigorous, noisy walk back to Keswick along the lake shore with white horses pawing at the little pebbly bays and wind roaring in the pines and shivering the water of ditches jellied with frogspawn as if to blow the last of the winter clean away.

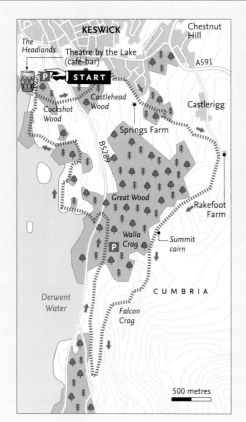

Start & finish Lakeside car park, Keswick, Cumbria CA12 5DJ (OS ref NY265229)

Getting there Bus: Service 554 (Carlisle), 555 and 556 (Lancaster, Carlisle) to Keswick (stagecoachbus.com). Road: M6 to Jct 40, A66 to Keswick.

Walk (6½ miles; moderate; Explorer OL4): Past theatre to lake; left; in 100m, left (fingerpost) along path. Over path crossing, up through Cockshot Wood. Cross field, then B5289 (269226). Bear left, fork immediately right uphill. Up and over Castlehead Wood; path to road (272229). Right, past Springs Farm; follow signed path through Springs Wood ('Castlerigg, Walla Crag'). In ½ mile, left over footbridge (283222) to road. Right; at Rakefoot fork right; follow path ('Walla Crag') over footbridge and steeply up beside wall. Near top, wall is broken by railings; right through gate here, left along crags to summit cairn (277213). Continue for 150m; stile through wall; don't turn right along wall, but head 'inland' on path heading for Bleaberry Fell. In 300m, bear right across beck on path along edge of escarpment. Follow this over Falcon Crag for ⅔ mile to meet wall (272198). Right downhill to gate; right along path towards Keswick for ¾ mile. At wall of Great Wood (271210), right uphill; left on footbridge across beck and fork left downhill on woodland path. In 200m, ahead over path crossing. Continue to car park (272214); follow slip road down to cross B5289; down steps; follow path. In 50m, left at footbridge to lake shore (270213); right along shore path for 1½ miles to car park.

Lunch Picnic; or the Stalls Bar in the Theatre by the Lake, Keswick CA12 5DJ (01768 772282)

Accommodation Littlefield, 32 Eskin Street, Keswick CA12 4DG (01768 772949; littlefield-keswick.co.uk) – quiet, welcoming, walker-friendly

Guidebook *Wainwright's Pictorial Guide to the Lakeland Fells*, Book 3 (Frances Lincoln)

More information Keswick TIC (0845 9010845), golakes.co.uk, ramblers.org.uk, satmap.com

Mellbreak and Crummock Water
CUMBRIA

"A grand hill in a beautiful situation with a character all its own and an arresting outline," says Alfred Wainwright of the fierce dark pyramid called Mellbreak. That neatly sums up this formidable-looking but actually quite manageable hill that lowers like a grumpy humped-backed monster over the western side of the long narrow lake of Crummock Water.

Setting out from the Kirkstile Inn, the northern face of Mellbreak looked so dark, sheer and forbidding that we wondered how on earth we were to get up there.

Yet once we'd reached the slippery screes that fan out down the mountain, it was easy enough — a bit of zigzag, a lot of hard breathing and upward effort, and we were standing proud at the northern summit cairn.

The view from the 508m (1668ft) northern peak of Mellbreak must be one of the best in the Lake District — back over Loweswater and north as far as the misty spread of the Solway Firth and the grey humps of Scotland's Galloway hills; east across Crummock Water to the pink screes of towering Grasmoor; north to the great mountain spine of Red Pike, High Stile and High Crag; west to the long green ridge of Hen Comb and Loweswater Fell rising across the deep, unpopulated valley of Mosedale.

A steep, skeltering path dropped us into Mosedale. Down there a green track skirted the western flank of Mellbreak in wonderful isolation and silence. If Mosedale ever had farms, fields and folk, they are long forgotten. Here were swaths of bog grazed by Herdwick sheep, and watery dells full of orchids, sundews and flowering sedges, all caught in a cradle of shapely fells. "Dreary and wet" was Wainwright's sour summing-up of Mosedale. The Master wasn't always right, was he?

Down on Crummock Water we turned north along the lake shore. What were the islet of Low Ling Crag and its tiny tombolo beach of grey shaley stones created for, if not for swimming in the cool lake water on a hot summer afternoon? That's what we did, and went on homeward with renewed springs to our heels.

On the grass verge outside the Kirkstile Inn sat a man with muddy hiking boots, a glass of beer and a very contented smile. "Oh," he winked as we went by, "it's shocking, this is! Wish I was at work!"

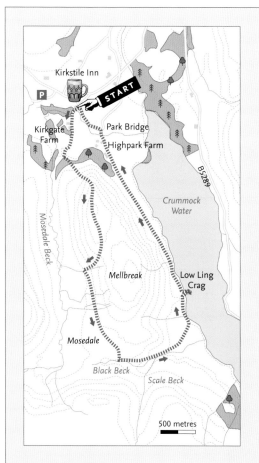

Start & finish Kirkstile Inn, Loweswater, Cumbria CA13 0RU (OS ref NY141209)

Getting there Road: Kirkstile Inn is signed from the Loweswater road, off B5289 (Buttermere-Cockermouth). Enquire at inn about local parking – official car parks at Maggie's Bridge (134210) and Scale Hill Bridge (149215).

Walk (6 miles, hard, OS Explorer OL4): From Kirkstile Inn fork right off left bend; immediately right ('No Through Road'). Country lane south for ½ mile past Kirkgate farm. At gate, lane curves right (139202); ahead uphill between trees. On open fell, keep ahead to bottom of scree (141199). Bear left; zigzag up (steep, skiddy!) to north summit of Mellbreak (143195). Ahead into dip. In 500m path bears right to a fork, 50m before rock outcrop on main path (145190). Fork right here on faint path, steeply down to track in Mosedale (141186). Turn left (south) for 900m, to pass metal gate. Shortly afterwards track curves left and follows the lower line of the bracken; keep ahead here (144178), aiming for curved peak of Red Pike. In 350m, go through gate in fence on bank (146175); descend to turn left along track by Black Beck (146174). Pass 3 footbridges (152174; 155175; 156178) but don't cross any of them. On reaching Crummock Water, bear left (north). Nearing north end of lake, in 1¼ miles, branch left (149197) up path through bracken which bisects angle with stone wall ahead. Reaching wall (148199), follow it to Highpark Farm. Turn right through gate in wall (145202); left through gate; on along stony lane. Cross Park Bridge (145205); fork left to Kirkstile Inn.

Lunch Kirkstile Inn (01900 85219; kirkstile.com)

Dinner/Accommodation Bridge Hotel, Buttermere CA13 9UZ (01768 770252; bridge-hotel.com) – friendly, well-run family hotel

Guidebook *Family Walks In The Lake District* by A. Wainwright/Tom Holman (Frances Lincoln)

More information Keswick TIC (0845 9010845; lakedistrict.gov.uk), visitengland.com, satmap.com, ramblers.org.uk

On a still morning of clearing skies over East Cumbria, the fields around Lupton lay quiet and green, soaked in overnight rain. A shepherd was calling a high-pitched summons from Newbiggin Crags. We watched his flock with their nosebands of white wool scampering towards him up the dark gorsy flank of the big limestone hill that overlooks the valley.

Beyond the chattering ford of Lupton Beck we climbed a steep track into the Access Land of Newbiggin Crags. The limestone pavement of this gently domed upland is cracked into deep grykes or channels, interspersed with naked clints of palely grey rock as rough to the touch as elephant hide. We followed an old quarry track up beside a stone wall with grand views spreading on all sides — north to the green shoulder of Scout Hill, west to Whitbarrow and the fells of South Lakeland, east towards the bulky hills of the North Pennines, and south-west to a gleam of Morecambe Bay with Black Combe hanging over it like a recumbent giant.

You're a bit of a fool if you rush past a prospect like this. We sat to admire it under a misshapen holly in a rock garden of pin mosses and crusty, pale-green lichens. Then we followed a flock of meadow pipits, swooping ahead with thin little squeaks, down into a broad, breezy upland of grass where a pair of shepherds fed their sheep as their dogs circled warily — a scene from the Hungarian plains rather than anything particularly English in character.

Newbiggin Crags form one of a pair of limestone domes. Hutton Roof Crags rises immediately to the south, a sprawling hill with a dwarf forest of juniper bushes clothing its northern flank. We pinched the hard green juniper berries as we climbed, but they were holding back their gin-and-tonic scent for a summer season.

Two free-climbers were scaling the block-like cliffs of The Rakes as we went past and down through Blasterfoot Gap towards the neat grey line of Hutton Roof village. The homeward path led through a bluebell wood, past Pickle and Sealford farms, and back by square-built old Lupton Tower and across the Lupton Beck meadows, where tiny black-legged lambs in plastic thermal macs went tottering and bleating after their newly delivered mothers.

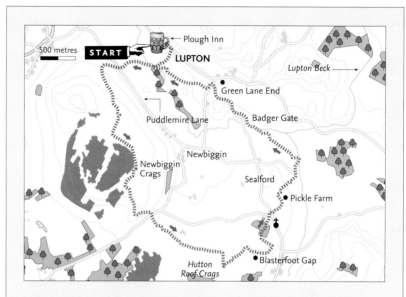

Start & finish Plough Inn, Lupton, Nr Kirkby Lonsdale LA6 1PJ (OS ref SD554812)

Getting there Road: M6, Jct 36; A65 towards Kirkby Lonsdale; Plough Inn on A65 in 1½ miles

Walk (7 miles, moderate, OS Explorer OL7): From Plough Inn, right (Kirkby Lonsdale direction) for 50m; right ('Lupton Beck') down track to cross beck (552809). Stony lane to Puddlemire Lane (547809). Cross road; diagonally right up track by stone wall. In 150m, stony lane hairpins back to left from track (546809); climb steep path that bisects these two, to meet old quarry track (545809). Left for ½ mile to meet stone wall (548803); right uphill by wall for 300m to meet crossing wall; left through gate (546800). Follow grassy track south, then SW, keeping crags on your right, for ⅔ mile to meet wall again (548793). Bear left downhill with wall on right for ⅓ mile to meet Limestone Link (LL) footpath just before road, at gate on right (549789).
Left along LL to cross road (552789; 'Hutton Roof' fingerpost). Follow path (it diverges to right from LL) up over Hutton Roof Crags for 1¼ miles, descending Blasterfoot Crags to rejoin LL on outskirts of Hutton Roof village at crossing of tracks beside house marked '1874' over the door (569784). Turn left uphill on LL, along wall past house. In 250m, right over stile (568785; yellow arrow/YA), through wood to lane by church (569788). Right to crossroads with road sign.
Through gate opposite; bear half left across field to Pickle farmhouse (571791). Left through gates (YAs); right along drive. Through gate by house, on over ladder stile (YA). Descend to Sealford Lane at Sealford Farm (573794). Over stile opposite ('Lupton Bridge' fingerpost; YA); bear left across field parallel to stream at bottom (crossing sheep wire halfway if in place). Keep curving left to cross stile by tree in far top corner of field (571798; YA). Cross next field, aiming for Badger Gate Farm; on by stiles and gates (YAs) to road by farm (565801). Right across bridge, follow road to Greenlane End. At sharp right bend (561806), left for 100m; right through stile (fingerpost) and follow YAs across fields to footbridge over Lupton Beck (552809). Right up lane to Plough Inn.

Conditions Paths can be muddy/slippery, especially on limestone pavement of crags

Lunch/accommodation Plough Inn, Lupton (01539 567700; theploughatlupton.co.uk)

More information Kendal TIC (01539 735891), golakes.co.uk, satmap.com, ramblers.org.uk

Seathwaite and Duddon
CUMBRIA

I've used the little weather-resistant guides published by Frances Lincoln in various locations, and learned to trust them. So setting out from Seathwaite (the Duddon Valley one, not the one under Scafell Pike) with Norman and June Buckley's guide, *Walking with Wordsworth in the Lake District*, promised a great afternoon's walking in the river valley that Wordsworth explored as a boy and immortalised in his *River Duddon* sonnets.

Not that it was easy to step from the Newfield Inn (cheerful fire, friendly folk, snoring dogs) into the spit and bluster of a wet old day. The Tarn Beck rushed noisily under its hazels and alders. The tops of the Seathwaite Fells were misted over, the trees dripped and the road was slick with water rills. A half-gale pushed me along northwards, past whitewashed Tongue House Farm and up a stony path on to the open moor between High Tongue and Troutal Tongue.

The Duddon's vale is full of tongues — high rocky knolls that give the valley a wild character that is unique in the Lake District. Along the wet grasses the golden busbies of bog asphodel shivered in the wind in their tens of thousands. What rhymes with asphodel? Wordsworth would have found something to encapsulate the damp shimmer of buttery bronze up here in the wind and rain.

Gradually the weather relented: the mist shredded off the Seathwaite Fells, revealing their high spine against patches of intense blue sky. The rain-swollen River Duddon came leaping and churning through a dark slit of a gorge, to jostle in a surge of bubbles under the single arch of Birks Bridge.

I lingered on the bridge, listening to the crashing of the river, then turned downstream. Pied wagtails bobbed on the rocks. A whinchat squeaked and clicked up the bank. The path rose and fell, a tricky stumble among slippery tree roots and rocks. One moment the Duddon was sluicing over flooded stepping stones at my elbow; the next it was hissing between rock walls 60m (200ft) below.

I threaded through a cathedral-like pine forest, skidded across a scree slope of red and grey boulders, and recrossed the roaring Duddon to follow its east bank down to Seathwaite. On the outskirts of the village I passed a pebbly strand where a couple of boys were skinny-dipping in the rampant river, risking life and limb as country boys have done since Noah — let alone William Wordsworth — was a lad.

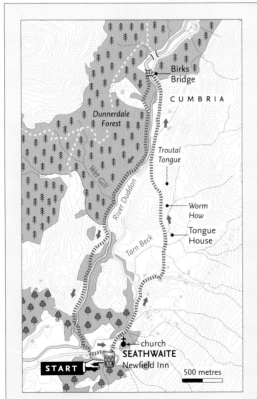

Start & finish Newfield Inn, Seathwaite, Cumbria LA20 6ED (OS ref SD227960)

Getting there Road: M6 to Jct 36; A590, A5092, A595 to Duddon Bridge; Ulpha & Seathwaite signposted from here

Walk (5½ miles, moderate grade, OS Explorer OL6): From inn, follow road past church and on. At Undercrag fork right (232967, 'Coniston'). In 300m, left ('No Through Road') past Hollin House. By Tongue House, left across footbridge (236974); ahead up slope, through gate (yellow arrow/YA), past Thrang Cottage, through wicket gate. In 50m, left up path through trees, across open fell for ½ mile past Troutal Tongue to road (234983). Ahead for ⅔ mile; left across Birks Bridge (234993); left along riverside path.

Soon path climbs right (white arrows) to top of knoll. Same line descending (NB indistinct path; beware rocks, roots and mud!) to woodland section by river. In ⅔ mile, ford Wet Gill by logs (229979); over stile; path climbs (YA) behind crag; descends to cross scree (224966). Left to cross Duddon by stone bridge (224963); right through gate; riverside path to cross Tarn Beck (225960); left to Newfield Inn.

Conditions Riverside path between Birks Bridge and Seathwaite is slippery and tricky underfoot with roots, stones and mud. Allow plenty of time. Boots are essential; stick helpful.

Lunch Newfield Inn, Seathwaite (01229 716208) – meals noon-9pm daily

Reading *Walking with Wordsworth in the Lake District* by Norman and June Buckley (Frances Lincoln)

More information Broughton-in-Furness TIC (01229 716115; lakedistrictinformation.com), ramblers.org.uk, satmap.com

Pendle Hill is the witchiest hill in England — mostly, but not entirely, on account of the notorious trials of 1612 when ten local men and women were hanged at Lancaster for practising the dark arts. Pendle is a massive presence, looming over the village of Barley. It always seems to have had an ominous reputation, probably because of the way it attracts dramatic weather.

Today it rode under a great breaking wave of cloud. As we climbed the steep, stone-pitched path to the summit, skeins of mist came drifting across, turning Pendle House farm below into a washy watercolour. A kestrel came swooping out of the cloud and cut down across the path with backswept wings, vanishing into the mist.

Runners, dog walkers and hill climbers materialised, passed us, and were swallowed up in cloud. At the top we followed a grassy track to find George Fox's well, a modest, urban-looking trapdoor in the hillside. Raising it revealed a silver tankard chained to the lid, ready to be lowered into the well. I drank a scooped handful from the spring below — ice cold, glass clear and sweet. Fox, young and full of spiritual zeal, refreshed himself here in 1652 having just experienced the epiphanic revelation on Pendle's summit that drove him to go forth and preach, and to establish the Quaker movement.

We forged south through the mist along the crest of Pendle, on a cairned track that soon turned and plunged down out of the murk. Big views opened eastward as we followed a rutted bridleway at the foot of the hill, down to where the Ogden Water's shallow flow wound out of steep-sided Ogden Clough to fill the twin reservoirs that lie above Barley.

Coming back into the village we passed the site of Malkin Tower, lair of the Pendle witches — according to their persecutors. Who knows what Alizon Device, Chattox, Old Demdike and Mouldheels were really up to? Whatever it was, their shadows still lie long across this beautiful valley and the hill that overhangs it.

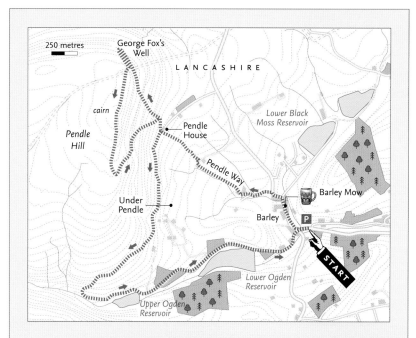

Start & finish Car park, Barley Picnic Site, nr Nelson, Lancs BB12 9JX (OS ref SD823403)

Getting there Bus: Service 7 (Clitheroe-Nelson). Road: M65, Jct 13; A682 ('Kendal'); in ¾ mile, left ('Roughlee'). From Roughlee, follow 'Barley'.

Walk (6¼ miles, moderate/hard, OS Explorer OL41): Turn right through village; left by Meadow Bank Farm; follow waymarked Pendle Way/PW across fields to Pendle House farm (809412) and up steep slope to top of Pendle Hill. Right over stile (806418) to visit George Fox's well (200m along path). Return over stile; right for 100m; left/south along PW for ½ mile, past trig pillar (805414). Where PW forks right (804409), keep ahead on grooved path, curving left to rim of escarpment (805408). Descend to Pendle House farm. Right along bridleway, with wall on left for ¾ mile, past Under Pendle (808404), to where bridleway turns left (807401). Keep ahead through kissing gate, down to Ogden Water (801397). Left along PW past Upper Ogden reservoir; road past Lower Ogden reservoir to Barley.

Conditions Sharp, steep climb from Pendle House to summit. Pendle Hill often windy, rainy, misty – hillwalking gear advised.

Lunch/accommodation Barley Mow, Barley, Pendle BB12 9JX (01282 690868; barleymowpendle.co.uk) – welcoming, walker-friendly pub with rooms.

More information The Cabin Café and Information Centre, Barley picnic site (01282 696937), Clitheroe TIC (01200 425566), visitlancashire.com, visitengland.com, satmap.com, ramblers.org.uk

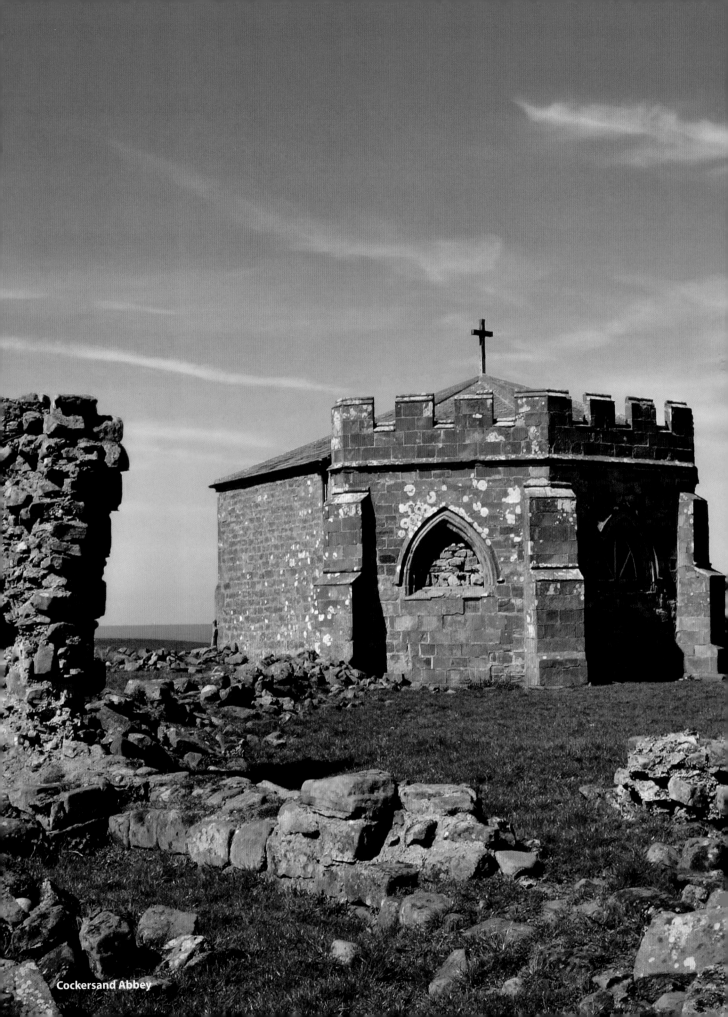
Cockersand Abbey

Cockerham to Conder Green

LANCASHIRE

A glorious afternoon on the west Lancashire coast under wall-to-wall blue sky. We walked the green fields of Cockerham with the Bowland moors rising in the east, Blackpool Tower tiny and familiar down in the southwest, and the Lake District fells around Helvellyn and Scafell Pike standing as if cut from pale blue card on the northern horizon.

Down at the sea wall a great flat apron of saltmarsh lay spread at the edge of Cockerham Sands, cut with wriggling channels. Brackish pools winked in the sun like a thousand bright eyes. The tide was on the make, advancing along the shore road and up the creeks in a frothy mini-tsunami, driving flights of loudly piping dunlin, oystercatchers and redshank shoreward in agitation. Further out on a vanishing sandbank, geese babbled together, a musical chiming across the water, reminiscent of sheep bells in Alpine pastures.

The seawall path ran past Bank End and Bank Houses, remote farmsteads among flat green pastures out at the edge of the land. As the coast turned north we came to Cockersand Abbey, or what remains of it — a curious semi-rectagonal chapter house among angles of walls, its soft

red sandstone rubbed into dimples and hollows by 800 years of wind and weather.

Cockersand Abbey was founded on this lonely shore as a leper hospital. When the site was excavated in the 1920s, archaeologists found fragments of lead and coloured glass from the windows that were smashed at the Dissolution of the Monasteries. The abbey ruin became a source of ready-worked building stone. Only the chapter house survived, because the local landowners wanted it for their family mausoleum.

From Cockersand Abbey we followed the windy coast path north to Crook Farm, with Heysham Power Station looming massively ahead like a 1950s suburban house designed by an ogre. Soon it was behind us, and we followed the grassy imprint of Marsh Lane over sheep pastures to Glasson Dock, a rare survival of a small working port. A dip into the cornucopia of goodies in the Port of Lancaster Smokehouse here, and a last stretch on a railway path into Conder Green above the golden marshes of the Lune Estuary.

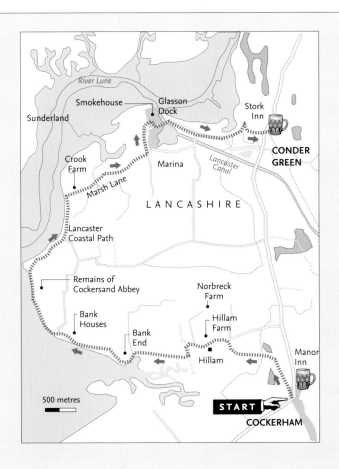

Start Manor Inn, Cockerham, near Lancaster LA2 0EF (OS ref SD465522)

Getting there Bus: Services 89, 89H (Lancaster-Knott End). Road: Cockerham is on A588 between Conder Green and Pilling (M6, Jct 33).

Walk (7 miles, flat and easy, OS Explorer 296): South from Manor Inn down A588; in 50m, right beside Old Mill House. Follow lane; through garden at top; through kissing gate at end of garden (464524, yellow arrow/YA). Follow fence on right downhill; follow YAs along field edges, round cottage (462529). Leave cottage garden over stile; ahead over field and footbridge (YA); follow ditch/fence on right for ½ mile to Hillam Lane (455531). Left past Hillam Farm; in ½ mile, right (449528) along sea wall. Follow Lancaster Coastal Path/LCP north for 3¾ miles via Bank End (441528), Cockersand Abbey chapter house (427537), Crook Farm (431550) and Marsh Lane to road at Glasson (443556). Left, then right to Glasson Dock. Cross swing bridge (445561); cross road by Victoria Inn; right along LCP. In ¾ mile, cross bridge (456560); right to Conder Green. Bus 89/89H or taxi (01995 607777) to Cockerham.

Lunch Picnic – provisions from Port of Lancaster Smokehouse, Glasson LA2 0DB (01524 751493; lancastersmokehouse.co.uk)

Accommodation The Mill at Conder Green, Lancs LA2 0BD (01524 752852; themillatcondergreen.co.uk) – really comfortable, superbly positioned

More information Lancaster TIC (01524 582394), visitlancashire.com visitengland.com, satmap.com, ramblers.org.uk

Whitendale & Dunsop Bridge

LANCASHIRE

A cool and cloudy morning over the Forest of Bowland, the moorland heart of Lancashire. As we walked the sheep pastures under the dun brown shoulder of Beatrix Fell, a curlew flew low past us, its long, downcurved bill quivering open to emit the familiar bubbling trill that haunts these northern hills.

In times past the Forest of Bowland lay under harsh laws of prohibition. The landlord's tenants were made to pass their dogs through a silver hoop and any animal big and powerful enough to scramble through it would be destroyed as a potential poaching asset. Grouse-shooting interests were paramount and ramblers strenuously discouraged. Times and tempers change, though. When the Countryside and Rights of Way Act was passed in 2000, this enormous wheel of bleak and beautiful country was opened to all walkers for the first time.

Bowland is properly wild country, with plenty of surprises for walkers. Up at Dunsop Head we found the springs of Dunsop Brook overflowing with stored rainwater. We floundered through soft, sloppy peat and moss. Jane went in knee-deep, emerging with a tremendous sucking sound as though the bog were smacking its lips over her like a tasty lollipop.

At last we reached firmer ground, where three birdwatchers were waiting. "See the male hen harrier?" inquired their leader. "Flew right across where you were." We'd been too preoccupied with our battle with the bog to spare a glance for anything else. "Yep, only three of them in Britain," the twitcher exulted.

Down in the hidden cleft of Whitendale, other ornithological celebrities are resident — a pair of breeding eagle owls, surprise incomers with six-foot wingspans, capable of taking out a young deer. We didn't spot these beautiful strangers on the way back to Dunsop Bridge, but there were grey wagtails and herons, white-chested dippers and black-capped stonechats and a crowd of jolly swallows hawking over the river, their white rumps and scarlet streaks a splash of colour against the grey of evening.

Start & finish Dunsop Bridge car park, Lancs BB7 3BE approx. (OS ref SD661501)

Getting there Bus: Service 10 (dalesbus.org), Clitheroe-Slaidburn. Road: M6, Jct 31a; B6243 ('Clitheroe') through Longridge; 1 mile past Knowle Green, left on minor road through Whitewell to Dunsop Bridge.

Walk (10½ miles, strenuous, OS Explorer OL41): Right along road; just before bridge, right ('bridleway') along drive. Pass terraced houses (658507); in 100m, right (yellow arrow/YA) through kissing gate, up steps, over stile; ahead along fence. At ruined wall, half-left to Beatrix Farm (664514). 100m past farmhouse, left through gate. Blue arrow/BA points ahead, but follow 2 YAs (pointing left) along right bank of stream (YAs). In ½ mile, at bottom of Oxenhurst Clough, cross stream (671518). Follow YAs, with fence on right, to farm drive (674521); on past The Hey to Burn House (682528). Through driveway gate and on down to lane (685522).

Left for ¾ mile. Left up drive (694530, 'Burnside Cottage'). Skirt Burnside Cottage through gates (690537); on up fellside beside stone wall (BAs). At top of wall (687540), through gate; bear right. 200m past conifer clump, path hairpins back left and climbs for 1 mile to Dunsop Head (676542). NB: deep, wet bogs across the path here! Bear left to stone wall on high ground to left of bogs; follow it to the right, to a fence curving away to left; follow this fence west, then north, keeping close to it, and treading with care, till you meet the wall again near a gate (675544).

From the gate, left along moor path (yellow-topped posts, arrows, cairns) for 1 mile, descending to Whitendale. By first stone wall of farmyard, left (662550, unmarked) on path with wall on right. In nearly 1 mile, horseshoe left across Costy Clough footbridge (659536). In 150m, right over stile, down to track; left for 500m; right across footbridge (654533), left along road for 2¼ miles to Dunsop Bridge.

Conditions: Deep, wet bogs at Dunsop Head. Hill-walking gear, boots, stick.

Lunch Picnic or Puddleducks café, Dunsop Bridge BB7 3BB (01200 448241; puddleduckscafe.co.uk)

Accommodation Inn at Whitewell, BB7 3AT (01200 448222, innatwhitewell.com) – a wonderful old inn; welcoming, full of character; 2½ miles from Dunsop Bridge

More information Clitheroe TIC (01200 425566), satmap.com, visitengland.com, ramblers.org.uk

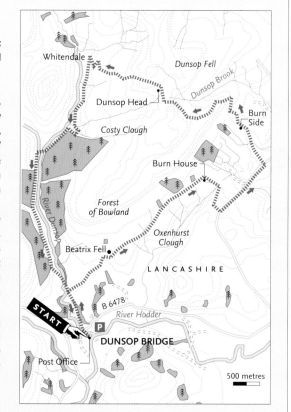

Lumb and Goodshaw Chapel

LANCASHIRE

A cool misty Lancashire day, with the sky as close-fitting as a grey cloth cap over Rossendale and its tributary valleys. A cheery milkman met us on the lane from Lumb to the moors, chinking two bottles in his hand. "G'morning – y'all right?"

The Pennine Bridleway ran as a hedged lane, winding and twisting past farmhouses and isolated cottages, all the buildings and field walls made of the same dark sandy stone and blotched with the green lichen so characteristic of these moors. Over the uplands a silence lay, broken by a crow call, a faint whistle of wind in the sedges, and the expressive fluting of a blackbird in the valley far below. As always when looking down from these moors, it was hard to relate today's smokeless factory chimneys, silent mills and empty terraced streets to the roar and rattle, smog and human movement of half a century ago in these once-industrial valleys.

The bridleway led on through deeply hollowed miniature canyons worn down by centuries of boots, hooves and farm wheels. Many old tracks tangle and ramify across the moors — limers' gaits along which laden carts jolted to bring lime fertiliser to the acid fields, packhorse routes and colliers' trods, a superb network for riders and walkers exploring the Rossendale uplands. At an old stone cross we swung west, crossing the sedgy moorland fields with glimpses north to the steely waters of Clowbridge Reservoir and the slopes of Nutshaw Hill.

Down at Goodshaw we found Kathy Fishwick — an old acquaintance and a key-holder of the remarkable Goodshaw Chapel. This ancient Baptist foundation looks like a house, and in fact it is one — a house of the Lord. Every square inch inside is crammed with high-sided box pews with hard benches and a good view of the minister's desk. Goodshaw Chapel could easily hold a congregation of three or four hundred. It frequently did so in times past, when the faith followed the wool and cotton trade. In 1760 the chapel-goers came singing over the hills, bearing these pews on their backs to furnish their new prayer house, which formed the heart of the community for the next 100 years.

We bade Kathy goodbye and went on up steep-sided Folly Clough with its millrace relics, out and over Swinshaw Moor where larks laid claim to each sedge clump in song and the black peaty pools reflected the racing sky.

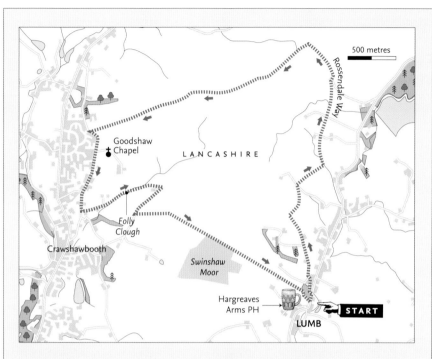

Start & finish Millennium Green, Lumb, Lancs BB4 9PN (OS ref SD838250).

Getting there Bus: Service 483 (Burnley-Bury) 63 (Rawtenstall circular route), rossendalebus. co.uk. Road: M66/A56 to Rawtenstall; A681 ('Bacup'); in Waterfoot, left on B6238 ('Burnley'); in 2¼ miles, park at Lumb Millennium Green.

Walk (6 miles, moderate, OS Explorer OL21): Follow Pennine Bridleway/PBW north. In 1¼ miles Rossendale Way/RW joins PBW beyond Near Pastures (840268). In 500m PBW turns right (841273), but keep ahead. At stone cross (838276) RW turns left across moor for 1²/₃ miles, descending to road in Goodshaw Chapel (815267). Left to pass chapel on left (815263). Ignore footpath fingerpost beside chapel; in another 70m, left up tarred path, through gateway (815262). Diagonally right on path; through gate by wood (816261); down through squeeze stile; on down walled lane (yellow arrow/YA). At bottom (816259), left past metal barrier, up grassy track in steep-sided valley on left bank of beck (YAs). In 400m cross beck; in 200m bear right up steps (820261), past farm at top. Right through kissing gate (822261); ahead down farm drive. In 350 m, left through stone kissing gate (820259; YA). Follow path up gully, past trees onto moor. In ½ mile, at edge of Swinshaw Moor Access Land (827256), YA points diagonally left; but keep ahead beside wall, then fence. Cross stile; on to waymark post with 3 YAs (832254). Ahead with wall on right past wind generator; then with wall on left. Through metal gate; skirt cottages (835252); down farm drive to Lumb.

NB: this walk is very muddy in parts; steep, awkward path beside beck (816259-820261); some sheep-wire hopping may be necessary

Lunch Picnic or Hargreaves Arms, Lumb BB4 9PQ (01706 215523)

Accommodation Ye Olde Boot & Shoe, Millar Barn Lane, Waterfoot BB4 7AU (01706 213828)

More information Rawtenstall tourism information point at Malachi Fitzpatrick's Temperance Bar (01706 231836), visitlancashire.com, satmap.com, ramblers.org.uk

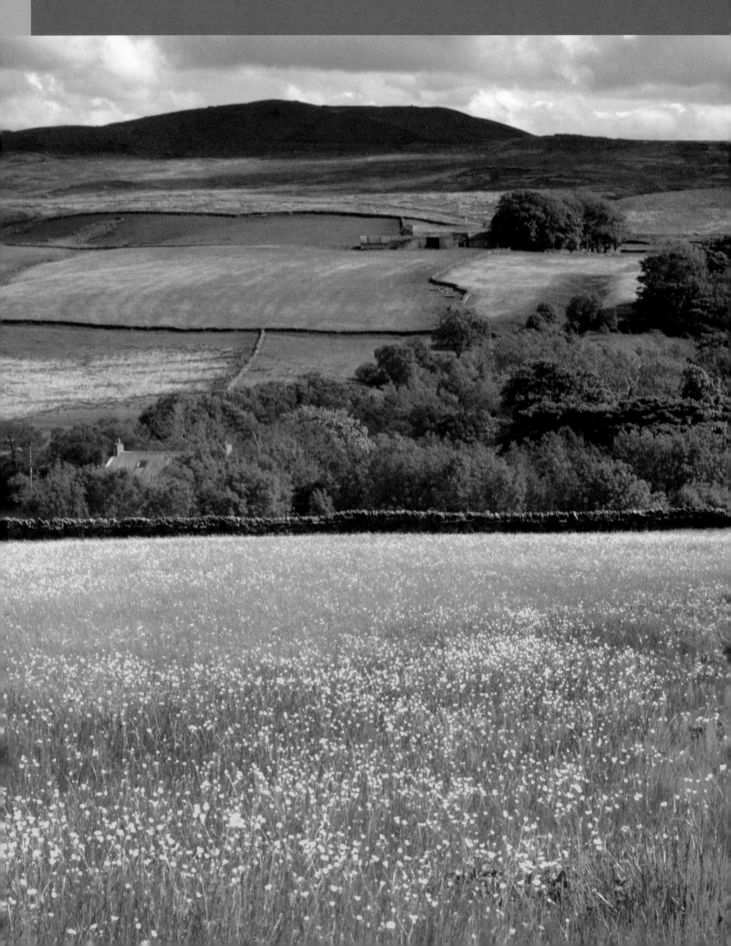

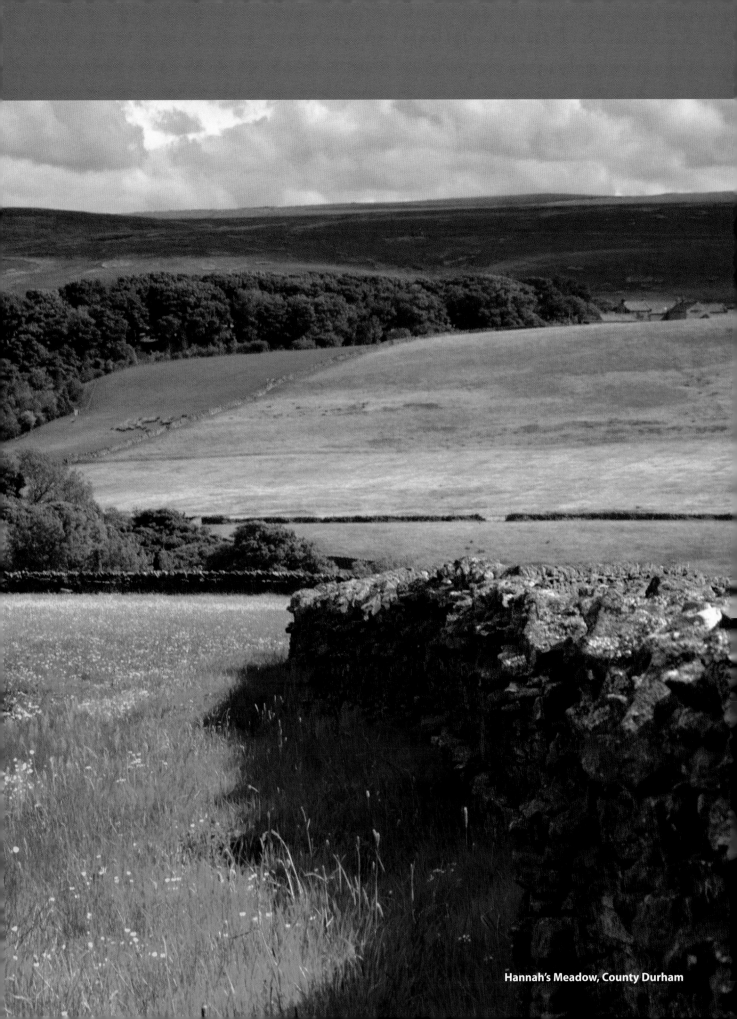

Hannah's Meadow, County Durham

Cauldron Snout and Cow Green
COUNTY DURHAM

"We've seen the dipper," enthused the woman we met under Falcon Clints, "and a black grouse in the rocks just along there." "And a grey shrike," put in her husband. "And you've seen the peregrine, have you? And the ring ouzel ... Ooh, thanks, we'll keep our eyes peeled."

How can one begin to list the richness of bird life in the breeding season around the meadows and moors of Upper Teesdale? And that's to say nothing of the wonderful Ice Age relict flora sprinkled across the limestone grassland and the bogs and heaths of this lonely cleft in the hills, where the young River Tees comes tumbling down its volcanic steps to sinuate through the dale.

Redshanks, lapwings and oystercatchers flew round us, piping and bubbling their anxious calls as we skirted their nests and young hidden in the sedges. Mountain pansies with purple and yellow petals, northern marsh orchids of royal purple, lipstick-pink lousewort and buttery gold kingcups spotted the grass and damp bog patches.

On through the narrowing throat of the dale, with the dolerite cliffs of Falcon Clints standing dark and hard-edged overhead. A slate-backed peregrine went darting out across the river from the crags, twisting like an acrobat before hanging in the sky on an invisible step. The only sounds were bird cries, wind rustle and the mumble of the shallow Tees. It was like lingering in some private corner of heaven.

The rush and roar of Cauldron Snout beckoned us on round the corner of the crags. The peat-charged waterfall came bouncing down its rock staircase in a series of foaming cataracts as brown as bottle glass. We scrambled up the rocks and found ourselves in another reality — wide uplands and the great wind-ruffled lake of Cow Green Reservoir.

The homeward way lay across the pathless hillside of Cow Rake Rigg, then back through the wide valley of Harwood Beck. Tiny pink bird's-eye primroses grew on the banks of the sikes (a local name for streams), and the creaking complaints of lapwings and the alarm calls of redshanks piped us out of their territory and on down the valley.

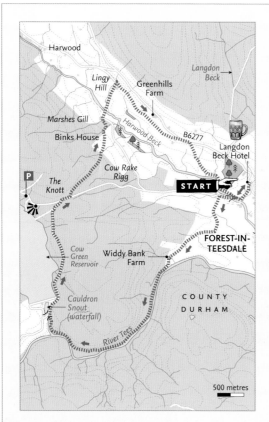

Start & finish Langdon Beck Hotel, Co Durham DL12 0XP (OS ref NY853312)

Getting there Road: B6277 from Middleton-in-Teesdale. Park in lay-by down side road opposite Langdon Beck Hotel ('Cow Green').

Walk (10 miles, moderate, OS Explorer OL31): On down Cow Green road. 250m after crossing Harwood Beck, left (847309, 'Moor House NNR') on stony track to Widdy Bank Farm (837298) and on under Falcon Clints. Scramble up crags to right of Cauldron Snout waterfall (815286) to road at top. Right to road at The Knott (817309); turn right. Either follow road back to Langdon Beck (2½ miles), or pass cottage on left and bear left ('footpath' fingerpost) north-east across Cow Rake Rigg (no track). Over first crest; aim right of fenced shaft; then aim for wall running uphill, a little to left of prominent white house on distant hillside ahead. In ½ mile, come over crest; head for Binks House below. Cross stone stile; skirt Binks House (825320); cross stile (yellow arrow/YA) in bottom left corner of field. Follow stream on left for 100m; left to cross it, then stile (YA); half left to ladder stile (YA); down through gate and through Marshes Gill farmyard to road (825324). Ahead over Harwood Beck.

On left bend at Lingy Hill farm (828320), right along field track for 1 mile to Greenhills (838320). Up drive to road (841319); right over stile. NB fingerpost points straight downhill, but bear half left down to wall stile (842316, YA). On in same direction to bottom left corner of next field (845313). Ladder stile; follow Harwood Beck to bridge (850304); left to Langdon Beck.

Conditions Tricky underfoot across boulders below Falcon Clints; rock scramble beside Cauldron Snout

Lunch Picnic or Langdon Beck Hotel (01833 622267; langdonbeckhotel.com)

Accommodation The Old Barn, Middleton-in-Teesdale, DL12 0QG (01833 640258; theoldbarn-teesdale.co.uk) – lovely warm and welcoming B&B

More information Middleton-in- Teesdale TIC (01833 641001), Moor House-Upper Teesdale National Nature Reserve (northpennines.org.uk), visitengland.com, ramblers.org.uk

A sunny day, clear and cold, had settled over Teesdale. The new leaves on the beech trees along the River Greta shone a sharp acid green as they filtered the morning sunshine. We followed a field path up the noisy Greta from Greta Bridge, walking against the flow of the river that sparkled over its bed of rocky slabs in the narrow west-east dale it has carved for itself.

A brief climb to the lip of the dale — seas of yellow oilseed rape rolling away to pale purple moors on the northern skyline — and then we were dipping down into the wooded cleft where the ruin of St Mary's Church lay in its walled graveyard. A wonderful peaceful spot to idle and wander among the old slanting gravestones, unsteadily lettered by local masons — 'Christopher Thwaites Postmaster of Greata Bridge 1693', 'Julian & Jane Sutton Bless ye The Lord Praise Him & Magnifie Him', and a low stone for a child, simply inscribed 'EH 1699'.

The path wound on, increasingly narrow and crumbly, through Tebb Wood, a world of white, blue and green with bluebells and wild garlic, bugle and wood anemones. Neither of us could remember any riverside walk so bright with wild flowers — the dusky purple nodding bells of water avens, false oxlips with multiple primrose heads on cowslip-like stalks, bold pink campion, white stars of stitchwort, early purple orchids. Blackcaps burbled musically in the scrub hawthorns, and wrens chattered. The sun poured over everything like a warm bath for the senses, just edged enough with cold fingers of breeze to remind us that we were in the Durham dales in springtime.

Down by the stone-built Brignall Mill we crossed the Greta, splodged through the muddy caterpillar tracks of a logging operation, and turned back along the south bank of the river. What a contrast! These north-facing slopes of the gorge were at least a month behind those facing south only just across the river, with bluebells not yet bloomed and celandines and delicate white wood sorrel still out in glory.

The path climbed to a precipitous ledge above the Greta, then turned south through the woods high over Gill Beck. At Gillbeck Bridge we took to a silent country lane and field paths through open uplands where young calves kicked and capered in the meadows. A stretch of road with far moorland views and then the homeward path through Mill Woods and by the water-sculpted churn holes of the Greta's gorge.

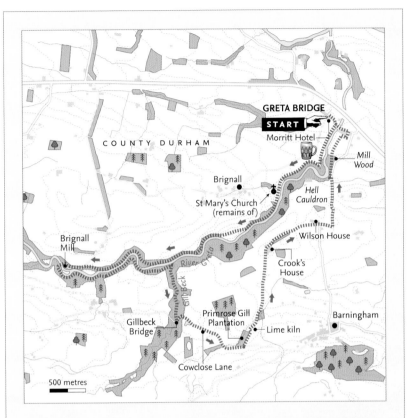

Start & finish Morritt Hotel, Greta Bridge, Co. Durham DL12 9SE (OS ref NZ085133)

Getting there Road: Greta Bridge is signposted off A66 between Scotch Corner (A1) and Bowes

Walk (9½ miles, moderate, OS Explorer OL30): Morritt Hotel – follow path along north bank of River Greta for 3½ miles to Brignall Mill (047112). Cross river (yellow arrows/YA); return along south bank path for 1¼ miles. Bear right (061112) up Gill Beck path to Gillbeck Bridge (062105). Cowclose Lane to corner of Primrose Gill Plantation (072101); left up byway past limekiln (073104). In 300m, left (blue arrow) up fields to Crook's House (075115). Farm drive to Wilson House (083118); ahead along road for ½ mile; left (085125; fingerpost) over stile; right through Mill Wood and on by Hell Cauldron to Greta Bridge.

Conditions For surefooted walkers – riverside paths are narrow, slippery and eroded in places

Lunch Picnic

Accommodation Morritt Hotel, Greta Bridge (01833 627232; themorritt.co.uk) – family-run, very friendly, helpful and well-kept

More information Durham walks and accommodation – thisisdurham.com, ramblers.org.uk, satmap.com

Hannah's Meadow
COUNTY DURHAM

There aren't many proper old upland hay meadows left in England, but the one at Low Birk Hatt farm in Baldersdale is an absolute beauty. That's thanks to Hannah Hauxwell, the lone woman who farmed these fields in an entirely traditional way until her retirement in 1988, and also to Durham Wildlife Trust — which took them on, renamed them 'Hannah's Meadow', and continued the good work.

We stepped into the sparse little exhibition in Hannah's Barn below High Birk Hatt farmhouse, and then followed the Pennine Way beside the meadow — not yet cut, its sweet vernal grass and sedges full of old hay meadow flowers such as yellow rattle, knapweed, moon daisies and the blue powder puffs of devil's-bit scabious. Miss Hauxwell became a TV star in the 1970s when a series of programmes followed her unadorned life through the seasons. A reluctant star, she never could quite understand what all the fuss was about, but what a wonderful treasure her decades of hard work left us in this Durham dale.

From Low Birk Hatt the squashy, puddled track of the Pennine Way led us up and out on to Cotherstone Moor. A half gale from the west shoved us around like a ruffian, then got behind us when we left the National Trail and struck out east across the moor. Curlews and golden plover piped plaintively, a great crowd of starlings went swooping all together, and a red grouse planed away on stubby scimitar wings. Swaledale ewes among the sedges stared incredulously in our direction, then averted their gaze like a pew full of spinsters at the sight of something unspeakably shocking — a vicar in cycling shorts, perhaps.

On a wild open upland, unfenced for miles under a gigantic sky, we found an alternative loop of the Pennine Way and followed it back north. Above the path the flat-topped granite outcrop of Goldsborough stood proud of the moor — a miniature table mountain, whose sheer southern crags are only seen by sheep and walkers. We lingered under the rocks, admiring their weather-cut striations and the brilliant purple heather lining their ledges, and then dropped back down over many stone stiles into sunlit Baldersdale and the homeward path. Lapwings creaked in the sedgy fields, oystercatchers zipped down the wind, and every blade of grass squeaked and sparkled underfoot.

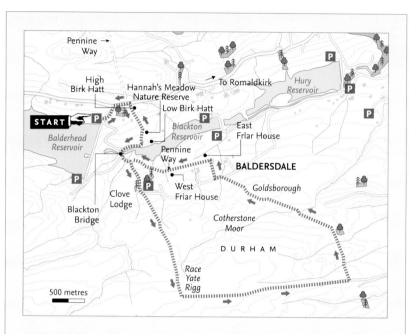

Start & finish Balderhead Reservoir car park, near Romaldkirk, Co Durham DL12 9UX approx. (OS ref NY929187)

Getting there Road: On outskirts of Romaldkirk, right off B6277 Cotherstone Road ('Reservoirs'). In 4½ miles pass 'High Birk Hatt, Hannah's Meadow' sign on gate on left (933190); in another 250m, left through gateway to Balderhead Reservoir car park.

Walk (8 miles, moderate, OS Explorer OL31): Walk back to 'Hannah's Meadow' gate; go through, and down lane ('Pennine Way'/PW). At gate (933190), right to Hannah's Barn exhibition. Return to PW; follow it past Low Birk Hatt (936184), across Blackton Bridge (932182). Fork left (no waymark) across beck. At triple PW fingerpost (934181), right up stony track to road beyond Clove Lodge Farm (935177). Ahead; in 200m, right (PW) across Cotherstone Moor. In 1 mile, at Race Yate, cross stile in fence (942161, PW). In 100m, left off PW through gate (blue arrow/BA); follow grassy track (sometimes faintly marked on ground) east for 1⅔ miles. At gate where wall and fence meet at Ladyfold Rigg, left (969164, BA) along Bowes Loop of PW. In ½ mile, at cross-wall by ruin (965171), go through left of two gates. In 20m fork left, aiming for crags of Goldsborough. Cross Yawd Sike (stream) by railed footbridge (960174); carry on below left slope of Goldsborough. At crest beyond (952178), fork left aiming for West Friar House Farm.

At road (948179, PW), left for 100m; right down drive to East Friar House. Down left side of byre (acorn, yellow arrow/YA); left over stile (946182, YA); follow PW/YAs west through fields and stone stiles to Low Birk Hatt and car park.

Lunch Picnic

Accommodation Rose & Crown, Romaldkirk, Barnard Castle, Co. Durham DL12 9EB (01833 650213; rose-and-crown.co.uk) – really comfortable, efficient and helpful

More information Middleton-in-Teesdale TIC (01833 641001), thisisdurham.com, visitengland.com, satmap.com, ramblers.org.uk

Hayfields of Upper Weardale

COUNTY DURHAM

"There was snow on them thar hills this morning!" said the cheerful man we passed in the street at Wearhead. He was right, too: we'd woken to what in Upper Weardale they call a "lambing storm": a sudden late spring fall of snow on a streaming north wind. Now, a couple of hours later, it had melted from the fells around Wearhead village. West Durham lay in sunshine, though white showers were already regrouping on the northern horizon.

A rough hillside grazed by inquisitive horses brought us up out of the dale bottom to the fell tops where lambs ran crying to the ewes and icy little balls of hail came battering round our ears. The squall whirled away south, revealing a wide bowl of moorland hills with stone-built farms scattered all down the dale sides.

The upland birds were in full nesting flow — lapwings tossing about the sky like paper kites, curlews trilling in the sedges, redshanks calling *pic! pic!*, and golden plovers standing with heads held high, piping to mates or rivals, a bright 's' of white feathers outlining their shapes, their backs shimmering gold in gleams of sun.

Lark song filled the air directly overhead as we found a high track between banks of mountain pansies, some entirely of rich purple, others with lower lips of yellow, and one or two a creamy yellow all over. The old lane wound among the spoil heaps of Weardale's long-defunct lead-mining industry, hummocks of green and red mosses and lichens where we picked up glittering gems of opaque purple fluorspar. The walled track slanted down the dale side through more humpy mining ground where a young semi-wild foal looked shyly over her mother's back.

From the grey stone settlement of St John's Chapel we climbed once more into a succession of unimproved, unspoiled hay meadows. There aren't many communities of proper hay meadows left in this country, and these, carefully nurtured by the farmers and monitored by North Pennines AONB, are the glory of the dale for their wild flowers. Green froths of lady's mantle, clovers, mauve heads of wood cranesbill, cowslips going over, yellow rattle not yet come in — there they all were, ready to burst into their full colourful pomp come June.

Another snow flurry came whipping across Weardale, and we told ourselves we'd be back to see the meadows in the heat and colour of a proper summer.

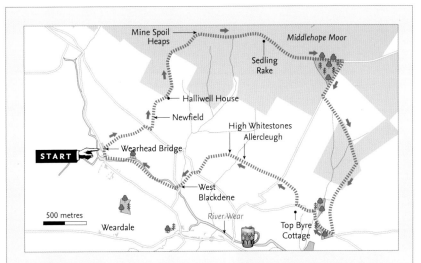

Start & finish Wearhead, DL13 1BE approx. near A689 bridge (OS ref NY858395)

Getting there Bus: Service 101 (Cowshill to Stanhope). Road: Wearhead is on A689 between Stanhope and Alston.

Walk (6 miles, moderate, OS Explorer OL31): From Wearhead Bridge, head north up A689 (Alston direction). Just before phone box, go right (bridleway fingerpost) along laneway. Bear left over stile ('Valley Crest'), on up steep path, curving right and aiming for notch in skyline. Through gate at top (861397); aim left of house; stone stile (fingerpost) onto road. Right; in 50m, left (863397; fingerpost) up stony lane past Newfield and Halliwell House for nearly 1 mile to crossing of walls by mine spoil heaps (868408). Turn right along Sedling Rake track for 1 mile, past wood to road junction (884405). Right; in ¼ mile, left (882401; 'bridleway') down walled moor track.
In ½ mile, at second crossing wall (886394), bear right along wall, down to go through gate (884391). Down beside wall; over next crossing wall (883390; no stile – scramble over wooden barrier); diagonally left aiming right of farmhouse (883388). Through stile left of gate; through gate below; diagonally left down to lane (884386). Sharp right up lane; opposite Top Byre Cottage (880390), right up field path, keeping close to wall on left (path narrow in places) for 3 fields to cross road (878392). On up drive opposite (fingerpost), past Allercleugh farm house and buildings (873394) with hay meadows on your left. In field by High Whitestones, follow permissive footpath diagonally down across field; left down walled lane to Whitestones farm (869394). Through gate (yellow arrow/YA) and down to cross road (869393). Ahead through stone stile (fingerpost) and garden; through gate (YA). Aim half right across field to upper end of wall; behind it, go through stile and gate (YA); down beside wall, then down steps, through stile (YA) and along alley to road in West Blackdene (867391). Cross River Wear; right along Weardale Way to Wearhead Bridge.
NB: Unsuitable for dogs – sheep country

Lunch Picnic (village shop in Wearhead)

Accommodation Low Cornriggs Farm, Cowshill, Weardale, Co. Durham DL13 1AQ (01388 537600; britnett.net/lowcornriggs farm) – fabulous home cooking and warm welcome

More information Durham walks/accommodation: thisisdurham.com
North Pennines AONB – events, guided walks, etc (01388 528801); northpennines.org.uk.
More guided walks (0191 3729100); durham.gov.uk/countryside

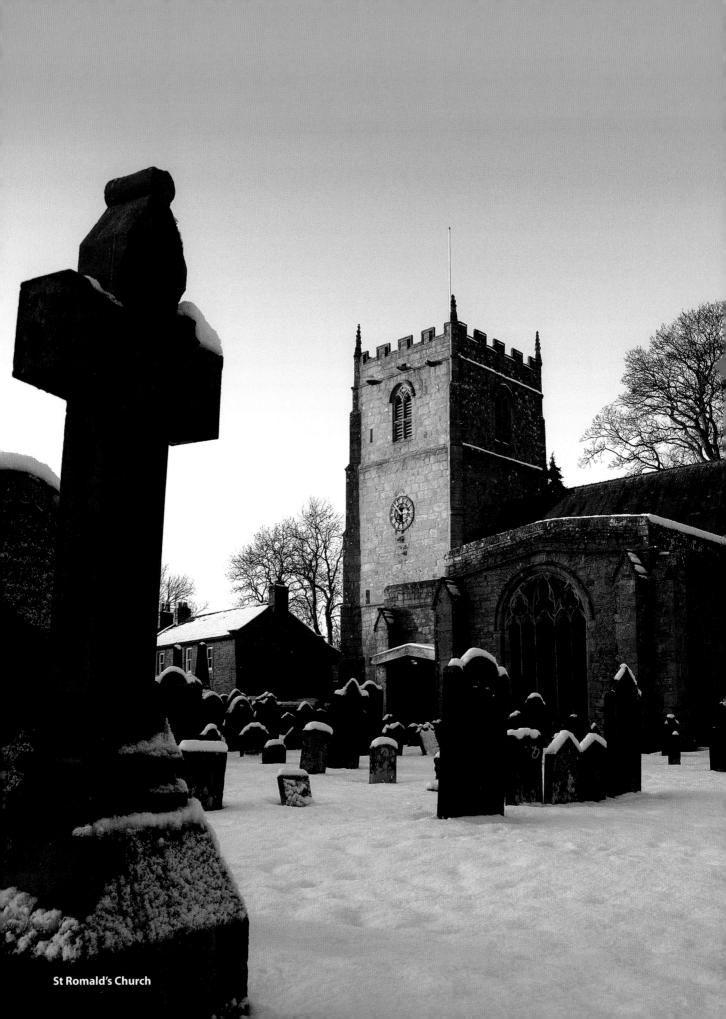

St Romald's Church

Romaldkirk and Cotherstone
COUNTY DURHAM

There was a blue sky over Upper Teesdale, and a darkly forested Pennine skyline heavy with bruised cloud. The two were due to come to blows later, with foul slated to triumph over fair. This early in the morning, though, autumn sunshine was spreading across the creamy grey stone houses of Romaldkirk and soaking the beeches about the village green with translucent splashes of lime and butterscotch.

In St Romald's Church, Sir Hugh Fitz Henry lay in the north chapel, his face smoothed by the patting hands of seven centuries. The Lord of Bedale, Ravensworth and Cotherstone was felled in battle with the Scots in 1305. He lies in chainmail, in the act of drawing his stone sword. No knight expected to die in his bed in these regions at the turn of the fourteenth century, especially not a participant in King Edward's wars against the Scots.

The Teesdale Way footpath led me from Romaldkirk over the fields towards the Tees. Near the river I skirted the handsome Dales longhouse of Low Garth, half dwelling and half byre, silent in an overgrown farmyard,

windows blanked and chimneys cold. In the woods the path ran carpeted with fallen oak leaves. I walked mesmerised by the sigh and rush of the bottle-brown Tees as it crashed down its flights of rapids, exuding that exhilarating smell of a river newly off the moors, stained with peat and rammed full of oxygen.

The Lord of Cotherstone, when he fancied something savoury after the roast heron and neat's-foot jelly, would have tucked into ewe's-milk cheese. But today there are milk cows in Teesdale, and beautiful crumbly Cotherstone cheese. At the post office in Cotherstone village I bought a fat truckle to take home, and an extra slice for pure greed's sake. With a full mouth and an eye on the rainclouds, I turned home along the Tees Railway Walk, a footpath along the trackbed of the former Tees Valley Railway by way of the mighty Baldersdale Viaduct. How would Hugh Fitz Henry have reacted to a sight of the iron horse? It made a great one-reeler for the skull cinema as I walked, the warrior astride his caparisoned destrier, charging the smoke-belching monster at full and reckless tilt.

Start & finish Rose & Crown, Romaldkirk, Co Durham DL12 9EB (OS ref NY995221)

Getting there Bus: (scarletbandbuses.co.uk) services 95/96 from Barnard Castle. Road: A1 to Scotch Corner; A66 to Barnard Castle, B6277.

Walk (5 miles, easy, OS Explorer OL31): From Rose & Crown cross road and grass; left along lane. Right by Rose Stile Cottage ('TeesdaleWay/TW' fingerpost). In ¼ mile, go through left-hand of two gates (998216); path crosses three fields to Low Garth (003216). Cross stile (TW); left down bank, stile into wood. Follow TW beside Tees, then up to gate. Left end of barn; in front of Woden Croft houses (008208), then through gate. Left down fence, through gate (009207); cross field, down to Tees. In ¼ mile pass footbridge over Tees (013202); in 100m cross River Balder; right into Cotherstone. Up lane by left side of Fox & Hounds (011198); cross stile and field; stile onto Tees Railway Walk (009194). Right for 2 miles to Romaldkirk.

Lunch and accommodation Rose & Crown, Romaldkirk (01833 650213; rose-and-crown co.uk), Fox & Hounds, Cotherstone (01833 650241; cotherstonefox.co.uk)

More information Barnard Castle TIC (01833 690909), visitnortheastengland.com, thisisdurham.com, ramblers.org.uk

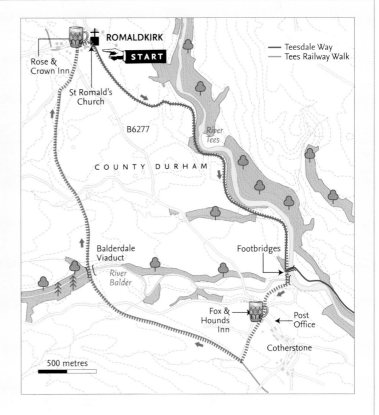

Yeavering Bell and Akeld
NORTHUMBERLAND

On a day like this, with strong sunshine and blue skies pouring across Northumberland, there isn't a more welcoming range of hills in these islands than the Cheviots. Bosomy, rounded and dressed in brilliant green and purple, they seem to beckon, especially to walkers.

In the farming hamlet of Akeld, just outside the regional capital of Wooler, stands a bastle, a reminder of a savage history. These fortified farmhouses — with their tiny windows, 'upstairs' doors and walls many feet thick — date from the days when the Scottish Borders were aflame with cattle-thieving and feuds. Back then, any man who wanted to live would barricade himself and his family into the upper floor of a bastle and hope to see out a siege.

Above Akeld, a winding path led us away through bracken and heather across the hunched back of White Law. We dipped into a hollow, then climbed past the circular foundations of ancient beehive huts to the summit of Yeavering Bell. This high and handsome hill is the king of the north Cheviots, its knobbly brow encircled by a great wall — once 3m (10ft) thick, now scattered — and crowned with a cairn.

Up there we sat, catching our breath and savouring the view — the chequerboard plain stretched north at our feet, a steel-blue crescent of North Sea, and the rolling heights of the Cheviots as they billowed away south into the heart of the range. Then it was down from the peak and on through the bracken to find the broad green road of St Cuthbert's Way striding purposefully through the hills.

The hard rock outcrop of Tom Tallon's Crag rode its heathery hilltop like a salt-brown ship pitching in a russet sea. We passed below the crag, then followed a grassy old cart track into the cleft of Akeld Burn. Suddenly all the birds of the air seemed to be flying about us — meadow pipits in undulating flight, kestrels and sparrowhawks hanging in their hunting stances, and a raven flapping with a disdainful 'cronk!' out over the northern plains before us.

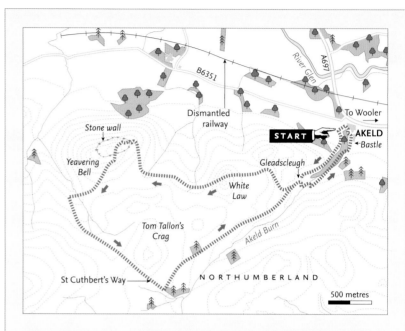

Start & finish Akeld, near Wooler, Northumberland NE71 6TA approx. (OS ref NT957297)

Getting there Bus: Service 267 (glenvalley.co.uk), Wooler-Berwick. Road: Akeld is on the A697, 2½ miles west of Wooler. Park carefully beside green: please don't obstruct entrances.

Walk (6 miles, moderate, OS Explorer OL16): Walk through farmyard; up track (blue arrow/BA). Pass to right of Gleadscleugh cottage (952290); through next gate; in 100m, right over stile (950288; yellow arrow/YA). Follow path, bearing right up left rim of stony Glead's Cleugh. Follow YAs on posts for 1¼ miles over White Law (943290) and down to stile and gate in fence under Yeavering Bell (932290). Path up to saddle to right of summit; at wooden pallet marker (931294), left on path to summit cairn (929293). Follow path half left off summit, through scattered stone wall (928292); here fork right (YAs, 'Hill Fort Trail') to St Cuthbert's Way/SCW at stile (923287). Left, following SCW for 1 mile. Pass Tom Tallon's Crag; through gate in wall (933278); in 300m, at near corner of conifer plantation, turn left off SCW through gate (935277); follow track to Gleadscleugh house. Right (951289, BA) on track to right of house; zigzag across burn; on by wall; follow yellow arrows to Akeld, passing bastle (958294) on your left.

Lunch Picnic

Accommodation Red Lion Inn, Milfield, Northumberland, NE71 6JD (01668 216224; redlionmilfield.co.uk) – cheerful village pub with rooms

More information Wooler TIC, The Cheviot Centre, 12 Padgepool Place (01668 282123), visitnorthumberland.com, visitengland.com, satmap.com, ramblers.org.uk

Allendale
NORTHUMBERLAND

It is a fantastically blowy morning over the Northumbrian moors. The night before, tucked up in a cosy bed at High Keenley Fell Farm high on its ridge, I heard the gale roaring like a monster in the larches and over the farm roofs. But down here in Allendale Town, sheltered in the cleft of its deep green dale, the wind sounds more of a continuous, mighty sigh in the racing heavens over Allendale.

On the fellside to the north of the compact little town, I look over to a great rise of stone-walled fields topped with broad dun-coloured moors and the upraised fingers of a couple of industrial chimneys. It's all sheep and cattle around here now, but Allendale Town once was a noisy, two-fisted settlement of 6,000 people, most of them employed in the lead mines on the moors. The chimneys poured out toxic sulphur fumes, brought through nearly a mile of stone-lined flues from the dale's big smelting mills. But the town's lead business all came sliding to a stop in the late nineteenth-century, and these days you can't find a quieter dale in these lovely northern hills.

Late-flowering cowslips and milkmaids dance crazily in the wind as I follow the hillside path past Housty and Stone Stile Farms towards Catton. A spine-tinglingly poignant bubble of curlew calls comes from the fields, and I catch a flash of white as the stout wading birds with their long down-curved bills settle themselves among the sedges with an ecstatic shiver of sabre-shaped wings.

Catton lies silent around its village green. In the fields beyond, fat lambs run riot, one prancing on top of its mother's back as she lies chewing. Below Old Town a bridge crosses the shallow, peat-brown River East Allen in its sheltered little gorge. Before following the riverbank path back to Allendale, I pause, leaning on the parapet to watch two white-breasted dippers bobbing on midstream stones while a flycatcher swoops out, up, over and back to its branch above their heads with a beak full of insect fodder.

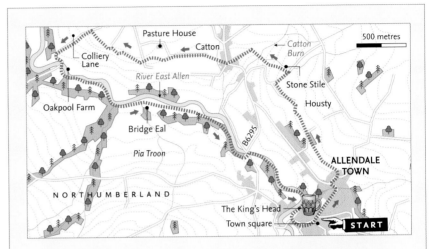

Start & finish Allendale Town square, Northumberland NE47 9BD (OS ref NY837558)

Getting there Bus: Service 688 (Hexham-Allendale). Road: Allendale Town is on B6295 between A69 (Hexham-Haydon Bridge) and A689 (Stanhope-Alston).

Walk (7 miles, moderate, OS Explorer OL43): From Allendale town square turn left (Hexham direction) along main road (pavement). In ¼ mile, cross Philip Burn (841562); in 50m, right up side road by 'Dene Croft'. In 100m, left up walled path, (842564; fingerpost 'Housty'); in 100m, left over ladder stile (fingerpost). Follow yellow arrows/YA across fields to Housty. Keep left of house and over stile (836572; YA); follow drive to road (834575). Right for 200m; left (836576; fingerpost 'Stone Stile, Catton'). Skirt left of barn, over stile (YAs); bear half left down field; through gate (833577; no YA). Bear right through next gate (no YA); bear left down to cross wall by stone step stile; cross Catton Burn footbridge (832578). Bear right up wall; in 100m, left over ladder stiles, through fields and farmyard (YAs) to road in Catton (829577).

Right; in 50m, left by 'Catton 2000' stone seat, down lane. Cross footbridge (827577; YA) and follow green lane (YAs) for ½ mile, past Pasture House to cross road (818578; fingerpost). Turn right through gate (fingerpost 'Old Town, Bishopside'; YA) across field above Struthers; then follow wall (step and ladder stiles) for ¼ mile to Old Town (814579). Through yard (YAs) and on across fields (YAs, stiles) to road (812581). Turn left downhill; descend Colliery Lane to cross River East Allen at Oakpool bridge (808577). Turn left (fingerpost 'Allendale Town'); don't bear right up waymarked field path, but keep ahead past front of Oakpool Farmhouse and on along track, then path, on right bank of river, over footbridges, through house garden at Bridge Eal (818573, YAs) to turn left across river on B6295 by weir (831566). Turn right along left bank (fingerpost 'Allendale Town'), sticking close to river. In 1 mile, opposite cricket pavilion, bear left up walled lane (836560) to road; left to town square.

Refreshments The King's Head, Allendale (01434 683681; www.thekingshead-allendale.co.uk), Forge Studios cafe (01434 683975; allendaleforgestudios.co.uk)

Accommodation High Keenley Fell Farm (01434 618344) – comfortable, good food and stunning view

Information Hexham TIC (01434 652220), visitnorthumberland.com, ramblers.org.uk, satmap.com

College Valley and Elsdonburn, Cheviot Hills
NORTHUMBERLAND

Our friend and walking companion Dave Richardson had only just taken delivery of his new concertina from Wiltshire master maker John Dipper after a decade of waiting, and had brought it down with him to Northumberland to play us a few tunes. But first some inspiration, in the form of a walk in the Cheviot Hills.

Those who know the Cheviots only from the pedestrian treadmill of the Pennine Way tend to associate them with mist, muck and misery. But walkers who head for their secluded northerly valleys are rewarded by open hills full of grand curves, with sensational views from their grassy heights.

On a morning of smoking cloud and pearly light we set off along the College Valley. This deep, sheltered cleft in the northern flank of the Cheviot Hills held several sheep farms not so long ago. These days, just two farms account for some 12000 acres of hill grazing. It was a stiff pull up the slope of Great Hetha to the Iron Age fort at the summit. We walked a circuit of the double ramparts of stone, looking out at hills folding to the south in steamy grey waves. Below us lay the lonely farmhouse of Trowupburn. Generations of Cheviot dwellers here lived with legends of grumpy giant trolls who would snatch unwary local musicians to entertain them in their caves.

Near the farm we crossed the Trowup Burn — the only way for a mortal to escape the trolls, who dared not go over running water. On the far bank a splendid bull in a cream-coloured coat was swinging his tail and murmuring in the ear of a young heifer. We climbed the bracken slopes beside Wideopen Burn, where whinchats were singing "wee-chit-chit!"

Up beyond Wideopen Head we found the Stob Stones, a pair of stumpy porphyry boulders where the local Gypsies once crowned their kings. Here we had a breathtaking view northwards over thirty miles of low, rolling border country. A long moment to stand and stare; then we cut east along the upland track of St Cuthbert's Way to the College Valley.

That night we feasted on wonderful music. The new concertina might have been made within sight of the Wiltshire downs, but it was pure Cheviot that Dave brought forth from it — the hornpipes, reels and jigs of these hills, while we sat and dreamed back over the day.

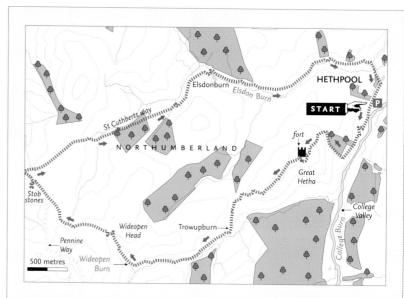

Start & finish College Valley car park, Hethpool, near Kirknewton NE71 6TW approx. (OS ref NT894280)

Getting there Road: A69 (Wooler-Coldstream); B6351 to Kirknewton; Hethpool signed just beyond, at Westnewton

Walk (8 miles, moderate/strenuous, OS Explorer OL16): From car park, left along road (detour to stone circle on right, 893278). In ½ mile, fork right (891275, 'Great Hetha') up left side of plantation. At top of wood (888277), left up to Great Hetha summit fort (886274). Don't turn right off summit towards Elsdonburn, but keep ahead (south-west) along green ridge (white arrow) till you look down on a white house. Half right here down grass track to stile (877269, 'Hilltop Trail'); left down farm track to Trowupburn (876265).

Past house, bear right through gate and up grassy lane with fence on left. In 600m, left across Trowup Burn (871262); in 500m, recross burn and a stile (867261), and turn left to continue through bracken. In 200m bear right at circular sheepfold into valley of Wideopen Burn. Follow path through bracken up right side of valley to Wideopen Head. Meet a fence here, and go through a gate (861265). Keep ahead on grass track for ½ mile to meet Pennine Way (854269). Right along PW for 500m (detour left to see Stob Stones, 851270), to 3-finger post (850272). Right here ('Elsdonburn 1½'), and follow waymarked St Cuthbert's Way for 3½ miles back to Hethpool.

Lunch Picnic

Accommodation Tankerville Arms, Wooler NE71 6AD (01668 281581; tankervillehotel.co.uk)

More information Wooler TIC, The Cheviot Centre, 12 Padgepool Place (01668 282123), visitnorthumberland.com, satmap.com, ramblers.org.uk

Doddington Moor
NORTHUMBERLAND

A blowy morning in Northumberland, with a light milky fret over the vale of the River Till. Across the sunlit farmlands, the Cheviot Hills stood up proud on the southern skyline, a patchwork of green and orange. Climbing the country lane from Doddington up to the moors, I kept turning round for another stare.

A noble view; perhaps that was why our distant ancestors chose Doddington Moor as the site for so many of their stoneworks. Northumberland is rich in sites with mysterious cup-and-ring markings — rounded depressions surrounded by a doughnut ring, gouged in the surface of flat rocks — and Doddington Moor is one of the best places to find them.

I followed a hill track past Wooler Golf Club, and on past a congregation of droopy-horned bullocks who jostled up to stand and stare like rude young men in a pub. The path led me around a vast field of oats, and then by map, compass and the pricking of my thumbs to stumble suddenly on

a fine cup-and-ring marked rock, a sandstone slab dimpled with man-made hollows that looked east towards the coastal hills. Was it sited here to face the rising sun? There's no telling now; but the slab still holds its power and presence.

Harebells trembled in the wind, which fought me like a foe past the seething firs of Kitty's Plantation. 'Stone Circle (rems. of)' the map said, and here it was: a big king-stone the size of a man, crusted with lichens and grooved by weather, lording it over a circle of recumbent stones.

I followed an escarpment path, smacked and elbowed by great blasts of wind. Before descending into Doddington village once more I sheltered by the lonely Shepherd's Cottage on the brink of the moor and tasted that mighty Cheviot prospect to the full. Whoever lives here is monarch of what must be one of the finest views in Britain.

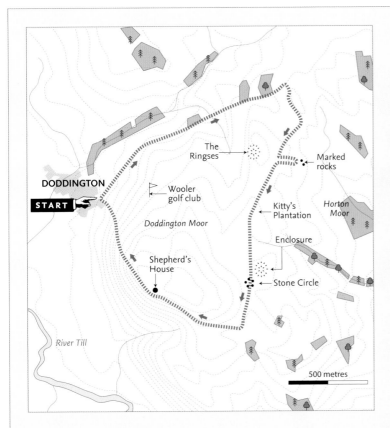

Start & finish Parking place on B6525 in Doddington, Northumberland NE71 6AN approx. (OS ref NT999324)

Getting there Air: easyJet (easyjet.com) to Newcastle from Bristol or Belfast. Bus: (glenvalley.co.uk) service 464 (Wooler-Berwick-on-Tweed). Road: A697 to Wooler; B6526 to Doddington. Parking for three cars just beyond foot of lane marked 'Wooler Golf Club'.

Walk (4 miles, moderate, OS Explorer 340): Climb lane towards golf club. At 'Welcome to Wooler Golf Club' notice, ahead along dirt road for ¾ mile. Left through gate (NU 016334; 'Weetwoodhill'); path south to crossing of fences (015327). Through gate; left over stile; left through gate; aim for right corner of plantation to find cup-and-ring stones in 250m, beyond lip of slope (018327). Return to cross stile; left past Kitty's Plantation (013322) and stone circle (013317) to reach gate (012313). Don't go through; right by fence for 350m. By gate (009313), bear right uphill on track. Left along escarpment to fence. Descend to cross stile; path to Shepherd's House (005316). Don't follow track behind house; keep ahead on path along escarpment, soon aiming for large farm below. Cross stile (001320); yellow arrows downhill to lane. Left into Doddington. NB: Last section from 012313 (gate beyond stone circle) is through thick bracken. This walk is for confident walkers with map, compass, GPS.

Lunch Picnic

More information Wooler TIC, The Cheviot Centre, 12 Padgepool Place (01668 282123), visitnorthumberland.com, ramblers.org.uk, satmap.com

Elsdon

NORTHUMBERLAND

The low-rolling Northumbrian hills enclose Elsdon in a loose embrace. The plain, dignified stone houses of the ancient community are scattered around their big, diamond-shaped village green which lies complete with a circular pound for stray animals (Elsdon was a famous stopover for cattle drovers on the long road south), and the broad and handsome Church of St Cuthbert (the monks who were carrying the saint's body away from Holy Island and its Viking marauders rested here more than 1000 years ago).

As we set out across the sheep pastures on a brisk morning, yet more bloody and stirring Border history looked down on us from the stark stone battlements of Elsdon Tower, a grim pele, or stronghold, built when the Scots and English raided each other's territory during a wild and lawless medieval era.

Near Folly Farm a big brown hare leapt up almost under my boots and went away like a miniature racehorse, its long black-tipped ears erect as it sped off. We pulled up for a breather and admired the blotchy tan and cream waves of heather and moor grass along the spine of the distant Simonside Hills. Frisky bullocks were cantering together in the fields at Fairneycleugh, and horses in red winter coats stood companionably nose to nose down at Soppit Farm.

This mid-Northumbrian landscape is all open country, big pasture fields, sedgy moorland and dark conifer blocks sitting together in a pleasing blend. You stride out more vigorously and breathe the clean air more deeply in such surroundings. At Haining farmhouse, the owners are making a superb job of restoring their stone field walls, and they have planted a wide new woodland of native species — alder, rowan, willow, hazel, cherry and hawthorn.

Above Haining we crossed the ragged knoll of Gallow Hill, looking down on a memorable view of Elsdon with the far-off Cheviot Hills standing grandly on the northern skyline. A notice board at Hillhead Cottage, warning of an application to build wind turbines six times the height of the Angel of the North on pristine Middle Hill just alongside, was a sharp reminder of how such views can be lost. It was a sobering thought to carry down the hill and back to Elsdon.

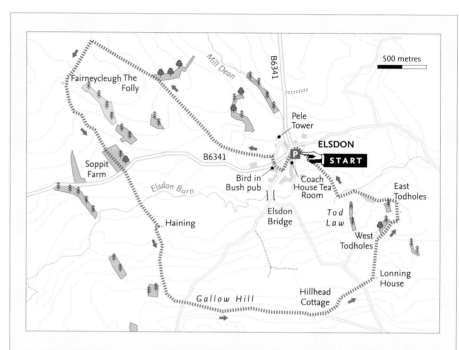

Start & finish Village car park, Elsdon, Northumberland NE19 1AB approx. (OS ref NY938933)

Getting there Road: Elsdon is signposted off A696 (Newcastle upon Tyne to Jedburgh) between Kirkwhelpington and Otterburn

Walk (6 miles, easy, OS Explorer OL42): From car park, left into Elsdon. Follow B6341 past church; in 100m, right over ladder stile (936933, 'The Folly'). Ahead over fields (stiles, yellow arrows/YAs). In 3rd field, steer right of reservoir with mast to junction of tarmac lanes at stile (926940). Ahead (fingerpost) up drive past The Folly; in almost ½ mile, left off drive (920944; fingerpost) to Fairneycleugh farm. Go through gate across track (917940). Left down grassy track to Soppit Farm (920934, blue arrows/BAs), then on through trees to cross B6341 (922932, fingerpost) and on to Haining (YAs). Keep right of farmhouse; at yellow arrow post (925927) right for 50m; left (YA) uphill through plantation on grassy track. Cross stile (926920). Left (BA) to cross road. On (fingerpost, 'Hillhead Cottage') over Gallow Hill (931919), keeping wall and fence close on left. 650m after crossing road, go through gate (933919) and follow wall on right to Hillhead. At waymark post (939919, BA) go right; in 50m, left through gate; cross cottage drive; through gate ahead (YA) along fence on left and through gate (940918, YA). Aim half right for Lonning House; cross next stile with 2 YAs; follow right-hand one towards Lonning House. Cross road; on down farm drive (943921, YAs). On across stable yard beside house (944921, YAs). In field beyond, aim diagonally left between electricity poles, descending to cross stile into lane at West Todholes (945925). Right to East Todholes. Just before farmhouse, left over ladder stile (946926, YA); in 50m, at post with 2 YAs, keep ahead, descending beside plantation and through gate (946928, YA). Left along fence, follow YAs to cross Elsdon Burn (943929) and bear left. Aim for the corner of the fence on your left; turn 90° right here (941929, YA), aiming a little away from fence on your right to cross ladder stile in a bend of the stone wall far ahead (940931). Aim ahead for Elsdon Tower to return to car park.

Lunch Impromptu Tea Room (01830 520389 – closed Thursdays). Bird in Bush PH due to re-open shortly (01830 520914; birdinbushinelsdon@gmail.com)

More information Alnwick TIC (01665 511333), visitnorthumberland.com, ramblers.org.uk, satmap.com

Hadrian's Wall and Haughton Common

NORTHUMBERLAND

A light dusting of snow over Hadrian's Wall, with the Whin Sill cliffs riding west from Housesteads, an iron-coloured tsunami breaking into the white wintry sky. Once I had topped the dolerite crags beside the old Roman fort, an answering wave stood in view over the moors beyond the crags — the low dark billow of Wark Forest, filling the northern skyline.

As I came clear of the sycamores on Housesteads Crags, the Whin Sill ran before me, a rollercoaster of sheer cliffs, with the snow-crowned strip of the Roman wall standing proud as it has done for 2,000 years. Down in a dip under Cuddy's Crags I struck out north along the Pennine Way into the barbarian badlands. Now the Whin Sill showed its harsher aspect as I looked back — pale green columnar crags in a dinosaur spine 30m (100ft) tall.

Sedgy and ice-crusted, the Pennine Way straggled towards the forest.

Out east beyond Broomlee Lough rose the King's and the Queen's Crags, outcrops of the Whin Sill where Arthur and Guinevere quarreled over a game of catch — if legend can be believed. Once in the forest, crags and moors were shut away by the dark, timeless shade of white-powdered conifers.

It wasn't long before I was out on the wide moors of Haughton Common, scratching my head for a sight of the footpath. Bless the Countryside and Rights of Way Act! Haughton Common is 'access land' these days — anybody's to wander over at will. I set a course along Crow Crags, then plunged across the moor towards Stell Green farmhouse on its lonely crag. The delight of tramping the whitened farm drive towards the bared teeth of Sewing Shields Crags, with the prospect of a final mile beside the Roman wall towards a gold and silver sunset, brings a retrospective rush of pleasure even as I write.

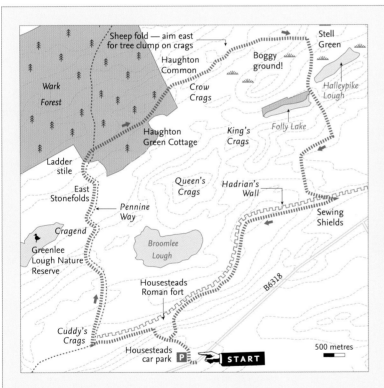

Start & finish Housesteads car park, Hadrian's Wall NE47 6NN approx. (OS ref NY714684) – £4 all day (coins)

Getting there Rail: (thetrainline.com) – nearest station Bardon Mill (4 miles). Bus: (01424 322002; hadrianswallcountry.co.uk/travel/bus); Hadrian's Wall bus AD122. Road: A69, Newcastle to Carlisle; at Hexham, A6079 to Low Brunton; B6318 Chollerford to Housesteads.

Walk (8½ miles, moderate/hard, OS Explorer OL43): Left along Hadrian's Wall from Housesteads Fort for ½ mile; at Cuddy's Crags, right on Pennine Way (781686; white acorn symbols, yellow arrows) for 1½ miles by Cragend (782700) and ladder stile near East Stonefolds (780707) into forest. In 300m (781709; 'Haughton Green' fingerpost), head off Pennine Way to Haughton Green Cottage (788713). Ahead ('Lonborough, Fenwickfield' fingerpost) for 100m; left across stream; follow yellow arrows to leave forest (791717) onto Haughton Common (access land, choose own path). Follow top of Crow Crags for ½ mile to sheep fold among trees (778722). Aim a little right (due east – boggy, some streams to ford) for ⅔ mile to Stell Green farmhouse, in tree clump on ridge (808722). Follow farm drive south for 1½ miles to Hadrian's Wall at Sewing Shields (811703); right to Housesteads.

Conditions Some boggy ground; trackless across Haughton Common. If inexperienced, keep walk for fine weather.

Lunch Twice Brewed Inn (on B6318 near Bardon Mill), NE47 7AN (01434 344534; twicebrewedinn.co.uk)

Accommodation Carraw Farmhouse, Military Road, Humshaugh, Hexham (01434 689857; carraw.co.uk).

More info Housesteads Roman Fort: english-heritage.org.uk, nationaltrust.org.uk, hadrianswallcountry.co.uk, visitnortheastengland.com, visitnorthumberland.com

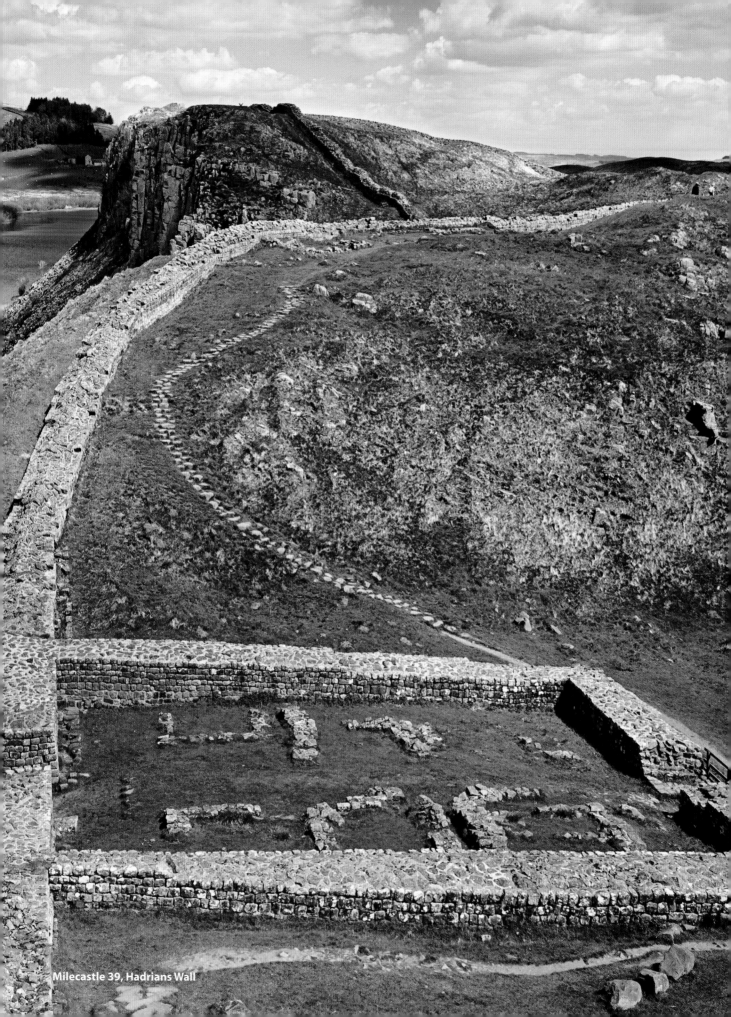

Milecastle 39, Hadrians Wall

Vindolanda and Hadrian's Wall

NORTHUMBERLAND

Hadrian's Wall retains, in greater or lesser ruin, its observation towers and guard-posts, and the roads and townships that served it. The Wall forms the most remarkable monument in Britain to those energetic, organised and life-loving invaders, the Romans. They wrenched our history forcefully out of its courses, and yet it's the tiny details of their everyday lives that fascinate us most.

How incredibly angry the tile-maker of Vindolanda must have been when that stupid pig walked all over the nice new clay flooring he'd left out to dry in the sun. A surviving tile from the spoiled batch, on display in Vindolanda's museum just south of the Wall, carries the prints of the pig's incurving toes, as sharp today as the hour they were dinted 2000 years ago. And here, alongside, are the hobnailed shoes and thong sandals of this Roman fort's inhabitants, their nose-picks and knives and scribe-written birthday invitations. Outside lie the foundations of the town they lived in, its houses, temples, wells and paved streets.

Walking the rushy meadows a mile or so to the south, I looked up at the thin line of Hadrian's Wall as it rode the rollercoaster crags of the Whin Sill, the volcanic rampart that strides across the neck of Northumberland. A magnificently muscled bull, lion coloured and sporting a leonine mane, watched me cross the broad grassy ditch or vallum and turn east along the wall. The stepped path swooped me up the crests and down into hollows of the dolerite sill, passing the sites of the milecastles and turrets where conscripts from the Low Countries paced and shivered and looked out into the debatable lands to the north from where the wild Picts might come screaming at any moment.

As I stared out from the wall to the looming black line of Wark Forest, the blue humps of the Cheviot Hills beyond, it was all too easy to imagine those young men sulkily clutching their cloaks around them and wishing they were down in Vindolanda where the latrines ran with clean water and the stew came hot to the table.

The old house and barns of Hotbank Farm lay huddled on the slope of Hotbank Crags, their walls much patched with Roman stones. Here I left Hadrian's Wall and headed across the vallum and down flowery meadow slopes, with Vindolanda spread below me in the evening sunlight.

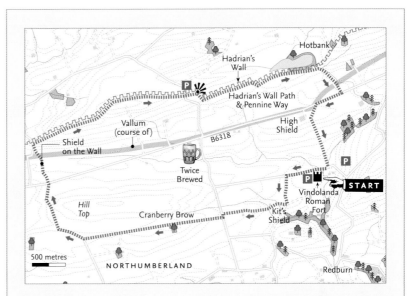

Start & finish Vindolanda car park, near Bardon Mill, Northumberland NE47 7JN (OS ref NY767664)

Getting there Bus: Service 685/85 to Bardon Mill. Road: signposted from B6318 at Once Brewed (north of A69, between Haydon Bridge and Haltwhistle at Bardon Mill).

Walk (8 miles, moderate, OS Explorer OL53): From Vindolanda car park, left along road; in 100m, left through gate, down track; in 400m, right (766660) on path (stiles, yellow arrows/YAs). NB After passing barn at Kit's Shield (764659), negotiate tree blocking path! Skirt Layside (760659, YAs); on to road (756658). Left, then right along lane ('Cranberry Brow') for 1⅓ miles to road (735655). Right (fingerpost) on drive to Hill Top; on to road (730659). Right to cross B6318 (729663, stile, 'Shield on the Wall').

Path along field wall, then diagonally left across Roman Vallum ditch to Hadrian's Wall (727669). Right along National Trail for 3 miles to Hotbank Farm (771680). Leave National Trail here; right down farm drive to B6318. Right along grass verge for 400m; left (770674, stile, 'Vindolanda') across field, aiming to cross stile on left of High Shield house (769672, YA). Left to stile (YA); down fields with fence on left. In 2nd field, fence trends away left, but keep a beeline ahead to stile and road at bottom (772665). Right to Vindolanda car park.

Conditions Short, steep ups and downs on Hadrian's Wall. Bulls, cows, calves may be in fields.

Refreshments Vindolanda Café

Accommodation Twice Brewed Inn (on B6318 near Bardon Mill), NE47 7AN (01434 344534; twicebrewedinn.co.uk) – very cheerful, walker-friendly stopover

More information Vindolanda (01434 344277; vindolanda.com), National Park Centre Once Brewed – on B6318 next to Twice Brewed Inn (01434 344396), visitengland.com, satmap.com, ramblers.org.uk

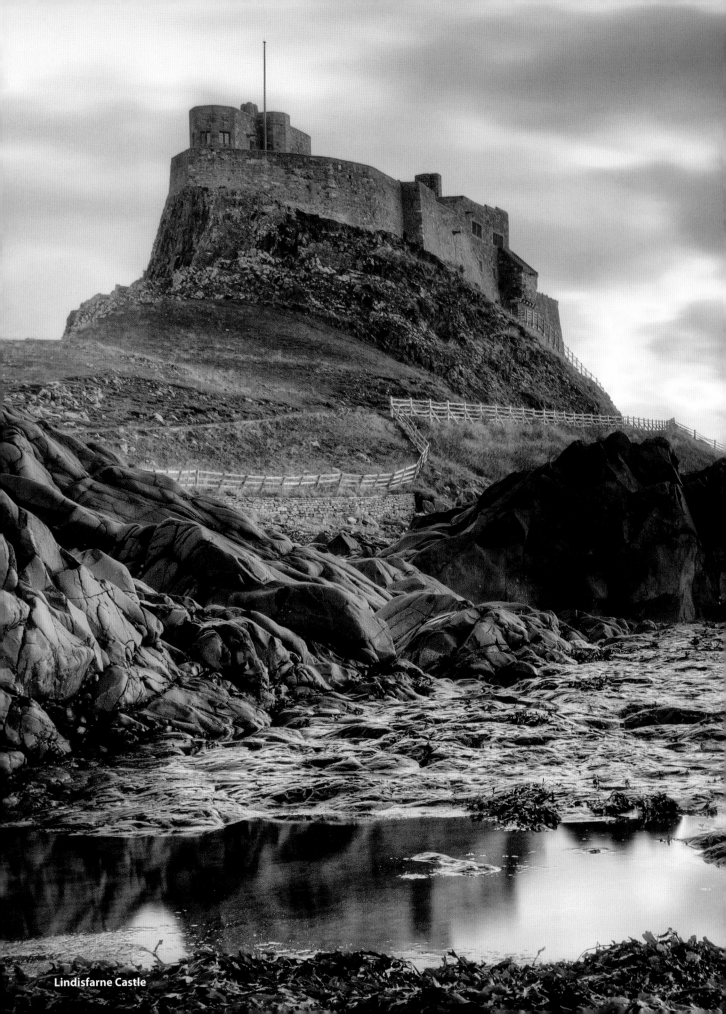
Lindisfarne Castle

Holy Island
NORTHUMBERLAND

I made out, approaching across the sands, a slow black dot (which) resolved itself into a Ford car. This indomitable thing, rust red, its mudguards tied with string, splashed and slithered towards me; and at the wheel was a handsome young girl with blue eyes and a soft Scots voice . . . So we splashed over the sands to Lindisfarne.

H.V. Morton in *The Call Of England*, 1927

Alas, the famous salt-rusted taxis of Holy Island that so entranced the ultra-romantic Morton are long rotted to pieces. But romantics of all kinds and conditions can do as I did this blowy day on the Northumberland coast – gird their loins and follow the ancient pilgrim path over the wide tidal sands. Tall rough poles mark the straight way, with barnacle-encrusted wooden refuge towers for foolish virgins to clamber into if beset by a rising tide.

The ribbed sands stretched away. Bladderwrack crunched underfoot. It was a good hour's walk. The green sandhills and huddled village of the island seemed to draw no closer until the last moment. But this was a heavenly way to cross to Holy Island, or Lindisfarne, to give it an older and lovelier name.

Holy Island village is still partly a fishing community, mostly for crab and lobster these days. Creels lean drying against house walls in the narrow lanes. People come to Lindisfarne for its peace, its small-scale beauty and its remarkable monastic history. St Aidan of Iona established a monastery in Lindisfarne in the seventh-century. St Cuthbert became its hermit bishop and saintly icon. The 'most beautiful book in the world', the illuminated *Lindisfarne Gospels*, was crafted here.

This little island off the Northumbrian coast kept alive the flickering light of Christianity during the Dark Ages; and when Holy Island was reoccupied after the Norman Conquest (the monks having fled Danish raids in AD 875) a wonderful new monastery was built here.

Lindisfarne is full of marvels. Wind and weather have sculpted swirling shapes in the red sandstone walls of the church, whose 'sky arch' springs 15m (50ft) in the air, seemingly unsupported. Down by the harbour old herring boats, sawn in half and upturned, make fishermen's huts. Lindisfarne Castle rides the basalt knoll of Beblowe Crag like a tall ship; Sir Edwin Lutyens redesigned it for drama, and Gertrude Jekyll laid out the walled garden ablaze with colour.

Inland, the humps of the Cheviot Hills began to fade under rain. The island's strollers vanished into the tea shops and I was left alone to walk the north shore dunes, savouring the wind and showers, the barking of pale-bellied brent geese newly arrived from Svalbard, and the eerie singing of seals on the sands.

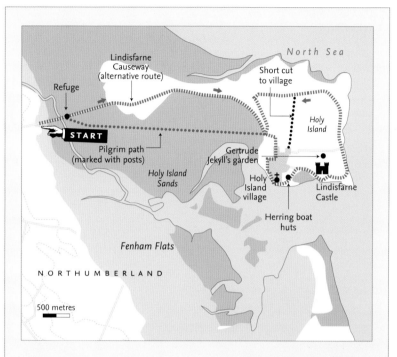

Start & finish Holy Island causeway car park, Northumberland TD15 2PB approx. (OS ref NU079427)

Getting there Air: easyJet (easyjet.com) to Newcastle from Bristol or Belfast. Rail: (thetrainline.com; railcard.co.uk) to Berwick-upon-Tweed (10 miles). Bus: Service 477 (perrymansbuses.co. uk) from Berwick-upon-Tweed. Road: Holy Island is signed off A1 between Belford and Haggerston

Walk (10 miles including sands crossing, 3½ miles island circular; easy; OS Explorer 340): From car park follow causeway, then pilgrim route posts, to Chare Ends on Holy Island (NB see below!). Follow road to Priory ruins (126418 – signposted). Return to Market Square; between Crown & Anchor and Manor House Hotel, follow path to shore. Left round harbour; on to castle (detour to Gertrude Jekyll's garden – 136419). Continue on coast path, past The Lough and National Nature Reserve notice. Follow path to left along line of dunes for ½ mile to meet fence at NNR notice (129433). For island circular, left through gate, ahead to village. For sands crossing, keep ahead for ½ mile; bear left (122433) with causeway on right, to rejoin posts at Chare End.

NB: Causeway is impassable for 2½ hours either side of high tide. Tide times are posted at both ends of the causeway; or visit www.lindisfarne.org.uk.

Lunch Plenty of options in the village

Accommodation Manor House Hotel (01289 389207; manorhouselindisfarne.com), Crown & Anchor (01289 389215; holyislandcrown.co.uk), Ship Inn (01289 389311; theshipinn-holyisland.co.uk)

More information Berwick-upon-Tweed TIC (01670 622155), www.lindisfarne.org.uk, visitnorthumberland.com, ramblers.co.uk, satmap.com

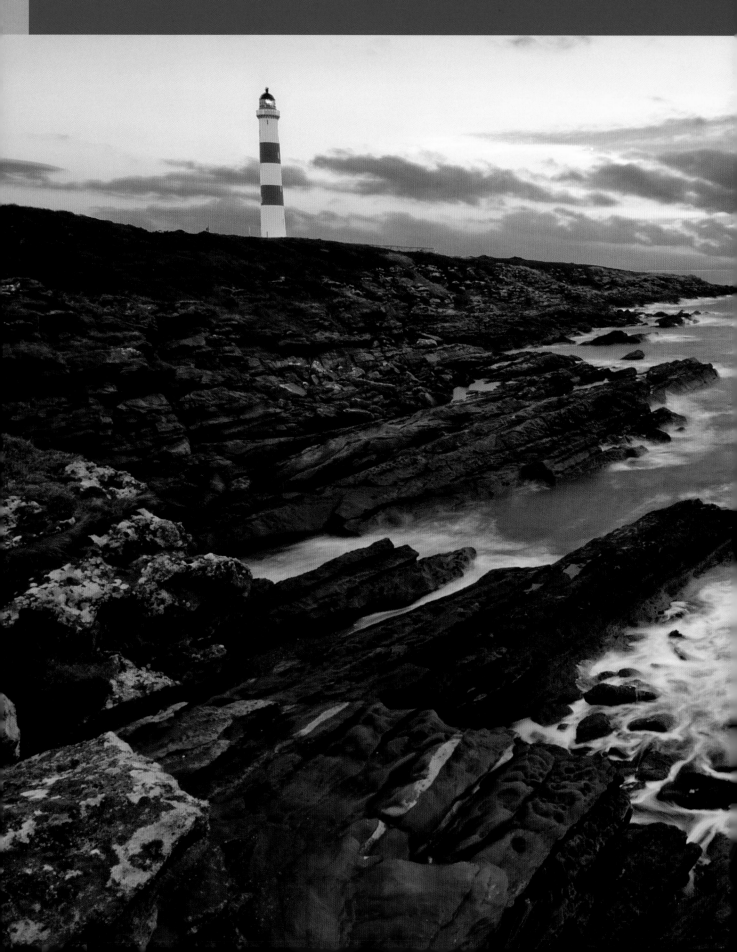

Scotland

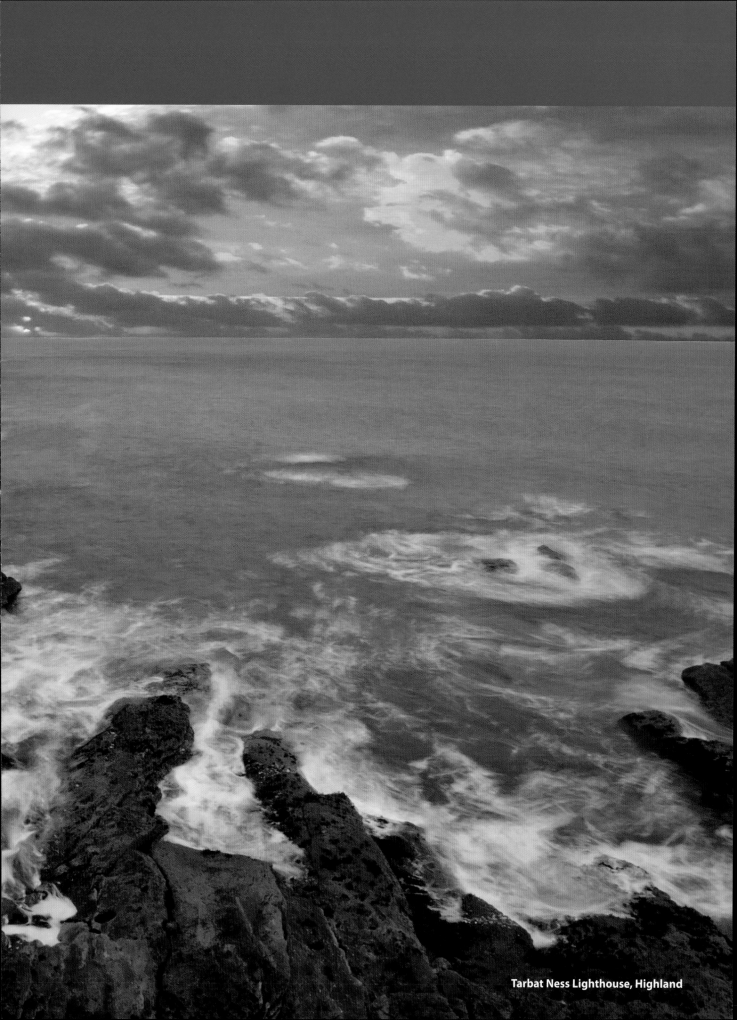

Tarbat Ness Lighthouse, Highland

Forvie National Nature Reserve

ABERDEENSHIRE

Forvie National Nature Reserve lies on the Scottish coast north of Aberdeen. This spectacular reserve contains nearly two thousand acres of sandy beaches, open moorland, estuarine mudflats and a great wilderness of ancient green sandhills that stretch away south from the Visitor Centre at Collieston.

On a brisk, windy day with a cloudy sky hurrying rain showers out to sea, the dunes looked dun and drab as we followed the coast path among their shaggy camel humps. But that first dull impression gave way to astonishment at the richness of their flora — spatters of white heath bedstraw, stout northern marsh orchids with richly purple flower heads, pink streamers of ragged robin, wild pansies with lower lips of cream and yellow. Lichens, mosses and heather combined to lay a subtly-coloured foundation for these floral glories of the sandhills.

At North Broad Haven a sour fishy whiff heralded a teeming colony of kittiwakes. We lay on the cliff edge above a guano-whitened sea stack where a row of cormorants sat on a line of untidy nests. The nestlings craned their heads up to rub the throats of their parents, stimulating them to regurgitate the fish they'd brought back in their crops.

Down on the beach at Rockend we strode south on firm sand to the boundary of the ternery. Here sandwich, common and little terns have their summer breeding ground; and once we had crossed the dunes and were perched looking down on the Ythan Estuary, we could see them lined up head to wind in hundreds on the mud flats. Beside our homeward path along the river a great congregation of eider ducks lay moulting, the males with green neck flashes and black toupés with centre-partings like 1920s cabaret cads.

Eiders flock to Forvie in their thousands in spring to nest on the moors behind the dunes. These handsome, bulky birds gobble the estuary's mussels whole, grinding them small in their gizzards. Forvie NNR offers the eider a place of safety, as it does the terns, the wild flowers and the dunes that have been growing and shifting along this coast since Stone Age man came hunting here.

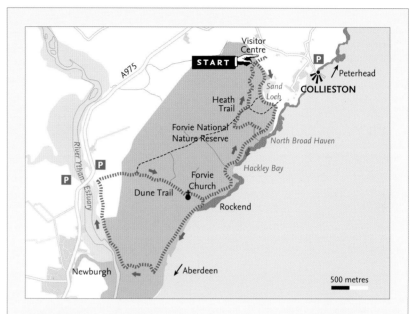

Start & finish Forvie NNR Visitor Centre, Collieston AB41 8RU (OS ref NK034289)

Getting there Bus: Service 63 (Aberdeen-Peterhead) to Collieston Cross (1½ miles). Road: Forvie NNR is signed off B9003 Collieston road (from A975 between Newburgh and Cruden Bay).

Walk (8½ miles, easy, OS Explorer 421): From Visitor Centre follow 'To The Reserve.' Through gate; turn left along gravel track towards line of cottages (Red Route or Heath Trail, with occasional waymark posts). Along right side of Sand Loch to coast (036281); right along dune path above sea. In 1½ miles, descend to beach at Rockend (023265). Continue along beach for ¾ mile to rope barrier at ternery (014253). Turn right into dunes past tern sign on pole; follow Dune Trail to Ythan Estuary (009254). Right up estuary path for 1 mile. Opposite info shelter, turn right (005269). Follow Dune Trail posts for 1 mile to Forvie Kirk ruin (021266); then follow 'Hackley Bay' to coast (023265). Left up coast for 1¼ miles. At Red Route post (033276), left inland on Heath Trail. At marker post at far side of small loch, don't turn right; keep ahead. At 'Shortcut' post bear left; at next post, fork left (032284) to return to Visitor Centre.

Lunch Picnic

Accommodation Jurys Inn Aberdeen Airport, AB21 0AF (01224 725252; www.jurysinns.com/hotels/aberdeen-airport)

More information Forvie NNR Visitor Centre (01358 751330; nnr-scotland.org.uk), visitscotland.com, satmap.com, visitaberdeen.com

Royal Deeside and Glen Girnock

ABERDEENSHIRE

At last, after days of rain over Scotland, a beautiful sunny morning of wind and high cloud and patches of brilliant blue sky. Around Balmoral Castle, the River Dee ran broad and sparkling, and the hills cradling the royal retreat were brushed green and gold with bright sunlight.

A couple of miles downriver, I made my way through the fields around Abergeldie, climbing over and wriggling under tall ladder stiles, following rickety fences and 4x4 tracks knee-deep in heather through the lonely valley that separates the rocky knolls of Creag Ghiubhais, 'hill of the fir trees', and Creag nam Ban, 'hill of the women'. The unaccustomed sunshine had called out the butterflies; meadow browns in clouds, leopard-spotted fritillaries and a beautiful royal blue creature that moved too erratically for me to fix its name for sure. I surprised a buzzard on a field wall; it stared round at me as though it had never seen a human being before, then jumped up and flapped with stiff wing-beats over the trees.

Near the Mill of Cosh I turned on to a stony track and made for the hills. These four-wheel-drive roadways have proliferated throughout the Highlands and they are a wonderful asset for walkers. But they haven't succeeded in keeping a population in the remote back country hereabouts. Beside the track, the house of Loinveg stood shuttered. Beyond lay the great dun-coloured bowl of Glen Girnock, the Girnock Burn snaking through its marshy bottom, heathery hills encircling it. Not a sheep, not a cow. Silence, a cold wind, and the exhilaration of striding out in empty moorland with a stunning view.

I passed a tiny stone-built whisky still, some long-forgotten amateur distiller's illicit pride and joy, and came to the abandoned farmstead of Bovaglie, windows boarded, ornate garden gate swinging in the wind, an eerie and haunted place. A final high stretch looking west into the heart of the Grampian Mountains, and a descent through a pine forest bearded with trailing lichens, down to the road and the broad Dee Valley once more.

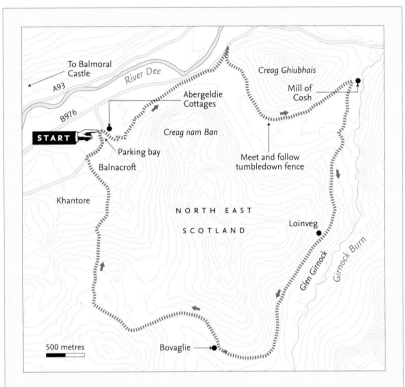

Start & finish Parking bay near Abergeldie Cottages, near Balmoral AB35 5TJ approx. (OS ref NO 287948)

Getting there Road: A93 Braemar-Ballater; at Balmoral, B976 ('East Deeside'). Cross River Dee; follow B976. Pass sign on left to Clachanturn; next right (unmarked); just past right bend, parking bay on right.

Walk (8½ miles, moderate, OS Explorer 388): Up driveway opposite, past Abergeldie Cottages and on up grass track. Dogleg left and right (289947); continue uphill, with stone wall and trees on right, to forestry fence. Right; follow fence down; cross two ladder stiles (291949); follow fence for ¾ mile, descending beside B976. Pass two locked gates; on through trees for 400m. At next locked gate by road (304958), hairpin back to right up grassy track through trees, then through open heather for ⅔ mile, passing between Creag nam Ban and Creag Ghiubhais, to meet tumbledown fence (310949). Left along it for ¾ mile to Mill of Cosh; right on stony track (320953). Follow track for 3 miles past Loinveg and Bovaglie. In another mile, right at junction (290923). In ⅓ mile, where track begins to descend, right at track crossing (285925). Stile into forest (286929); at fork in ¼ mile (286934) keep ahead (left); down to Khantore (288938); road to Balnacroft (285944); right to car.

NB: Faint track skirting Creag Ghiubhais – some heather wading!

Lunch Picnic

More information Ballater TIC (01339 755306; royal-deeside.org.uk), Ballater Walking Festival in May: walkballater.com

Devon Way and Dollar Glen

CLACKMANNANSHIRE

On this cloudy spring day, Tillicoultry looked just as I remembered it: a neat, proud Clackmannanshire mill town, with the Ochil Hills rearing 600m (2000ft) behind in a dramatic green wall. The mills have long fallen silent along the River Devon, but sheep still dot the slopes like flecks of snow.

St Serf, Tillicoultry's sixth-century miracle worker and missionary, would have enjoyed the sight. The saint, a keen shepherd, had his own flock under special protection. A rustler stole, roasted and ate Serf's pet ram. He then boldly denied the crime, but the very mutton was heard bleating inside the guilty party's stomach.

Nowadays the winding River Devon runs at the feet of the Ochils in company with the Devon Way, a beautifully landscaped footpath and bridleway established along a disused railway line.

I walked briskly, trying to work off a bacon-and-haggis breakfast, with the slow-flowing Devon on my right and the tremendous green and black rampart of the hills on the left. Along the old railway the ash buds were clamped shut and hawthorns stood thick with last autumn's shriveled berries, but a song thrush in an elder bush was busy trying to charm the laydeez.

Along the valley in Dollar, the Dollar burn came sparkling from its steep glen through the town. I climbed a steep and slippery pathway up the rocky cleft of Dollar Glen where the burns of Care and Sorrow sluiced down black rock chutes to mingle in the stream of Dolour. Gloomy names, and a doom-laden history to the castle that blocks the throat of the glen on a formidable bluff.

Impregnable it must have seemed to the Campbells who built it, warmed themselves before its enormous stone fireplaces and shut their captured enemies away out of sight and mind in its cruel and terrible pit prison.

Bonnie Montrose couldn't take Castle Campbell — Castell Gloum was its ominous nickname — when he tried during the Civil War. But the Macleans destroyed it in 1654, firing the stronghold with flaming arrows while the garrison was out scouring the hills for food.

I climbed the spiral stair, to a roof-top view that had me gasping: Dollar below, a gleam of the Firth of Forth amid southern hills thirty miles off, Saddle Hill and King's Seat towering to the north, seemingly just overhead.

Then I descended from Castell Gloum down the Burn of Sorrow, back along the old railway line where mating frogs filled the ditches and wrens trilled their song as if man and his bloody inclinations had never been invented.

Start & finish Sterling Mills car park, Tillicoultry FK13 6HQ (OS ref NS 920965).

Getting there Bus: (www.traveline.info) from Glasgow, Stirling, Alloa, St Andrews.
Train: (www.trainline.com) to Alloa (3 ½ miles).
Road: A91 from Perth or Stirling to Tillicoultry; car park is just off A91, on A908 Alloa road.

Walk (8 miles, easy/moderate grade, OS Explorer 366): From car park, left up A908; right along Devon Way for 3 miles to Dollar. Just past Dollar station platform, left (963976) beside Dollar Burn to clock tower (973908); on up East Burnside, then Dollar Glen, following path and walkways to Castle Campbell (962993).

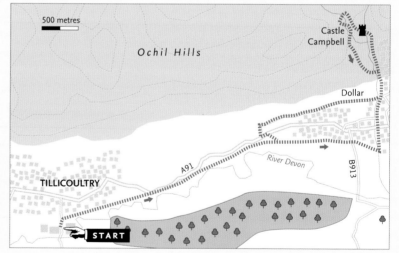

Leaving castle, go through gate; in 15m, left up path to cross Burn of Sorrow (959995) and turn left. In 200m, at 'Dangerous Cliffs' notice, left downhill, cross 2 bridges, uphill for 100m, then down across 2 more bridges opposite castle (961993). Follow West Glen signs. At top of slope, white arrow points left down glen path. In 500m descend to cross Dollar Burn (963988); continue to bridge at top of East Burnside (963983). Right along lane past Dollar Golf Club for 1 mile to corner by Belmont House (947979); left to A91 (947978). Cross (take care!). Left for 100m; right down road; right (950977) along Devon Way to Tillicoultry.

NB: Steep, slippery paths in Dollar Glen. Dogs on leads in Dollar Glen.

Lunch Plenty of places in Tillicoultry and Dollar

More information www.visitscotland.com

Loch Trool

DUMFRIES AND GALLOWAY

A warm day of sun and cloud over Galloway, the forgotten corner of southwest Scotland. Finch and warbler song echoed in the woods of alder and silver birch along the Water of Trool. A good squirt of Avon Skin-so-Soft, incomparable deterrent to the midges, and we were off along the river with the high hills of Galloway cut sharply against white cumulus and blue sky, the crumpled-bed profile of Mulldonoch standing tall across Loch Trool, the grey-green teeth of Cambrick Hill beyond.

Up beside the roughly squared lump of Bruce's Stone we gazed across the head of the loch to the slopes where Robert Bruce's ragged guerrillas had whipped the mail-clad asses of the English in 1307, rolling great boulders down on them and charging the demoralized remnants into flight. The tumbled hills around Glen Trool lay in mild sunshine today, as peaceful as could be. We crossed a miniature gorge of black rock walls by way of Buchan Bridge and followed a hill path through the bracken into the lonely side cleft of the Gairland Burn.

The Galloway hills hold many secret places, especially in these foothills of the wonderfully named Range of the Awful Hand. You would never suspect it from down in Glen Trool, but a string of beautiful peat-dark lochs with white quartzite-sand beaches lies above the Gairland's glen.

The hillside track led us up among boggy patches jumping with tiny green and yellow frogs, upstream beside the glassy oxygenated waters of the burn. We skirted steely dark Loch Valley and climbed beside ancient animal pens of massive boulders to reach imperial-blue Loch Neldricken, its waters bright with bog bean, its white and salmon-pink beaches etched in crescents under the shoulder of The Merrick.

"Ony sauchle o' a body can write a book," a local shepherd growled to the rural writer Rev C. H. Dick at the turn of the twentieth century, "but it tak's a man tae herd The Merrick."

Looking at the great whaleback of Galloway's highest mountain, we saw exactly what he meant.

Down in Glen Trool once more we crossed the head of Loch Trool and turned back along a swooping path through the forest. Cuckoos made call and response across the sunny valley, and the loch waters sparkled as though a generous, invisible hand had scattered diamonds there.

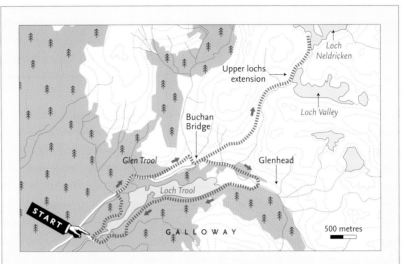

Start & finish Car park at foot of Loch Trool; nearest postcode DG8 6SU (OS ref NX297791)

Getting there Bus: Service 359 (Newton Stewart-Ayr) to Glentrool village (www.dumgal.gov.uk) Road: A714 Newton Stewart-Girvan. In 8 miles, right to Glentrool Visitor Centre. Follow 'Bruce's Stone'; in 1½ miles, right ('Start of Loch Trool Trail') to car park.

Walk (5½ miles circuit of Loch Trool, or 10 miles including upper lochs, moderate, OS Explorer 318): Follow woodland path past 'green waymarks'/GW sign. NB: GWs are posts with green bands; they carry white waymark arrows (on their reverse sides) for clockwise walkers! In ½ mile enter conifer forest; in 200m, look for GW on left; climb track to road (402799). Right past Bruce's Stone car park (416804); descended rough road to cross Buchan Bridge (418804); fork left and continue (GW; 'Gairland Burn').

In 200m, at right bend (420805), Loch Trool Trail continues along road. For Gairland Burn and upper lochs extension, go through gate and up hillside path ('Loch Valley, Gairland Burn'). Follow track to Gairland Burn; continue up left bank. Near top, cross side burns (436818); keep near Gairland Burn to Loch Valley. Keep left of loch, then follow stone wall by burn up to Loch Neldricken. Return to gate near Buchan Bridge; rejoin Loch Trool Trail by turning left along road (GW).

In ⅓ mile cross Gairland Burn and continue; go through gate, and in 150m bear right off road (430801; 'National Cycle Network 7'). Follow path to cross burn (430800); forward up side of forestry ('Southern Upland Way/SUW'); left along SUW beside Loch Trool for 1¾ miles, to cross Caldons Burn footbridge and reach T-junction (399789) with SUW post, GW post and a blue post marked '7 Stones'. Bear right here to footbridge and car park.

Lunch Picnic. Glentrool Visitor Centre (01671 840302) – light meals, maps, midge repellent.

Accommodation Creebridge House, Newton Stewart DG8 6NP (01671 402121; creebridge.co.uk)

More information visitscotland.com

John Muir Country Park
EAST LOTHIAN

Dunbar lies on the rugged East Lothian coast, round the eastward curve from Edinburgh. The town's most famous son, John Muir (1838-1914), was a hugely influential, pioneering conservationist, who founded the national parks movement in his adoptive United States. Muir acknowledged as a lifelong inspiration the wild coast "around my native town of Dunbar by the stormy North Sea".

The day lay cold and still, a pearly January morning with sea light slanting across wide freshwater marshes, shaggy dunes of pale green marram grass and long, tan-coloured sands. The red sandstone houses of Dunbar crowded to their headland across Belhaven Bay, backlit by the sun. Its muted glow picked out the details of the volcanic lumps and bumps that litter this low-lying East Lothian coast — the hollow-backed cone of North Berwick Law, triangular Traprain Law and, out in the Firth of Forth, the flat wedge of the Isle of May and the white rectangle of the lighthouse on the looming dark face of the Bass Rock, rising from a white collar of breaking waves.

Stefan Sobell, Dave Richardson and I strolled the dunes away from the town, talking of citterns (Stefan makes them, Dave plays them) and bitterns, holy fools and godwits. A small brown bird with a dark head and yellow bill went hopping among the empty snail shells of the dunes. "Twite?" "Yep." A plump little bird with dark green legs and a china-white belly stooped and probed the mud of the Tyne estuary among a crowd of grey plover. "Greenshank?" "Yep."

To landward lay the long, dark bar of coniferous Hedderwick Hill Plantation, cover and concealment for birds of prey. Suddenly one was overhead — "Peregrine!" — a little dark hunter flying with quick wingbeats round a flock of 200 knot. The waders formed themselves into a dense, defensive ball; then one of their number panicked and made a break, quitting the safety of numbers in a desperate dash towards the open sea. Pursuer and prey chased out over the firth, the knot managing to keep out of the peregrine's clutches with a series of last-second jinks and swerves. "Who'll win?" I asked Dave. "The one that's got more fuel on board," was his reply.

Wartime tank traps leaned at the edge of the trees, green-topped and crumbling. Beyond them rose the candlesnuffer turrets and fantasy roofs of Tyninghame House, a Mad King Ludwig extravaganza of a country pile. In a mossy forest hollow we ate our ham, mustard and spelt bread sandwiches, then headed back along the John Muir Way. Would Dunbar's celebrated son have enjoyed the morning's walk in our company? I'd like to think so.

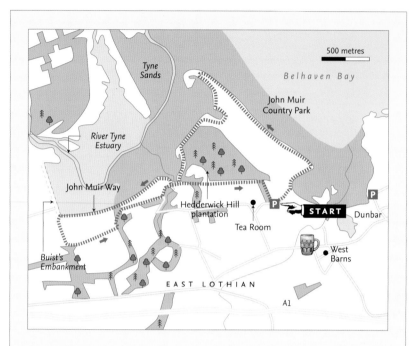

Start & finish Linkfield car park, John Muir Country Park, West Barns, Dunbar, East Lothian; nearest postcode EH42 1XF (OS ref NT652785)

Getting there Train: (thetrainline.com, railcard.co.uk) to Dunbar (2½ miles by John Muir Way coast path). Bus: Services X6, X8 or 106 Edinburgh-Dunbar (firstgroup.com). Road: A1 to Dunbar; follow brown John Muir Country Park signs to car park.

Walk (5½ miles, easy, OS Explorer 351): From car park turn left (NW) along shoreline for 2¼ miles, to Tyne estuary (642800) then inland along shore, then edge of Hedderwick Hill Plantation to cross footbridge (640788). Join John Muir Way (JMW) here; follow it along shore for ¾ mile; leave JMW where it angles sharp right along estuary basin at noticeboard (627784). Left here for 300m, then left again (628781) along field edge, following 'Hedderwick Hill' fingerposts. In ¾ mile at right bend (639787), go left to recross footbridge (640788); follow JMW back to car park/Dunbar.

Lunch East Links Family Park Café (01368 865070; eastlinks.co.uk)

More information www.dunbar.org.uk, visitscotland.com/surprise, John Muir Trust (01796 470080; www.jmt.org), ramblers.org.uk, satmap.com

Creag a' Chalamain
HIGHLAND

The last time I had seen mountain leader Andy Bateman he'd navigated a group of us off the high Cairngorm plateau in thick mountain mist, after a not entirely restful night spent in a self-dug snowhole in midwinter. A fantastic feat, I'd thought at the time — but to a mountain expert like Andy just another day at the office.

It was great to see Andy again. We set off from the Cairngorm ski area's car park — on a bright summer's morning this time — for a circuit of the unjustly neglected 'lesser peaks' that stand a little away from the classic Cairngorm corries and high tops. "Terminal moraine," said Andy as we followed a long, rubble-strewn ridge, "pushed up by a glacier on its way into these mountains."

The moraine led to a rocky little gorge, Eag a' Chait, the 'notch of the wildcat', a jumble of rough granite and sparkly mica schist, where a meadow pipit fluttered and piped to lead us away from the nest.

Now came sightings of mountain hare, roe deer and a tiny grouse chick as we climbed a succession of three peaks, each steeper and higher than the last — Castle Hill, Creag a' Chalamain and then the long, stony back of Lurcher's Crag. Up among the weather-sculpted rocks of its summit we sat to have our sandwiches and stare round at the view — southwest to the dark wall of buttresses under Sgòr Gaoith; east to the corrie scoops below Cairn Lochan and Stob Coire an t-Sneachda, the 'corrie of the snows'; south through the extraordinarily steep and deep cleft of Lairig Ghru.

Beyond the jaws of Lairig Ghru jutted a great black crag. "John Brown told Queen Victoria it was called the Devil's Point," Andy said. "He knew she'd ask him, and he couldn't very well give her the proper translation from the Gaelic — the Devil's Dick!"

We turned back through alpine meadows spattered with tiny pink flowers of dwarf azalea, paused for a drink of icy cold, peat-flavoured snowmelt water, and crunched back down the long track home.

Start & finish Cairngorm Mountain car park above Glenmore Lodge, Aviemore PH22 1RB (OS ref NH989061)

Getting there Bus: Service 31 from Aviemore. Road: A9 to Aviemore; B970 to Coylumbridge; signs to Glenmore; continue up to road end

Walk (8½ miles, strenuous, OS Explorer 403): At top of car park, right down steel steps. Along lower car park to stone pillar ('Parking Donations' notice) and post ('Allt Mhor Trail'). Path between them to bottom of gorge. Cross Allt a' Choire Chais by footbridge (984071); up stone-pitched path. In 200m, just before lone Scots pine on right, turn left (984072) up pitched path. Follow crest of moraine ridge west for 1 mile before descending to Caochan Dubh a' Chadha stream. Just before reaching it, turn right (974063) on peaty path through narrow Eag a' Chait gully for ¾ mile. Where view ahead opens out, just before gate in fence on right (963066), turn left opposite last crag on left, up faint path through heather. Keep bank with rock outcrops on left, and ascend south to the ridge, then south-west to summit of Castle Hill (958058). Now head south-south-east to craggy top of Creag a' Chalamain (962053).
Path descends and heads right along Chalamain Gap towards Lairig Ghru cleft. In ½ mile, where path begins to descend and bear left into Lairig Ghru, look for small cairn on left (960046). Follow obvious path south-east for 1 mile, at first at edge of Lairig Ghru, then steeply up over stony hillside to rocky summit of Lurcher's Crag (969033). Leaving summit, continue south along left rim of Lairig Ghru to edge of plateau and sensational view (970028). Bear left along edge, then further left to contour the opposite hillside. Keep same contour for ½ mile to meet broad, well-maintained track on ridge of Miadan Creag an Leth-choin (977035). Left along it for 1¾ miles back to car park.

Conditions Steep, boggy and rough in places. For experienced, well-equipped hill walkers with stamina. Allow 5-6 hours.

Lunch Picnic

Accommodation Fraoch Lodge, Boat of Garten, PH24 3BN (01479 831331; scotmountainholidays.com) or Moorfield House, Boat of Garten, PH24 3BN (01479 831646; moorfieldhouse.com), Scot Mountain Holidays (01479 831331; scotmountainholidays.com)

More information Cairngorm Mountain (01479 861261; cairngormmountain.org), visitscotland.com/natural, satmap.com, ramblers.org.uk

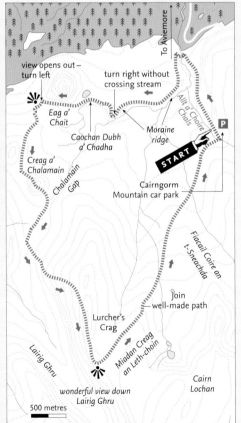

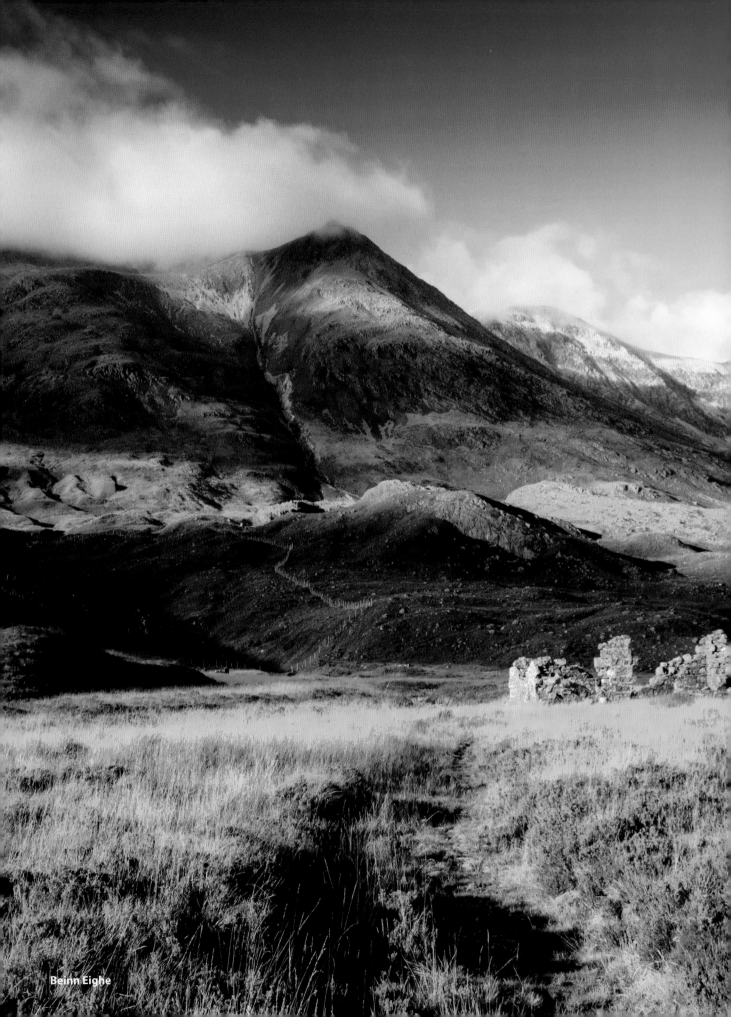

Beinn Eighe

Coire Mhic Fhearchair, Beinn Eighe, Torridon

HIGHLAND

Beinn Eighe, pride of the Torridon region of western Scotland, is a noble mountain — or is it a series of mountains? The map shows it rising over the tumbled country between the lochs of sea Maree and Torridon in a ghostly swirl like a four-fingered hand, the contours so tightly bunched to indicate the steepness of its crags and promontories that it looks impenetrable to an ordinary walker. There is a path, however, that reaches the core of Beinn Eighe without any trials or terrors.

It was a beautiful warm morning when we set off from the car park on the Torridon-Kinlochewe road. The stony path led up between the white screes of Coinneach Mhor and the blocky grey cliffs of Stuc a' Choire Dhuibh Bhig. We crossed a mountain torrent by way of stepping stones to reach an otherworldly upland. Great rugged tents of mountains stood pitched on a green plateau where a constellation of steely lochans lay glinting. This is the heart of Wester Ross, a roadless wilderness whose eagles and otters outnumber its human inhabitants.

A rush-choked lochan quivering with water boatmen and dragonflies showed where we were to turn off for the climb round the dark bulk of Sail Mhor, the most westerly 'finger' or buttress of Beinn Eighe. The path rose steadily, with enormous views of sea-like waves of hills, till we came in sight of the waterfall sluicing down the rock wall that underlies the hanging corrie in the palm of Beinn Eighe.

A last upward scramble, and we were looking into a giant geological crucible. On the left, the pale shattered rock of Ruadh Stac Mhor; in the centre at the back of the horseshoe, three great grey buttresses in the face of Coinneach Mhor; and on the right, Sail Mhor's purple-black wall of pinnacles and columns. At their feet, the long dark lake of Loch Coire Mhic Fhearchair, reflecting the peaks that hung more than a thousand feet above. It's a view to give anyone a proper sense of their own insignificance in the scale of time and change, as these mountains experience such things.

We stripped off and crept into the shallows of the loch, cold and refreshing after the long hot climb, as smooth as olive oil on the skin. Among the rocks we found delicate white saxifrages, bulky spiders with tiny scarlet parasites attached, mountain frogs as motionless as stones, glossy black crowberries and red bearberries. A world of wonders.

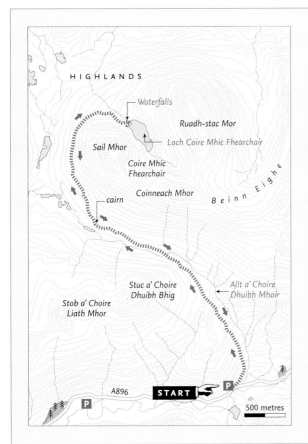

Start & finish Car park on A896, 6 miles SW of Kinlochewe (OS ref NS959568)

Getting there Road: A896 Torridon road from Kinlochewe; car park is on right beside a bridge, ½ mile after passing 'Torridon Estate' sign.

Walk (7 map miles, about 9 miles actually walked, strenuous, OS Explorer 433): Start of path is marked 'Public Footpath to Coire Mhic Nobaill'. Follow this well-maintained path. In 1¾ miles, cross stepping stones (947589). In another ¾ mile, at the far end of a rushy lochan, fork right at a cairn (935594) and follow path for 1¾ miles up to Loch Coire Mhic Fhearchair (940611). Return same way.

Conditions Rocky, uneven path climbs 500m (1650ft approx). Wear good walking boots, hill-walking gear.

Lunch Picnic

Accommodation Kinlochewe Hotel, By Achnasheen, Ross-shire IV22 2PA (01445 760253; kinlochewehotel.co.uk) – cheerful stopover, handy for Beinn Eighe National Nature Reserve

More information visitscotland.com, satmap.com, ramblers.org.uk
Walking in Torridon by Peter Barton (Cicerone) – see Walk W1

Camasunary Bay, Isle of Skye

HIGHLAND

Strathaird is one of the least known peninsulas of the Isle of Skye, much shorter and more slender than its big southerly twin of Sleat, much less dramatic in its geology than the basalt masterpiece of northerly Trotternish. Yet it has one advantage that the others lack: Strathaird is rooted at the foot of the mighty Black Cuillins, so that walking north from its tip one has those tall and savage mountains, the pride and heart of Skye, constantly in view. And Camasunary Bay, the destination of the precarious coast path running north from the remote community of Elgol, is a wild gem, a strand of grey, wave-pounded pebbles backed by a green sward whose two houses, one each end of the bay, stand dwarfed by the mountains behind them.

I had forgotten just how tricky the path from Elgol actually is: a narrow ribbon of pebbly mud in the hillside, whose seaward edge drops in several places a hundred feet sheer to the rocky shore. Shoved along by a good stout southwesterly wind, I needed all my head for heights, and a sure foot into the bargain, because apart from the hazards of the path itself there was the wonderful forward view as a constant distraction. The two tiny white dots of Camasunary's houses, three miles away when I first caught sight of them, grew only slowly, but their guardian peaks—the

shark's tooth of Bla Bheinn to the east, the blockier pyramid of Sgurr na Stri in the west — seemed to rear higher and closer each time I glanced towards them.

Behind the bay other rounded hills lumped in the middle distance, a telling contrast in shape and atmosphere to the jagged black spine of the Cuillin proper as it gradually revealed itself halfway up the sky beyond.

The coast path dropped to traverse the pebbles of Cladach a'Ghlinne bay before rising again in another precipitous stretch. At last it set me down on the boggy moorland that forms the eastern flank of Camasunary Bay. Seals bobbed in the sea, kittiwakes and fulmars planed by, and the pebbles and rushy hinterland of the bay lay spattered with bright primary colours — not clusters of rare flora, alas, but the fractured remains of plastic fish boxes cast up by wind and tide.

My final view of Camasunary Bay was from high on the stony track back to the road — a sea-fretted pebble strand, the two tiny houses far apart, and that mighty backdrop of crumpled mountains.

Start & finish Car parking bay opposite Cuillin View Gallery & Coffee Shop, Elgol IV49 9BJ approx. (OS ref NG519137)

Getting there Train: (www.thetrainline.com) to Kyle of Lochalsh, bus service 55 via Broadford to Elgol. Road: A87 via Skye Bridge to Broadford; B8083 to Elgol

Walk (9 miles, moderate/hard grade, OS Explorer 411): From parking bay opposite coffee shop, walk back uphill to start of Camasunary path on left (OS ref: 520139). Walk north for 3 miles to Camasunary Bay (518137); bear right up stony track to B8083 (545172); turn right to return to Elgol.

Conditions Elgol-Camasunary is a very narrow hillside track above steep drops; possibility of vertigo. Camasunary-B8083 is a rough hill track. Walking boots and waterproof clothing recommended.

Lunch Cuillin View Gallery & Coffee Shop, Elgol (01471 866223) – friendly folk, home baking, great coffee, stunning views

Accommodation Hotel Eilean Iarmain, Sleat, Isle of Skye (01471 833332; eileaniarmain.co.uk) – very traditional, welcoming atmosphere; next to the sea.

More information Portree TIC (01478 612992; www.visithighlands.com), www.visitscotland.com/perfectwalks

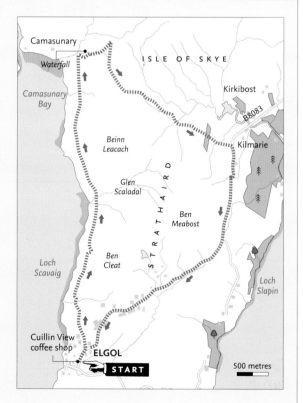

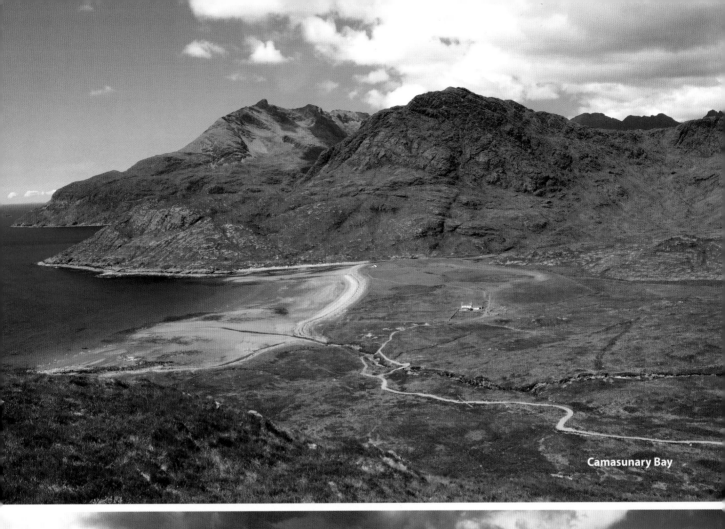

Camasunary Bay

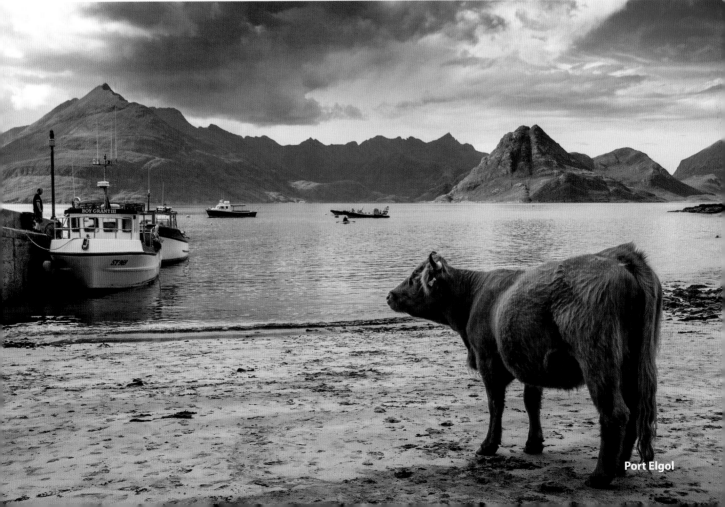

Port Elgol

Creag Meagaidh Nature Reserve
HIGHLAND

Long-horned Highland cattle put their heads up from the lush grazing in the floor of Aberarder Forest to peer through their luxuriant fringes and watch us go by. We were heading for one of the most fascinating nature reserves in Scotland. Creag Meagaidh National Nature Reserve, centred around the great sombre cliffs and corries of the Creag Meagaidh range, has embarked on an ambitious programme to encourage the recolonisation of this rugged mountain landscape by the native flora and fauna that have been destroyed by overgrazing, deforestation and other manifestations of the heavy hand of man.

We walked a rising path through woods of young birch, oak and alder, free to grow now that the sheep have been removed and the deer controlled. The boggy hill slopes were a silent riot of wood cranesbill's purple-blue flowers, intensely blue milkwort, stubby white heath spotted orchids, the yellow Maltese crosses of tormentil, and the roll-edged leaves of insect-eating butterwort in lime-green sprays. Rocks along the path were inscribed with a phrase from a Sorley MacLean poem: "I saw the little tree rising, in its branches the jewelled music" — and that fitted the growing trees, the flower-starred banks and the exuberant singing of chaffinches, meadow pipits and skylarks.

A tiny brown frog bounced away as we brushed against the sprig of heather he was using as a springboard. At the top of the rise the path left the trees and curved west across open moorland tufted with bog cotton. Below in the glen the Allt Coire Ardair snaked and sparkled in its rocky bed. Northwards rose the flattened pyramid head of Coire a' Chriochairein, and round in the west hung the high, rubble-filled notch called The Window that marks the northern edge of cliff-hung Coire Ardair. A lichened rock lay by the way, the parallel lines in its flat surface gouged out 10 000 years ago by the glacier that formed the precipitous glen.

The top of the glen was blocked by a low barrier of heath and grass, concealing the moraine or mass of rock and rubble that the head of the glacier had pushed before it up the valley, like dust before a broom. From its ridge we looked down to Lochan a' Choire, suddenly revealed like a conjurer's trick — a little glass-still lake under black, snow-streaked cliffs. I ran down and scampered a quick, slip-and-slide circuit of the lochan. Then we sat on a ledge of mica-sparkling rock and ate our sandwiches to the glide and plop of small fish — Arctic char, residents of Lochan a' Choire since they were isolated up here in the great melt at the end of the last glaciation. May they thrive another 10 000 years in this most beautiful mountain nature reserve.

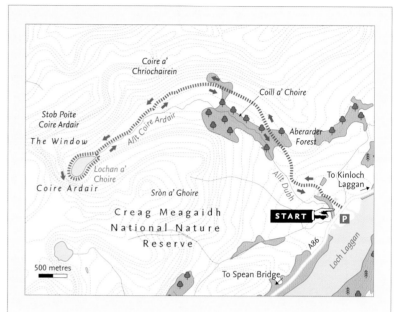

Start & finish Creag Meagaidh NNR car park, PH20 1BX (OS ref NN483873)

Getting there Road: Creag Meagaidh NNR car park is signposted on the A86 between Spean Bridge and Kinloch Laggan

Walk (8½ miles, moderate, OS Explorer 401): From car park follow red trail (otter symbol). In 500m pass to right of toilets/buildings (479876). Follow path on the level, then up steps; fork right at top (474879; 'Coire Ardair') on clear stony path for 3 miles to Lochan a' Choire (439883). Return same way.

Don't forget midge repellent!

Lunch Picnic

Accommodation Spean Lodge, Spean Bridge, Inverness-shire PH34 4EP (01397 712004; speanlodge.co.uk)

More information Creag Meagaidh NNR (01528 544265; www.nnr-scotland.org.uk/creag-meagaidh), visitscotland.com/natural, satmap.com, ramblers.org.uk

Forsinard Flows
HIGHLAND

The two-car train clacked and rattled its way up the Strath of Kildonan from the Sutherland coast, the landscape on either side becoming increasingly high, wide and wild. Brown and grey bogland swept away to hilly horizons on all sides. No green fields, no cosy farms, no settlements. Stepping down onto the platform at Forsinard station, way out in the middle of these vast peatlands, I watched the train groan off towards Wick and felt a very long way from anywhere familiar.

The Flow Country occupies about a million acres of the northernmost Scottish mainland. This is the wettest and wildest landscape in Britain, lumpy with mountains and overspread with enormous swaths of sphagnum bog, apparently dead and bare, in fact seething with rare and extraordinary wildlife.

The RSPB's Forsinard Flows National Nature Reserve, based on its visitor centre in the former station buildings at Forsinard, preserves nearly 40 000 acres of this fragile and sombrely beautiful country from encroachments that threaten it in the shape of forests planted for investment purposes, agricultural 'improvements', windfarms and other disturbances.

It's the pleasure of the Forsinard warden to take visitors out walking across the reserve and give them a precious insight into an ecosystem whose treasures might escape the notice of uninstructed wanderers.

"Greenshank, greylag goose, cuckoo…" The warden recited the 'recently spotted' list as we tramped west towards the dark peak of Ben Griam Beg, closely watched by three red deer hinds. "Golden plover, osprey, black-throated and red-throated divers, and golden eagle, though I haven't seen that one myself." The divers are rarities nationally, but nothing unusual to birdwatchers in the Flows.

Meadow pipits flitted from sprig to sprig of the heather, common scoter (not so common, actually) and teal bobbed on the dark lakelets or 'dubh lochans' that formed a watery maze on the top of the rise.

The dubh lochans get their name from their peat-shaded water, and peat is the keynote here — 3m (10ft) of unrotted vegetation that has been lying on the acid rock below since the last Ice Age. From the flat bog surface rose tuffets of emerald and ruby sphagnum.

I bent to plunge my fingers deep into a pale grey velvet cushion of woolly fringe moss, and found myself looking at a tiny scarlet sundew, an insectivorous plant with a marbled fly trapped fast in its sticky hairs.

Up on the ridge we crept towards Gull Loch. There were no divers there today; just a solitary greenshank who flew quickly away, the streak on his back making a dazzling spot against the slate-grey clouds, his piercing *"tew-tew-tew!"* coming back to us — a perfect expression of the wild spirit of this haunting and remarkable place.

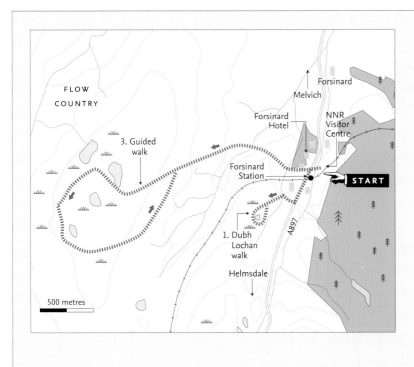

FLOW COUNTRY

Forsinard
Melvich
Forsinard Hotel
NNR Visitor Centre
3. Guided walk
Forsinard Station
START
1. Dubh Lochan walk
A897
Helmsdale

500 metres

Start & finish Forsinard Flows National Nature Reserve Visitor Centre, Forsinard station, Sutherland KW13 6YT (OS ref NC891425)

Getting there Train: (thetrainline.com) to Forsinard. Road: A897 Helmsdale-Melvich road to Forsinard.

Walks 1. Dubh Lochan Trail (1 mile, easy grade, leaflet guide): paved walkway to pools near Visitor Centre. **2.** Forsinard Trail (4 miles, easy grade, leaflet guide): self-guided circular walk – fields, bog, pools, woods – riverbank, from car park on A897 (904485), 4 miles north of Forsinard. **3.** Guided Walk (3-4 miles, moderate grade, Tuesdays, May 1-August 31 each year): walk with Reserve Warden to pools west of Visitor Centre. Wet and boggy – wear wellingtons/waterproof shoes.

Lunch Forsinard Hotel KW13 6YT (01641 571221; theforsinard.co.uk)

More information Forsinard Flows NNR visitor centre (01641 571225, rspb.org.uk; nnr-scotland.org.uk), visitscotland.com

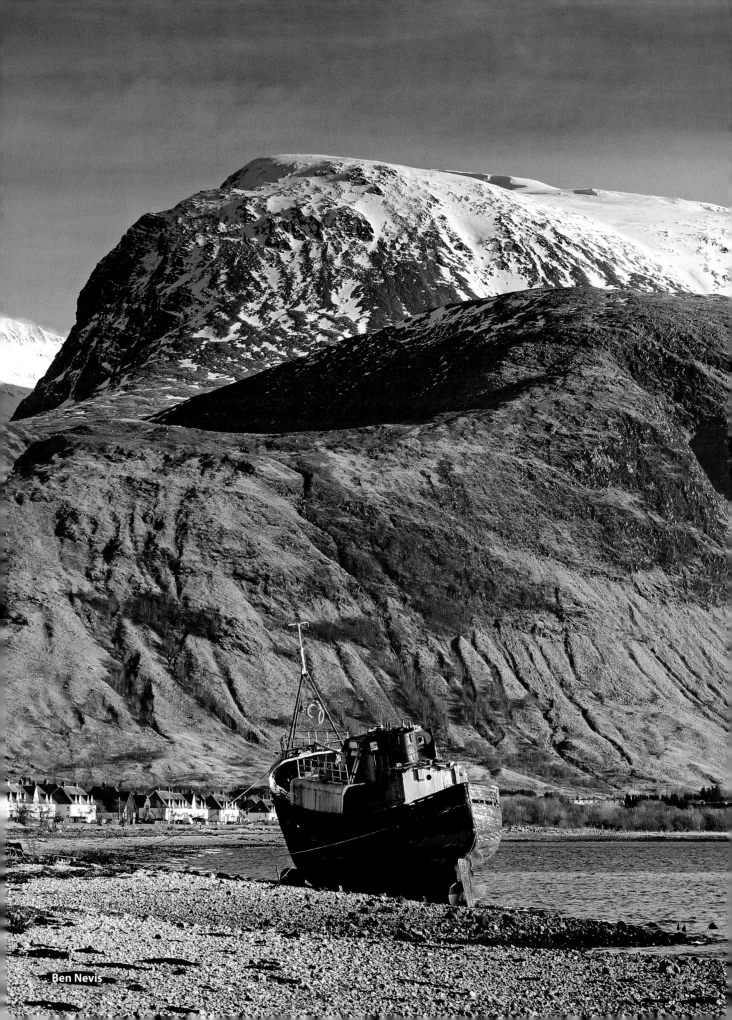
Ben Nevis

Glen Nevis

HIGHLAND

Well lathered in Avon Skin-So-Soft (kind to your skin, but also a proven defence against the bluidy midgies), Jane and I set out from Glen Nevis Visitor Centre on one of those west of Scotland mornings when the high tops have shawled themselves up in misty cloud after days of stair-rod rain, and only a fool, or a walker with X-ray specs, is headed for the summits. Ben Nevis would have been a temptation in any other conditions, but what's the point of getting all the way up there if you can't see your hand in front of your face, let alone the view from the highest point in the British Isles?

Luckily for us there was a good alternative, a low-level circuit of the glen where the River Nevis pours seaward at the feet of the mighty Ben Nevis range from the heart of Lochaber. The river ran dimpling over pebbly shallows and round bushy islets in a tunnel of alder, sycamore and ash. Sandpipers darted upriver with silvery calls and a flash of white rump.

The flank of Ben Nevis rose into smoking grey cloud, great purple buttresses cut with gullies where white strings of rain-swollen torrents came tumbling — Red Burn, Five Finger Gully, Surgeon's Gully. The forward view showed the river winding from its gorge under twin rugged peaks streaked with pale quartzite: Sgùrr a' Mhàim and Stob Bàn. This must be one of Scotland's greatest low-level prospects.

We passed an ancient graveyard, a square of immaculate sward inside mossy walls, guarded by wonderful old beech trees, silent and peaceful. The squelchy path dipped past Highland cattle with ferocious horns and mild manners.

We crossed the roaring Lower Falls of the River Nevis and hit the homeward stretch — a forest track running north, its verges thick with heath bedstraw, crimson and emerald sphagnum, and lime-green rosettes of insectivorous butterwort, the royal blue flowers nodding above on hair-like stalks. Good smells of wet rock, water, earth and pine resin followed us back up the glen, as sunlight broke through across the northern hills and Ben Nevis shrugged its shoulders free of the clinging cloud shawl at last.

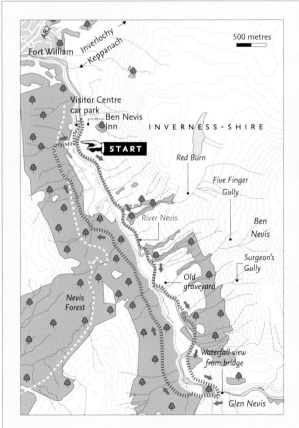

Start & finish Glen Nevis Visitor Centre, Glen Nevis, near Fort William PH33 6ST (OS ref NN123730) – paid parking at Visitor Centre

Getting there Train: (thetrainline.com) to Fort William (1½ miles). Road: A82 to Fort William; follow 'Glen Nevis' signs.

Walk (8 miles, easy, OS Explorer 392); From visitor centre follow river downstream to cross suspension bridge (123731). Right upstream along left bank of river. In 1 mile pass bridge to youth hostel (128718); keep on by river for 2½ miles to pass cottages at Polldubh (142687). In 350m pass sheep pens; bear right to road. Right to cross Lower Falls (145684); along road for 300m; left by bus stop opposite cottages (143684) on broad forest track. Follow it for 2¾ miles to pass West Highlands Way (WHW) spur descending on right (122717). In 350m join main WHW route (121721; thistle symbols). Follow it to road; left, then right to Glen Nevis Visitor Centre.

Conditions Riverside path is rocky and muddy in places. Many streams to ford.

Lunch Snacks in Glen Nevis Visitor Centre. Ben Nevis Inn PH33 6TE (01397 701227; ben-nevis-inn.co.uk) – above Achintee House, across river.

Accommodation Glentower Lower Observatory, Achintore Road, Fort William PH33 6RQ (01397 704007; glentower.com)

More information Glen Nevis Visitor Centre (01397 705922; ben-nevis.com), visitscotland.com, satmap.com, ramblers.org.uk

Little Wyvis
HIGHLAND

It's one hell of a climb to the pride of mid-Ross, the 1046m (3432ft) crown of the great whaleback mountain called Ben Wyvis — too much, really, for this scorcher of a summer's day. But Little Wyvis, a couple of miles to the southwest, looked just the job at 764m (2507ft), a good upward pull on a fine stony track and no one else to share the mountain with us.

Grasshoppers ticked in the grass, bees were busy in the wild thyme and bird's foot trefoil flowers. The thistles were out in royal purple, with dark green fritillary butterflies opening their black and burnt orange wings over the brushy blooms as they delicately sipped the deep-sunk nectar. Halfway up the mountain we stopped for a water break and sat on a rushy bank to watch a meadow pipit perched on a fence post as it preened its speckled breast and dark wing coverts.

The zigzag track rose up the flank of Little Wyvis, the sun striking a million diamond winks out of its mica-sheathed rocks. We plucked juicy bilberries, sweet and sharp on the tongue, beautifully refreshing to the upward climber. The delicate white flowers of starry saxifrage dotted the acid-green sphagnum in the wet ditches along the track.

At the summit of Little Wyvis we found a small rocky cairn infested with scores of bees. Ben Wyvis rose to the north, a double hump with precipitous slopes facing in our direction. Through binoculars we saw the red and yellow dots of walkers sweltering in the sun as they struggled up the leg-twanging ascent. Rather them than us. Standing by the cairn we took in a truly stupendous view, from the lumpy mountains of Torridon way out west to the long sea lochs at Dornoch in the east, a vista of green mountains and steely waters that might fittingly have been labelled 'Heart of Scotland'.

On the way down two plump birds stood on a rock, staring us down. White patchy bellies, feathery feet, salt and pepper backs, and a bold red eyebrow on the male. A pair of ptarmigan, no less — my first ever sighting of these elusive birds of the high mountains. And just beyond them a mountain hare motionless under a peat bank, his ears short and neat, his pelt ridged. What a thrill.

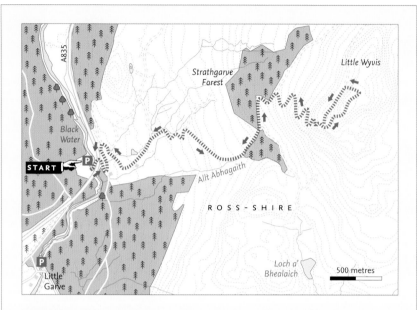

Start & finish Car park on A835 Inverness-Ullapool road (OS ref NH402639)

Getting there Road: A835 towards Ullapool from Inverness; 1 mile north of Garve, pass A832 turning; in another 1½ miles, car park signed on left just before bridge

Walk (7 miles there and back, strenuous, OS Explorer 437): Cross A835 (take care!); left for 100m; right up roadway. In 50m, left past gateway post (ignore warning sign – it's aimed at 4x4 drivers). Follow gravel track. In ½ mile pass barn (407640); on through deer gate. In another mile, at second gate, left up track (418640). In another ½ mile, track forks (422646); continue to right here, up zigzag track. In ¾ mile, just below summit at 700m, rough track goes left (427643); ignore this and keep ahead upwards. Go through remains of fence, and on up to summit cairn (430645). Return same way. NB: this is a mountain walk with 650m of climb; take hillwalking boots, clothes, equipment.

Lunch Picnic

Accommodation Aultguish Inn, By Garve, Ross-shire, Scotland IV23 2PQ (01997 455254; aultguish.co.uk) – cheerful, welcoming inn; also budget rooms and bunkhouse

More information Inverness TIC (01463 252401)

Monadhliath Mountains

HIGHLAND

It rained cats and dogs in the night, and well on until mid-morning. So what else is new in the Scottish Highlands? At last, the sky began to brighten — enough to make a kilt for a wee sailor. I'd been looking forward so much to getting up high and wild into the back country of the Monadhliath Mountains that a little bit of spit wasn't going to put me off.

When the glaciers had finished with the Monadhliath, they'd created a hauntingly beautiful range with ice-smoothed flanks, deep sided glens and thick moraines of rubble through which streams and rivers push. Today, the River Calder in the flat lower strath of Glen Banchor and its tributary Allt Fionndrigh were rumbling and roaring, rain-swollen torrents shifting boulders and pebbles from their glacial banks by the ton. Rain moved in rippling curtains through the vees of the side glens, hanging in the throat of Fionndrigh's cleft before moving away on the west wind to allow a gleam of sun.

I passed the old cattle-raising and raiding settlement of Glenbanchor, now nothing more than mossy stones, and made north up the stony track where Glenbanchor's cattle were driven each spring to sweeter grass high in the mountains. The Allt Fionndrigh came crashing down out of the hills, loud and chaotic over its boulders, and I walked upstream to find a footbridge. Red deer stags moved along the ridge a thousand feet overhead, only their antlers visible against the grey sky.

Under the rocky bluffs of Geal Charn I found a flimsy wooden bridge and crossed the river. Sodden and squelchy, a path led up and over a saddle of high moorland. I followed a line of old fence posts, descending a long slope towards the hissing torrent of Allt Ballach. On the far side, the hills rose to hump-back peaks — Carn Dearg and Carn Macoul, with a jumble of darkly magnificent mountains to the edge of sight beyond.

Down by the River Calder again, I turned for home. A frantic squealing in the upper air drew my binoculars. A pair of slate-grey peregrines swooped down from the clouds and circled me, driving the intruder on and out of their private wilderness.

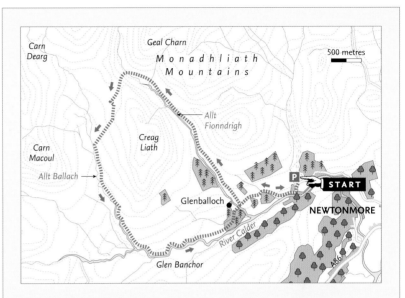

Start & finish Shepherd's Bridge car park, Glen Road, Newtonmore; nearest postcode PH20 1BH (OS ref NN693998)

Getting there Train: to Newtonmore. Road: A9 to Newtonmore. From village main street, follow Glen Road to Shepherd's Bridge car park.

Walk (8 miles, hard, OS Explorer 402): From car park continue across Shepherd's Bridge; on for ½ mile, passing abandoned cottage. Just before footbridge to Glenballoch (681993) turn right up Allt Fionndrigh river to join track up Fionndrigh glen. In 2 miles, descend left to cross footbridge (659019); follow track up cleft for 500m. At top (657015), more easily visible track swings right, but continue 50m, then bear left up faint grassy 4 x 4 track, aiming for Creag Liath peak. In 100m, track swings right; in 200m it reaches old fence posts (657012). Follow them to right (tricky underfoot – keep well left of the posts until past peat hags). Follow posts down to Allt Ballach river (652005); left beside river for 1¼ miles to confluence with River Calder (652986). Left by river to Glenballoch and car park. NB: Trackless and boggy from footbridge in Fionndrigh glen onwards. Take map, compass, GPS, hillwalking gear, stick.

Lunch Picnic or The Wild Flour, Newtonmore, PH20 1DA (01540 670975)

Accommodation Greenways B&B, Newtonmore PH20 1AT (01540 670136)

More information Wildcat Centre, Main Street, Newtonmore PH20 1DD (01540 673131). Aviemore TIC (01479 810930), visitscotland.com, ramblers.org.uk, satmap.com

Not many who venture the Road to the Isles are lucky enough to have fellow walkers as seasoned and reliable as Richard and Guy Spencer. While I'd been enjoying a plate of lamb casserole and a pint of bitter, followed by eight hours' deep and dreamless sleep, in the companionable comfort of Corrour Station House (a matchless walkers' guesthouse right on the railway platform) Richard and Guy had been bivouacking on hard tack in Staoineag Bothy out on Rannoch Moor. That's the way Richard, a former soldier, likes it. As for Guy, being a black Labrador he generally goes along with Richard's say-so.

Corrour calls itself the loneliest railway station in Scotland. The Station House shines a tiny beacon of light, warmth and good cheer in the vast wastes of Rannoch. Richard and Guy knocked on the door not long after sunrise. We set out early, descended to the shores of beautiful Loch Treig and turned west through a narrowing pass below the tumbled slopes of Creag Ghuanach, walking against the flow of the peat-stained Abhainn Rath river.

Out here it's true wilderness, one of the few places in Britain that can properly claim that label: bog, loch, rock and water — an elemental scene. A couple of bothy huts, Staoineag and Meanach, lie along the banks of the Abhainn Rath, but other than that you can hardly believe anyone has ever come here. Yet this modest, muddy track, snaking around as it climbs gently west to the watershed of Abhainn Rath and Water of Nevis, was once a famed cattle-droving route, known as the Road to the Isles, along which the hardy drovers herded Highland cattle towards the great fairs of Crieff and Falkirk.

We strode on across heather and bog to ford the Abhainn Rath where it came bouncing and chattering down from its high corrie under Stob Ban, the White Point. A few minutes for a sandwich and cuppa, and we were following the track below the mighty shoulder of snow-streaked Ben Nevis. The Road to the Isles dropped to thread through the gorge of the Water of Nevis with its 60m (200ft) Steall waterfall, a breathtaking spectacle. A final mile on a flywalk ledge above the gorge and I was easing the boots from my steaming feet in the Glen Nevis car park and giving Guy a congratulatory pat.

This is a tough walk, but not a daunting one. Do it with a friend, plan properly and pick decent weather. You'll never forget it.

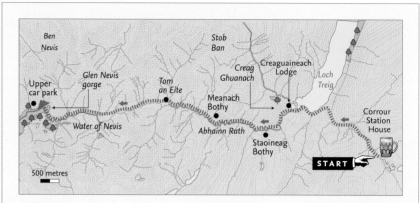

Start Corrour Station House, Corrour Estate, by Fort William PH30 4AA; (OS ref NN356664)

Finish Upper car park, Glen Nevis

Getting there Train: (thetrainline.com; railcard.co.uk) to Corrour station

Getting back Taxi: (Jamie's 01397 701778; Fort William Taxis 01397 700000; plenty more)

Walk (14 miles to Upper car park/15¾ miles to Lower Falls car park, allow 8-10 hours, hard grade, OS Explorers 385, 392): From Corrour Station House, cross railway line; right (NW) along west side of the railway; follow track down to turn left along shore of Loch Treig. Cross footbridge at Creaguaineach Lodge (309689); left (west) along north bank of Abhainn Rath for 5 miles to ford it by Tom an Eite (242695). Continue west for 5 miles on north bank of Water of Nevis, through Glen Nevis gorge to car park (167691). NB The route is wet, boggy and trackless in places. A tough, lonely walk for map-readers with stamina, experience and proper equipment, including food.

Lunch Picnic

Accommodation Corrour Station House (01397 732236; corrour-station-house-restaurant. co.uk) – unique, very welcoming café/restaurant (open 8.30 am – 9 pm daily, March-October) Accommodation in the refurbished Signal Box. Staoineag and Meanach Bothies: (mountainbothies.org.uk) Other Corrour Estate accommodation (01397 732200; www.corrour.co.uk)

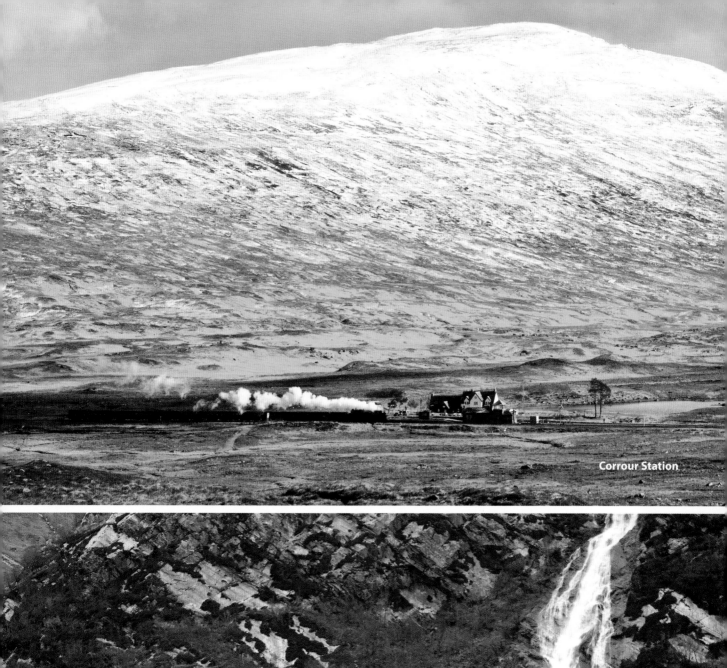

Corrour Station

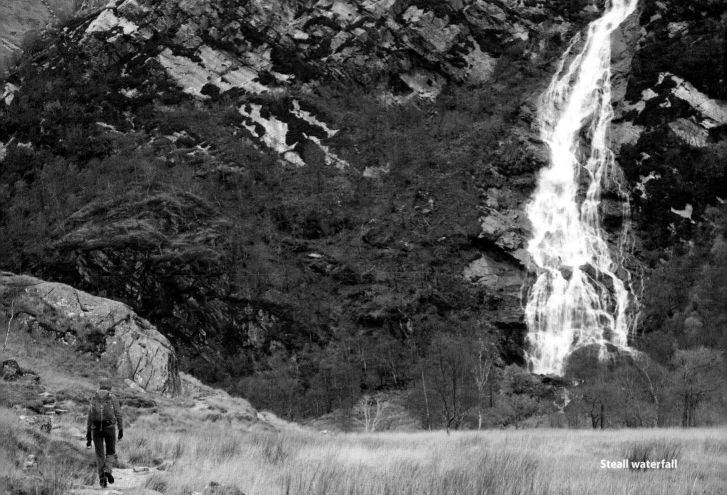

Steall waterfall

Tarbat Ness
HIGHLAND

The Tarbat Peninsula juts northeastwards into the North Sea in the throat of the Moray Firth, just north of Inverness. The Picts, those mysterious Scots of the first millennium AD, were very active around this small tongue of land. They carved beautiful and enigmatic figures and symbols to embellish the early Christian monastery on the outskirts of what is now the remote fishing village of Portmahomack.

We lingered in Tarbat Old Church on the monastery site, admiring its exhibition of Pictish sculpture, and when we emerged, it was into the soft grey blanket of a proper Easter Ross haar, or sea mist. Portmahomack's crescent of sandy beach, its neat strip of fishermen's cottages and stumpy pier lay wreathed in cold vapour. Walking the grassy path northwards towards Tarbat Ness, we passed fishing boats' nets hung out to dry on tall poles, and entered a misty world of low gorsy cliffs, sea-sculpted sandstone rocks in whorls and sandwich layers, and a grey wrinkled sea whispering on a shore now pebbly, now sandy.

Young herring gulls in shabby brown plumage, not quite mature enough to fend for themselves, wheezed sulkily on the shore rocks like resentful teenagers: "Mum! Mum! Gimme something to eat!" A great herd of bullocks came blowing and sighing out of the mist to inspect us. One word of admonition and they all plunged aside and went cantering off together.

The red-and-white striped lighthouse at the point of Tarbat Ness was hidden in the mist until we were almost upon it. Beyond the tower the uneasy sea seethed in out of the fog to burst against the rocks of the headland. It is extraordinary to think that any plant community could survive in such an environment of salt spray, wind and exposure, but the maritime heath, the ragwort and fireweed, harebells and marsh orchids of Tarbat Ness seem to thrive in adversity.

Our homeward path down the east coast of the peninsula skirted a succession of bays under crumbling sandstone cliffs. There was something truly magical about this walk with the evening closing in, oystercatchers and curlew piping from the shoreline, and the lonely little bays emerging one after the other from the otherworldly driftings of the mist and the unseen pulsings of the tide.

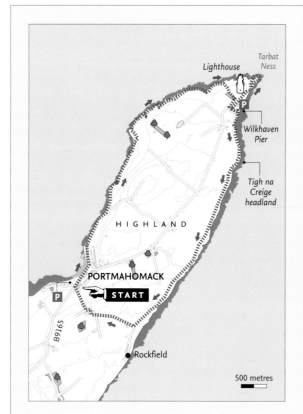

Start & Finish Tarbat Discovery Centre, Portmahomack IV20 1YA (OS ref NH916845)

Getting there Bus: Service 24 from Tain. Road: Portmahomack is at the end of B9165 (signed from A9 between Invergordon and Tain)

Walk (8½ miles, easy/moderate, OS Explorer 438): North along west-coast path for 1¾ miles; 200m beyond fishing bothy and anchors, right up gorsy bank (925870), through gate, on along cliffs. In 1½ miles, near lighthouse, where fence crosses path into sea, right through gate (942876). Up fence past plantation to wall; right to road (943872); left to lighthouse and Tarbat Ness. Return past lighthouse and car park; left to Wilkhaven Pier (945871). Right through gate ('Rockfield 5 km'); follow shore path south. In ½ mile, right up waymarked diversion (945864) over Tigh na Creige headland; back to shore. Continue along shore for 2½ miles to Rockfield (924832); right along road to Portmahomack.

Conditions Frisky cattle may be about

Lunch Oystercatcher restaurant/B&B, Portmahomack IV20 1YB (01862 871560; the-oystercatcher.co.uk): Wed-Sun, April-Oct. Booking recommended.

Accommodation Ross Villa, Knockbreck Road, Tain IV19 1BN (01862 894746; rossvilla.co.uk) – beautifully kept

More information Tarbat Discovery Centre, Portmahomack (01862 871351; tarbat-discovery.co.uk), Dornoch TIC (01862 810594), visitdornoch.com, visitscotland.com, satmap.com, walkhighlands.co.uk

Upper Loch Torridon and Inveralligin
HIGHLAND

"I award this walk," wrote Peter Barton in his wonderful guidebook *Walking in Torridon*, "the Golden Rose for its beauty, variability and grandeur. I have walked widely in the Torridon region and have been to the summits of all its mountains, but I still rate this walk the loveliest of all."

Powerful words. You could go a long way on them; all the way out to Torridon in western Scotland in my case, spurred there by the promised magic of mountain, loch and wide, empty country.

I was lucky enough to be walking with Jim Sutherland, of the Nineonesix mountain adventure company, who with his co-author, Chris Lowe, has updated what is certainly the best guidebook a hill walker in the sublime Torridon region could want. The weather might have been better (wind and rain — a typical summer's day in west Scotland), but at least it kept the midges at bay, and it didn't interfere with our enjoyment of the day.

Inveralligin village sits isolated on the north shore of Upper Loch Torridon, a sea loch that lies under beautiful towering hills. The walk started with a mountain view of impossible majesty: the three summits of the Beinn Alligin horseshoe standing tall and formidable to the north, and across the racing white caps of the loch a dark uplift of ridges, corries and peaks centred on Beinn Damph.

On a sunny day that prospect could easily have you trapped like a fly in a silken web; but not with half the North Sea trying to reach the Atlantic in the form of rain on a tree-shaking easterly. We got down to the loch shore and were soon in the shelter of big beeches and limes, walking seaward with the rain at our backs.

On a promontory beyond Torridon House stood a little church and a tall Celtic cross to the memory of Duncan Darroch, a Victorian laird of Torridon. His tenants thought well of their landlord; after his death a hundred of them escorted his body over the mountains to its burial, a courtesy normally reserved for a clan chief. From the headland in the loch, more mountain heads revealed themselves: Sgorr Ruadh, the Red Peak; Beinn Liath Mhor, the Big Grey Mountain; Sgurr nan Lochan Uaine, the Peak of the Green Lakelet.

Inveralligin lay beyond, a handful of white houses scattered along the shore, a tiny pier stacked with creels. There are communities even more remote than this along the coasts of western Scotland, but on this wild day we could have been well on the way to the end of the Earth. A Golden Rose of a walk: Peter Barton had it just right.

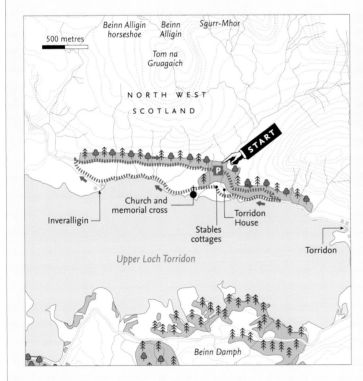

Start & finish Beinn Alligin car park, Torridon IV22 2HA (OS ref NG869576)

Getting there Road: Follow Inveralligin signs from Torridon village (on A896 between Kinlochewe and Shieldaig). Car park on left, 2½ miles west of Torridon.

Walk (7½ miles, easy, OS Explorer 433): From car park, right along road, down to loch shore. Right along loch. In ¾ mile, fork left (870572, 'Stables Cottage'); follow track past houses. Left in front of Stables Cottage (868573); over stile and on to pass track to church (863572). Continue to Inveralligin. Fork right by phone box; right along upper road (837579) to car park.

Refreshments Torridon Stores and Café (01445 791400) – try their amazing cakes

Accommodation Kinlochewe Hotel, by Achnasheen IV22 2PA (01445 760253; kinlochewehotel.co.uk)

More information Nineonesix mountain guiding (01520 755358; www.nineonesix.co.uk), visitscotland.com/surprise; *Walking in Torridon* by Peter Barton, updated by Chris Lowe and Jim Sutherland, published by Cicerone (cicerone.co.uk) – Walk EW7

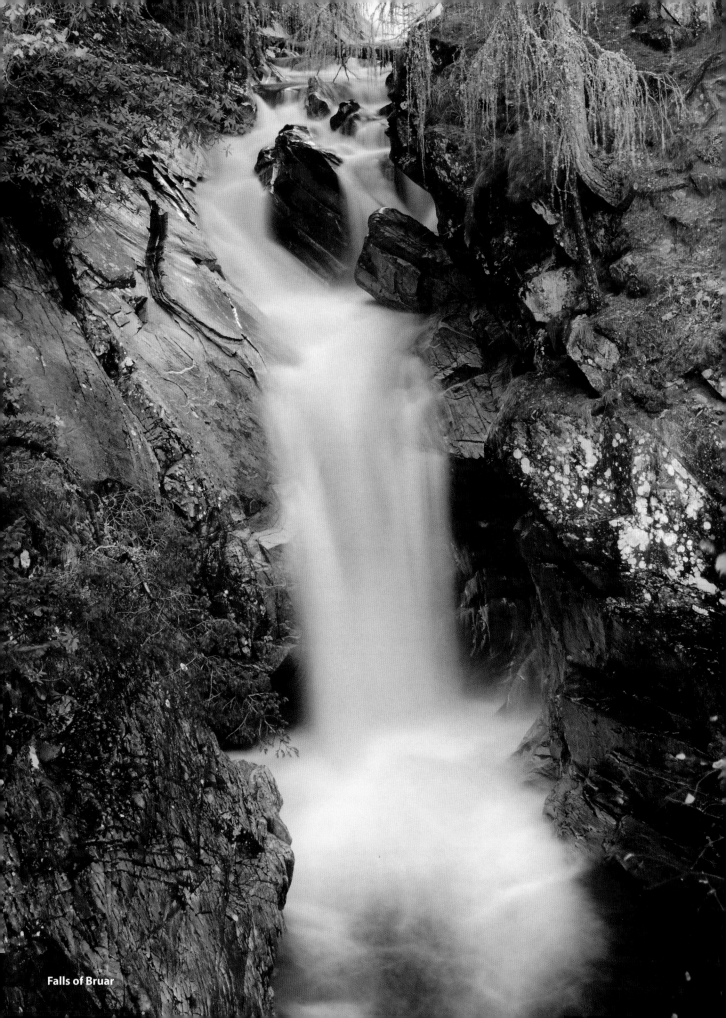

Falls of Bruar

Falls of Bruar

PERTH & KINROSS

Young men and women in white helmets and blue jumpsuits were throwing themselves over the Falls of Bruar like salmon in reverse. I stood on the brink of the flood-sculpted gorge and watched them leap from a ledge under the none-too-tender persuasion of their gung-ho instructor, plummeting down to smack into a pool 9m (30ft) below.

What would John Murray, 4th Duke of Atholl, one of the grandest of eighteenth century Highland lairds, have made of such forward behaviour on his estate? He suffered a bit of teasing from Robert Burns after the poet visited the Bruar Water in 1787. Burns was dismayed at the bareness of the moorland that enclosed the famous falls, and composed The Humble Petition of Bruar Water to give His Grace a respectful push in the silvicultural direction:

> *"Would then my noble master please*
> *To grant my highest wishes,*
> *He'll shade my banks wi' tow'ring trees,*
> *And bonie spreading bushes.*
> *Delighted doubly then, my lord,*
> *You'll wander on my banks,*
> *And listen mony a grateful bird*
> *Return you tuneful thanks."*

These days, forests of larch, silver birch and Scots pine shade the Falls of Bruar, and a good stretch of mountainside beyond. I crossed the upper of two ornate bridges over the roaring falls, and found a woodland path that climbed steadily up towards the open moor. Roe deer fled away between the pines, and a red squirrel lingered at the end of his branch to watch me out of his territory.

The track left the trees, running for miles on the fringe of the wide moorlands around Glen Banvie. Ahead the rugged blue profiles of Carn Liath and Beinn a' Ghlo stood tall and seductive on the eastern skyline. Then it was back into the forest, down to Old Blair and the ancient ruined kirk of St Bride. John Graham of Claverhouse, 'Bonnie Dundee', was buried here in July 1689 after dying of the wounds he received while leading his Highlanders to victory over government troops at the Battle of Killiecrankie a few miles away.

A stretch across the beautiful parkland of Blair Castle, a final mile through the forest, and I was crossing the Falls of Bruar once more — the only river in creation to boast in prideful verse:

> *"Here, foaming down the skelvy rocks,*
> *In twisting strength I rin;*
> *There, high my boiling torrent smokes,*
> *Wild-roaring o'er a linn:*
> *Enjoying each large spring and well*
> *As Nature gave them me,*
> *I am, altho' I say't mysel',*
> *Worth gaun a mile to see."*

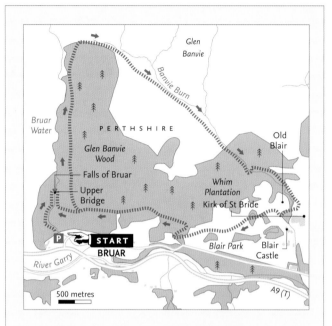

Start & finish Falls of Bruar car park, Bruar, near Blair Atholl, Perthshire PH18 5TW (OS ref NN820660)

Getting there Road: At junction of A9 and B8079, at Bruar, 3 miles west of Blair Atholl

Walk (11½ miles, moderate, OS Explorers 386, 394): Follow Falls of Bruar Walk (signed behind House of Bruar) to cross Upper Bridge (820669). Path returns down opposite bank. In 350m, at seat in clearing, 2 paths fork left (820666). Follow left-hand path to T-junction (826666); left up forest road. In ⅓ mile, fork left on grassy track (824670; post with red arrow). Follow it for 3¾ miles north through Glen Banvie Wood, then south-east down Glen Banvie to enter Whim Plantation (853677); descend to tarmac road (868667). Right past Old Blair; walled road to T-junction on avenue (864665). Left; follow road for 1¼ miles to enter woodland. In 200m, at 5-way junction, hairpin back right (843660). In ¼ mile follow track round left bend (846663). Continue for 1¼ miles through forest to pass through gateposts (827666); in 100m, left ('Falls of Bruar'); cross Lower Bridge (819664); return to car park.

NB Steep unguarded drops beside falls!

Lunch Picnic

Accommodation Moulin Hotel, Moulin, Pitlochry PH16 5EW (01796 472196; moulinhotel.co.uk)

More information atholl-estates.co.uk, visitscotland.com/surprise, ramblers.org.uk, satmap.co.uk

Melrose to St Boswells
SCOTTISH BORDERS

The cowled face of the nun stared down from the dusky red wall of Melrose Abbey. There was an upward curl at the corners of her sandstone lips, a smile of quiet amusement put there by a long-forgotten stone carver 600 years ago. I was smiling myself, having just heard the tale of what archaeologists found inscribed on the container that held Robert the Bruce's heart when they unearthed it at the abbey in 1996. There were no inspiring last words or ringing exhortations from the iconic Scottish king, but a splendidly prosaic note: "Found beneath Chapter House floor, March 1921, by His Majesty's Office of Works."

The town of Melrose is a charming huddle of red sandstone buildings along the windings of the River Tweed. St Cuthbert's Way rises southward out of the town, and from its sloping track on Gallows Hill I looked back to see the lacy stonework of the abbey's arches lit by the sun against the whaleback hills to the north.

The broad green path climbed to a saddle between the dramatic camel humps of the Eildon Hills. A short, steep upward haul — perfect for sorting out a post-Hogmanay heid — and I was standing at the peak of Eildon Mid Hill, looking across to the multiple ramparts on Eildon Hill North, where the Romans once built a signal tower.

These abrupt, conical hills are thick with legend. The best and most extraordinary is an early medieval ballad concerning Thomas the Rhymer, a poetical youth who meets a beauteous lady on the Eildons. She is the Queen of Elfland, and Thomas is whirled away for an adventure full of blood, sex and magic.

On the summit of Mid Hill I gazed from the distant Cheviots in the east to the low blue ridges of Ettrick Forest along the western skyline. Then I skeltered downhill, out of the cold wind and on down St Cuthbert's Way past boggy hollows and grazing meadows to Bowden and a sheltered green lane that led through flat pastures east to Newtown St Boswells. The River Tweed wraps a couple of snaky coils around the edge of town, and I followed a bushy path along the south bank. The water rushed noisily over shallows and shillets, sucking at the opposite shore.

Behind a screen of trees, Dryburgh Abbey and its glories of architecture lay hidden. That was for tomorrow — today I was content to walk beside the softly roaring Tweed, looking back to the high humps of the Eildon Hills and thinking of Thomas the Rhymer and his elfin lover.

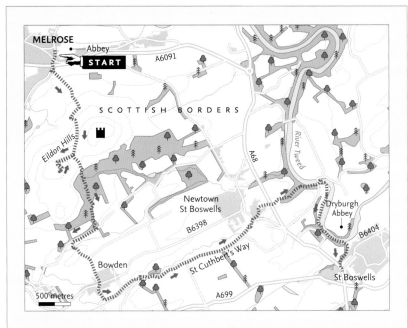

Start Market Square, Melrose TD6 9PL (OS ref NT548340)

Getting there Train: Borders Railway (scotrail.co.uk) to Tweedbank; taxi (07929 232923), or Border Abbeys Way (2½ mile walk) to Melrose. Bus: Service 95 Edinburgh-Galashiels, 68 Galashiels-Melrose. Road: Melrose is signed from A68 (Jedburgh-Lauder).

Walk (7½ miles, moderate, OS Explorer 338): From Market Square, south uphill, under A6091. In 100m, left (547339; 'St Cuthbert's Way'/SCW); bear left on edge of woodland. Up steps; up gravel path (SCW); uphill for ¾ mile to saddle between North and Mid Hills (551325). Climb either/both; back to saddle; south (SCW) for 1½ miles to B6398 in Bowden (554305). Dogleg right/left across road, down lane ('Bowden Kirk'); in 250m, left (555303). Follow SCW for 1⅔ mile into Newtown St Boswells. Cross B6398 (578315); ahead, following SCW/Border Abbeys Way under A68 (581317). Follow SCW, ascending and descending steps, for ½ mile to reach suspension bridge over River Tweed (589320). Don't cross bridge; continue along south bank for ¾ mile to B6404 (594311). Right for bus 67 or 68 to Melrose.

Lunch/accommodation Buccleuch Arms, The Green, St Boswells TD6 0EW (01835 822243; www.buccleucharms.com)

More information Peebles TIC (01721 728095), visitscotland.com, satmap.com, Melrose Abbey (01896 822562, historicscotland.gov.uk)
Ballad of Thomas the Rhymer: sacred-texts.com/neu/eng/child/ch037.htm

The Loch of the Lowes
SCOTTISH BORDERS

Tibbie Shiels Inn stands beautifully positioned on the isthmus that separates the Loch of the Lowes from its bigger sister, St Mary's Loch. James Hogg, the Scottish Borders shepherd-poet born in the nearby Ettrick Hills, would call into the inn from time to time around the turn of the nineteenth century.

Hogg, who left school at seven, was often dismissed as a rough-arsed yokel, a boozy buffoon and a bit of an oaf. But today a handsome statue of the man looks past the inn towards the Captain's Road, a stony old track that carried Jane and me up into the hills on a blowy morning.

The rounded hills bulged on all sides, dotted with circular stone sheepfolds — evidence of the sheep farming that once dominated these borderlands. The old pens down by the Crosscleuch Burn lay so neatly walled into compartments that they could have been built as an example of good practice. But there's little shepherding as Hogg would have recognised it in the back hills today.

In a roadless valley beyond Earl's Hill we found Riskinhope Hope, once the home of a shepherd and his family, now a hollow square of stone walls under tattered shelter pines. We sat and munched our sandwiches, trying to imagine life in this isolated cleft with only the trickle of the sike and bleating of sheep to break the silence.

Up on the ridge beyond, the views were immense, out over sombre brown hills under an enormous sky. We followed a grassy track down towards the main farm of Riskinhope, still flourishing in the valley of the two sister lochs, its farmer striding with stick and dog among his flock.

Along the lochside path grew monkey flowers, broad yellow trumpets spotted with scarlet. There were early purple orchids and ragged robin, butterworts and milkmaids, mint and thyme — a floral carpet laid alongside the Loch of the Lowes. Here is a scene of absolute stillness, caught by Hogg in his poem 'Caledonia':

> *"Sweet land of the bay and wild-winding deeps*
> *Where loveliness slumbers at even,*
> *While far in the depth of the blue water sleeps*
> *A calm little motionless heaven"*

The Ettrick shepherd helped his lifelong friend Sir Walter Scott to collect ballads for the latter's hugely successful 1802 collection, *Minstrelsy of the Scottish Border*. Hogg, a lifelong fiddle player and singer, later lamented that setting down the old Border ballads in print had killed them off as a living oral tradition. I hope his shadow attends the music sessions that flourish at Tibbie Shiels Inn. It would give the old shepherd pleasure to find out just how premature his judgment was.

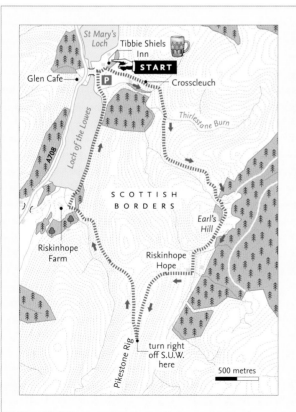

Start & finish Tibbie Shiels Inn, St Mary's Loch, Selkirkshire TD7 5LH (OS ref NT240205)

Getting there Road: Signposted off A708 (Yarrow-Moffat)

Walk (5 miles, moderate, OS Explorer 330): Follow Southern Upland Way/SUW waymarks up Captain's Road (waymarked 'Ettrick via Captain's Road') for 3 miles via Thirlestane Burn crossing (247200), Earl's Hill, Riskinhope Hope abandoned farm (250183) and on for ⅔ mile. On ridge, opposite end of forestry down on your left, pass SUW post; in 400m, on Pikestone Rig, come to two SUW posts 20m apart (244176). Descend to lower post (yellow arrow/YA pointing left); bear right here on grass path, down to Riskinhope Farm. Through gate in fenced field; down through lower gate; ignore YA pointing ahead past farm, and bear right through trees along lochside path for 1 mile to Tibbie Shiels Inn.

Lunch/accommodation Tibbie Shiels Inn (01750 42231; www.tibbieshiels.com)

Tea Glen Café, St Mary's Loch (01750 42241; sites.google.com/site/glencafestmarysloch/home)

More information Selkirk TIC (01750 20054), visitscotland.com/surprise ramblers.org.uk, www.satmap.co.uk

Hermaness
SHETLAND ISLANDS

The bonxie surveyed me coldly, raising dark wings and issuing a harsh double croak from its hooked, half open beak. These fierce inhabitants of the Shetland Isles (known as great skuas to the outside world) are not at their sweetest during the chick-rearing season. Instead of launching itself at me and skimming my head with outstretched feet, however, the bonxie contented itself with a good hard stare until I had walked on out of its personal space. The chicks must still be in the egg, I realised. Last time I had climbed the Hill of Hermaness — the northernmost point of Unst, the northernmost island in the entire British archipelago — a bonxie had swooped so close that it had parted my hair. I'd smelt the fishy reek of its breath as it screamed in my face, and instantly conceived a deep respect for the fearless great skua.

Dodging the bonxies is only one of the many thrills of Hermaness. As you climb the path past the peat-brown lochans there's the chance of spotting snipe and golden plover, and perhaps a rare red throated diver sailing the water. On your right the craggy cliffs of Burra Firth dissolve in and out of the mist. And as you crest the hill and start down the last slope in Britain, ahead are the skerries that close off these islands, a line of canted, gleaming rock stacks with cumbersome, enchanting names: Vesta Skerry and Rumblings, white with nesting gannets; Tipta Skerry; Muckle Flugga with its high perched lighthouse. A little farther off rises the round blob of Out Stack, prosaically named, romantically situated: the end of the end.

Down there in the thrashing water, sometime around 1850, Lady Jane Franklin scrambled from a tiny boat up the slippery flanks of Out Stack and cried a prayer for her missing husband into the wind. The Arctic winter of 1845 had swallowed Sir John Franklin and his 142 companions as they searched in vain for the Northwest Passage, and Lady Jane was left to weep and mourn in public, raising funds for fruitless rescue expeditions with her tears and imploring.

I had it all to myself, the whole magical place. Fulmars circled, puffins scurried, gannets wheeled and plunged, the wind blew like a challenge. I dropped to the turf, grinning all over my face, and stared out north to where, 1000 miles beyond the curve of the sea, the Arctic ice begins.

Start & finish The Ness parking place, Burrafirth, Isle of Unst (OS ref HP612147)

Getting there Air: Flybe (www.flybe.com) or Loganair (www.loganair.co.uk) fly from Inverness and Glasgow to Shetland. Bus and ferry: (www.zettrans.org.uk/bus/documents/NorthIslesLeaflet.pdf), Lerwick-Haroldswick, Isle of Unst. The Ness is another 3 miles (bicycle hire (01957 711254/711393), Dial-a-Ride service, 01957 745745). Road with ferries: A968, B9086.

Walk (5 miles, moderate, OS Explorer 470): From Ness parking place at end of road, follow marked circular path (green-topped posts) round Hermaness. Allow 2-3 hours. Remote, windy, boggy and slippery underfoot: dress warmly and in waterproofs; walking boots. Take great care on cliff edges. Bring binoculars and a stick. Information leaflets in metal box at start of path. NB: great skua dive-bombs during chick-rearing season, late May until July, coming close but rarely striking. To deter, hold stick above head. Avoid Sothers Brecks nesting area, May-July.

Lunch Picnic

Accommodation Irene and Tony Mouat, Clingera, Baltasound, Unst ZE2 9DT (01957 711579) for self-catering at North Dale (sleeps four: 3½ miles from Hermaness) or Baltasound (sleeps six)

Information Lerwick TIC (01595 695807), www.shetland.org, visitscotland.com
Cruises to Muckle Flugga: Contact Tony Mouat, above
Hermaness information: Scottish National Heritage, Lerwick (01595 693345; www.snh.org.uk)

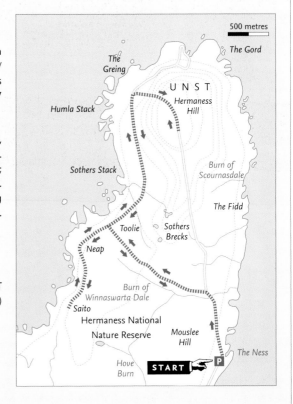

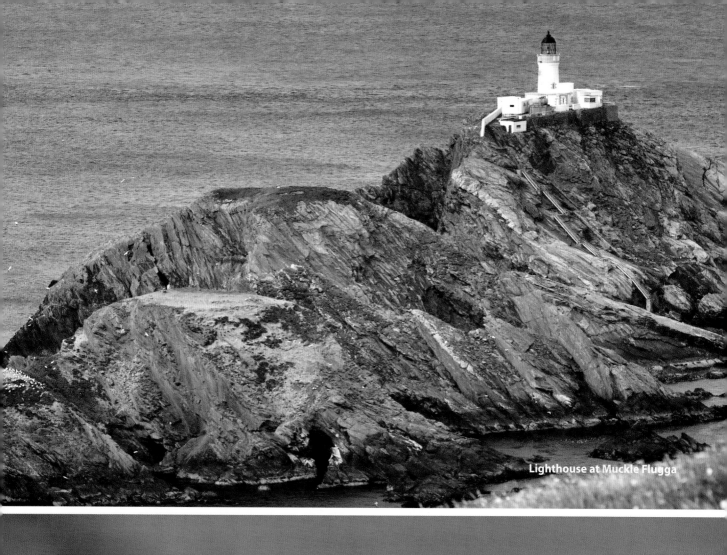
Lighthouse at Muckle Flugga

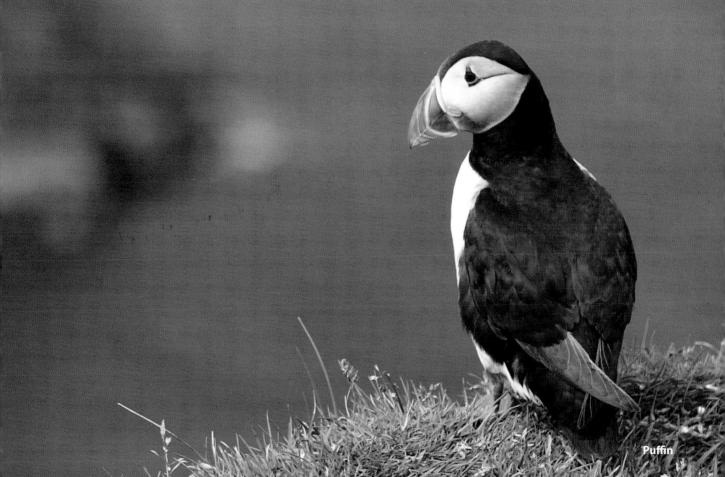
Puffin

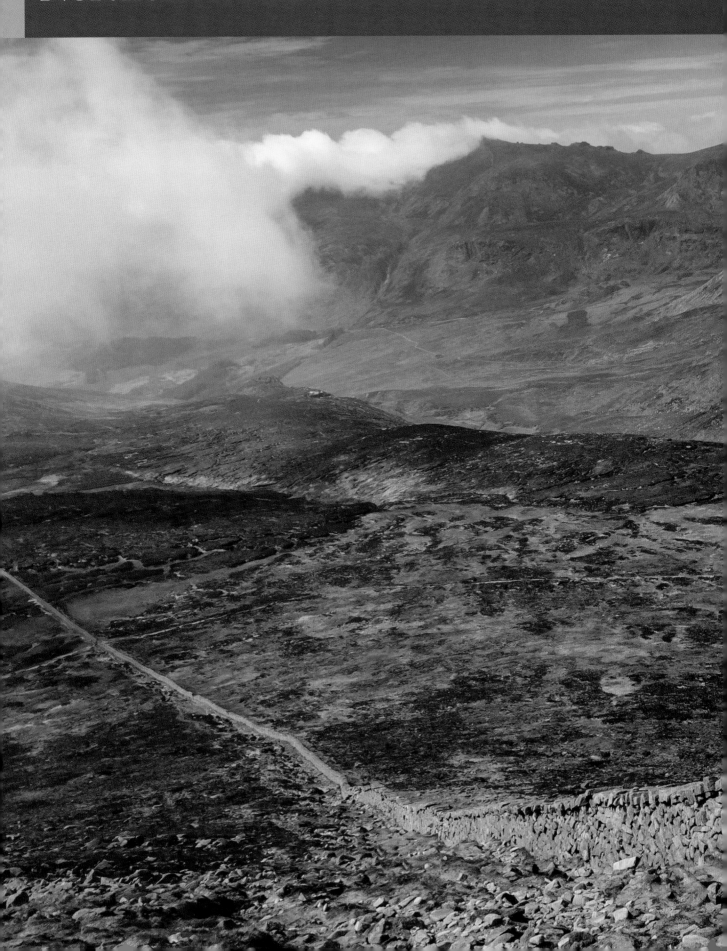

Northern Ireland

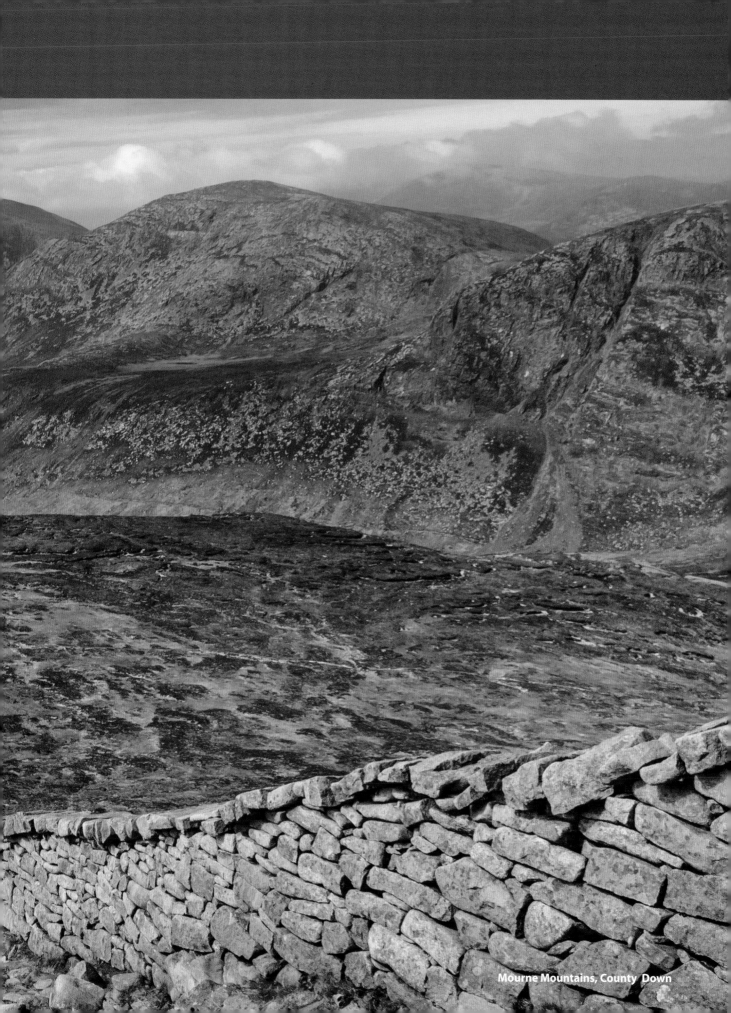

Mourne Mountains, County Down

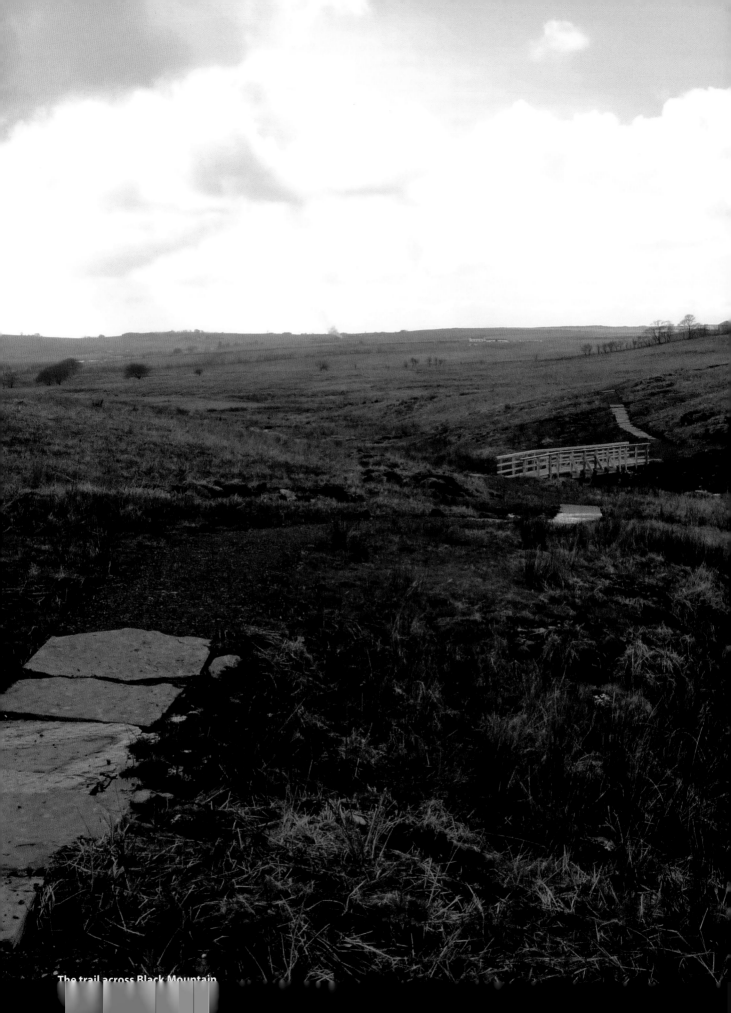

The trail across Black Mountain

Heavy cloud hung over Belfast. After a couple of days' sightseeing in the city we were itching to get up high and cram some hilltop air into our lungs. To the west of Belfast the cloud had cut the city's heights off at the knees, but when we set off from the National Trust's visitor centre on Divis Mountain, the murk was already drifting clear of the tops.

NT warden Dermot McCann filled us in on the network of walks the trust has established up here, where all Belfast comes when it wants a good blow-through. "From Divis on a good day you can see, well ... Cumbria and the Scottish coast across the sea, Belfast Lough, the Mourne Mountains, Donegal — and of course the whole of Belfast city laid out below."

Divis is a wild place, amazingly so when you consider how close to the city it is. Moorland and blanket bog, bright with flowers in season, stretch off in all directions. The shoulder of Black Mountain shut Belfast away as we made our way up the hillside towards the summit masts on Divis Mountain. Meadow pipits flitted, crying *chee-chee-chippit!* Skylarks sprang up from sedgy clumps to climb their aerial staircases, tiny shapes fluttering frantically in a grey sky filled with their sweet continuous song.

From the summit of Divis the view was still a green-grey blur, but down at the trig pillar on the crown of Black Mountain we sat and took in the clearing prospect — Belfast Lough narrowing to push inland past the docks towards the city centre, Cave Hill a dark ominous bulk hanging over the northern sector; a faint hint of the Ards Peninsula hills to the south east; and 20 miles away in the south the hunched back of Slieve Croob with the dramatic cones of the Mourne Mountains looking over its shoulder, palest grey against a white horizon. Of all the features in the city below us, the great yellow shipbuilding cranes Samson and Goliath and the silver ships' prow shape of the Titanic Belfast museum stood out most clearly, picked out together in one concentrated beam of intense sunlight.

We followed the Ridge Trail southwest with Belfast on our left shoulder; then the whole city vanished like a dream as we turned for home across the boggy mountain under celestial lark song that had never let up the whole walk through.

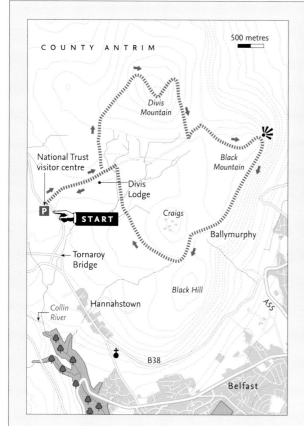

Start & finish National Trust visitor centre, Divis Lodge, near Hannahstown BT17 0NG (OS of NI ref J273744)

Getting there Road: M1 south from Belfast, Jct 2. A55 past Andersonstown; in 1½ miles, left on B38 (Upper Springfield Road). Just past Hannahstown, right (Divis & Black Mountain); in ½ mile, right opposite Long Barn car park (free parking) to NT visitor centre car park (moderate charge – coins).

Walk (6 miles, moderate, OS of NI Discoverer 15; walk maps downloadable at nationaltrust.org.uk or walkni.com): Right along road through gate; left (Summit & Heath Trails) up track. In ½ mile at fork, follow Summit Trail. Just before circular butt (276755) right up rock-studded trail to Divis summit trig pillar (281755). Follow access road down to road (285749). Left; before masts, right (Ridge Trail) up boardwalk, then gravel path to Black Mountain summit trig pillar (294748). On southwest along Ridge Trail (gravel, boardwalk, flagstones) for 2½ miles back to road (275745); left to NT centre.

Lunch Picnic, or snacks at NT centre café

More information NT Visitor Centre, Divis Lodge (02890 825434; nationaltrust. org.uk/divis-and-black-mountain), discovernorthernireland.com, satmap.com, walksireland.com

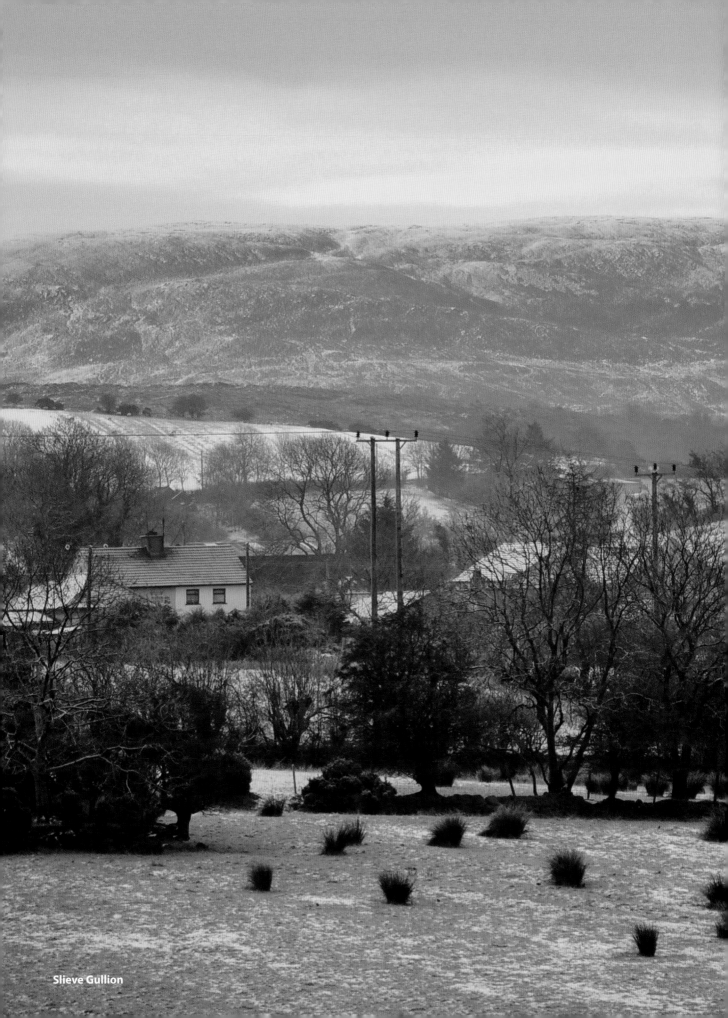

Slieve Gullion

Slieve Gullion
COUNTY ARMAGH

"Ever smelt pine needles properly?" inquired my companion, walker and naturalist Ron Murray, as we strolled the Forest Drive along the southern flank of Slieve Gullion. "Crush 'em like this between your finger and thumb." I suited action to words and sniffed deeply: a spicy blast of orange as pungent as a marmalade factory.

We left the trees and climbed, short and sharp, to the southern peak of Slieve Gullion. This big dark hump of a mountain forms the centrepiece of a remarkable volcanic landscape set in the green farmlands of South Armagh. Powerful subterranean convulsions sixty million years ago caused the ancient Slieve Gullion volcano to collapse, sending a ripple of molten rock outwards like a stone thrown in a pond. The circular ridge solidified, then weathered over ages into the guardian hills of the Ring, a ten-mile wide circle of craggy mini-mountains encircling Slieve Gullion like courtiers around a king.

Surprisingly few walkers venture into the countryside southwest of Newry to climb the mountain and savour for themselves one of the most spectacular high-level views in Ireland, a 100-mile circle from the Mountains of Mourne to the tumbled hills of Antrim and the billowy Sperrins, the green-and-brown mat of the Midland plain and the Wicklow Hills beyond Dublin, as tiny and pale as tin cut-outs.

I turned away from the breathtaking prospect at last to find Ron beckoning from a little low doorway of stone set deep into the side of the cairn. On hands and knees I followed him inside to find a chamber walled with stones neatly shaped and fitted. A Neolithic passage grave under a Bronze Age cairn, say the archaeologists. Not at all, retort the romantics. Here is the house of the Cailleach Beara, the unspeakably wicked witch who turned the mighty hero Fionn MacCumhaill into a feeble old man when he dived into the Lake of Sorrows to retrieve her golden ring.

Ron and I strode the windy summit ridge past the Lake of Sorrows. A huge half-finished millstone lay half in and half out of the water. "A miller pinched it from the Cailleach Beara's house," said Ron, "but it brought him such bad luck that he decided to put it back. When his donkey had got it this far, the poor thing fell down dead. That's where it stayed from then on. No one quite fancies moving it ..."

Start & finish Slieve Gullion Forest Park car park, Drumintee Road, Killeavy, Newry, Co Armagh BT35 8SW (OS of NI ref J040196)

Getting there Bus: Service 43 (Newry-Forkhill) to Forest Park entrance. Road: N1/A1 Dublin-Newry; B113 ('Forkhill'); in 3½ miles, right ('Slieve Gullion Forest Park') to car park.

Walk (8 miles, moderate, OS of NI Discoverer 29; Ring of Gullion Way/RGW blue arrows): Top-left corner of car park, left up path through trees. In ¼ mile join Forest Drive (038191), up slope, then level, for ¼ mile to RGW post on left (035190). Right up drive, past metal barrier; left uphill for 1½ miles to car park (018200). Beyond picnic table, right at white post, steeply uphill. South Cairn (025203) – Lake of Sorrows – North Cairn (021211). Aim north for Sturgan Mountain (left of Cam Lough), then white house between you and lake. Fork right at grassy 'lawn' with boulder beyond, aiming for house. At road (025230), right for 3 miles, passing Killeavy Old Church (040221), to Forest Park entrance (046199). Right to car park.

Lunch Slieve Gullion Courtyard coffee shop, or picnic by Lake of Sorrows

More information Slieve Gullion Courtyard (02830 848084), discovernorthernireland.com ✓

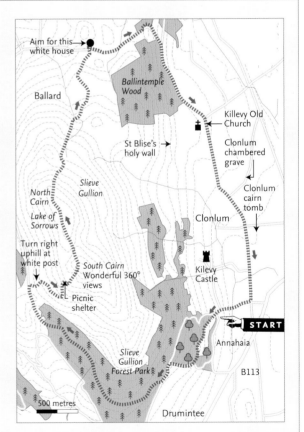

The shapely hummocks of the Mourne Mountains stood muted and insubstantial under a cloud-blotched sky and a pale sun. Wrens sang in the flowering gorse bushes along the lane from Meelmore Lodge. The western face of the Mournes rose before us, the jagged profile of Slieve Meelmore and the rounder bulk of Slievenaglogh framing the hollow where the Trassey Track snaked in its long climb to the Hare's Gap. Generations of quarrymen forged the track and its tributary paths to the granite quarries that floored and walled the industrial north of England in the nineteenth century.

The zigzag path rose steeply to where the flat saddle of the Hare's Gap was seamed by the long dark line of the Mourne Wall. This remarkable construction of roughly squared granite blocks, built by hungry men in the early twentieth century to earn themselves a crust, circles the high top of the Mourne Mountains for 22 miles, swooping up and down all the major peaks. Once across the wall we got a breathtaking prospect of the heart of the range, from the castellated crags of Slieve Bearnagh and the knobbed peak of Ben Crom overhanging its namesake reservoir to the long graceful nape of Slieve Donard, tallest of all.

Smugglers, ne'er-do-wells and travellers in a hurry used to cut across the high Mournes from the sea by way of a rough path known as the Brandy Pad. We followed it towards Slieve Donard along the slopes of Slieve Commedagh, through a high bleak landscape where meadow pipits fluttered and cheeped, and a solitary raven croaked a warning *ark-ark-ark-ark* to his mate invisible among the rocks.

Clouds built and melted, rain spat and subsided, and Slieve Donard pulled a shawl of thick mist over her head. Under the mountain we recrossed the Mourne Wall and went stumbling and splashing down towards Newcastle in the company of the Glen River, a noisy little chute of rapids and cascades. A walk in a Mourne heaven — nothing soft or accommodating about it, everything stark, hard and beautifully wild.

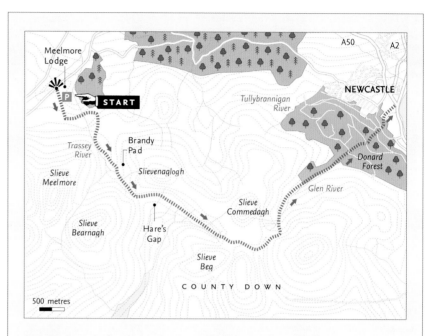

Start Meelmore Lodge, Trassey Road, near Bryansford, Co Down BT33 0QB (OS of NI ref SB305307)

Getting there Bus: Mourne Rambler bus service in the summer (mournemountains. com). Road: Meelmore Lodge is signed off B180 Newcastle-Hilltown road. Car park: pay and display

Walk (7 miles, moderate/strenuous, OS of NI 1:25 000 Activity Map 'The Mournes'): From car park, left up stony lane ('Mountain Walk' sign on wall): Through right-hand of two gates; follow lane to cross field wall (308302). Left ('Mourne Way') for 500m; right up stony Trassey Track. In 1 mile track crosses river and bears right; but keep ahead here, steeply up to cross Mourne Wall at Hare's Gap (323287). Left at cairn along Brandy Pad path for 1½ miles to cairn on saddle between Slieve Commedagh and Slieve Beg (342278). Bear left at cairn, under The Castles crags. At end of crags (348277), fork left, up to cross Mourne Wall (350279). Descend beside Glen River. In 1½ miles, pass Ice House (364295). In 200m at dirt road/concrete bridge, descend left bank of river. In 400m, right across bridge (379299); descend right bank. In 350m, left across Donard Bridge (372302). Descend left bank; through Donard Park into Newcastle.

Conditions Some steep parts; slippery underfoot in woods. Walking stick advisable. Dogs on leads.

Lunch Meelmore Lodge café (02843 726657); Villa Vinci, Newcastle (02843 723080)

Accommodation Slieve Donard Resort and Spa, Newcastle BT33 0AH (02843 721066; hastingshotels.com), Meelmore Lodge hostel/camping, 52 Trassey Road, Bryansford BT33 0QB (02843 725949; meelmorelodge.co.uk)

More information Newcastle TIC (02843 722222), walkni.com, discovernorthernireland.com, walksireland.com, satmap.com

It can be a wet old place, Co Derry, after a month of good solid rain. Down in the glen of the Altkeeran River below Carntogher Mountain, all was sedgy. But the old coach road along the glen gave firm footing through the turf. Streams ran orange from the iron minerals of the mountain, up whose green flank Jane and I went climbing.

Pink conquistador helmets of lousewort clashed with virulent red sphagnum in the banks of the tumbled wall that we were following. It lifted us to the shoulder of the mountain, and a track where we met two walkers from a local townland.

They pointed out Slieve Gallion ten miles to the south ("a Derry mountain, despite what you might hear") with great precision and pride. "I've walked this path since I was a boy," one said, "and by God I will do it till the day that I die!".

Up at the Snout of the Cairn, Shane's Leaps lay just off the path — three innocuous-looking rocks. Did Shane 'Crossagh' O'Mullan, the light-footed outlaw with the scarred face whom all the ladies sighed for, once escape the lumbering English soldiery up here? So old tales say.

At the Emigrants' Cairn just beyond the Leaps we found a heart-stopping view to the hills of Donegal, the last prospect of their native land that those walking over the mountains to the ships in Lough Foyle would carry with them to "far Amerikay".

Back across the slopes of Carntogher we went, following the boggiest of upland tracks, half peat and half puddle, past black heaps of iron-mining spoil to the top of the ridge and another most tremendous westward view across the silver fishtail of Lough Foyle, on beyond the pale humps of Barnesmore and the Blue Stacks to the jagged spine of Errigal out at the edge of sight in western Donegal. Between Errigal and Mourne there cannot be fewer than a hundred miles.

All Northern Ireland lay spread out for us and we lingered long over this extraordinary feast. On the way down we passed a Bronze Age cist grave. There was something about the little dark hole in the bank, slab-lined and secretive, that simply invited a tall and wild tale. But no one was there to tell it to us today.

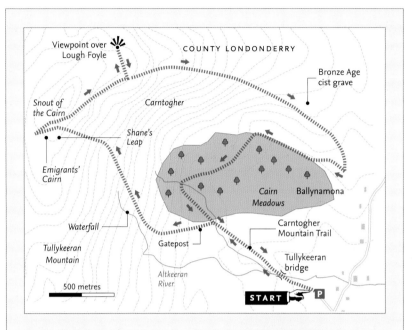

Start & finish Tullykeeran Bridge, near Maghera (OS of NI ref C819045)

Getting there Bus: Ulsterbus (www.translink.co.uk) to Maghera (3 miles) or Swatragh (3½ miles). Road: A29 (Coleraine-Maghera); minor roads to parking place by ruined cottage at Tullykeeran Bridge.

Walk (5½ miles, moderate grade, OS of NI 1:50 000 Discoverer 8 – red trail): Follow road 100m beyond third bridge, left over stile by gatepost (red/blue arrows); follow track for ½ mile into Altkeeran Glen (805407 approx). Right up path by tumbledown wall (red/blue arrows). In ¾ mile, stony track crosses path (800058 approx); left (red arrow) to Emigrants' Cairn and Shane's Leaps (796058). Return for 50m; left at post (red arrow) along grassy track to marker post on saddle of ground; walk 400m left here to ridge viewpoint over Lough Foyle and Donegal hills; return to marker post. Continue downhill along track for 2 miles, past cist grave (824061), through gates, down to road (823055). Right (red arrow) for 2 miles to car park.

Lunch Rafters, Swatragh (02879 401206) – food all day, open fire, warm welcome

Accommodation Laurel Villa guesthouse, Magherafelt (02879 301459; www.laurel-villa.com) – friendly, well-run 'house of poets'. From £70 double B&B

More information Magherafelt TIC (02879 631510), midulstercouncil.org/Things-To-Do/Tourism-Heritage; discovernorthernireland.com Downloadable map/instructions at http://www.walkni.com/d/walks/320/Carntogher%20History%20Trail%20Guide.pdf Trail map at car park

Downhill and Benone Strand
COUNTY LONDONDERRY

Frederick Hervey, 4th Earl of Bristol, Bishop of Londonderry from 1768 to 1803, was a remarkably broad-minded man. In that intolerant era of Penal Laws against Catholics, the bishop allowed the local priest to celebrate Mass in the Mussenden Temple, one of the follies that he erected around his preposterously extravagant Downhill Estate on the cliffs outside Castlerock. Hervey was red-blooded and eccentric, fond of his wine and the ladies, addicted to foreign travel and apt to have himself borne around in a palanquin and to drop spaghetti on the heads of pilgrims passing below his balcony in Rome.

Jane and I entered Downhill on a brisk windy morning under the knowing grins of the mythic lynx-like beasts that guard the estate's so-called Lion Gate. Beyond lay the Bishop's enormous Palace of Downhill in poignant ruin, its grand fire places hollow and stark, its windows blank, state rooms carpeted with grass and open to the sky. In the heyday of Downhill this incredible centre of luxury high on the cliffs had an entrance façade flanked by Corinthian pilasters, with a double stair leading to the door. There was a State Dining Room, a State Drawing Room, and a two-storey gallery for the Bishop's superb art collection, all covered by a magnificent dome. Façade and double stair still stand, but now the interior walls, once beautified with exquisite plasterwork, are sealed with functional concrete. The elaborate mosaics are gone from the chimney breasts, and buttercups and clover have taken the place of Wilton and Axminster. It's a strange, uncanny and altogether haunting atmosphere in the empty shell of the Palace of Downhill.

Down on the brink of the basalt cliffs beside the domed Mussenden Temple, we looked out on a most sensational view: the sea shallows creaming on seven clear miles of sand that ran west in a gentle curve towards the mouth of Lough Foyle, with the clouded hills of 'dark Inishowen' beckoning from far-off Donegal.

That proved an irresistible call. Down on the strand we pushed into the wind. Waves hissed on the tideline, sand particles scudded by. Surfers rode the waves like water demons. The black and green rampart of the cliffs was cut vertically by white strings of waterfalls, the falling cascades blown to rags in mid-plummet. All this vigour and movement whipped us onwards to where the preserved sand dunes of Umbra rose between strand and cliff foot. It was a complete change of tempo here, sheltered among the sandhills, down on our hands and knees amid pyramidal orchids of blazing crimson, yellow kidney vetch, lady's bedstraw sacred to the Virgin Mary, and tall spikes of common spotted orchids.

Lying prone in the dunes, looking back through a screen of marram grass and clovers, we saw the dark pepper pot shape of the temple on the brink of Downhill cliff. Had the bold Bishop of Londonderry kept a mistress in there, as stories say? I rather hope he had, and his palanquin and spaghetti-tureen, too.

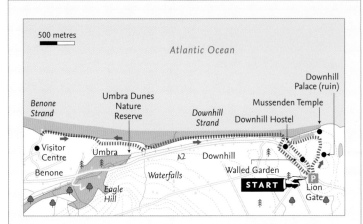

Start & finish Lion Gate car park, Downhill Estate, Castlerock BT514RP (OS of NI ref C757357)

Getting there Train: (www.translink.co.uk) to Castlerock (½ mile). Bus: Ulsterbus service 134. Road: On A2 between Castlerock and Downhill Strand.

Walk (6 miles, easy grade, OS of NI Discoverer 04). From Lion Gate car park explore Downhill Palace ruin, then Mussenden Temple (758362). Return anticlockwise along cliff and take in the Walled Garden. From Lion Gate cross A2 (take care!); right downhill beside road on pavement. Short stretch with no pavement leads to foot of hill. Right under railway; left along Downhill Strand. After 1¼ miles, where river leaves dunes, look left for Ulster Wildlife Trust's Umbra Dunes notice (732359). Follow fence through dunes to descend on Benone Strand. Continue to Benone (717362 – lavatories, Visitor Centre). Return along beach and A2 to Lion gate car park.

Lunch Picnic or seasonal café at Benone Bistro, Benone Tourist Complex (028 7775 0555)

Accommodation Downhill Hostel (02870 849077; downhillbeachhouse.com) at foot of hill – dormitory or private rooms available. Whole hostel bookable.

More information Downhill (NT) (02870 848728; www.nationaltrust.org.uk); Coleraine TIC (02870 344723); discovernorthernireland.com.

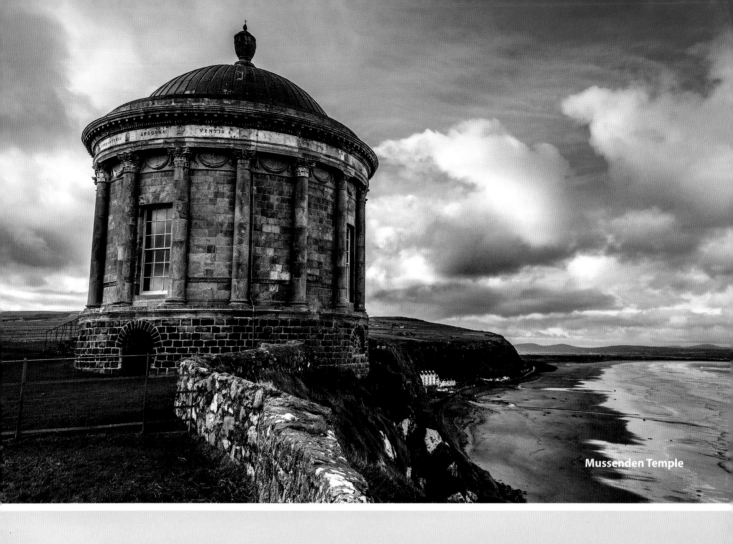

Mussenden Temple

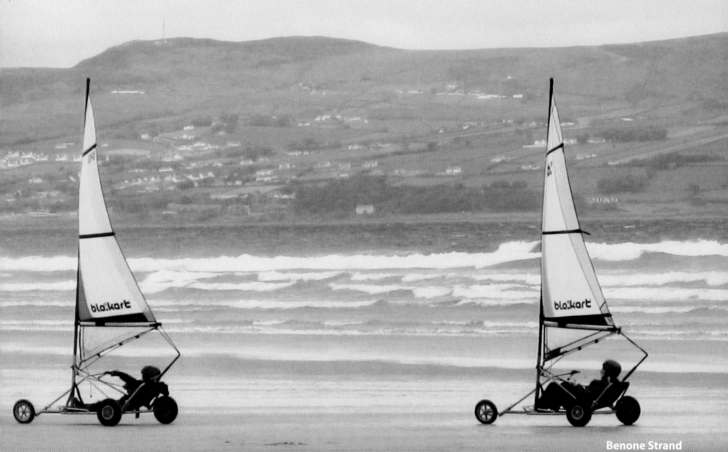

Benone Strand

Drumderg Road runs west out of Moneyneany, shedding tarmac and houses as it gains height, with the eastern fells of the Sperrin Hills rising ahead. On this muggy midsummer day the verges were bright with vetches, foxgloves, speedwell and buttercups. The sharp yellow of tormentil and a white froth of heath bedstraw heralded the switch from rushy lowland sheep pastures to peat moors as the road lifted into a dark, wild upland of blanket bog under heavy grey clouds.

We reached the saddle between Crockmore ('The Big Hill', in actuality a flattened dome) and Crockbrack ('The Speckled Hill', a dun-coloured ridge). The far views were tremendous — Slieve Gallion lumping up in the south-east, Benbradagh raising a snub snout in the north-west, and all round a roll call of Sperrin heights — Craigagh and Spelhoagh, Slievavaddy with its winking eye of a lough, Sawel Mountain's dominant 678m (2224ft) cone.

These rolling, peat-blanketed hills seem wilder than any other range in Northern Ireland, because you rarely see another walker up here. So Jane and I were saying to each other as we descended from Crockbrack, muffled against wind and rain, towards the deep cleft where the Drumderg River springs. Then a vision in T-shirt and shorts shot by. Noel Johnston from Belfast was doing a sponsored expedition to raise money for a charity bringing divided communities together. He'd tramped a long way, sleeping rough, and had a long way to go —another of those admirable youngsters putting their time and energy into making a better post-Troubles Northern Ireland.

By the time we'd got down into the dell, Noel was long gone over the horizon. We sat there on two picnic rocks, munching wheaten bread and chocolate mints like lords, savouring lark song and the soft hushing whisper of wind in rushes. Then we went steeply and boggily up to our third summit, Craigbane ('The White Hill', a sombre swelling) and found the long road home, a mountain track that fell gently away towards Moneyneany. The plains of Antrim lay spread in sunshine at our feet, cradled by the slopes of Craiagagh and Crockmore, with a silvery gleam of Lough Neagh to beckon us down from the hills.

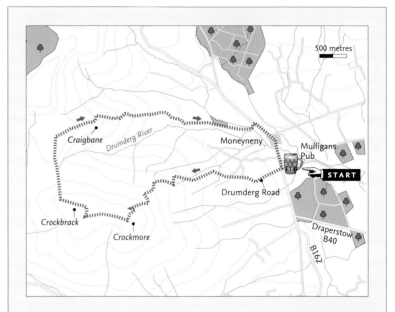

Start & finish Trailhead info board at Mulligan's pub, Moneyneany, Co. Londonderry BT45 7DU (OS of NI ref H754965)

Getting there Road: A6, A31 to Magherafelt; B40 to Draperstown and Moneyneany

Walk (7½ miles; moderate hillwalk, sometimes boggy, well waymarked; OS of NI Activity 1:25 000 'Sperrins' map. Walk downloadable at walkni.com): From pub car park, right along B40; in 30m, left up Drumderg Road (occasional yellow arrows/YAs, and 'Crockbrack Way'/CW waymarks) for 2½ miles. At first cattle grid, tarmac changes to stones; at 2nd one, keep ahead; at 3rd one, at Crockmore summit, ignore stile on right and keep ahead (725956, CW, YA). In 100m at T-junction, right (YA) on bog road towards Crockbrack. In ½ mile, right (717955, YA) up grassy track. In 200m, left (YA) to cross stile. Descend beside fence on left for 600m to fence running right (712959, YA). Follow it to right, steeply down to cross Drumderg River's headwaters. Continue up fence on far side (sloppy, boggy!) to cross stile at top (711970). Right (CW, YA) down stony road, then tarmac, for 3¼ miles to B40 (749974). Right to Mulligan's pub.

Lunch Picnic or Apparo Hotel, Draperstown (4 miles) – (02879 628100; apparorestaurant.com)

Accommodation Laurel Villa, Magherafelt, BT45 6AW (02879 301459; laurel-villa.com) – homely, helpful, spick-and-span B&B

More information Magherafelt TIC (02879 631510), discovernorthernireland.com, satmap.com

Vinegar Hill
COUNTY TYRONE

Martin McGuigan is exactly the man you want with you in the Sperrins Hills of Northern Ireland. This wild range of fells, straddling the waist of Co Tyrone, is his native ground.

"We would never have had this view if it wasn't for the Ice Age," Martin says, pointing out the landscape features of the Sperrins from the heights of the narrow Barnes Gap. "The glaciers scraped and shaped all the hills that you can see; and then, when they were melting, they formed a huge lake. When that overflowed it simply burst through a weak spot in the rock and formed the Gap itself."

A landscape with dynamic origins, and an exceptionally beautiful one. An old stony road, part of the new Vinegar Hill Loop walk that we are following, winds like a scarf around the upper shoulders of Gorticashel Glen. We look down into a silent bowl of fields, some green with good grazing, others hazed under bracken and sedge. Abandoned farmsteads lie dotted across the slopes, each rusted roof of corrugated iron an orange blob among tattered shelter trees — eloquent testimony to the hardships faced by small country farms.

"Lazybed strips." Martin's finger pointed out the corduroy rows on the slopes of the glen. We tried to imagine the work involved in wresting a family's living out of a lazybed. "I've dug rows like that myself," Martin observed. "It's hard enough work. You dig a trench and turn the soil over onto the next ridge,

grass to grass, to make a domed top and undercut sides. Spuds and cabbages. The biggest crop I had was half a ton out of ten rows, each maybe twenty yards long. So lazybeds are very effective — but they'd break your back."

On Vinegar Hill stands a tumbledown cottage, its rafters half smothered with fuchsia and Himalayan balsam, its fireplace choked with tendrils of ivy that feel their way blindly, like pale tentacles, out into the room. Martin fingers the balsam, ruminating: "These flowers were a big thing in my childhood. The bees would go crazy for them, and we'd see how many we could catch in a jam jar before we got stung."

Down where the Gorticashel Burn runs under a bridge, a ferny old mill house stands hard against the bank, with an ancient potato-digging machine on its mossy cobbles. Sparrows flock through a cotoneaster bush on a farmhouse wall. At Scotch Town we find the crossroads guarded by a handsome rooster in a tippet of gleaming ginger feathers. Near Garvagh, as we turn for our homeward step, a great roadside shed stands provisioned for the winter with dried sods of turf.

This whole glen speaks eloquently of the life and work of family farms, present and past. Now, with the opening of the Vinegar Hill Loop, cheerful voices will be heard around the abandoned steadings and boots will tread the forgotten green roads of Gorticashel once more.

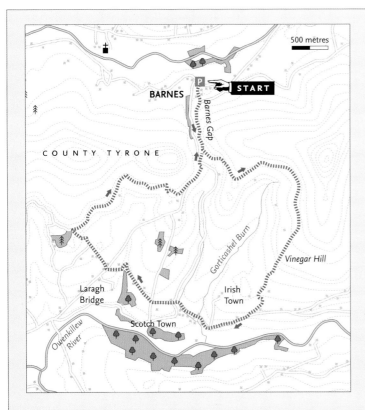

Start & finish Barnes Gap car park/toilet/picnic area at foot of Mullaghbane Road (OS of NI ref H551905)

Getting there Road: From B47 between Plumbridge and Draperstown, follow brown 'Barnes Gap' tourist signs to car park at foot of Mullaghbane Road, beside 'Plumbridge 5' sign

Walk (7 miles, moderate, OS of NI 1:50 000 Discoverer 13; walkni.com; purple arrow way marks): Walk up the higher of the two Barnes Gap roads ('Craignamaddy Circuit'/CC, 'Ulster Way' sign) past farm (barking dogs!). Right along Magherbrack Road for ⅓ mile; left (552896; CC) along dirt road. Follow it round Gorticashel Glen for 2 miles to road near Irish Town (558873). Right for ⅔ mile to crossroads in Scotch Town (548875; 'Gortin' left, 'Plumbridge' right). Straight across here and over next two crossroads (544875 and 538880) for 1 mile, to pass turning on left (536883 – tarmac stops here). Ahead for 300m; at stand of conifers, right (534885; 'Vinegar Hill Loop') on stony lane. Follow it for just over 1 mile to road (550892). Forward to Barnes Gap road; left to car park.

Lunch Picnic

More information Omagh TIC, Strule Arts Centre, Omagh (02882 247831), discovernorthernireland.com, ramblers.org.uk, satmap.com, sperrinstourism.com

Index

Publisher: Jethro Lennox
Project manager: Craig Balfour
Designer: Kevin Robbins
Layout: Davidson Publishing Solutions
Maps: The Times and Gordon MacGilp
Editorial: Sonia Dawkins, Rachel Grocott and Ewan Ross

Image Credits